DICTIONARY OF LABOUR BIOGRAPHY, Volume VIII

The *Dictionary* has been planned as a many-volumed project, with each volume organised on a self-contained basis. The time-span covers the period of modern industrialisation, from the closing decades of the eighteenth century to the present. Living persons are excluded.

Entries are on the same pattern as those for the *Dictionary of National Biography* and are intended to include persons active in the organisations and institutions of the British labour movement as well as those who influenced the development of radical and socialist ideas. Bibliographical sources (including writings) are attached to individual entries; and each volume includes a comprehensive subject index and a consolidated list of names.

The first seven volumes covered a wide range of entries from most periods of labour history, with the sixth specialising on the radical movements of the early nineteenth century and the seventh mainly concerned with personalities of the twentieth century.

This eighth volume spans two centuries of radicals, trade unionists and socialists. We have now begun to cover the early history of radicalism from the 1790s; and the Spencean concern with the land question is taken up a century later with biographical entries related to the movements stimulated by the writings of Henry George. These include some well-known personalities in the late nineteenth-century Christian Socialist movement. For the years between the two world wars there is a concentration on several individuals in Britain concerned with the growing nationalist movements in Africa. The emerging role of women in the British trade union and labour movements is well represented.

The Special Notes, begun in volume V, provide information on a random sample of organisations, movements and events which have been somewhat neglected in the general literature. They are continued here with entries on: The Guild of St Matthew; The Church Socialist League; The Twentieth Century Press; and the British Labour Delegation to Russia, 1920.

The editors

Joyce M. Bellamy is a Fellow of the University of Hull. Her publications include *Yorkshire Business Histories: A Bibliography* and *The Trade and Shipping of Nineteenth-Century Hull.*

John Saville is Emeritus Professor of Economic and Social History at the University of Hull. His previous books include *Ernest Jones: Chartist*; *Rural Depopulation in England and Wales, 1851–1951*; and three volumes of *Essays in Labour History,* edited with Asa Briggs. Forthcoming is his study *1848. The British State and the Chartist Movement.*

DICTIONARY
OF
LABOUR BIOGRAPHY

Volume VIII

Edited by

JOYCE M. BELLAMY

Fellow of the University of Hull

and

JOHN SAVILLE

Emeritus Professor of Economic and Social History, University of Hull

with assistance from

DAVID E. MARTIN

Lecturer in Economic and Social History, University of Sheffield

M

First published 1987

Published by
THE MACMILLAN PRESS LTD
Houndmills, Basingstoke, Hampshire RG21 2XS
and London
Companies and representatives
throughout the world

Typeset by
Latimer Trend & Company Ltd, Plymouth

Printed in Hong Kong

British Library Cataloguing in Publication Data
Dictionary of labour biography.
Vol. VIII
1. Labour and labouring classes – Great
Britain – Biography   2. Socialists –
Great Britain – Biography
I. Bellamy, Joyce M.   II. Saville, John
335′.1′0922   HD8393.A1
ISBN 0–333–38782–1 (vol. VIII)
ISBN 0–333–42757–2 (8-vol. set)

Contents

Acknowledgements

The research for this volume was made possible in part by our grant from what was formerly the Social Science Research Council (now the Economic and Social Research Council). We have, however, in these last three years had to exercise considerable financial economies, and, with much regret, we have lost the services of our part-time research assistant in Hull, Mrs Barbara Nield. We are indebted to her for the admirable competence she showed over many years while working with us, and we offer her our warmly-felt gratitude. We have been able to retain for this volume the part-time research services of Mrs Vivien Morton, who has dealt with many of our London queries, and we acknowledge once again her valuable help. To Dr David Martin of the University of Sheffield we offer our thanks for his careful reading of our entries and we have now felt it appropriate to recognise his assistance by including his name on the title page. To the Lipman Trust we are obliged for small grants over the three years 1984 to 1986.

As always, we have been helped by many individuals and institutions all over Britain, and in the outside world; in particular we are grateful for the help provided by Miss Audrey Hebb in Hull and Miss Allegra Dawe in London. Some work undertaken by Dr Helen Corr when she was financed by an SSRC grant to Professor C. Smout of the University of St Andrews has also been included in this volume. We also wish to thank all our contributors and the many individuals and organisations whose names are listed in the sources at the end of each biography.

We remain constantly indebted to our colleagues in the Brynmor Jones Library, and we share with them our grief at the death of Philip Larkin. He was always immensely helpful to us, and the special grant that the Library Committee gave for the purchase of Labour History material for many years was the result of his consistent support for our work. Among his colleagues we would especially mention Miss Maeve Brennan, Mr Brian Dyson, Mr Norman Higson, Mrs Ann Holbrook, Miss Wendy Mann, Mr John Morris, Mr Derek Orton and Mrs Joan Sargerson. We are much indebted to the University of Hull in general and the continued interest and support of our senior colleagues for the *DLB* project.

Of the many other librarians and archivists who have assisted us we would particularly record our debt to the British Library, London and Boston Spa, and the Newspaper Library, Colindale; Mr S. Bird, archivist, the Labour Party, London; Edmund and Ruth Frow of the Working Class Movement Library, Manchester; Mr R. Garratt, Co-operative Union Library, Manchester; Dr Angela Raspin, British Library of Political and Economic Science; Mr T. D. W. Reid, Stockport Public Library; and the Library of the Religious Society of Friends, London. We are grateful also for the information supplied by the staff of the General Register Office in London, the Registry of Wills at Somerset House, and the Public Record Office.

We also wish to thank the Virago Press and the London School of Economics for their permission to reproduce some extracts from *The Diary of Beatrice Webb*, ed. Norman and Jeanne MacKenzie, 4 vols (1982–5); and Mrs P. Kirwan, Great Missenden, for permission to include extracts from the letters in the Passfield Coll., BLPES, written by Margaret Harkness to her cousin, Beatrice Potter.

We further acknowledge the help given in proof-reading by Miss Audrey Hebb, Dr David Martin and Mrs Barbara Nield, and the work of Miss Wendy Mann and Mr V. J. Morris in the final stage of the index. We are also grateful to our copy-editors, Mrs V. Rose and Mr G. Eyre, for their careful reading of the entries. Finally we wish to thank our publishers and in particular Mr T. M. Farmiloe in the London office of Macmillan.

University of Hull   JMB
July 1986   JS

Notes to Readers

1. Place-names are usually quoted according to contemporary usage relating to the particular entry.
2. Where the amount of a will, estate value or effects is quoted, the particular form used is normally that given in *The Times*, or the records of Somerset House, London, or the Scottish Record Office, Edinburgh. For dates before 1860 the source will usually be the Public Record Office.
3. Under the heading **Sources**, personal information relates to details obtained from relatives, friends or colleagues of the individual in question; biographical information refers to other sources.
4. The place of publication in bibliographical references is London, unless otherwise stated.
5. All theses and dissertations cited were submitted to universities, unless otherwise stated (for example, 'London PhD' signifies a PhD thesis submitted to the University of London).
6. 'P.' indicates a pamphlet whose pagination could not be verified. Where it is known, the number of pages is quoted if under sixty.
7. The *See also* column which follows biographical entries includes names marked with a dagger and these refer to biographies already published in Volumes I–VII of the *Dictionary*; those with no marking are included in the present volume, and those with an asterisk refer to entries to be included in later volumes.
8. A consolidated name list of entries in Volumes I–VIII will be found at the end of this volume before the general index.
9. In Volume VI, pp. xix to xxxi, there are additions and corrections to Volumes I–V.

List of Contributors

Dr John L. Baxter	Adult Education Tutor, Sheffield City Council
Miss Margaret Bell	Cottingham, North Humberside
Miss Marjorie Bucke	Theberton, Suffolk
Mrs Maureen Callcott	Lecturer, Department of Humanities, Newcastle upon Tyne Polytechnic
Dr Malcolm Chase	Lecturer, Department of Adult and Continuing Education, Leeds University
Dr David Clark, MP	London
Simon Cordery	Research Assistant, American Historical Association, Washington, DC, USA
Dr Helen Corr	Douglas Knoop Research Fellow, Department of Economic and Social History, Sheffield University
Professor F. K. Donnelly	Department of History, University of New Brunswick, Canada
Peter Drake	Social Sciences Department, Birmingham Reference Library
Dr Tom Gallagher	Lecturer, School of Peace Studies, Bradford University
Dr Ian Goodfellow	Senior Counsellor, the Open University, South Western Region, Plymouth
Robert Griffiths	Cardiff
Dr June Hannam	Lecturer in History, Bristol Polytechnic
Laurence Jacobs	Research Student, King's College, Cambridge
Graham Johnson	Research Student, Department of Economic and Social History, Hull University
Fraulein Beate Kaspar	Teacher, Schlossgymnasium, Künzelsau, West Germany
Stephen F. Kelly	Journalist, Manchester
Dr John E. King	Senior Lecturer, Department of Economics, Lancaster University
Dr Richard Lewis	Senior Lecturer in History, Teesside Polytechnic
Dr Iain McCalman	Research Fellow in History, Research School of Social Sciences, the Australian National University, Canberra
Dr David E. Martin	Lecturer, Department of Economic and Social History, Sheffield University
Mrs Barbara Nield	Formerly Research Assistant, Department of Economic and Social History, Hull University

x

Trevor Peacock — Third Secretary, Australian Embassy, Athens

Dr Robin Pearson — Lecturer in Modern Economic History, Department of Economic and Social History, Hull University

Dr Naomi Reid — Stockport

T. David W. Reid — Reference Librarian, Stockport Public Library

Cllr John J. Rowley — Lecturer in General and Communication Studies, Dudley College of Technology

Professor James A. Schmiechen — Department of History, Central Michigan University, USA

Dr John S. Shepherd — Principal Lecturer (Adviser for Staff Development), Cambridge College of Arts and Technology

Richard Storey — Archivist, Modern Records Centre, Warwick University Library

Bob Turner — Tutor Organiser, West of Scotland District (Renfrew Division) of the Workers' Educational Association

Ken Weller — London

Andrew Whitehead — Journalist and broadcaster, London

Professor Diana Wylie — History Department, Yale University, New Haven, USA

List of Abbreviations

Omitted from this list are abbreviations for degrees (PhD, MA, etc.), and abbreviations for American states and British counties (used only in references).

ADB	*Australian Dictionary of Biography*
AEU	Amalgamated Engineering Union
AGM	Annual General Meeting
Anon.	Anonymous
App.	Appendix
AST	Amalgamated Society of Tailors
BISAKTA	British Iron and Steel and Kindred Trades Association
BL	British Library
BLPES	British Library of Political and Economic Science, LSE
Boase	F. Boase, *Modern English Biography ... 1851–1900* (Truro, 1892–1921; repr. 1965)
BSP	British Socialist Party
Bull.	*Bulletin*
Bull. Soc. Lab. Hist.	*Bulletin of the Society for the Study of Labour History*
c.	*circa* (Lat.): about
CAB	Cabinet Papers, PRO
CB	Companion of the Bath
CBE	Commander of the British Empire
Cd/Cmd	Command Paper
Ch.(s)	Chapter(s)
CI	Communist International
CL	Central/City Library
Cllr	Councillor
CMG	Companion of the Order of St Michael and St George
CO	Conscientious Objector
col.(s)	column(s)
Coll.	Collection
Cont. Rev.	*Contemporary Review*
Co-op.	Co-operative
CPGB	Communist Party of Great Britain
CRO	County Record Office
CSL	Church Socialist League
CSU	Christian Social Union
CWS	Co-operative Wholesale Society
d	old pence

Dept	Department
DLB	*Dictionary of Labour Biography*
DNB	*Dictionary of National Biography*
Dod	*Dod's Parliamentary Companion*
EC	Executive Committee
Econ. J.	*Economic Journal*
ed.(s)	edited/edition(s)/editor
EEC	European Economic Community
ELRL	English Land Restoration League
ELTLV	English League for Taxation of Land Values
Engl. Rev.	*English Review*
esp.	especially
et al.	*et alia/et alii* (Lat.): and others
ff.	pages following
fo.(s)	folio(s)
Fortn. Rev.	*Fortnightly Review*
Gaz.	*Gazette*
GRO	General Register Office
GSM	Guild of St Matthew
GUTW	General Union of Textile Workers
Hist. J.	*Historical Journal*
HL	House of Lords
HMG	His (Her) Majesty's Government
HMS	His (Her) Majesty's Ship
HMSO	His (Her) Majesty's Stationery Office
HO	Home Office
ibid.	*ibidem* (Lat.): in the same place
ICWPA	International Class War Prisoners' Aid
idem	(Lat.): the same; author as mentioned in previous entry
IISH	International Institute of Social History
ILEA	Inner London Educational Authority
ILP	Independent Labour Party
imp.	impression
Int. J. of Ethics	*International Journal of Ethics*
Int. Q.	*International Quarterly*
Int. Rev. Social Hist.	*International Review of Social History*
Int. Soc. Rev.	*International Socialist Review*
Int. Rev. Missions	*International Review of Missions*
IWMA	International Working Men's Association
J.	*Journal*
J. Cont. Hist.	*Journal of Contemporary History*
JP	Justice of the peace
Kelly	*Kelly's Handbook to the Titled, Landed and Official Classes*
Lab. Mon.	*Labour Monthly*

LCC	London County Council
LKG	The League of the Kingdom of God
LP	Labour Party
LRC	Labour Representation Committee
LRPU	Leeds Radical Political Union
LSE	London School of Economics
LTC	London Trades Council
Mag.	*Magazine*
MBE	Member of the British Empire
MFGB	Miners' Federation of Great Britain
M of E	*Minutes of Evidence*
MP	Member of Parliament
MRC	Modern Records Centre, Warwick Univ.
MS(S)	manuscript(s)
MVO	Member of the Victorian Order
n.	note
NAC	National Administrative Council
NATO	North Atlantic Treaty Organisation
Nat. Rev.	*National Review*
NCB	National Coal Board
NCF	No-Conscription Fellowship
n.d.	no date
NEC	National Executive Council
19th C.	*Nineteenth Century*
NLS	National Library of Scotland
no.(s)	number(s)
n.s.	new series
NSP	National Socialist Party
NUT	National Union of Teachers
NUWC	National Union of the Working Classes
NUWM	National Unemployed Workers' Movement
NUWSS	National Union of Women's Suffrage Societies
NY	New York (city or state)
OBE	Order of the British Empire
Obit.	Obituary/obituaries
PAC	Public Assistance Committee
P.	pamphlet (*see* Notes to Readers)
p.a.	per annum
PC	Privy Council(lor)
PL	Public Library
PLP	Parliamentary Labour Party
PMG	*Poor Man's Guardian*
PM Gaz.	*Pall Mall Gazette*
Pol. Q.	*Political Quarterly*
PRO	Public Record Office
pseud.	pseudonym
pt(s)	part(s)
Q(s)	question(s)

Q. Rev.	*Quarterly Review*
R. C.	Royal Commission
repr.	reprinted
rev.	revised
Rev.	*Review*
Revd/Rev.	Reverend
RIBA	Royal Institute of British Architects
RG	Registrar General
RILU	Red International of Labour Unions
RO	Record Office
RSDLP	Russian Social Democratic Labour Party
s	shilling(s)
SAC	Scottish Advisory Council
S. C.	Select Committee
SDF	Social Democratic Federation
SDP	Social Democratic Party
ser.	series
SOAS	School of Oriental and African Studies
Soc. Ann.	*Socialist Annual*
Soc. Rev.	*Socialist Review*
Spec.	*Spectator*
SSC	Society of Socialist Christians
STUC	Scottish Trades Union Congress
SWMF	South Wales Miners' Federation
SWTC	*Schoolmaster and Woman Teacher's Chronicle*
TCP	Twentieth Century Press
TLS	*Times Literary Supplement*
Trans.	*Transactions*
trans	translated/translator
TS	Treasury Solicitor
TUC	Trades Union Congress
UCTLV	United Committee for the Taxation of Land Values
U. D. C.	*Journal of the Union of Democratic Control*
UDC	Union of Democratic Control
U. F. Church Mag.	*United Free Church Magazine*
UNRRA	United Nations Relief and Rehabilitation Administration
Univ.	University
vol.(s)	volume(s)
WEA	Workers' Educational Association
WIL	Women's International League
WLL	Women's Labour League
WO	War Office
WSPU	Women's Social and Political Union
WWW	*Who Was Who*
YFT	*Yorkshire Factory Times*

List of Bibliographies and Special Notes

Bibliographies

The subject bibliographies attached to certain entries are the responsibility of the editors. The entries under which they will be found in Volumes I–VI are as follows:

Special Notes in Volume V

The Parliamentary Recruiting Committee and the Joint Labour Recruiting Committee in the First World War *see* **BOWERMAN, Charles William**

The 1917 Club *see* **HAMILTON, Mary Agnes**

The Mosely Industrial Commission *see* **STEADMAN, William (Will) Charles**

Special Notes in Volume VI

Woman's Industrial Independence (1848; reprinted) *see* **BARMBY, Catherine Isabella**

Boggart Hole Clough and Free Speech *see* **BROCKLEHURST, Frederick**

Ca'canny *see* **DAVIS, William John**

Special Note in Volume VII

The League Against Imperialism, 1927–1937 *see* **BRIDGEMAN, Reginald Francis Orlando**

The Gateshead Progressive Players, 1920–1980 *see* **DODDS, Ruth**

The Meerut Trial, 1929–1933 *see* **GOSSIP, Alexander (Alex)**

The Execution of Francisco Ferrer and the Labour Movement *see* **WARD, George Herbert Bridges**

Special Notes in Volume VIII

The Guild of St Matthew *see* **HANCOCK, Thomas**

The Church Socialist League *see* **MOLL, William Edmund**

The Twentieth Century Press *see* **QUELCH, Henry (Harry)**

The British Labour Delegation to Russia, 1920 *see* **TURNER, Sir Ben**

ALLSOP, Thomas (1795–1880)
RADICAL BUSINESSMAN

Allsop was born on 10 April 1795 at Stainsborough Hall, near Wirksworth, Derbyshire. His family were landowners but Allsop abandoned rural life when he was seventeen and went to London. There he entered the drapery business of an uncle and he seems to have flourished. He later acquired considerable skill on the Stock Exchange, of which he was a member, and generally prospered. He did particularly well during the early period of railway building. In 1818 he had become friendly with Samuel Taylor Coleridge, his friendship with whom lasted till Coleridge's death; and he also became well known in London literary circles, numbering Charles Lamb, William Hazlitt and 'Barry Cornwall' (Bryan W. Procter) among his friends. When Coleridge died, Allsop edited two volumes of *Letters, Conversations and Recollections of S. T. Coleridge*, published in 1836.

When Allsop began to adopt radical ideas is not clear from the few details of his early life that have survived. It would appear that he first became influenced by Robert Owen, and there exist in at least three archives a considerable collection of letters between Owen and Allsop and his wife, Anna. They begin in the early 1830s and continue until Owen's death in 1858. Allsop was a warm supporter of the Owenite Labour Exchanges, and among the most interesting section of the correspondence is that written during the year 1848, when Owen spent some time in Paris, interviewing a number of leading personalities on the Left.

Allsop was one of the few wealthy men in the British radical movement, and he seems to have been generous with financial help. He gave money for Owen's schemes, made bail available for many arrested Chartists, supported the Land Plan, and provided Feargus O'Connor with the title to freehold property worth £300 a year in order to allow him to qualify for Parliament. Ernest Jones was probably helped by him in the 1850s; certainly Allsop was recommending Jones to Owen for financial aid.

Allsop, benevolent though he was, must not be thought of simply as a wealthy man of goodwill. His Ultra-Radicalism was firm and steadfast and he remained faithful to radical causes to the end of his life. In 1838 there occurred a most interesting and unusual incident which illustrated very well Allsop's adherence to principle and his courage in taking a public stand on matters he felt deeply about. He was called to serve on the jury at the Central Criminal Court in London, and he objected, arguing that he could not under any circumstances find any person guilty. It was impossible for the poor to avoid crime given the circumstances of their social condition. It was Owenite principles applied to the practices of the law and the operation of the penal code. Allsop produced a written statement of his position but was not allowed by the Recorder to read it out in court; and it was published in full in the *Operative*, 9 December 1838, with a summary in the *New Moral World* on 15 December 1838. After arguing that the general environment encouraged crime with the Government making no provision for the rehabilitation of criminals, Allsop summed up:

With these convictions, with no sympathy for crime, or indifference to the security of property; but rather with a hatred of the one and a desire that the other may be efficiently protected, by measures adapted to the present state of society, instead of endangered by cruelties inflicted upon men who are made criminal by society itself, I do not consider myself justified in sending for punishment any prisoner arraigned at the bar.

In spite of his acceptance of much of Robert Owen's approach to social questions, Allsop would appear to have supported the Chartist movement and to have developed a considerable respect and affection for Feargus O'Connor. There is an important letter from Allsop to O'Connor, written on the eve of the Kennington Common meeting in 1848 (10 April), which illustrates Allsop's own radicalism as well as his attitude towards O'Connor.

The letter is quoted by J. G. Holyoake in his *DNB* entry for Allsop. It is not known whether the original is extant.

> Nothing rashly. The government must be met with calm and firm defiance. Violence may be overcome with violence, but a resolute determination not to submit cannot be overcome. To remain in front, *en face* of the government, to watch it, to take advantage of its blunders, is the part of an old general who will not be guided like a fish by its tail. Precipitate nothing, yield nothing. Aim not alone to destroy the government, but to render a class government impossible. No hesitation, no rash impulse, no egotism; but an earnest, serious, unyielding progress. Nothing for self, nothing even for fame, present or posthumous. All for the cause. Upon the elevation of your course for the moment will depend the estimation in which you will henceforth be held; and the position you may attain and retain will be second to none of the reformers who have gone before you.

There is another letter from this same year that has survived. Allsop wrote to Robert Owen on 3 May 1848 when the latter was in Paris, observing the development of the revolution. Allsop advised him to see Lamennais, Flocon, Ledru-Rollin, and Lamartine. Of the last named he wrote presciently, 'the aristocrats there, doomed as they are, cling to Lamartine and . . . if he harkens, he is lost'. He continued:

> I tell you *advisedly* that money is being used lavishly . . . to produce a reaction. . . . If Property-Capital ever gets its hook into the Public nose again the Revolution is lost for this generation. I believe that the only hope is in the utter, the *immediate* destruction *or* division of Capital as such & the making public property of real immovable wealth at an early period. Where one man is rich & another poor, the motto of the French Republic is a falsehood, a fraud – stark, staring nonsense, a self-contradiction [quoted Tsuzuki (1971) 26].

The most sensational episode of Allsop's life was connected with the unsuccessful attempt by Felice Orsini on the life of Louis Napoleon on 14 January 1858 in Paris when the Emperor and the Empress were driving down the Rue Lepelletier on the way to the opera. Three bombs were thrown, and although the two Sovereigns were unhurt, some twenty persons were injured, of whom six died. The incident caused serious differences between France and Britain. Although Orsini was an Italian, and the conspiracy essentially related to Italian politics, the bombs had been manufactured in England. Orsini had gone there on release from his imprisonment by the Austrians, and had made contact with British radicals, including G. J. Holyoake and Allsop; and it was the latter who arranged for the bombs to be made in Birmingham. There is no doubt about Allsop's involvement. There are unpublished letters between Holyoake and Allsop [McCabe, vol. *1* (1908) 247–56], and there are further references to Allsop in the Orsini letters published after the latter's death [*Letters*, vol. *2* (1861) 191–214 *passim*]. Orsini travelled on the Continent using Allsop's passport. A later anonymous French work, *La Vérité sur Orsini*, which Joseph McCabe quoted [vol. *1* (1908) 254], suggested that Orsini had seen some bombs in a Belgian museum, persuaded a carpenter to make a model of them, and gave them to Allsop, who in turn ordered five to be manufactured by a man called Taylor, in Birmingham. They were delivered to Allsop at the beginning of November, and taken by Orsini to Brussels. Allsop's part in the conspiracy was discovered by the British police when inquiries began after the Rue Lepelletier attempt, and Allsop left Britain in February 1858 for Mexico. The British Government offered the sum of £200 for his apprehension, but political pressure on the Home Office led to charges being withdrawn, and Allsop returned to Britain in September of the same year – wholly unrepentant.

The Orsini affair aroused considerable passion among British radicals. W. E. Adams wrote a famous eight-page pamphlet justifying the attack on the French Emperor:

Tyrannicide: is it justifiable?, published by Edward Truelove. The Government decided to prosecute, and a defence committee was established which included Joseph Cowen and John Stuart Mill [Adams (1903) 353 ff., and Introduction to 1968 ed., 14]. The prosecution was, however, withdrawn, but another conspirator, Dr Simon Bernard, was brought to trial in England, and acquitted: a considerable triumph for the radical cause [ibid., 325–6]. The affair also had reverberations at a national level. In response to French pressure, Palmerston introduced a Bill to amend the law of conspiracy, and on the second reading the Bill was defeated and the Government resigned. The episode is discussed in Paul [vol. *2* (1904) 143 ff.] and in all standard histories.

Allsop was a secularist and anti-clerical. The Orsini case brought him into contact with Charles Bradlaugh, and they remained friends for the remainder of their lives until Allsop's death. He supported Bradlaugh in the Northampton elections of 1868 and 1874, and again in 1880, although by this time he was very old and very frail. Allsop seems to have been in personal contact with most of the radicals of his day, and he supported, morally and financially, most of the radical causes of the time. In July 1871, when the General Council of the IWMA established a sub-committee to issue appeals and collect money for Communard refugees, Allsop became a member, along with the Positivists Edward Beesly and Frederic Harrison, and with both Marx and Engels. Allsop was a personal friend of the Marx family and of Engels, and there are a number of references to him in their correspondence.

Allsop became very deaf in later life; and it was a great affliction. He died on 12 April 1880 and his body was taken from Exmouth to Woking in Surrey, where he was buried on 17 April in unconsecrated ground. G. J. Holyoake pronounced the funeral address. Allsop's wife had died three years earlier. There were at least four children of the marriage: the eldest son, Robert, became a stockbroker; two other sons emigrated to the United States and, according to the obituary in the *Daily News* (copied in *Freeman's Exmouth Journal*), lived in Colorado; and a daughter married a Spanish diplomat who became Governor of the Philippines.

Thomas Allsop was an unusual man in many ways, and it is likely that there are parts of his private and political life that remain to be written. This interim biographical entry may provide encouragement for further research.

Writings: (ed.) *Letters, Conversations and Recollections of S. T. Coleridge*, 2 vols (1836; repr. 1858 and 1864); *California and its Gold Mines: being a series of recent communications upon the present condition and future prospects of quartz mining* (1853).

Sources: (1) MS: Allsop–Owen correspondence: John Burns Coll., BL, and Owen Coll., Co-operative Union, Manchester. Allsop–Engels correspondence: IISH, Amsterdam. (2) Other: *Operative*, 2 and 9 Dec 1838; *New Moral World*, 15 Dec 1838; K. Marx and F. Engels, *Collected Works*, vol. *38: 1844–51* (1982); *Times*, 25 Jan 1858; *Hansard*, 19 Feb 1858; K. Marx and F. Engels, *Werke*, bds *29, 30, 33, 34, 35* [for correspondence in the years 1858, 1862, 1871, 1877 and 1881 and see also index to bds *29* and *30*] (Berlin, 1966–79); C. A. Dandrant, *Procès Orsini, contenant les debats judiciaires devant la Cour d'assises de la Seine, la Cour de cassation etc.* (1858); *Lettere edite ed inedite di Felice Orsini, Garibaldi, E. Mazzini*, vol. *2* (Milan, 1861); *Vita e memorie de Felice Orsini, precudute dalla storia dell' attentato del 14 gennaio 1858 e seguite dagli interrogatori e documenti del processo*, Edizione nuovissima (*Firenze*, 2 vols 1863–4); Anon., *La Vérité sur Orsini. Le secret de l' affaire par un Ancien Proscrit* 4 pts (Paris, [1878–80?]); A. S. Headingley, *The Biography of Charles Bradlaugh* (1880; later eds); J. McCarthy, *A History of our own Times*, vol. *3* (1880); G. J. Holyoake, *Life of J. R. Stephens* (1881); *DNB 1* (1885) [by G. J. Holyoake]; H. B. Bonner, *Charles Bradlaugh: a record of his life and work* ..., 2 vols (1894; 7th ed. in 1 vol. 1908);

Letters of Samuel Taylor Coleridge, 2 vols, ed. E. H. Coleridge (1895); W. E. Adams, *Memoirs of a Social Atom*, 2 vols (1903; repr. in 1 vol. with an Introduction by J. Saville, NY, 1968); G. J. Holyoake, 'Unpublished Correspondence of the Robert Owen Family', *Co-op. News*, 11 June 1904, 705–6; H. Paul, *A History of Modern England*, vol. *2* (1904); G. J. Holyoake, *Sixty Years of an Agitator's Life* (1906); F. Podmore, *Robert Owen*, 2 vols (1906; repr. in one vol., NY, 1968); J. McCabe, *Life and Letters of George Jacob Holyoake*, 2 vols (1908); *Unpublished Letters of Samuel Taylor Coleridge*, vol. *2*, ed. E. L. Griggs (1932); D. Read and E. Glasgow, *Feargus O'Connor* (1961); *Dictionnaire biographique du Mouvement Ouvrier Français*, vols *1* and *3*, ed. J. Maitron (Paris, 1964 and 1966) [for Allsop, Bernard and Orsini]; *Minutes of the General Council of the First International 1871–72* [1964?]; *Boase 1* (1965); *The Harney Papers*, ed. F. G. and R. Black (Assen, 1969) [very brief references to Allsop in three of Harney's letters]; D. Tribe, *President Charles Bradlaugh M. P.* (1971); C. Tsuzuki, 'Robert Owen and Revolutionary Politics', in *Robert Owen: prophet of the poor*, ed. S. Pollard and J. Salt (1971) 13–38; Y. Kapp, *Eleanor Marx*, vol. *1: Family Life (1855–1883)* (1972); *The Daughters of Karl Marx: family correspondence 1866–1898*, trans. F. Evans with an Introduction by S. Rowbotham (1982); D. Thompson, *The Chartists* (1984). Obit. *Daily News*, 14 Apr 1880, repr. in *Freeman's Exmouth J.*, 17 Apr 1880; 'Rough Notes', *National Reformer*, 18 Apr 1880, 251.

JOHN SAVILLE

See also: †Charles BRADLAUGH; †George Jacob HOLYOAKE; †Robert OWEN.

BARNES, Leonard John (1895–1977)
SOCIALIST AND ANTI-IMPERIALIST

Leonard Barnes was the only son of John Albert Barnes, a senior civil servant, and his wife Kate (née Oakeshott). He was born in London on 21 July 1895, and went first to Colet Court Preparatory School and then as a scholar to St Paul's. He won an Open Scholarship to University College, Oxford, but the First World War intervened and he entered the Army, serving in the King's Royal Rifle Corps and ending up with the rank of Captain. He was three times wounded, and was awarded the Military Cross with bar. After a year in hospital he entered his Oxford college in 1919 and read Greats, gaining a first in the final examination. He then sat the Higher Civil Service Examination, in which he came out top of the list, but chose to enter the Colonial Office, as his father had done before him.

The war, inevitably, had a profound effect upon his personality. He wrote in his unpublished autobiography,

> By September 1918 my total was twenty four months on the front line, unusually long for a company officer in the infantry. Marks imprinted on the character by front-line service of this duration are ground so deeply as to become ineradicable, never to be overlaid by any later experiences whatsoever [McAdam (1977) 42].

The war also gave him an 'immunity from the great human delinquency of lust for amassed wealth, and thus was guarantee given, whatever might in the end destroy my character, it would not be cupidity or luxury' [ibid.]. He was about to experience the second important influence in his life. He entered the Colonial Office in the autumn of 1921 when Winston Churchill was Colonial Secretary and his early duties ranged from Ceylon to the East African department to the West Indies. In the course of his work he met T. E. Lawrence, Gertrude Bell and Lionel Curtis; and during the 1923 Imperial Conference he was given the job of acting as liaison officer to the South African delegation, and specifically to General Smuts.

Barnes provided a remarkable description of the Colonial Office in the early 1920s in the first volume of his unpublished autobiography. His disillusionment with its practices came fairly slowly: it was partly his growing realisation of the character of the war he had just fought in, partly his widening political and social horizons – he had among other things begun attending Hugh Dalton's lectures at the LSE; but, above all, it was the personal influence of Norman Leys, who began to inject moral doubts into Barnes's thinking about the nature and meaning of colonial rule.

Barnes resigned from the Colonial Office early in 1925 and went cotton farming with Eric Gibb in Zululand. Gibb was a friend from the war years, and his farm of 2000 acres was part of the South African Government's settlement scheme for ex-servicemen. Barnes could not yet be described as an anti-imperialist, and it was only quite slowly that his understanding of the character of white rule in South Africa began to be critical. It was discovering the land he was jointly farming had formerly been part of a scheduled black reserve that precipitated him into abandoning his partnership with Gibb and going into journalism and political opposition. Until he left South Africa in 1932 he had a range of jobs on various newspapers and journals, including the *Natal Witness*, the *Cape Times* and the Johannesburg *Star*; and these inevitably brought him into contact with the many different parts of South African society. He found ways of keeping in touch with black Africans, and he became close to the radicals and Socialists of the Opposition. With Margaret Hodgson and William Ballinger (they later married) Barnes investigated conditions in the protectorates of Bechuanaland, Basutoland and Swaziland, and Ballinger, through Winifred Holtby, tried to interest the members of the 1929–31 minority Labour Government in their ideas. Barnes had been commissioned to write a series of articles on the protectorates for the Johannesburg *Star* and later provided an account of his findings in *The New Boer War*, which the Hogarth Press published in England in 1932. Officials in the Dominion Office were evidently impressed by his book [Gupta (1975) 140, n. 37]. Before this Barnes had published what has become an important text of colonialism: *Caliban in Africa*. The book not only provided a brilliantly perceptive view of the Afrikaner's attitude to society, but at this early date Barnes was quite clear that, on all the crucial questions of class and colour, the English-speaking whites were at one with those who spoke Afrikaans. It was an unusual position to adopt for those days, and has been abundantly justified in the decades which followed. He wrote in his Preface (the book was published in 1930):

> My Afrikaner is simply a personification of the general will of white South Africans as a class towards natives as a class. . . .
>
> For the modes of Afrikaner thought upon such matters [the colour question] I have no admiration. But I am not in the least concerned to apportion between Briton and Boer the blame for what appear to me its abysmal failures. Such divergences of view as exist among the white people of South Africa do not seem to be either localised or racialised. In the Cape a ghostly tradition of liberalism still flits *per ora vivum*; but it is less and less honoured in practical observance. In the Transvaal, the Orange Free State, and Natal the intensity of anti-native sentiment is about equal. The predominantly British parts of the country today are not more reasonable than the predominantly Dutch.

Barnes prophesied a future that was irreversibly catastrophic; and, while his time-scale will have to be lengthened and historical complexities have become more difficult to unravel, his basic conclusions are not likely to be falsified:

> If the country holds to its present course, violent strife is, one would judge, at most a couple of decades off, probably less. But the solidity and compound mass of its colour-

prejudice are so huge that, even if a changed intention suddenly flashed into the Afrikaner mind, it could not transmit itself to the unwieldly weight in time to avert collision. Apparently South Africa must now proceed straight to disaster by mere force of inertia [Barnes (1930) 241–2].

Barnes returned to England towards the end of 1932, and immediately made himself available to the Labour Party. The Party had established an Advisory Committee on Imperial Questions in the 1920s, with Charles Roden Buxton as chairman and Leonard Woolf as secretary [Gupta (1975) 225 ff.]. Creech Jones, who became Secretary of State for the Colonies between 1946 and 1950, was a member. In the 1930s the Committee was joined by four voluntary exiles from South Africa – Barnes, W. M. MacMillan, Julius Lewin and Frederick Noble. Norman Leys and MacGregor Ross were already members; and the African group became an important influence upon Labour Party thinking.

Barnes' own political opinions were moving to the left in the years of Fascism and appeasement. In the 1935 general election he stood unsuccessfully as Labour candidate against J. H. Thomas at Derby. During the campaign he was reported in the local paper as saying that:

it was quite wrong to talk of a National Government in the real sense. The only thing that could be said about it was that it united practically all the anti-Socialist elements in the community. It was a coalition of those people who believed in profit and privilege rather than the welfare of the wage-earners. The capitalist system had had its historic importance, but it was decaying and ought to be abolished and a Socialist system set up in its place [*Derbyshire Advertiser*, 8 Nov 1935].

During the years after he returned to Britain, Barnes published a number of influential books. The British labour movement was much less aware in general of African problems than Indian, and Barnes' writings were among those which contributed towards a more balanced appreciation of the problems of Empire. He produced *The Duty of Empire* in 1935; *The Future of Colonies* in 1936; and the widely circulated Left Book Club *Empire or Democracy* in 1939. Towards the end of the war he published, as a Penguin Special, *Soviet Light on the Colonies*: a work of considerable imagination. It reflected, for instance, the widespread optimism on the Left in the matter of the Russian attitude in theory and practice to its former subject territories, although it was not a position which Barnes subscribed to in later years. But the book was an ingenious approach to the colonial problems of Africa, and this, it must be emphasised, was its main purpose.

In 1935 Barnes was appointed Lecturer in Education at the University of Liverpool. His head of department was Professor E. T. Campagnac, who retired in 1938. 'There were many', wrote Professor G. H. Rawcliffe, in an obituary notice (1977) 'who thought Leonard Barnes should have succeeded Campagnac [in 1938], but his political views were not everywhere palatable.' Barnes also became a successful Warden of Rankin Hall, a men's hall of residence.

His contact with the national Labour Party was now somewhat reduced, but he remained on the Advisory Committee, and he was present at the important meeting between Jawaharlal Nehru and leading Labour politicians in June 1938 when there was reached an agreement by which power would be transferred to India when Labour came to office. Those present included Attlee, Aneurin Bevan, Cripps and Harold Laski, and, without revealing its source, Barnes included the main terms of the agreement in his *Empire or Democracy* – they were also reproduced in the journal *Empire* in March 1939 [Gupta (1975) 258, n. 164]. Barnes, with Norman Leys, Frank Horrabin and Julius Lewin, had started the monthly *Empire* in June 1938 (he was in effect its editor), and it was handed over to the Fabian Colonial Bureau in March 1941. The reason for this, Julius Lewin explained much later, was that Herbert Morrison warned Barnes – through Creech Jones – 'that if *Empire* continued to expose so frankly the shortcomings of imperial rule, it would be banned' [*Third World*, May–June 1975, 16].

When the Second World War ended, Barnes resigned from Liverpool University, and two years later, in 1948, he was appointed secretary and director of the Delegacy for Social Training at Barnett House, University of Oxford. Before his appointment at Oxford he undertook two field studies for King George's Jubilee Trust: the first was published under the title *Youth Service in an English County* (1945) and the second as *The Outlook for Youth Work* (1948). He also visited Malaya as a member of the Carr-Saunders Commission on the founding of a university for that country (the Commission's report was published in 1947); and he went again to Malaya in 1950 as chairman of a committee of inquiry into the primary education of the Malay community.

The main work of the last stage of his public career was at Barnett House. His task there was not an easy one, for there was considerable doubt at the time within the University as to its standing as an academic department. Barnes set himself the aim of raising academic standards, and by the end of the 1950s the Delegacy had become a full department and was then renamed the Department of Social and Administrative Studies. Barnes remained director. He was especially interested in psychology and sociology, at a time when the latter subject was little studied in British universities. He retired at the age limit in 1962 and was succeeded by A. H. Halsey.

In 1964 Barnes was asked by the head of the United Nations Economic Commission for Africa to undertake four studies on the social and economic progress of the independent black African states. Barnes visited thirty-two African countries between 1964 and 1969 and produced four reports for the Commission. They were not for general publication but many of his findings were published in two books: *African Renaissance* (1969) and *Africa in Eclipse* (1971). In 1973 he further visited Zambia, at President Kaunda's invitation, and in a private capacity Botswana and Kenya.

Barnes was a radical scholar to the end of his days, and his influence, especially in the formative years of the 1930s, was wide-ranging and substantial. His *Caliban in Africa* was only slowly appreciated, but it was a work of major significance, and his activity within the Labour Party was a reflection of his grasp of the practical politics of his day. Barnes had great charm – 'one of the best-looking men I have ever known' (Laurens van der Post); and he was highly articulate. He was married twice: first in 1928 to Beatrice Davis, the daughter of Peter Davis of Pietermaritzburg, Natal, who died in 1943 and then, in 1943, to Margaret Blackburn, daughter of J. D. Blackburn, of Kendal. There were no children of either marriage.

Barnes wrote one novel, *Zulu Paraclete*, published in 1935, and two volumes of poetry. After his retirement from Barnett House he produced three volumes of autobiography, 'Radical Destination', which unfortunately remain unpublished. Anthony McAdam put them together into one volume with the title 'Let them scratch' and they are on microfilm in the library of the School of Oriental and African Studies.

In his last years he became increasingly concerned with the problem of human aberration in industrial society, and above all with the overriding question of human survival in a nuclear age. His later writings on non-African themes were often profoundly pessimistic, but always expressed with powerful logic and his deeply felt humanism. He died at Oxford on 10 March 1977, his wife surviving him. He left an estate valued at £9036.

Writings: *Caliban in Africa: an impression of colour-madness* (1930); *The New Boer War* (1932); *Youth at Arms* (poems) [war experiences 1914–18] (1933); 'Art and the Collective Life', *Virginia Q. Rev. 9*, no. 2 (Apr 1933) 195–207; 'A Soldier on War and Peace', *Engl. Rev. 56* (May 1933) 535–43; 'The Negro in the British Empire', *Virginia Q. Rev. 10*, no. 1 (Jan

1934) 78–93; *The Duty of Empire* (1935); *Zulu Paraclete: a sentimental record* [a narrative of farming life in South Africa] (1935); 'Socialism and Colonial Policy', in *New Trends in Socialism*, ed. G. E. G. Catlin [1935] 229–44; (with others), *Peace and the Colonial Problem* (National Peace Committee, 1935) 52 pp.; *The Future of Colonies* (Day to Day Pamphlet no. 32: 1936) 46 pp.; *Skeleton of the Empire* (Fact, no. 3: 1937); 'The Future of Imperialism', Ch. xi in *The League and the Future of the Collective System* (Geneva Institute of International Relations, 1937) 180–97; 'The Colonial Service', in *The British Civil Servant*, ed. W. A. Robson (1937) 231–50; 'The Empire as Sacred Trust: the problem of Africa', *Pol. Q. 9*, no. 4 (Oct–Dec 1938) 503–15; *Empire or Democracy?: a study of the colonial question* (Left Book Club, 1939); 'The Uprising of Indian and Colonial Peoples', in *Where stands Democracy?*, ed. H. Laski (1940) 63–84; 'Honesty about the Colour Bar' [review], *Lab. Mon. 23* (Nov 1941) 467–8; 'Debate on Africa' [review], ibid. *26*, no. 9 (Sep 1944) 285–6; *Soviet Light on the Colonies* (Penguin Special no. 131: 1944; repr. 1945); 'A Policy for Colonial Peoples', in *What Labour could do?*, ed. C. Latham (Fabian Society, 1945) 64–81; *Youth Service in an English County* (King George's Jubilee Trust, 1945); 'Trusteeship and the Colonial Question', *Lab. Mon. 29* (Jan 1947) 18–22; *The Outlook for Youth Work* (King George's Jubilee Trust, 1948); 'Freedom as a Social Quality', *Rationalist Annual* (1948) 31–8; 'The Texture of Social Welfare' [review], *Social Service 26*, no. 3 (Dec 1952–Feb 1953) 102–5; 'East Africa' [review], *Lab. Mon. 36* (Sep 1955) 430; 'Adult Education: ends or means?', *Listener*, 31 Jan 1957, 178–9; 'The Meaning of Social Health', *Modern Churchman* n.s. *5*, no. 1 (Oct 1961) 13–22; *The Homecoming* [poem] (1961); 'Authority in Oxford', *Oxford Mag.*, 25 Oct 1962, 20–1; *Répertoire des activités de protection sociale en Afrique . . .*, no. 1 (United Nations, NY, 1964); *African Renaissance* (1969; 2nd ed. 1971); *Africa in Eclipse* (1971); 'A Report to Dr K. Kaunda, Zambia 1973: comment and appraisal' [typescript report presented to Dr Kaunda at his request, 1973] 57 pp. [copy in Barnes papers, SOAS]; 'Radical Destination' [a three-volume autobiography, abridged 1976, is on microfilm at SOAS; Anthony McAdam edited this to one volume, the typescript of which is at SOAS under the title of 'Let them scratch']; *The Glory of the World* [Sonnets] (posthumous publication in Rotterdam, 1979).

Sources: The principal sources for a study of the career and philosophy of Leonard Barnes are his own writings and the work of Dr Anthony McAdam, whose article 'Leonard Barnes and South Africa', published in *Social Dynamics 3*, no. 2 (1977) 41–53, provides biographical material. The editors also wish to acknowledge the assistance given by Mrs Peggy Barnes, the late Professor Julius Lewin and the library staff at SOAS, London, where the Barnes papers are located. The papers include copies of Barnes' published and unpublished works, notebooks on his African visits and personal correspondence. They also include the correspondence and diaries of Barnes' friend Dr L. M. Jackson when the two men toured Nigeria, the Congo, Greece and Sicily together. Other sources include: *Derby Evening Telegraph*, 4–14 Nov 1935, especially the issue of 6 Nov, which has an article entitled ' "Sinister Figure of Hitler" watching Mussolini Move; Mr L. J. Barnes repeats War Warning; "Ostrich-like" Attitude of Mr Thomas'; *Derbyshire Advertiser*, 8 Nov 1935; Sir Cosmo Parkinson, *The Colonial Office from Within 1909–45* (1947); *Report of the Commission on University Education in Malaya* (1948); *Report of the Committee on Malay Education* (Kuala Lumpur, 1951); W. C. F. Plomer, *Turbott Wolfe*, with an Introduction by Laurens van der Post (1965); M. Wolfers, *Black Man's Burden revisited* (1974); P. S. Gupta, *Imperialism and the British Labour Movement, 1914–1964* (1975); J. Lewin, 'Starting Empire', *Third World*, May–June 1975, 15–16; idem, 'Leonard Barnes, the Man and his Books' [review article], *African Affairs 74*, no. 297 (Oct 1975) 483–4; C. J. Sansom, 'The British Labour Movement and Southern Africa 1918–1955: labourism and the imperial tradition' (Birmingham PhD, 1982). Personal information: A. Atmore, Tiptree, Essex; Mrs

P. Barnes, Great Haseley, Oxford, widow; the late Professor J. Lewin; Dr A. McAdam, Chelsea, Victoria, Australia; and B. Willan, London. OBIT. *Times*, 14 and 18 Mar 1977; *Oxford Times*, 19 Mar 1977; *Lab. Mon. 59* (May 1977); *University of Liverpool Recorder*, no. 75 (Oct 1977) 13–14.

JOHN SAVILLE

See also: *Arthur Creech JONES; Norman Maclean LEYS.

BARR, James (1862–1949)
LABOUR MP

James Barr was born on 26 July 1862 at Beanscroft, Fenwick, Ayrshire, on a farm that had been in the hands of his family since 1778. He was the eldest child of Allan Barr and his wife, Elizabeth (née Brown). Fenwick, he told the House of Commons in 1926, was 'the most celebrated Covenanting parish in Scotland', where he 'was nursed in the Covenanter's spirit' [*Hansard 200*, col. 1588]. Throughout a long public career, Barr regarded his religious faith as the guide in all he undertook. Although he was later described as 'a tall brawny man, a farmer to all appearance' [Johnston (1952) 240] Barr did not follow his father's occupation (though he did have an abiding interest in the land question). Instead he distinguished himself educationally and trained for the ministry. At the age of eight he became a pupil at Waterside Elementary School and there remained until February 1877, when he entered Kilmarnock Academy. At Kilmarnock he won the gold-medal prize in mathematics and was dux of the school. He went on to Glasgow University, where he again excelled, winning the Gartmore Gold Medal for an essay on political economy and prizes in all seven of the subjects that made up the arts course. In 1884 he graduated with first-class honours in mental philosophy. His efforts, however, affected his health and on medical advice he broke with study for eighteen months and took a trip to the United States and Canada to recuperate.

On returning to Scotland he was awarded a scholarship at the Free Church College, Glasgow. In 1889 he was ordained on taking up his first ministerial charge at the Johnstone and Wamphray Free Church and later received his Bachelor of Divinity degree. In 1896 he became minister of Dennistoun Free Church (afterwards the Rutherford United Free Church), Glasgow. From 1907 to 1920 he was minister of St Mary's United Free Church, Govan. In Church circles he was soon noted for his eloquent and scholarly preaching and for his fervent opposition to the liquor traffic. Barr also became known for his pacifist views. 'This pulpit', he told his congregation in 1901, 'stands against all war.' On this occasion he was speaking against the war in South Africa, which he blamed on a conspiracy of capitalists. He published his views in a penny pamphlet, *Wild War's Deadly Blast* (a phrase from Burns, Barr's favourite poet). Two years later, in a series of lectures which appeared under the title *Christianity and War*, he developed his arguments in greater detail. Again he expressed sympathy for the Boers, a people he regarded as exemplars of Protestant virtues.

In 1903 he was elected to the Glasgow School Board as one of four candidates endorsed by the United Free Church. After three years, however, it was decided that the Church would not formally support candidates and Barr stood as an Independent. He was returned at the top of the poll and remained a member of the Board until 1914. His election address of March 1906 indicates some of his attitudes at that time; his remarks included the following:

I have always stood for well-equipped schools and well-paid teachers. A Voluntary of the

Voluntaries, I have ever defended *on educational grounds*, the teaching of the Bible in Public Schools. I have always been in favour of the teaching of Scientific Temperance in our schools, and I have taken a prominent part in providing each teacher under the Board with suitable text books on the subject. Warmly approving, as I do, of the present physical exercises, I am opposed to all military drill in Public Schools and I am keenly averse to the compulsory proposals of Lord Roberts [Barr (1949) 283].

Three years later his address to the electors ended with an appeal in language that was characteristic of the fervour he brought to public life:

My watchword is – Forward Yet! Let us concur with heart and hand in ever bettering, ever uplifting, the masses of the people, in building the old wastes and repairing the waste cities, the desolations of many generations, till the child's sob in the silence shall give place to the peal of merry laughter, and happy, tended boys and girls shall play in the streets of our new Jerusalem.

> *'I will not cease from mental fight*
> *Nor shall my sword sleep in my hand*
> *Till we have built Jerusalem,*
> *In Scotland's green and pleasant land'*

[ibid., 284]

He often quoted Blake's lines, adapted to fit the purpose of Scottish nationalism, in election and other addresses.

In these years Barr was known as a radical Liberal and he spoke from the platform at Liberal rallies during the general elections of 1910. At the same time he worked with ILP members of the School Board. For example, he seconded W. M. Haddow's motion that school meals should be provided for necessitous children, a proposal that aroused keen opposition. In December 1910 he moved a resolution that pupils be provided with free school books. His position on the School Board also enabled him to press for a chair of Scottish literature and history at Glasgow University and to deplore the 'landed monopoly' that made for costly school sites and rents.

Barr's reputation as a radical led the boilermakers of Govan to approach him during a lock-out of 1910 and ask that he put their case. He and a fellow clergyman, A. J. Forson, addressed a public meeting at the City Hall. Barr called upon the shipbuilding employers to take a more enlightened attitude towards their workers, quoting the adage 'if you would make men trustworthy, trust them; if you would make men true, believe them' [ibid., 288]. In June 1913 Barr and Forson had life membership of the Boilermakers' Society conferred on them in recognition of their efforts.

Within a few years Barr moved from radical Liberalism to membership of the Labour Party. He opposed the declaration of war in August 1914 and joined other Liberals and Socialists with similar views in the Union of Democratic Control. The war, he wrote, in the September 1914 issue of St Mary's Church magazine, was the result of the system of alliances and the race of armaments that had divided the European nations into two hostile camps. He believed that the 'headlong rush into war' might have been checked had there been 'more public diplomacy and fuller Parliamentary discussion' [Barr (1914) 2]. He countered the argument that the war would end German militarism by pointing to Britain's alliance with the 'Russian Autocracy ... the most illiberal, oppressive, and reactionary in Europe' [ibid., 3]. Barr spoke at a number of meetings organised by the UDC and in the autumn of 1916 delivered two speeches in support of the Revd Humphrey Chalmers, a Christian pacifist and the Independent, 'peace by negotiation' candidate at the North

Ayrshire by-election. When some Church elders in Glasgow were critical of his action, Barr met them full on in a masterly statement before the Presbytery in November 1916 (which he later reprinted in *Lang Syne*, pp. 57–66). He summarised his speech to the electors and went on to maintain his right to express his views freely, a position that was accepted by the Presbytery. Also in 1916, he published a pamphlet, *The Conscientious Objector*, which examined the case of those individuals who had refused to fight and the obligation of the State to tolerate such an exercise of conscience.

In February 1915 Barr was appointed a member of the Royal Commission on the Housing of the Industrial Population of Scotland, to replace W. F. Anderson, who had died. The Commission had sat since 1912 and reported in 1917. By drawing attention to the wretched housing conditions in many Scottish towns the report helped to pave the way for the Housing, Town Planning (Scotland) Act of 1919, which brought a limited improvement in standards. The experience strengthened Barr's concern with questions of housing and increased his knowledge of a subject in which he was to specialise on entering the Commons.

As well as an advocate of housing reform, Barr was a prominent figure in campaigns to control the liquor trade. In 1916 he was appointed as convenor of the temperance committee of the United Free Church and toured Scotland during 1920 to urge total prohibition of the drink traffic. His efforts in this area were, however, largely unsuccessful; those of his own religious persuasion were impressed by his eloquence, but most Scots rejected or ignored the call for total abstinence. In 1920 he left St Mary's to become Home Mission Secretary of the United Free Church of Scotland, a position he held until 1925.

Meanwhile Barr had become active in the ILP, which he joined in 1920. He was adopted as candidate for Motherwell and was elected to the House of Commons at the general election of 1924 with a majority of 1040 in a straight fight with a Conservative. His election address included a call for the public ownership of mines, railways and 'the principal means of production, distribution and exchange' as well as the need 'to restore the land to the people, and the people to the land'. Declaring his pacifist principles, he emphasised his wish to improve the working of the League of Nations and to see better relations with Russia and Germany. He favoured home rule for Scotland, improved housing and education and the curbing of the liquor traffic. Some of the phrases quoted above from his school board address of 1909 were repeated, and he concluded with lines from Blake's 'Jerusalem'.

On biblical grounds, and as an expression of religious liberty, he affirmed, instead of taking, the oath at the beginning of parliamentary sessions. His parliamentary speeches, other than when concerned with day-to-day constituency problems, were usually expressions of his support for moral and social reform. He urged that more be done to improve housing, with special schemes for the most badly affected areas; he spoke of the need to encourage small farmers at the expense of large landowners; and he called for better standards in education. Recognising the obstacles in the way of complete prohibition, he favoured the control of alcohol through strict regulation and use of the local option. He also spoke against the importation of liquor into the colonies where he believed the traffic was doing great harm. His other main concern was the peaceful settlement of international disputes.

On 10 February 1925 Barr made his maiden speech, which lasted for seventy minutes and filled eighteen columns of *Hansard*. His purpose was to oppose the Church of Scotland (Property and Endowments) Bill, which aimed to facilitate the reunion of the Scottish Church. When union took place in 1929 he was among a minority of United Free Church members who continued as a separate body. In 1929 he was the first Moderator of this reformed United Free Church, a position he held again in 1943, five years after he had been appointed Senior Principal Clerk of the Church's Assembly. He was unbending in his conviction that the Church should be independent of the State.

In 1927 Barr introduced a Bill to provide for Scottish home rule which would have involved 'Dominion status and the withdrawal of Scottish MPs from Westminster' [Keating and Bleiman (1979) 102]. Many Scottish Labour MPs were sympathetic to their country having greater control over its affairs but they were not prepared to allow Westminster to pass legislation affecting the whole of the United Kingdom in the absence of Scottish representatives. The Bill was talked out at second-reading stage. At Westminster Barr was listened to with respect, though his style of speaking was probably more suited to the pulpit and the platform. Powerfully built, and always dressed in clerical garb, he was an impressive figure at public meetings. Tom Johnston noted that his speeches were sometimes considered 'too meticulously exact and precise' with over-use of elaborate quotation, but nevertheless he was a speaker who 'possessed the spiritual power and passion to rouse audiences' [Johnston (1952) 241]. He had a powerful memory for political data as well as biblical texts and poetry, especially that of Burns. He was proficient in shorthand, which he regarded as an invaluable aid in speaking and in study.

Barr was easily re-elected at the general election of 1929, receiving more votes than the Conservative, Liberal and Communist candidates put together. His platform was similar to that of 1924, although his election address included sections critical of the Conservative's record and of the methods of the CPGB. He concluded by saying, 'we are now on the verge of the Promised Land . . . let Motherwell march well in the front of the triumphal procession to Westminster'. Back in the Commons, much of his time was taken up as chairman of the Select Committee on Capital Punishment. Barr was an opponent of the death penalty, and when the Committee reported its chief recommendation was that there should be a five-year experimental period during which the penalty should be abolished. There was some support for this proposal, but not as much as he had hoped, and the Labour administration failed to arrange a debate on the Committee's report. Barr probably underestimated the strength of opinion in favour of capital punishment, as he did in a lecture given on 12 November 1936 when he remarked, 'the report still holds the field, and I venture to predict that a decade will not pass until the Committee's recommendation becomes the law of the land' [Barr [1936?] 3].

In 1931 he was chairman of the Consultative Committee of the PLP and officiated at the critical meeting of 24 August, the day MacDonald announced his intention of forming a National Government. Barr remained with the Labour Party and was one of the many MPs to be defeated at the general election of October 1931; Thomas Ormiston, the Conservative candidate, received 15,515 votes against Barr's 14,714. He contested the by-election at Kilmarnock in November 1933, but obtained 2653 votes fewer than K. Lindsay, the National Labour candidate.

Out of Parliament, Barr devoted more time to religious matters, publishing *The United Free Church of Scotland* in 1934 and taking up the post of minister of Shieldhall and Drumoyne Church in the same year. In 1932 the *Forward* publishing company of Glasgow issued Barr's pamphlet *The Church and War*, in which he made a historical survey of militarism and its opponents. Having criticised modern instances of the spirit of militarism, such as could be found in the official handbook of the Boy Scouts, he appealed for the establishment of a more Christian social order, 'based not on self-interest but on service, not on aggrandisement but on ministry, not on the will to power, but on the will to betterment' [p. 48].

At the general election of 1935 Barr was returned as MP for Coatbridge, with a majority of 4414 in a straight fight with T. D. K. Murray (Conservative). He again voiced his old causes, including that of Scottish nationalism. In 1937 he became chairman of the London Scots Self-Government Committee, which Tom Johnston had taken the leading part in establishing. Its members saw home rule as a means of bringing about major social change, but with the outbreak of war and Johnston's appointment as Secretary of State for Scotland in February 1941 it ceased to function. Other issues on which Barr spoke included the abolition of the death penalty and the need to prevent blood sports. He also stuck fast to his pacifism. One of the thirty-six sponsors of the Peace Pledge Union, he was associated with those Labour MPs, including Lansbury, Messer, Salter, Sorenson and George Hardie, who came together as the Parliamentary Pacifist Group in 1936.

His principles would not allow him to support the United Front, as he objected to Communism's espousal of armed insurrection and revolutionary violence, its opposition to parliamentary institutions and its hostility to religion. At the same time he recognised that the Soviet Union had made advances, and he approved of the restrictions placed on the drink traffic and the abolition of brothels in Russia. In considering the regime in Germany, Barr expressed unqualified opposition. He denounced the Erastianism of the Nazis in matters of religion, and characterised German Fascism as 'Neo-paganism' [Barr (1938) 47].

In spite of his opposition to totalitarianism, Barr's pacifist beliefs kept him from identifying with the war effort. In November 1939, along with nineteen other Labour MPs, he signed a 'Memorandum on Peace Aims' which called for an immediate conference to end the war and to secure 'a negotiated peace at as early a date as possible'. From the death of Lansbury in 1940 to the dissolution of 1945 he was convenor of the parliamentary Committee on the Position of Conscientious Objectors.

By then in his eighties, Barr did not contest the general election of 1945; Coatbridge was retained for Labour by Jean Mann. In his last years he saw through the press a study of the Scottish Covenanters and compiled *Lang Syne*, a book of reminiscences and reprinted lectures and addresses. He died in Glasgow on 24 February 1949, having, as Tom Johnston recorded, 'played many parts in his day – scholar, preacher, church moderator, home ruler, pacifist, educationist, temperance and Robert Burns orator, and Member of Parliament, but above all, and always, he was a fighter for spiritual and political freedom' [Johnston (1952) 240]. Johnston wondered whether it was a mistake that Barr should have entered Parliament, with all its pressures to compromise, instead of serving his generation through the Church. But for Barr a belief in the Gospel could not be separated from political action. As he had written in a tract, he held that 'Christ's great social and industrial Parables' dealt with such issues as the living wage and the tragedy of unemployment [Barr [1926?] 2]. It was the duty of the Christian, as Barr understood it, to proclaim Christ's social message, and, to do this, involvement in political life was unavoidable. His opposition to all forms of gambling and his advocacy of total abstinence and Sabbatarianism – in December 1942, for example, he addressed the Commons at some length on the Sunday opening of cinemas and related matters – were founded on religious principles. Though not all of his supporters shared the same attitudes, the idealism and crusading spirit of 'Jimmy' Barr, as he was sometimes known, commanded widespread approval.

In 1890 Barr had married Martha Wilson Stephen, daughter of A. H. Stephen, hosier, of Kilmarnock. They had five children: Mary, who died in infancy; James who became ill and died while a member of the Royal Navy in July 1918; Andrew, who practised as a doctor of medicine; Allan, who followed his father into the Church and became a professor at the training college of the United Free Church of Scotland; and Elizabeth, who also became a minister. After a service at North Woodside Church, Barr was buried alongside other members of his family in Fenwick Cemetery. His estate was valued at £1378.

Writings: *Wild War's Deadly Blast: a lecture on the war in South Africa, delivered in Rutherford United Free Church, Glasgow, on Sabbath Evening, 24th February 1901* (Glasgow, 1901) 23 pp.; *Christianity and War: a series of lectures delivered in Rutherford United Free Church, Glasgow, during the course of the South African War* (Glasgow, 1903); 'The War', *St. Mary's U. F. Church Mag.* no. 67 (Sep 1914) 1–4; *The Conscientious Objector* [1916] 32 pp.; *The Scottish Church Question* (1920); *The Freeing of Scotland* (Glasgow, 1921) 15 pp.; *Scotland Yet: an oration on Sir William Wallace and Scottish freedom* (Glasgow, 1921) 16 pp.; Foreword to W. Murray, *Home Rule for Scotland: the case in 90 points* (Glasgow, 1922); *Origin, Nature and Destination of the State* (Dundee, 1924) 39 pp.;

Democracy and the Gospel: an appeal to working people (Glasgow, [1926?]) 4 pp.; 'The Church's "Inalienable Right" ', *Spec. 141*, 21 July 1928, 83; *The Bible and the Working Class* (Glasgow, 1930) 16 pp.; (with R. J. Davies), *Report on the Polish–Ukranian Conflict in Eastern Galicia ... House of Commons ... September 1931* (Chicago, 1931) 23 pp.; *The Church and War* (Glasgow, 1932) 48 pp.; *The United Free Church of Scotland* (1934); *Capital Punishment from the Christian Standpoint* (Third Roy Calvert Memorial Lecture, 12 Nov 1936 [1936?]) 17 pp.; *Religious Liberty in the Totalitarian States: the challenge to the Church of Communism, Fascism, Nazism* (1938); *The Centenary of the Disruption and a Century of Progress: address delivered to the General Assembly* (1943) 20 pp.; *The Scottish Covenanters* (Glasgow, 1946); *Lang Syne: memoirs*, with a Foreword by T. Johnston (Glasgow, 1949).

Sources: W. I. Anderson, *A Roll of Graduates of the University of Glasgow* (Glasgow, 1898); R. C. on the Housing of the Industrial Population of Scotland Rural and Urban, *Report*, 1917/18 XIV, Cd 8731; election addresses, 1924 and 1929; *Hansard*, 1924–31, 1935–45; *Labour Who's Who* (1927); S. C. on Capital Punishment in Great Britain, *Report* and *M of E*, 1929/30 V, 1930/31 VI, *Scottish Biographies* (1938); M. A. Hamilton, *Arthur Henderson* (1938); H. Macpherson, 'James Barr: champion of the common man' [review], *Weekly Scotsman*, 7 Apr 1949; *WWW* (1941–50); T. Johnston, *Memories* (1952); E. O. Tuttle, *The Crusade against Capital Punishment in Great Britain* (1961); H. J. Hanham, *Scottish Nationalism* (1969); J. Brand, *The National Movement in Scotland* (1978); M. Keating and D. Bleiman, *Labour and Scottish Nationalism* (1979); M. Ceadel, *Pacifism in Britain 1914–1945: the defining of a faith* (Oxford, 1980); C. Harvie, 'Labour in Scotland during the Second World War' in *Hist. J. 26*, no. 4 (1983) 921–44; *Scottish Labour Leaders 1918–39: a biographical dictionary*, ed. and with an Introduction by W. Knox (Edinburgh, 1984) 61–5. Personal information: Revd Dr Allan Barr, Edinburgh, son; Revd Elizabeth Barr, Glasgow, daughter; Peter Dempsie, Bellshill, Lanark; Robin C. B. Stirling, editor *Motherwell Times*. OBIT. *Scotsman* and *Times*, 25 Feb 1949; *LP Report* (1949). NOTE. The editors wish to acknowledge an earlier draft of this biography written by Dr W. Knox, Heriot-Watt University. The entry on the Revd James Barr in *Scottish Labour Leaders* is inaccurate in minor details; these have been corrected for the present version by a daughter, the Revd Elizabeth Barr.

DAVID E. MARTIN

See also: †George LANSBURY; †Jean MANN.

BELL, Letitia (1890–1981)
LABOUR PARTY ACTIVIST

Letitia Bell was born in Scunthorpe, north Lincolnshire, on 5 February 1890. She was one of the six children of William Driffill and his wife Ellen (née Hollingsworth). Her paternal grandfather, Ralph Driffill, was a local shoemaker who, like many of his trade, was also a Radical; in the evenings groups of people gathered in his workshop to hear him read political literature.

Lettie or Tisha, as she was often known, was brought up in Brigg, where her father, an insurance agent, had moved with his family. Like his father, William Driffill was a Radical and a supporter of the Liberal Party. Although her parents were Primitive Methodists, she attended the local Church of England school – there being no other – but the Methodist chapel also provided part of her education and she was an avid reader of books from the

Sunday-school library. Letitia enjoyed school but she was already aware of political issues such as the refusal by Nonconformists to pay rates for the upkeep of Church of England schools. A respected local Methodist, father of one of her school friends, went to prison in this cause, and henceforth was known as 'Martyr' Clarke. Letitia occasionally demonstrated her own independence at school by a refusal to recite the Creed or to attend Ascension Day services.

When she was thirteen her father died. Ellen Driffill was a remarkable woman, and to keep the family together and in food began to earn a living as a midwife (unqualified) and by going out sewing, carrying her heavy sewing machine and a Gladstone bag containing scissors, needles, buttons, patterns and so on. She lived to the age of ninety-four, remaining mentally alert to the end of her days and always interested in politics.

At fourteen Letitia left school to become a dressmaker, only for the shop to close down before she finished her apprenticeship. She was then employed by a Brigg family as a 'mother's help'. In the meantime and in keeping with the family tradition, she had developed an interest in politics. About 1906, or perhaps earlier, the family became Socialist, largely through the influence of Will Kelford, who had come from Sheffield to live and work in Brigg. He was already a member of the ILP and later married Letitia's elder sister Susannah. In about the year 1908 Letitia and her brother Edward joined the ILP branch at Barton-on-Humber (later her younger brother, John, kept a left-wing bookshop in Bradford). She attended many meetings organised by the Clarion Cycling Club in north Lincolnshire and her family often gave hospitality to visiting speakers. On one occasion, she later recalled, Katharine Bruce Glasier spoke in Brigg market-place, only to be pelted with banana skins and orange peel.

In 1910 the Brigg family for whom she worked went to Alloa in Scotland and Letitia accompanied them for about three years. She became active in the ILP in Glasgow, collected at meetings, sold *Forward* and was for a time secretary of the Maryhill branch. She was also a delegate to the Socialist Sunday Schools' Union. With Jessie Stephen, Agnes 'Geordie' Hardie (sister-in-law of Keir Hardie) and others she tried to organise domestic servants into a trade union. All her spare time was devoted to Labour politics. In 1913 she moved to Bradford, where her brother Edward was active in the ILP, and there too she threw herself into the cause. She took part in the meetings of the Clarion Club, helped to run the Laisterdyke Socialist Sunday School and – something she remembered all her life – was on the platform to hear Keir Hardie speak at a meeting to celebrate Oastler Sunday. She was an advocate of women's suffrage and a member of the Women's Social and Political Union, though she did not adopt militant methods.

In 1914 she moved to Hull and in the following year married Joseph Spalding Bell, whom she had known since meeting him at the Barton-on-Humber branch of the ILP. He too had been brought up as a Methodist, but they were now both humanists and were married at Brigg Register Office. Letitia Bell lived in Hull for over forty years and for most of the time worked for the Labour Party in the capacity, as she saw it, of a rank-and-filer. She always enjoyed elections and would gladly address envelopes, canvass (her claim was that, although occasionally answered rudely, she always 'left a door in such a way that she could go back to it'), help at committee rooms and scrutinise at the count. She also held various offices in her ward, North Newington, and was treasurer of the South West Hull division. Between elections she collected funds from families who had pledged to pay 'a penny a week for Labour', becoming known as 'the Labour Lady'.

Her knowledge of working-class life led to her nomination as a trade union representative before the court of referees at which appeals against the refusal of public assistance were heard. In 1933 she became a non-corporate (co-opted) member of Hull City Council, serving on the health and public assistance and the education committees – subjects in which she was particularly interested. As a member of the public assistance committee she was involved in especially arduous work. The Labour Party had recently gained control of the

City Council, and were concerned to ensure that all claimants for assistance were receiving the maximum amounts to which they were entitled: and the committee undertook a complete review of all the public assistance claims in the city. Her concern with education lasted for many years. She was a member of the governing body of a number of schools, and she took a keen personal interest in the work and problems, visiting them and always, whenever possible, attending their special occasions. Her education committee service continued until 1957.

In December 1935 her husband died in his early fifties, leaving her with three children, aged twelve, fourteen and eighteen. He had worked as a manager for a firm of family grocers, but had been discharged in March 1935, almost certainly because his employer disapproved of his and Lettie's politics. He was offered a job with the Hull Co-operative Society, and for the last few months of his life canvassed for grocery orders. His main interests, apart from politics, were playing the piano, reading and gardening. He was less active politically than Letitia but he was especially interested in the internationalist aspects of Socialism, and after the Russian Revolution he learned Esperanto and corresponded with a Russian in that language. He fully supported his wife in her suffragette and Socialist politics, and was always willing to look after the children while Letitia went to her political meetings, or attended the many WEA classes on social history, local government and economics that helped to enlarge her knowledge and political expertise.

When her husband died, their son John had just completed his first term at Cambridge University, where he had gone on scholarships. The widow's pension for Letitia and the two girls was 18s per week, reduced to 15s when the elder daughter reached the age of sixteen (in 1937). Letitia was determined that the children's education should not suffer, and she had taken the only work that was available: part-time cleaner and dinner server at the newly opened North Hull clinic. She then had to leave the City Council in 1936 and moved to North Hull, although she maintained contact with the Labour Party in South West Hull until early in the war, when she joined the North Hull branch. She became treasurer of Greenwood ward and secretary of the women's section. One of her principal concerns was that women should be more involved in politics, and towards this end she arranged programmes of afternoon meetings at the homes of members. She was a member of the Hull and District Women's Advisory Committee and a regular attender of Labour women's summer schools – virtually the only holidays she had for some years after her husband's death. True to the Clarion Club tradition, she regarded social activities and companionship as important aspects of political life.

Letitia Bell made only two attempts to be elected to public office, both within four weeks of each other. On 1 November 1946 she was defeated, by 4565 votes to 4291, as the Labour candidate for Pickering ward in the municipal elections. On 28 November, at a by-election in Botanic ward, she polled 1929 votes, 279 fewer than her opponent. In both her election addresses she emphasised the improvement of housing, health and education as matters deserving priority.

For several more years she continued her rank-and-file activities in the Labour politics of Hull, until in 1957 she moved to Cottingham to live with her daughters. Finding that the local branch of the Labour Party had fallen into abeyance, she set about reviving it and served in the posts of secretary and treasurer. She also joined the Campaign for Nuclear Disarmament and took part in its marches. On completing seventy years' work for the Labour Party, in 1976 she was the guest of honour at a party to present her with a signed photograph of James Callaghan (who was Prime Minister at the time) and other gifts. In these later years she attended what meetings she could, often being taken by younger members of the Labour Party, whom she always sought to encourage. Though increasingly frail, she maintained an optimistic and humorous attitude to life and never lost her early political beliefs, voting by post in the local election of May 1981. She died at home in Cottingham on 15 August 1981. The funeral took place at the Hull Crematorium. She was survived by her daughter, Margaret, a retired schoolteacher, and John, a compensation officer for the General and Municipal Workers' Union. Barbara, her other daughter, who was also a schoolteacher, died in 1976.

At the age of eighty-nine, Letitia Bell reflected on the period covered by her life, and a few sentences of what she wrote will stand as a statement of her political outlook:

> Hull has been a good place to live, politically speaking. I have been active in the Party through all the years and have held one office or another for over 50 years. There has never been a shortage of good, capable leaders and many important changes have been brought about. The Labour Women's Sections have been hard-working and well-organised with a good spirit of comradeship.
>
> It is a long way to look back. To know what is past, the mistakes and successes, can help us to plan the future. I can think of a life with no pensions or family allowances. No educational opportunities for the majority, no maternity or child welfare services and many other amenities which we take for granted. And then I remind myself (and others) that none of these advantages have come to us as rewards for good conduct. They have come about because men and women and young people have been able and willing to fight injustice and poverty. The greatest thing in these days is that there is opportunity for individual development and a fuller life.
>
> I owe a great debt to the Labour Party for the many good friendships I have enjoyed and for the many exciting occasions when we have 'won the fight'. I think it is a great privilege to have taken a small part in bringing about some good changes and I have great faith in the future of the Party.

Letitia Bell was small, less than five feet tall. Her manner was quiet, her opinions definite, and she was not easily intimidated. She had a great capacity for enjoyment and a zest for new experiences. She always remembered with pleasure and delight the miners' demonstrations in Alloa in 1910 and the May Day demonstration in Glasgow in 1912. And she was always an optimist: not with an easy-going optimism but with a belief in the possibility of bringing about change by the efforts of ordinary people themselves.

Letitia Bell is not likely to be recorded in the general histories of the British labour movement. She was one of the many thousands who laboured in their own villages, towns, and cities – mostly unsung except by their immediate fellow citizens but without whose devoted and self-sacrificing efforts the local and national movements they served with such loyalty and devotion would never have happened.

Writings: 'A Few Thoughts of a Rank-and-Filer: some changes in a lifetime' [1979] 6 pp. [copy in *DLB* Coll.].

Sources: Election addresses, Nov 1946; *Hull Sentinel*, July 1957. Biographical information: G. W. Oxley, City Archivist, Hull. Personal information: Miss Margaret Bell, Cottingham, N. Humberside, daughter. OBIT. *Hull Daily Mail*, 20 Aug 1981.

MARGARET BELL
DAVID E. MARTIN

BRIGGS, William (Billy) Layton (1876–1957)
LABOUR ALDERMAN AND TRADE UNIONIST

'Billy' Briggs, as he was often known, was born in Cambridge on 15 September 1876, the eldest son of William John Briggs, a railway worker, and his wife Sarah (née Layton). He attended St Philip's, the local elementary school, where he had hopes of training to become a teacher, but his father's early death made it necessary for him to begin work. Soon after leaving school and at the age of fifteen he joined the London and North Eastern Railway as a clerk, and later became an active member of the Railway Clerks' Association. He continued to be employed with the London and North Eastern (later the Great Eastern Railway) until his retirement in 1935.

As a young man he was a member of St Philip's Church; and he became active in the Church of England Young Men's Society, a debating club which provided many Cambridge citizens with an introduction to political and social ideas. It led on, for Briggs, to the WEA and courses in European history, economics, biology and psychology. He lived in the working-class district of Cambridge known as Romsey Town, and helped the Romsey Boys' Mutual Help Club on the clerical side. In 1912 Briggs became a foundation member of the Cambridge Labour Party. Labour in Cambridge was, for the greater part of Briggs's active political life, a minority party in a Conservative town, although from 1945 to 1951 the town had a Labour MP, A. L. Symonds; and it was always a party of moderate Socialists. Briggs himself, in his political views, epitomised the average Labour activist in the area. He supported, for example, the First World War and, as a delegate from the Railway Clerks' Association, he became a member of the local Food Control Committee. He had been rejected for active service on health grounds and during the war he organised a National Savings group among Cambridge railway employees.

Soon after the war ended Briggs became chairman of the divisional Labour Party and served from 1919 to 1922, when he was succeeded by Leah Manning. The Cambridge party put up a candidate in the 1918 general election – a Welsh Nonconformist parson, the Revd Rhondda Williams, who polled under 4000 votes against Sir Eric Geddes's total of some 11,500 [Manning (1937) 25 and (1970) 54–6]. Hugh Dalton was adopted as candidate in February 1920, and provided a lively account of the 1922 general election in the first volume of his memoirs [(1953) 129 ff.]. He came second, pushing the Liberal into third place, and the Labour vote up to nearly 7000.

In November 1920 Briggs was elected to the Borough Council for Romsey, and he continued to hold the seat until he became an alderman in 1929. He served on a wide range of council committees, including finance, education and, during 1923 and 1924, the housing committee, where he took an active part in debates on the provision of municipal housing. For a number of years Briggs was chairman of the Romsey Labour Party and as such was president of the Cambridge Romsey Labour Club and Hall Ltd, which was responsible for building (by voluntary labour) and running a Labour club in the town. He also served for a period as chairman of the Trades Council and in that capacity during the General Strike he played a major role as a spokesman for the Strike Committee in organising strike centres, and providing entertainment for strikers. Subsequently the Chief Constable was quoted in the *Cambridge Chronicle* (19 May 1926) as saying, 'There has not been the slightest trouble and that was largely due to the lead given by Councillor Briggs and his colleagues.' However, he was downgraded by the railway company for his part in the strike, although he was later promoted to chief clerk in the general section of the locomotive department, a post he held up to retirement. It was as chairman of the Trades Council that he accepted an invitation to discuss trade unionism and economics with the Duke of York and Duke of Gloucester when they were undergraduates at the University.

He was twice mayor of the borough. His election in 1937 attracted particular attention as he was Cambridge's first Labour mayor. He served for a second time in 1943–4. On both occasions he brought to the office his particular qualities of level-headedness, common sense and a forthright and complete honesty to which council colleagues and local press reports paid full tribute. There was considerable mutual respect between Briggs and members of other political parties. He declined an invitation to attend the coronation in 1937 in Westminster Abbey in favour of participating in local celebrations and also to save the cost to the town's mayoral expenses fund. An event he was particularly pleased to be associated with during his first mayoral year was a large meeting, at which he presided, called to raise funds for a hostel to be opened at Pampisford for Basque refugee children from the Spanish Civil War. In the 1941 New Year Honours he was awarded the OBE.

In addition to his duties as a councillor, Briggs played an active part in other spheres of Cambridge public life. He was appointed to the magistrates' bench in 1918 and for a number of years from 1933 he was chairman of the panel of JPs concerned with juvenile cases. From 1945 to 1951, when he retired, he served as chairman of the full bench. During the war years he was the chairman of the Civil Defence Committee. For a long period he was on the management committee of Coleridge School and he continued to take a close interest in the work of the WEA, filling at different times various offices within its organisation. In 1951 he received an honorary MA from Cambridge University, a recognition of his work that gave him much pleasure.

Briggs resigned from the City Council in April 1956 because of ill health, and he died at his home in Greville Road on 28 December 1957. The funeral, which in addition to family mourners was attended by the Mayor and Corporation of Cambridge and a number of University officials, was conducted at Great St Mary's Church and was followed by cremation. He left an estate of £8239. His widow, Elizabeth Mary Ann Briggs (née Cornwell), came from Bury St Edmunds and before their marriage in 1905 had been a dressmaker. During the 1920s she had been active on behalf of the League of Nations Union and was a voluntary worker for the War Pensions Committee for the Romsey Town area, a manager of several schools and a member of the library committee. She died in 1960. There were two daughters of the marriage: Grace, who became secretary to the Master of Peterhouse, and Lilian, who became a schoolteacher and later a headmistress.

Sources: *Cambridge Chronicle*, 12 Dec 1923, 13 Feb 1924, 12, 19 May 1926; *Cambridge Daily News*, 9 Sep 1930, 9, 11 Nov 1936, 2, 10 Nov 1937, 9, 13 Nov 1943, 3 Mar, 15 Sep 1951, 21 Apr 1956; L. Manning, 'Some Recollections of 1918 in the Cambridge Labour Party', in *Silver Jubilee 1912–1937: twenty-five years in the history of the Cambridge Labour Party*, ed. D. Hardman (Cambridge, 1937); H. Dalton, *Call Back Yesterday: memoirs 1887–1931* (1953); L. Manning, *A Life for Education* (1970). Personal information: Mrs Lilian Fletcher, Andover, Hants, and Mrs Grace Ray, Cambridge, daughters; Mrs Sallie Purkis, Cambridge. OBIT. *Cambridge Evening News*, 30 Dec 1957.

BARBARA NIELD

See also: †Elizabeth Leah MANNING; *Clara Dorothea RACKHAM.

BROWN, Alfred Barratt (1887–1947)
CHRISTIAN SOCIALIST AND PRINCIPAL OF RUSKIN COLLEGE

Alfred Barratt Brown was born in Leeds on the last day of 1887. His father, Alfred Kemp Brown, and his uncle, Francis Henry Brown, were joint secretaries of the Flounders Institute in Leeds, which provided opportunities for higher education for Quakers and other

Nonconformists, who were excluded from University entrance. The Institute was absorbed into Leeds University, but funds were retained in a Trust to help Quakers attending universities when these were opened to them. Frank Brown became secretary of this Trust and Barratt Brown took over from him on his death. Barratt Brown's mother was Emma Barratt, who came from Essex and died when he was six. He claimed that he read *The Times* to her during her last illness. The Browns, Barratts and Kemps were all Quaker families and there are family trees of the Browns going back to seventeenth-century Quakers in Hertfordshire and later in Sussex.

Barratt Brown went to Bootham School, the Quaker school in York, at which his father had earlier been a master, and from Bootham to the University College of Bristol. His father had by this time moved to Bristol and was active on a number of committees of the Society of Friends. At Bristol, Barratt Brown became a friend of Clifford Allen, a close association which continued throughout their lives. Both of them worked in the University Settlement Movement and in the Student Christian Movement in Bristol. Both of them studied classics and took London University degrees (Bristol did not gain University status until 1909) and went on to other universities – Barratt Brown to Merton College, Oxford, and Clifford Allen to Peterhouse, Cambridge. Barratt Brown's political background was Liberal, Allen's Conservative, but at university both joined the Fabian Society and later the ILP. Barratt Brown, however, retained his Quakerism, while Allen, under the influence of Goldie Lowes Dickinson, became an agnostic.

In 1912 Barratt Brown, who had been studying classics (Literae Humaniores) obtained his degree (a second) and married Doris Eileen Cockshott, a student at Somerville and daughter of a Southport solicitor. His wife joined the Society of Friends just before the marriage. In the same year, Barratt Brown was appointed a lecturer in psychology at Birmingham University and deputy warden of Woodbrooke, the Quaker Settlement at Selly Oak, Birmingham. By this time, the threat of a major war hung over Europe and Barratt Brown's views as a Quaker pacifist and Christian Socialist led him into much activity in the ILP and outside, writing and speaking against the arms race and then against the war itself. In 1915 Barratt Brown became one of the first members of the No-Conscription Fellowship (NCF), which was organised by Fenner Brockway, editor of the *Labour Leader*, and with Allen as chairman. The NCF became an extensive national organisation with branches and federations of branches and a complex communications system, which was based on lessons learned from the suffragettes, who were represented by Catherine Marshall.

As a result of the NCF campaign the Government's first Conscription Bill, introduced early in 1916, allowed for 'conscientious objection' with exemption of three types: (1) absolute, (2) exemption from combatant service and (3) exemption conditional on doing some 'work of national importance'. Tribunals were set up, and, while some Quakers and others with religious objections were given exemption, most of those presenting themselves to the Tribunals had their objections rejected and were passed over to the military authorities. Barratt Brown insisted that his objection was political as well as religious and joined Allen and others in proposing that their work in the NCF was 'work of national importance'. There was a real danger that, if they were transferred from Britain to France, objectors might be executed, and some were actually sentenced to death. The efforts of the NCF, however, persuaded Asquith, the Prime Minister, to require that the military authorities after court martial should hand back their victims for punishment in civil prisons.

Thus it was that Barratt Brown spent two and a half years in various prisons – Wormwood Scrubs, Dartmoor and Canterbury. There is a photograph in the family album of Walter Ayles, J. P. Fletcher, W. J. Chamberlain, Barratt Brown, Allen and Fenner Brockway each with a small attaché case on their way to serve their first prison sentence. Thereafter, the military authorities played cat and mouse, letting objectors out for a time and then taking them back, and, when they refused once more to put on uniform, sentencing them to further periods in gaol. Barratt Brown was not finally released until early in 1919. It was typical of his disregard for his own person that he argued strongly inside the NCF that more time should be spent on anti-war propaganda and less on releasing COs from gaol. He was in Wormwood Scrubs when Sir Roger Casement was hanged, an incident that was evidently so distressing to all the prisoners that Barratt Brown found no mention of it in his diaries when he came to consult them while preparing evidence for a Select Committee on Capital Punishment in 1930. Prison was a searing experience, although, unlike Allen, Barratt Brown was physically strong. It was typical that, since he normally took a cold bath every morning, he requested the warders to hose him down each day while in gaol.

Barratt Brown returned in 1919 to Woodbrooke and to lecturing in Birmingham and took up again his writing and speaking for the Labour movement, especially in the local Labour paper, the *Town Crier*, edited by W. J. Chamberlain in Birmingham. In 1921 he was invited to become vice-principal of Ruskin College, Oxford. The principal was Sanderson Furniss, who had been a lecturer at the College since 1907. Furniss was by this time quite blind and in 1923 Barratt Brown moved into the principal's lodgings at Ruskin and became acting principal in November 1925 and principal in 1926. Ruskin had reopened in 1919 as a 'College of the Labour Movement' – in direct challenge to the same claim made by the Central Labour College, which had been founded out of the student strike and breakaway of 1909. The labour movement as a whole had been greatly strengthened by the war, trade union funds were more easily available and the College was recognised for grant by the Board of Education. Two-year courses leading to an Oxford University diploma in Politics and Social Science were the norm, but nearly half of the fifty or so students in residence stayed only for a year and took no examinations.

For the ten years after 1923 Ruskin went through an exceedingly difficult period. Slump followed boom, trade union membership declined sharply and with it union funds. In spite of some local authority and TUC grants there were not enough scholarships to fill all the available places. In the year of the General Strike, a proposal was made for the TUC to take over both Ruskin and the Central Labour College [Griggs (1983) 197 ff.)]. The initiative came from the Socialist Countess of Warwick, who offered to give Easton Lodge, her stately home in Essex, to the movement. The offer came to nothing through lack of funds, but it was Barratt Brown's strong conviction that the isolation – from libraries and the whole community of learning of Oxford – would be a serious drawback. His own links with the University, his close friendship with A. D. Lindsay, the Master of Balliol, with G. D. H. Cole and others, had enabled him to establish a measure of integration of Ruskin with the University which gave access to libraries and to lectures, and entrance to colleges for Ruskin students who were able to follow University degree courses.

The breakdown of the Easton Lodge proposals, however, left Ruskin with a burden of debt and a group of unsafe wooden buildings at the back of the brick building on Walton Street. These ramshackle outhouses served for dining, library, tutors' studies and offices. The TUC monthly cheque frequently arrived late. The College lived on the goodwill of Arthur Gillett, the Oxford Quaker banker, a close friend of Barratt Brown, and since the take-over of Gillett's Bank, a director of Barclays. Barratt Brown set out to raise money, stumping the country to find supporters in the midst of the Depression. In this he was remarkably successful, drawing on funds from far outside the labour movement.

By this time Barratt Brown had become a relatively well-known local and even national figure. He was treasurer of the Oxford City Labour Party and had been serving as secretary of a group of men and women 'of all Parties and of none', who had come together in 1933 to sign a Manifesto on Liberty and Democratic Leadership. The dangers to Britain of the trend towards Fascism, already seen on the Continent, was combined for this group with antipathy towards the Soviet Union. Barratt Brown had side-stepped the problem of the use of Ruskin College hall for public meetings by Fascists and Communists, insisting only that no uniforms should be worn by any organisation using the hall.

The 'Liberty and Democratic Leadership' grouping was chaired and largely inspired by Clifford Allen, Barratt Brown's close friend and associate of student days and of the war years. In 1931 Allen had become Lord Allen of Hurtwood, for what he believed was the desperate need for a *national* response to the economic and political crisis. 'Liberty and Democratic Leadership' attracted a wide range of Liberals, some Conservatives (including Harold Macmillan) and many prominent members of the Labour Party, together with academics, journalists and some wartime civil servants, among the most prominent being Geoffrey Crowther and Arthur Salter. In 1935 the group launched itself as the Next Five Years Group, with Allen as chairman, Barratt Brown as secretary and Geoffrey Crowther as editor of the book *The Next Five Years*. This publication followed in 1936. At the same time, *New Outlook* was published as a monthly journal. *A Programme of Priorities* appeared in 1937, with a wide range of signatures for quite openly collectivist principles.

The group was divided, however, on the issue of the Popular Front and on the need for the League of Nations to operate military sanctions. Salter was returned to Parliament on the 'Next Five Years' ticket for Oxford University in 1937. A year later Barratt Brown found himself estranged from his old friend A. D. Lindsay, who stood as a Popular Front candidate in a famous Oxford by-election when Quintin Hogg was returned to Westminster. Barratt Brown was a firm supporter of the Republican Government in the Spanish Civil War, although as a pacifist he would not have fought. When his son Michael considered going to Spain in an ambulance unit he was encouraging, but relieved when the plan fell through.

Barratt Brown and Clifford Allen were both, for their own ethical and political reasons, opposed to a military alliance against Hitler, and it led them to be accused of appeasement. Allen supported collective security through the League of Nations, but his opposition to military sanctions associated him with the policies which culminated in Munich. Barratt Brown attempted a version of direct action. Believing that non-violent intervention of thousands of people could deter Hitler, he collected volunteers to go to the Sudetenland in 1938 and place themselves physically between the German tanks and Czech people. They failed to obtain visas.

In all this pressure of public activity Barratt Brown was able to find just the people who could help Ruskin out of its financial difficulties. He had already an extraordinarily wide circle of friends, and funds were raised from a number of Trusts as well as private persons, including a major donation from Sir Malcolm Stewart, who was a Commissioner for the Depressed Areas. As a result of the monies raised, all the debts were paid off and new study bedrooms, a vice-principal's flat, a new students' common room and an extensive library were built to replace the old wooden buildings. The new buildings were opened by Lord Sankey in 1936, with A. D. Lindsay, the Master of Balliol, presiding.

To have achieved such a success in the slump years of the early 1930s must be regarded as a remarkable victory over adversity, and one which has gone sometimes quite unrecognised by Ruskin historians. Before the Second World War the links of the College with the University were firmly established through the University's Extra-mural Delegacy and its Adult Education Centre, set up in 1927 at Rewley House and by which Ruskin students entered the University degree courses. Links with social-work courses were also established through Barnett House and the Oxford diploma in Public and Social Administration. The greatest tribute to the Ruskin of the 1930s was, however, that two new colleges were founded on the Ruskin model, one in Wales at Harlech and the other in Scotland at Newbattle Abbey. In both cases the driving force came from the associates of Barratt Brown – at Coleg Harlech, Tom Jones, Lloyd George's Cabinet chief, and, at Newbattle, Lord Lothian, another appeaser and later Ambassador to the United States, who gave his house at Dalkeith to found the College.

Ruskin College had been closed from 1940 to 1945 and the buildings were used as a maternity hospital. Barratt Brown became a welfare officer of the Ministry of Labour in the

Southern Region, helping to accommodate and support the thousands of men and women, mostly women, who were moved southwards into war work, and especially in the build-up to the D-Day landings. He resigned from Ruskin in 1943, to allow for a new appointment to be made at the war's end, but continued to help with the work of the College's Correspondence Department, which expanded greatly to meet the demands of members of the armed forces. Throughout his years at Ruskin he had not only lectured regularly and taken his full share of tutorials, but he always had a programme of evening classes for the Oxfordshire WEA and corrected each week his stint of correspondence course papers for Ruskin's Correspondence Department. He established and maintained personal relationships with many of these external students and encouraged them in their activities. At the end of the war, Barratt Brown was retired from the Ministry of Labour and took up a post funded by the Rowntree Trust with the old association of his student days, the Educational Settlements Association. It was while visiting the Settlement at Rhondda in South Wales in 1947 that he was struck by a heart attack, and died on 2 October. He was cremated at Newport and a memorial meeting was held at the Friends Meeting House, Oxford, on 11 October.

Apart from his work at Ruskin and with the Next Five Years Group, Barratt Brown was a considerable scholar. His more substantial writings – *The Naturalness of Religion* (written with his lifelong friend John Harvey in 1924), *The Machine and the Worker* (1935) and *Democratic Leadership*, the Swarthmore Lecture of 1937 – and his editing of *Great Democrats* (1934) reveal a wide range of scholarship and a lapidary style. His regular contributions to the *Hibbert Journal* show also the breadth of his interests – in the new machinery, in leisure, in poetry and music, in social and industrial psychology, in what he liked to call the 'laughter of God'. His poems were regularly published in the *Observer*, especially at Christmas, and his book reviews were an almost weekly feature of the Quaker paper, the *Friend*.

Barratt Brown is probably best understood as a Christian Socialist who was not afraid to involve himself deeply in the actual day-to-day problems and arguments of the labour movement. When asked about the potential incorporation of Ruskin students into the capitalist establishment compared with the supposedly clear stand on working-class education made by the breakaway Labour Colleges, his answer was forthright, if not, perhaps, entirely accurate: 'I notice that Labour Cabinets are staffed by the products of the Labour College, while my students are to be found in the committee rooms of the unions and constituency parties and I would not have it otherwise.' His acceptance of war work in the Second World War showed that the absolutism of his pacifism had been somewhat relaxed in his later years.

His widow, who had been very active in Quaker affairs, survived him for thirty-seven years, a longer time than she had lived with him. She died in 1984 at the age of ninety-seven. His son Michael became the first principal of the newly established Northern College in 1977. There were one other son and two daughters of the family who also survived him. He left an estate valued at £8559.

Writings: 'Intuition', *Int. J. of Ethics 24*, no. 3 (Apr 1914) 282–93; *The Universal Light: a statement of Quaker faith* (1905 Committee of Yorkshire quarterly meeting of the Society of Friends, 'A' series, no. 32: Harrogate [1917?] 16 pp., 4th imp. Friends' Book Centre, 1933); 'The Dark Night of the Soul', *J. of Religion 3*, no. 4 (Sep 1923) 476–88; (with J. W. Harvey), *The Naturalness of Religion* [1929]; 'Machinery – Blessing or a Curse', *Hibbert J. 28* (Oct 1929) 1–12; 'The Leisure Problem', ibid. (Apr 1930) 455–64; evidence with Carl Heath before the S. C. on Capital Punishment, *M of E*, 1930–1 VI, Qs 4268–375; 'Education for Leisure', *Hibbert J. 31* (Apr 1933) 440–50; *Democracy and Education* (National Adult School Union, Frank Metcalfe Memorial Lecture, 1934) 20 pp.; (ed.) *Great Democrats*

(1934), trans. into Spanish by R. Loskill as *Grandes demócratas* (Buenos Aires, [1942]); *The Machine and the Worker* (1934); 'In Defence of the Machine', *Spec. 157* (21 Aug 1936) 300–1; *Democratic Leadership* [Swarthmore Lecture] (1938); Barratt Brown had poems published in the *Observer* and book reviews in the *Friend*.

Sources: *Labour Who's Who* (1927); *WWW* (1941–50); J. A. Venn, *Alumni Cantabrigienses*, pt 2, vol. *3* (Cambridge, 1947); W. W. Craik, *The Central Labour College* (1964); A. Marwick, *Clifford Allen: the open conspirator* (1964); M. Gilbert, *Plough my own Furrow: the story of Lord Allen of Hurtwood as told through his writings and correspondence* (1965); M. Cole, *The Life of G. D. H. Cole* (1971); C. Griggs, *The Trades Union Congress and the Struggle for Education 1868–1925* (Lewes, Sussex, 1983); H. Pollins, *The History of Ruskin College* (Ruskin College Library Occasional Publications, no. 3: Oxford, 1984). Personal information: M. Barratt Brown, Baslow, Derbys, son. OBIT. *Times*, 4, 7, 10, 13 October 1947; *Friend*, 10 Oct 1947. NOTE. Mr Michael Barratt Brown provided a detailed sketch of his father's life, from which this entry has been produced, although he must not be held responsible for any errors of fact or evaluation. The editors wish to express their appreciation for his generous help and co-operation. No personal papers for the Ruskin years seem to have survived.

JOHN SAVILLE

See also: †Reginald Clifford ALLEN; †Walter Henry AYLES; †Frances Evelyn (Daisy) WARWICK.

CHAMPION, Henry Hyde (1859–1928)
SOCIALIST PUBLISHER AND PROPAGANDIST

Born on 22 January 1859 at Poona, India, the son of Major-General James Hyde Champion and his wife Henrietta Susan (née Urquhart), Champion was sent to England to be educated when 'quite a little boy'. At Marlborough, Champion – on his own account – failed to distinguish himself. He enrolled as a cadet at the Royal Military Academy in September 1876, and was commissioned as a lieutenant in the Royal Artillery in January 1878. Later that year, Champion's battery was sent to Bombay. During the Afghan War of 1880, he served in the Quetta garrison and was awarded a campaign medal. He caught typhoid and in the summer of 1881 was invalided home. While recuperating, a friend showed Champion round the slum districts of London. Champion wrote in his reminiscences published initially in the Melbourne *Trident* (May–Nov 1908):

> What I saw in London during those few weeks completely changed the course of my life. Whatever I have done that seems to me, in the retrospect, to have been worth doing – that was the beginning of it [repr. *Bull. Soc. Lab. Hist.*, no. 47 (1983) 23].

He visited the United States in the company of the same friend, and while there read the works of Henry George, and was particularly impressed by George's *Progress and Poverty*. The identity of Champion's friend is uncertain: it may well have been R. P. B. (Percy) Frost, Champion's contemporary at Marlborough and later his close colleague in the Land Reform Union and the SDF and possibly the best man at Champion's wedding when, on 9 August 1883, he had married Juliet Bennett, then twenty-eight years old.

Returning from sick leave, Champion had a spell of duty at Woolwich and then as an adjutant at Portsmouth. During this time, he read widely on economic issues, including works by Adam Smith, J. S. Mill, Ricardo and Marx. He became a convinced Socialist, but his intention of leaving the Army was frustrated by the outbreak of the Egyptian War. On the day he learned of the British victory at Tel-el-Kebir in September 1882, he handed in his resignation to his commanding officer. The next night, so Champion recalled, or thought he recalled, 'I was preaching Socialism' on Clerkenwell Green. Champion joined the Democratic Federation (which in 1884 became the Social Democratic Federation) and began a close association with its leader, H. M. Hyndman. He became the Federation's honorary secretary at its 1883 conference.

Champion had £2000 from his father which he put into the publishing business of Kegan Paul, Trench and Co. At the end of three months he resigned and took his money out, to put it as a half-share in a printing plant owned by J. C. Foulger, who was a radical and possibly a Socialist. It is not clear whether Foulger was already publishing under the imprint of the Modern Press or whether it was founded when Champion joined the business; either way from 1883 until 1889 the Modern Press published a wide range of journals and pamphlets from the office in Paternoster Row. The first Socialist statement of the Democratic Federation, *Socialism made Plain*, was published by Champion in June 1883, and on 19 January 1884 the Modern Press published the first number of the weekly *Justice*. When Hyndman debated with Charles Bradlaugh on 17 April 1884 'Will Socialism benefit the English People?', Champion and his small staff published the full text in *Justice* within thirty-six hours. In the same year, 1884, Champion had subsidised the taking-over of the monthly *To-day*, which was thereafter to be a Socialist journal, edited by E. Belfort Bax and J. L. Joynes. In August 1885 Champion began employing H. W. Lee, then a young man of twenty, who took Champion's place as secretary of the SDF in November 1885, a position he held until 1913. Champion's resignation from the position of secretary may have been connected with the 'Tory Gold' episode, for which see below.

Champion's publishing activities were always run at a loss. The last issue of *Justice* printed by the Modern Press appeared in June 1887, and the Modern Press itself was finally wound up in 1889 [Frow (1975) 62–3]. Champion later recalled:

Altogether I had £4000 from my father. It took me about seven years to get through this, because, although the printing business swallowed a great deal, I always managed to make a respectable amount by my pen; writing for newspapers, magazines, reviews of all sorts. And I lived inexpensively [Champion in *Trident*, repr. *Bull. Soc. Lab. Hist.*, no. 47 (1983) 24].

During the 1880s, Champion was active in many causes. He was the founding honorary treasurer in 1883 of the Land Reform Union, which later became the English Land Restoration League and a member of the Fellowship of the New Life. There appear to be minor differences between historians as to whether Champion joined the Fabian Society, but if he did it seems that he soon left [Pelling (1952–3); MacKenzie (1977 and 1979)]. His main political activity was as a leading figure in the SDF. With him in his first year were Edward Aveling, Harry Quelch, Jack Williams and, very soon, William Morris. When Morris and Aveling seceded to form the Socialist League, Champion stayed with Hyndman, with whose views at this time he was in general accord. Champion helped to establish the Clerkenwell branch of the SDF, took part in the unemployed agitation and stood unsuccessfully as a candidate in the School Board elections in October 1885. The episode which did much to throw some doubts on Champion's politics was the 'Tory Gold' affair during the general election of the late autumn of 1885, when Champion passed on money provided by Maltman Barry to be used for election purposes. [For bibliography on Barry see below.] The incident was commented on in a letter from J. Hunter Watts, treasurer of the SDF, published in the *Pall Mall Gazette* of 4 December 1885. Pelling [(1965 ed.) 41] writes that Hunter Watts 'had been left in the dark' and he also characterises Watts's letter as 'angry'. This is not perhaps the correct reading. Watts does not mention either Champion or Maltman Barry by name in this *Pall Mall Gazette* letter, and, while he uses the phrase 'ill-advised' to describe the acceptance of the money, he goes on to characterise the electoral campaign as one which Socialists regarded 'as a battle of frogs and mice'; and he ended, 'I make known these facts in justice to those who condemn the action of my comrades, who thought it right, however, to take ammunition from the enemy in order to blaze it in their faces.'

There were resignations from the SDF, but the main, rather small, core of militants continued their political activities. During the winter of 1885–6 the London branches of the SDF were involved in the unemployed agitation. On 8 February 1886 – later to be known as 'Black Monday' – there was first a meeting in Trafalgar Square organised by the Fair Trade League and in part 'captured' by the SDF. After the meeting John Burns led a demonstration down Pall Mall. Windows were smashed and a number of shops looted. As a result Burns, Hyndman, Champion and Jack Williams were charged with seditious conspiracy. William Morris and Belfort Bax went bail, and the trial opened on 8 April 1886 with the Attorney-General prosecuting. After four days before a liberally minded judge, the jury returned a verdict of not guilty, adding a rider that Burns and Champion had used 'highly inflammatory language' [Tsuzuki (1961) 72 ff.].

The commonly accepted view is that Champion, along with the other defendants, was firmly against lootings. He certainly made very critical comment of the looting, but, in his analysis of the reasons for the acquittal of himself and his comrades, Champion ascribed it to the fear of mobs, sympathy with the poor, and political cunning in avoiding martyrdom for the accused [*Justice*, 24 Apr 1886]. While Champion later appeared to rule out civil disturbance as a political strategy [e.g. 'Street Fighting', ibid., 14 Aug 1886], as late as January 1887 Champion was arguing that, should revolutionary force be necessary, 'the swifter and heavier the blow struck, the better in the long run for the side that takes the initiative'. This latter article ['Mobs and Revolutions', ibid., 15 Jan 1887] was submitted by the Metropolitan Police to the Home Office for legal consideration [HO 144/183, A45225]. Meanwhile, on 17 March 1886 – while Champion was waiting to stand trial at the Old Bailey – his wife, Juliet, had died. Her death certificate records that she had suffered from alcoholism and from menorrhagia and syncope.

After the acquittal Champion continued his propagandist activities for the SDF, but his ideas were beginning to change. He became increasingly dissatisfied with the SDF's lack of political influence. The last of his many signed editorials in *Justice* appeared in January 1887 and in May 1887 he started his own monthly, *Common Sense*. In June he gave a series of lectures on Socialism which he published in pamphlet form. In one of these, *Social-Democracy in Practice*, he underlined his adherence to a constitutional position:

No Social Democrat in England advocates a resort to physical force revolution, so long as we enjoy even our present somewhat limited right of free discussion, meeting and combination, and so long as our imperfectly representative form of government is not rendered less representative [p. 5].

Champion had already begun to turn his attention to industrial questions, and he became closely associated with Tom Mann. In 1886 the Modern Press published Mann's *What a Compulsory Eight-Hour Working Day means for the Workers*; and in October of the same year an Eight Hours League was formed with branches in London and Newcastle. At the same time as Champion was developing his interest in industrial questions he was also revising his ideas on political matters. The TUC had established a Labour Electoral Committee (later Association) in 1886 and Champion began to move towards the strategy of a broad-based 'Labour Party' within which all committed to Socialist principles could work together. He further advocated the intervention of Socialists in parliamentary by-elections in order to develop and extend their agitation and propaganda. In September 1887 in *Common Sense* Champion published an article entitled 'The Future of Socialism in England' in which he criticised the 'vacillating tactics and absence of definite policy' of the SDF. The struggle inside the SDF dominated the annual conference in the following year, in August 1888. John Burns and Champion were among the most bitter critics and the breach was made permanent when Hyndman attacked Champion in *Justice* (20 Oct 1888) and specifically mentioned Champion's relations with Maltman Barry as one further proof of the unsuitability of Champion to remain in the leadership of the SDF.

Champion, with Burns and Tom Mann, left the SDF. Champion himself was actually expelled from the Federation in November 1888 and retorted by stating that the expulsion was invalid and then submitted his resignation [*Labour Elector*, 1 Dec 1888]. They already had another journal for the presentation of their policies. This was the monthly *Labour Elector*, which Champion began in June 1888 (*Common Sense* having closed down in March 1888). The *Labour Elector*, which in November became a fortnightly and in January 1889 a weekly, was intended to have a wider appeal to the movement and to concentrate especially upon industrial questions. An early issue was that of the grievances of the match girls employed by Bryant and May in East London – also being publicised by Annie Besant in the *Link* – and later in 1888 Champion encouraged Tom Mann (under the name of 'Joe Miller') to obtain employment in Brunner's chemical factory at Northwich [Mann (1923) 77–8]. Mann's reports were published in the *Labour Elector* between November 1888 and March 1889.

Throughout late 1887 and the whole of 1888 Champion also endeavoured to develop new forms of political organisation. He announced himself as a candidate at a Deptford by-election in January 1888, but withdrew when the Liberal made some concessions. In the spring of 1888 came the famous mid-Lanark by-election when Keir Hardie stood as miners' candidate against the Liberals. T. R. Threlfall of the Labour Electoral Association, urged on by Champion, went north to assist Hardie, but, when the latter refused an alternative seat offered by the National Liberal Association, Threlfall withdrew. Champion, with other Socialists and radicals, continued and again the question of Champion's finances became an issue. It was widely rumoured that 'Tory Gold' was again being accepted, an allegation that Margaret Harkness, a Socialist novelist and friend of Champion, firmly denied. She made her own financial involvement explicit in two letters to the *Star*:

I think it is pretty well known that I paid my friend Mr Keir Hardie's election expenses at Mid-Lanark; also that I am not a Conservative but a Socialist. . . . Tory gold is a myth. John Burns knew this when he became treasurer of the *Labor* [*sic*] *Elector* some months ago; he was satisfied that the money of the Labor party had come from Socialists. I will not speak of the sacrifices which have been made for the party by Mr H. H. Champion. Ever since he left the Social Democratic Federation he has been a target for the abuse of Socialists [20 Sep 1889]

and in a second letter a few days later (25 Sep 1889) she specifically denied that 'Mr Champion has any political intimacy with Mr Maltman Barry': a statement that was unlikely to be accurate in view of later developments. It is also not wholly certain that Margaret Harkness was giving a true account of what happened in the Mid-Lanark election; and it is likely that some of the details of the financial transactions will always remain unknown. [See Webb (1982) 302; Reid (1978) 115; Morgan (1975) has only a brief account of the episode, on p. 25.]

After the election Hardie formed the Scottish Labour Party; and in London the Champion group left the Labour Electoral Association and considered seriously the possibility of establishing a 'National Labour Party'. A National Labour Party did, in fact, come into existence, with Champion as honorary secretary, and H. Harford as honorary treasurer; but it does not seem to have lasted very long [Pelling (1952–3) 228–9]. What gave new life to independent Socialists such as Champion and Tom Mann was the upsurge of New Unionism from the summer of 1889. During the great Dock Strike, Champion helped to advise on tactics, assisted in negotiations and did much to encourage sympathetic newspaper coverage. The *Labour Elector* for a time became the official organ first of Will Thorne's Gasworkers' Union and then of the Dockworkers. The paper was now under a stronger political group in its management committee. Thorne also brought Champion into closer contact with the Avelings and to a more limited extent with Engels. 'If our lot here', Engels wrote to Lafargue on 17 October 1889,

> – I mean Champion especially – don't make mistakes, they will soon have it all their own way. But I confess I cannot get myself to have full confidence in that man – he is too dodgy. He used to go to Church Congresses and preach socialism there, and now he has formed a committee for organizing the East End women with a lot of middle class philanthropists who held a meeting with the Bishop of Bedford in the chair – and of course of this business they took good care to exclude Tussy [Eleanor Marx]! Now I don't like that, and if they go on that way I shall soon leave them alone. Burns is too fond of popularity to be able to resist such things and goes in with Champion – if I once see him alone, I shall speak to him [Engels and Lafargue (1956) 342].

Within a few months of the London dock strike, controversy arose over Champion's editorial attacks on Liberals and Progressives. Champion was outside the mainstream radical tradition, which had close historical links with the Liberal Party; and his trade union allies became increasingly uneasy with his denunciations of Liberals and radicals as 'mere party hacks and at bottom the most treacherous enemies of the working class' [*Labour Elector*, 1 Mar 1890]. A major dispute on the management committee led to Champion closing down the paper, and he sailed for Australia in the summer of 1890, returning to England in the following year. He was, it must also be added, recuperating from an illness when he left England.

Champion arrived in Melbourne on 12 August 1890. His reputation, for his work in the London Dock Strike, had preceded him. He brought a letter of introduction from John Burns and was warmly welcomed by the Trades Hall Council. Almost immediately he became involved in the maritime strike. He made some unfortunate interventions, in particular his description of Australian trade unionists as 'an army of lions led by asses' [*19th C.*, Feb 1891, 226] – a remark bitterly remembered down the years; and when the strike ended on 13 November he was denounced as a 'traitor and capitalist stooge' [*ADB* vol. 7 (1979) 604]. It was an episode he was constantly reminded of in later years.

After Champion returned from Australia he immediately tried to take up again his political activities. He worked for a time as assistant editor and then acting editor of the *Nineteenth Century*, to which he had previously been an occasional contributor. He became quite well known in literary circles and in 1892 he edited a short-lived literary monthly, the *Novel Review*. Champion contested Aberdeen South in the general election of 1892 and polled almost 1000 votes. He had strong personal and family links with Aberdeen – he belonged to the Urquhart family – and published a local weekly paper, the *Aberdeen Standard*, for five months in 1893–4. He wrote extensively for the paper, including a nine-part series entitled 'Men I have met', and a number of leading articles deploring illegal violence. It was in Aberdeen that he made the acquaintance of Frederick Rolfe ('Baron Corvo') who gave a favourable account of Champion (under the guise of a character named Dymoke) in his novel *Hadrian the Seventh*.

Champion had revived the *Labour Elector* in January 1893 as a weekly publication under the editorship of Maltman Barry. Champion's continued association with Maltman Barry and the dubious source of his political funds, and also his unremitting hostility to Liberalism and Lib-Labism, earned him the enmity of Keir Hardie and others of his former political colleagues. Champion arranged to attend the founding conference of the Independent Labour Party in Bradford in January 1893 as a delegate of the Aberdeen Labour Party, but was prevented from doing so by illness. Although speakers at the conference criticised Champion for supposed links with the Conservative Party, a number of his followers were elected to the ILP's Council. But when, a few weeks later, Champion attempted to act on behalf of the ILP at a by-election in Grimsby, the majority of the Party's Council signed a letter specifically repudiating him.

In May 1893 the *Labour Elector* became a monthly – in consequence it was explained, of 'the continued and serious illness of Mr Champion – and the following month, in an apparent act of defiance, the journal adopted the sub-title of 'the organ of the Independent Labour Party'. Champion continued to attempt to rally his remaining followers, and in August 1893 he attended the International Socialist Congress in Zurich, but his influence was sharply declining. He closed down the *Labour Elector*, the last full issue appearing in January 1894, and shortly after sailed for Australia, arriving in Melbourne in April. He apparently never returned to Britain. Persistent ill health was a factor in both his decision to emigrate and his choice of destination. The nature of Champion's illness is unclear. Havelock Ellis, in his autobiography published after Champion's death, alleged that Champion's health had been 'affected by venereal disease' – something which, apparently, Champion's second wife disputed vigorously after his death.

Champion remained an active Socialist in Victoria, although he continued to be the subject of almost perpetual political controversy. He was prominent in women's suffrage and anti-sweating movements and as a Fabian. He stood unsuccessfully for the Victorian Legislative Assembly in 1894 (in this instance actually withdrawing before the poll), in 1896 and again in 1900. He remained in contact with many of his one-time political colleagues in Britain. And he was a leading member of the Victorian Socialist Party, and again a colleague of Tom Mann between 1906 and 1909, holding office at various times as president and treasurer of the Party and as acting editor of its paper, the *Socialist*. He spent much of his time and effort on various co-operative projects, including a co-operative farming venture.

Champion was employed for a number of years as a leader writer on a Melbourne daily newspaper, the *Age*, though on the self-imposed stipulation that he would not be required to write about local politics. He wrote a book dealing with social questions in which he restated his proposal for an Imperial Customs Union. From 1895 to 1897, he published a weekly political and literary journal, the *Champion*, and for the succeeding two years published the *Sun*, a weekly society paper. From 1907 to 1909 he edited a Melbourne literary monthly entitled the *Trident*. It was in this journal that he serialised his reminiscences of aspects of his life before emigrating to Australia, entitled 'Quorum Pars Fui' (a quote from the *Aeneid*). These reminiscences are self-justificatory and at times flippant, but are nevertheless by far the most substantial of Champion's autobiographical writings. A later typescript autobiographical sketch – obviously written for publication – covers much the same ground as 'Quorum Pars Fui'.

He had married, on 8 December 1898, Elsie Belle Goldstein, then twenty-eight, a younger sister of the noted Australian suffragist Vida Goldstein. For many years Elsie ran a Book Lover's Library in Melbourne. In May 1899, Champion started his most enduring publishing venture, the *Book Lover*, a monthly journal of news and reviews about books and the literary scene which continued publication until August 1921. He also established the Australasian Authors' Agency in 1906, and published a number of successful novels by aspiring young Australians. These various literary undertakings must be judged as successful on all but commercial grounds, for Champion was declared bankrupt in 1922. His health had been indifferent ever since he settled in Australia. He suffered a stroke in 1901 which left him partly paralysed and with his speech impaired. It was further illness in 1909 which finally obliged him to withdraw from an active role in the Victorian Socialist Party. Nevertheless, Champion lived to within a few months of his seventieth birthday. He died at 462 Punt Road, South Yarra, Victoria, on 30 April 1928. He was cremated the following day after a Christian Science service, the religion of the Goldstein family. Champion had addressed the Church Congress in England in 1887, but, although he seems to have regarded himself as a Unitarian, his specific commitment, if he had one, is not known. As for his beliefs in later life, within the Goldstein milieu, it would appear that at the least – and no doubt for family reasons – he gave token allegiance to the Christian Science position. He was survived by his wife, who died in 1953; there were no children of the marriage.

Colleagues of Champion in the Socialist movement in Britain commented on his aristocratic appearance, his military disposition and his outspokenness and lack of patience. These shortcomings, compounded by an injudicious choice of associates and a habit for political intrigue, undermined his political career. Champion's fierce antipathy to Lib-Labism could be taken for a disguised sympathy for the Conservatives. Yet few people ever doubted the sincerity and sacrifice with which he promoted Socialist ideas. He must have had some cause to reflect on what might have been when he received a letter from G. B. Shaw in January 1924 on the formation of the first Labour Government, even though Shaw was much exaggerating what could have come about in Champion's career: 'I suppose you have seen the names of the new Cabinet. Think of what you have missed by emigrating! The secretaryship for War, or a peerage, at least' [quoted in Kellock (1971) 95].

Champion left behind him no institutional legacy or group of followers. He was already outside the main developments of British Socialists in the 1890s, and his contempt and hatred of the Liberal Party, and those who worked within its traditions, was unusual as well as somewhat isolating. But he was a considerable influence in the early Socialist movement; 'brilliant and restless' as the *New Leader* obituary described him; and he certainly retained the affection and respect of some of his old comrades, including, it would seem, Tom Mann.

Writings: Champion earned his livelihood from his writing. The journals in Britain and Australia with which he was most closely associated have been mentioned in the text. The following list includes, in addition to Champion's political pamphlets, a selection of his most important signed articles in British journals: 'Surplus Value I: for workers who are not Socialists', *Christian Socialist*, no. 10 (Mar 1884) 154–5; 'Contemporary Socialism', *To-day 3*, no. 17 (May 1885) 229–36; 'Force a Remedy', *Justice*, 9 Jan 1886; '1848 and 1886', ibid., 24 Apr 1886; 'Street Fighting', ibid., 14 Aug 1886; 'The Procession of the Proletariat', ibid., 9 Oct 1886; 'Socialists of the Armchair', *To-day 6* (Oct 1886) 146–51; contributor to A. White, *The Problems of a Great City* (1886) 184–8; *The Facts about the Unemployed: an appeal and a warning* (1886) 16 pp.; 'Mobs and Revolutions', *Justice*, 15 Jan 1887; 'The Future of Socialism in England', *Common Sense 1*, no. 5 (15 Sep 1887) 65–70; 'Socialism and Christianity' [text of address to Church Congress], ibid., no. 6 (15 Oct 1887) 89–93; Introduction to G. Bateman, *Socialism and Soldiering* (1887) 16 pp.; *Wrongs that require Remedies* (1887) 16 pp.; *The Theories of Socialism* (1887) 16 pp.; *Social-Democracy in Practice* (1887) 16 pp.; *Co-operation v. Socialism: being a report of a debate between Mr H. H. Champion and Mr Benjamin Jones* (Manchester, 1887) 36 pp.; 'Reasons for our Existence', *Labour Elector*, June 1888, 1; 'The New Labour Party', *19th C. 24* (July 1888) 81–93; 'An Eight-hour Law', ibid. *26* (Sep 1889) 509–22; 'The Great Dock Strike', *Universal Rev. 5* (Sep–Dec 1889) 157–78; *The Great Dock Strike in London, August 1889* [1890] 30 pp.; *The Parliamentary Eight Hours Day* [1890] 16 pp.; 'The Federation of Labour', *New Rev. 2* (Jan–June 1890) 524–33; *The Late Strike in Australia: what a British labour leader has said about the use and abuse of trades unionism* [1890?] 16 pp.; 'The Crushing Defeat of Trade Unionism in Australia', *19th C. 29* (Feb 1891) 225–37; 'A Labour Inquiry', ibid. *30* (July 1891) 89–99; 'The Labour "Platform" at the Next Election', ibid. *30* (Dec 1891) 1036–42;

'The Origin of the Eight Hours System at the Antipodes', *Econ. J. 2* (1892) 100–8; 'Protection as Labour wants it', *19th C. 31* (June 1892) 1027–31; 'Mr Chamberlain's Programme', ibid. *32* (Dec 1892) 875–82 [a reply to an article by J. Chamberlain, ibid. (Nov 1892)]; 'Charles Stewart Parnell', *Aberdeen Standard*, 14 Sep 1893; 'Joseph Chamberlain', ibid., 19 Oct 1893; 'Socialists and Anarchists' [from the *Aberdeen Standard*], *Labour Elector*, Jan 1894, 9–10; *The Root of the Matter* (Melbourne, 1895); *The Claim of Women* (Sydney, 1895) ?P.; Preface to S. A. Byrne, *The Turn of Fortune's Wheel* (Melbourne, 1907); 'Quorum Pars Fui: an unconventional autobiography', *Trident* [Melbourne] (May–Nov 1908) [repr. in full in *Bull. Soc. Lab. Hist.*, no. 47 (Autumn 1983) with an Introduction by A. Whitehead, 17–35].

Sources: (1) MS: Correspondence and an autobiographical sketch (typescript, 9 pp. and undated), Mitchell Library, State Library of New South Wales, Australia; John Burns Coll., BL. (2) Other: J. H. Watts, 'The Man in the Moon again', *PM Gaz.*, 4 Dec 1885; 'From the Social Democrat Point of View', ibid., 9 Feb 1886; S. Olivier, 'A Champion of the Perverse', *To-day 6* (Nov 1886) 175–8; 'The Parliamentary Representation of Mid-Lanark', *Scotsman*, 23 Mar 1888, 6; *Justice*, 20 Oct 1888; *Labour Elector*, 1 Dec 1888; M. E. Harkness, 'Letters' [relating to Keir Hardie's election expenses], *Star*, 20 and 25 Sep 1889; *Labour Elector*, 1 Mar 1890; J. D. Fitzgerald, 'Mr H. H. Champion on the Australian Strike', *19th C. 29* (Mar 1891) 445–53; *Labour Annual* (1896) 197–8; *The Encyclopaedia of Social Reform*, ed. W. D. P. Bliss (1897) 218–19; *Marlborough College Register from 1843 to 1889 Inclusive*, 4th ed. (1900); G. B. Shaw, Preface to *Cashel Byron's Profession* (1901); H. Quelch *et al.*, *How I became a Socialist* [1902?]; J. Burgess, *John Burns* (Glasgow, 1911) [Chs 3 and 4 give some account of Champion's friend the soap-manufacturer R. W. Hudson, who *may* have put up funds for Burns at Nottingham in the general election of 1885]; H. M. Hyndman, *The Record of an Adventurous Life* (1911); E. B. Bax, *Reminiscences and Reflexions of a Mid and Late Victorian* (1918); T. Mann, *Tom Mann's Memoirs* (1923); M. Roberts, *W. H. Hudson: a portrait* (1924); J. Clayton, *The Rise and Decline of Socialism in Great Britain, 1884–1924* (1926); J. Burgess, *Will Lloyd George supplant Ramsay MacDonald?* (Ilford, Essex, [1926?]); J. Macdonald, 'A Few Memories of H. H. Champion', *Social Democrat 45* (June 1928) 2; H. S. Salt, *Company I have kept* (1930); H. W. Lee and E. Archbold, *Social-Democracy in Britain* (1935); Havelock Ellis, *My Life* (1940; repr. 1967); H. Pelling, 'H. H. Champion: pioneer of labour representation', *Cambridge J. 6* (1952–3) 222–38; idem, *The Origins of the Labour Party, 1880–1900* (1954; 2nd ed. 1965); F. Engels and P. and L. Lafargue, *Correspondence*, tome *2: 1887–1890* (Paris, 1956); C. Tsuzuki, *H. M. Hyndman and British Socialism* (Oxford, 1961); A. E. P. Duffy, 'Differing Policies and Personal Rivalries in the Origins of the ILP', *Victorian Studies 6*, no. 1 (Sep 1962) 43–65; L. E. Fredman, 'A Note on Henry Hyde Champion and the Maritime Strike of 1890', *Labour History* [Canberra] *11* (Nov 1966) 62–5; P. Thompson, *Socialists, Liberals and Labour: the struggle for London, 1885–1914* (1967); H. Pelling, 'Corvo and Labour Politics', *TLS*, 6 Feb 1969; P. Kellock, 'H. H. Champion: the failure of Victorian Socialism' (fourth-year thesis, Dept of History, Monash, 1971); B. Walker, *Solidarity Forever!* (Melbourne, 1972); *Gissing: the critical heritage*, ed. P. Coustillas and C. Partridge (1972); P. Coustillas, 'Three Letters from Gissing to H. H. Champion', *Gissing Newsletter 8*, no. 1 (Jan 1972) 12–15; idem, 'People Gissing knew: II – H. H. Champion', ibid., *11*, no. 3 (July 1975) 11–18; L. M. Henderson, *The Goldstein Story* (Melbourne, 1973); S. Pierson, *Marxism and the Origins of British Socialism* (Ithaca, NY, 1973); V. Bailey, 'The Dangerous Classes in Late-Victorian England: some reflections on the social foundations of disturbance and order with special reference to London in the 1880s' (Warwick PhD, 1975); R. and E. Frow, 'The Modern Press and the Social Democratic Federation 1883–87', *Bull. Soc. Lab. Hist.*, no. 31 (Autumn 1975) 62–3; K. O. Morgan, *Keir Hardie: radical and socialist* (1975); K. D. Brown, *John Burns* (1977); N.

and J. MacKenzie, *The First Fabians* (1977); F. Reid, *Keir Hardie: the making of a socialist* (1978); *Australian Dictionary of Biography*, vol. 7 (Melbourne, 1979); N. MacKenzie, 'Percival Chubb and the Founding of the Fabian Society', *Victorian Studies 23*, no. 1 (Autumn 1979) 29–55; F. Boos, 'William Morris's Socialist Diary', *History Workshop J. 13* (1982) 1–75; B. Webb, *The Diary of Beatrice Webb*, vol. *1: 1873–1892*, ed. N. and J. MacKenzie (1982). Biographical information: Australian High Commission, London; Dept of History, Monash Univ.; National Army Museum; Royal Artillery Institution; State Library of New South Wales; Miss M. Creightmore, South Yarra, Victoria; J. Holroyd, Windsor, Victoria; Prof. N. MacKenzie, Lewes, Sussex; Dr H. Pelling, Cambridge; Dr G. Serle, Hawthorn, Victoria; K. Weller, London. Personal information: Mrs Inez Bell, Melbourne, Victoria and Mrs Keile Hinde, South Yarra, Victoria. OBIT. *Age* [Melbourne] and *Herald* [Melbourne], 1 May 1928; *Argus* [Melbourne], *Daily Chronicle, Daily Herald, Daily Telegraph, Star* and *Times*, 2 May 1928; *New Leader*, 4 May 1928; *Australian Worker* [Sydney], 9 May 1928.

ANDREW WHITEHEAD

See also: †Annie BESANT; †John Elliott BURNS; Margaret Elise HARKNESS; James Leigh JOYNES; Henry (Harry) QUELCH; †William James THORNE; †John (Jack) Edward WILLIAMS.

Maltman Barry: a bibliography

The principal source on the career of Barry is P. Martinez, 'The "People's Charter" and the Enigmatic Mr Maltman Barry', *Bull. Soc. Lab. Hist.*, no. 41 (Autumn 1980) 34–45, but the following works contain some details of his activities, although a number of basic facts of his life remain undiscovered. See C. M. Davies, *Unorthodox London or Phases of Religious Life in the Metropolis*, 2nd ser. (1875) 272–5; F. Kitz, 'Recollections and Reflections', serialised in *Freedom* (1912) [published in a limited edition by C. Slienger in 1976]; W. Collison, *The Apostle of Free Labour* (1913); J. Burgess, *Will Lloyd George supplant Ramsay MacDonald?* (Ilford, [1926?]); M. Beer, *Fifty Years of International Socialism* (1935); H. W. Lee and E. Archbold, *Social-Democracy in Britain* (1935); H. Pelling, *The Origins of the Labour Party, 1880–1900* (1954; 2nd ed. 1965); H. Collins, 'The English Branches of the First International', in *Essays in Labour History*, vol. *1*, ed. A. Briggs and J. Saville (1960) 242–75; C. Tsuzuki, *H. M. Hyndman and British Socialism* (Oxford, 1961); H. Collins and C. Abramsky, *Karl Marx and the British Labour Movement* (1965). NOTE. The editors wish to acknowledge the assistance given by Andrew Whitehead in the compilation of this bibliography.

CHATTERTON, Daniel (1820–95)
ATHEIST AND COMMUNIST

Born on 25 August 1820 at 6 Dorrington Street – now part of Mount Pleasant – in the Clerkenwell district of London, Dan was the eldest child of Daniel Chatterton and his wife. Chatterton described his parents as in 'a fair position' [*Biography* [1891?] 1]. His mother was a Christian, but he was much more influenced by his father, an atheist, who worked as a japanner. Chatterton recalled that as a young boy he accompanied his father to the Rotunda in Blackfriars Road, a venue for radical and free-thought meetings. His health during childhood was poor, and for this reason he was twice sent away to school. He was brought home at the age of twelve after an accident befell his father which apparently forced him to give up japanning and work as a coal merchant. By the age of fourteen, Dan was apprenticed to a bootmaker and he ascribed at least some of his intellectual development to 'mixing with Workmen who are proverbialy [sic] thinkers' [ibid., 2]. He later set up in business on his own account but was unsuccessful and so was obliged, as he put it, to earn a 'precarious crust' as a journeyman.

Nothing is known of Chatterton's involvement in Chartism beyond his own statement that he was badly injured during a police attack on a Chartist meeting on Clerkenwell Green in 1848 – a misfortune in which he rather gloried. In March 1855, during the Crimean War, Chatterton enlisted in the 77th Foot Regiment, receiving a bounty of seven pounds. He was not well suited to military life, a diminutive figure at just over five feet and four inches, and was repeatedly ill. He was discharged after two years' service. Dan Chatterton's occupation on enlistment was recorded as shoemaker, and he appears to have resumed this trade on his return to London. He married Emma Cook, the illiterate daughter of a labourer, in St Pancras Parish Church in July 1857. Emma died of pneumonia in St Pancras Workhouse in February 1865 at the age of thirty-two. Chatterton married again in July 1867 to Emily Scott, the daughter of a tailor and at twenty-one less than half Dan's age. It is not clear when she died, but she is believed not to have outlived her husband. He often spoke at Malthusian League meetings about the poverty and miseries that a large family and the resultant overcrowding had inflicted on him:

He was a Communist, and more than that a strong Neo-Malthusian. He advised the poor to marry if they pleased, but to have as few children as possible until they were better off. He himself had drunk deep of the cup of human misery, having been the father of ten children, eight of whom were dead, and having witnessed sights enough to drive him into despair [*Malthusian*, June 1884, 518].

His personal sufferings were clearly an important factor behind the temper of his political propaganda.

Two of the issues to which Chatterton devoted particular attention – slum housing and family limitation – reflected what must have been very personal concerns. He was once reported as referring 'in a vehement and unreportable manner to the condition of the poor, remarking that he lived in a house in which every brick was loose, and yet the rental of it was £126 per year [shame], and not fit for a pig to live in' [*Malthusian*, Feb 1884, 483]. This was a recurring theme in his pamphlets, as was his emphasis on the sufferings of women and their role in overthrowing the established institutions of society. One of his titles, *Babies and Bunny Rabbits* [1883?], has been described as 'what appears to be the first birth control tract of the nineteenth century written by a worker for other workers' [McLaren (1978) 175]. In it Chatterton republished details of various contraceptive methods, including the sheath and the vaginal syringe. Although he was associated with the Malthusian League, the arguments he advanced in this pamphlet were not the standard neo-Malthusian ones, for he advocated contraception on the grounds that sexual love should be enjoyed without risking penury and starvation.

The extent of Chatterton's political activity in the first fifty years of his life is something of a mystery. He recalled that he was hurt, though apparently less seriously than in 1848, during a Reform demonstration in 1866. He first achieved prominence in the republican and extreme radical organisations which developed out of the Reform League. He was a leading figure in the Land and Labour League, a member of its council, and proprietor of the copyright of the *Republican* (1870–2), a journal closely associated with the League [Harrison (1965) 226–7]. Chatterton was also on the general committee of the Anti-Game Law League, which had been established in 1872 [Hopkins (1985) 254], and in the same year he was briefly involved with the Universal Republican League, an offshoot of a seceding group from the International Working Men's Association. He was active in the National

Education League, but withdrew because he supported secular rather than simply non-sectarian education. Chatterton was a frequent speaker at meetings of the Patriotic Society, and once this body had obtained premises on Clerkenwell Green – where it developed into one of the foremost radical clubs in London – he served briefly on the club committee. He appears not to have been connected with any of the specifically O'Brienite organisations, but his political ideas at this time – with their emphasis on land nationalisation and currency reform – reflect the prevalent influence of Bronterre O'Brien's teaching among artisan radicals in London.

Chatterton's first pamphlet, which appeared without attribution, was about the victimisation in 1872 of Metropolitan Police constables involved in an agitation for more pay. In a style which came to be the hallmark of Chatterton's writings, he argued that if the police and armed forces began to think for themselves, they would join the people in a revolution:

> in fact, an entire smashing-up of kings, queens, princes, priests, and policemen, land and money mongers, and rascality of all sizes and degrees – in a word, an entire re-organisation of Society on the basis of Liberty, Equality, and Fraternity [Chatterton [1872] 4].

The first of the pamphlets written under his own name appeared three years later, and like all those that followed it was robustly, even rudely, atheistic, denouncing 'priestcraft' and 'kingcraft'. His tracts became increasingly intemperate and insurrectionary. He poured invective on the Queen and the Royal Family and on politicians and political organisations of all hues. He incited the downtrodden to bloody revolution which would sweep away their oppressors, and he was angered by the apathy of his intended audience. The most cogent presentation of his political programme is to be found in *The Commune in England* [1882?]. In this he put forward a People's Programme by which a Senate would be elected by all men and women over twenty to establish secular, free and compulsory education, the nationalisation of the land and all natural resources and public utilities, the creation of a national system of credit, banking, pensions and retailing, and other far-reaching reforms.

The style and more particularly the appearance of Chatterton's publications changed markedly in the mid-1880s, when he commenced his most extraordinary venture, *Chatterton's Commune: the atheistic communistic scorcher*. This unorthodox and sometimes barely legible publication appeared more or less quarterly from September 1884 until Chatterton's death. 'Old Chat' wrote all the articles, composed the ill-matching type, and printed without a press using just his hands to get an impression on the cheap yellow tissue which he used as paper. The print run was about one hundred, and production was further handicapped by Chatterton's ill health and failing eyesight. He was proud to describe his paper as the 'most Unique Production of the Nineteenth Century' [*Chatterton's Commune*, no. 14 [Jan 1889?] 4].

Chatterton described himself as an atheist and communist. He was a proselytiser for free-thought and delighted in enticing clerics into debate, even succeeding in drawing an exchange of letters from the Archbishop of Canterbury [*Times*, 27 Mar 1880]. He was not associated with any particular organisation, though in his last years his closest links outside the secular movement were probably with the anarchist groups. He was a familiar figure at open-air meetings and demonstrations, expounding his views and selling his publications; and his regular interventions at public meetings of all kinds reinforced his reputation as a political maverick. H. H. Champion recalled how, in the 1880s, Chatterton had disrupted a meeting of the Clerkenwell branch of the Social Democratic Federation at which Lord Brabazon was propounding the merits of emigration:

> Chatterton struggled on to the platform and poured out his indignation. Gaunt, ragged, unshaven, almost blind he stood, the embodiment of helpless, furious poverty, and

shaking his palsied fist in Brabazon's face, denounced him and his efforts to plaster over social sores, winding up with a lurid imaginative account of the Uprising of the People and a procession in which the prominent feature would be the head of the noble lecturer on a pike [*Book Lover*, Aug 1899, 25–6].

On the other hand, Stewart Headlam's biographer recorded the story of how Chatterton once rounded on a fellow atheist who was giving Headlam a hard time at a public meeting: 'You let him alone. I've been turned out of every public-house debating society in London for saying things which this here parson let me say at his meetings without a murmur' [Bettany (1926) 55].

Anecdotes about Chatterton abound, and there are also several more considered and substantial descriptions of him. The individualist John Henry Mackay included a lengthy pen sketch of Chatterton – 'a strange old man whose face certainly no one ever forgot after having once seen it' – in his documentary novel *The Anarchists* [(1891) 51–5]. Richard Whiteing provided a fascinating but more fanciful portrait of him, under the guise of 'Old 48', in his popular novel *No. 5 John Street*. Another detailed description appears in the reminiscences of the writer W. Pett Ridge [[1925?] 66–71].

Chatterton lived variously in St Pancras, Somers Town and King's Cross, and for the last ten or so years of his life in the notorious slums around Drury Lane. One of Charles Booth's informants, a City Missionary, encountered Dan and his handicapped son, both of 'good character', in the second floor of a house off Drury Lane:

The man is a notorious Atheist, one who holds forth on behalf of his creed under railway arches, saying that if there be a God he must be a monster to permit such misery as exists. This man suffers from heart disease, and the doctor tells him that some day in his excitement he will drop down dead. His room is full of Freethought publications [Booth (1902) vol. *2*, 65].

Chatterton made his living in his old age as a bill-sticker and vendor of free-thought and left-wing papers. He may also have received grants from a benevolent fund of the National Secular Society [*Star*, 10 July 1895].

Chatterton died of pneumonia and asthma at 29 Goldsmith Buildings, Drury Lane, on 7 July 1895. He was buried three days later in a common grave in the St Pancras Cemetery at Finchley. The funeral was conducted by a prominent secularist and radical, Robert Forder. Chatterton's wish to be cremated, for which he had tried to raise money by selling cabinet photographs of himself at a shilling (two photographs survive in the Nettlau Collection), was not realised. The obituaries paid tribute to Chatterton's personal integrity and the courage with which he promoted his political beliefs. A sympathetic piece in the London evening paper the *Star* was accompanied by a drawing of Chatterton. 'His well-known figure will be sadly missed', wrote the anarchist journal *Freedom*, 'for he had no enemies – not even amongst the police. His seventy-five years of poverty and struggle endured mostly in the gutters of London streets, fighting in his own way the battle against social injustice, is a piece of heroism which will carry his name down to future generations.'

Writings: A number of Chatterton's pamphlets, including his autobiography written in the third person, were reprinted in *Chatterton's Commune*. The BL has all forty-two issues of this journal, available for consultation both in original format and on microfilm. Pamphlets: *The Revolution in the Police* [1872] 8 pp.; *Hell, Devils and Damnation* [1875?] 8 pp.; *The Fruits of a Philosophical Research* [1877?] 8 pp.; *Blood, Bullets and Bayonets* [1879?] 8 pp.; *The Homes of the Poor and the Board of Works* [1879?] 8 pp.; *Chatterton's Letter to the Prince of Wales* [1882?] 8 pp.; *The Commune in England* [1882?] 8 pp.; *The Existence of God* [1882?] 8

pp.; *Babies and Bunny Rabbits* [1883?] 8 pp.; *God and Gold* [1886?] 8 pp.; *Impeachment of the Queen, Cabinet, Parliament and People* [1886?] 8 pp.; *What is Life? What is Death?* [1886?] 8 pp.; *The Franchise Swindle* [1887?] 8 pp.; *The Homes of the Poor and the Royal Commission Swindle* [1887?] 10 pp.; *Impeachment of the Queen, Cabinet, Parliament and People* [1887?] 8 pp.; *The Wail of the Worker* [1887?] 8 pp.; *Merry England, so-called* [1888?] 8 pp.; *Biography of Dan Chatterton* [1891?] 8 pp.; *Where are you going to when you die?* [1892?] 8 pp.

Sources: (1) MS: Nettlau Coll., IISH, Amsterdam; quarterly paylists for the 77th Foot Regiment, PRO. (2) Other: London directories, 1805–46; *Republican*, Mar and Nov 1871; *Clerkenwell News*, 22 Mar 1871 and 17 Jan 1872; *National Reformer*, 26 May 1872; E. D. J., 'Red London: V. The London Patriotic Society', *Weekly Dispatch*, 6 July 1879, 12; *Malthusian*, July 1879, Feb and Aug 1880, Jan 1881, Feb 1883, Feb and June 1884; *Times*, 27 Mar 1880; *Observer*, 28 Mar 1880; *Justice*, 15 Jan 1887; *Star*, 31 July 1888; *New York Herald* [London], 1 June 1890; *Clerkenwell Chronicle*, 1 Nov 1890; J. H. Mackay, *The Anarchists: a picture of civilization at the close of the nineteenth century* trans. from the German (Boston, Mass., 1891); R. Whiteing, *No. 5 John Street* (1899); *Book Lover* [Melbourne] *1*, no. 4 (Aug 1899); C. Booth, *Life and Labour of the People in London*, 17 vols (1902); W. Pett Ridge, *I like to remember* [1925?]; F. G. Bettany, *Stewart Headlam: a biography* (1926); B. Webb, *My Apprenticeship* (1926); M. Nettlau, *Anarchisten und Sozialrevolutionäre ... in den Jahren 1880–1886* (Berlin, 1931); M. Kavanagh, 'Some Little-known Anarchists: Dan Chatterton', *Freedom*, Feb 1934, 4, repr. in rev. form in *War Commentary*, 10 Feb 1945, 2; E. P. Thompson, *William Morris: romantic to revolutionary* (1955); R. Harrison, *Before the Socialists: studies in labour and politics, 1861–81* (1965); R. Harrison, G. B. Woolven and R. Duncan, *The Warwick Guide to British Labour Periodicals, 1790–1970* (Hassocks, Sussex, 1977); A. McLaren, *Birth Control in Nineteenth Century England* (1978); J. Quail, *The Slow Burning Fuse: the lost history of the British Anarchists* (1978); N. Walter, 'Community and Commitment', *Freedom*, 2 Sep 1978, 9–11, 15; 16 Sep 1978, 9–13, 15; 30 Sep 1978, 9–12, 16; E. Royle, *Radicals, Secularists and Republicans: popular freethought in Britain, 1866–1915* (Manchester, 1980); H. Shpayer, 'British Anarchism, 1881–1914: reality and appearance' (London PhD, 1981); L. Barrow, 'Determinism and Environmentalism in Socialist Thought', in *Culture, Ideology and Politics*, ed. R. Samuel and G. Stedman Jones (1982) 194–214; H. Oliver, *The International Anarchist Movement in Late-Victorian London* (1983); J. Burnett, D. Vincent and D. Mayall, *The Autobiography of the Working Class*, vol. *1* (1984); H. Hopkins, *The Long Affray: the poaching wars in Britain* (1985); A. Whitehead, 'Forgotten Freethinkers (1): "Old Chat" ', *Freethinker*, Sep 1985, 136–7, 140. Biographical information: H. Becker, Münster, Germany; Bishopsgate Institute, London; Bodleian Law Library, Oxford; BL, London; Dr D. Englander, Milton Keynes, Bucks; W. Fishman, London; Dr D. Goodway, Leeds; St Pancras Cemetery, Finchley, London; N. Sinnott, Yarraville, Victoria, Australia; K. Weller, London. OBIT. *Star*, 10 July 1895; *Freethinker*, 14 July 1895; *Torch*, 18 July 1895; *Anarchist* [Sheffield] *2*, no. 20 (Aug 1895); *Freedom*, Aug 1895.

ANDREW WHITEHEAD

See also: Henry Hyde CHAMPION.

COMSTIVE, William (1792–1834)
RADICAL AND GRANGE MOOR INSURGENT

Born at the tiny hamlet of Myerscough, north of Preston in Lancashire, and baptised at

Garstang Parish Church on 10 June 1792, Comstive was the son of Ann Comstive, whose social position in the community was recorded in a single word: 'poor'. His father, whose name does not appear in the parish register, was a soldier who died in battle in the early years of the war with France. Later in life William Comstive's letters reveal that he was aware he was 'base born'. Ann Comstive was not able to maintain her child, so young William was sent to live with various relatives, including an aunt who lived at Kirkham and an uncle, William Comstive senior, who in 1820 was a master dyer at the Catteral works near Garstang in Lancashire. Throughout his life Comstive seems to have harboured bitter feelings against his mother for her inability to raise him and in a letter he mentions that she had not seen him since he became a man.

In 1811, at the age of nineteen, Comstive enlisted in the 29th Regiment of Infantry and in the next seven years he served in the Peninsular War and was at the battle of Waterloo. In 1813 he was demoted from corporal and in 1815 from sergeant for 'unsteady conduct'. After completing his military service in 1818 he returned to Kirkham before moving on to Barnsley in Yorkshire, where he became a journeyman weaver in the still-expanding linen trade. It was there in 1819 that he got involved in the radical politics of the Barnsley Union Society, and, when in early 1820 that organisation decided to participate in a general rising or insurrection, Comstive was chosen to act as their military commander. He and Richard Addy, a Yorkshireman who had also served in the Army, were thought to have the necessary military experience to lead armed men. At the same time it should be noted that Comstive was not part of the inner circle of veteran Barnsley radicals, known as the Secret Acting Committee. He was too recent an arrival in Barnsley to be entrusted with the decision to rebel; instead he was told to march the men to Huddersfield.

On the night of 11 April 1820, after he had drawn up a plan of attack, Comstive led a group of 300 or 400 ill-armed Barnsley area radicals on a twelve-mile march to Grange Moor outside Huddersfield. According to eyewitnesses, the men were armed with pikes and a few guns, they marched in military fashion and many had knapsacks on their backs. A man familiar with the route went ahead and pointed out those houses where guns could be seized. The Barnsley area rebels planned to capture Huddersfield in concert with thousands of other armed radicals from the entire West Riding of Yorkshire. They reached Grange Moor at 5 a.m. on the morning of 12 April and Comstive drew the men up in a line. They unfurled their radical banners and then some Huddersfield radicals came out to inform them that the rising was off. The men began to break ranks, discard their weapons and generally flee as best they could. Comstive was one of the last to leave the field and he was captured by a contingent of soldiers as he tried to slip into Huddersfield. The rising was a fiasco, but most of the rebels managed to escape. Comstive and twenty others were apprehended and sent to York Castle to be charged with High Treason.

While in prison he sought consolation in the Bible and his letters indicate a familiarity with Scriptures. He was a 'good penman' and often acted as a spokesman for the rebels during their incarceration and at the subsequent trial. When the men petitioned for better prison conditions, Comstive's bold signature headed the list of names. Like many early nineteenth-century political prisoners, Comstive tried to bargain with the authorities by offering to give and to obtain information about radical conspiracies. The Home Office refused to make any deal with him, as it was aware that he was holding back information on the Yorkshire unrest of 1820.

At a special Yorkshire Assize in September 1820, the Grange Moor rebels were found guilty of High Treason and sentenced to death. This was later commuted to transportation (for life in Comstive's case) and he, along with ten other rebels, was sent to Van Diemen's Land (Tasmania) aboard the convict ship *Lady Ridley* in 1821. His conduct in the hulks and during the voyage was reported to be good.

Once in Australia this pattern changed and between 1823 and 1832 Comstive was convicted eight times on charges of drunkenness. He was sent to labour on the docks in the

Launceston and George Town areas in the north of Tasmania. In spite of his problems he was entrusted with the position of overseer. Other offences committed by him included: 'Using improper language to overseer McClure' (1825), assault (1831), and 'absent from church muster' (1833). This type of behaviour caused him further difficulties, and in 1827, for example, he was sentenced to work in 'irons' for one month. In 1834 he was implicated in the forging of a bill and his death on 9 May 1834 is noted in the convict records.

While other convicts, including some political exiles, seized the opportunities offered by the Australian convict system and obtained pardons, Comstive was never awarded his freedom. He died as he had arrived some thirteen years earlier – a convict. There is no record that he ever married or that he had any children.

Sources: (1) MS: Lancashire CRO, Preston: Garstang Baptismal Register, 1792. PRO: WO 12/4505–9, W. Comstive's service record; HO 20/1, letters and petitions of prisoners in York Castle, 1820; HO 40/12, Yorkshire Insurrection papers, 1820; HO 41/6, H. Hobhouse to S. Corbett, 26 Feb 1821; HO 44/2, W. Comstive to W. Comstive senior, Aug 1820; TS 979/3573, depositions concerning the Grange Moor rebellion, Apr 1820. Barnsley PL: J. H. Burland, 'Annals of Barnsley' [c. 1881]. Tasmanian State Archives, Hobart: convict records, CON 31/6. (2) Other: J. L. and B. Hammond, *The Skilled Labourer* (1919; later eds); E. Hoyle, *History of Barnsley* (Barnsley, Yorks, 1924); E. P. Thompson, *The Making of the English Working Class* (1963; 2nd ed. 1968); F. Peel, *The Risings of the Luddites, Chartists and Plug-drawers*, 4th ed. with an Introduction by E. P. Thompson (1968); F. K. Donnelly and J. L. Baxter, 'The Revolutionary "Underground" in the West Riding: myth or reality?', *Past and Present*, no. 64 (1974) 124–32; F. K. Donnelly, 'The General Rising of 1820' (Sheffield PhD, 1975); J. Stevens, *England's Last Revolution: Pentrich 1817* (Buxton, Derbys, 1977).

F. K. DONNELLY

See also: Thomas FARRIMOND; Benjamin SCHOLES.

DAVENPORT, Allen (1775–1846)
SPENCEAN, CO-OPERATOR, SECULARIST AND CHARTIST

Allen Davenport was born on May Day 1775 in Ewen, a village on the Gloucestershire–Wiltshire border. One of the ten children of an impoverished domestic weaver, he received no formal education, but taught himself to read principally by studying broadsheet ballads he had already learned by ear. He worked from the age of twelve, first as a groom for a local gentleman farmer, then as a groom and horse-breaker for a veterinary surgeon named Lawrence, in nearby Cirencester. At nineteen, however, he ran away to Bristol intending to become a sailor; but instead he was recruited into the Windsor Foresters, a light cavalry regiment. In spite of his seven years' enlistment, from 1794 to 1800, Davenport never saw service overseas and spent most of his time in Scotland. It was while stationed in Aberdeen that he learned, with the assistance of two friends, the trade of shoemaker. This he followed for the rest of his life, commencing at Cirencester on his discharge from the Army. After four years working for a master at what he later described as 'starvation prices', Davenport moved to London. He never again returned to his native Gloucestershire.

In his youth Davenport had been 'a staunch Tory', but he had by now become a supporter of Charles James Fox. He was disgusted, though, by the Foxites' performance in office. However, shortly after arriving in London, Allen Davenport read *The Important*

Trial of Thomas Spence, the Newcastle-born agrarian reformer imprisoned in 1801 for seditious libel. The trial proceedings reprinted his offending book, *The Restorer of Society to its Natural State*, in its entirety. The effect of reading this was akin to religious conversion for Davenport:

> I read the book and immediately became an out and out Spencean. I preached the doctrine to my shopmates, and to everybody else, wherever and whenever I could find an opportunity. I had been a sort of Whig reformer before; but I now saw clearly, that all Whig, Tory, or even Radical Reformers were as rushlights to the meridian sun, in comparison with that proposed by the clear headed, and honest hearted Thomas Spence. And I told all the reformers that I met with, that no other reform was worth fighting for, but they generally laughed at me, and called me a visionary. This was in 1805 [*Life* (1845) 42].

Davenport was not at this time involved in any trade politics: his early years in the capital were spent working in non-society shops. But about 1810 he joined a large Holborn shop, Bainbridge's, in Southampton Court, Queen Square. His wife, whom he had married in 1806, was already employed in Bainbridge's workshop as a shoe-binder. Davenport remained here until 1828, specialising in the production of women's shoes. He immediately joined the fifth section of the 'ladies' men', which met at the York Arms, Holborn, and shortly became a delegate to the society's executive. His period of service coincided with the peak of the ladies' men's power, with fourteen London divisions, an extensive provincial correspondence, and the confidence and means to enforce wage demands and the exclusion of non-apprenticed labour at law. In 1813, however, the society overreached itself: a strike in support of a detailed price-list having been successful, further action was taken, prematurely in Davenport's view, by 'some of the more turbulent of the members'. This brought into being an employers' association which successfully resisted the strike and imposed wage reductions. Davenport dated the decline of his union from this event. It was this perhaps that imbued him with a lasting scepticism as to the efficacy of trades combinations, for in 1825 he was to argue in the *Trades' Newspaper* (4 Dec) that workers' combinations served only to encourage retaliatory action by employers: 'what do they produce, generally speaking, but discontent and misery?' There is no record of Allen Davenport having taken part in the prolonged strike of the 'ladies' men' in 1826. Surplus labour, in his view, undermined the every effort of trades combinations, and it was therefore upon efforts to eliminate the former that he concentrated his political energies, very much in accordance with his initiation into radical politics through the writings of Thomas Spence. He was inclined to see in employers a potential ally with whom to oppose the landed interest (his own employer, Bainbridge, was a close friend), and he adhered to this view even as a class leader in the National Union of the Working Classes.

In spite of the fact that reading Thomas Spence had constituted such a watershed in his life, Davenport did not become involved in political activity outside his trade society until the post-war period. These depressed years, he later recognised, turned him into a 'desperate politician'. He attended all the reform meetings of 1816–17, and in 1818 joined the Spenceans at their new meeting-room in Archer Street, Soho. Henceforward he was to be consistently active in the metropolitan radical movement, and his prolific career as a writer dates also from the same time.

Davenport had started writing in 1814 with a satirical poem in a Sunday paper, the *News*, on the peace celebrations of that year: a sequel attacking the Prince Regent, however, was declined as libellous and it was nearly four years before he recommenced serious writing. William T. Sherwin, in whose [*Weekly*] *Political Register* much of his early work appeared, was particularly encouraging, decisively so in respect of his prose writing. Davenport was by inclination a poet, however, and his first major publications in his own right were both lengthy poems, *The Kings, or Legitimacy unmasked* (1819), a spirited republican drama; and *Claremont* [1820?], a satirical elegy on the death of Princess Charlotte, daughter of the Prince Regent, written during the radical agitation over Queen Caroline.

Davenport deserves recognition, however, for more than his radical writing. With the appearance of his work in print came increasing confidence upon the platform. By the autumn of 1819 he had cast off the alias of Ferguson, hitherto used by him in public speaking. In the spring of that year, following a split in the Spencean leadership, Davenport joined the more pragmatic Robert Wedderburn (a mulatto tailor) at another Soho chapel, in Hopkins Street. The news of Peterloo completed what might be termed Davenport's political apprenticeship: 'War . . . has already been declared against us why then should we hesitate, for my own part I am ready now. . . . I compare the present time to the crisis of the French Revolution, we must arm ourselves as they did' [HO 42/197, 18 Oct 1819]. At Hopkins Street, Davenport fast made his mark as a spirited and incisive political orator; here also he and Wedderburn led a branch of the Watsonite 'General Union of Non-Represented People'. In the closing months of 1819 the chapel became a significant centre of both radical debate and armed drilling. Infiltrating the covert movement which inelegantly culminated in the Cato Street affair, a Home Office spy reported, 'Thislewood [*sic*] says he depends more on Wedderburn's division for being armed than all the rest' [ibid.]. These reports, as well as the fact that shoemakers' societies were poised to lend considerable support, suggest that Davenport must be regarded as having been implicated in the Cato Street conspiracy. It is not surprising that his autobiography is silent about his personal connections with Wedderburn and Thistlewood, or that he maintained a low profile for almost the next three years.

During this period, however, Davenport's poetic contributions to the Queen Caroline episode achieved a quite wide currency. His personal affairs also took a new turn when he was appointed by his employer, William Bainbridge, to oversee a building development in Tollington Park, Finsbury Park. Davenport lived in a cottage on the site from 1822 to 1828. Here, largely through gardening, he rediscovered something of the rural pleasures of his youth, which in turn 'rekindled in my mind [a] fond and ardent passion for the Muses' [*Life*, 54]. His enthusiasm for agrarian reforms was likewise stimulated. In September 1823 he returned to political journalism with the first of twelve articles in Richard Carlile's *Republican*. During the same period Davenport proposed a scheme for statutory wage rises in step with bread prices, and commenced a lifelong advocacy of co-operation and Owenite socialism. He described his acceptance of Owenism in the following terms:

> Though I still adhered to the '*Spencean system*', I conceived that the arrangements proposed by Robert Owen, were still more extensive and more complete, than merely causing the land to be made public property, seeing that the social system embraces all the powers of production and distribution of wealth, as well as holding the land in common, by an equitable administration of which would place all mankind *in a state of equality of condition* [ibid., 58].

In 1830 he became a founder member of the First Co-operative Manufacturing Community in Old Street, Finsbury. The group was a modest, but in retrospect highly significant, attempt to put into practice the precepts of the better known British Association for Promoting Co-operative Knowledge.

For a short period Davenport acted as storekeeper for the Community, for whom he composed a 'Co-operator's Catechism' [*British Co-operator*, July 1830], which is an invaluable insight into grass-roots Owenism. A dramatic indication of his enthusiasm for the cause was the decision, made by him and Charles Jennison (another former Spencean) to move house in 1831 in order to live closer to Robert Owen's Gray's Inn Road 'Labour Exchange'. Davenport's description of it is one of the most fascinating passages in his autobiography. About the same time he became founder member of another Finsbury radical society meeting at the Optimists' (later Philadelphian) Chapel. His associates here included James Watson, and the prominent trades leader John Gast. The Chapel and its successor, the Finsbury Forum, were the headquarters of the local NUWC group, of which Davenport was a class leader. The Finsbury radical–secularist axis was the principal focus for the energies of former Spenceans, and in 1833 the same group set up a lively radical forum at the Bowling Square Chapel, which doubled as a 'Society for Scientific, Useful and Literary Information'. Allen Davenport was a frequent lecturer here, and later at the Finsbury Hall of Science, City Road.

Davenport never lost sight of the call for the public ownership of the land which had first attracted him into radicalism. In the 1830s he, more than any other, presided over the revival of interest in Thomas Spence, a biography of whom he published in 1836. His advocacy of land reform, however, did not blind him to the merits of other causes. He was insistent, for example, that the principle of public ownership should be extended to machinery as well. He was also among the earliest and most forthright *male* supporters of feminist causes. His advocacy of birth control was founded, significantly, on a specific appreciation of a woman's desire to control her own fertility [*Republican*, 25 Aug 1826]. His views on marriage were those of Robert Owen, but he was no slavish follower of the latter and belonged rather to that often overlooked group of working people who, while being socialists, chose to distance themselves from Owen. Davenport regarded him as admirable but essentially unworldly, and criticised in particular his doctrine of the formation of character and what he perceived to be over-fastidiousness in setting up practical community experiments. In 1839 he unsuccessfully applied to join the Manea Fen community in Cambridgeshire, a group which was completely independent of the main Owenite movement and without Owen's personal sanction. The same sense of frustration at the direction of the socialist movement led him later to support warmly the Chartist Land Plan, believing that it was more effective than Owenism in promoting a widespread redistribution of property and the establishment of agrarian communities. He fully appreciated the shortcomings of the Plan from the socialist point of view.

The measure of Davenport's standing as a metropolitan reformer can be seen in his close involvement in radical activities throughout the capital: in Soho, in Finsbury, and occasionally south of the river, where he addressed both NUWC meetings, and those of the Borough Female Society. Yet he was dogged by ill health and increasingly defective sight, which made working and writing difficult. In 1834 he very nearly died and was for a time dependent on the assistance of his trade society, and on a public subscription organised by Henry Hetherington and James Watson. He now went to live with an old friend and fellow Finsbury radical, Charles Neesom, and his wife at 5 Moor Lane in the City. Upon his recovery Davenport became actively involved in East End politics. With Neesom and Charles Jennison, he was instrumental in setting up a workers' mutual education society, the Eastern Institution, in Shoreditch. The three were also co-founders of the East London Democratic Association, of which Davenport was the first president. The association was the more radical of the two organisations from which metropolitan Chartism principally grew; it was here that Davenport met the young George Julian Harney, who became a close friend. Davenport was elected to the executive of the Central National Association, an abortive attempt to unite the factions within London radicalism; but his application to join the London Working Men's Association was initially blocked. He was a supporter of the City Charter, and Shoreditch Democratic, Associations; but, in the light of the successive rebuffs sustained by Chartism during the years 1839–42, Davenport's position, like that of his friend Neesom, moderated. Both men, for example, joined Lovett's National Association, of which Davenport was made an honorary member in 1844.

Now in his seventies, Davenport concentrated mainly on secularist and educational activities. Since 1836 he had been president of the Great Tower Street Mutual Instruction

Society, Covent Garden; and he became president also of the Gould Square Mechanics' Institute, and was instrumental in setting up the Finsbury Mutual Instruction Society in Bunhill Row. He was a frequent patron of the Cornish Coffee House in the same street, and a keen participant in public discussions there: 'I have always considered', he wrote at the end of his life, 'this house a sort of second home' [*Life* (1845) 72]. In 1843 he was elected auditor to the Anti-Persecution Union, recently formed to assist free-thinkers facing prosecution or imprisonment, and their families. Though writing less frequently for the radical press, Davenport continued with his own publications. *English Institutions* (1842), a poem extolling the virtues of Mechanics' Institutes, mutual instruction societies and Halls of Science, reflected his abiding interest in education. *The Origin of Man and the Progress of Society* (1846) was based on his popular lecture series, tracing the development of the institution of private property. In the previous year he had published his *Life and Literary Pursuits*, an autobiography not unnaturally suffused with its author's pride in his achievements as an autodidact. A copy of this work, long believed lost, has recently been discovered and reveals the full force of Davenport's commitment to popular education. It was membership of mutual instruction societies and the like, rather than of political organisations, which Davenport chose especially to emphasise. His part in the Chartist movement is nowhere mentioned; but his faith in educational progress as the guarantor of real reform is everywhere apparent.

Davenport had not, though, withdrawn from involvement in Chartism. His continued association with Harney, (who promoted renewed interest in the *Life of Spence* through the *Northern Star*) is an indication of this. Virtually Davenport's last contribution to the press was a poem 'O'Connorville' [*Northern Star*, 29 Aug 1846], written to celebrate the opening of the first Chartist Land Company estate. Davenport wrote only one other poem, in fact dictated on his deathbed, expressing his readiness to die a free-thinker. He died on 30 November 1846. In accordance with his express wishes he was buried in the unconsecrated section of Kensal Green Cemetery, after a procession from the Finsbury Hall of Science. George Harney and G. J. Holyoake were among the principal mourners, and the graveside oration was delivered by William Devonshire Saull, a veteran free-thinker and patron of radical causes. Allen Davenport was interred in an unmarked common grave (plot no. 6386/7). Subsequently Saull himself, and Henry Hetherington, were buried opposite him. His wife had died in 1816, ten years after their marriage; Mary Ann, apparently their only child, died some time after 1824. The final medical and burial expenses for Allen Davenport were met by appeals in the *Northern Star* and *Reasoner*. Throughout his life he had been constrained by poverty and attendant ill health. Holyoake remarked that, 'had he been less poor he would have been more famous' [*Reasoner*, 29 Jan 1847, 18]. Davenport did not, however, aspire to fame. It was as an educator, rather than as a leader, that he made his particular contribution, distinctive not least because of his commitment to the values of Spencean agrarianism throughout a political career spanning forty years, and to the broadening of his social and political horizons within the changing context of English radicalism.

Writings: Among the pseudonyms used by Davenport were 'Alphus' and 'Economicus'. The following bibliography, however, only covers signed articles, and those that can be positively ascribed to him. 'A Last Thought on the Fete', *News*, no. 476 (28 Aug 1814); 'To Mr. Wm. B——t M——ll' [poem], *Diligent Observer 1*, no. 4 (23 Aug 1817) col. 126; 'The Topic', *Sherwin's [Weekly] Political Register 2*, no. 15 (3 Jan 1818) 106; 'To the Patriots of Westminster', ibid. *3*, no. 5 (13 June 1818) 78–9; 'To the Editor of the *Political Register*', ibid., no. 12 (25 July 1818) 191–2; 'To the Editor of the *Political Register*', ibid., no. 15 (15 Aug 1818) 234–9; 'The Devil out-devilled', ibid., no. 17 (29 Aug 1818) 271–2; 'To the Editor', ibid., no. 18 (5 Sep 1818) 283–8; 'To the Editor', ibid., no. 20 (19 Sep 1818) 313–18;

'Reflections on Revolutions', ibid., no. 24 (17 Oct 1818) 373–80; 'A Hint to the Congress', ibid., 383–4; 'An Ode to Major Cartwright', *Medusa 1*, no. 14 (22 May 1819) 109; 'A Song', ibid. no. 16 (5 June 1819) 130; 'To the Editor on his Recent Death, his Subsequent Resurrection, and his Final Ascension into the Comet', *Theological Comet*, no. 3 (7 Aug 1819) 21; 'To the Editor, Letter I', ibid., no. 4 (14 Aug 1819) 28–9; 'To the Editor, Letter II', ibid., no. 6 (28 Aug 1819) 47–8; 'Hunt Triumphant', *Radical Reformer and People's Advocate*, no. 3 (29 Sep 1819) 21; 'To the Champion of Liberty', ibid., 21–2; 'Ministerial Plots and Royal Thanks', ibid., no. 6 (20 Oct 1819) 41–2; 'The Retrospect, or Bloody Buoy', ibid., no. 8 (3 Nov 1819) 61–2; 'St. Ethelstone's Day', *Theological Comet*, no. 16 (6 Nov 1819) 125; *The Kings, or, Legitimacy unmasked: a satirical poem* (1819) 12 pp. [copy in PRO, HO 42/220]; *Claremont, or the Sorrows of a Prince: an elegiac poem* [1820?] P. [copy in the Guildhall Library, City of London]; *Queen of the Isles* [1820?]; 'The Poet's Mite', *Republican 6*, no. 17 (20 Sep 1822) 516; 'To Mr R. Carlile', ibid., 515–16; 'Reflections on Agrarian Justice, being a Reply to Mr Carlile's Objections to an Agrarian Government', ibid., no. 21 (18 Oct 1822) 655–62; 'Congratulations to the Hero of the Press, Mr Carlile', ibid. 7, no. 4 (24 Jan 1823) 100–2; 'Sonnet', ibid., no. 11 (14 Mar 1823) 352; 'Monarchy, or Political Reflections, Part I', ibid., no. 18 (2 May 1823) 565–73; 'Monarchy, or Political Reflections, Part II', ibid., no. 25 (20 June 1823) 785–91; 'Monarchy, or Political Reflections, Part III', ibid. 8, no. 7 (22 Aug 1823) 212–18; 'The Captive', ibid. 9, no. 2 (9 Jan 1824) 63–4; 'Agrarian Equality', ibid. 10, no. 13 (1 Oct 1824) 390–411; 'Ghosts', *Republican 12*, no. 5 (5 Aug 1825) 155–7; 'Proposal for Bread Wages', *Trades' Newspaper and Mechanics' Weekly J.*, no. 9 (11 Sep 1825) 135; 'Bread Wages', ibid., no. 21 (4 Dec 1825) 322; 'Unions', ibid., no. 35 (12 Mar 1826) 517; 'To the Editor', *Republican 14*, no. 7 (25 Aug 1826) 220–3; 'Co-operation', *Co-op. Mag. 1*, no. 10 (Oct 1826) 329–30; 'Co-operation', ibid., no. 11 (Nov 1826) 356–7; 'The Gods, or Theological Reflections', *Republican 14*, no. 19 (17 Nov 1826) 579–87; 'Remarks on the Genius and Writings of the late Mr Percy Bysshe Shelley', ibid., no. 23 (15 Dec 1826) 715–17; *The Muse's Wreath: composed of original poems* (1827); 'The Co-operators Catechism', *British Co-operator*, no. 4 (July 1830) 73–6; 'The Co-operator's Catechism', *Associate and Co-operative Mirror*, nos 10, 11 and 12 (1830) [whole issues]; 'Co-operation', *Prompter*, no. 19 (19 Mar 1831) 311–12; '*Vox Populi, Vox Dei*', *Penny Papers for the People*, no. 26 (27 May 1831) 7; 'Hints to Judges and Juries', *Prompter*, no. 48 (8 Oct 1831); 'To the Lady of the Rotunda', *Isis*, no. 7 (24 Mar 1832) 112; 'Reflections on the Doctrine of Necessity, in a Letter to Robert Owen, Esq.', ibid., no. 8 (31 Mar 1832) 122–4; 'A View of Society', ibid., no. 11 (21 Apr 1832) 169–70; 'Liberty and Reason', *Cosmopolite 1*, no. 26 (1 Sep 1832); 'Female Patriotism', ibid., no. 29 (22 Sep 1832); 'The Magpie and the Wood Pigeon', *Crisis 1*, no. 30 (29 Sep 1832) 116–17; 'Sonnet to Henry Hetherington', *PMG*, no. 79 (8 Dec 1832) 638; 'The Ocean and the Mountain Stream', *Crisis 2*, no. 19 (18 May 1833) 151; Letter to the Editor, *Working Man's Friend and Political Instructor*, no. 24 (1 June 1833) 191; 'To the Editor of the *Man*', *Man 1*, no. 3 (21 July 1833) 20; 'The Agrarian System', ibid., no. 4 (28 July 1833) 26–7; 'The Origin of Man', ibid. 32; 'First Principles', ibid., no. 7 (18 Aug 1833) 51; 'Character of the Middle Classes', *PMG*, no. 116 (24 Aug 1833) 275; 'The Origin of England', *Man 1*, no. 9 (1 Sep 1833) 72; 'Character of the Middlemen', *PMG*, no. 118 (7 Sep 1833) 291–2; 'The Working Classes come to their Senses', ibid., no. 120 (21 Sep 1833) 308; 'Exclusive Dealing', ibid., no. 121 (28 Sep 1833) 315; 'The Golden God', ibid., no. 123 (12 Oct 1833) 331; 'The Promised Land', *Man 1*, no. 14 (23 Oct 1833) 112; 'Exclusive Dealing', *PMG*, no. 125 (26 Oct 1833) 346; 'Mr Hunt, the Reform Bill, and the Working Classes', ibid., no. 128 (16 Nov 1833) 370–1; 'Property in Danger', ibid., no. 189 (17 Jan 1835) 397–8; 'Unions – Causes of Failure – how might they be substituted?', ibid., no. 206 (16 May 1835) 533; 'Grounds for the Assembling of the People', ibid., no. 208 (30 May 1835) 547–8; 'Simultaneous Meetings', ibid., no. 215 (18 July 1835) 605–6; *The Life, Writings, and Principles of Thomäs Spence, Author of the Spencean System, or Agrarian Equality* [1836] 24 pp.; 'Universal Suffrage', *London Democrat*, no. 9 (8 June 1839); 'The

Rise, Progress, and Probable Results of the Social System', *Working Bee* n.s. *1*, no. 20 (17 Oct 1840) 158; 'Self-love', ibid., no. 21 (24 Oct 1840) 163; 'Self-love' [part two], ibid., no. 22 (31 Oct 1840) 171–2; 'Divine Providence', ibid., no. 25 (21 Nov 1840) 195; 'The Rise, Progress and Probable Results of the Social System' [part two], ibid., no. 26 (28 Nov 1840) 202–3, and [part three], ibid., no. 30 (26 Dec 1840) 234; 'The Question answered; or what is God?', *New Moral World* n.s. *2*, no. 4 (23 Jan 1841); 'The King of the Barricades', *National Association Gaz.*, no. 14 (2 Apr 1842); 'Frost's Farewell, or, the Exile of Cambria', ibid., no. 24 (11 June 1842); *English Institutions* (1842; reissued 1846 [copy of latter in Vanderbilt Univ. Library, Tenn.]); 'An Elergy on Mr. Shelley, written soon after his Death', *Oracle of Reason 2*, no. 98 (28 Oct 1843); *The Life and Literary Pursuits of Allen Davenport . . . written by himself* (1845) [copy in Vanderbilt Univ. Library, Tenn.; for a review of the *Life* see *Trades' Weekly Register and Apprentice*, Oct 1845, 156, and Nov 1845, 180]; 'The Patriot', *Northern Star*, 24 Jan 1846, 3; 'The Poet's Hope', ibid., 11 Apr 1846; 'Ireland in Chains', ibid., 25 Apr 1846; 'The Land, the People's Farm', ibid., 27 June 1846, 3; 'The Iron God', ibid., 3 July 1846, 3; 'The Social Sun', *Reasoner 1*, no. 10 (6 Aug 1846) 157–8; 'O'Connor-ville', *Northern Star*, 29 Aug 1846, 3; 'Hail Glorious Hades!', ibid., 3 Oct 1846, 3; *The Origin of Man and the Progress of Society* (1846) 15 pp. [copy in Goldsmiths' Library, London Univ.].

Sources: (1) MS: HO 42/197 (18, 27 Oct 1819), 42/198 (1, 15 Nov 1819) and 64/11 (27 July 1831), PRO; letterbook, 1845–8, G. J. Holyoake Coll., Bishopsgate Institute, London. (2) Other: 'To Correspondents', *News*, no. 479 (18 Sep 1814); *British Co-operator*, no. 4 (July 1830); *PMG*, 1831–5, esp. nos. 9 (3 Sep 1831), 12 (24 Sep 1831), 22 (19 Nov 1831), 64 (1 Sep 1832), 90 (23 Feb 1833), 111 (20 July 1833), 134 (28 Dec 1833), 184 (13 Dec 1834), 216 (25 July 1835) and 228 (17 Oct 1835); *Cosmopolite*, nos 52 (2 Mar 1833) and 56 (30 Mar 1833); *Movement*, no. 30 (6 July 1834) 240; *Cleave's Weekly Police Gaz.*, 30 July 1836; *London Mercury*, no. 4 (18 June 1837); *London Dispatch*, nos. 38 (4 June 1837), 52 (10 Sep 1837), 58 (22 Oct 1837) and 74 (11 Feb 1838); *Working Bee*, no. 20 (30 Nov 1839); *Northern Star*, 21 Nov 1840; *Oracle of Reason 2*, no. 95 (7 Oct 1843) 341; *Northern Star*, 30 Aug 1845, 3, 5; ibid., 20 Sep 1846, 1; ibid., 27 June, 3, 17, 24 Oct, 7 Nov, 5 Dec 1846; *Reasoner 1* (1846) 245, 264, 271, 307; G. J. Holyoake, *The Life and Character of Richard Carlile* (1849) 29–31 ['Why should the Unbeliever fear to die?', the author's address at the meeting in memory of Davenport held at the Finsbury Hall of Science, City Road]; *National Co-operative Leader*, no. 17 (8 Mar 1861); ibid. no. 18 (15 Mar 1861); W. Lovett, *Life and Struggles . . .* (1876; repr. 1967) 214; J. M. Wheeler, *Biographical Dictionary of Freethinkers* (1889); G. J. Holyoake, *Sixty Years of an Agitator's Life*, vol. *2* (1892) 263; idem, *Bygones worth remembering* (1905) vol. *1*, 22; Y. V. Kovalev, *An Anthology of Chartist Literature* (Moscow, 1956) 122–4, 382; R. Harrison, 'Labour Notes and Queries: Allen Davenport', *Bull. Soc. Lab. Hist.*, no. 2 (Spring 1961); E. P. Thompson, *The Making of the English Working Class* (1963; rev. ed. 1968); J. F. C. Harrison, *Robert Owen and the Owenites in Britain and America* (1969); E. Royle, *Victorian Infidels* (1974) [for Anti-Persecution Union, *passim*]; I. J. Prothero, 'Allen Davenport (1775–1846)', in *Biographical Dictionary of Modern British Radicals*, vol. *1*, ed. J. O. Baylen and N. J. Gossman (Brighton, 1979) 111–13; idem, *Artisans and Politics in Early Nineteenth Century London: John Gast and his times* (Folkestone, Kent, 1979) *passim*; D. Goodway, *London Chartism* (1982); M. S. Chase, 'The Land and the Working Classes: English agrarianism *c.* 1775–1851' (Sussex DPhil, 1985). OBIT. *Northern Star*, 5 Dec 1846; *Reasoner 2*, no. 29 (Jan 1847) 16–18; *Utilitarian Record 2* (Jan 1847) 1, 4–5. A portrait of Allen Davenport is the frontispiece of both his *Life, Writings and Principles of Thomas Spence* [1836] and his autobiography, *The Life and Literary Pursuits of Allen Davenport* (1845). NOTE. The editors wish to acknowledge the helpful comments by Dr I. J. Prothero, Dept of History, Manchester Univ., on an earlier draft of this biography and assistance given also by Dr David Goodway, Dept of Adult and Continuing Education, Leeds Univ.

MALCOLM CHASE

See also: † Richard CARLILE; †Robert OWEN.

DAVIES, Stephen Owen (1886–1972)
MINERS' LEADER AND SOCIALIST MP

There is an unresolved query about the date of S. O. Davies' birth. There is no record at the GRO. When he completed his registration form for entry to University College, Cardiff, he entered his date of birth as 27 November 1883; but throughout his life – for example in *Who's Who*, which is the responsibility always of the individual concerned – date of birth was always given as 1886.

Davies, who was known during his adult life as 'S. O.', was born in Abercwmboi, near Aberdare, South Wales. His mother, Esther Owen, had been a shop assistant and was a strong and resourceful woman with a prize-winning singing voice. His father, Thomas Davies, left farm labouring to become a miner in the Rhondda valley; he helped organise miners' trade unions in the 1870s, but his most celebrated activity was his radical journalism. Under the pseudonym 'Llwynog o'r Graig' ('the Mountain Fox') he wrote a weekly column in *Tarian y Gweithiwr* ('The Worker's Shield') beginning with the issue of 6 October 1876. The area of circulation was entirely Welsh-speaking, and his attacks on excessive drinking, religious bigotry, the Aberdare School Board and above all the coal-owners and their supporters and especially the 'gaffers' (overmen or foremen) all led to an intensive search for the identity of the author. His last letter was on 30 August 1878, and the revelation that the 'Fox' was Thomas Davies was to lead to years of victimisation from the pits. He later became an insurance agent.

The family were ardent chapel-goers and, although Thomas Davies was highly critical of the narrowness and sectarianism of the churches in general, he was eventually elected a deacon of Soar Chapel in Mountain Ash. During the Welsh revival of 1904–5 he was, however, excommunicated by his fellow deacons, many of them colliery officials.

There were six children in the Davies family. Both parents could speak English, although Welsh was the language of the home as it was of the whole village in which they lived. It was within this environment of loving parents and an intensely Welsh cultural life of music, the chapel and the pits that S. O. developed his own radicalism. He went to the local school, where there was serious controversy over the teaching of English and Welsh, and at the age of twelve he joined his brothers in the Cwmpennar pit. When the coal reserves here were exhausted, the family moved to Mountain Ash, and S. O. began studying mining engineering at night classes in Aberdare. He worked and studied to the point of nervous exhaustion, and recuperated with his father's relatives in Carmarthenshire, going underground in Caebryn and Emlyn collieries. He began his studies again, this time at the renowned Gwynfryn Academy in Ammanford – a 'progressive' theological college. He eventually passed examinations in mining and colliery management, and won a travelling scholarship to the coalfields in Western Europe.

When he returned home – already with a strong social conscience – it was agreed that he should apply to enter the Nonconformist ministry. In 1908 he secured sponsorship from the Brecon Memorial College (the Independents or Congregationalists, the second largest of the Welsh Nonconformist denominations). Under the scheme he would obtain a BA at University College, Cardiff, and would then study theology at the Brecon College; and as a student he would be expected to preach in local chapels. S. O. was much influenced by the 'new theology' of R. J. Campbell, and before his first year was concluded the Brecon authorities had set up a sub-committee to inquire into what were rumoured to be S. O.'s heretical theological views. The conflict with Brecon was to spread over the year January 1909 to February 1910, when the College finally decided to end their sponsorship [Griffiths (1983) Ch. 2]. His father had died in August 1909, and his mother and Mary, one of his sisters, had moved to Cardiff; they both insisted that he should continue with his degree. During his first year he had studied Greek, Latin, Hebrew and the Scriptures and now moved over to the social sciences, obtaining a BA in the summer of 1913.

During his year as a student he had become increasingly active in Socialist politics through the ILP, and while still at University College he stood as an ILP candidate for the Cardiff Board of Guardians; and, although unsuccessful, his Socialist vote was regarded as an important advance in the city. Later in 1913 he returned to mining, and began work in the Great Mountain Colliery, Tumble, Ammanford, where his brothers David and Gibbon were also employed. Within a few months he was elected checkweighman, and his career as a miners' official had begun.

S. O. Davies was a committed Socialist all his life. His Socialism developed out of his family's radical tradition fortified by the revolutionary events of the twentieth century: above all the Bolshevik assumption of power in Russia in 1917. He remained a Christian, albeit notably unorthodox, and, while he became well-read in Socialist, including Marxist, literature, it is important to underline the crucial influence of the native Welsh radicalism which has produced so many outstanding Socialists, of whom S. O. was to be one of the most remarkable examples. He quickly made his Socialist mark in his own area, and he began lecturing to ILP evening classes as well as the usual round of trade union engagements. He was opposed to the war on Socialist grounds, and was especially active in the opposition to military conscription. It was during the war that he was adopted as parliamentary candidate for the Llanelli division. When the first Russian revolution of 1917 took place, public meetings throughout South Wales celebrated the overthrow of the Tsarist autocracy; and the famous Leeds Convention of 3 June 1917 [Graubard (1956) 36 ff.] called for similar meetings all over the country. The South Wales Workers' and Soldiers' Council was to be established after a Swansea conference fixed for 29 July, but the meeting was broken up by jingoists and 'bit-badge' men (the local branch of the Discharged Soldiers' League [Egan (1975) 22–3]). S. O. Davies was present.

In October 1918, just before the war ended, S. O. was elected the full-time agent for the Dowlais district of the SWMF. On the first count he had come in the top three along with W. H. Mainwaring, from the Rhondda, already a well-known personality in the South Wales area. S. O. and Mainwaring had a public debate one Sunday afternoon in the Oddfellows Hall; and in the deciding ballot S. O. gained 1245 votes to Mainwaring's 1142. He quickly developed a reputation for militant action. His early struggles centred upon accident compensation, home evictions and concessionary coal, and in 1919 he led several successful local strikes in support of a minimum wage and the re-employment of demobilised soldiers. He worked closely with the neighbouring miners' agent for Merthyr, Noah Ablett [DLB 3], and between them they organised a high level of Socialist activity in and around the borough of Merthyr. In the coupon election of December 1918 James Winstone, vice-president of the SWMF, stood as ILP candidate, and was defeated by the sitting Liberal MP by only a small majority: a good result for the Socialists in what was generally a run-away victory for the jingoists and those who had supported the war. In February 1919 a Merthyr alderman had lamented, 'Merthyr gets an opprobrious name throughout the whole country, and people think we are a hot-bed of Bolshevism and Socialism of the most violent kind' [Merthyr Express, 15 Feb 1919]. On May Day 1919 thousands of people met in Cyfartha Park to hear Ramsay MacDonald, James Winstone, Noah Ablett and S. O. Davies.

S.O.'s general political approach tended towards a syndicalist position, dismissive of parliamentary action with a concentration on industrial struggles. He derived commitment and inspiration from the revolutionary movements on the European continent, and he was especially active in the 'Hands off Russia' campaign in 1919–20, and later against British troops in Ireland. His activities in concert with Ablett and A. J. Cook (the Rhondda Miners' Agent) alarmed the Intelligence Services; and they warned the Cabinet in 1920 that the trio had set up Councils of Action in Merthyr and the Rhondda, and that they intended to 'use the movement as a preliminary to the establishment of the Soviet system of government' [CAB 24/110/1793, quoted in Davis (1978) 51 and 61, n. 87]. When the coal crisis of 1919 forced Lloyd George to offer what became known as the Sankey Commission, the delegates of the SWMF argued for a boycott; and when the Commissioners' first-stage findings were published, Ablett and S. O. Davies still proposed rejection. The national ballot, however, even in South Wales, was heavily in favour; and it was only later in the same year, when Lloyd George rejected nationalisation, that the two agents were proved correct in their estimate of the coal politics of the immediate post-war period.

S. O. was involved in all the struggles of the years up to the General Strike of 1926. He played an especially important part in the solution of the problem of 'non-unionism' which had become a serious matter in Wales with the economic depression of the early 1920s [Griffiths (1983) 58–61]. In 1924 he was elected to the executive of the MFGB where he joined Noah Ablett; and later in the same year he defeated Arthur Jenkins to become vice-president of the SWMF, a position he held for nine years.

The Communist Party of Great Britain was formed in 1920, and S. O., while in sympathy with much of its policies and objectives, took a clear decision to remain in the Labour Party. He argued that many miners had only recently been weaned away from support of the Liberal Party and that to imbue the mass of those who supported the Labour Party with Socialist ideas would not be accomplished easily. He regarded the ILP as the Socialist vanguard within the Labour Party, and that to move outside was to risk isolation and a decline of political influence. Nevertheless, he was a lifelong supporter of Communist affiliation to the Labour Party, and he opposed bans and proscriptions on Communists and their organisations. He aligned himself in South Wales with the Unofficial Reform Committee and the Minority Movement, and at the 1922 MFGB Conference, he proposed the South Wales motion for affiliation to the Red International of Labour Unions. A. J. Cook seconded the resolution, which was defeated, every other district voting against.

The RILU was established at a Congress in Moscow in July 1921, and a British Bureau was set up in London. The South Wales miners were the only significant affiliation to the Bureau [Martin (1969) Ch. 1] and in October 1922 S. O. Davies took the chair at a special conference in Cardiff of trade unionists convened by the British Bureau. A week later he went to attend the second World Congress of the RILU in Moscow as the representative of the Dowlais District of the SWMF. After the Congress ended he spent two weeks touring the Don mining district, and at the request of the Soviet Government wrote a book on mining techniques, management and trade unionism. Lenin personally thanked him. He returned to South Wales in January 1923 and published an account of his visit in the February 1923 issue of the *Colliery Workers' Magazine*, the official journal of the SWMF. He wrote in ecstatic terms, and this record is an important illustration of the effect and influence of Soviet society upon many militants from Western Europe. For his part, S. O. never changed his mind:

Who can hope to picture to the mind of the Welsh miner the depths of that spiritual revolution that the consciousness of freedom has wrought in the Russian people? How the breaking of ages-old shackles of cruel, debasing servitude has given such splendid expansiveness to the mind and let loose boundless energy for creative work? The supreme pleasure that is felt by these emancipated people as they jealously and proudly watch the growth of a new culture, the spontaneous expression of those creative energies pioneering a new world of thought and a new material civilisation? Here, at last, you have a people who know much, indeed, of the 'zest for living', who stand confidently and exultingly facing the future, proud of the eternal honour bestowed upon them as pioneers of a new civilisation. The British worker, grounded down in penury at his uninspiring toil, has been left behind by the Russian worker. To the latter the whole material world, with all its unrevealed mysteries, exists, awaiting the application of man's all-conquering mind.

The serious economic problems of the mining industry inevitably involved S. O. in a ceaseless struggle on behalf of his members. 'Red Friday' of 31 July 1925 was recognised by S. O. as only a temporary respite, and he warned forcefully against complacency. Growing unemployment led S. O. to advocate branches for unemployed miners, and this brought him into conflict with the National Unemployed Workers' Movement, whose organiser, Wal Hannington, criticised S. O. for organising an alternative to local unemployed committees. S. O. defended himself vigorously in the *Sunday Worker* for 20 September 1925, arguing that keeping miners together after a colliery closure – as a non-contributory branch of the SWMF – reminded employed miners of their responsibilities to the workless. It also enabled the unemployed to remain active in the trade union movement and allowed them to sit on welfare and other local government committees. The controversy did not deter S. O. from future co-operation with the NUWM.

In the early months of 1925 there had been established the International Class War Prisoners' Aid, an international organisation with national groups formed to give legal, material and moral support to all workers and their families who were prosecuted for industrial and political activities. The ICWPA was a Comintern body and the secretary of the British Bureau was first Wal Hannington and then Bob Lovell. S. O. Davies chaired a meeting in Cardiff on 6 February 1926 to set up a South Wales district of Prisoners' Aid, and was involved in its work thereafter.

In the months between 'Red Friday' and the beginning of the General Strike in May 1926, S. O. was concerned to develop a militant strategy of aggression. He supported the slogan of the Left – All Power to the General Council—but in an article of September 1925 he explained the context in which he understood the slogan:

Our immediate duty is obvious: a fundamental reorganisation of the Trades Union Movement; the centralisation of all Trade Unions in the General Council; the abolition of our cumbersome and slowmoving sectional constitutions; the realisation that even the days of comparative peace in the economic world are gone by, and that the decline of British Capitalism has reached a point that makes every wage demand on any considerable scale a revolutionary issue. Hence our slogans must be: Mass attacks must be met by Mass attacks; sectionalism is suicidal; Our Hope is in a mobile, centralised, scientifically organised industrial army, which means all power to the General Council [*Colliery Workers' Mag.*, Sep 1925].

Throughout the months leading to the General Strike S. O. continued to warn the miners and the TUC that the Government had bought time only to prepare its forces for a successful confrontation. He presented evidence on behalf of the MFGB to the Samuel Commission – making the case both for higher wages and for nationalisation of the industry – but he was wholly realistic about the Commission's likely Report. His own views on the situation were contained in a pamphlet he wrote with Cook and Ablett: *Our Present Plight*. During the General Strike and the seven-month lock-out which followed, the Merthyr borough central strike committee was a model of a disciplined and effective organisation. S. O. himself toured the coalfields during the lock-out as part of what a hostile press termed 'Cook's Travelling Circus', and he remained to the end an advocate of the hard line towards the coal-owners and the Government. He led the Welsh efforts to persuade the

MFGB to intensify the struggle and reject district-by-district negotiations or settlements. His analysis of the reasons for defeat was widely recognised as cogent: the slogan of 'All Power to the General Council' had ignored too easily the necessary preconditions, namely the abolition of unions' sectionalism; the need for a new fighting TUC leadership; the establishment of a 'mobile, centralised, scientifically-organised industrial army', which S. O. had been urging from the summer of 1925. Instead, the miners and other workers had entrusted decision-making and negotiations to a General Council that was dominated by a cautious reformism and which proved cowardly, unwilling to prepare for a real confrontation, and afraid to accept Russian and other offers of international support.

With the defeat of the miners the problem of non-unionism and the growth of company unionism became serious once again; and it was not to be resolved until the later 1930s. S. O. gave unconditional support to the first hunger march in 1927 from South Wales, against the decision of the TUC and the executive committee of the SWMF. This was a period, however, when there developed much bitterness within the Left of the labour movement. In 1927 the General Council of the TUC decided to excommunicate Trades Councils who identified themselves with the Minority Movement. S. O., who was clearly identified with the National Left Wing Movement as well as the Minority Movement, opposed all these bans and proscriptions, but this did not prevent attacks upon him from the Communist Party. The 'Class against Class' strategy which the international Communist movement had adopted led the British Communist Party, and its associated organisations, to attack all those outside its own ranks and among them left-wing members of the Labour Party. The most bitter issue for S. O. was the expulsion of the Mardy Lodge in 1930 from the SWMF. It was a complicated story which has been told in a number of places [Francis and Smith (1980) Ch. 5; Griffiths (1983) 85 ff.] and it led to unpleasant vilification of S. O. by the local, regional and national bodies of the Communist Party. Arthur Horner's autobiography, *Incorrigible Rebel* [(1960) 109] goes some way towards setting straight the record, the complete reading of which absolves S. O. from any duplicity. S. O. himself always appreciated. with a remarkable saneness of view, that the need for unity on the Left was paramount.

S. O.'s wife, Madge, died of cancer in February 1932. They had been married for thirteen years and there were three young daughters below the age of fourteen. With the help of co-operative neighbours and a wonderful housekeeper, Letty Davies, S. O. came through his personal crisis; and in August 1934 he married again: this time to Sephora Davies, a schoolteacher from Gwaun-cae-Gurwen in Carmarthenshire. It was to be a very happy relationship, with two sons being added to the family.

In the same year, 1934, Richard Wallhead died. He had been MP for Merthyr since 1922 [*DLB 3*] and the competition for the seat was intense. The final list included H. B. Lees-Smith, who had already been a minister in the 1929 Labour Government, and Sam Jennings, a much respected local alderman. S. O. had three votes over the latter and won the selection. The ILP, now disaffiliated from the Labour Party, put up Campbell Stephen [*DLB 7*] and the Communist Party the much more formidable Wal Hannington. Polling was on 5 June, and Hannington's candidature came just when the political line of the CPGB was beginning to change towards the policy of the United Front. S. O. attacked the ILP for its political irrelevance and the CPGB for its sectarianism towards the left-wing of the Labour Party as well as for its advocacy of 'bloody revolution'. The voting was: Labour (S. O. Davies), 18,645; Liberal, 10,376; ILP, 3508; and CPGB, 3409. In the 1935 general election, S. O. had a majority of nearly 11,000 over the ILP candidate – no one else stood – and from 1945 to 1970 his majority never fell below 17,000.

The main political and industrial events of the 1930s for S. O. were the successful fight over company unionism, the continued struggle of the unemployed as carried on both inside Westminster and outside, and the civil war in Spain. S. O. was continuously critical of the Labour and trade union leadership throughout these years, and he supported the initiatives for greater unity on the Left and for a Popular Front. As with the overwhelming majority of the Left and the centre of the Labour Party he was consistently hostile to the appeasement policy of the Chamberlain Government. When war came in September 1939 he remained highly critical of the Conservative Government's approach and policy. He did not take the Communist line of outright opposition and his name did not appear among the long list of signatories to the People's Convention, for he recognised the central threat that Fascism offered to political democracy; but he was always exceedingly wary of the actions and policies of the ruling class. His attitude towards the formation of the Coalition Government in the spring of 1940 was instructive. He had grave misgivings about the Labour leaders joining the new administration of Winston Churchill; and he ended his House of Commons speech with these words:

We shall watch this Government critically and anxiously. Their task presumably is to mobilise the men and resources at our disposal; but will they be able to do it? I am confident that they will not be able to do it unless the dead hand of the past is removed, and until the crippling weight of organised profiteering is lifted and the 'patriotism limited' of high finance, of the money changers and gamblers on our stock exchanges is completely eliminated. . . . We on these benches are as prepared to fight Nazism as is any representative in any part of this House, whether that Nazism is partially concealed in this country or blatantly open elsewhere. We shall do so, but not at the price of sacrificing the principles which have ever been dear to us, namely, the interests of our own people who have placed us in this House [*Hansard*, 13 May 1940].

Two years later, on 4 April 1942, he wrote in similar vein to a Welsh miners' agent:

The manner in which this war is conducted will determine the nature of the Peace. They are inseparable. Private ownership, with its rabid profit-seeking, is as arrogant and insolent in the saddle these days as ever it was in the past. In fact, it is more deeply entrenched now than it was in pre-war days. How can the class in power, deriving its sustenance, its pomp and splendour, from human exploitation, ever establish the basis of permanent peace? Our class has already been deprived of most of its cherished achievements. Its freedom has been whittled away to an alarming degree. A Labour Home Secretary, who has been in the past notoriously keen in suppressing minority and progressive views within our own Movement, is now most evilly engaged in restricting the freedom of the Press and of opinion. Are these facts not of supreme and urgent importance? Is not the vast drama at this moment being enacted in India, with its 400 million souls, a matter of profound interest to all of us? I could go on enumerating life and death issues arising from the corrupt heart of modern Imperialism [S. O. Davies papers, Swansea].

S. O. Davies voiced his opposition to almost all the foreign policy decisions of the Churchill Government: to the failure to grant India independence – he had a bitter exchange over India with Sir Stafford Cripps in the House of Commons on 11 September 1942 – and above all, in the last year of the war, against British intervention in Greece. When the war in Europe ended, in May 1945, with the general election which followed, S. O. found himself in a House of Commons dominated by Labour members, and just as quickly found himself in opposition to much that the Attlee Government was proposing. Labour's foreign policy S. O. denounced, and on issue after issue he was arguing that basic Socialist principles were being pushed aside.

On one important matter, however, S. O. found himself welcoming with enthusiasm the actions of the Government. He had sat on Merthyr Borough Council since 1931, and had been mayor in 1945; and he was deeply concerned with the working and living conditions of his constituents. In 1935 a Royal Commission had recommended the withdrawal of county borough status, and in 1939 a Political and Economic Planning Report had suggested that the town should be shut down, and its population resettled elsewhere. S. O. fought hard, and successfully, against such policies, and during the war years persuaded Whitehall to build 'shadow' factories in Merthyr and Dowlais. After 1945 he found great support from Hugh Dalton ('the greatest friend that I and the Merthyr Borough ever had' [Griffiths (1983) 117]); and throughout the years after 1945 S. O. was assiduous in his efforts to encourage industrialists to establish themselves in his area.

The growing coldness of international relations between East and West in the 1950s found S. O. firmly allied with the Soviet Union and the world Communist movement. In a number of crucial issues he has since been proved correct, notably his denunciation of South Korea at the time of the beginning of the Korean War in the summer of 1950 and over the highly emotive question of germ warfare – a matter now (1986) much more open to argument and analysis than at the time. In November 1950 Sephora Davies, an executive member of the World Peace Council, read her husband's greetings to the World Peace Congress in Warsaw. S. O. brushed aside Labour National Executive warnings and an inquiry by the Welsh Regional Council of Labour (whom he called 'a conglomeration of nonentities') and he continued to address rallies of the British–Soviet and Britain–China Friendship organisations and other proscribed bodies, and write articles in *Labour Monthly*, the *Daily Worker* and *Socialist Outlook*. This uncompromising stance differentiated him from the 'Keep Left' MPs and *Tribune*; indeed, he never regarded himself a 'Bevanite'.

The expulsion of Sephora Davies from the Labour Party in 1951 did nothing to curb S. O.'s rebelliousness. The execution ('cold-blooded murder') of Julius and Ethel Rosenberg in the USA in 1953, as alleged Soviet spies, prompted S. O. to demand that the US Embassy and military bases in Britain be shut down and their personnel deported; in the ensuing Commons uproar, Clement Attlee publicly disowned S. O. on behalf of the Parliamentary Labour Party. In June that year, S. O. praised the Socialist Unity Government's handling of the crisis in East Germany: Will Lawther, president of the National Union of Mineworkers, issued a statement saying that S. O. was 'well-known as a fellow-traveller of the Communist Party' who should resign or be sacked as Merthyr's MP.

In 1954 the Whip was withdrawn from S. O. again, for voting against the rearming of West Germany as a member of NATO. Later that year he savagely denounced Winston Churchill, following revelations that the war leader had been prepared to rearm captured Nazis to fight the Soviet Red Army in 1945. S. O. was one of the few MPs who refused to sign Parliament's birthday commemoration book to Churchill. From the outset of the Suez crisis in 1956, he upheld the rights of the Egyptian people and President Nasser; he opposed Britain's nuclear weapons policy, launched well-informed parliamentary assaults on 'futile' civil defence against atomic war, and severely criticised Aneurin Bevan's about-turn on nuclear disarmament. On the important question of the Soviet invasion of Hungary, S. O. had an equivocal position, and he maintained, in public, a silence. He was deeply conscious of the issues involved and well appreciated that much of the outcry in the West came from professional anti-Communists. But he also understood Magyar nationalism and their desire for freedom. What S. O. never did was to act as an apologist for the show trials in Eastern Europe in the immediate post-war years. But he also declined to voice any criticism of the Communist authorities, preferring to keep his unease to himself rather than – as he saw it – lending the slightest aid or comfort to anti-Socialist propaganda. He regarded the long-term security and stability of the international Socialist system to be of supreme importance, of ultimately being a greater 'good' than the short-term desires or interests of a just or well-meaning cause. To the end of his life, S. O. remained a staunch defender of the Soviet Union and its policies, and his own Socialist commitment is impossible to appreciate without this recognition of the central importance in his political belief of 1917 and all that followed. In 1962, in greetings to *Pravda*, he recalled meeting the Russian philologists, musicians and geologists who had done so much to develop the national cultures and natural resources of the Soviet peoples. He also told Radio Moscow that year:

> To any, if they exist, who doubt the enormous success of your revolution I would advise them to study conditions existing in pre-revolutionary days and compare them with life in the Soviet Union today – its dazzling successes in the scientific world, its vast educational and productive achievements, and its social system in which the overwhelming emphasis is placed on the sacredness of human life. And please remember, particularly you my young Soviet friends, that all this has been achieved in a hostile, jealous, and an extremely dangerous world.
>
> It is only in a Socialist State that war and the preparations for war bring profit to no-one. Nor do you profit on the hunger and oppression of others. Hence, may your Socialist State, your classless society from which the profit-monger has been eliminated, be the inspiration of the working-classes the world over to fight with you for World Peace and world comradeship [S. O. Davies papers, Swansea; 1A, ii].

In the midst of Cold War controversies, S. O., in the House of Commons, voiced the connection between Socialist internationalism and his own nationality:

> The Wales we have been discussing all day strongly objects to this Parliament irrevocably dragging it into the abyss of destruction. We have no quarrel with any people or nation in this world. We are instinctively hospitable and we are a nation of workers. We can feel no enmity against any other people or nation, whatever their colour, creed or religion. We abhor the swashbuckling fire-eating speeches which we have had in this House, and as a Welsh nation we repudiate their sentiments. The heart of our hospitable country goes out to those who are struggling against tyranny and against obstruction, because we know that obstruction has been placed in the way of this little country to which I am proud to belong [*Hansard*, 22 Jan 1953].

S. O.'s cultural background, the Welsh people's political loyalties, and the callous treatment of South Wales in the 1930s, combined to make him a passionate advocate of Welsh self-government. He accused Tory and Labour governments alike of neglecting Welsh interests. In 1953 he urged Welsh Labour MPs to turn the annual Welsh Day debates in Parliament into 'days of protest by the Welsh people against the subjugation of our country by a people of alien tradition, alien culture and alien tongue'. He sponsored and played an active part in the campaign and petition for a Parliament for Wales between 1950 and 1956. In 1955 S. O. pushed his Private Member's Bill for Welsh Home Rule to a full-day second-reading debate, although it was eventually voted out. His appearance on a Plaid Cymru (Welsh National Party) platform and other Home Rule activities led to disciplinary appearances before the Welsh Regional Council of Labour and national executives, but did not modify his stance. In the 1960s he continued to call for a law-making Welsh Assembly, sponsored Plaid Cymru MP Gwynfor Evans in Parliament, and boycotted the investiture of the Prince of Wales in 1969. Throughout his life he was a fervent patron of Welsh cultural and educational institutions, holding numerous public offices, including governorships in the University of Wales. On the Irish question, too, S. O. took a lifelong stand in favour of Irish independence and unity; in 1949 he came close to expulsion from the PLP for voting against the Ireland Bill and its Unionist veto on Irish reunification.

The Left in the PLP had a chequered history of support and opposition on armaments and defence questions. Early in 1961 opposition began to build up against the Polaris nuclear submarine programme. On 16 March 1961 five Labour back-benchers forced a division over the Conservative Government's military budget, and then voted against, registering thereby their opposition to the Polaris agreement with the Americans. The five were Michael Foot, Emrys Hughes, Sydney Silverman, William Baxter, and S. O. The PLP voted 90 to 63 to withdraw the Whip, and the five therefore sat in the Commons as independent Socialists. When Harold Wilson was elected leader of the Labour Party after Gaitskell's death, S. O. applied for readmission to the PLP. After three months his application was accepted following an undertaking not to defy the PLP in Commons votes. But Wilson's second Government, between 1966 and 1970, caused S. O. and his constituents great distress. S. O. rebelled against public spending cuts, trade union controls and the wages freeze; he narrowly escaped expulsion from the PLP after refusing to endorse Harold Wilson in a 'No Confidence' vote in 1968, and again the following year when he abstained during Budget divisions as a protest against further increases in Selective Employment Tax. On a positive note, however, S. O. succeeded in reforming National Insurance law in 1967 with a Private Member's Bill: his measure secured extra compensation for dust-afflicted miners who had also contracted emphysema or chronic bronchitis. This pioneering step crowned a long-time interest and involvement in social legislation; his efforts had won him a reputation many years before as a champion of old people's rights.

The single greatest tragedy in S. O.'s political life struck in October 1966, when the pit village of Aberfan was overwhelmed by a sliding tip of colliery waste. One hundred and forty-four of his people perished in the avalanche, 109 of them schoolchildren. S. O.'s testimony at the subsequent Tribunal was characteristically courageous and controversial: although he and other community leaders had complained about the menacing tips, nobody had insisted upon their removal for fear the National Coal Board would carry out its veiled threat to close the colliery altogether. This terrible dilemma was circumnavigated by the Tribunal, which merely censured NCB employees for negligence and the Board itself for perpetuating the bad practice of former coal-owners. Prime Minister Harold Wilson insisted that the Aberfan Disaster Fund contribute towards the cost of removing the tips above the village; S. O. resigned from the Fund committee in disgust at this 'blackmail'. In March 1970, he boycotted the Merthyr ceremony that bestowed the Freedom of the Borough upon Wilson.

This last gesture – together with S. O.'s previous attacks on the Wilson Government, and his advanced years – finally determined the Merthyr constituency party's decision to replace S. O. as the official Labour Party candidate for the 1970 general election. But on 18 June he confounded all forecasts when, standing as an 'Independent Socialist', he defeated the official Labour man by more than 7000 votes. Spending less campaign cash than any other victorious candidate in Britain, S. O.'s appeal was heart-rendingly straightforward: 'YOU KNOW ME – I'VE NEVER LET YOU DOWN. DON'T FORGET S.O.' Over the next eighteen months he voiced his opposition to the European Common Market, apartheid in South Africa, the Industrial Relations Bill, internment in Northern Ireland, local government reform and the withdrawal of free school milk; he applauded the local campaign for Welsh-language education. Then, on 25 February 1972, at the age of eighty-eight, he died peacefully in his sleep at Merthyr General Hospital. He was survived by his widow and four of his five children. One of his daughters, Margot, who pre-deceased him, qualified in medicine; another, Mary, qualified as a physical education teacher. One son, Alyn, became principal of Bretton Hall College of Education and then a chief inspector with the ILEA. His second son, Stephen, trained as a computer operator. His third daughter attended the LSE and subsequently married. S. O.'s funeral service was at Soar–Ynysgau Chapel and he was buried at Maesyrarian Cemetery, Mountain Ash. He left effects valued at £1945.

The tributes that followed were fulsome, from old enemies as well as friends; they came from trade unionists, academics, Socialists and Communists, Welsh Nationalists and even the Tory press. Long before the end of his life, S. O. had become a legend. He had created a larger-than-life image – and then lived up to it; his dress was Edwardian, his gestures were exaggerated, his speech rich in accent and anecdote; he referred to himself habitually in the third person, as 'old S. O.' Jim Griffiths, a contemporary of S. O. in Parliament, gave his own personal tribute which was published in the *Merthyr Express*, 3 March 1972:

[S. O.] was gifted with a pleasing presence and an impressive personality, and had he found it possible to work with the team would probably have attained ministerial office.

However, he always was a lone figure. He did not knit easily and seemed to like being in isolation. The one place where he would relax was at the Welsh Table in the Members' Tea Room at the House of Commons. Many a talk he and I had at that table – always in Welsh – homespun Carmarthenshire Welsh. He would always begin the conversation by asking: 'Shwd mae pethau lawr 'co?' ['How are things over there?'] – lawr 'co meaning the anthracite area . . . and with the miners of Glo Carreg who launched him on his career in the South Wales Miners' Federation – and eventually on the road to St. Stephen's.

S. O. and I were the only survivors of the miners' leaders in South Wales who led the miners during those heroic months of 1926 – and through the long, heartbreaking years of the aftermath.

With the passing of S. O. and the loss of a seat in the Rhondda, it now seems inevitable that for the first time since Mabon became Rhondda's M. P. in 1885 South Wales will not have a single M. P. who will have made the journey from the coalface to Parliament. We are nearing the end of an era in Welsh politics . . . .

Writings: Articles in the *Llanelly Mercury*, 1914–17, included 'An Open Letter to the Carmarthenshire Education Committee', 23 Sep 1915; 'Education, Progress and Economy', 2 Dec 1915; 'Why Conscription should be opposed by the Workers!', 17 Feb 1916; 'Maladministration of the Military Service Act', 9 Mar 1916. Articles and reviews by S. O. Davies appeared in the *Amman Valley Chronicle* over the same period and he also wrote for the *South Wales Daily News*. Other articles: 'Russia in December 1922', *Colliery Workers' Mag.* Feb 1923; 'The Industrial Armistice', ibid., Sep 1925; 'On organising the Unemployed', *Sunday Worker*, 20 Sep 1925; evidence with Frank Hall before the R. C. on the Coal Industry [Samuel Commission] 1926 XIV pt A, vol. II Qs 12876–13332 [non parliamentary]; (with N. Ablett and A. Cook) *Our Present Plight* (1926) P; 'On the General Strike', *Sunday Worker*, 23 Jan 1927; 'On reorganising the SWMF', *Miners' Monthly* (Apr 1934); [on the future of Wales], *Western Mail*, 29 July 1936; [on the Popular Front], ibid., 14 Mar 1939; 'Press Freedom in Wartime', *Lab. Mon. 23* (Mar 1941) 122; 'Withdraw British Forces from Korea!', *Socialist Outlook*, Aug 1950, 1; 'Labour and War', *Lab. Mon. 32* (Sep 1950) 400–4; 'Labour and Rearmament', ibid. *33* (June 1951) 253–6; 'Labour's New Fight', ibid. (Dec 1951) 559–61; [on the Korean War], *Western Mail*, 7 Apr 1952; [on the Rosenbergs and East Berlin], *Merthyr Express*, 6 Apr 1953; 'Need the Miners fear a Welsh Parliament?', *Western Mail*, 10 May 1954; [on NATO], *British–Soviet Friendship*, Feb 1958; 'Signposts – or Windmills?', *Lab. Mon. 43* (Oct 1961) 465–7; [on the EEC], *South Wales Echo*, 9 Aug 1971. Selected parliamentary speeches from *Hansard*: on the Portal Report, 14 Nov 1934; on the Unemployed Assistance Board, 22 June 1936; on war aims, 12 Oct 1939 and 27 Jan 1942; on Coalition Government, 13 May 1940; on India, 11 Sep 1941; on the coal industry, 10 June 1942; on the Beveridge Report, 17 Feb 1943; on Welsh affairs, 24 Nov 1948; on the Korean War, 5 July 1950 and 13 Sep 1950; on germ warfare in Korea, 23 Oct 1952; on self-government for Wales, 22 Jan 1953; on the Government of Wales Bill, 4 Mar 1955; on unemployment and depopulation, 4 Apr 1961; on the Industrial Diseases Bill, 2 Dec 1966; on Aberfan, 26 Oct 1967.

Sources: (1) MS: S. O. Davies papers, Univ. College, Swansea, and Glamorgan RO, Cardiff. (2) Other: *Labour Who's Who* (1927); *Kelly* (1955); S. R. Graubard, *British Labour and the Russian Revolution 1917–1924* (Cambridge, Mass., 1956); Joseph Redman [pseud.

Brian Pearce], *The Communist Party and the Labour Left 1925–1929*, with an Introduction by J. Saville (Reasoner Pamphlets, no. 1: Hull [1957]) 31 pp.; A. L. Horner, *Incorrigible Rebel* (1960); *Dod* (1966); R. Martin, *Communism and the British Trade Unions: a study of the National Minority Movement* (Oxford, 1969); P. Tinniswood, 'Old S. O. will not pull his Punches', *Western Mail*, 16 Apr 1969; 'Should S. O. stay on?', *Times*, 25 Feb 1969; G. Mathias, 'This Man S. O.', *South Wales Echo*, 9 Apr 1970; *Sunday Express*, 12 Apr 1970; 'Labour MP gets ready for his Last Struggle', *Times*, 15 Apr 1970; *Y Cymro*, 13 May 1970; 'S. O. Davies refuses to be Freeman', *Times*, 30 July 1970; 'S. O. Extra', *Observer Colour Supplement*, 25 Oct 1970; *WWW* (1971–80); D. Egan, 'The Swansea Conference of the British Council of Soldiers' and Workers' Delegates, July 1917', *Llafur 1*, no. 4 (Summer 1975) 12–33; P. Davis, 'The Making of A. J. Cook', ibid. *2*, no. 3 (Summer 1978) 43–63; H. Francis and D. Smith, *The Fed.* (1980); E. and R. Frow, *Bob and Sarah Lovell: crusaders for a better society* (Manchester, [198-?]) 25 pp.; R. Griffiths, *S. O. Davies: a Socialist faith* (Llandysul, Dyfed, 1983); idem, 'Ail-Gloriannu S. O. Davies', *Y Faner*, 26 Aug 1983. Biographical information: *Merthyr Express* [Celtic Newspapers Ltd, Merthyr Tydfil]. Personal information: Dr Peter Jackson, Hull Univ. OBIT. *Guardian*, 26 Feb 1972; *Times*, 26 and 29 Feb 1972; *Western Mail* and *Yorkshire Post*, 26 Feb 1972; *Guardian*, 2 Mar 1972; *Merthyr Express*, 3 Mar 1972; R. Page Arnot, 'Courageous Leader', *Lab. Mon. 54* (Apr 1972) 168–72.

ROBERT GRIFFITHS

See also: †Noah ABLETT; †Arthur James COOK; †Arthur Lewis HORNER; Arthur JENKINS; †William (Will) LAWTHER; †Campbell STEPHEN; †Richard [Christopher] Collingham WALL-HEAD; †James WINSTONE.

DIAMOND, Charles (1858–1934)
LABOUR POLITICIAN AND NEWSPAPER PROPRIETOR

Born on 17 November 1858 in the parish of Gortade, Magnera, County Derry, Charles Diamond was the third of a family of six children. His father, a tenant farmer, was evicted from his holding while Diamond was a boy. The family, who were devout Catholics, then moved to the next township, Upperlands. Charles attended the national school there for a time and was then taught classics by a tutor, John M'Cluskey, who was later described by a schoolfellow as 'a ripe scholar and capable teacher' [*Glasgow Herald*, 10 Mar 1934]. Following attacks on local Catholics mounted by the Orange Order, on 12 July 1878, the family left the area. Diamond himself migrated to Newcastle upon Tyne, where he displayed early talent as a journalist and business man and was soon running a newspaper which catered for the Irish community in the North East of England. In 1882 he married Jeannie McCarthy, the sister of a future Catholic bishop of Galloway. Throughout his life Diamond was an ardent Irish nationalist and a devout Roman Catholic, and these beliefs animated his career as a newspaper proprietor and reformist politician over a period of fifty years.

In 1884 he founded the *Irish Tribune*, but not long afterwards he shifted his base from Newcastle to Glasgow. There he joined the *Glasgow Observer*, which had been launched in April 1885 to cater for the Catholic Irish and their descendants, who, by 1900, made up almost 8 per cent of the population of Scotland, most of whom were concentrated in the Glasgow region and in certain mining districts. Diamond acquired the *Glasgow Observer* outright in 1894 and he revolutionised its appearance. He adopted the latest methods in what was a period of rapid innovation in press development. A few years later his was the first newspaper in Scotland to use linotype machines and by 1910 the paper was installed in a modern three-storey building in North Frederick Street, Glasgow.

Diamond created a press empire which encompassed forty publications at its height, thirty-seven of which were in existence at the time of his death in 1934. His newspaper group had editions in all the major British cities with Catholic populations of Irish descent, his best-known organ being the *Catholic Herald*, published in London. He wrote editorials on party political and religious topics which were duplicated in his chain of weekly papers. In a sense they were separate publications, although Diamond has been characterised as the head of a news and features syndicate rather than a chain of newspapers [Edwards (1979) 171]. He also had other business interests, including membership of the board of directors of the English Sewing Cotton Company and, as chairman, of the English Insurance Company.

While still only in his early thirties, Diamond was a power in the Irish National League, the British section of the Irish Home Rule Party, which had an influence in all the major industrial cities where the migrant Irish had settled. He was also on close terms with leaders of the Home Rule Party and, with the recommendation of Michael Davitt, he was nominated as Home Rule candidate for North Monaghan. At the general election of 1892 he received 3697 votes, a majority of 1437 over his Conservative opponent. He was not a very vocal MP, and his interventions in the Commons were mostly on minor issues. Diamond, who described himself as an 'anti-Parnellite', was embroiled in the internecine warfare which gripped the Irish parliamentary party following the downfall of Charles Stewart Parnell in 1891. It was a period when Irish nationalist fortunes were at a low ebb, and Diamond declined to stand in the 1895 general election.

In conducting his newspapers he usually endeavoured to deliver the votes of his readers to the Liberals, principally because they were considered sympathetic to Home Rule for Ireland. Undoubtedly Diamond's press empire helped to keep alive a strong interest in Irish affairs even among the descendants of emigrants who would never visit Ireland. Sometimes he instructed his local editors to back Labour candidates in municipal elections if they were sounder on the Home Rule issue or in the absence of a Liberal. He demonstrated an early sympathy for some Labour aspirations when he allowed the Glasgow Socialist John Wheatley to use the pages of the *Glasgow Observer* to press his claim that there was no inherent contradiction in being both a practising Catholic and a committed Socialist. The debate between Wheatley and his religious detractors occurred between 1906 and 1910, and although Diamond never shared Wheatley's standpoint he drew closer to the Labour movement thereafter.

Diamond's leftward swing resulted from growing disillusionment with the Liberals over Ireland rather than from a positive acceptance of radical politics in the British domestic sphere. As a self-made man of humble origins, he also resented the fact that the Liberals were unwilling to provide political openings for working-class activists in cities where the immigrant vote was numerous. He eventually became a member of the Labour Party after the Dublin Easter Rising of 1916. Initially hostile to de Valera and the other Easter insurgents, he swung rapidly into the full separatist Sinn Fein camp following the execution of the leaders of the rebellion. In 1918 he was Labour candidate for Peckham in London and during the election campaign his newspaper chain enthusiastically embraced the Labour cause. Even John Maclean, recently appointed by Lenin as a Soviet consul, was supported at Glasgow, Gorbals. In Peckham Diamond was bottom of the poll in a three-cornered contest. Convinced that a strong Labour Party would bring Irish independence, he offered to find £100,000 to establish pro-Labour newspapers in different parts of the country. In April 1919, at a public meeting held in Glasgow with James Maxton in the chair, he criticised the behaviour of the police during the recent industrial unrest in the city. He opposed the formation of an Irish Labour Party in Glasgow, which might have divided the labour movement, on the grounds that accentuating religious and nationalist differences would be against the interests of Catholics in Britain.

A few months later Diamond's Roman Catholicism and Irish nationalism led him to express views that resulted in his imprisonment. The *Catholic Herald* of 27 December 1919 contained a long article by Diamond under the title 'Killing no Murder'. It appeared in thirty-four local editions, printed in Manchester and Glasgow and with a total circulation of 125,000 copies. The article was prompted by a recent attempt on the life of Field Marshal Lord French, Lord-Lieutenant of Ireland. French, he wrote, represented 'foreign rule, physical force, tyranny, and brutality', and the Irish had a moral right to sweep him and their other oppressors into the sea. He examined various instances of tyrannicide, showing how English public opinion had often supported nationalist movements. Moreover, he argued, the law recognised that an individual could justifiably kill an attacker in self-defence; it was the same with the Irish who were fighting for their liberty.

The authorities decided that the article contravened section 4 of the Offences Against the Person Act of 1861 and a warrant was issued for Diamond's arrest. On 9 January 1920 he was arrested at his office in Bouverie Street and remanded in custody. Eventually he obtained bail until his trial at the Old Bailey in March. For the Crown the Attorney-General argued that passages in the article were 'a calculated and deliberate incitement . . . to make a further, and this time successful, attempt upon the life of the Lord-Lieutenant'. In support of his plea of not guilty, Diamond stated he had never advocated violence. Evidence as to his good character was given by twelve witnesses, including the Earl of Clarendon, a director of the English Insurance Company, and Lieutenant-General Sir Arthur Slogett, who thought the article was 'journalistic gas'. The views of this 'plain soldier' were referred to in his address to the jury by the defence counsel, R. Barrington-Ward, who argued that Diamond had the right of free speech and that he was commenting on historical events, not encouraging unconstitutional activities. The jury found Diamond guilty. In passing sentence Lord Justice Coleridge stated the defence had 'rightly failed' to persuade the jury and that Diamond would go to prison for six months in the second division.

During his trial Diamond held that the reactionary forces of Dublin Castle had instigated the prosecution, and his conviction does not appear to have reduced his standing in the rest of the United Kingdom. In June 1920 the Scottish Catholic hierarchy petitioned the Home Secretary for his release. There is no evidence that Diamond wished to see the Irish troubles transferred to England or Scotland; his object was to present the case for his co-religionists. As a consequence of this priority it was in Catholic rather than Labour circles that his influence was greater and he never seems to have had other than a marginal position relative to the Labour Party. His political views were probably regarded as based too narrowly on Irish and religious factors. Even in the general election of November 1922, when he was Labour candidate for the Rotherhithe division of Bermondsey (and was only 46 votes behind the successful Conservative), he struck discordant notes by insisting that Labour was not a Socialist party and by using his papers to criticise 'pro-Bolshevik' elements in it. He did not contest the general election of 1923, though he supported Labour candidates (with the exception of secularists such as H. G. Wells, who, campaigning for the seat at London University, drew Diamond's fire for opposing separate education for Catholics). Diamond urged that more attention should be given to land reform, an issue which again reflected his Irish background and his antipathy to the English aristocracy.

It was in Scotland, where Diamond's papers had their best circulation, that his support for Labour was most significant. It is never easy to measure the impact of the press on political attitudes and voting behaviour, although in one sphere Catholic voters do seem to have followed Diamond's advice. Until 1929 triennial elections for local school boards were held in Scotland on a system of proportional representation. Shortly before each election the *Glasgow Observer* published lists of candidates together with minute instructions as to the order of preference that the voters should adopt. The turnout of Catholic voters in these contests was high and in areas where Catholicism was strong the results were often close to the recommendations of the *Glasgow Observer*. In the elections of 1919 and 1922 the paper urged that second-preference votes should go to candidates who stood as Socialists. In 1922

James Maxton was elected to the Glasgow Education Board, though with far fewer votes than a local Catholic canon. Later the *Glasgow Observer* (27 Mar 1926) used this example to drive home the message that where a priest and a Socialist were in contention Catholics were more likely to put their religion first. Such was also Diamond's position. In 1923 he quarrelled with the *Daily Herald* over an allegedly anti-Catholic article it had published, and in 1926 he called its editor, George Lansbury, 'a political hypocrite and slanderer' for suggesting that the British secret service was encouraging Catholic clerics to foment discontent in the Soviet Union [*Glasgow Observer*, 27 Nov 1926]. On the other hand, he apparently sought to allay the fears of some leading Catholics about the Labour Party. In April 1923 he had a private audience with Pope Pius XI, who had issued a number of interdicts against Socialist parties in Europe. Though he afterwards wrote an article for the Vatican newspaper *Osservatore Romano* declaring he would leave the Labour Party if so required by his Church, he perhaps also used the visit to emphasise his belief that the Party included many non-Socialists.

His attitude to the Labour Party was summed up in a short book he brought out in 1925, *Why Socialism cannot come and remain*. Based on a series of weekly columns he had published in his papers between April and July 1924, it was in part a reply to Ramsay MacDonald's pamphlet *Why Socialism must come* (ILP, 1924). Diamond's main theme was that the Labour Party should be helped 'to carry out a multitude of drastic changes that will give the disinherited masses a fair show in the battle of life.' But, he continued, Socialism was 'an illusion, an impossibility . . . a desperate remedy, worse than the disease for which it pretends to be a cure' [Diamond (1925) 99]. He identified Socialism with the godlessness of the Soviet Union, which he bitterly criticised. In the general election of 1924 he stood, for the third and last time, as a Labour candidate, on this occasion in the Clapham division of Wandsworth, a safe Conservative seat. His papers, however, opposed Labour candidates who were regarded as pro-Communist; thus Ben Tillett was mentioned with the comment, 'no Catholic vote in the division where he is a candidate should be given to this man' [*Glasgow Observer*, 18 Oct 1924]. His papers also criticised the Labour Government's term of office for its timidity over the Irish question and for attempting too few social reforms. At Clapham, where he was defeated in a straight fight, there was press comment about the way he toured the constituency in a Rolls-Royce, to which the *Glasgow Observer* (25 Oct 1924) made a characteristic rejoinder: 'Why not? There was a time when the automobile was the monopoly of the Capitalist candidate but that day has gone for good.'

After 1924 Diamond withdrew somewhat from Labour politics and made his support for the party even more conditional. He quarrelled with John Wheatley, Labour MP for Glasgow Shettleston, over his bid to integrate Socialism with progressive aspects of Catholicism, and fiercely criticised supporters of the General Strike in 1926. He took up the issue of proportional representation, since he thought that with such a system Catholics, thanks to their disciplined voting habits, could return a phalanx of Catholic Labour MPs from multi-member constituencies. Given Britain's electoral system, he never went so far as to advocate a separate Catholic party. Instead questionnaires on moral, religious and international topics became a feature of his newspapers' coverage of local and national elections. If candidates failed to reply or else gave unsatisfactory answers, readers were urged to repudiate them at the polls. Sometimes the *Catholic Herald* backed Conservatives while still acknowledging that the Labour Party had benefited its working-class readership in material terms. In the 1931 general election his papers endorsed Labour candidates of differing hues, including the radical ILP members who were returned for Glasgow constituencies.

During the 1922–3 Irish civil war Diamond had used ferocious language to condemn the Republican side of the conflict, its leader Eamon de Valera being described in the *Catholic Herald* as 'a hybrid Spaniard of alleged Jewish extraction'. Hostile references to the Jews regularly featured in Diamond's papers. He was often temperamentally incapable of distinguishing between his opponents' ideas and their personalities and this led to a series of costly libel actions which absorbed most of his profits in later years; with advertisers increasingly reluctant to support unpopular vendettas, revenue from the *Catholic Herald* dropped by almost half between 1924 and 1932.

For the remainder of his life Diamond continued to run his newspapers and it was on a working visit to Glasgow in January 1934 that he fell ill with heart disease. He returned to his London home, 22 Prince's Gate Court, Kensington, where he died on 19 February at the age of seventy-five. Following a Requiem Mass at Brompton Oratory he was buried at Kensal Green Cemetery on 21 February. He was survived by his wife and left effects to the value of £6034. Among the numerous tributes published in the *Glasgow Observer* (24 Feb 1934) one commented that Diamond's 'attitude towards modern Labour politics was practically that of the Catholic Social Guild of which he was a constant and munificent benefactor'.

Writings: *Why Socialism cannot come and remain* (1925).

Sources: *Catholic Herald*, 27 Dec 1919 and 13 Mar 1920; *Glasgow Herald*, 9 and 10 Mar 1920; *Scotsman*, 9 and 10 Mar 1920; *Glasgow Observer*, 18 and 25 Oct 1924, 27 Mar and 27 Nov 1926; *WWW* (1929–40); J. Handley, *The Irish in Modern Scotland* (Cork, 1947); D. McRoberts, 'Charles Diamond', *New Catholic Encyclopaedia*, vol. 4 (Washington, DC, 1967) 849; G. C. Gunnin, 'John Wheatley, Catholic Socialism and Irish Labour in the West of Scotland' (Chicago PhD, 1973); O. D. Edwards, 'The Catholic Press in Scotland since the Restoration of the Hierarchy', in *Modern Scottish Catholicism*, ed. D. McRoberts (1979) 156–82; T. Gallagher, 'Catholics in Scottish Politics', *Bulletin of Scottish Politics*, no. 2 (Spring 1981) 21–43; idem, 'Scottish Catholics and the British Left 1918–39', *Innes Rev. 34*, no. 1 (Spring 1983) 17–42; G. P. Maguire, 'Charles Diamond reappraised', *Irish Post*, 7 May 1983. OBIT. *Glasgow Herald*, *Scotsman*, and *Times*, 20 Feb 1934; *Glasgow Observer*, 24 Feb and 10 Mar 1934.

TOM GALLAGHER

See also: †John WHEATLEY.

EVANS, Thomas (1763–182–?)
SECRETARY OF THE LONDON CORRESPONDING SOCIETY AND SPENCEAN

Apart from his date of birth in 1763 nothing is known of the early life of Thomas Evans. He appeared as a delegate from Division 40 on 6 August 1795 to the general committee of the London Corresponding Society. Within three weeks he had switched divisions, and would do so again, though this was by no means unusual. Far more notable, however, was his rapid rise to senior office in the Society: secretary of Division 28, later president of the seventh; a member of the executive and finally, by the summer of 1797, its secretary. Evans' introduction to, and achievement within, the London Corresponding Society were quite possibly due to the friendship and influence of one James Powell, a customs clerk of Somers Town in the north of the capital. At the time he was first noted in the records of the Society, Evans lodged with Powell, a member of the general and executive committees who also assisted John Bone when the latter was secretary. Powell was also a government spy, a skilled dissembler responsible for providing the authorities with a constant stream of detailed and accurate intelligence on the London Corresponding Society during the years 1795 to 1798. His deceit was known to no one in the Society. Powell clearly found it useful to have a friend highly placed in the Society who could supply news of its deliberations when he was unable to attend; and on at least one occasion Evans unwittingly enabled Powell to furnish the Secretary of State's office in Whitehall with detailed intelligence, when the spy was forced to remain at home due to a heavy cold. That Evans was innocent of the situation is clear from Powell having to delay sending his report, because, as he told the Bow Street magistrate to whom it was sent, he 'had nobody I could trust to put it into the Post on account of the Direction' [PC 1/23/A38, 12 Jan 1796].

Evans was not without ability, however, and Powell's patronage alone (particularly given the latter's sometimes buffoonish front) would not have been enough to secure for him the secretaryship of the London Corresponding Society. Thomas Evans was diligent in his attendance at meetings, and, precarious though his personal finances were, he lent the Society small sums of money. He was deputed to launch a new Division, the 50th, in January 1796, and became president of the 7th in 1798. In the summer of the previous year he had assumed the post of secretary at a time when government persecution was notably punitive. Almost his first task on taking office had been to assume responsibility for organising a controversial mass public meeting in the face of a magistrates' prohibition, and the possibility therefore of it being forcibly dispersed. This open rally was seen by Evans and its other supporters not only as a crucial test of liberty of speech and assembly, but also as a means of reviving flagging public support and outflanking Foxite ambitions; but it was a strategy from which other members strongly dissented, including Francis Place and John Ashley (a former secretary) both of whom in consequence resigned from the Society. Undeterred, Evans was energetic in trying to organise simultaneous provincial rallies, and in suggesting ways of circumventing the Seditious Meetings Acts. The London meeting went ahead on 31 July 1797, troops in the capital being alerted and police leave cancelled. In the event the meeting, which was attended by some 3000, dispersed peaceably after the intervention of magistrates strongly backed by police. Six speakers were arrested. 'After this meeting', observed Place, 'the Society declined.' Presiding over this political deterioration in the Society's position did nothing to enhance Evans' subsequent reputation, though one should also recognise the risks he took in so public an involvement.

Among those arrested on 31 July was the plumber Benjamin Binns, another former assistant secretary to the Society and one of Evans' Plough Court neighbours. Binns, brother of the better-known John, was Evans' main point of contact with the growing Irish revolutionary movement, and their association was an important one for the radical underground in the capital. Evans seems to have at first believed that the London Corresponding Society could by itself initiate revolution. The month before the meeting of 31 July, for example, a spy at a meeting in Furnival's Inn Cellar, a frequent haunt of revolutionaries, recorded, 'one Thomas Evans said it would not be long before there would be a Revolution, that all the Corresponding Societies would meet together in three Weeks – he believed in a Fortnight, that a Field was engaged already for the purpose & the precise time would be known about Thursday next' [PC 1/40/A132, Thomas Milner to the Lord Mayor, 24 June 1797].

The disappointments of 31 July 1797 would seem to have moved Evans both towards a more overtly revolutionary stance, and to growing sympathy with Irish radicalism, whose fortunes he recognised as crucial to the English popular movement. His support for the Irish cause led him to agree readily to act as signatory to the London Corresponding Society's *Address to the Irish Nation* early the following year. This, the last publication of consequence by the Society, was apparently circulated in 'samizdat' form. It is interesting to note that Place believed Evans at least to have co-authored the *Address*, though it was actually written by the United Irishman John Binns. About the same time Evans was centrally involved in the formation of cells of United Englishmen, in imitation of the Irish revolutionary organisation, in various parts of London. In early April, at a meeting of the United Englishmen at Evans' home, it was proposed to organise in four 'Grand Districts' covering the compass points of the capital and metropolitan Surrey. 'Evans assured them, that when they had so collected their Members they would form a Junction with the United Irishmen who are in London, & undertake together some great Design' [HO 42/42, 'Secret Information', n.d.]. Members solemnly swore 'to defend my country should necessity require for which purpose [I] am willing to Join the society of True Britons & to learn the use of arms – in order that equal rights and Laws should be established and Defended' [HO 42/ 42, 29 Mar 1798]. 'True Britons' was the group's alternative title, perhaps chosen to avoid invidious comparison with the already notorious United Irishmen, and therefore may be indicative of growing unease in the London Corresponding Society about the direction in which Evans and his closest associates sought to take it. One plausible reading of the patchy documentary sources for this period is that attempts were made to oust Evans as secretary. As early as 9 November 1797 one source curiously refers to him as having resigned; by early March the following year a Grubb Street calenderer (cloth finisher), John Morgan, appears acting as 'Provisional Sec.' while a few weeks later the election of a new secretary was being openly canvassed in the general committee. At a meeting of the latter on 5 April an attack by Evans on 'the internal condition of the French nation, which he stated to be widely remote from the enjoyment of liberty', was 'heard with universal attention', until he proposed that the Society collectively arm itself as a volunteer military corps. The suggestion was regarded, correctly, as disingenuous.

The issue of Evans' secretaryship was resolved for the Society when, on 18 April 1798, he was arrested with twelve others at a meeting of the United Englishmen in the Queen of Bohemia public house, Clerkenwell. Pike-heads were allegedly found, while in Evans' pocket was discovered an oath 'of the society of True Britons'. The purpose of the meeting seems to have been to convert members of several divisions of the Corresponding Society into a cell of the United Englishmen. Evans' neighbour Benjamin Binns was arrested at his home the next morning; later the same day fifteen more Corresponding Society activists were taken at a meeting of the general committee, while another raid yielded further United Englishmen together with an abstract of correspondence between them, provincial groups and Ireland, 'the whole in Evans's Hand writing'. Later arrests included Thomas Spence, Alexander Galloway (a leading United Englishman and Evans' brother-in-law), and almost everyone calling at Evans' home and inquiring after him. This series of pre-emptive arrests effectively contained the revolutionary movement in the metropolis.

Thomas Evans was detained without trial for nearly three years, first in Winchester and then in Chelmsford gaol. Much of this time was passed in solitary confinement. During his imprisonment he was visited by Sir Francis Burdett, in the course of the latter's investigation into the conditions of detention of state prisoners. With Burdett's encouragement, Evans campaigned to be released, both petitioning the House of Commons and demanding an immediate trial to establish his innocence of High Treason. Janet, his wife, had given birth to their only child, Thomas John, very shortly after Evans' arrest. In spite of his earlier political differences with her husband, Francis Place helped support Janet Evans and her son during what were clearly difficult years. Evans' activities in the period immediately after his release in March 1801 are obscure. James Powell, in a letter to the Home Office shortly before the 'Despard Conspiracy' was exposed, offered the view that Pendrill, Hodgson, Galloway and Evans 'appear to have attached themselves to the conspiracy'; but, while this intelligence is readily verifiable in the case of the others mentioned, for Evans corroborative detail is wanting. The precariousness of his economic position in the early years of the nineteenth century may have contributed to his apparent inactivity. Certainly, the range of Evans' occupations suggests a broken and uneven life beset with financial difficulties: baker, bawdy print-colourer, failed publisher (with John Bone, 1796–7), 'manufacturer of spiral springs and patent braces', coffee-house keeper and printer. To this list should perhaps be added professional criminal, for, in the company of several petty offenders he had first encountered in gaol, Evans was one of a highly organised group attempting the blackmail of members of the royal family and, *inter alia*, Francis Place, in the years 1810–13. Place had continued to assist the family following Evans' release in 1801, but parted company from him over £20 lent in 1806 and used, in Place's words, 'for a dishonest purpose'. With Jonathan 'Jew' King, Davenport Sedley and Patrick Duffin, Evans was involved in attempts to blackmail Place over his involvement in the notorious Sellis affair of 1810. Joseph Sellis, valet to the Duke of Cumberland, had died in mysterious circumstances – murdered, some felt, by his master. At a Coroner's Inquest the jury, of which Place was foreman, brought in a verdict of suicide: an implication widely drawn at the time was that they had been commissioned to obscure Cumberland's part in the affair. This, along with allegations that he was a spy, formed the basis for the attempt to blackmail Place. The allegations were printed in the *Independent Whig*, whose editor, Henry White, played a prominent part in the extortion.

Just how central Evans was in this gang is impossible to determine, as the source of information on his involvement is primarily Place himself. What is clear, though, is that nearly all Place's judgements on Evans, which have greatly influenced subsequent historians, were the product of a highly embittered hindsight. Within the space of a few years Evans passed from a place among the 'leading' and 'cleverest' Corresponding Society members [BL Add MS 27808, fo. 30] to 'a fanatic of a peculiar description, ignorant, conceited, and remarkably obstinate. Such a man could only have been secretary when the society had proceeded a long way in its decline and had greatly changed its character' [ibid., fos 105–6]. A charitable, yet not entirely implausible, explanation for Evans' conduct is that he acted on genuine suspicions, and maybe sought also to fund underground political activity on the strength of them. Place was naturally circumspect in public about his enmity with Evans. Notwithstanding his criminal connections, Thomas Evans' links with 'respectable' radicalism remained strong. He took his responsibilities as an elector for Westminster seriously, being appointed with Thomas Hardy, for example, to a committee organising Cochrane's and Burdett's election campaign in 1812. Along with Arthur Thistlewood, a newcomer to metropolitan radicalism, Evans sought nomination to the committee of the leading Nonconformist educational body, the West London Lancasterian Association: in spite of Burdett's support, both men failed. Increasingly, however, Evans' political energies were directed at a new sphere of radical politics – Spenceanism.

The extent, if any, of the association between the agrarian reformer Thomas Spence and Evans in the 1790s is unknown. Evidence links neither Spence with the United Englishmen, nor Evans with Spence in this decade; though John Smith, a printer working for the latter, was another Corresponding Society activist who, like Benjamin Binns, was a neighbour of Evans. Yet when Spence died in September 1814 Evans immediately and without opposition assumed the leadership of the Society of Spencean Philanthropists, suggesting both a previous involvement with its founder and a close association with him. Several active conspirators from the 1790s were closely involved with Spence, including Evans' fellow prisoners Galloway and Charles Pendrill – the latter a key figure in the national revolutionary network. The Spenceans deliberately chose a 'free and easy' format for their meetings, so it is difficult to trace any individual's involvement with precision. Isolated events afford occasional glimpses of Evans involving himself in the activities of the Spencean group. In October 1803 the Corresponding Society veteran Arthur Seale, Spence's printer, was prosecuted for publishing a defence of Colonel Despard which Galloway had commissioned for delivery to Evans. During his imprisonment in 1812, Daniel Isaac Eaton was supported by a subscription whose organisers included Evans and George Cullen: the latter, one of the most enthusiastic admirers of Spence, had stood bail for him in 1801. It was probably Evans who supplied copy on the Rappite community of Harmony, Indiana, for Spence to use in his last publication, *Giant Killer or Anti-Landlord*, in 1814. A few months later Evans junior was sent to France with instructions from his father to strengthen links between the Spenceans and British radical exiles in Paris. Accompanied by Thistlewood (whose business was apparently gambling), the sixteen-year-old travelled armed with a parcel of Spence's works to distribute, and a strict paternal instruction 'that I consider you the agent of mankind and that no oppertunities [*sic*] are to be lost of propagating the true Philosophy of Nature' [HO 42/168, letter to his son, 18 Sep 1814]. Galloway provided a letter of introduction for his nephew to Richard Hodgson, a veteran Jacobin arrested in 1798, and T. J. Evans was to seek out especially William Putnam McCabe, a United Irishman, and Benjamin Binns. The trip was ill-starred, Thistlewood quarrelling with Hodgson over his handling of property belonging to the latter in England. Spence himself died while Thistlewood and Evans' son were in France.

While the French mission met with indifferent results, at home Spenceanism enjoyed increasing numerical and political strength. Like Spence, Evans was unwavering in his faith in the 'Progress of Reason aided by the Art of Printing'; but Evans was no slavish disciple and, largely through his influence, Spenceanism broadened its political agenda, at the same time revealing a growing sense of urgency. This is evident in much Spencean writing about this time, most notably in a series of five letters Evans contributed to the *Independent Whig*, commencing in August 1815, on economic and constitutional issues. Evans also drafted an *Address and Regulations of the Society of Spencean Philanthropists*, printed by Seale the same year; this was followed by a *Journal* of which, unfortunately, copies do not appear to have survived. Numerous broadsides were also issued by the Spencean group, an *Essay on Printing* (possibly by Evans' close associate of this time, Robert Wedderburn), and two editions of Thomas Evans' major political work, *Christian Policy, the Salvation of the Empire*. This fifty-six-page pamphlet encapsulates the ideology of the Spencean Philanthropists in the years immediately following Spence's death, as well as providing a vivid insight into a distinctive version of the Jacobin tradition. The context of Spence's millenarian development was one that Evans shared: poverty, metropolitan sectarianism, and the cross-fertilisation of popular religious and political movements. The post-war depression renewed millenarian speculation among the Spenceans. Successive editions of the *Address and Regulations* of their Society emphasised with growing urgency 'the calamitous condition of the great majority of mankind'. In *Christian Policy* Evans foresaw, 'a dread crisis . . . a whole people paralysed and in danger':

> These nations are arrived at a crisis the most tremendously awful to contemplate, brought upon us by the mistaken policy of our rulers, the avarice of our landholders and merchants, the influence of a corrupted press . . . the great body of the people . . . drained by taxation, of their rightful share of the national property and the only source of power [(1816) iii, 1].

The language was apocalyptic, but the essence of Evans' argument was secular even when bolstered by scriptural reference:

> The sacred records declare, that such establishments shall not endure in peace, and the awful visitations arising therefrom in our own days are evidence, that till we put away the abomination of desolation, paganism; and return to a just administration of that property which is equally the natural right of all, by abolishing lordship of the soil, the earth will be filled with violence, and will continue to be deluged with blood. Christian policy would make the world a paradise, the prevailing pagan system constitutes a hell [ibid., 15].

Scriptural elements were more evident in Evans' ideas than in those of Spence, who had made little reference to Christ, or the New Testament generally, preferring the Old Testament for inspiration, support and analogy, in keeping with his Calvinistic background.

Under Evans' influence, however, the Spenceans placed considerable emphasis on their being Christians, though in a manner consistent with the overall tenor of deism they shared with Spence himself. Evans denied the divinity of Christ while emphatically affirming his historicity: in his view Christ was a radical reformer, dedicated to restoring the Old Testament agrarian laws of jubilee (Leviticus 25). The true essence of his teaching was first subverted by Paul, and then by 'the pagan Greeks, that made this man a divinity' [*Christian Policy*, 10]. The true Christian therefore denies Christ's divinity, and upholds the laws of God and Nature so conspicuously flouted in the pagan institution of private property. Evans emphasised the parallels between Spenceanism and the early Christians, and drew particular attention to what he held to be residual elements of true Christianity in the organisation of the Church. Essentially this was to demonstrate the viability and veracity of the 'joint stock principle' whereby members of a community can hold property jointly and in perpetuity, unaffected by deaths or fluctuations in numbers. For all its faults, therefore, the Church provided a paradigm for organising public ownership of the land. By analogy private property was pagan. Interwoven with this argument was another element of the English radical tradition, one which Spence had largely ignored: the Norman Yoke. In Evans' view Saxon society was purely Christian, its system of property holding broadly in line with Levitical law and natural rights: Alfred the Great, 'a philosopher, a philanthropist and law-giver', had 'established in this island the agrarian commonwealth'.

The populist thrust which Evans' adoption of the Norman Yoke gave to Spenceanism may partly be seen as a bid, typical of the flurry of Spencean publications in the years 1814–16, to widen the constituency of appeal for agrarian radicalism. The Society of Spencean Philanthropists met with sufficient success in this way to expand its activities by 1815. Originally meeting as a 'free and easy' in the Cock public house Grafton Street, Soho, the Society now divided into three further sections meeting at public houses in Carnaby Market, Moorfields and the Borough (Southwark). A 'conservative committee' comprising two delegates from each section, plus the librarian, treasurer and secretary, was formed. A purchasing fund backed the 'library of useful books for the instruction of members'. The librarian (Evans) was the chief officer of the Society, reflecting its collective faith that 'Printing is the best gift that Nature, in its clemency has granted man. It will ere long change the face of the Universe' [Wedderburn, *Essay on Printing*, [1818]]. However, Evans' desire to widen the appeal and influence of Spenceanism was constrained by a strong sense of the need to guard its original purity, as he saw it. When the Society organised mass public rallies, to be addressed by Henry Hunt, in November and December 1816, Evans withdrew suddenly when Hunt declined to endorse any specifically agrarian demands in the petition due to be presented by the assembly to the Regent. The Spa Fields meetings, as they became known, therefore went ahead without either Evans or his son participating, even though the elder's *Christian Policy* had been clearly intended by the Spenceans as central to their preliminary propaganda. This was the book that was hawked round the taprooms of London in the weeks leading up to the meeting of 16 December; and this was the work which Robert Southey seized on to review when commissioned by the Government to attack the radical movement in the *Quarterly Review*.

The withdrawal of Evans from active participation in the Spa Fields conspiracy effectively isolated him from the mainstream of revolutionary politics. In the opinion of the Home Office, however, Evans was still as important a figure as he had been in the 1790s: on 9 February 1817 both Evans and his son were arrested on a charge of High Treason. This ostensibly arbitrary act deterred many from attending the third Spa Fields meeting the following day; it also removed from circulation one who, in spite of withdrawing from the organising group, had nevertheless headed subscription lists to defray the legal costs of those who had been arrested immediately after the meeting of 2 December. By a savage irony, presumably not unintended by a Government with a vested interest in sowing dissension in radical ranks, Evans was now detained yet again without trial for almost a year, while the core group of conspirators went free, following the acquittal of Dr Watson. Janet Evans campaigned vigorously to free her husband, who on his release pursued an unsuccessful case for compensation. Imprisoned first in Cold Bath Fields and then in Horsemonger Lane gaols, Evans was again removed from the central role in metropolitan radicalism to which he had been long accustomed. Furthermore his recently established business as a brace- and spring-maker collapsed while he was in prison. The episode, immediately following as it did his estrangement from the Spenceans over Hunt's views, deeply embittered Evans. None of his subsequent attempts to re-establish himself in either business or politics was successful.

Following the arrest of the two Evanses, formal meetings of the Spenceans resumed as a 'free and easy' at an old haunt, the Mulberry Tree in Moorfields, with Wedderburn playing a leading role. The group adopted the title of Polemic Society, first used by the Society in 1816, and resumed the Spencean strategy of achieving revolution through the growth of knowledge and press agitation. Galloway was rumoured to have financed its short-lived journals, the *Forlorn Hope* and the *Axe laid to the Root*. To help re-establish their presence in London radicalism, a chapel was hired by sympathisers in Evans' name, in Worship Street, Shoreditch, in October 1817. There was a considerable overlap between its congregation and Mulberry Tree regulars, to which in any case services were often adjourned. However the chapel was patronised in addition by several prominent Unitarian businessmen in the City, along with members of the Freethinking Christians (a universalist sect whose members later included Henry Hetherington). Meetings at this location were short-lived, though. They had ceased by June 1818: by this time, having been released, Evans had hired larger premises in Archer Street, Soho. Business here was conducted as a debating society, though the hall was licensed for worship and two Sunday 'services' were held in addition to a crowded mid-week meeting. Evans usually acted as chairman, but Wedderburn increasingly dominated proceedings. It was at about this time that divisions among the members of the Spencean circle became irreconcilable. Evans appears to have tried hard to dissuade John George, Preston and Wedderburn from participating in any way in Watson's activities. Wedderburn resigned from Watson's White Lion group in consequence. George, though he continued to attend, gave in to Evans' veto on reforming the Spenceans on the Surrey side of the Thames. Preston seems to have ignored him. While the Evanses, father and son, resented the adulation Preston and the other Spa Fields conspirators received, the latter in their turn accused Galloway (chairman of a prisoners' relief committee) of partiality in the distribution of relief to his brother-in-law and nephew. In May 1818 Evans made the rift completely public, attacking Dr Watson in a letter to the *New Times* and branding him and his circle renegades who courted government repression of all radical activities. In reply Watson accused Evans of 'putting forward mistatements [*sic*] with a view of obtaining a little popularity'. Stressing the need for 'the most determined co-operation ... to overthrow a system destructive to people's freedom and happiness', Watson alleged Evans did the opposite, not least through presuming to monopolise the title 'Spencean Philanthropist' now the Society had folded. Spencean Philanthropy, declared Watson, was a general creed 'founded in truths unanswerable but by acts contrary to natural justice' [*Shamrock, Thistle and Rose*, 29 Aug 1818]. The Westminster by-election the following March found the two men supporting opposing sides.

Evans was now preferring the title 'Christian Philanthropists' and he revised the original Address and Regulations of the Spenceans for reissue about the same time as the dispute with the Watsonites reached its climax. He also produced a wholly new work, based on John Mellish's *Account of a Society at Harmony* (1815), a description of the Philadelphian Rappite community. Its contents illustrate just how little Evans, unlike Watson, was adapting his politics to the post-Spa Fields situation and how far he was seized by a Utopian idealism strikingly at variance with his beliefs during the 1790s or the early years of the Spencean Philanthropists. Evans was now engaged in a new business venture, a radical coffee house and newsroom in Moorfields – where he employed as shopboy Robert George, son of the veteran Jacobin John George, and later a central member of the Cato Street group, fortunate to escape prosecution. This new commercial venture was, however, short-lived, Evans being evicted from the premises in December 1818, probably for debt. He faced problems, too, from an unexpected quarter – the Archer Street Spencean group itself. Wedderburn's stridently impious oratory had been causing the two Evanses increasing unease, indicative probably of a deeper social and political incompatibility between them and Wedderburn. In March 1819 a squalid dispute arose, ostensibly over the ownership of furniture and effects in the chapel, which Evans wished to close and Wedderburn to continue. As in the earlier dispute with Dr Watson, the mantle of true Spenceanism was disputed, with Evans being branded an 'apostate' by his erstwhile associate. Wedderburn carried the majority of the congregation with him, first at Archer Street and then from August at larger premises in Hopkins Street. Evans briefly led a splinter group to a chapel in Wood Street, Cripplegate, but finally had to content himself with only the chair at the Mulberry Tree meetings.

As far as revolutionary politics was concerned, Evans was now effectively marginalised, though in 1820 he did team up with Thomas Preston once more to organise relief work for the families of those arrested after Cato Street. Increasingly, however, it was his son Thomas John Evans who made a mark in radical circles. Described by Place as 'a very worthy young man', the younger Evans had sights firmly set on a career as serious journalist. It was apparently he who drew his father into the company of T. J. Wooler, John Cartwright and other members of the demoralised Westminster Committee to form a short-lived 'Liberal Alliance'. Through these contacts, and backed financially by Galloway, T. J. Evans secured the proprietorship of the *Manchester Observer* early in 1820. He assumed control with the issue of 19 February, promising investigative journalism, unflinching support for universal suffrage, annual parliaments and the secret ballot, better news from the capital and the expulsion from the paper's columns of adverts for venereal disease cures. All this was in keeping with the aspirations to respectable radicalism of his father. For a while the latter remained in the capital, but in the late spring of 1820 he joined his son in Manchester, doubtless seeking new political pastures. The pair acted as northern administrators of a subscription raised in London in support of political prisoners, beneficiaries of which included Samuel Bamford. But the elder Evans' main preoccupation at this time was a biography of his mentor, Thomas Spence. This he printed and published from an address in Short Street, off Oldham Street, Manchester, in May 1821. As the earliest biography of Spence it is particularly valuable, though a great deal of it is taken up with extracts from Spence's works and a 'selection of Spencean Songs'.

In a short appendix to the *Brief Sketch of the Life of Mr Thomas Spence*, Evans tartly noted the circumstances that had swiftly ended his son's editorship of the *Manchester Observer*. In April 1821 T. J. Evans had been prosecuted for 'libelling the army' in a report of a public-house brawl between weavers and soldiers in Oldham the previous year. T. J. Evans was gaoled in Lancaster Castle, and his interest in the paper sold. For a while his father tried to support himself and his son from the proceeds of his printing enterprise but, shortly after the younger Evans' release in April 1822, they returned to London. Both were involved in the formation of the London Mechanics' Institution, the originating group for which met in the British Forum debating rooms at Lunn's Coffee House, Clerkenwell Green. T. J. Evans, meanwhile, had begun to work for the radical daily paper the *British Press*. In early February 1824 the elder Evans appeared on a public platform with Gale Jones at a meeting marking the birthday of Thomas Paine. There his known career ends, no less abruptly than it had began. Presumably Thomas Evans had died some time before 1831, when his son was in correspondence with Francis Place about the latter's projected biography of Spence.

There is little surprising about a figure in the early labour movement either being born, or dying, in complete obscurity. Yet the absence of any information about these aspects of Evans' life does underline his somewhat enigmatic quality. His life had about it something of a character of a picaresque novel; but his connections with the underworld, though real, need to be kept in perspective, not least because of Place's (understandable) partisanship, but also in view of the pervasiveness of low life in the London where Evans lived and worked. First through his revolutionary fervour, then through his attachment to Spencean-ism, Thomas Evans rose out of the rank and file to positions of responsibility in the radical movement: just how much responsibility, in the revolutionary movement of 1797–8, may never be clear. One of Place's allegations about Evans was that his only motive in becoming secretary of the London Corresponding Society was to siphon off money meant for John Binns, in order to settle a personal debt. Evans' examination before the Privy Council in March 1798 offers equivocal evidence, though he had very good reason to devalue his radical fervour before that particular audience. Evans' commitment to the Society, like the responsibilities he held within it, extended far beyond the constraints of personal interest. Before the Sellis affair, and in spite of publicly dissenting from Evans' politics, Place had recognised this and supported Evans' family during his first lengthy imprisonment. During his second detention, in 1817, Evans actually refused an offer of release that entailed being bound over to refrain from political activities. Among the visitors Evans received at this time was Alexander Boswell MP, a Government supporter checking on the conditions in which state prisoners were held. He found no fault with them, but in his report to Sidmouth, the Home Secretary, he provided a description of Evans to set against those of Place: 'He is a man of a strong acute mind and who had read and remembered a great deal' [HO 42/168, 4 July 1818].

Without Evans, Spence's posthumous influence might well have dwindled: instead Evans' vigorous prose captured for Spenceanism an extended hearing. When Robert Southey, at the Government's behest, analysed the radical movement for the *Quarterly Review*, it was as much the work of Evans as that of Spence with which he was concerned. Richard Carlile noted how Evans' *Christian Policy* had been the medium through which Spencean ideas had influenced moderate reform proposals for a single property tax. Finally, with no less emphasis than his treatment of Owen, it was Spencean Philanthropy as construed by Evans upon which the Revd Thomas Malthus seized to ridicule 'systems of equality' in the extensively revised fifth edition (1817) of his *Essay on Population*. Evans' political writing was important in popularising Spencean ideas of social and economic reform, and in general his approach constituted an important transitional stage between English Jacobinism and Owenism.

Writings: 'Particulars of the Arrest of T. Evans' (1798), Burdett papers, MS. Eng. Hist. c296/63–6, Bodleian Library, Oxford; contribution to *Spence's Songs: part the first* [1812?], untitled poem, 'on reading' [Spence's] "Address to POSTERITY, Warning them against the LANDLORD JUDAS"'; contributions to *Spence's Songs: part the second* [1812?], 'An Address to the Fair, celebrating the Day on which the Rents of the Lands are divided among the People, to Every Man, Woman and Child', 'The Spencean System, or the Way to be Happy and Free', 'The Inefficacy of the French Revolution' and 'The Spencean Plan for a'that'; contribution to *Spence's Songs: part the third* [1812?], 'The Rose and the Shamroc [*sic*]'; *A Humorous Catalogue of Spence's Songs* [1812?]; letter to Thomas John Evans, 18 Sep 1814, HO 42/168, PRO; letters to the editor, *Independent Whig*, nos 504 (27 Aug 1815), 507 (17 Sep 1815), 512 (22 Oct 1815), 537 (14 Apr 1816) and 549 (7 Sep 1816); *Christian Policy, the Salvation of the Empire, being a Clear . . . Examination into the Causes that have produced the Impending, Unavoidable National Bankruptcy*, 2nd ed. (1816) 48 pp.; 'Petition of Thomas Evans', 10 Apr 1817, HO 42/163, PRO; *The Petition of Thomas Evans, Librarian to the Spencean Philanthropist Society, and Author of 'Christian Policy, the Salvation of the*

Empire', *to the Honourable House of Commons* (1817) [against his imprisonment without trial on suspicion of treasonable activities] 8 pp.; *Christian Policy in Full Practice among the People of Harmony* ... (1818) 16 pp.; petition against the suspension of the Habeas Corpus Act, HO 42/182, n.d., PRO; *A Brief Sketch of the Life of Mr Thomas Spence, Author of the Spencean System of Agrarian Fellowship or Partnership in Land* ... (Manchester, 1821) 24 pp.

Sources: (1) **MS:** Bodleian Library, Oxford: Burdett papers, MS. Eng. Hist. c296/63–6. BL, Dept of MSS: Place papers, Add. MSS 27808, fos 30, 91, 98 ff., 225–9; 27809, fos 95–9; 27812, London Corresponding Society minute book; 27813, fos 113–21, 126–9; 27815, 29 Apr 1796; 27816, fo. 540; 27840, fos 6–7, 85, 95, 99; 35143, fos 62–3; 35152, fos 60–3; 36457, fo. 93; 36623, fo. 52; 37930, 17 July 1830. BL, Dept of Printed Books: Place Coll., Set 38, fos 108, 187, 203. Irish State Paper Office, Dublin Castle: Rebellion papers, 620/18A/11, Wickham to Cooke, 19 Apr 1798. PRO, Chancery Lane: PC 1/23/A38, 12 and 29 Jan, and 8 and 29 Dec 1796; PC 1/40/129; PC 1/40/A132; PC 1/41/A138, 9 Nov 1797, 30 Jan, 26 Feb, 7 and 29 Mar 1798; PC 1/3526; PC 1/3535, 25 Dec 1800 [*sic*; should read '1801']; TS 11/122; TS 11/41/148, 14 Mar 1813; TS 11/689/2187; TS 11/697/2210, *Rex* v. *T. J. Evans*; TS 11/1071/5075, 6 Jan. 7 and 19 May, 26 Nov 1810. PRO, Kew: HO 40/3 (3), fo. 890; HO 40/7 (4); HO 40/8 (4); HO 40/9 (4); HO 40/15, fos 18, 20, 26, 31–2; HO 40/16, fos 22, 28; HO 41/26, p. 10; HO 42/30, 14 May 1794; HO 42/42, 8 and 29 Mar, Apr 1798; HO 42/73, 7 Sep 1803; HO 42/143; HO 42/158, 9, 27 and 29 Jan 1817; HO 42/159; HO 42/163, 10 Apr 1817; HO 42/166, 1 May and 2 June 1817; HO 42/167, 26 and 30 June 1817; HO 42/168, 4 July 1817; HO 42/172, 2 Dec 1817; HO 42/172, 'A Statement of the Grounds on which Several Persons apprehended under Lord Sidmouth's Warrants and detailed under Acts of 57 Geo. III c. 3 and 55 were so arrested and detained', 22 Jan 1818; HO 42/174, 4 Feb 1818; HO 42/177, Hunt to Thistlewood, 19 June 1818; HO 42 /180; HO 42/181; HO 42/190, 29 Dec 1818 and 15 Apr 1819; HO 42/192, 19 Aug 1819; HO 44/4, fo 255; HO 44/5, fo. 176; HO 59/1, fo. 75.

(2) **Theses:** T. M. Parssinen, 'Thomas Spence and the Spenceans: a study of revolutionary Utopianism in the England of George III' (Brandeis PhD, 1968); I. D. McCalman, 'A Radical Underworld in Early Nineteenth Century London: Thomas Evans, Robert Wedderburn, George Cannon and their circle, 1800–1835' (Monash DPhil., 1984); M. S. Chase, 'The Land and the Working Classes: English agrarianism *c.* 1775–1851' (Sussex DPhil., 1985).

(3) **Other:** London Corresponding Society, *Proceedings at a General Meeting of the Nottingham Corresponding Society* (1797); idem, *The London Corresponding Society's Answer to a Member of Parliament's Letter* (1797) 8 pp.; idem, *Proceedings of the General Committee of the London Corresponding Society on the 5th, 12th and 19th April 1798, relative to the Resistance of a French Invasion. Stated in a letter to a friend: intended to have been inserted in the Morning Chronicle* (1798); idem, *Address to the Irish Nation* (1798) – not extant, but repr. in the *Report of the Committee of Secrecy ... relating to Seditious Societies* (1799); *Giant Killer and Anti-Landlord*, 2, 13 Aug 1814; *Address and Regulations of the Society of Spencean Philanthropists* (1815); J. Melish, *Account of a Society at Harmony* ... (1815); *Polemic Fleet of 1816* (1816); [R. Southey], 'Parliamentary Reform', *Q. Rev.*, Oct 1816, 225–78; [*First*] *Report of the Committee of Secrecy on Papers which were presented to the House by Viscount Castlereagh on 4 February* 1817 IV, I; R. Wedderburn, *Essay on Printing, by a Spencean Philanthropists* [*sic*] [1818]; *Address of the Society of Spencean Philanthropists to all Mankind* (1819); T. R. Malthus, *Essay on the Principle of Population*, 5th ed. (1817); *Axe laid to the Root*, no. 1 (1817) cols 15–16; ibid., no. 2 (1817) cols 17–18; *Forlorn Hope*, no. 1 (1817) cols 6–10; *Reformist's Register*, Oct 1817, 426; *Independent Whig*, 18 Jan 1818, 36–8; *Black Dwarf*, 21 Jan 1818; *Shamrock, Thistle and Rose, or the Focus of Freedom* 1, 29 Aug 1818; *Address of the Society of Christian Philanthropists* [1819?]; R.

Wedderburn, *A Few Lines for a Double-faced Politician* [1819?]; *Manchester Observer*, 19 Feb 1820; T. Preston, *Letter to Lord Viscount Castlereagh* (1820); *Republican 4*, no. 4 (22 Sep 1820); *Cobbett's Weekly Political Register 39*, no. 3 (21 Apr 1821); ibid. *40*, no. 3 (4 Aug 1821); *Republican 9*, no. 6 (6 Feb 1824); A. Davenport, *The Life, Writings and Principles of Thomas Spence* ... [1836]; R. R. Madden, *The United Irishmen: their lives and times*, vol. *1* (1842); S. Bamford, *Passages in the Life of a Radical*, vol. *2* (1844; later eds 1967, Oxford 1984); A. Davenport, *The Life and Literary Pursuits of Allen Davenport ... written by himself* (1845); J. W. Hudson, *The History of Adult Education* ... (1851); B. B. Jones, 'The People's First Struggle for Free Speech and Writing', *Reasoner*, 5 June 1859; G. Wallas, *The Life of Francis Place, 1771–1854* (1898, 4th ed. 1925); O. Rudkin, *Thomas Spence and his Connections* (1927); H. Collins, 'The London Corresponding Society', in *Democracy and the Labour Movement*, ed. J. Saville (1954) 103–34; A. W. Smith, 'Irish Rebels and English Radicals, 1798–1820', *Past and Present*, no. 7 (Apr 1955) 78–85; C. Hill, 'The Norman Yoke', in *Puritanism and Revolution: studies in interpretation of the English Revolution of the 17th Century* (1958); E. P. Thompson, *The Making of the English Working Class* (1963; 2nd ed., 1968); J. M. Main, 'Radical Westminster, 1807–1820', *Historical Studies 12* (1966) 186–204; *The Autobiography of Francis Place*, ed. M. Thale (Cambridge, 1972); M. Elliott, 'The "Despard Conspiracy" reconsidered', *Past and Present*, no. 75 (1977) 46–61; E. J. Evans, 'Thomas Evans (1763–?)', in *Biographical Dictionary of Modern British Radicals*, vol. *1*, ed. J. O. Baylen and N. J. Gossman (Brighton, 1979) 164–6; I. J. Prothero, *Artisans and Politics in Early Nineteenth Century London: John Gast and his times* (Folkestone, Kent, 1979); J. Ann Hone, *For the Cause of Truth: Radicalism in London 1796–1821* (Oxford, 1982); R. Wells, *Insurrection: the British experience, 1795–1803* (Gloucester, 1983); M. Thale, *Selections from the Papers of the London Corresponding Society, 1792–1799* (Cambridge, 1983); G. Claeys, 'Thomas Evans and the Development of Spenceanism, 1815–16: some neglected correspondence', *Bull. Soc. Lab. Hist.*, no 48 (Spring 1984) 24–30; J. Belchem, *'Orator' Hunt: Henry Hunt and English Working Class Radicalism* (Oxford, 1985).

MALCOM CHASE

See also: †Richard CARLILE; Thomas PRESTON; Thomas SPENCE; Robert WEDDERBURN.

FARRIMOND, Thomas (1766–1828?)
RADICAL AND GRANGE MOOR INSURGENT

The son of William Farrimond and Jane Simpkin, both weavers of Pemberton, Thomas Farrimond was born at Lamberhead Green, near Wigan, and baptised at the Wigan Parish Church in Lancashire on 11 October 1766. Thomas Farrimond learned the hand-loom weaving trade in his father's shop and later set up house with his wife, Mary, at Pemberton. They were Methodists and attended the Lamberhead Wesleyan Chapel at Wigan, in whose records for the years 1796–1806 were registered the births of their children, George, Ann, Mary, Iris and Thomas. An older son John, born about 1795, is not listed in this source, and this may indicate that the couple were converted to Methodism in the mid-1790s.

Like several other poor weavers from Wigan, Farrimond migrated to Barnsley in Yorkshire, where the expansion of linen weaving had created a demand for labour. He arrived in Barnsley in May 1810 to work as a linen weaver and part-time barber. On Saturdays and Sundays men came to his house to get a shave, to read the papers and to talk politics. Farrimond was a radical in both politics and religion. He belonged to the New Street, Methodist New Connexion (or Kilhamite) Chapel in Barnsley, in whose records the baptism of his daughter Betty is listed for 6 May 1812.

Reform meetings were held in Barnsley late in December 1816 and soon afterwards a Barnsley Union Society was founded. Farrimond became its secretary and in this capacity wrote to the veteran Yorkshire reformer, John Payne of New Hall Hill, and to Major John Cartwright. The Major provided the Barnsley men with the rules of London union societies as well as books on reform. According to Farrimond, this society was disbanded in April 1817 when the Government placed restrictions on public meetings and suspended the Habeas Corpus Act. Farrimond was involved in the conspiracy of May–June 1817 that ultimately resulted in the arrest of dozens of radicals as well as in the uprisings at Pentrich and Holmfirth. From his own testimony as well as that of the notorious 'Oliver the Spy' it is known that Farrimond attended a meeting of radical delegates at Wakefield on 5 May 1817.

A second Barnsley Union Society was set up in January 1818 and its members paid one penny a week to subscribe to the *Manchester Observer*, *Leeds Mercury* and the *Black Dwarf*. Meetings were held on Monday nights at Farrimond's house, where 'every person had liberty to stand up and give his opinion on what was read'. Radical literature was then distributed to leaders who took them back to their 'sections' for further discussions. On 12 July 1819 the Barnsley Union Society demonstrated its strength by organising a public meeting on reform which was attended by several thousand persons. Farrimond was called to the chair and he addressed the crowd on three occasions that day. He claimed he had been a reformer for twenty years and his speeches consisted of appeals to reason and justice, attacks on corruption, as well as numerous scriptural references. In millenarian style he warned his listeners, 'in a little time, there will be a National union of the three Kingdoms, when we shall make a manly demand by the voice of reason and justice, of our rights as Englishmen' [Burland [c. 1881] 388]. Although Farrimond sometimes apologised for his lack of oratorical skills, a hostile informer suggested otherwise:

Who is this Thomas Farrimond I hear you ask? Why he is an operative weaver; more bit with politicks, than ever Don Quixot was with knight errantry. . . . He has an eye in his head, such as I never saw to. Talk politicks, and his eye connacts and dilates like a catty eye. He can speak, and his hearers know how bountiful Providence has been – how enviable this nation once was. Now how cursed!! The common people hear him with admiration [Harewood papers, 5 Dec 1819].

He spoke with a Lancashire accent and also had to overcome a slight speech impediment in his public addresses.

In 1819 Farrimond was twice a delegate to radical meetings in Leeds and once to a meeting in Stockport. At the latter he was held for two days by local radicals who suspected him of spying. He was released when a former Barnsley resident came forward to identify him.

On 8 November 1819 the Barnsley Union Society held a large demonstration to protest against the Peterloo massacre, but thereafter was more clandestine in its activities. Government restrictions on public meetings and drilling exercises passed in December 1819 made open activities more difficult. The several hundred members of the Barnsley Union Society were organised in sections which sent delegates to meetings of an inner circle of radicals known as the 'Secret Acting Committee'. The latter consisted of eight to ten experienced and trusted radicals. Farrimond was its secretary and weekly meetings were held in his house. This group corresponded with other radicals, sent delegates to radical meetings, and in the early months of 1820 made plans for an armed rising.

This Secret Acting Committee agreed to participate in a general rising to take place on the night of 11 April 1820. They were to meet with thousands of West Riding radicals outside Huddersfield and to attack that town. Accordingly, at the appointed hour some 300–400 armed men marched from Barnsley to Grange Moor outside Huddersfield. On arrival they discovered that something had gone wrong and the expected support from other districts was not there. Farrimond was one of the first to admit they had been betrayed. The Grange Moor rebels then fled in every direction and the authorities were able to arrest only a few dozen men, twenty-one of whom they tried at York in September 1820 for High Treason.

Much to the dismay of the authorities, Thomas Farrimond escaped from Grange Moor and a reward of £100 was offered for his arrest. Farrimond went to Royton in Lancashire, then on to Whitfield, Liverpool, Kendal and Ulverstone. There he was spotted by a constable, but escaped by leaping through a window. He was finally caught at Whitehaven on 16 September 1820 and sent back to York on a charge of High Treason. After lengthy negotiations an agreement was reached by which Farrimond was to make a full statement of his activities in exchange for immunity from the death sentence. During the trial on 12 March 1821, Farrimond appeared to have suffered a breakdown, he cried and made an extremely moving appeal for mercy on behalf of his dependants. The judge pronounced him guilty of a crime punishable by death, then added for good measure a graphic description of the decapitation of the body of a traitor. Farrimond's sentence was later commuted to transportation for life and in May 1821 he was marched to the hulks at Sheerness. He was not transported, but instead spent the next seven and a half years confined to the hulks. There he was reported to be 'A remarkable well behaved man'. He was released with a pardon on 20 November 1828, at the age of sixty-two. No further records of his life have been located, and it is not known when he died.

His daughter Ann was married in 1818 to James Lowe, another member of the Secret Acting Committee and a Grange Moor insurgent. Farrimond's son John was also a weaver and a participant in the Grange Moor rising. He was found guilty of High Treason at York in September 1820 and spent two years in the hulks before obtaining a pardon in October 1822.

Sources: (1) MS: Lancashire CRO, Preston: Wigan Parish Records. PRO: RG 4/1771, Wesleyan Chapel Records, Wigan; RG 4/3645, Methodist New Connexion Records, New Street Chapel, Barnsley; HO 40/9 (2), narrative of Oliver, 1817; HO 40/15, T. Farrimond to Lord Sidmouth, 5 Dec 1820; HO 40/16, T. Farrimond to Lord Sidmouth, 15 Feb 1821, and examination of T. Farrimond, 8 Mar 1821; HO 42/200, extract of a letter from Stuart Corbett to Stuart Wortley MP, 8 Dec 1819; TS 11 979/3573, depositions of Michael Downing and Thomas Morgan, Apr 1820; HO 9/6 and 9/7, 979/3573; Hulk reports, HO 9/6 and 9/7. West Yorkshire Archive Service, Sheepscar, Leeds: Harewood papers, anonymous information enclosed in J. Beckett to Earl Harewood, 5 Dec 1819. Barnsley PL: J. H. Burland, 'Annals of Barnsley' [c. 1881]. St Mary's Parish Church, Barnsley: marriage register, 1818. (2) Other: *Wakefield and Halifax J.*, 16 July 1819, 16 Mar and 1 June 1821, 11 Oct 1822; J. L. and B. Hammond, *The Skilled Labourer* (1919; later eds); E. Hoyle, *History of Barnsley* (Barnsley, Yorks, 1924); E. P. Thompson, *The Making of the English Working Class* (1963; 2nd ed. 1968); F. K. Donnelly and J. L. Baxter, 'The Revolutionary "Underground" in the West Riding: myth or reality?', *Past and Present*, no. 64 (1974) 124–32; F. K. Donnelly, 'The General Rising of 1820' (Sheffield PhD, 1975); F. J. Kaijage, 'Working-Class Radicalism in Barnsley, 1816–1820', in *Essays in the Economic and Social History of South Yorkshire*, ed. S. Pollard and C. Holmes (Barnsley, Yorks, 1976) 118–34; J. Stevens, *England's Last Revolution: Pentrich 1817* (Buxton, Derbys, 1977).

F. K. DONNELLY

See also: †William ASHTON; William COMSTIVE; Benjamin SCHOLES.

FORD, Isabella Ormston (1855–1924)
SOCIALIST, TRADE UNIONIST AND CAMPAIGNER FOR WOMEN'S RIGHTS

Isabella Ormston Ford was born at St John's Hill, Leeds, on 23 May 1855. She had two brothers and was the youngest of six daughters (of whom two died in infancy) of the Leeds solicitor Robert Lawson Ford and his wife Hannah (née Pease). Isabella Ford grew up in a household immersed in radical liberal politics, women's rights and humanitarian causes. Her father was a close friend of John Bright, and a succession of European liberals, including Mazzini, stayed with the family when she was a child. Hannah Ford had a particularly important influence on her daughters. Along with many other Quakers she worked for the emancipation of slaves, joined Josephine Butler's campaign against the Contagious Diseases Acts and was active in the movement for women's suffrage. Isabella Ford described her mother, who supported Kossuth, as 'quite a revolutionist' [*Leeds Weekly Citizen*, 12 June 1914] and recalled that she taught her daughters that they should 'never laugh at what is new' [Mallon (1908) 251].

All the Ford children were encouraged by their early family life to taken an active interest in political and social questions. Isabella Ford's brother, J. Rawlinson Ford, was a solicitor in his father's firm and served as a councillor, and then alderman, on Leeds City Council. He was the leader of the Liberal group on the Council between 1912 and 1919. His wife took an interest in women's rights as a member of the Yorkshire Ladies' Council of Education. Isabella Ford's other brother, T. Benson Ford, was trained as an engineer. He gave up this career because he thought that it might involve him in the manufacture of armaments, and became the owner of a silk-spinning mill instead. In the years immediately preceding the war he was chairman of both the Health Committee of the West Riding and the West Riding Insurance Committee. Shortly before his death in 1918, he approved of the introduction, by his son Charles, of a co-partnership and profit-sharing scheme at their silk-spinning firm, Ford, Ayrton and Co. Ltd [*Times*, 20 Sep 1926; *Co-partnership*, no. 516 (Apr 1964) 18; and Pafford (1974) 14].

The eldest daughter, Mary, married Richard Smith of London and she died in 1894. Of the three younger daughters, Emily was a well-known church artist, and Bessie was very musical. Bessie was always close to Isabella, who was the youngest daughter and the outstanding public personality of the family. The girls were encouraged by their parents from an early age to become active in social work. Hannah Ford was a member of the Education Board of the Yorkshire Ladies' Council of Education and helped to organise a series of lectures on health for working women in the 1870s. From their middle teens her three youngest daughters taught for many years in a night school for mill girls which she helped to establish with her husband and a local shoemaker in the East End of Leeds.

During the 1880s and 1890s the involvement of all three sisters with working women broadened from reform and educational work to trade union organisation. Isabella, who had read about the industrial conditions of women workers in the *Bee-Hive*, a weekly paper taken by her mother, became first involved in practical organisation in 1885 through Emma Paterson, who was a friend of the family. Isabella Ford was encouraged to help establish a Tailoresses' Society in Leeds under the auspices of the Women's Protective and Provident League; and, although the Society collapsed the following year, in 1886, it brought her into contact both with working women and with members of the Leeds Trades Council. She became a close friend of John Bune, secretary of both the Trades Council and the Brushmakers' Society, who was a staunch supporter of the Liberal Party. By 1888 she felt confident enough to take the initiative in setting up a new organisation, the Workwomen's Society. This was to be open to all women workers, but was aimed in particular at women employed in the rapidly expanding factory sector of the ready-made tailoring trade. The Society emphasised friendly benefits, and members insisted on the inclusion of a no-strike policy in the rules; but by 1889 it still had only 109 members.

A new impetus was given to the organisation of female workers in Leeds during the labour unrest which was widespread in the city between 1888 and 1890. It was Isabella Ford's activities during this period that brought her to prominence as a trade union organiser, and she became the acknowledged advocate of working women's rights in the West Riding. In September 1888 two hundred Leeds weavers came out on strike in protest against a reduction in prices. After reading adverse reports about the strike in the press, Isabella Ford went among the women to find out the facts for herself and stayed to help in the dispute. In the following year she again gave help to female textile workers who were on strike in nearby Alverthorpe. These disputes brought her into contact with the leaders of the West Yorkshire Power-loom Weavers' Association and was the start of long-standing friendships with Ben Turner and Allen Gee.

In October 1889 mounting discontent among tailoresses in Leeds prompted Isabella Ford to call a public meeting to establish a Tailoresses' Union which would be based on sound trade union principles. She was assisted by members of the Socialist League, who had already made contact with her in 1887 because of her work on behalf of tailoresses. At a well-attended public meeting Clementina Black, representing the Women's Trade Union and Provident League, spoke of the victory achieved by the London dockworkers and the encouragement this should give to all less skilled workers to improve their conditions. A few days after the meeting seven hundred female machinists employed by Messrs Arthur and Co., wholesale clothiers, went on strike to obtain a reduction in the charge made for power. The firm claimed a victory after four weeks, but many of the strikers stayed out until the end of December.

The tailoresses received help from all sections of the labour movement, but the most energetic leadership came from Isabella Ford and the Socialists. Isabella Ford gave rousing speeches at public meetings, helped to organise the collection and distribution of relief and publicised the women's case in the press. She was made an honorary life member of the Trades Council in 1890 in recognition of her work during the strike.

Throughout the 1890s Isabella Ford gave most of her time to the organisation of tailoresses and wool and worsted workers in Leeds and the West Riding. She was president of the Leeds Tailoresses' Union, which had recruited 2000 members during the enthusiasm of strike action. Numbers fell away dramatically once the strike was over and never again rose above 300. Along with the working women on the committee of the union, Isabella Ford made great efforts to gain more members. She attended numerous factory meetings, spoke at recruiting drives and helped out in disputes. She also gave material assistance to the union by providing the money to employ a full-time secretary. Agnes Close, a tailoress, was appointed to the post in 1896 and became a close friend of the Ford sisters. Isabella and Bessie Ford also financed the establishment of a Women's Trade Union Club in 1897, which was to be a focal point for all groups involved in the organisation of women workers in Leeds. The club provided space for meetings, a reading-room and a place for women workers to have tea together. Although the Tailoresses' Union remained small, its active members were able to keep issues affecting women workers to the front in the Leeds labour movement in the 1890s. The union sent two delegates to the Trades Council and was always represented at labour rallies; and Ben Turner's friendship with Isabella Ford ensured that the union's activities were given widespread coverage and sympathetic support in the *Yorkshire Factory Times*.

In 1899, on the verge of collapse, the Tailoresses' Union merged with the men's organisation, the Amalgamated Union of Clothing Operatives. Isabella Ford had worked hard to achieve a mixed-sex trade union in the clothing trade, although she feared that women's specific interests would not necessarily be safeguarded in the new organisation: fears which were realised in the policies pursued by the union in the years preceding the war.

From the late 1890s to the end of her life Isabella Ford gave her services to the textile workers' union. She had been active in the famous Manningham Mills dispute in Bradford in

1890 and 1891 and spoke on behalf of the union at countless meetings in towns throughout the West Riding. In her speeches she always emphasised the need for unity between the sexes and she was not afraid to criticise male workers who used married women workers as scapegoats for all their industrial problems. In 1913 the union used the occasion of the implementation of the National Insurance Act to launch a recruiting drive among female workers; and Isabella was once again active in helping to arrange meetings and in speaking to female textile workers in Leeds. She also represented women workers at numerous International Textile Workers' Congresses, where her fluency in French and German enabled her to act as an interpreter for the other union delegates.

The interesting and remarkable quality of Isabella Ford's approach to the difficulties of the female worker was her opposition to the typical concerns of the philanthropically inclined which had dominated Victorian charity. She was scathing in her attacks on philanthropists who dealt with the consequences, not the causes, of women's subordinate position at the workplace, arguing that higher wages would make rescue work unnecessary. She had an unusual understanding of the way in which industrial work had psychological and social, as well as material, effects on workers' lives. She emphasised that she in no way underestimated the 'well-known hardships working women have to endure – such as, defective or indecent sanitary accommodation, overcrowding, non-ventilation &c.' and their very low level of wages:

> But what is in some respects more important than these matters, and is, therefore, what I particularly wish to describe, is the effect produced on the general morality of the workers, the deadening and warping of their humanity, by the ordinary regulations imposed upon them in their industrial lives by most factories (with some few exceptions) good and bad alike [*Humane Rev. 2* (1901–2) 198; published initially in the *Friends' Q. Examiner 34* (Apr 1900) and revised for the *Humane Rev.* article].

Isabella Ford further argued that conditions within the factory failed to give women any moral sense, while underpayment robbed their lives of beauty and happiness.

Her attempt to understand why women workers thought and acted in the way that they did made her, unlike many of her contemporaries, unwilling to pass moral judgements on their actions. Referring to the Manningham Mills dispute she said:

> I have never felt absolute hunger . . . but these girls did. We found some of them desperate with hunger, and supplied a breakfast of tea and bread and butter every morning. One poor girl with a drunken father and an invalid sister collected 10s and ran away with it. To her it represented wealth, and I was only sorry there was not more in the box. She had awakened to the right to possess something [*Leeds Weekly Citizen*, 12 June 1914].

She displayed similar understanding in relation to married women workers, arguing that they were forced to work through economic necessity and that she was 'heartily tired of hearing so much abuse of the married woman worker'. The married working woman could never rest and, if she neglected her home and children, 'who could blame her?' [*Labour Leader*, 2 Sep 1904, 262].

Isabella Ford also attacked philanthropists for teaching women workers that true femininity implied submission to authority. She took the opposite view, arguing that women must revolt and act independently to change their own conditions. She was quite clear that 'when the working woman does awake and desire her true salvation, she must, as all of us must, work it out for herself'. All that could be done by middle-class outsiders was to 'help awaken that desire' [*Humane Rev. 2* (1901–2) 196–7]. It was this approach that led Isabella Ford in the 1890s to emphasise trade union organisation as the key to any change in women's industrial position. She insisted that trade unionism not only brought material benefits but was also the essential and necessary means whereby women would realise their humanity, a theme to which she returned again and again. Trade unions fostered a sense of collectivism in place of individual competition and gave women a higher sense of their industrial worth and enhanced their personal dignity [*YFT*, 17 Mar 1893 and 1 Mar 1895]. She argued that women's resistance to trade unionism was deeply rooted in the contemporary definitions of femininity, and that it was the task of trade unions to 'fight against every form of conventional thought ... particularly among the women themselves' [*Women's Trade Union Rev.*, Jan 1900, 12]. She also insisted that trade unionism should be linked with the vote. Political emancipation would raise the status of industrial women and give them a voice, making it more difficult for employers to exploit their weaknesses.

Isabella Ford naturally campaigned in the 1890s to make existing factory legislation more effective. She was one of the first women to argue the case for employing female factory inspectors and was instrumental in obtaining an extension of the particulars' clause to the tailoring trade in 1895. At the same time, she had an ambivalent attitude towards factory legislation which differed from the views expressed by the Women's Trade Union League. She often opposed the introduction of protective legislation for women, not on the grounds of equal rights or the defence of individual liberties, but because she was sceptical of the impact of such legislation when women were unorganised and afraid to complain. She noted how woman workers frequently connived with their employers to deceive inspectors, who were seen as interlopers at the workplace. She was particularly critical of legislation which aimed to restrict women's employment (such as minimum wages legislation) and which thereby benefited male workers. She was also incensed that women were not consulted about such proposals. Her stand on these issues brought her into conflict with the Trades Council and with Ben Turner, although it did not damage their friendship.

When she first began to organise women workers Isabella Ford was still involved with Liberal Party politics. In February 1889 she helped to found a Leeds branch of the Women's Liberal Association and expressed the hope that educated women would assist those with fewer advantages. It was her involvement in the tailoresses' dispute and growing friendship with local Socialists that brought a change in her political views. She later wrote, 'I found it quite impossible to obtain any help, politically, from either of the two parties.' The Liberal Party was 'the avowed advocate of trade unionism, but the Liberal employers were quite as bitter against any of their female employees who dared to join a union'. The tone in which they spoke to women workers showed that 'sex hatred, or what is even worse, sex contempt on the part of men towards women, was underlying our social structure' [*Labour Leader*, 1 May 1913].

In the early 1890s Isabella Ford began to address labour clubs and churches in the West Riding on the subject of women's rights and Socialism. She found a natural home for her views in the Independent Labour Party, became a member in 1893, and always spoke of the ILP with affection. She believed that it was the only party which offered full equality to women, for they had been elected on to the National Administrative Council almost immediately and had never been expected to act just as unpaid canvassers or dignitaries on platforms. During the First World War she wrote that she was 'proud' of the ILP's stand on the war. 'I have always been thankful that I had the good sense to be a Socialist and now am more so than ever. No other party has stood ... for common sense and civilisation, to say nothing of the principles of Christianity and humanity' [*Leeds Weekly Citizen*, 15 Jan 1915].

Her political work was of both a propagandist and a practical nature. She was always available to speak at labour meetings and was elected a parish councillor in 1895. She gave financial assistance to the ILP and in the late 1890s she helped to clear considerable debts left by Joseph Burgess, who had edited the *Workman's Times*, while Bessie Ford provided finance and editorial assistance for the pamphlet *A Remembrance to Tom Maguire* (1895). Her contribution to the labour movement was made at a national as well as at a local level. After the formation of the Tailoresses' Union she became a member of the central committee of the Women's Trade Union League. Between 1903 and 1907 she served on the NAC of the ILP and went from there as a delegate to the Labour Party conferences of 1903, 1904 and 1905. She was the first woman to speak at a Labour Party conference when, in 1904, she supported a motion that women should be given the vote on the same terms as men [*Conference Report* (1904) 47–8]. Her work for the ILP made her a close friend of Philip Snowden and Keir Hardie.

Socialism naturally meant a change in the quality of life as well as material reforms. Bessie Ford was a talented musician and organised a series of free concerts in Leeds each winter, while Emily was known not only for her church murals but also for her Yorkshire sketches. Isabella – in addition to numerous short stories, wrote three novels, one of which, *Mr Elliott*, dealt with industrial life in Yorkshire and Lancashire – and was a member of the Leeds Arts Club. Her broad vision of Socialism led her to become part of the circle of West Riding Socialists who gathered around the writer Edward Carpenter. Bessie and Isabella were influenced by the writings of Walt Whitman – as was Carpenter – and through Carpenter they sent several sums of money to Whitman between the years 1885 and 1891 [see *W. Whitman: the correspondence* vols *3, 4* and *5* (1964–9)]. Whitman in return sent a signed copy of his complete works, published in 1890, to both Carpenter and the Ford sisters. Isabella Ford made close and lasting friendships with members of this Socialist group, in particular Edward and Alice Carpenter, Tom Maguire, Katharine Conway and Alf Mattison, and she also corresponded regularly with Olive Schreiner. The Ford sisters, who were also interested in psychical research, introduced their cousin, Edward Pease, to Frank Podmore at a seance [MacKenzie (1979) 44].

Along with many in the ILP, Isabella Ford believed that Socialism would bring a 'moral regeneration of society of the most complete and searching kind', one which would be founded on 'justice that demands freedom for all' [*Women and Socialism* (1906) 2]. She did not look to class conflict to provide the motive force for social change, but argued in this pamphlet that the education provided by involvement in trade unionism and labour politics would convince individuals of the justice and superior values of Socialism. Where she differed from many of her colleagues in the ILP was in her emphasis on the importance of women's emancipation for the achievement of Socialism. She believed it was essential for the Labour Party that both sexes worked together from a position of equality, for 'there can never be anything worthy until it is built on men and women together, neither claiming superiority to the other' [*Leeds Weekly Citizen*, 12 June 1914].

She placed great emphasis on the importance of family life, arguing that the relationship between men and women formed the core around which society would grow and change, for 'the family, the home, is the very heart of a nation' [(1906) 3]. At first glance this statement seems to accord with ILP rhetoric which evinced a sentimental attachment to the image of a stable family life with the woman at the centre, but Isabella Ford had a different conception of the nature of this family life. She believed that fathers were as important as mothers in contributing to the well-being of the next generation and argued against any attempts to idealise women's role within the family. She constantly referred to the poor facilities in working-class homes and emphasised that in reality motherhood was not always 'honourable' and voluntary. She thought that women's caring role in the family made them ideally suited to work for Socialist aims, in particular the achievement of love and beauty, but in order for women to do this without a 'sickliness of sentiment' they had to be politically free. This alone could wipe out the view that 'women are naturally more angelic than men, and somehow possess more firsthand knowledge about heaven' [*Labour Leader*, 1 May 1913]. Once women had the vote their intelligence would be awakened and household matters would sink to a proper place, enabling and encouraging them to take a greater part in public affairs. Aware of the difficulties working-class women faced in this, she advocated co-operative housekeeping, but recognised that they were not yet ready to accept such a plan.

After 1906 Isabella Ford's energies were directed more fully to the campaign for women's suffrage. Her mother had given her an early interest in women's rights and her first public speech had been made on the subject of women's suffrage. It was the increased vigour of the suffrage movement in the years before the First World War, however, that encouraged her to believe that other issues should take second place until the vote had been won. The decision to change the emphasis of her activities was not taken lightly and by 1906 she was divided between her loyalty to the labour movement and her growing conviction that women's suffrage had to take priority [Gawthorpe (1962) 216].

With her Quaker background, Isabella Ford was opposed to the use of violence and worked for the more constitutionalist National Union of Women's Suffrage Societies (NUWSS). Isabella and Emily Ford were vice-presidents of the Leeds Women's Suffrage Society, while Bessie was the treasurer. Isabella played a key role in the formation of the West Riding Federation of Women's Suffrage Societies, of which she was chairman. She provided much-needed financial support for the Federation, and the Yorkshire movement appeared less vigorous during her absences. She spoke tirelessly on the subject of women's suffrage to labour rallies, Socialist meetings and a variety of women's groups throughout the West Riding as well as taking her share of the more mundane day-by-day tasks of fund-raising and petitioning.

Her suffrage work took her increasingly to London. She was elected to the executive of the NUWSS every year between 1907 and 1915, with the exception of 1911, when ill health forced her to stand down. She represented the NUWSS at most of the large demonstrations in London, took part in deputations to the Government and attended international congresses on women's suffrage in a variety of European countries. Isabella Ford had a boundless optimism and hope for the future in these years. After the Trafalgar Square suffrage meeting of 1906 she wrote that she wished the pioneers 'could have been there to see the splendid progress our cause has made, and how near, how very near, we are now to obtaining that freedom they so ardently desired' [*Labour Leader*, 25 May 1906]. She later wrote to Edward Carpenter that the new comradeship between women made her 'burst with joy' [Carpenter correspondence, 25 Aug 1913].

When war broke out in 1914 Isabella Ford continued to work for women's suffrage. As a pacifist she had worked all her life for peace between nations, to protect individual liberties and to uphold the rights of persecuted national minorities. In the 1890s she had opposed the Trade Council's resolution to restrict Jewish immigration and a succession of political refugees stayed in her home, including the Russian Stepniak, who sent his congratulations when her novel *Miss Blake of Monkshalton* was published by John Murray in 1890 [letter from Stepniak, Ford papers, West Yorkshire Archive Service]. The First World War posed a severe challenge to her ideals and she could not give the same degree of support to the war effort as many other suffrage workers. She thought that the women's movement, being international and democratic, should be at the forefront of any attempts to gain a speedy end to the war. Her views were at odds with those of her close friend Millicent Fawcett, and Isabella Ford felt compelled to explain her position in the following terms: 'I hate Prussianism as heartily as you do – and I long for it to go – But I do not think that war ever destroyed war – and real salvation can only come to people and nations from within' [Fawcett correspondence, Oct 1914]. At first Isabella Ford tried to suppress her 'tiresome war opinions' for the sake of unity [ibid., n.d.], but in 1915, along with a number of other women, she resigned from the executive of the NUWSS. The immediate cause was the refusal of the executive to support the International Women's Congress to be held at The Hague. Isabella Ford was one of a number of British delegates allowed visas by the Government to attend the conference. But when the women arrived at Tilbury docks they found that the North Sea had been closed to shipping and they were unable to complete their journey [Liddington (1983) 181].

Isabella Ford did not neglect the material interests of working women during the war, spending many hours in tedious committees dealing with separation allowances and wage assessments. None the less, most of her energies were devoted to the growing campaign by women of all nations to bring a speedy end to the war by negotiation and to build the foundations for international co-operation in the future. This campaign was spearheaded by the Women's International League for Peace and Freedom, formed after the conference at The Hague. Isabella Ford was an executive member of the British section of the League and also established a Leeds branch of the Women's Peace Crusade, a more popularly-based movement. She spoke at all the Labour May Day rallies in the war and post-war period on the theme of international peace, and supported Labour Party resolutions for an end to secret diplomacy. She also gave her support to a variety of groups, including the Union of Democratic Control, the wartime National Council for Civil Liberties and the movement against the extension of conscription, which sought either to gain peace by negotiation or to protect individual liberties against the encroachment of state power.

When it became clear that the Government intended to introduce a franchise Bill towards the end of the war, she renewed her activities on behalf of women's suffrage. She found the proposal to give the vote only to women over thirty an insulting one, but argued that women had to take what they could get in order to achieve more in the future. In the post-war years her age and poor health limited the extent of her public activities, but she continued to work wherever she could for women's rights, international peace and Socialism, and, like so many radicals of her generation, she joined the 1917 Club. After the Armistice she visited Germany to make personal investigations into conditions there and helped to relieve distress by working through the Friends' Relief Committee. She continued to attend international congresses on peace and women's rights and was a delegate to the International Peace Conference at The Hague in 1922. She was excited about a planned visit to a women's conference in Washington in 1924, but was prevented from going because she fell ill. On several occasions she had been asked to stand as a parliamentary candidate for the Labour Party, but always declined on the grounds of poor health. Nevertheless, she continued to work for the Labour Party until the end of her life, putting a great deal of effort into Philip Snowden's election campaign of 1923. She wrote to Millicent Fawcett that 'I am greatly moved when I think that the Labour men I have known so well like Snowden are in power. But I hear from him in particular, how immense their difficulties are – both amongst their own MPs and constituents and the other parties ... their inexperience makes things hard' [Fawcett correspondence, 16 Mar 1924].

Throughout her life Isabella Ford's contribution to the labour movement and to women's suffrage was a public and propagandist one, whereas her sisters worked from behind the scenes. She was a good speaker, entertaining her audiences with witty and humorous speeches. She sometimes found public speaking an effort. Mrs Swanwick, a fellow suffragist, recalled that when physically weary she would say, 'They will expect me to be funny and it is not always easy' [Women's Leader, 1 Aug 1924]. She had a wide circle of male and female friends who were active in either the labour or the women's movement. Her commitment to Socialism, working women's rights and international peace brought her frequently into conflict with one or other of these friends, but in the long term the friendships survived. One contemporary thought that this was because Isabella Ford was broad and well balanced, lacked stridency in her manner and was willing to listen to others. She also had a sense of humour and could laugh at herself [Mallon (1908) 251].

In spite of her many friends, Isabella Ford's involvement in the labour movement also brought isolation. She found that it was difficult to maintain friendly relations 'with those on both sides of the gulf, capital and labour' [Women's Industrial News, Mar 1898, 31–2]. Some of her middle-class contemporaries called her 'mannish' and accused her of 'unfeminine behaviour' when she spoke in public [YFT, 5 Aug 1892 and 21 Apr 1893]. At the same time, some working-class men could also be suspicious of her motives. In 1904 she wrote to the press to refute the accusation that she was still a member of the Women's Liberal Association. She wrote the letter because 'I find evil reports are sometimes easily, and I regret to say, gladly, believed of middle-class women' [ibid., 11 Mar 1904]. She attracted almost the opposite reaction from working men who supported her. They tended to place her on a pedestal and described her activities on behalf of working women in reverential terms, emphasising her gentle and loving personality. At her funeral, the keynote of her character was given as 'keen pity for all suffering creatures' [ibid., 24 July 1924]. Such remarks can, however, give a distorted impression of Isabella Ford's personality, for they emphasise her gentleness at the expense of her undoubted political toughness. Mary Gawthorpe recalled how she was taken to task by Isabella Ford and Ethel Snowden for writing an article in the local press on women's suffrage without asking permission. She contrasted her own political innocence with Isabella Ford's experience of national political intrigues and leadership struggles [Gawthorpe (1962) 215–16]. Isabella Ford had to withstand 'pelting and stoning' for her stand on women's suffrage and peace and she could make fighting speeches for causes that she held dear. In 1914, at the annual conference of the NUWSS, she spoke against any co-operation with the Government for war purposes 'with a pugnacity of word and gesture which took everyone's breath away, and then, having had her say, stamped off the platform and down the hall in almost ferocious style' [New Leader, 25 July 1924].

Isabella Ford never married and lived most of her life at Adel Grange with her two sisters. They were always comfortably off and were able to maintain lodgings in London and to take holidays in Europe. Isabella received considerable emotional and intellectual support from her sister Bessie, and she never fully recovered from Bessie's death in 1919: 'a piece of myself has gone', she wrote to Edward Carpenter (2 Aug 1919). In 1922 she moved with her sister Emily to Adel Willows, a smaller property near the Grange. It was here that she died on 14 July 1924, survived by Emily and her brother, J. Rawlinson Ford. Her funeral took place at the Friends' Burial Ground, Adel, and a memorial gathering organised by the Women's International League and the National Union of Societies for Equal Citizenship was held at the Guildhouse, Eccleston Square, London, on 28 July. She left an estate valued at £24,540, which, apart from a legacy to her parlourmaid, was shared among her relatives.

In her writings Isabella Ford made a significant contribution to feminist and Socialist ideas. Her early feminism was rooted in her radical liberal and Quaker upbringing. From this she derived a commitment to women's equal rights and a sympathy with the needs of working women. Throughout her life she put great faith in the power of the vote to bring sweeping changes, not only in the material conditions of women's lives but also in their self-awareness. She never thought that emancipation would come from institutional change alone but that real freedom also required a change in the hearts and minds of individuals. She argued that a denial of the franchise meant that women were ignored as human beings and only political equality could restore their full humanity [Women's Trade Union Rev., Jan 1900, 12]. She argued consistently that there could be no economic freedom for women unless they had political freedom. The vote would give all women, but particularly working-class women, a greater sense of responsibility and confidence in their own worth. This would raise their industrial status and give them a voice in legislation which affected their lives. She thought that political enfranchisement would help women to know that they were men's equals: 'No Trade Unionism can flourish as long as women say, "Well, I'm only a woman and so I can't expect to get a man's wage"' [Labour Leader, 1 May 1913].

Isabella Ford combined a demand for equal rights with the view that women had a unique contribution to make to public life because of their caring role within the family. She thought that the involvement of women in any movement tended to 'strengthen and purify it' [YFT, 17 Mar 1893] and argued that enfranchisement of women would lead to demands for social legislation to benefit their sex. The vote, however, meant more than the passing of discrete reforms. It was part of the march of civilisation in which women's involvement in politics would change the whole tenor of society. A belief in women's special qualities informed Isabella Ford's analysis of the relationship between feminism and peace. Women, she believed, naturally sought peace because:

> Women have more to lose in this horrible business than some men have; for they often lose more than life itself when their men are killed; since they lose all that makes life worth living for ... the destruction of the race too is felt more bitterly and deeply by those who through suffering and anguish have brought the race into the world [*Leeds Weekly Citizen*, 12 Mar 1915].

She thought that women were more likely than men to co-operate across national boundaries, for, as 'the mothers and the educators of the human race, the bond which unites us is deeper than any bond which at present unites men' [ibid., 28 May 1915].

In her emphasis on equal rights, on women's special qualities and on the power of the vote, Isabella Ford shared many of the objectives and concerns of the late-nineteenth-century women's movement. However, her Socialist beliefs and unique understanding of the problems of working women brought a new dimension to her feminist ideas. This enabled her to depart from the liberal framework of argument which predominated in the suffrage movement. She rejected individualism in favour of collectivism and co-operation, and located the source of women's oppression in their subordinate economic position within industry and the home as well as in their political subjection.

From the 1890s onwards, in her activities and in her ideas, Isabella Ford saw no distinction between trade union organisation, Socialism and women's emancipation. Her speeches returned again and again to the same theme: that working women could only improve their industrial position by trade union organisation and by the achievement of the vote. This would place the sexes on an equal footing and only then could they work together for Socialism. The most systematic statement of her views on the relationship between women's emancipation and Socialism was put forward in her pamphlet *Women and Socialism*. (Originally published by the ILP in 1904, revised and reissued in 1906.) Although her analysis lacked depth in many places and tended to avoid areas of conflict between women's needs as a sex and the question of class unity, the pamphlet did recognise and attempt to explore the relationship between sex and class oppression.

Isabella Ford argued that the women's movement and the labour movement were linked because both arose from economic dependence and both demanded 'a State founded on the highest justice and the consequent reform of the home' [*Women and Socialism*, 3]. She quoted Karl Pearson's view that 'the status of woman and the status of labour are intimately associated with the manner in which property is held and wealth inherited' [ibid., 3]. Drawing examples from history, she tried to show that the economic position of both women and workers had deteriorated over time, reaching its nadir under industrial capitalism. She wanted to convince the suffrage movement that women could only achieve full emancipation as part of a Socialist transformation of society, for only Socialism stood for justice, co-operation and 'equality and opportunity for the whole race' [*Labour Leader*, 1 May 1913]. She felt optimistic that the women's movement and the labour movement were drawing closer together, for the labour movement had lost its old class hatred and the women's movement was extending its appeal to all classes.

Along with Socialists such as Olive Schreiner, Isabella Ford refused to draw a boundary between personal and political life, arguing that the home was the heart of the nation. It was the starting point from which men and women developed a sense of citizenship and the ideals of justice and humanity. However, under industrial capitalism the relationship between the sexes in the home had been distorted. Women were economically and politically dependent on men, making men into their oppressors. Unless this oppression was undermined it would be impossible for either sex to be free. Her analysis of women's economic dependence was hampered by the separate spheres ideology which permeated the women's movement of the period. She advocated trade union organisation as a solution for the economic dependence and inequality of working women. However, in the case of married women who did not work for wages she fell back on the panacea of the vote, arguing that political freedom would result in a more equal companionship between the sexes. This failure to tackle head-on the economic dependence of married women arose from an unwillingess to challenge the sexual division of labour in the family.

Isabella Ford minimised the conflicts that could arise around issues of sex and class. She was able to do this because she believed that sex hatred and class war were no longer important concepts. She echoed the views of ILP leaders in arguing that men and women from all classes would be drawn to work for Socialism once they realised that it implied a higher state of civilisation. Where she made a specific contribution to the Socialism of the ILP was in her insistence that women's contribution to social change was essential and in her focus on the needs of working women. Her influence on the ILP, in particular on its leadership, was frequently noted by contemporaries. Sylvia Pankhurst claimed that Philip Snowden was converted to support for a limited franchise for women by 'the witchery of the genial old Isabella Ford', while Katharine Bruce Glasier argued that Isabella and Bessie Ford's influence on Yorkshire labour leaders helped to create an atmosphere favourable to women's equal rights in the county [Pankhurst (1931; 1977 ed.) 203; *Labour Leader*, 9 Apr 1914]. Joseph Clayton, who was himself active in Socialist politics, recognised in his history of the Socialist movement that women were not just helpers of men in the ILP but co-leaders. He concluded that the contribution of women such as Isabella Ford was to give the ILP a 'tendency to look upon Women's Suffrage as a reform of vital need, and the equal co-operation of men and women in politics not as an ideal but an everyday business' [Clayton (1926) 84]. This understanding of the importance of women's contribution and feminist issues to the early Socialist movement has been largely lost in later histories of the ILP.

Writings: (i) MS: Correspondence with (i) MILLICENT FAWCETT, NUWSS papers, Fawcett Library, City of London Polytechnic, and Millicent Fawcett papers, Women's Suffrage Coll., Archives Dept, Manchester CL; (ii) EDWARD CARPENTER, Carpenter Coll., Sheffield CL; (iii) KEIR HARDIE and FRANCIS JOHNSON, Francis Johnson ILP Coll. on microfilm; (iv) KATHARINE GLASIER, Glasier papers, Sydney Jones Library, Liverpool Univ.; (v) CHARLOTTE JACKSON, a relative of her personal maid, 1914 [copies in *DLB* Coll. from Mrs J. Micklethwaite, Leeds, granddaughter of Charlotte]. (2) Other: *Miss Blake of Monkshalton* [novel] (1890); 'Legislation for Women' [letter], *YFT*, 10 Apr 1891; letter on women's wages, ibid., 4 Sep 1891; 'Leeds Tailoresses Union: important questions', ibid., 24 June 1892; 'Women Inspectors of Factories and Workshops', *Women's Herald*, 16 Mar 1893; 'Industrial Conditions affecting Women of the Working Classes', *YFT*, 17 Mar 1893; 'The Labour Question' [report of a talk by Isabella Ford at Huddersfield Labour Club], ibid., 21 Apr 1893; *Women's Wages and the Conditions under which they are earned* (Humanitarian League pamphlet, no. 8: 1893) 17 pp.; *On the Threshold* [novel] (1895); 'Particulars for the Tailors', *Women's Trade Union Rev.*, Apr 1897, 9; *Women as Factory Inspectors and Certifying Surgeons* (Women's Co-operative Guild, 1898) P.; 'Unsatisfactory Citizens', *Women's Industrial News*, Mar 1898, 29–32; contribution to the views of leading trade unionists on the potential of women workers for organisation, *Women's Trade Union Rev.*, Jan 1900, 12; 'Industrial Women, and how to help them', *Friends' Quarterly Examiner 34*, no. 134 (1900) 171–84, rev. and repr. in the *Humane Rev. 2* (Apr 1901–Jan 1902) 196–207, and as a pamphlet by the Humanitarian League [*c.* 1900] 12 pp.; *Mr Elliott* [novel] (1901); 'Collecting Information at the Girls' Club: a sketch from life', *Humane Rev. 3* (Apr 1902–Jan 1903) 314–19; letter on her membership of the Liberal Party wrongly reported in the *Leeds Mercury*, *YFT*, 11 Mar 1904; 'Woman as she was and is', *Labour Leader*, 13 May 1904; 'In Praise of Married Women', ibid., 2 Sep 1904; 'Exeter Hall and Trafalgar Square', ibid., 25 May 1906; 'Life in a Swiss Village', ibid., 13 July 1906; 'Women and the Transvaal

Constitution', ibid., 10 Aug 1906; *Women and Socialism* (1906) 16 pp.; 'Women Workers in the Wholesale Clothing Trade', *Englishwoman 2* (July 1909) 637–45; 'Of Witches', ibid. *6* (May–July 1910) 73–9; 'Wages in the Textile Trade', *Standard*, 9 Nov 1911; 'The Gold Fish', *Englishwoman 18* (Apr–June 1913) 327–34; 'Why Women should be Socialists', *Labour Leader*, 1 May 1913; 'On the War', *Leeds Weekly Citizen*, 15 Jan 1915; 'Women plead for Peace' [letter], ibid., 12 Mar 1915; 'The Hague Peace Conference', ibid., 28 May 1915.

Sources: (1) MS: NUWSS papers, Fawcett Library, City of London Polytechnic (including executive committee minutes); Alf Mattison Coll., Brotherton Library, Leeds University (including diaries, 1893–1920); Alf Mattison's letterbook, in the possession of E. P. Thompson, Upper Wick, Worcestershire; Women's Trade Union League papers, TUC Library, London; Leeds Trades Council minute books and scrapbook of Isabella Ford's book reviews and some correspondence, including letter from Stepniak, dated 2 Jan 1890. West Yorkshire Archive Service, Leeds. (2) Other: *Women's Union J.*, 1884–90; *YFT*, 1889–1920; 'I. O. Ford', ibid., 1 Nov 1889 [with portrait]; M., 'To the Misses Ford', ibid., 13 Dec 1889; *Women's Trade Union Rev.*, 1891–1914; *Labour Leader*, 1895–1914; LP, *Conference Report*, 1903, 1904, 1905; J. J. Mallon, 'Isabella Ford', *Woman Worker*, 7 Aug 1908; *Leeds Weekly Citizen*, 1911–24; *The Suffrage Annual and Women's Who's Who* (1913); K. B. Glasier, 'The Part Women played in founding the ILP: reminiscences of the time when it was hard for a woman to be a Socialist', *Labour Leader*, 9 Apr 1914, 6–7; 'Some Eminent Trade Unionists no. 8. Miss Isabella Ford', *Leeds Weekly Citizen*, 12 June 1914; E. Carpenter, *My Days and Dreams: being autobiographical notes* (1916); B. Turner, *The Heavy Woollen District Textile Workers' Union* (Dewsbury, Yorks, 1917); 'A History of the Leeds Labour Party, 2', *Leeds Weekly Citizen*, 11 Jan 1918; 'Miss I. O. Ford, *Jus Suffragii 14*, no. 8 (1920) 142; B. Turner, *Short History of the General Union of Textile Workers* (Heckmondwike, Yorks, 1920); B. Drake, *Women in Trade Unions* [1920]; M. G. Fawcett, *The Women's Victory and After: personal reminiscences, 1911–18* (1920); 'Ben Turner looks back', *Clarion*, 28 Mar 1924; *Labour Who's Who* (1924); J. Clayton, *The Rise and Decline of Socialism in Great Britain, 1884–1924* (1926); 'Co-partnership for Industry. Leeds Conference: successful Yorkshire scheme', *Times*, 20 Sep 1926; R. Strachey, *The Cause: a short history of the women's movement in Great Britain* (1928; repr. with a new Preface by B. Strachey, 1978); E. E. Crossley, 'Isabella Ford', *Leeds Weekly Citizen*, 28 June 1929; B. Turner, *About myself 1863–1930* (1930); E. S. Pankhurst, *The Suffragette Movement* (1931; repr. with a new Introduction by R. Pankhurst, 1977); R. C. Strachey, *Millicent Garrett Fawcett* (1931); P. Snowden, *An Autobiography*, vol. *1* (1934); J. Thomas, *A History of the Leeds Clothing Industry* (Yorkshire Bull. of Economic and Social Research Occasional Paper no. 1: Jan 1955); R. Fulford, *Votes for Women: the story of a struggle* (1957); E. P. Thompson, 'Homage to Tom Maguire', in *Essays in Labour History*, vol. *1*, ed. A. Briggs and J. Saville (1960) 276–316; J. F. C. Harrison, *Learning and Living 1790–1960* (1961); M. Gawthorpe, *Up Hill to Holloway* (1962); Anon., 'R. C. Ford – 1879–1964: Ford, Ayrton & Co. Ltd', *Co-partnership*, no. 516 (Apr 1964) 18–19; P. Gunn, *Vernon Lee [pseud.]: Violet Paget, 1856–1935* (1964); *W. Whitman: the correspondence*, vols *3, 4*, and *5*, ed. E. H. Miller (NY, 1964–9); J. Hendrick, 'The Tailoresses in the Ready-Made Clothing Industry in Leeds, 1889–99: a study in labour failure' (Warwick MA, 1970); S. Rowbotham, *Hidden from History: 300 years of women's oppression and the fight against it* (1973; 2nd ed. 1974); E. R. and J. H. P. Pafford, *Employer and Employed: Ford, Ayrton & Co. Ltd, silk spinners with worker participation, Leeds and Low Bentham 1870–1970* (Pasold Research Fund, Edington, Wilts, 1974); C. Pearce, *The Manningham Mills Strike, Bradford, December 1890–April 1891* (Hull, 1975); *Women in the Labour Movement: the British experience*, ed. L. Middleton (1977); J. Vellacott Newberry, 'Anti-War Suffragists', *History 62*, no. 206 (Oct 1977) 411–25; S. Rowbotham and J. Weeks, *Socialism and the New Life: the personal and sexual politics of*

Edward Carpenter and Havelock Ellis (1977); J. Liddington and J. Norris, *One Hand tied behind us: the rise of the women's suffrage movement* (1978); N. MacKenzie, 'Percival Chubb and the Founding of the Fabian Society', *Victorian Studies 23*, no. 1 (Autumn 1979) 29–55; C. Tsuzuki, *Edward Carpenter: 1844–1929* (1980); T. Woodhouse, 'The Working Class', in *A History of Modern Leeds*, ed. D. Fraser (1980) 353–8; D. Clark, *Colne Valley: Radicalism to Socialism* (1981); J. Liddington, 'The Women's Peace Crusade: the history of a forgotten campaign' in *Over our Dead Bodies: women against the bomb*, ed. D. Thompson (1983) 180–3; idem, *The Life and Times of a Respectable Rebel: Selina Cooper* (1984); O. Banks, *The Biographical Dictionary of British Feminists*, vol. *1: 1800–1930* (Brighton, 1985) 82–4. Biographical information: Dr M. E. Currell, Birmingham Univ.; Fawcett Library, City of London Polytechnic; Mrs A. Heap, Local History Librarian, Leeds CL; A. J. Kerry, Ford and Warren, solicitors, Leeds; Dr Gail Malmgreen, Univ. of Massachusetts; Mrs J. Micklethwaite, Leeds; C. Pearce, Golcar. Personal information: Mrs U. O. Ford, Leeds, and Mrs E. Pafford, Bridport, Dorset, great-nieces of Miss Ford. OBIT. *Yorkshire Evening News*, *Yorkshire Evening Post* and *Yorkshire Post*, 15 July 1924; A. Mattison, 'The Late Miss I. O. Ford', *Yorkshire Evening Post*, 16 July 1924; *Yorkshire Observer*, 16 July 1924; *Leeds Mercury*, 17 July 1924; *YFT*, 17 July 1924; *Times*, 18 July 1924; J. Arnott, 'Isabella O. Ford: an appreciation', *Leeds Weekly Citizen*, 19 July 1924; B. Turner, 'I. O. Ford: an appreciation', *YFT*, 24 July 1924; *Woman's Leader*, 25 July 1924, 208–9 [by M. G. Fawcett]; *New Leader*, 25 July 1924; *Daily Herald, Daily Telegraph* and *Times*, 29 July 1924; *Friend* and *Woman's Leader*, 1 Aug 1924.

JUNE HANNAM

See also: †Edward CARPENTER; †William Henry DREW; †Allen GEE; †Emma Anne PATERSON; Ben TURNER.

GIBB, Margaret Hunter (1892–1984)
LABOUR PARTY ACTIVIST

Margaret Gibb was born on 31 July 1892 at Dunston, near Gateshead, the only daughter of William Harrison, a commercial traveller and his wife Susan (née Hunter). Her father, who died in December 1893, had been a radical Liberal, but her mother, grandmother and aunt with whom she grew up were not politically involved. An interest in politics was something which developed in Margaret in an individual fashion. She was one of the first scholarship holders at the new Blaydon Secondary School and recalled attending, as a schoolgirl, important political meetings in Newcastle upon Tyne and hearing Keir Hardie and the Foreign Secretary, Sir Edward Grey. She was much more impressed with the teaching at Blaydon than that at St Hild's College, Durham, where she trained as a schoolteacher for two years from 1910. She found the regime at the College highly restrictive, narrowly Anglican and the curriculum limited and shallow, but the friendship made there with Molly Thompson lasted until Molly's death in 1981 and they shared their home at Cambo village in Northumberland for almost thirty years. It was during her years as a young teacher at Crookhill that her political interests developed. During the First World War she was a pacifist, and refused, for instance, to go into the school yard to celebrate Empire Day.

Soon after the general election of 1918 she attended her first Labour Party meeting in response to a notice inviting women to be addressed by Lilian Anderson Fenn, a newly appointed Labour Party organiser. Only four women attended, but a Women's Section was established and Margaret Gibb allocated the role of secretary. This marked the beginning of a lifetime of political commitment and activity. Until 1924 this was centred on the

ILP which she became a member of soon after joining the Labour Party, and on the growing organisation of Women's Sections in Durham County. In 1921 Margaret was a founder member of the Durham Labour Women's Advisory Council. The local centre for ILP activity was the Westfield Hall, Gateshead, and weekends and many evenings were spent there involved in all kinds of political, cultural and social activities. It was here, practising public speaking, that she met Tom Gibb, an ILP organiser and Labour Party agent from Jarrow, and they married in 1923.

Marriage meant resignation from Margaret Gibb's teaching post because that was the usual rule in the teaching profession. Her husband's job as Morpeth agent came to an end because of shortage of funds, and they moved to Blyth, the Hartlepools and then to Stevington in Bedfordshire, all within a year. In Bedfordshire a more liberal local authority employed married women and Margaret obtained the headship of the village school at Stevington. The Gibbs lived here for three years, during which Margaret started a Labour Women's Section which met in the school house. At the end of 1926 Tom became agent for Central Sheffield and she joined him in February 1927. He died at the end of July and she was offered and accepted his post, helping P. C. Hoffman to win the seat for the first time for Labour in 1929. In that year she herself was elected to Sheffield City Council as member for Moor ward and served on the education committee and four sub-committees. She resigned after a year when she was selected from 127 applicants for a post on the Labour Party's national staff organisation as one of two organisers for what was then the North-East region, consisting of eighty-six constituencies in Yorkshire, Durham and Northumberland. The other regional organiser was Will Lewcock. Margaret Gibb succeeded Harriet Fawcett, who had only been in the post a few months and had followed Lilian Fenn, who had worked in the North East from 1919 to 1929. The salary of £260–£320 a year was similar to the one Margaret Gibb had received as a headmistress, and she retained her post for twenty-seven years, until her retirement in 1957. In 1942 the region was reorganised, the East and West Ridings of Yorkshire being removed and Cumberland and Westmorland added to form the new Northern region. The same year, Margaret moved from Sheffield to a flat in Saville Row, Newcastle upon Tyne. Nine years later she moved to the house in the Riding in the Trevelyan estate village of Cambo in Northumberland where she lived until her death in 1984.

When Margaret began her work the second Labour Government was halfway through its brief life, and the previous decade had seen rapid advances in Labour's local and national organisation, reflected in its electoral success. But a year later, in August 1931, the Labour Government resigned and in the ensuing election Labour's parliamentary seats were reduced from 288 to 46. The background to this catastrophic result was severe economic and social depression; the North East in the 1930s was especially hard hit, with long-term unemployment in the major industries of mining, iron and steel, shipbuilding and textiles. Labour Party organisers were expected to identify the needs of their area and plan the work appropriately. All organisers were supposed to send weekly reports to Transport House, attend annual staff conferences, numerous training and briefing sessions and the annual Labour Party Conference. Local and parliamentary elections in the region and assistance at by-elections elsewhere were naturally part of the work, but otherwise Margaret Gibb spent much of her time advancing the organisation of the Women's Sections which had begun to develop since individual Labour Party membership was introduced in 1918.

The North East region was particularly important for its extensive activity among working-class women. The first meeting of the elected Women's Advisory Council for Durham (at which Margaret Gibb was present) was in February 1923, under the direction of Lilian Fenn, and it was there decided to organise a Durham Women's Gala at Wharton Park, Durham City, along the lines of the well-established Durham Miners' Gala. The date chosen was 9 June 1923; and about 6000 attended, having marched from New Elvet through the city to the Park. Seven bands took part on this first occasion. Ada Gilliland was the Gala secretary, and among the speakers were Dr Marion Phillips, the Labour Party's chief woman officer, Sidney Webb (MP for Seaham) and Jack Lawson (MP for Chester-le-Street). The Gala remained a central point of the Labour women's year from that date and celebrated its Diamond Jubilee in 1983, with Margaret Gibb as the only survivor of the original founders.

When Margaret Gibb became regional organiser in 1930 the Women's Sections were already well established. In many areas they were already the backbone of the Labour Party organisation and activity. The majority of women were full-time housewives, many were miners' wives, and money was scarce. Margaret Gibb said in 1970 in a tape-recorded interview:

> I still remember the Jarrow meetings of women. A huge hall, just packed, jammed with women . . . and they were all paying a penny a week to the Labour Party. There was no question of 12s a year or anything like that – a penny a week. I don't know that it was so much a matter of coming to a meeting as that it was getting out, getting with other people for perhaps a couple of hours.

And she also recalled a meeting in the village of Lingdale in the North Riding of Yorkshire, where, in a room full with about eighty people, there was not one woman whose husband was at work.

Usually a Women's Section held fortnightly meetings, and as great a variety of activities as the organiser's ingenuity could conceive was attempted. Margaret Gibb was, of course, already familiar with the Durham constituencies, and she also knew something of Northumberland, since she had lived there in the early days of her marriage. She was much less familiar with Yorkshire and Cumberland. Her approach in these early years was to concentrate on the areas she knew well, and to experiment first with these groups. Social activities included play productions, attempted originally in Northumberland and then introduced into Yorkshire. There was the usual run of socials, whist-drives and dances, but these in the 1930s had to be carefully costed. Margaret Gibb's great contribution, however, was to go beyond the everyday activities and the usual 'meetings' and develop as varied a programme as practical imagination could devise. There were adaptations for the women's groups of local festivities, such as the traditional Cutlers' Feasts. There were 'family reunion' evenings; 'round table conferences'; 'question and answer' sessions; sports days with trophies presented by local MPs and miners' lodges, and, in Northumberland, Lady Trevelyan presented a silver cup for the County Labour Women's Sports. The Women's Gala in Durham was followed by galas in Northumberland and Yorkshire, and in Northumberland it always coincided with the famous Miners' Picnic.

The main objective of Labour Party organisers was, however, the development of political support for Labour through political education and political activity. Margaret Gibb began a monthly letter which was circulated to all the Women's Sections in her region. It included news of activities, books recommended for reading, and each issue set out questions for discussion at future meetings. She continued the annual 'Schools' begun by Lilian Fenn and regarded these as very important. The first was held in 1930 at Barrow House, Keswick, when twenty-nine women from the Durham sections attended for a week. Subsequent annual Schools were on a larger scale, with sixty or seventy women from the whole region attending centres at Matlock, Middleton, Cloughton, Otterburn and Keswick. Expenses for the Schools were paid at first by the County Advisory Councils and later, additionally, there were scholarships from various supportive groups. The Schools were very popular and, as there was great competition for places, tests were used for selection, usually consisting of a number of questions on a set book or pamphlet, and a general knowledge paper. At the Schools there were daily talks by local MPs and outside speakers. Grace Colman lectured regularly at the schools from 1932 until 1945, and among the later popular speakers were Horace King (Speaker of the House of Commons from 1965 to 1970) and Ernest Armstrong (MP for North-West Durham from 1964; he continued to hold the seat until the 1983 election). A central part of the programme of these annual Schools was the emphasis placed upon training for the administrative and political work of local Labour Parties. The women learned the nature of the duties of taking the chair, or acting as secretary or treasurer.

Among the other activities developed by Margaret Gibb were the occasional 'propaganda' tours. The first went from Gateshead soon after the electoral débâcle of 1931. Seventy-two bus-loads carrying about 1300 women and two former MPs who had lost their seats went from Gateshead down to Harrogate, distributing literature on the way, and ending with a meeting on the 'Stray' in Harrogate. On a lesser scale, similar 'tours' went into southern Scotland from Northumberland and down along the Yorkshire coast from Staithes to Whitby, and from Hull to Withernsea and Hornsea. By 1939 in Durham County, the best organised area of her whole region, there were 196 Women's Sections and 4000 paid-up members.

During the Second World War apart from the annual galas most activities continued as usual, though membership and attendance declined. Travel through the huge region was very difficult, because of petrol rationing, late trains and the black-out. But Margaret Gibb was determined to keep things in working order as far as possible. There was more money in circulation and she was at a school in Cumberland when the end of the war with Germany was announced. Labour's success in the 1945 general election provided a stimulus to increased activity in the constituencies. Margaret described a general euphoria with offers of help 'pouring in' and membership numbers increasing again to peak in 1947. In 1946 the women's galas restarted and at the Durham Women's Gala in 1947, she recalled, 'you couldn't see a blade of grass in Wharton Park'. New activities in the post-war period included the extension of gala-type meetings and rallies in Cumberland at Wigton and Keswick. For a few years homecraft exhibitions, Women's Institute style, were organised on a county basis. An annual Speakers' Forum was inaugurated, with representatives from the women's groups from North Yorkshire, Cumberland, Durham and Northumberland competing for a silver shield. In 1955 the Northern Region Women's Rest Fund was established. Margaret formed a committee from three members of each area's advisory committee and sections were asked to pay 3d per member per year. Every year since, eight women have been sent for a fortnight's holiday, either at the Mary Macarthur house in Stansted, Essex, or Cober Hill Guest House near Scarborough.

By the time Margaret Gibb retired in 1957 the rapidly changing social and economic pattern was having its effect on the membership and attendance of political organisations of all kinds. Far more women were employed outside the home, where, in any case, the arrival of television and improved comfort generally made the alternative of a political meeting less attractive. But the first generation of Labour women in the Northern region, particularly in urban and industrial centres, had been introduced to the possibility of influence and participation in the affairs of their local community, with many becoming politically literate and with skills which equipped them to act as local councillors and magistrates. Many of these women acknowledge the impact on their lives of Margaret Gibb, who gave them inspiration and confidence to take their first steps in public life. The quality of her methods, her training and organisation of the Women's Sections, her wide range of contacts at national level in the Labour Party and her persuasive personality have been important in four counties.

Margaret Gibb's services in this respect were acknowledged at a dinner and presentation given for her by the Northern group of Labour MPs and in 1965 she was awarded the OBE. While her major work was with the women's organisations, Margaret participated in a wide range of Labour Party activity. The ILP was central until the mid-1920s. In the late 1930s she joined the Fabian Society, becoming vice-chairman of the Tyneside branch and a life member. From 1951 to 1984 she was an active member of the Morpeth Labour Party. In retirement she threw her energies into reviving the ailing Berwick constituency, a part of the region which was not a Labour Party stronghold, and which had always returned a Liberal or Conservative MP. She was election agent in the constituency in 1959 and 1964, and played a very full part in helping to organise the general elections there of 1966, 1970 and 1974. In 1968 she became honorary life president of Berwick Constituency Labour Party. She retained an optimistic interest in the details and difficulties of the Labour movement until her death and never turned down an invitation to a meeting or event in spite of the difficulties of travel from Cambo. In 1977 she was a guest speaker at the Durham Labour Women's Advisory Council Annual Gala and in 1983 was the only founder member present at its sixtieth anniversary, for which she wrote a recollection of the first Gala.

Margaret Gibb's talents as a highly gifted teacher were noted in her pupil–teacher reports between 1908 and 1910. Her training, experience and natural gifts in this respect were invaluable in her Labour Party work. She was a tall woman, always well-groomed and distinguished-looking; to some, she was formidable in appearance and manner. She used her deep, resonant voice with professional skill sometimes emphasising its soft Northumberland quality, at others revealing the crisp, precise traits of the skilled manager. She was a remarkable raconteur with an instinct for the dramatic and a sense of humour that was often impish. Her interests were wide-ranging, but above all she retained a genuine unaffected curiosity and interest in people. Everyone she met felt her friendship and knew that she was as interested in them personally as in their political usefulness. She maintained contact with hundreds of people from all the districts to which her work took her and remembered with remarkable clarity many others who had crossed her path. Throughout her working life she was sensitive to the problems faced by women, their economic difficulties, personal qualities (and limitations) and domestic situations; and to almost the end of her very long life she was absorbed in political issues and affairs. Her conversation remained lively and stimulating in her very old age and she died in Hexham General Hospital on 27 January 1984 after a short illness. Her funeral took place at West End Road Crematorium, Newcastle, on 6 February.

Writings: (1) MS: autobiographical notes, *DLB* Coll. (2) Other: 'The Story of Twenty-five Years' Work', in *Silver Jubilee 1920–1945: Durham County Labour Women's Advisory Council* (1945) [5 pp.]; 'Dr Marion – an inspiration to so many of us', *Labour Woman*, Sep 1965, 148 and 160; 'The Labour Party in the North East', *North East Labour History*, no. 8 (1974) 9–15; 'Memories from the Past. No. 1: the first Durham Labour Women's Gala', ibid., no. 17 (1983) 40–1; 'Diamond Jubilee Gala – 1983: a memory' [typescript of 3 pp.].

Tape recordings: 1970 between N. McCord, M. Callcott and M. Gibb, copy with N. McCord and M. Callcott; 1979 between J. Saville and M. Gibb, copy in Brynmor Jones Library, Hull University, A/T 543; 1982 between M. Callcott and M. Gibb, copy with M. Callcott, and 1983 between Liz Kemp, M. Callcott and M. Gibb, copy with E. Kemp and M. Callcott.

Sources: (1) MS: Durham Labour Women's Advisory Council, minute books 1923–58, and Northumberland Labour Women's Advisory Council minute books 1924–8 and 1928–35, North Regional LP Headquarters, Gateshead; letters from Tom Gibb to Margaret Gibb, Dec 1926–Feb 1927, with her personal and political papers in the Northumberland CRO, Wideopen. (2) Other: Durham County Education Committee, *Pupil Teachers' Report Book* (1930); 'Margaret Gibb retires', *Labour Woman*, Sep 1957, 137; M. Callcott, 'Parliamentary

Elections in County Durham between the Wars: the making of a Labour stronghold', *North East Labour History*, no. 8 (1974) 15–19; idem, 'The Organisation of Political Support for Labour in the North of England: the work of Margaret Gibb 1929–1957', ibid., no. 11 (1977) 47–58; 'MPs to join Birthday Party', *Newcastle J.*, 31 July 1982; 'Celebrations for Party Woman', *Morpeth Gaz.*, 6 Aug 1982; 'Many celebrated 90th Birthday at Cambo', *Morpeth Herald*, 6 Aug 1982; M. Callcott, 'Labour Women in North East England', *North East Labour History*, no. 17 (1983) 35–99. Personal information: Dr Martin Bulmer, LSE; Dr Pauline Dower, Cambo, Northumberland; Ald. Margaret Murray, Newcastle; Mrs Joan Robinson, Darlington, Co. Durham; Cllr Ethel Sprintall, Hartlepool, Cleveland; Mrs Ivy Spry, Seaham, Co. Durham. OBIT. *Morpeth Herald*, 9 Feb 1984.

MAUREEN CALLCOTT

Editorial Note: Our association with Mrs Gibb arose from a letter she sent in 1972 to Dame Margaret Cole, whose review of *DLB 1* she had read in the August issue of *Socialist Commentary*. In her letter she suggested further names for inclusion, and from that time until shortly before her death she was regularly in touch with us, sending details of local labour personalities eligible for inclusion. She also commented most helpfully on draft entries of people she had known personally. Her enthusiasm for the *DLB* was stimulating and much appreciated.

JS
JMB

GUEST, Leslie Haden (1st Baron Haden-Guest of Saling) (1877–1960)
LABOUR MP

Haden Guest was born at Oldham, Lancashire, on 10 March 1877, the son of Alexander Haden Guest, a surgeon and physician of Manchester, a radical in politics at whose home visitors included Annie Besant, Herbert Burrows, H. M. Hyndman and J. M. Robertson. The young Haden Guest was also influenced by his own experience of poverty and deprivation in the cotton towns, and he became radicalised at an early age. He was educated at William Hulme's Grammar School and at Owens College, where he studied medicine.On the death of his father he moved to London to complete his medical training at the London Hospital. When he qualified in 1900 he went to South Africa, served in the war against the Boers, and then continued in practice there from 1902 to 1905.

When he returned to London he began work as a children's doctor in Southwark, just south of the Thames, and he developed what was really the beginning of the school clinic movement in London. He established, for instance, the first dental clinic for schoolchildren. His work at the premises in Pocock Street (between Blackfriars Road and Southwark Bridge Road) attracted much attention and there was a constant stream of visitors. He wrote a good deal on problems of child health, including a 1911 Fabian pamphlet, *The Case for School Clinics*, which was revised and reprinted in 1922. Haden Guest in these years before the First World War was a young man in a hurry: 'a fiery young Welsh doctor' as he has been described [Thompson (1967) 219]. He was elected to the EC of the Fabian Society in 1907 at the same time as Aylmer Maude. They were part of the reform movement inside the Fabian Society that was associated with H. G. Wells. Haden Guest was much influenced by Wells's writings; he had reviewed *Anticipations* enthusiastically in the March 1902 issue of *Fabian News*, and in general he supported Wells's abortive efforts against the founders of the Fabian Society [Cole (1961) 117 ff.]. Haden Guest was also very active in the City branch of the ILP, which was established in 1908. It specialised in industrial and financial problems and ran midday meetings for businessmen. Its members included R. C. K. Ensor, Clifford Allen, Emil Davies and H. H. Schloesser, all of whom were also Fabians.

When the war came Haden Guest was engaged in organising hospitals and Red Cross work. He was a prime mover in the foundation in 1914 of the Anglo-French Hospitals Committee of the British Red Cross Society and the Order of St John (and for many years was a member of its medical group). His Army rank was Captain and he was awarded the Military Cross in 1916 for bringing in wounded under fire at Passchendaele Ridge. At the conclusion of hostilities he returned to his medical and political work in London. In 1919 he was elected to the LCC as Labour member for Woolwich East, and served until 1922; and in December 1923 he was returned to Parliament for North Southwark. In April 1920 he went with the British Labour Delegation to Russia, serving, with C. R. Buxton, as joint secretary, and probably drafting most of the official *Report* [see **Special Note** attached to the Ben Turner entry]. Haden Guest, like all the members of the Delegation, was unequivocally against British military intervention and the economic blockade, but he was highly critical of many aspects of the Communist regime, and he especially emphasized the failure of the Bolsheviks to win over the peasantry. He summarised his views on Russia and the countries of Eastern Europe in a book published in 1923, *The Struggle for Power in Europe 1917–21*.

Haden Guest was parliamentary private secretary to John Wheatley during the months of the first Labour Government, and it was during this period that he took the initiative in forming the Labour Commonwealth Group of MPs: the first organised effort within the House of Commons to develop a coherent policy for the Empire. Haden Guest at this time was imperialist in his attitudes towards the Empire, and he believed that a more positive approach to Empire development would help to improve Britain's economic problems. He publicised the work of the Imperial Economic Committee, and during the winter of 1925–6 entered upon negotiations with some leading Tories who were active in the Empire Industries Association. Nothing came of the talks, W. A. S. Hewins being among those who opposed any contact with Labour people [Gupta (1975) 64–9]. Haden Guest's general ideas at this time were moving steadily to the right and he was becoming increasingly disillusioned with the Socialists in the labour movement. In 1927 he resigned his parliamentary seat and membership of the Labour Party. The immediate reason was over the Labour Party's opposition towards the China policy of the Conservative Government, which included a firm stand on the issue of Shanghai as an international port controlled by Western powers, including Britain. The Parliamentary Labour Party had called for the withdrawal of British troops, a move which Haden Guest wrote would be 'a long step in the direction of the triumph of Bolshevism in China and the spread of "world revolution" to 400 million people'. These words are taken from a small book Haden Guest published in 1929 – *Is Labour leaving Socialism?* [p. 25] – in which he set down the arguments that accounted for his rejection of his former Socialism. The book was shot through with anti-Communism, and his main themes were the incompetence of the moderate leaders of the labour movement, and the constant threat coming from the Left. He particularly attacked the ILP, and used the involvement of the ILP leadership in the League Against Imperialism as an example of the success of Moscow-inspired initiatives in the contemporary world. We must, he said in the final paragraph of the book, drive home 'the lesson that the theories of Socialism are outworn, that the attempt to practise Socialism has proved a failure, and that men must return to the roads of realism and experience in their search for an improvement of their social and economic conditions' [p. 132].

After resigning his seat at Westminster he stood as an Independent Constitutionalist in the by-election which followed, and was supported by the local Conservative Association. He lost to the Liberal candidate, E. A. Strauss, who beat George Isaacs, the Labour candidate, by a thousand votes. In June 1928 Haden Guest wrote to Stanley Baldwin asking to join the Conservative Party and he was warmly welcomed.

He fought North Salford as a Conservative in 1929 and was defeated, but by 1931 he had returned to the Labour Party. He was defeated decisively at Wycombe in the general election of that year and again in 1935, when he opposed his namesake (but no relation) the Hon. Ivor Guest at Brecon. He was returned in the Labour interest at a by-election at Islington North in 1937, a seat he retained until 1950.

His political ideas were radicalised during the 1930s. Economic depression and mass unemployment at home, with international Fascism becoming steadily more menacing as the decade advanced, were powerful influences upon many; and Haden Guest had family reasons in addition. David Guest, one of his two sons by his second marriage, became a Communist at Cambridge, and fought in the International Brigade in Spain. He was killed on the Ebro in July 1938. David's sister, Angela, was in an ambulance unit, and his mother, Carmel, visited Spain during the Civil War and was immensely active in Spanish Medical Aid in Britain [Alexander (1982) 229].

Haden Guest's political attitudes in this decade were illustrated in an interesting way by his public statements on the Moscow trial of 1936. Like so many of his contemporaries who were not Communists, Haden Guest nevertheless accepted fully and completely the Russian version of the guilt of the accused: at least, that was true of the first of the series of trials in 1936–7 of leading Bolsheviks. He was an eye-witness to the trial of Zinoviev and Kamenev and wrote a long account for the *Spectator* which was published on 4 September 1936. The last paragraph of his letter summed up his argument:

The trial shows very clearly the great danger to the Soviet Union of the concentration of power in a very few hands. This danger has however been foreseen by the Communist leaders for some years past, and they have endeavoured to divide and decentralise that power as much as possible. The new constitution which will come into operation at the end of this year will establish the foundations of the Soviet Union more firmly because it will widen the basis of that power in an essentially democratic way [p. 381].

Haden Guest returned to the House of Commons in 1937. He was connected with the Leverhulme Foundation for many years and had been appointed a member of the Commission established by the Leverhulme Research Fellowship Committee to investigate conditions in West Africa shortly before the outbreak of war in September 1939 (he was secretary of the Fellowship Committee from 1933 to 1951). He was also appointed a member of the parliamentary committee on the evacuation of the civil population. During the war years he played an active and critical part on the back benches. On 25 June 1942 a motion of no confidence in the central direction of the war was placed on the Order Paper of the House of Commons. The most important Conservative signatures were those of Sir John Wardlaw-Milne, Admiral of the Fleet Sir Roger Keyes and Leslie Hore-Belisha. The debate commenced on 1 July and ended the following day. Aneurin Bevan spoke late in the debate and delivered one of the major speeches of his career. Churchill wound up the debate and won an overwhelming victory by 475 to 25. Bevan and seven other Labour MPs–F. J. Bellenger, F. G. Bowles, L. Haden Guest, B. V. Kirby, S. S. Silverman, R. R. Stokes and Neil Maclean – voted for the censure motion. They were all 'carpeted' by Attlee, not because they had voted against the Coalition Government, of which Attlee was Deputy Prime Minister, but because they had defied his party line, already agreed at a meeting of the PLP [Foot (1962) 371–9; Harris (1982) 198–9].

Haden Guest accepted a peerage in 1950 and in 1951 became a Labour Whip. His considerable literary output covered the many areas of his interests: medical and scientific matters, international relations, child life and health, and education. He married three times: first in 1898 to Edith Low, of London, by whom there were two sons. The marriage was dissolved by divorce in 1909, and in 1910 he married Muriel Carmel, daughter of Colonel Albert Goldsmid MVO. There were two sons and a daughter. After his second wife's death he married, in 1944, Dr Edith Macqueen, of Braintree, Essex. He died on 20 August 1960 and his funeral took place at Islington Crematorium on 25 August. He left an estate valued at £1249.

Writings: (with others) *The Charter of the Child* (1910) 32 pp.; 'The Administration of the Law relating to the Medical Inspection and Treatment of School Children', *Trans of the Medico-Legal Society 8* (1910–11) 58–73; *The Case for School Clinics* (Fabian Tract no. 154: 1911; rev. and repr. 1922) 15 pp.; *Theosophy and Social Reconstruction*, with a Foreword by Annie Besant (Riddle of Life Series, no. 3: 1912); *Votes for Women and the Public Health* (Women's Freedom League, [1912]) 8 pp.; *The Nation of the Future* (1916); (ed.) *The New Education: a critical presentation of the education scheme of the London Education Authority October 1920* (1920); (ed.) *British Labour Delegation to Russia 1920: Report* (1920); *The Struggle for Power in Europe 1917–1921* (1921); *The Care and Nursing of Babies and Children* (1922); (with Sir H. Johnston), *The Outline of the World Today*, 3 vols (1923–4); 'Turkey as it is', *Spec. 134* (13 June 1925) 962–3; 'Labour's Imperial Policy', *Outlook 57* (5 June 1926), vi–vii; 'Empire and Fruit', ibid. (3 July 1926) 30–1; 'Turkish Babies and Turkish Petroleum', ibid. (10 July 1926) 43–4; 'An Empire Cabinet', ibid. (7 Aug 1926) 146–7; 'Migration and Prosperity', ibid. (4 Sep 1926) 223–4; *The Labour Party and the Empire* [1926]; *The New Russia* (1926); *Canada as a Career* (1927); *Where is Labour going?: a political pamphlet* (1927); 'Will Canada stay in the Empire? I', *Outlook 61* (3 Mar 1928) 282–3, and II (7 Apr 1928) 455–6; *The New British Empire* (1929); *Is Labour leaving Socialism?* (1929); 'The Egyptian Situation', *Engl. Rev. 50* (Mar 1930) 298–304; 'The Moscow Trial' [letter], *Spec. 157* (4 Sep 1936) 381; 'Medicine in the Soviet Union', ibid. (2 Oct 1936) 539–40; 'Religion in the USSR', ibid. (16 Oct 1936) 627–8; 'Standards of Life in Russia', ibid. (13 Nov 1936) 847–8; (ed. with an Introduction) *The Writings and Diary of Chester Jones* (1936); (ed.) *The Next Steps in Educational Progress* [report of the proceedings at a conference held in 1914] (1936); *If Air War comes: a guide to air raid precautions and anti-gas treatment* (1937); 'The A. R. P. Services', *New Statesman and Nation 14* (27 Nov 1937) 900–1; 'The Crimea Conference IV', *Lab. Mon. 27* (Apr 1945) 108–9.

Sources: 'Red Cross War Notes', *The Red Cross*, 15 Nov and 15 Dec 1914, Jan and Apr 1915; *Reports of the Joint War Committee and the Joint War Finance Committee of the British Red Cross Society and the Order of St John, 1914–1919*, pt XVI: *France and Belgium* (HMSO, 1921) 350–1; *Labour Who's Who* (1924); *Medical Directory* (1936); *David Guest: a scientist fights for freedom 1911–1938*, ed. C. Haden Guest (1939); *Medical Register* (1939); M. Bondfield, *A Life's Work* (1948); G. D. H. Cole, *A History of the Labour Party from 1914* (1948); *WWW* (1951–60); M. M. P. McCarran, *Fabianism in the Political Life of Britain 1919–1931* (Washington, DC, 1952; 2nd ed. Chicago, 1954); Lord Woolton, *Memoirs of the Rt Hon. the Earl of Woolton* (1959); S. R. Graubard, *British Labour and the Russian Revolution 1917–1924* (Cambridge, Mass., 1956); R. W. Lyman, *The First Labour Government 1924* (1957); G. D. H. Cole, *The Story of Fabian Socialism* (1961); M. Foot, *Aneurin Bevan*, vol. 1: 1897–1945 (1962); A. M. McBriar, *Fabian Socialism and English Politics 1884–1918* (1962); A. Marwick, *Clifford Allen: the open conspirator* (1964); P. Thompson, *Socialists, Liberals and Labour: the struggle for London 1885–1914* (1967); P. S. Gupta, *Imperialism and the British Labour Movement* (1975); Bill Alexander, *British Volunteers for Liberty: Spain 1936–1939* (1982); K. Harris, *Attlee* (1982). Biographical information: Mrs M. Poulter, archivist, the British Red Cross Society, Wonersh, Guildford, Surrey; Miss J. E. Bennett, Leverhulme Trust, London. OBIT. *Times*, 22 Aug 1960; *LP Report* (1960).

JOHN SAVILLE

See also: †Reginald Clifford ALLEN; †Charles Roden BUXTON; Richard Rapier STOKES; Ben TURNER for the British Labour Delegation to Russia, 1920 **(Special Note)**; †John WHEAT-LEY.

HANCOCK, Thomas (1832–1903)
CHRISTIAN SOCIALIST

Thomas Hancock, the third son of Charles and Rebecca Hancock (née Hunt), was born in London on 19 June 1832. His father was an animal-painter at the time of Thomas's birth, but by 1848 had opened a gutta-percha works. One of Charles Hancock's brothers, Thomas, is regarded as the father of the india-rubber industry, while another, Walter, was an inventor and promoter of steam locomotives for use on roads. The young Thomas Hancock attended four schools, the last two being Merchant Taylors' and Clarendon House. He left the latter in 1847 and, after undertaking several months of study at a London School of Design, became an apprentice wood-carver at his father's factory. He did not complete the apprenticeship.

Hancock's late adolescence was characterised by two preoccupations. One was art, especially drawing. The greatest influence in his life at this time was his cousin, John Hancock, a sculptor of some note whose works included the statue *Il Penseroso*, commissioned for the Egyptian Hall at the Mansion House. Undoubtedly Thomas's main ambition was to follow in his cousin's artistic footsteps. The second predominant influence was secularism; he became an avid reader of the *Reasoner* and *Cooper's Journal*, and in 1850 pronounced Shelley's *Queen Mab* his favourite book.

Both of these concerns were superseded in 1852, when Hancock first encountered Frederick Denison Maurice, the theologian of the Anglican Christian Socialist Movement, founded in 1848. Maurice at this time drew huge congregations to weekly Sunday afternoon services in the chapel of Lincoln's Inn. The circumstances that first prompted Hancock to attend these services are not clear, but he soon became a regular worshipper at them. Maurice had an enormous impact upon Hancock, whose regard for Maurice became almost adulatory.

During 1856 Hancock became convinced that he was called to the priesthood, but his parents, who were Anglicans but not of a religious disposition, warned him to expect no financial assistance from them. The following year his father terminated his employment at the gutta-percha works; relations between Hancock and his parents, whom he despised as having been 'bitten with the disease of our Century, the Commercial epidemic' [MS 'Diaries and Letters'], had been cold for some time.

Unemployed, and receiving no income from his parents, Hancock eked out a living by writing stories for literary magazines, usually published anonymously. Most of his time, however, he spent in the British Museum, studying Latin, Greek, patristics and English religious history. This last interest prompted him to enter in March 1858 a prize-essay contest on the decline of Quakerism. He was awarded second place, and the following year his composition was published as *The Peculium*.

Contrary to the expectations of the anonymous Quaker who had sponsored the competition, Hancock argued that it was not only inevitable but desirable that Quakerism should decline. In doing so he drew heavily on the ideas of Maurice, who distinguished between the Church and sects and claimed that all human organisations were bound eventually to decay. The only invincibly endurable body was that which could be identified as *the* Catholic and Apostolic Church, and Hancock argued that the Society of Friends could not thus be identified even within the terms of its own confession.

Quakerism had thrived in the seventeenth century, Hancock asserted, because God had raised it up to testify to a 'great and godly principle' which Christians in England were at that time neglecting: namely, the doctrine of the Light of Christ within all people. In making this claim Hancock was applying for the first time a conviction which he took originally from Maurice, but which he was to develop in his own writings and make a cornerstone of his Christian Socialist theology. This was the idea that whenever the Church was failing in its responsibilities God would cause some other group of people to perform his work. It was in this light that Hancock acclaimed the Socialist movements of the 1880s.

On the basis of the scholarship displayed in *The Peculium*, together with Maurice's recommendation, Samuel Wilberforce, the Bishop of Oxford, agreed in 1861 to ordain Hancock to the Anglican ministry. Wilberforce's decision to ordain someone who had studied neither at a university nor a training college was extraordinary and indicates that he must have been highly impressed by Hancock.

From 1861 to 1875 Hancock served four curacies, at St Leonard's, near Wendover, Buckinghamshire (1861–5); St Mary's, Leicester (1865–6); Holy Trinity, Westminster (1866–7); and St Stephen's, Lewisham (1867–75). In January 1865 he married Kate Farmer, a friend's sister, to whom he had been engaged since 1857. After 1875 he again became unemployed, and was forced once more to resort to literary work. During this period, which lasted until 1883, he was offered only one post in England, the living of Hickleton in Yorkshire. This he declined, because the practice of patronage under which the offer was made by Charles Wood, later Lord Halifax, was in Hancock's eyes a major fault of the Victorian Church, and one against which he was to fight for much of his life.

By the time he left Lewisham in 1875, Hancock had become profoundly depressed with the practices of the Victorian Church, although he remained devoted to an ideal of the national Church as the predominant vehicle for social change in accordance with God's will. Like Maurice, Hancock believed that the primary responsibility of the Church was to realise and make manifest the Kingdom of Christ on earth, a mission which necessitated the eradication of commercialism, of the ideal of competition, of selfishness. The trouble for Hancock was that in an industrial society which made virtues of these vices, the Church of England was failing ignominiously to challenge the existing social order. Early in his ministry, Hancock made it his mission to bring the Church into conformity with his ideals.

The elucidation of these ideas can be found in *Christ and the People*, a volume of twenty-eight sermons preached by Hancock at Lewisham. In the theology there expounded, Hancock identified the Church as 'the organized Unity of those who confess the Fatherhood of God' [(1875) 304]; since God was the Father of all, in a relationship embodied for Hancock as for Maurice in the doctrine of the Incarnation, the Church was ideally coextensive with the whole of humanity. Baptism, available to all, was the recognition of this common fatherhood, and from the rights of all men and women to this 'baptismal citizenship' [ibid., 38] Hancock argued, originally if obscurely, a case for universal suffrage. It was because the Church should embrace the whole of humanity that Hancock was so hostile to Protestant sects, which seemed to him to use narrow forms of doctrine or notions of the elect as measures of exclusiveness. The Salvation Army, for example, was 'a separatist, not a common army' [*The Pulpit and the Press* (1904) 170], and Hancock's absolute rejection of sects was implicit in his persistent refusal to identify himself as a Christian rather than a Churchman; 'I do not remember that I have ever dared to use the vague word "Christianity" in a good sense', he once reflected [*Church Reformer*, Dec 1889].

The proper response to God for any individual, Hancock maintained, was to practise self-sacrifice in one's dealings with other people. This was by no means an original conviction, but Hancock was distinctive in his extension of this principle to the Church itself. He was especially censorious of any actions in which the Church appeared to set itself against the rest of society. One such case which drew his anger was the School Board elections after the passage in 1870 of the Forster Education Act, which enabled each board to determine whether religious instruction should be taught in its school. Hancock attacked the consequent attempts by Christians to win control of the boards as a 'godless and infidel' act

[*Christ and the People*, 63] which appeared to set God against the people. Hancock was a firm opponent of any Church involvement in education, and an undisguised supporter of Joseph Chamberlain's National Education League.

Hancock's more fundamental criticism of the Church of his day, however, was that it had allied itself with the middle classes of Victorian England in worshipping 'the two idols of property and respectability' [ibid., 313]. Respectability was sinful, Hancock contended, because its essence was an evaluation of oneself above the rest of humanity; it set class above common fellowship. As for private property, in a theological sense it did not exist, for the world belonged to God; it was not ownership but stewardship that men and women really exercised. This was the meaning with which Hancock invested Proudhon's dictum 'property is theft' when he quoted it with enthusiasm from his pulpit. Because property was God's, its earthly 'owners' sinned against Him when they used it for their own ends, rather than for the common good.

The solution continually urged by Hancock upon the Church of England, in order to restore it to its proper mission, was the abolition of patronage. He judged that the Church would remain a tool of capital so long as its livings and episcopal sees were distributed by wealthy individuals or by governments and he advocated a return to the kind of democracy that he perceived to have characterised the primitive Church. He envisaged a system in which Church appointments would be contested at elections, in which all people in the relevant area, not only churchgoers or even only baptised Anglicans, would have the right to vote.

Hancock's criticisms were thus very largely directed at the Church from within, and this certainly limited the scope of both his activities and his appeal when he identified himself as a Socialist in the 1880s. His apparent preoccupation with the Church, however, was itself a reflection of his concern for the whole of society; Hancock simply ascribed to the Church a greater responsibility for effecting social change than most Socialists or most Christians could find reasonable.

Hancock found a new vehicle for the expression of his ideas when he returned to England late in 1880 after spending a year in Germany, where he had held a temporary chaplaincy, under the auspices of the Society for the Propagation of the Gospel, in Axenstein; he had held similar appointments in Germany during 1875 and 1876. This vehicle was the Guild of St Matthew which, under the leadership of Stewart Headlam, had been transformed from a parish group in Bethnal Green to an organisation of Anglican Christian Socialists, determined to 'justify God to the people' by promoting the social criticism which they believed to be the true responsibility of the Church.

Hancock lectured for the Guild in its early years, on topics such as 'The Church and Democracy', 'Church and State' and 'Church Property', and probably became a member in 1881. Two years later he at last regained employment in the Church of England, when Henry Shuttleworth, also a prominent GSM member, was appointed rector of St Nicholas Cole Abbey, in the City of London. Immediately Shuttleworth offered Hancock a 'lectureship' which was attached to the living; Hancock gratefully accepted, and held the position until his death.

Hancock was a skilled theologian, and brought to the GSM a comprehensive structure of religious thought within which its members could better understand their convictions, and develop them further. The part that he played in the life of the Guild was, accordingly, that of theological teacher, a role something like that of Maurice in the earlier days of Christian Socialism. The impact that Hancock made in fulfilling this role was doubtless due in part to the caustic eloquence with which he expressed himself in all his polemical compositions. By virtue of his sermons in St Nicholas Cole Abbey, his lectures, and his numerous articles in Headlam's *Church Reformer*, he became, as F. Lewis Donaldson was to put it, 'the prophet of the Guild, its intellectual spiritual father-in-God' [*Church Times*, 2 Oct 1903].

The nature of the pronouncements which so inspired younger members of the Guild, like

Donaldson, can best be gauged from *The Pulpit and the Press*, Hancock's second major volume of sermons, preached during the 1880s. The Magnificat he called 'the hymn of the universal social revolution', observing that in it Our Lady 'rejoices in the vision' of a 'catastrophe of wholesale confiscation. She has not a word to say on behalf of the rights of property and class, or of a fair compensation' [*The Pulpit and the Press*, 27]. His best-known writing, however, was a sermon of this period entitled 'The Banner of Christ in the Hands of the Socialists'. In it, Hancock welcomed the occupation of London churches by the unemployed as the reclamation by 'the Son of Man Himself' of his Church, which had been carried into captivity in Babylon by 'the capitalists and landlords' [ibid., 39–40].

Although a loyal member of the Guild of St Matthew until his death, Hancock disagreed in at least two important respects with its dominant ideology, particularly as enunciated by the Guild's warden, Stewart Headlam. First, Hancock did not share the dedication displayed by Headlam and other members of the Guild to the theories of Henry George concerning the restoration of land values. Although a firm advocate of land nationalisation, he certainly did not consider land value to be the most important question facing Socialists, as Headlam did, and he rarely mentioned George in his sermons or articles. The second matter on which Hancock stood alone was in not identifying himself as a High Church Anglican. Headlam was an exuberant ritualist, once going so far as declaring himself and others like him to be 'Socialists because we are sacramentalists' [*Church Reformer*, Oct 1891], and his enthusiasm in this regard characterised the Guild as a whole. It was not shared by Hancock, who throughout his life as an Anglican refused to ally himself with either the ritualist or the evangelical wing of the Church of England, and who was a Socialist because of the implications he drew from his conception of the Fatherhood of God.

Hancock did, however, stand with Headlam on two questions which caused dissension within the Guild early in the 1890s. The first such division occurred in 1891, when Headlam issued in the name of the Guild a manifesto on education, in which he called for the abolition of Church and other voluntary schools. His view was not shared by GSM members such as Shuttleworth, who led a vigorous though unsuccessful attempt to have the relevant part of the manifesto rescinded, but it was identical with Hancock's own approach to education. Defending Headlam, Hancock restated the case he had argued many times that the Church's intrusion into education, though once necessary, was now anachronistic, and that 'fifty years hence, in every thoroughly civilized and progressive State, the clergy will possess no schools' [*The Pulpit and the Press*, 157].

The two were also in agreement, but again at odds with other Guild members, when they repudiated the early Independent Labour Party in 1893. Headlam's reasons for doing so, like those of many of his fellow Fabians, were bound up with his attachment to, and hopes of, the Liberal Party. Hancock's opposition was based on his conviction that only the Church, because of its essentially universal nature, was capable of building a Socialist society. All political parties, like all religious sects, he viewed as necessarily exclusivist; the concern of a Socialist must be for the whole of humanity, and such a comprehensiveness was irreconcilable with loyalty to a party.

Hancock spent the last few years of his life writing history; a leaflet on the Act of Uniformity, a measure of which he approved, was published in 1898, and a work entitled *The Puritans and the Tithes* was published posthumously in 1905. Hancock had an exhaustive knowledge of English Church history, particularly of the seventeenth century, and he employed it in numerous historical notes that he contributed mostly to Anglican newspapers. He was also adept in handling historical evidence to sustain polemical points and, indeed, never attempted objectively to separate his understanding of history from his own opinions and convictions. The aim of his pamphlet on the 1664 Act of Uniformity, for example, was to denounce the organisation of English religious affairs prior to the Restoration, when the allocation of livings and other practices had been tightly controlled to sustain the Protestant sectarian character of the Protectorate; and he hailed the Act as having liberated England from this 'sectarian tyranny'. He believed that Protestant sectarianism had been so firmly grounded that it could be considered 'established' itself; and with conscious irony he attacked it in the same terminology and with the same complaints used by the Dissenters of his own day in their attacks upon the Church of England. Most of his efforts as an historian went into the preparation of a substantial ecclesiastical and social history of the Commonwealth, which was unfinished when he died; the mass of notes and documents that he left was destroyed by his family, who found them illegible. This work, which occupied him periodically for most of his life, would have represented Hancock's major contribution to historical research and since no record of it survives it is impossible accurately to evaluate his abilities as an historical scholar. Eduard Bernstein, the German Social Democrat, who came to England in 1888 has an interesting comment about Hancock in *My Years of Exile* [(1921) 236]. Hancock, he wrote, 'by the labour of decades had amassed an enormous amount of material' on the English revolution of the seventeenth century, and his vast collection of manuscripts were made freely available to Bernstein: an act of generosity which quite overwhelmed the German scholar.

Hancock continued throughout his last years to attend GSM meetings, although his acute deafness from about 1895 prevented him from participating effectively. He was also increasingly troubled by neuralgia and rheumatism, both of which had plagued his health intermittently for most of his life. In September 1903 he was re-elected to the GSM Council, and a few days afterwards, on 24 September, he died suddenly at Dover. On 29 September he was buried in Harrow Cemetery, close to his home. He was survived by his wife, Kate, their son, Aidan, and four daughters. Kate subsequently put in order many of Hancock's diaries, letters and other papers, transcribing others, and eventually produced a manuscript collection of eleven volumes. Aidan, himself a Christian Socialist priest and a GSM member at the time of his father's death, joined the more militant Church Socialist League in 1906.

Thomas Hancock cut something of a solitary figure in the late Victorian Church, and among other Socialists. His singular achievement was to propound a theology, and a social criticism, which made the Church of England ultimately responsible for the entire state of English society. It was not an outlook which most Socialists could find pertinent, or Anglicans appealing, or other Christians relevant. Yet the tributes later paid by younger Christian Socialists such as Donaldson and Conrad Noel testify to the enormous impact Hancock made upon their ideas, and his real achievement may have been in providing a theology which gave Christian Socialists such as these an intellectual framework within which their own work could develop.

Writings: (1) MS: 'The Diaries and Letters of Thomas Hancock', compiled by Kate Hancock. This collection is held by the Hancock family of Bombay, New Zealand. (2) Other: *The Peculium: an endeavour to throw light on some of the causes of the decline of the Society of Friends, especially in regard to its original claim of being the peculiar people of God* (1859; repr. 1907); *Lessons learned from the Marriage of the Prince of Wales: a sermon preached in the Church of S. Leonard's, Bucks., on the Fourth Sunday in Lent, 1863* (Tring, Herts, 1863) 8 pp.; *A Bishop must have the Good Report of those who are without the Church: a sermon preached on the Sunday after the confirmation of Dr. Temple, (being the Ember-Sunday in Advent, December the 12th, 1869)* (1869) 16 pp.; *The Resurrection of Jesus Christ the Hope of Mankind: a sermon preached on Low Sunday evening, April 4th, at S. Stephen's Church, Lewisham* [1869] 13 pp.; *The Return to the Father: seven sermons on a part of the parable of the prodigal son, preached at S. Stephen's Church, Lewisham, on the Sunday mornings in Lent, and on Easter Day, 1872* (1873; repr. 1904); *Christ and the People: sermons chiefly on the obligations of the Church to the State and to humanity* (1875); *Salvation by Mammon: two sermons* [repr. from the *Church Reformer*, Dec 1890 and Jan 1891] [1891] 24 pp.; *The Act of Uniformity: a measure of liberation* (1898) 54 pp.; Contributed to *Henry Cary*

Shuttleworth: a memoir, ed. G. W. E. Russell (1903) 36–65; *The Pulpit and the Press and Other Sermons, most of which were preached at S. Nicholas Cole Abbey* (1904); *The Puritans and the Tithes* (1905). Also numerous articles in the *Church Reformer* and, many unsigned, in *Church Times, Church Work, Churchman's Family Mag., Clerical J.*, the *Echo, London Society, St James's Mag., Saturday Rev., Westminster Gaz.*; also many short stories, almost all unsigned, in *Chambers's Edinburgh J., Hedderwick's Miscellany*, the *Rose, the Shamrock and the Thistle* and *Titan*.

Sources: (1) MS: see Writings. (2) Other: A. V. Woodworth, *Christian Socialism in England* (1903); Introduction by W. E. Collins to Hancock's *The Peculium*, (1907 ed.) 9–30; E. Bernstein, *My Years of Exile* (1921); F. G. Bettany, *Stewart Headlam: a biography* (1926); D. O. Wagner, *The Church of England and Social Reform since 1854* (NY, 1930); G. C. Binyon, *The Christian Socialist Movement in England: an introduction to the study of its history* (1931); S. C. Carpenter, *Church and People 1789–1889: a history of the Church of England from William Wilberforce to 'Lux Mundi'* (1933; rev. ed. 1959); H. M. Lynd, *England in the Eighteen-Eighties: toward a social basis for freedom* (1945; repr. 1968); M. B. Reckitt, *Maurice to Temple: a century of the social movement in the Church of England* (1947); editorial in *Sobornost*, ser. 3, no. 5 (Summer 1949) 165–74; S. G. Evans, *Christian Socialism: a study outline and bibliography* (1962) 31 pp.; A. M. Allchin, *The Spirit and the Word: two studies in nineteenth century Anglican theology* (1963); S. G. Evans, *The Social Hope of the Christian Church* (1965); O. Chadwick, *The Victorian Church*, pt 2 (1966; 2nd ed. 1972); S. Mayor, *The Churches and the Labour Movement* (1967); P. d'A. Jones, *The Christian Socialist Revival 1877–1914: religion, class and social conscience in late-Victorian England* (Princeton, NJ, 1968); S. Yeo, 'Thomas Hancock, 1832–1903: "The banner of Christ in the hands of the socialists"', in *For Christ and the People: studies of four socialist priests and prophets of the Church of England between 1870 and 1930*, ed. M. B. Reckitt (1968) 1–60; G. K. Clark, *Churchmen and the Condition of England, 1832–1885: a study in the development of social ideas and practice from the old regime to the modern state* (1973); T. Peacock, 'The Call of the Kingdom: Thomas Hancock and Anglican Christian Socialism' (dissertation for Queensland BA, 1979). OBIT. *Church Times*, 2 Oct 1903; *Commonwealth*, Nov 1903.

TREVOR PEACOCK

See also: †Stewart Duckworth HEADLAM; William Edmund MOLL for Church Socialist League **(Special Note)**; †Conrad le Despenser Roden NOEL; and below: The Guild of St Matthew.

The Guild of St Matthew

The Guild of St Matthew began humbly in 1877, after an enthusiastic member of the parish of St Matthew, Bethnal Green, a girl named Carrie Hatch, suggested to Stewart Headlam, curate of the parish, that he institute a communicants' guild to encourage a better attendance at Holy Communion. The charter which Headlam gave to the Guild had somewhat larger implications, though its full potential was not immediately exploited:

(i) To get rid, by every possible means, of the existing prejudices, especially on the part of Secularists, against the Church, her sacraments and doctrines.

(ii) To promote frequent and reverent worship in the Holy Communion and a better observance of the teaching of the Church of England, as set forth in the Book of Common Prayer.

(iii) To promote the study of social and political questions in the light of the Incarnation.

The Guild was inaugurated at a meeting and service on St Peter's Day, 1877; the objects that it adopted were to stand almost unchanged throughout its history.

Headlam was ejected from his Bethnal Green curacy the following year. The Guild of St Matthew thereupon shed the local, parochial outlook it had assumed at first, and resolved to transform itself into a pressure group for the promotion of Christian Socialism. To mark the change of direction, the Guild's constitution was amended in one small but important respect: to the first objective was added the intention 'to justify God to the people'. The phrase was Charles Kingsley's, and by adopting it the Guild laid claim to the succession of the movement of 1848. Apart from this extension the original constitution was maintained, as was the patronage of St Matthew, and the early stress on the importance of the Church's sacraments remained a feature of the Guild throughout its life.

It was with the first of its objects, meeting the challenge of secularism, that the revamped Guild was at first occupied. Its aim here was not to condemn the secularist movement, but to demonstrate, in debate with secularists, the emancipating and liberating nature of the Church, or at least of the GSM's concept of what the Church should be. This approach was in conspicuous contrast to the furious denunciations usually levelled against the secularist movement by Christian groups, and in practice the Guild often found itself defending secularists and siding with them against the assaults of such organisations as the Christian Evidence Society. 'How much nearer to the Kingdom of Heaven are these men in the Hall of Science than the followers of Moody and Sankey!', Headlam considered [Bettany (1926) 50], and he insisted in his harangue to the Leicester Church Congress of 1880 that 'it is because the Christian Church has not got itself recognised as a society for the promotion of righteousness in this world that the Secular Society is so strong' [Binyon (1931) 120].

Apart from Headlam, the clerical nucleus of the Guild in its early years included his close friend George Sarson, and Sarson's brother-in-law John Elliotson Symes, who subsequently became an academic economist at University College, Nottingham. They were soon joined by Henry Shuttleworth and Thomas Hancock. Shuttleworth, a friend of Annie Besant, was president of the anti-Sabbatarian National Sunday League, which campaigned for the opening of museums, art galleries and libraries on Sundays. In 1890 he was appointed to the chair in Pastoral and Liturgical Theology at King's College, London. Another early clerical member, though not so prominent in the affairs of the Guild as these others, was W. E. Moll, who in the early years of the twentieth century was a leader of the labour movement on Tyneside, and a member of the Independent Labour Party's NAC.

The Guild of St Matthew secured a potent vehicle for the dissemination of its propaganda in 1883, when Headlam purchased the monthly *Church Reformer* from another Guild member, R. H. Hadden. Although the paper was not officially the organ of the Guild, the GSM's affairs and concerns dominated its pages. Its subtitle was 'An organ of Christian Socialism and Church reform', its motto the last four lines of Blake's 'Jerusalem'. Headlam, besides being editor, was the paper's chief contributor, followed by Hancock, whose sermons were regularly printed. Other writers included Selwyn Image, Sidney Webb and Ramsay MacDonald. The *Church Reformer* was highly regarded in Socialist circles, not only among Christian Socialists. Bernard Shaw thought it 'one of the best of the Socialist journals of that day' [Bettany (1926) 104]. Shaw was a frequent attender at GSM meetings, though not a member; his humorous recollections of an address on Socialism by Bishop E. S. Talbot of Rochester, sponsored by the Guild in 1888, are to be found among his published correspondence [*Collected Letters 1874–1897* (1965) 199–201].

The administrative work of the GSM fell upon its executive secretary, Frederick

Verinder, who also sub-edited the *Church Reformer*. A layman, Verinder was one of the original members of the organisation when it was formed as a communicants' Guild. He was an extremely talented bureaucrat and publicist, but had little intellectual originality; more than any other member of the Guild, he was a disciple of Headlam. Like the warden, he kept his position throughout the Guild's history.

Until 1883, arguments with secularists in lectures, debates and printed propaganda constituted the main work of the Guild. In that year, however, social and economic reform replaced secularism as the Guild's primary concern, so noticeably that an evangelical journal called the *Rock* protested, with some exaggeration no doubt, that, 'If insurrection should break out in England, . . . it will be due, and largely indeed, to the clerical and other firebrands, Mr. Shuttleworth and his friends, who are seeking to propagate what they call Christian Socialism' [Reckitt (1974) 122].

The Guild's social and economic aspirations were embodied in its Socialist programme which was adopted at its annual meeting in September 1884, and again at a public demonstration in Trafalgar Square the next month:

That whereas the present contrast between the condition of the great body of the workers who produce much and consume little, and of those classes who produce little and consume much is contrary to the Christian doctrines of Brotherhood and Justice: This Meeting urges on all Churchmen the duty of supporting such measures as will tend –

(a) To restore to the people the value which they give to the land;
(b) To bring about a better distribution of the wealth created by labour;
(c) To give the whole body of the people a voice in their own government; and
(d) To abolish false standards of worth and dignity.

The year 1884 was an eventful one for British Socialists. The Democratic Federation became the Social Democratic Federation and the Fabian Society was formed. In the same year Hancock preached a sermon on 'The Social Democratic Pentecost', in which he expressed the solidarity with which the GSM approached secular Socialist bodies:

That which is anti-social, separatist, or sectarian . . . is fundamentally anti-spiritual. Socialism, however materialist or 'sensual' its temporary manifestations may be, 'is born of the Spirit'. . . . The apostles of Jesus were the first internationalist socialists (Hancock (1904) 92–3].

The issue pursued most vigorously by the GSM was the land question, as developed by the American Henry George in *Progress and Poverty*, the British edition of which appeared in 1880. Many of its members were involved in the land restoration movement that developed rapidly, though with limited influence, among British Socialists after George's Irish tour of 1882. Headlam became a close friend of the 'man sent from God whose name was Henry George' [Lynd (1945) 142], and he was a leading member of the Land Reform Union from its inception in 1883; other members of the Union, which subsequently became the English Land Restoration League, included Sarson, Shuttleworth, Symes, Shaw, Webb, Tom Mann and Sydney Olivier.

Headlam, like George, saw land as the issue upon which all aspirations for social justice must be founded, and the Guild was identified with the land issue in the eyes of many contemporaries. However, in common with many other British Socialists, Headlam took from George a conviction of the importance and urgency of the land issue while implicitly rejecting or ignoring the accompanying strictures of his theories. In the first place, Headlam did not accept that taxation should be restricted to rents. He differed in this respect from some other members of the Guild, such as Sarson and Symes, who were both doctrinaire

Single Taxers, and in 1888 Headlam launched a furious assault on Symes's *Political Economy*, which, with its opposition to the taxation of capital, was virtually a Georgeite textbook. So hostile was Headlam's attack that Symes resigned from the GSM Council. Further, Headlam advocated, as did Hancock, the nationalisation of land, a measure explicitly rejected by George. Thus, while the Guild played a major role in publicising George's theories in Britain, its members were by no means unanimous in their response to them.

While the land question and the means for resolving it whether by taxation or by nationalisation, consistently dominated the GSM's political prescriptions for English society, a broader indication of more immediate reforms for which Guild members hoped was provided by a document issued by Headlam during the 1885 general election campaign. In it he advised that candidates be urged to support the following proposals:

1. Free education
2. The rating of unoccupied land in towns
3. An increase in the land tax
4. The conferring on municipalities of the power to rate the dwellings of the poor
5. An eight-hours bill
6. A bill shortening the hours in shops
7. Increased power for municipalities to undertake industrial work for the purpose of relieving distress   [Jones (1968) 129].

The membership of the Guild was never high, and in spite of a steady growth throughout the 1880s it remained below 200. Approximately one third of the members were Anglican clerics. However, its numbers were at least comparable with those of other Socialist groups. The Social Democratic Federation, for instance, had fewer than 700 members in 1885, and the Socialist League fewer than 150; the Fabians numbered below 700 as late as 1903. It is true of the GSM as of these other bodies that it attracted attention and publicity far outweighing its numerical membership, mainly because of the vigour of its leading members.

The GSM certainly displayed an enthusiasm to compensate for its size. In 1884 it distributed a list of twenty-four lecturers, all of whom were available to speak anywhere on a total of 130 subjects. Members, especially Headlam, made extensive speaking tours thoughout Britain, carrying the GSM gospel as far afield as Glasgow, Liverpool and Plymouth. Articles from the *Church Reformer* were reprinted in India by the Madras *Philosophic Enquirer*, and in Australia by the *Kapunda Herald*, the paper of the radical South Australian Land Nationalisation Society.

At various times during the 1880s the GSM had four different branches in London, a number of British branches outside London, and some abroad: for example, in New York, Canada, the West Indies, Bloemfontein (South Africa) and New South Wales. Outside London, however, the only centres where the GSM functioned healthily were Bristol and Oxford; the other branches were small and insignificant.

The Guild was particularly successful in establishing for itself a place in the public's attention during the years 1886 and 1887, when economic distress brought mass actions of thousands of unemployed workers in the streets of London. In 1886 the Guild organised a series of public meetings on Christian Socialism, and in June participated in the conference of 'progressive organisations' which was held at the South Place Chapel on the initiative of Annie Besant and was attended by the delegates of virtually every British Socialist and anarchist group except the SDF. In the next year the Guild's Socialist programme was again put to a Trafalgar Square rally; subsequently, when the Home Secretary banned political gatherings in that venue, a GSM deputation asked to talk to him, its request was refused, and Headlam immediately retaliated by holding a demonstration in the Square illegally. He was prevented by the police from proposing any resolutions. In November 1887 he officiated at the funeral of Alfred Linnell, who was killed by being run down by the police, and led the long funeral procession through London, itself an imposing show of united Socialist strength [Thompson (1955) 579 ff.].

The 1880s were the Guild's heyday. In the next decade it was fraught with division, first in the dispute of 1891 in which Headlam was attacked by Shuttleworth for urging the abolition of Church schools, and then two years later, when Hancock and Headlam opposed the new Independent Labour Party. It was also forced to contend, from 1889, with a rival for the hearts and minds of politically progressive Anglicans. This was the Christian Social Union, of which Charles Gore, Scott Holland and Brooke Foss Westcott were the leading members. It was more broadly based than the Guild in terms of both ecclesiastical and political opinion; socially concerned Church people who found either the political radicalism or the High Churchmanship of the GSM not to their taste made their home in the new organisation. Guild members differed in their attitudes to it. Shuttleworth, Moll and Donaldson, for instance, saw no contradiction in membership of both groups, but Headlam and Hancock were scathing in their criticisms of the more moderate body.

The GSM faced a crisis of unprecedented gravity in 1895, after Headlam provided half the bail during Oscar Wilde's trial, and drove Wilde to and from the Old Bailey each day of the trial, through jeering mobs. Twelve members immediately left the Guild; another, Charles Marson, led a call for Headlam to vacate the office of warden, declaring that he was all for building a new Jerusalem here on earth, but not for 'wading through a Gomorrah first' [Church Reformer, Oct 1895]. Later that year the Church Reformer ceased publication, and the writing was on the wall for the Guild.

Paradoxically, in 1895 the Guild had its highest recorded membership, 364, but this number dropped severely as the decade drew to a close. The divisions of the early 1890s left their mark and, while no new controversies erupted among its members, the Guild never regained the vitality it had experienced during the previous decade. By 1903 Shuttleworth, Sarson and Hancock had all died, Headlam's interests in London education were increasingly absorbing his attention, and a number of the Guild's younger members found they could muster less and less enthusiasm for an organisation which had shown little enthusiasm for the political labour movement. Many such members, including Moll, Donaldson and Conrad Noel, felt more comfortable from 1906 in the Church Socialist League (CSL) which arose in the wake of the Labour Party successes in the 1906 election and which required its members to be committed Socialists.

The foundation of this High Church Anglican Socialist body left the GSM with little subsequent purpose, and in 1909 Headlam dissolved it. Throughout Headlam had been its leading personality. There had been attempts to unseat him, and he did himself offer to stand down; but his occupancy of the wardenship was tenacious and the success and the decline of the Guild were certainly more his responsibility than that of any other individual. The Guild, moreover, was financially dependent on him, especially in its last years. The accounts for 1906 revealed that roughly a quarter of the Guild's total income came from a loan he made [GSM, Occasional Paper no. 35 (Sep 1906) 6].

Headlam wound up the GSM with a melancholy sense of failure, lamenting that 'we have not been able to induce the parish churches themselves to regard the work we do as part and parcel of their ordinary Christian duty' [Binyon (1931) 147]. The Guild had, however, been successful in showing for the first time in Britain the possibility of a system of thought in which Christian beliefs were shown not only to be compatible with modern Socialist principles, but to lead unavoidably to them. Its own appeal as a body was limited by its rigorous Churchmanship, and more particularly by its predominant sacramentalism, but this limitation was also its strength, helping to produce a distinctive outlook which gave the movement a singular coherence. It is no coincidence that the Church Socialist League, many of whose members had matured under the Guild's influence, retained a High Churchmanship no less vibrant. The Guild's fatal weakness, on the other hand, was its deliberate aloofness from the political labour movement at a time when Anglicans who might otherwise have been drawn to it perceived an allegiance to Labour to be the correct way forward for Christian Socialists. It was this deficiency that the Church Socialist League was, in its early years, to make good.

Sources: The principal sources comprise the publications of the Guild, together with contemporary writings and a number of academic studies which contain references to its activities. The bibliography which follows has been divided into works published under the auspices of the council of the Guild and those of contemporary and later writers.

(1) Guild Publications: Occasional Papers nos 1–44 (1896–1909) contain information on Church services, forthcoming lectures, texts of sermons and the annual reports and statements of account of the Guild. No. 22 (13 Feb 1901) is devoted to the London County Council elections, no. 25 (June 1902) relates to the Education Bill, and no. 35 (Sep 1906) reports on the Guild's financial problems and includes a letter from Stewart Headlam on the possible dissolution of the Guild in view of the formation of the Church Socialist League. Other Guild works included: *To the Right Reverend Fathers in God, the Archbishops and Bishops of the Church of England* . . . [with reference to their votes in the House of Lords on the Parish Councils' Bill, 1894] (1894) [3] pp.; *The Relation of the Labourers to the Church: an address to the . . . Archbishops and Bishops assembled in Conference at Lambeth, 1897* [1897] 8 pp.; *The Church and the Teacher: an urgent plea for the organisation of a body of Church people trained in the art of teaching children* . . . [1904] [2] pp. [issued under the names of S. D. Headlam, warden, and Conrad Noel and Cecil Chesterton, honorary secretaries]; *The Church and the Polling Booth, being the Manifesto of the Guild of St Matthew to the Christened People of England* (Women's Printing Society, 1905) 12 pp.

(2) Contemporary Works: The most useful contemporary source is the *Church Reformer*. See also A. V. Woodworth, *Christian Socialism in England* (1903); T. Hancock, *The Pulpit and the Press and Other Sermons* . . . (1904); Conrad Noel Coll., Brynmor Jones Library, Hull Univ., DNO 5/3, which includes articles from the *Church Times*, 25 July 1903 and 30 Sep 1904, and some GSM literature, with several circular letters to Guild members from Headlam, in one of which, dated 25 June 1903, and addressed to Council members, he offers to resign from his wardenship.

(3) Other: Substantial accounts of the Guild can be found in the following works: F. G. Bettany, *Stewart Headlam: a biography* (1926); D. O. Wagner, *The Church of England and Social Reform since 1854* (NY, 1930); G. C. Binyon, *The Christian Socialist Movement in England: an introduction to the study of its history* (1931); H. M. Lynd, *England in the Eighteen Eighties: towards a social basis for freedom* (1945; repr. 1968); M. B. Reckitt, *Maurice to Temple: a century of social movement in the Church of England* [Scott Holland Memorial Lectures 1946] (1947); S. G. Evans, *Christian Socialism: a study outline and bibliography* (1962) 31 pp. [for bibliographies of the major writings of Guild members]; P. d'A. Jones, *The Christian Socialist Revival 1877–1914: religion, class and social conscience in late-Victorian England* (Princeton, NJ, 1968); *For Christ and the People: studies of four Socialist priests and prophets of the Church of England between 1870 and 1930* ed. M. B. Reckitt (1968). *See also*: E. P. Thompson, *William Morris: romantic to revolutionary* (1955; rev. ed. 1977); G. B. Shaw, *Collected Letters*, vol. *1: 1874–1897*, ed. Dan H. Laurence (1965). NOTE. The editors wish to acknowledge the helpful comments given by Dr I. Goodfellow, The Open University, Plymouth.

TREVOR PEACOCK

See also: William Edmund MOLL for Church Socialist League **(Special Note)**; Frederick VERINDER.

HARKNESS, Margaret Elise (1854–1923)
SOCIALIST AUTHOR AND JOURNALIST

Margaret Harkness was born on 28 February 1854 at Upton on Severn, Worcestershire, the second of five children of Robert Harkness (1826–86), who was an Anglican priest – as were his four brothers, and also the husbands of two of his sisters. Margaret's mother, Elizabeth Bolton Toswill (née Seddon) – a widow with a daughter, Mary, at the time of her marriage – was the daughter of William Seddon, a lace-manufacturer of Leicester. The Harkness family originated in Ireland and had upper-class connections. By the marriage of Robert Harkness's father to Jane Waugh Law, daughter of George Henry Law, Bishop of Bath and Wells (1761–1845), they were distantly related to the English aristocracy as far back as Edward I. On her mother's side of the family Margaret was related to Richard Potter (1817–92), whose nine daughters included Beatrice, who married Sidney Webb. Beatrice and Margaret were second cousins. By contrast with the high-society connections, which were more prestigious than useful, the maternal link with the moneyed classes was later of direct importance to Margaret, as the material situation of her family appears not to have corresponded with its social status. From 1865 to his death in November 1886, Robert Harkness was rector of Wimborne St Giles, Dorset. Margaret Harkness sometimes complained of her family's poverty in letters to her cousin Beatrice, although her father's estate at death was not insubstantial (he left £9678).

Robert Harkness, according to Margaret's letters, was of conservative inclinations, in both religious and social matters. Although – or perhaps because – Margaret Harkness grew up in the sheltered atmosphere of a country parish where nothing very exciting took place, she was unhappy and discontented as a young girl. Beatrice Potter wrote of her:

> When I first remember her at St Giles she was an hysterical egotistical girl with wretched health and still worse spirits. Her clerical and conventional parents tried to repress her extraordinary activity of mind, causing a state of morbid sensibility and fermentation which gave almost a permanent twist to her nature [24 Mar 1883, Webb, *Diary*, vol. *1* (1982) 79].

Margaret herself had earlier written in a letter to Beatrice:

> You scarcely know how difficult it is to me to express myself or arrange my ideas, I am all alone, and thoughts come and no one cares, and if I speak, I am simply thought wrong or idiotic. I envy you very much being in the society of people who can help you [letter to Beatrice, 13 Aug 1876, item 37, Passfield Coll.].

Whatever formal education was considered necessary for Margaret within the limits of the convention of the time must have taken place at home. She was finally sent to Stirling House, 'a smart finishing school in Bournemouth' at the age of twenty-one to obtain the final polish to her feminine skills. It was there that she met her seventeen-year-old cousin Beatrice, who became her close friend.

Margaret's slow groping towards a more definite agnostic and socially critical attitude took place in the face of increasing opposition from her family. From her letters a picture is built up of an intelligent young woman anxious to gain experience and deeply dissatisfied with the conditions of her life, but not finding it easy to formulate and order her thoughts and feelings.

On her return from Bournemouth, Margaret was faced with the problem of determining her future. 'I am years older than you are and I have not chosen my life', she wrote to Beatrice [letter, n.d. [*c.* 1876], ibid., item 36]. It was obvious from her letters that she was prepared to submit to the wishes of her family, although for herself she rejected the possibility of marriage. But since her father was presumably neither able nor willing to support his daughter in the long run, the search for an occupation suitable to her position was unavoidable. It was, therefore, with the approval of her parents that she was sent to London in 1877 to be trained as a nurse at Westminster Hospital. For Margaret this hospital training soon became daily routine. In addition to an almost ten-hour day as a nursing assistant she was expected to go to lectures and observe individual 'cases'. Margaret Harkness did not find this life particularly satisfying. She lived in a sort of 'boarding house' in Broad Sanctuary, with 'two ladies ... one a ritualist, the other a quakeress [*sic*]. The others are uneducated women. I only see these people at meals, and then their crude ideas amuse me immensely' [ibid.]. Even her change of circumstances failed to relieve her feeling of intellectual and emotional isolation; she also felt pressurised by the demands of her family. For the time being, however, Margaret Harkness was still prepared to submit to the wishes of her parents. In January 1878 she did not return to Westminster Hospital but began as an apprentice dispenser for a Miss Granville. Since her senior was an 'out and out ritualist' and fiercely opposed Margaret's freer religious attitude, she did not get on with her well. By May 1878 she was confronted with the problem of deciding whether to prolong her training for another eighteen months or to obey her parents' wishes yet again and go to Dorset for a few months to look after her sick mother. The latter alternative would be on the assumption that she would subsequently leave Wimborne St Giles again. She decided to do her duty, but at home she was continuously confronted with the same problems: 'I wish I could take interest in my own life. I used to do so, but I am tired of it now, and find it hard work to go on living' [letter to Beatrice, 24 Aug 1878. ibid., item 45]. Finally there appeared to her no other alternative except to continue the training she had begun. Therefore she returned to Kensington and took up a post at Guy's Hospital in Southwark.

At the beginning of 1880 various vague opportunities for the future offered themselves. She mentioned in a letter the possibility of taking on the post of private nurse to 'some little cousins ill with fever in Florence' whose mother had offered to pay all her expenses; and she also wrote that she was encouraged to apply for the post of secretary in a women's hospital [letter to Beatrice, 3 Feb 1880, ibid., item 49]. All the letters written during these first years in London give the impression that Margaret Harkness experienced them above all as a continuation of her depressing youth in Wimborne St Giles. She was in a state of continual depression which was only made endurable by her strong sense of duty. At the same time her awareness of politics appears to have been increasing: 'Do you care for politics? If I were in your place I would very much. It's rather slow work in my place. I read the papers and have a little political world of my own – anyhow it amuses me' [ibid.].

The prospect of having to continue leading a hard and frustrating life and having to give up any hope of developing her personal talents further eventually became so unbearable for Margaret Harkness that the break with her family's wishes and therefore with the family itself became inevitable. She decided not to continue in the profession she had trained for but to attempt to earn her living as a journalist and authoress. It is not possible to set a precise date to this decision but it must have been around the New Year of 1881. Since no personal details on Harkness have been preserved for this period, it is not known where she lived or who supported her to begin with. But it is probable that Kate or Beatrice Potter assisted her financially and introduced her to the circle of intellectuals, whose central meeting-place was the Reading Room of the British Museum. Margaret Harkness's acceptance in this group was for her a means of personal liberation.

Her first known publication was an article titled 'Women as Civil Servants' in the reputable liberal monthly *Nineteenth Century*. In it she described the existing opportunities for women to earn a 'safe and respectable' living in the State Civil Service and particularly in the Post Office. Her subsequent articles also proved her ability to make herself familiar with a subject previously unknown to her and to present it in clear and matter-of-fact terms, if somewhat lacking in brilliance of style or content. At the same time she began writing books and novels for which she could not find a suitable publisher and of which nothing is known. She wrote the following in a letter to Beatrice Potter about her work:

I have tried literature now for nearly three years and have worked very hard. I have written in many magazines and papers including the *Nineteenth Century* and *National*. Also two books of which I was forced to sell the copyright to an inferior publisher; and am preparing a book for Macmillan. I have also written an M. S. which Bentley refused because it was directed against Capital Punishment, and which has been read by a good novelist and pronounced full of promise. . . . My income last year was £150. I made it by working almost night and day; and wrote the M. S. on Capital Punishment in three months doing other work all the while [letter to Beatrice, 29 Feb 1884, ibid., item 51].

The continual financial worry mentioned here helps to explain the surprising fact that during this period Margaret Harkness produced two books for the Religious Tract Society. At the beginning of 1884 her monetary situation was so hopeless that she was forced to ask Beatrice Potter for financial help. It is not proved that the Potters did lend her the money, but it is probable given the close contact between Margaret and her relations at this time. Having broken with her own family, she had spent Christmas 1882 with the Potters; in 1883 she was present as a nurse at the death of Lawrencina Potter, Beatrice's mother; in the summer of 1884 she went on an extended tour of Bavaria with Beatrice and at various times she stayed at Kate Potter's house after her marriage to Leonard Courtney. At any rate, it was possible from then on for her to survive, if somewhat precariously, as a freelance author and journalist.

Apart from her literary work Margaret Harkness began in the early 1880s to become particularly interested in the problems of the East End of London, and her social and political ideas grew more radical. She began to see in Socialism the desired alternative to the English social system and in the Socialist movement the social group capable of realising this alternative. This was the result of her direct experience of poverty in the East End, her research inquiries for her articles and essays and her friendship with women such as Eleanor Marx and Annie Besant. At some indefinite date between 1885 and 1887, Margaret Harkness became a member of the SDF, but her membership was, apparently, short-lived. In 1889 in a letter to the editor of the *Star* she claimed, 'I joined the SDF and discovered it to be a dead body in a few months. Then I left it' [*Star*, 25 Sep 1889, 4]. But it was in this organisation that she met Henry Champion, John Burns and Tom Mann, with whom she was to be closely associated during the London Dock Strike.

It was not until after her father's death in 1886 that she began to use the pseudonym 'John Law'. All her subsequent books and some of her later articles carried this name, which could have had a family connotation but is more likely to have been taken from the eccentric John Law of Lauriston (1671–1729), to whom her book *Out of Work* (1888) was dedicated. Lauriston, a director of finance in France – although unsuccessful – was regarded by some French historians as the precursor of modern State Socialism. In letters to *Justice*, the *Labour Elector* and the *Star*, in the years 1888–90, however, Harkness used her own name, as she also did for two articles in *Justice*: 'Girl Labour in the City' – an account of her own researches – and 'Salvationists and Socialists', in March and April 1888 respectively. The latter article was the outcome of her developing interest in the work of the Salvation Army, which she had portrayed in the first of her novels about social injustice, *A City Girl* (1887), as being the only organisation really prepared to provide help for the underprivileged. She sent a copy of this to Engels through her publishers, Vizetelly, and received a reply which praised her work but offered some helpful criticism:

What strikes me most in your tale besides its realistic truth [it related to a proletarian girl being seduced by a middle-class man] is that it exhibits the courage of the true artist. . . . If I have anything to criticise it would be that perhaps, after all, the tale is not quite realistic enough. Realism, to my mind, implies beside truth of detail, the truth of reproduction of typical characters under typical circumstances. Now your characters are typical enough, as far as they go; but the circumstances which surround them and make them act, are not perhaps equally so. In the *City Girl* the working class figures as a passive mass, unable to help itself and not even showing (making) any attempt at striving to help itself. . . . Now if this was a correct description about 1800 or 1810, in the days of Saint-Simon and Robert Owen, it cannot appear so in 1887 to a man who for nearly fifty years has had the honour of sharing most of the fights of the militant proletariat. . . . I am far from finding fault with your not having written a point-blank socialist novel . . . to glorify the social and political views of the authors. . . . The realism I allude to may crop out even in spite of the author's opinions. Let me refer to an example. Balzac whom I consider a far greater master of realism than all the Zolas *passés, présents et à venir* gives us a most wonderfully realistic history of French 'Society' . . . from which . . . I have learned more than from all the professed historians, economists and statisticians of the period together. . . .

I must own, in your defence, that nowhere in the civilised world are the working people less actively resistant, more passively submitting to fate, more *hébétés* [stupefied] than in the East End of London. And how do I know whether you have not had very good reasons for contenting yourself, for once, with a picture of the passive side of working class life, reserving the active side for another work? [Letter Engels to Harkness, beginning of Apr 1888, *Marx and Engels: selected correspondence* (2nd ed. 1965) 401–3.]

Harkness's second novel, *Out of Work* (1888) featured the famous 'Bloody Sunday' fracas in Trafalgar Square on 13 November 1887 when John Burns and Cunninghame Graham were arrested and later sentenced to six weeks' imprisonment. It showed, according to John Goode [(1982) 57], 'many signs of a sophisticated response to Engels's critique' and it offered 'a picture, not like *A City Girl* of a social *section*, but of a social *situation*, the consequences of unemployment' [ibid.].

During 1887–8 Harkness edited a series of unsigned articles in the *British Weekly: a journal of social and Christian progress* published under the title 'Tempted London: young men' and 'Tempted London: young women' which were reprinted by Hodder and Stoughton as *Tempted London: young men* (1888) and *Toilers in London or inquiries concerning female labour in the metropolis* (1889). A reviewer of the 'Tempted London' articles writing in the *Christian* recommended that a copy 'be placed in the hands of and read by, every country youth who arrives in the metropolis. They would then be fully armed with knowledge as to the snares that are set for the feet of the unwary . . .' [*British Weekly*, 19 Oct 1888, 409].

Harkness directed her sympathy towards the very poorest classes – the 'slummers': 'My principal interest is with a class below the unskilled labourers; I mean the scum of our population that haunts the slums of our great cities' [*New Rev. 5* (1891) 377]. She had already portrayed the Salvation Army in her novel *A City Girl* as the only organisation really prepared to provide help for the underprivileged. She challenged the SDF when she wrote in *Justice* (24 Mar 1888), 'The two organisations ought to work more together than they do at present, for they have many points of common interest. For our respect the army teaches us a great lesson. It has never split up. It is one large labour union.'

The book for which she is perhaps best known was first published in 1889. This, like

Toilers in London, began in serial form in the *British Weekly* but was then published, also by Hodder and Stoughton, as *Captain Lobe: a story of the Salvation Army*. When she wrote this novel she had become frustrated with the divisions she had encountered among those professing Socialist principles and she castigated the labour movement. She was criticised for her chapter 'Among the Socialists' and admitted in a letter to the editor of *Justice* (20 Apr 1889), that she had tried to get it back but the book had gone to press. In defence of her comments, however, she wrote:

> We are not a happy family, and sometimes our quarrels make it difficult for us to 'sacrifice without cursing' as Mazzini puts it. To find oneself without a relation or a friend, because one is by conviction a Socialist, and then to have vials of wrath poured on one's head, by Socialists, makes one inclined to curse [p. 3].

Harkness's direct involvement with the Socialist movement was during the years from 1887 to 1891. Apart from a short stay in Manchester which probably gave rise to her book *A Manchester Shirtmaker* [1890] (dedicated to Cunninghame Graham), she lived most of the time at various addresses in London, although in 1887 and 1888 she worked in Scotland as a contact for Champion with the Scottish miners' leader, Keir Hardie. She took part in Hardie's election campaign when he contested Mid-Lanark at a by-election [see biography of H. H. Champion in this volume]. It is likely that Harkness was offering only part of the story concerning election expenses and it is possible that some of the money came from Champion – with whom her relations were close, and possibly intimate – and that Champion himself may have obtained funds from Maltman Barry. Her claim to have paid Hardie's election expenses was disputed by Beatrice Potter, who was coming to distrust her 'more and more' [14 Nov? 1889, Webb, *Diary* (1982) 302].

During the London Dock Strike of 1889, Harkness involved herself in a mediation attempt. Cardinal Manning, in an autobiographical note dated 16 September 1889, acknowledged that Harkness had visited him on 5 September with a message from the strike leaders to the effect 'that the coal heavers who had returned to work would strike again at noon the next day, if the Dock Directors did not grant the demands of the men' [Purcell (1895) 662]. It is possible that the Harkness visit was one of the factors which encouraged Cardinal Manning to intervene. When Harkness wrote of her experiences in the labour movement in *George Eastmont: wanderer* (1905), she dedicated her book to 'the memory of His Eminence Cardinal Manning with whom the author was associated during the Great Dock Strike of 1889'.

After her involvement with the Dock Strike, Harkness was still in touch with Beatrice Potter, who herself was feeling very depressed in early 1890. Living at home, where her father was only partly conscious, she was unable to carry out the work she had earlier begun as a social investigator. Miss Potter had helped her cousin Charles Booth with his inquiry into the life and labour of London and she had become an ardent supporter of the co-operative movement, on which she was in the process of collecting material for a book. Anxious to get some advice, she sought her cousin Margaret's help and the latter suggested Sidney Webb, who 'knows everything ... he literally pours out information' [Webb, *Diary* (1982) 319 (Introduction to pt V)]. So on 8 January 1890 Sidney Webb was introduced to Beatrice Potter at her cousin's lodgings, 45 Great Russell Street, near the British Museum. Sidney Webb immediately drew up a list of sources and their relationship later developed into the well-known partnership.

Harkness then left England for a visit to Germany in order to study the Continental labour movement. There she met August Bebel and other German Social Democrats [letter from 'John Law', *PM Gaz.*, 21 Oct 1890]. Hyndman, in an article in *Justice* (28 Feb 1891) entitled 'The Marxist Clique', listed 'the prominent members of the little Marxist clique and mutual admiration society in London' who 'are or were: Friedrich Engels, H. H. Champion,

Edward Aveling, Eleanor Marx, Maltman Barry, John Burns, Tom Mann, Keir Hardie, W. Parnell, and Margaret Harkness ("John Law"); with them has been closely associated though happily he is opposed to their methods, in some particulars, Cunninghame Graham'. But it was unlikely that Harkness was still associated with many of her former friends by that date. Her friendship with Engels had ended when she refused to enter his house if Edward Aveling were present, a decision also taken by a German feminist, Gertrud Guillame-Schack. Both women 'flatly refused to give Engels any further reason for their desire to avoid Aveling' [Bernstein (1921) 202]. She had also severed her relationship with Beatrice Potter [9 Sep 1890, Webb, *Diary* (1982) 341]. Harkness had also written critically about the Socialist leaders in an article, '"Salvation" vs Socialism – in Praise of General Booth', in the *Pall Mall Gazette* (21 Oct 1890):

I had discovered to my bitter disappointment that the Socialist leaders were the strongest individualists of my acquaintance, and that, although six of them could do the necessary work if united, no six could work together for six months without a quarrel. They talked Socialism, but practised Individualism; and all the time the slummers were starving . . . the Salvationists have hit on the right thing – I mean labour colonies. . . . I saw labour colonies on the Continent. . . . In the history of England the Salvation Army will, I believe, be set down as 'The Slum Saviour'; as the religious body that said the curses of starving men and despairing women shall not rest on God, for not God but MAN is responsible for the poverty of England.

To counter criticism of her article, Harkness wrote in a (supposedly anonymous) letter 'From one who knows John Law' to the editor of the *Pall Mall Gazette* (29 Oct 1890):

Very naturally, John Law's interest is in the workers, not their leaders; but no one ever spoke more warmly of these men, or praised in higher terms John Burns's physical courage, Tom Mann's unselfish enthusiasm and H. H. Champion's power of self-sacrifice for the good of the people. In talking of the labour leaders as individualists she wanted probably to find an excuse for their misunderstandings; for her faith in Socialism was sorely tried by what she saw while working as a Socialist. She showed me before she went away some of the letters she had received during the two years she worked with the Socialists. Most of the letters were anonymous, but in them she was accused of every imaginable sin. The mildest said she ought to be shot as a Tory spy and hung for taking money from the Tories. One letter spoke of 'vulgar intrigues', another of 'disappointed ambition'. But it was not these things that made her write a farewell letter in your columns last spring; it was the conviction that the vote was the weapon that the workers would use, and that the new trade unions would prove a broken reed when capitalists united.

Harkness's book on the Salvation Army had been well received, with requests from Germany, Russia and Sweden for translation rights [letter, *Justice*, 20 Apr 1889] and in 1891 a new edition of *Captain Lobe* was published with the title *In Darkest London*, followed by a further edition two years later which Harkness dedicated to her brother William Bathurst Harkness. She supported the work of the Salvation Army primarily, however, for rational reasons and not because she had been 'converted'. And this was confirmed by General Booth in his Preface to the 1891 edition: 'I am quite aware that the author of this volume, is in many respects very far from accepting our discipline, or subscribing to our theology.'

Harkness had become weary of the conflicts she had encountered and, in order to convalesce after a serious illness, she went on a world tour during 1891 which took her to Australia, New Zealand and the United States. Although she had told Beatrice Potter she intended to leave England for 'always', she did, in fact, return from time to time. She had arrived in Australia a few months after Champion had left it and when the workers were recovering from the bitter maritime strikes during which Champion had intervened; and, like Champion, she returned to Australia in 1894, visited one of the Government's newly initiated workers' colonies and had an account of her week on a labour settlement published in the *Fortnightly Review* in 1894. But nothing, so far, is known of her activities in the years from 1895 until the publication of her partly autobiographical book *George Eastmont* in 1905. In that book she depicted, in novel form, characters and events from her own life in the labour movement – something which she had told Beatrice Potter in 1889 she intended to do: '"I can tell you nothing now, but I shall get out of the whole thing someday – then I can tell you all." ... She is going to bring it all out in a book' [14 Nov? 1889, Webb, *Diary* (1982) 303].

Margaret Harkness then turned her attention to life in the Indian sub-continent and Ceylon where she appears to have spent the years between 1906 and the First World War. It is known from her writings that she left Ceylon late in 1906 for India and spent Christmas in Madras. Her earlier friendship with Annie Besant enabled her to attend the Theosophists' annual convention at Adyar, Madras, where she had hoped for introductions to Mohammedans and Hindus as she did not wish 'to become a unit of the governing community' [Harkness [1909?] 3]. But she did not find the Theosophists helpful with introductions, although she visited the Central Hindu College at Benares, started by Annie Besant, and was also invited to her home. She was in Delhi in July 1907 for the fiftieth anniversary of the Indian Mutiny and she also visited Cawnpore, where the massacre of the women and children had taken place. She spent some time in Hyderabad in the same year and in 1908 she was in Bombay during the sedition trial of B. G. Tilak, the Indian nationalist leader and founder of the Home Rule for India League [Gupta (1975) 410].

She recounted her travels in *Glimpses of Hidden India*, first published probably in 1909 with a revised third edition three years later and a new title: *Indian Snapshots*. This was followed in 1914 by *Modern Hyderabad*. All these works were published by Thacker of Calcutta, but her next book, *The Horoscope* [1914/15?], which concerned two brothers in Ceylon, one a Christian, the other a Buddhist, was published in both Calcutta and London. Another edition of *Captain Lobe* also appeared in 1915, but with the 1893 dedication to her brother William deleted. From Harkness letters in the Dorset Record Office it was apparent that Margaret and her brother were estranged. In 1912 William Bathurst Harkness, a Lieutenant-Colonel in the Royal Marines and a CB, had married Evelyn Dauntesey, and under a name and arms clause in the Robert Dauntesey Settlement, changed his name to Dauntesey to enable his wife to become tenant in tail. According to their daughter, Mrs Patricia Kirwan, Margaret's father would not have her name mentioned and William did not mention her either, nor was she included in his will, dated 5 April 1913, although he had left £2000 jointly to his other sisters [letters, Harkness to the Revd J. A. Bouquet, St Giles Rectory, 12 and 25 June 1917, Dorset CRO; letter from Mrs P. Kirwan to Miss I. Snatt; and W. B. Dauntesey's will at Somerset House, London].

Her long absences abroad may be why she does not appear to have visited her other brother, Robert, in the years between 1901 and 1924. A staunch Conservative, he had left the Wimborne area in 1901 to settle at Penyard House, Weston, near Ross on Wye, Herefordshire, where he became a local squire. He died in 1914 and his widow, Mary Robina, ten years later, on 27 April 1924. Her visitor's book for the years 1901–24 includes signatures of all the Harkness family – except Margaret – but in her will, dated 1919, she included her three sisters-in-law, Margaret, Katherine and Constance, who were to inherit income from a trust fund.

Following her mother's death at the age of ninety-five in 1916, Margaret Harkness was living temporarily in London before returning to France, where she had been working – although the nature of this work is not known. But she was concerned about the care of her father's grave, previously undertaken by her mother, and was in correspondence with the rector of Wimborne St Giles about the possibility of help being obtained from her brother

William. She also indicated her intention of making a will to include a request that a window be erected in the Wimborne St Giles church in memory of her parents [letters, Dorset CRO]. This was not to be undertaken until after her own death, however [letter from Toller to Revd J. A. Bouquet, ibid.]. Her mother, whose net estate was valued at £989, had left Margaret and her sisters some investments in her will.

Margaret Harkness's last known publication, *A Curate's Promise: a story of three weeks, September 14–October 5 1917* (1921) told of a curate's decision to join the Salvation Army instead of the armed forces as a chaplain. She did not live to inherit the trust fund income from her sister-in-law, as she predeceased her when she died at the Pensione Castagnoli in Florence on 10 December 1923. No record of her own will has been located, but following her wishes a window dedicated to the memory of her parents and designed by Ninian Comper was installed in the church at Wimborne St Giles in 1934. She was survived by her brother William, and her sisters Katherine and Constance.

Very few details of Margaret Harkness's private life appear to have survived. One incomplete and undated letter to Beatrice Potter suggests that she had a love affair with a man who was probably married:

> I feel I shall always be grateful to Mr. . . . , for he came into my life when I might have become bitterly sceptical. He has many faults, but his invariably sweet temper, and his affection have helped me. I have helped him too, I think. . . . I shall never see him again, of course [letter to Beatrice, n.d., item 52, Passfield Coll.].

Margaret Harkness was only moderately interested in the economic foundations of Socialist theory and in an analysis directed towards revolutionary social change. She supported the views of Champion, who rejected the use of violence after the unemployment riots in the 1880s, and she advocated the establishment of an independent Labour Party. Like Champion she saw the basic principle of Victorian liberal capitalism – 'free' competition – as being the reason for the exploitation, unemployment and suffering of the working classes.

Her true interests lay in the victims of the social system and in the possibilities of giving practical aid to those groups in British society who seemed a long way from political self-help. She was motivated by a general 'sympathy for wretchedness and suffering' [letter to Beatrice, 10 Dec 1875, ibid., item 34] and by her feeling of moral obligation to help and care for others. In a letter to the editor of *Justice* (24 Mar 1888) she wrote, 'Socialism must be looked at from its moral as well as its economic aspect. Men and women cannot be left to starve while Socialists are waiting for a social Revolution, or laying siege to the ballot box.' She felt slummers needed to be taught basic moral values before any attempt at their political organisation could be successful, and 'no Labour Party can supply improved conditions for the slummers until the slummers rise in the social scale and make their demands effective' she wrote in her *New Review* article in 1891. P. J. Keating [(1971) 242] considered Margaret Harkness's novels *A City Girl, Out of Work* and *In Darkest London* to be 'a curious hotch-potch of literary influences and revolutionary ideas' and there is little doubt that for many years her ideal remained a society organised along anarcho-Communist lines as propagated by Kropotkin and portrayed in her book *George Eastmont*.

Margaret Harkness's complaints about personal attacks and the lack of unity in the movement were presumably not solely projections of an ambitious and hysterical intriguer, as Beatrice Potter suggested, but rather the expression of her difficulty in finding a political and personal home within the many different contemporary trends of ideas and social currents. The problem of living without social and personal recognition was particularly intense for the 'independent woman', as Margaret Harkness considered herself to be. She was involved in the transition from the traditional feminine role of housewife and mother to a new feminine independence; and, as with so many, it caused her severe emotional problems.

Writings: Margaret Harkness's known published writings comprise books, articles in the periodical and labour press, and letters to the editors of these and other papers. Some were written in her own name, others using her pseudonym, 'John Law', and on at least one occasion she wrote as 'One who knows "John Law"'. For this bibliography her works are grouped chronologically in the various categories. Her known MS writings comprise: (i) twenty-one letters to her cousin Beatrice Potter between 1875 and 1887 (from internal evidence), Passfield Coll., section II, 1 (ii), items 34–54, BLPES; and (ii) five letters to the Revd J. A. Bouquet, rector of Wimborne St Giles, between 4 June 1917 and 2 July 1917, PE/WMG IN 12, Dorset CRO, Dorchester.

(1) Works in her own Name: 'Women as Civil Servants', *19th C. 10* (Sep 1881) 369–81; 'Railway Labour', ibid. *12* (Nov 1882) 721–32; 'The Municipality of London', *Nat. Rev. 1* (May 1883) 395–407, and *2* (Sep 1883) 96–105; *Assyrian Life and History* (Religious Tract Society [1883]); *Egyptian Life and History according to the Monuments* (Religious Tract Society, 1884); 'Girl Labour in the City', *Justice*, 3 Mar 1888, 4–5; 'Salvationists and Socialists', ibid., 24 Mar 1888, 2; 'Letter to the Editor' [in reply to a comment on her article of 24 Mar 1888], 14 Apr 1888, 6; 'Home Industries', ibid., 25 Aug 1888, 2; 'Letter to the Editor', *Labour Elector*, Oct 1888, 8; 'Letter to the Editor', *Star*, 20 Sep 1889, 4; 'Letter to the Editor', ibid., 25 Sep 1889, 4; 'Letter to the Editor', *PM Gaz.*, 7 Mar 1890, 7.

(2) Works in the Name of 'John Law': *A City Girl: a realistic story* (1887; 2nd ed. [1890]); (ed.) unsigned articles in the *British Weekly* on 'Tempted London: young men', Oct 1887–20 Apr 1888, published in book form as *Tempted London: young men* (1888) by Hodder and Stoughton, and a similar series on young women, 27 Apr–28 Dec 1888, published in book form (again by Hodder) as *Toilers in London: or inquiries concerning female labour in the metropolis*, being the second part of 'Tempted London' (1889); *Out of Work* (1888); 'Captain Lobe: a story of the East End', *British Weekly*, 6 Apr–14 Dec 1888, published as *Captain Lobe: a story of the Salvation Army* (1889; new ed. under the title of *In Darkest London*, with an Introduction by General Booth, Bellamy Library, no. 8: 1891; reissued in 1893 and repr. as *Captain Lobe* in 1915); 'Letter to the Editor', *North British Daily Mail*, 25 Aug 1888, 2; 'Impressions I: Herbert Spencer', *British Weekly*, 11 Jan 1889, 175; 'Letter to the Editor' [on *Captain Lobe*], 20 Apr 1889; '"Salvation" vs. Socialism – in praise of General Booth', *PM Gaz.*, 21 Oct 1890, 1–2; *A Manchester Shirtmaker: a realistic story of to-day* [1890] [published in Dutch [1891]]; 'A Year of my Life', *New Rev. 5* (Oct 1891) 375–84; 'Roses and Crucifix', *Woman's Herald*, 5 Dec 1891–27 Feb 1892; 'The Children of the Unemployed', *New Rev. 8* (Jan 1893) 228–36; 'A Week on a Labour Settlement', *Fortn. Rev.* n.s. *56* (Aug 1894) 206–13; *George Eastmont: wanderer* (1905); *Glimpses of Hidden India* (Calcutta, [1909?]; 3rd rev. ed. published in Calcutta in 1912 with the new title of *Indian Snapshots: a bird's-eye view of India from the days of the Saib Company to the present time*); *Modern Hyderabad* (Calcutta, 1914); *The Horoscope* (Calcutta and London, [1914/15?]); *A Curate's Promise: a story of three weeks (September 14–October 5 1917)*, with an Introduction by General Bramwell Booth (1921).

(3) In the Name of 'One who knows "John Law"': '"Salvation" and Socialism', *PM Gaz.*, 29 Oct 1890, 2.

Sources: (1) MS: In addition to Margaret Harkness's own MS writings the following have been used for this biography: (i) 'The Diary of Beatrice Webb 1873–1943', 57 vols (Cambridge, 1978) [on microfiche]; (ii) visitor's book covering the years 1901–24 of Mrs Mary Robina Harkness, in the possession of Mrs N. E. Lowth, Ross on Wye, Herefords, whose late husband was a cousin of Mrs Harkness; (iii) letter from Toller, Burgess and Pochin, solicitors, Leicester, to the Revd J. A. Bouquet, St Giles's Rectory, Wimborne St Giles, Dorset, PE/WMG IN 12, Dorset CRO; (iv) Harkness family trees supplied by Rear-Admiral James Harkness CB, Lymington, Hants, and Peter Harkness, Letchworth, Herts. (2) Other: *British Weekly*, 19 Oct 1888, 409 [refers to a notice of 'Tempted London' in the *Christian*]; 'The Marxist Clique', *Justice*, 28 Feb 1891; E. S. Purcell, *Life of Cardinal Manning Archbishop of Westminster*, vol. *2: Manning as a Catholic* (1895); *Chambers's Biographical Dictionary*, ed. W. and J. L. Geddie (1897; later eds); *Burke's Landed Gentry of Ireland* (1899); *Hereford Times*, 27 June 1914 [obit. of Robert Harkness]; S. Leslie, 'Cardinal Manning and the London Dock Strike', *Dublin Rev. 167*, no. 335 (Autumn 1920) 221; E. Bernstein, *My Years of Exile: reminiscences of a Socialist*, trans. B. Niall (1921); M. Warrender, *My First 60 Years* (1933); *Karl Marx and Friedrich Engels: selected correspondence* (Moscow, 1955; 2nd rev. ed. 1965); F. Engels and P. and L. Lafargue, *Correspondence*, vol. *2*: 1887–1890 (Moscow, 1960); A. Stafford, *A Match to fire the Thames* (1961); E. W. Domville, 'The Presentation of the London Working Classes in Fiction 1880–1914' (London PhD, 1965); C. Tsuzuki, *The Life of Eleanor Marx 1855–1898* (Oxford, 1967); H. Gemkow *et al.*, *Friedrich Engels: a biography* (Berlin, 1970; English trans. Dresden, 1972); P. J. Keating, *The Working Classes in Victorian Fiction* (1971); P. S. Gupta, *Imperialism and the British Labour Movement 1914–1964* (1975); *The Letters of Sidney and Beatrice Webb*, vol. *1: Apprenticeships 1873–1892*, and vol. *3: Pilgrimage 1912–1947*, ed. N. MacKenzie (1978); F. Reid, *Keir Hardie* (1978); W. J. Fishman, 'Tower Hamlets 1888', *East London Record*, no. 2 (1979) 19–27; J. Goode, 'Margaret Harkness and the Socialist Novel', Ch. 3 in *The Socialist Novel in Britain: towards the recovery of a tradition*, ed. H. G. Klaus (Brighton, 1982); *The Diary of Beatrice Webb*, ed. N. and J. MacKenzie, vol. *1: 1873–1892. Glitter around and Darkness within* (1982), vol. *2: 1892–1905. All the Good Things of Life* (1983), and vol. *4: 1924–1943. 'The Wheel of Life'* (1985); B. Kaspar, *Margaret Harkness. A City Girl: eine literaturwissenschaftliche Untersuchung zum naturalistischen Roman des Spätviktorianismus* (Tübingen, 1984); E. Sypher, 'The Novels of Margaret Harkness', *Turn of the Century Women* [Univ. of Virginia] *1*, no. 2 (Winter 1984) 12–26; R. Gray, *Cardinal Manning: a biography* (1985); D. E. Nord, *The Apprenticeship of Beatrice Webb* (1985). Biographical information: the British Architectural Library, RIBA, London; Michael Bouquet, South Molton, Devon; Allen T. P. Cooper, Wimborne St Giles, Dorset; W. J. Corney, Hurstpierpoint, Sussex; P. Dickinson, Rouge Dragon Pursuivant, College of Arms, London; William Fishman, London; Mrs M. E. Griffiths, Archivist, Shaftesbury Estates, Wimborne St Giles; Revd J. Hackett, Sutton, Surrey; K. D. D. Henderson, Steeple Langford, Wilts; H. Jaques, County Archivist, Dorset; T. G. O'Neill, School of Agriculture and Forestry, Melbourne Univ.; Mrs G. T. Pearson, Milton Regis, Kent; Robinson, Till and Oakley, solicitors, Beverley, Humberside; D. I. Roots, Rochester, Kent; *Ross Gazette*, Ross on Wye, Herefords; Salvation Army, London; Miss Irene Snatt, London; Revd A. Symondson, London; Revd R. Thomson, Gillingham, Kent; Toller, Burgess and Pochin, solicitors, Leicester; Warner, Goodman and Streat, solicitors, Fareham, Hants; Andrew Whitehead, London. Personal information: Mrs Patricia Kirwan, Great Missenden, Bucks, niece; Mark Lowth, Westerham, Kent; Mrs N. E. Lowth, Ross on Wye. NOTE. The editors wish to record their thanks to the many people who have been consulted and especially to Miss Irene Snatt for her invaluable assistance.

JOYCE BELLAMY
BEATE KASPAR

See also: †Annie BESANT; †John Elliott BURNS; Henry Hyde CHAMPION; †Robert Bontine CUNNINGHAME GRAHAM; †Beatrice WEBB; †Sidney James WEBB; and Editorial Note below.

Editorial Note: The file on Margaret Harkness was begun in 1980 when Professor Norman

MacKenzie sent us a draft entry based on research undertaken by Fräulein Beate Kaspar for a German university dissertation. Nothing was known of the date and place of her death, and the search for these details has provided us with a large-scale cautionary tale over some five years.

Miss Harkness's last publication appeared in 1921. Inquiries to the publishers provided no relevant information. The death and will registers [for England and Wales] were searched from 1919 to 1954 and there was no trace. We then began to search for other members of the family, and our correspondence became considerable. We gained detailed knowledge of the extended family, but were still no nearer to the basic facts we were seeking. In early 1984, however, through several contacts, we learned that Miss Irene Snatt of London was also working on Margaret Harkness for a biography and we pooled our information. She, too, had also failed to discover the date of death, although she had been in touch with a niece.

Miss Snatt had also discovered that a window in the church at Wimborne St Giles – the Revd Robert Harkness's last parish – had been bequeathed by his daughter Margaret. This window led to some degree of mystification. It had been installed in 1934, and although all the appropriate Church and diocesan records were explored, there were no documents that offered any clues for our search. On learning that the window had been designed by Ninian Comper, we therefore began to correspond with the RIBA and with scholars working on the Comper papers, but there was no mention of the arrangements for this particular window. We then wrote to the Shaftesbury Estates, whose area covered Wimborne St Giles, and this led us to the Dorset CRO and its small collection of Harkness correspondence. From these letters we learned of Miss Harkness's intentions in 1917, to have a window placed in the church after her death.

The problem was finally solved for us following an inquiry to the College of Arms. Mr Patric Dickinson, who had earlier offered information to the *DLB*, decided, since he happened to be at the GRO on one occasion, to check the Consular death registers for 1921 to 1925 and found the reference to Miss Harkness's death in Florence.

We ourselves were under the impression that these had already been checked. Obviously, when the GRO death registers revealed nothing, the first thing to be investigated was the possibility of death overseas, and the possible record of death in the Consular files. Our own research worker in London had made a check at an early stage of the inquiry at a time when one volume was missing, as she later recalled. Miss Snatt's approach was dominated by the 1934 date for the church window, and she went back in the Consular records to about 1927, although she too had looked for an earlier volume which was missing at the time.

The search for the date of death of Margaret Harkness involved a very large correspondence. We are obliged to add that the error we made – in not going back, at various stages of the search, to first principles – is easier to state than to be certain it will be avoided in the future. Family research is notoriously a landscape filled with distorting perspectives and misleading impressions for all travellers, however experienced they may feel themselves to be. But it should also be said that, if we had succeeded earlier in establishing the date of death, the details of Miss Harkness's family and her bequest would not have been discovered.

JMB
JS

HOBSON, Joshua (1810–76)
RADICAL PRINTER, EDITOR AND REFORMER

Joshua Hobson was born in Huddersfield, Yorkshire, in November 1810, the youngest of four children. His father, a building labourer, died shortly after his birth, leaving the young family in the charge of their mother. The only formal education Hobson received consisted of short terms at a local dame school and at the Seedhill National School, where he obtained a rudimentary grasp of reading and writing. As a teenager he moved across the Pennines to Oldham, and found work as a cotton hand-loom weaver, from which he evidently learned much. His fellow weavers were obviously militant radicals, and Hobson wrote a series of letters to the Lancashire newspapers under the pen-name 'Whistler at the Loom'. He did not remain long in Oldham, returning to Huddersfield before he was twenty to be apprenticed to a local cabinet-maker.

In Huddersfield he became active in the working-class Short Time Committee. On 19 June 1831 Hobson and five other Short-Timers met Richard Oastler, the Tory land steward whose 'Yorkshire Slavery' letters had opened the debate on factory regulation. Oastler and the Short-Timers agreed to ignore their religious and political differences for the sake of factory reform, and the Fixby Hall Compact, as this agreement became known, exerted a profound influence on Hobson's thinking. Oastler's benign paternalism solidified Hobson's belief in a past Golden Age, which, in conjunction with contemporary programmes for political and social reform, served as his model of an ideal, just society [Driver (1946) 86–8].

As the issue of parliamentary reform gained momentum, the Huddersfield radicals established a Political Union in November 1831 to counter the influence of the Ramsden family, the Whig landowners who dominated local politics. Hobson and two other Fixby Hall radicals, John Hanson and John Leech, became joint secretaries of the Political Union, and, at a public meeting in December, Hobson condemned both Whigs and Tories as 'being not for the rights of all, but for the plunder of all' [PMG, 10 Dec 1831]. With the passage of the 1832 Reform Bill Huddersfield gained a seat in the House of Commons and the Political Union decided to continue agitating for a broader franchise. Early in 1833 a second-hand printing-press was purchased. Hobson constructed a frame and ancillary tables and then operated it as the Union Free Press. Housed by the Political Union in Swan Yard, its output reflected the need for a reliable local working-class press, serving the immediate needs of both Political Unions and Short Time Committees. In June 1833 a more lasting publication appeared in the form of an eight-page unstamped newspaper, the weekly Voice of the West Riding.

The Voice was owned by a group of radicals who rented the Union Free Press from the Political Union but exerted little control over the editor or editors. Editorial decisions were made on the basis of a wide-ranging eclecticism: factory and parliamentary reforms were advocated, workers were warned to eschew militant trade unionism in favour of negotiation, abuses of power were criticised, and the first editorial asserted, 'we want everyone to be fully and thoroughly satisfied that there is little to choose between Whig and Tory, and that the being IN or OUT of Place, constitutes the principal difference' [Voice of the West Riding, 1–8 June 1833]. The language of the Voice generally echoed Robert Owen's conciliatory tones, but these could not mute its inherent antagonism towards capitalism and the aristocracy. The eight-hour day propounded by the Society for Promoting National Regeneration was supported and the worker co-operatives established by the Grand National Consolidated Trades Union were applauded, not as ways of mediating class conflict, but as means for workers to establish an alternative economy.

The Voice published a variety of different views. As with most other papers of the day, articles and editorials were generally unsigned, and the task of uncovering the identities of the writers and editors is almost impossible. As the mast indicated, Hobson printed and published the Voice, but there is no evidence to support the generally accepted contention that he was editor. Other prominent individuals played leading but undefined roles: Oastler was a frequent contributor, as were the Leeds trade unionist and radical William Rider and the Bradford republican Peter Bussey.

Hobson was, however, undeniably the person most prominently associated with the paper. In August 1833 he was imprisoned in the Wakefield House of Correction for six months for selling the *Voice*. Recognising the political motives behind his summons, Hobson defended himself on the grounds 'that the printing and publishing of such a paper, is not a violation of any moral principle, but, on the contrary, one of the most virtuous actions that man can do, that of doing good to his species' [ibid., 10 Aug 1833]. Hobson was replaced as printer by John Francis Bray (then at the beginning of his radical career) [see *DLB 3*], and there were many signed contributions of Rider and Bussey. For Hobson imprisonment meant national attention, with his defiant defence speech being reprinted in newspapers around the country and with William Cobbett bringing his case before Parliament. When he returned to Huddersfield in January 1834 Hobson received a hero's welcome, and he toured the West Riding as a celebrated victim of the war of the unstamped press. When he resumed his duties on the *Voice*, he renewed his contacts with the Manchester newsagent Abel Heywood and the London printer John Cleave, and for the following decade these three men constituted an informal but close-knit partnership responsible for the production and distribution of many leading Chartist and Owenite writings.

The *Voice* folded in June 1834 and two months later Hobson, Rider and Oastler brought out the *Argus and 'Demagogue'*. The *Argus*, a four-page unstamped devoted to castigating local Whigs, lasted for little more than a month but cemented Hobson's links with the radicals of Leeds. In the autumn he moved to that town and opened a newsagency, set up a press and was twice again imprisoned for selling unstamped papers. Hobson became prominent in the local movement: in December 1835 he chaired a series of meetings called to hear Feargus O'Connor, a missionary from the Great Radical Association of Marylebone, which resulted in the revival of the Leeds Radical Association; and on 28 August 1837 he chaired a meeting on Woodhouse Moor addressed by Cleave and Henry Vincent at which the Leeds Working Men's Association was formally constituted. Hobson and Bray, another founder member of the Working Men's Association, proceeded to establish links with the Leeds Owenites, committing the Leeds radicals to education and peaceful agitation until Rider and George White brought the Working Men's Association into the more militant Great Northern Union in July 1838.

Hobson's organisational skills were not limited solely to these proto-Chartist groups, for as 'Parson' of the Leeds Owenites he chaired the first meeting of the local branch of the Association of all Classes of all Nations on 1 October 1837 and continued to take an active interest in Owenism both locally and nationally. He maintained close links with the Huddersfield Owenites through Lawrence Pitkethly, another Fixby Hall radical, and represented the Leeds branch at West Riding delegate meetings. In conjunction with Cleave and Heywood, Hobson printed innumerable books, pamphlets and periodicals, including for a short time the *New Moral World* (the official weekly Owenite journal) and the works of Robert Owen and Robert Dale Owen. In 1838 he championed Owenism against the Revd J. E. Giles, a Leeds Baptist minister who preached a series of well-advertised sermons accusing Owen of promulgating an immoral atheistic creed. Hobson replied to Giles in five lectures, which he published as *Socialism as it is!!!*, refuting criticisms of Owenite marriage arrangements and asserting the right to religious freedom in any society, including the projected New Moral World. The Hobson–Giles debate was one of the earliest episodes in what was to become a national issue in January 1840, when the Bishop of Exeter launched a series of attacks on the Owenites in the House of Lords and began a period of political persecution of secularists.

As a body the Leeds Owenites were handicapped less by clerical opposition than by their own inability to secure a permanent meeting place. From December 1837 until February 1841 they used the Leeds Music Saloon as their Social Institution and, with a capacity of about 500, prospered. However, the Music Saloon proved irreplaceable after it was converted into a Mechanics' Institute, and a series of smaller rooms could not compensate for this loss. Proposals for a Hall of Science were rejected because, observing the financial difficulties of their brethren in Huddersfield, the Leeds Owenites felt they could not guarantee an adequate return on their initial investment. Hobson for his part consistently supported calls for independent working-class institutions and gave scientific lectures and demonstrations in the Huddersfield Hall of Science and in aid of the building fund of the Leeds Oddfellows.

Hobson's Owenite activities were parallel to his work for the Chartists. He was an organiser and speaker on behalf of both movements, but he was above all a printer and publisher, a professional radical whose income was derived from his printing press and newsagency. The bulk of his work was for the Chartist and Owenite movements, although he was not limited in his output: from June 1835 until July 1838 he was Oastler's printer; and for about six years he was the main West Riding printer for the Anti-Poor Law movement. Although Hobson did not himself write extensively, he did compile and print a series of almanacs, initially as the *Social Reformers' Almanack* (1840–1) aimed specifically at Owenites, and later as a more general work, the *Poor Man's Companion*, to which Chartist lecturers referred for statistics in their debates with the Anti-Corn Law League.

To his contemporaries Hobson became best known as the printer, publisher and sometimes editor of the *Northern Star*. O'Connor's dealings with the provincial press had made him realise that a national stamped newspaper was needed to unite the myriad of separate working-class groups behind a single objective. The latter he was to find in the Charter; the former was to become the *Northern Star*. O'Connor first suggested the idea to Hobson at an Anti-Poor Law rally in May 1837. The idea slowly took root, replacing Hobson's plan for a more modest, unstamped paper, and emerged six months later with O'Connor as proprietor, Hobson as printer and publisher, and the Revd William Hill as editor. Production problems abounded, including financial and time constraints which combined to limit the first number to 3000 copies, but enough shares were sold to finance the venture, sureties were obtained, and the *Northern Star and Leeds General Advertiser* rapidly established itself as Britain's most widely circulated provincial paper. Hobson printed and published the *Star* from 18 November 1837 until it was transferred to London in November 1844, and he became editor when O'Connor fired Hill in July 1843. Hobson's office was an important centre of communications for the Chartists, allowing regional organisations to overcome the barriers represented by the Corresponding Societies Act of 1799 and drawing the movement together through the many local agents who handled the *Star*.

Hobson and his clerk, John Ardill, were chiefly responsible for establishing this network of over a hundred agents around the country: it contributed in no small degree to the unprecedented success of the paper. Weekly circulation reached a peak at about 36,000 in 1839, and Hobson once again became active in local Chartism. He took part in various demonstrations which showed the readiness of the workers of Leeds for the vote, peaceful public protest and local political participation. Hobson led the Chartists into a number of public meetings, particularly those of the Leeds Parliamentary Representation Association and its successor, the Complete Suffrage Association. These intrusions followed a set pattern: the Chartists would enter the meeting place en masse, call for their own candidate (invariably Hobson) to take the chair, move resolutions supporting the Charter, and energetically denounce leading Whigs.

Hobson was equally prominent in local political campaigns, a strategy of participation at the municipal level which the Leeds Chartists attempted unsuccessfully to implement on a national basis. In December 1841 Hobson and Ardill were elected to the Board of Improvement Commissioners as part of a Chartist list, and in the following March both were elected to the first Chartist Board of Churchwardens. When the Improvement Commission was dismantled in August 1842, the Leeds Chartists turned their attention to the Town Council, and in November 1843 Hobson was elected councillor for Holbeck ward, carried by a combination of Chartist and Tory voters. He and another Chartist councillor,

John Jackson, raised issues such as parliamentary reform, freedom of speech and fiscal retrenchment at Council meetings, defending working-class interests whenever possible but with little influence upon municipal policies.

Hobson's experience in Leeds politics proved valuable when the town of Huddersfield faced the task of reforming the separate committees responsible for administering public services. At a public hearing on 19 July 1844 he suggested replacing these individual bodies with a single Board of Improvement Commissioners, and was appointed to a public committee charged with applying to Parliament for the necessary legislation. An Improvement Bill was drafted, and when it became law four years later Hobson was appointed Clerk to the Board of Works.

This work on the Improvement Bill was a prelude to Hobson's permanent return to Huddersfield in 1845, but his focus had already been narrowing from national issues to local concerns for some time. He had nominally edited the *Star* since July 1843, but he increasingly allowed G. J. Harney, his sub-editor, a free hand to run the paper, devoting his own energies to putting together a weekly column of extracts from *Punch* and answering critics who accused him of a slavish devotion to O'Connor. After O'Connor moved the *Star* to London, Hobson used a variety of pretexts to remain in the West Riding, and when in the metropolis spent his time attending the numerous meetings associated with the slow demise of the Owenite community in Hampshire.

Hobson left the *Star* in October 1845, turning away from national issues. He concentrated on building up the newsagency and bookshop he had purchased in Huddersfield in 1842. His partner in this enterprise was Benjamin Brown, a local printer who was to play an important role at the outset of this second stage of Hobson's career. Brown was a member of the local executive of the National Charter Association and an outspoken critic of the Chartist Land Scheme. When O'Connor rejected a land colonisation plan drafted by Hobson for the National Association of United Trades – a plan which Hobson argued would enable the Chartists to apply for protection under Friendly Society legislation – Hobson joined Brown in openly criticising O'Connor. Hobson's retreat was complete by 1847 when he denounced O'Connor in a series of articles for the *Manchester Examiner* (which he reprinted as *The Land Scheme of Feargus O'Connor*), earning a bitter rebuke from O'Connor in the pages of the *Star*.

In 1846 Hobson again entered the agitation for factory reform, this time in an extended argument with T. P. Crosland, a local factory owner. Crosland and Hobson debated at a rally in support of the Short Time Movement, when Crosland argued that Parliament had no right to interfere in the natural compact between master and man. Hobson replied that the relationship between employer and employee in the factory was an unnatural one, unlike that existing in a small workshop between masters and journeymen, and that without legislative protection factory workers were at the mercy of their employers. The argument spilled over into a series of broadsides and letters, with Hobson warning Crosland not to victimise those among his employees who supported factory reform. This particular disagreement ended amicably, for in 1855 Crosland hired Hobson to edit the *Huddersfield Chronicle* and allowed him to use it as a vehicle for his Oastlerite Toryism.

After the quarrels with O'Connor and Crosland, Hobson concentrated on his role as a municipal politician. He served two terms as a member of the Board of Highway Surveyors before becoming Clerk to the Board of Works in 1848. Here he was responsible for the construction of a new cemetery and the conversion of a warehouse into a model lodging house, the first use of the Labouring Classes Lodging Houses Act of 1851. Acrimony again characterised Hobson's working relationships, however, and he resigned amid charges of corruption and favouritism.

For a year he lived in semi-retirement on a small farm on the outskirts of Huddersfield, but in April 1855 he was asked to edit the *Huddersfield Chronicle* by his old antagonist T. P. Crosland. Hobson accepted, and for the next sixteen years he pursued a vigorous policy of supporting local Tories and warning his readers against the Whigs. In 1860 he became secretary to the Huddersfield Tenant Rights Association, formed when a proposed alteration of the leases on the Ramsden estates threatened to divest tenants of the right to claim compensation for improvements made to their holdings. Hobson used the *Chronicle* to support the lessees' cause and linked Ramsden's proposals with a Whig conspiracy to impoverish the working man. Ramsden capitulated after seven years of arguments, and Hobson described the tenants' victory as a victory for workers everywhere. He also found time to serve as an Improvement Commissioner and a Poor Law Guardian before rejoining Benjamin Brown on a new project, the *Huddersfield Weekly News*.

At the beginning of 1871 the *Chronicle* became a daily paper, a change Hobson did not welcome. When Brown invited him to join the *Weekly News* Hobson accepted, viewing the opportunity as a chance to continue serving those who could not afford the time or money necessary for a daily paper. The *Weekly News* was owned by Brown and N. Learoyd, a lawyer who had worked with Hobson while the latter had been Clerk to the Board of Works, and who was to write a detailed eulogy when Hobson died. Hobson for his part continued to mix public issues with private grievances, engaging and enraging his political opponents, particularly the conductors of the Whig *Examiner*, in one argument after another; and fighting for the erection of a memorial to the younger Peel.

The Peel memorial was one of Hobson's last campaigns, a fitting conclusion to the life of one so precariously balanced between the forces of Toryism and the unified working class of the future. Hobson died on 8 May 1876 at Huddersfield, a sixty-five-year-old bachelor. He left effects valued at less than £200. Never an entirely consistent Chartist or Owenite, he generally remained true to the moral outlook of his Oastlerite Tory roots. He always advocated broadening the franchise and usually linked it with the need for the secret ballot. He frequently spoke of the need for working-class institutions, from Halls of Science to modest meeting-rooms, to enable workers to gather unhindered. As a municipal reformer he appealed for the construction of town halls to give workers a single regular meeting place, which he believed would encourage them to stop wasting their energies in an illusive search for national solutions to what he perceived as local problems. This belief was characteristic of the second stage of his career, after he had turned away from what he perceived as the failure of the Owenite communal and Chartist mass political programmes. As a speaker, organiser, writer and publisher Hobson had contributed to what can only be called a radical culture, a system of norms and expectations which used conventional symbols and accepted literary and journalistic forms to teach the workers their rights and to inform them of the means by which a just society would be created. There were a number of contradictions in Hobson's simultaneous advocacy of Chartism and Owenism, but he was by no means alone in this; and the same was true of his Tory radical sympathies. What Hobson was concerned with was equality and justice, and it was these aims that allowed him to resolve the ambiguities and the apparent conflicts in his intellectual position.

Writings and Editorial Works: Most of the works Hobson published are included in *Bibliography of the Chartist Movement, 1837–1976*, ed. J. F. C. Harrison and Dorothy Thompson (Hassocks, Sussex, 1978), and in the extensive bibliography to J. F. C. Harrison, *Robert Owen and the Owenites in Britain and America: the quest for the New Moral World* (1969). Hobson's two major works are his pamphlets *Socialism as it is!!!* (Leeds, 1838) and the *Land Scheme of Feargus O'Connor* (Manchester, 1848). He also edited and published *The Social Reformers' Almanack* (Leeds, 1840 and 1841), the *Poor Man's Companion* (Leeds, 1842) and the *Poor Man's Companion and Political Almanack* (Leeds, 1843). He was best known for – and is best preserved in – the newspapers he printed, published and/or edited. These were the *Voice of the West Riding* (1833–4), the *Argus and 'Demagogue'* (1834), the *New Moral World* (1834–45; printed by Hobson, 1839–41), the *Northern Star* (1837–54;

printed by Hobson, 1837–44), the *Huddersfield Chronicle* (1855–71), and the *Huddersfield Weekly News* (1871–6). For details of most of these publications, see *The Warwick Guide to British Labour Periodicals: a check list*, compiled by R. Harrison, G. B. Woolven and R. Duncan (Hassocks, Sussex, 1977). Broadsides, posters and handbills from Hobson's various presses are to be found in the Goldsmiths' Library, London Univ.; Kirklees Library, Huddersfield; and Tolson Memorial Museum, Huddersfield.

Sources: (1) MS: Limited to a letter from William Cobbett to Hobson, 24 Aug 1833, in the Tolson Memorial Museum, Huddersfield. (2) Other: *PMG*, 5 Nov 1831 and 10 Dec 1831; *Leeds Mercury* (later the *Yorkshire Post*), 1833–71; *Leeds Times*, 1835–43; *Fleet Papers*, 30 Jan 1841 and 13 Jan 1844; *Huddersfield Chronicle*, 8 Apr 1854; W. R. Croft, *The History of the Factory Movement, or, Oastler and his Times* (Huddersfield, 1888); D. F. E. Sykes, *The History of Huddersfield and its Vicinity* (Huddersfield, 1898); C. Driver, *Tory Radical: the life of Richard Oastler* (1946; repr. NY, 1970); J. F. C. Harrison, 'Chartism in Leeds', in *Chartist Studies*, ed. A. Briggs (1959) 65–98; J. T. Ward, *The Factory Movement 1830–1855* (1962); M. Brook, 'Lawrence Pitkethly, Dr. Smyles and Canadian Revolutionaries in the United States, 1842', *Ontario History 57* (1965) 79–84 [*Note*. There are variations in the spelling of Pitkethly's name, the most frequent form being 'Pitkeithly', but 'Pitkethly' is the form found in signed contributions of his to the *Northern Star* and in the official index to wills at Somerset House]; J. H. Wiener, *The War of the Unstamped: the movement to repeal the British newspaper tax* (Ithaca, NY, 1969); A. M. Hadfield, *The Chartist Land Company* (Newton Abbot, Devon, 1970); P. Hollis, *The Pauper Press: a study in working-class radicalism of the 1830s* (1970); A. Booth, 'A Radical Ranker', *Co-op. Rev.*, Nov 1971, 2; E. Royle, *Victorian Infidels: the origins of the British Secularist Movement 1791–1866* (Manchester, 1974); A. Chadderton, 'Joshua Hobson, A Huddersfield Radical Leader', *Saddleworth Historical Soc. Bull.*, Summer, Autumn, Winter 1975, 25–9, 49–52, 60–4 respectively; S. Chadwick, *'A Bold and Faithful Journalist': Joshua Hobson 1810–1876* (Huddersfield, 1976); J. Epstein, 'Feargus O'Connor and the "Northern Star"', *Int. Rev. Social Hist. 21* (1976) 51–97; J. Saville, 'Robert Owen on the Family and the Marriage System of the Old Immoral World', *Rebels and their Causes: essays in honour of A. L. Morton*, ed. M. Cornforth (1978) 107–21; D. Fraser, 'Politics and Society in the Nineteenth Century', in *A History of Modern Leeds*, ed. D. Fraser (Manchester, 1980) 270–300; E. Yeo, 'Culture and Constraint in Working-class Movements, 1830–1855', in *Popular Culture and Class Conflict 1590–1914: explorations in the history of labour and leisure*, ed. E. and S. Yeo (Brighton, 1981) 155–86; S. Cordery, 'Voice of the West Riding: Joshua Hobson in Huddersfield and Leeds, 1831–1845' (York MA, 1984). OBIT. *The Late Mr. Joshua Hobson, with a Tribute to his Memory by N. Learoyd* (Huddersfield, 1876), repr. from the *Huddersfield Weekly News*, 13 and 20 May 1876; *Huddersfield Chronicle*, 13 May 1876; *Huddersfield Examiner*, 13 May 1876. NOTE. The editors wish to acknowledge helpful comments from Dr Edward Royle, York Univ.

SIMON CORDERY

See also: †John Francis BRAY; †John CLEAVE; †Abel HEYWOOD; †Robert OWEN; †Henry VINCENT.

IRVING, David Daniel (Dan) (1854–1924)
SDF ORGANISER AND LABOUR MP

Dan Irving was born in Birmingham on 31 October 1854, the son of Samuel Irving, a commercial traveller, and his wife Susannah. He was educated at Dawson's National School, Birmingham, and at thirteen went to sea. After seven years as a merchant seaman he settled in Bristol in 1875. At first he worked for about a year as a warehouseman before obtaining a post with the Midland Railway Company. He rose to the position of foreman shunter. In politics he was a radical Liberal, in religion a Baptist. Though he came into contact with Socialists during the late 1880s, he still advocated thrift and temperance as the best means of abolishing poverty and regarded the Liberal Party as the only vehicle of political progress. An able organiser, he was chairman of a branch of the Liberal Operatives' Association which numbered 2000 members.

A railway accident in which he lost a leg helped to change his views. His employers found him another job but reduced his wage by eight shillings a week [*Labour Annual* (1896) 204]. This practical lesson, as he saw it, in the workings of the capitalist system also led to disillusionment with his Church. He sampled other sects until at a Sunday-morning discussion class he came into contact with Socialist workmen who tried to win him over to their beliefs. According to his own account, his first Socialist meeting was a lecture by Edward Carpenter on 'Justice, not Charity' which so enraged him that he decided to study the subject in order to repudiate it. Gradually, however, he was converted:

and finally found – Socialism! Socialism, which to me means more than economics, or ethics, which stands for the science and philosophy of life. From that day . . . I have never wavered in my allegiance to its principles, doubted its truth, or feared for its ultimate triumph as the guiding principle on which the Commonweal will yet be founded [*Justice*, 30 Dec 1911].

At about the same time the working class was becoming better organised. In Bristol, the centre of a vigorous labour movement, a gas workers' union was formed. Irving became its secretary (and he remained a member of the union, which was later incorporated into the National Union of General Labourers, until his death). He also took an active part in helping the local miners' agent in organising that district of the MFGB and was involved in the formation of the Bristol branch of the General Railway Workers' Union. In 1890, as a member of the Bristol Socialist Society, he was elected chairman of its workers' organising committee, which sought to bring workers, particularly the unskilled and women, into trade unions. He was considered as the Socialist candidate for the Bristol East by-election held in May 1890, but eventually Havelock Wilson was nominated.

In 1892 Irving and his family, together with Enid Stacy, who was also active in the Bristol labour movement, joined the Starnthwaite home colony in Westmorland [Hardy (1979) 114]. The Unitarian minister Herbert V. Mills had projected and financed the community. However, by the spring of 1893 trouble had developed to such an extent that Irving wrote a letter to the *Clarion* complaining about Mills's 'autocratic spirit' and the way the colony was conducted as 'an outdoor workhouse' [*Clarion*, 1 Apr 1893, quoted Hardy (1979) 114]. Subsequently, amid bitter recriminations, Mills expelled Irving and Stacy. The affair also brought to an end Irving's friendship with Katharine Conway, who, though previously regarding herself as Irving's 'spirit wife', sided with Mills [Thompson (1971) Ch. 3]. To support himself Irving turned to itinerant lecturing and in this way seems to have come to the notice of the Burnley branch of the SDF which appointed him as its full-time secretary. He held the post for twenty-four years, until 1918. Burnley was the base from where he helped to build a strong local organisation as well as becoming a leading figure in the SDF.

In January 1898 Irving was elected to the Burnley School Board. He issued an advanced programme, which included raising the school-leaving age to sixteen, and to general surprise he polled more votes than any other candidate. He had a deeply held and abiding conviction that education was a vitally important means of social progress. It was the subject of many of his lectures and he attended the opening of Ruskin College in 1899. As a member of the

School Board he argued that the whole community benefited if children were better educated and therefore the community should pay to compensate families who kept their children at school (as a textile town, Burnley had many children working in factories as 'half-timers'). The physical well-being of schoolchildren was also important: school meals, medical inspection and open-air schools were all causes that he pioneered in Burnley.

In 1903 school boards were disbanded, but by then Irving held other public offices from which to put his views. In 1899 he was elected as a borough auditor. From 1901 to 1904 and from 1907 to 1910 he was a member of the Burnley Board of Guardians. Attempts were made to stifle his criticisms of the way the workhouse was managed, and on one occasion the police were called in to eject him from the workhouse, where he was persisting in demands for information. Eventually the operation of the tramp ward was reformed and inmates were provided with a better diet – improvements which Irving claimed had resulted at least in part through his agitation.

His major local platform was the Town Council. After a number of unsuccessful attempts to gain election he was returned in November 1902 for Gannow ward. His election bill described him as 'the children's friend & workers' champion' and pledged that he would work for improved sanitary conditions, the equal treatment of corporation workers, the provision of a free library and an extension of the tramway system. Irving was a fervent advocate of municipal Socialism, which he believed could transform the worker's life. His most substantial piece of writing was a pamphlet in which he argued that local authorities should make themselves responsible for the provision of a wide range of goods and services. He regarded housing as the most important responsibility of a town council, after which he discussed how medical treatment might be provided municipally. Among the other things he advocated were municipal lodgings and a theatre, the supply of milk, bread and coal and the management of public houses by local authorities. Irving emphasised not only that a council should be comprehensive in its functions but also the political consequences of such a system:

> there is no limit, except that of the necessities and enjoyments of human life, to the avenues whereby the citizen in his corporate capacity may not minister to his own well-being. He may become his own banker, his own holiday-provider, may order arrangements either for his wedding or his funeral, far better than all these things are at present provided by so-called private 'enterprise'. .... A right conception of corporate life will make you understand that the Council is but your corporate self – the expression of your corporate *being*. .... A realisation of this truth would at once revolutionise the whole condition of life in all our large centres of population [Irving [1906?] 15].

Apparently the communitarian ideals that had taken Irving to Starnthwaite later found expression in his municipal work.

He was a member of the Town Council until November 1922, with the exception of the year 1905–6. Education was his principal interest but he was also active on the tramways, health and maternity committees, as well as sitting at various times on other committees and sub-committees. He was the Council's representative on other bodies and became widely known in the Burnley area as an advocate of reform.

In addition to his local government activities he was constantly involved in the work of the SDF, and was a member of its executive committee from 1897 to 1915. His powerful voice addressed innumerable meetings and he organised lecture tours for other Socialists. He became an experienced campaigner at elections, acquiring a detailed knowledge of electoral law and procedures. He was first a parliamentary candidate at the general election of 1906, when he unsuccessfully contested the Accrington division of Lancashire. In April 1908 he stood on behalf of the SDF in the Manchester North-West by-election solely as a propagandist exercise and polled only 276 votes [Morris (1982) 236]. At Rochdale he was bottom of the poll in both the general elections of 1910. In Burnley he worked for the election of H. M. Hyndman, who unsuccessfully contested the constituency in the general elections of 1895, 1906 and January and December 1910.

On the whole Irving's views were close to those of Hyndman, although, in part due to the nature of Burnley politics, he was less sectarian than some of the other SDF leaders. The Burnley branch of the SDF had been established in 1891 and by 1894 had a paying membership of 900. This growth was associated with various strikes in the local textile and coal-mining industries. A number of trade union officials were also members of the SDF, with the result that the political and industrial movements developed close ties. In particular, the Textile Trades Union helped to fund the local SDF branch. Irving, who had already been involved in Bristol trade unionism, became a firm advocate of the need for Socialists to work with the unions. As he told the SDF annual conference in 1897, their aim should be not to 'capture the trade unions in any offensive sense, but to capture the intelligence of their members, so as to cause them to see the limitations of their own movement'. He was also convinced of the benefits to be gained from co-operation with Socialists who were not members of the SDF. He had close connections with the Clarion movement and spoke as a Clarion vanner in 1894–5. With the ILP relations were more complicated because of the existence for a few years of an ILP branch in Burnley. However, the formation of the Burnley Labour Representation Committee led to practical co-operation between 1905 and 1909 and good relations existed with ILP branches elsewhere in Lancashire, notably in Nelson.

Irving regretted the decision taken by the SDF conference of 1901 to withdraw from the Labour Representation Committee. With the support of his Burnley colleagues he campaigned for reaffiliation to the Labour Party and unsuccessfully proposed several motions to this effect at SDF conferences. His work at the local level and his fervent belief in the possibilities of municipal Socialism made him a persistent critic of the centralised organisation of the SDF. Although he seems to have avoided quarrelling with Hyndman, he tried to reduce the influence of the London leadership. In 1904, for example, he called for the EC to hold quarterly meetings in different towns, and in the same year he wrote that 'what is wanted to make our organisation grow in numbers and in power, is more of a spirit of loyalty to the decisions of the majority' [*Justice*, 15 Oct 1904]. The Burnley delegation to the 1905 SDF conference proposed a resolution that a joint conference be held with the ILP to discuss common action. When the EC tried to avoid a vote, Irving demanded that the delegates should decide, and the motion was narrowly defeated. A few years later he developed his position more fully in a letter replying to Harry Quelch's arguments against affiliation to the Labour Party. Opposing what he regarded as an isolationist posture, Irving wrote:

It is largely because we abandon this policy of isolation in various localities where we enter into active political work that we hold as favourable a position as we do; were we to carry out logically our national policy locally, I am of opinion that we would suffer severely as an organisation and lose much of the influence with the trade unions that we undoubtedly possess, and that to the detriment of Socialism [ibid., 7 Apr 1908].

Similarly, he preferred to speak of the 'class struggle' rather than of 'class war', a term which was favoured by many SDF activists but which he regarded as too dogmatic.

With the prospect of realignment of the Left he modified his approach to the Labour Party and worked for the formation of a new Socialist body made up of disaffected ILP branches, Clarion Clubs and his own party. At the unity conference held in September 1911 he was elected to the provisional EC and in the following May at the first conference of the British Socialist Party he retained his seat on the executive. Within a short time, however, the question of affiliation with the Labour Party had again arisen, and with the outbreak of war in 1914 the new party suffered deeper divisions. The differences between the 'internatio-nalists' and the 'militarists' within the BSP had surfaced in December 1912 when a majority of the EC had passed an anti-militarist resolution. A temporary compromise was reached whereby the question was referred to the party conference in May 1913. Irving, who was the conference chairman, helped to avoid a split when the matter was passed over without a vote being taken. Such tactics were not possible once the war started. Though Irving had been attending a meeting of the International Socialist Bureau on the eve of declaration of war, like Hyndman he adopted a vigorously anti-German position. This led to conflict within the ranks of the BSP. On one occasion, after John Maclean, a BSP member, had been convicted of making statements prejudicial to recruiting, Irving wrote to the press dissociating himself from the 'scandalous imputation' of Maclean's remarks [*Manchester Guardian*, 13 Nov 1915, quoted Kendall (1969) 98].

At the Salford conference of 1916 the BSP split. When Albert Inkpin announced that the proceedings would take place behind closed doors, Irving unsuccessfully tried to speak against the decision. The discontented delegates – including many of the 'old guard' – then withdrew and subsequently issued a statement. This declared that Socialism would not come 'if we deliberately sever ourselves from the mass of our countrymen while the United Kingdom, our Colonies, and our Allies, are engaged in a life and death struggle against German militarism and German atrocities' [quoted Lee and Archbold (1935) 238n.]. Irving signed this statement and joined like-minded colleagues in a new body, the National Socialist Party (which at its third annual conference reverted to the old title, the Social Democratic Federation). He was active in encouraging men in the Burnley area to enlist and gave his full support to the war effort.

By the end of the war he had arrived at a political position close to that of the mainstream of the Labour Party, to which the NSP was affiliated. With Hyndman no longer a candidate for Burnley, Irving's reputation was such that the local labour movement adopted him to contest the general election of December 1918. He polled 15,217 votes as against 12,289 for the Coalition Conservative candidate and 8,825 for the Liberal. At the general elections of 1922 and 1923 he retained the seat with similar majorities. Irving made relatively little impression during his five years in the Commons. After over forty years of Socialist agitation he found he had to adjust to the atmosphere of Parliament, as on an occasion when the Speaker called on him to withdraw the charge that another MP had spoken a 'damned lie'. He was a Labour spokesman on fisheries and maintained his interest in education – which he referred to in one debate as 'the finest investment in human happiness' [*Hansard*, 12 Apr 1921, col. 1004]. His last speech was an exposition of Socialism which filled ten columns of *Hansard* with the sort of arguments and appeals that he had been making for most of his life. When he had finished speaking Lloyd George commented, 'There is no man in this House who is better entitled to speak Socialism than he. For 40 years he has put up a very consistent, gallant and courageous fight for the principles he has expounded now' [ibid., 16 July 1923, col. 1941].

In later years Irving was a somewhat venerable figure. His shock of hair was completely white, as was his full beard, while rimless glasses gave him a studious appearance. He had a tendency to reminisce about his career and on occasion reminded the House of Commons that he spoke as a former member of the Burnley School Board. Some within the labour movement regarded him as a narrow plodder – 'What a dull dog Irving is', commented Bruce Glasier in 1914 [Thompson (1971) 203] – but others admired his persistent efforts as an organiser and speaker. To many he was known as 'Honest Dan'; at the numerous elections he contested, the simple slogan of his supporters was 'Dan's the Man'. In north-east Lancashire his political work received wide acknowledgement, and it was in this area that he did most to assist the emergence of Labour as an independent movement.

In November 1922 Irving was disappointed to lose his place on the Town Council, but 'in recognition of his long and valuable services to the town of Burnley' the honorary Freedom of the Borough was conferred on him on 2 January 1924. On 25 January he suffered a fatal heart attack at his home in London. He was buried in Burnley Cemetery on Saturday 2 February. During the funeral factories were closed and business suspended. The route to the cemetery was lined by thousands of spectators, who saw the mayor and members of the Town Council, magistrates' bench and socialist and labour bodies follow the funeral procession, which was headed by the municipal band. A service conducted by the Revd Canon Winfield concluded with the singing of 'The Red Flag'. Irving was survived by his wife – he had married Clara Brock, the daughter of a Bristol house decorator, in 1879 – and two daughters. He left effects to the value of £471. The subsequent by-election, held on 28 February, enabled Arthur Henderson to resume his parliamentary career.

Writings: 'Some Thoughts on the Labour Movement', *Justice*, 28 Jan 1893; 'Some of our Foes', *Burnley Socialist*, 1 June 1894; 'The Textile Operatives and Child Labour', *Justice*, 20 Nov 1897; 'Twelve Months' Work on a School Board', ibid., 4 Mar 1899; 'Child Labour and Education', *Social Democrat 3* (Sep 1899) 271–4; 'Dan Irving and his Work: as borough auditor and School Board member', *Justice*, 19 May 1900; 'The Physical Basis of Education', *Social Democrat 4* (June 1900) 180–4; 'Socialism and the Labour Party', *New Age*, 18 Dec 1902; *The Municipality, from a Worker's Point of View*, with an Introduction by the Countess of Warwick [1906?] 16 pp.; 'Tragedy of Toil', *Justice*, 7 Jan 1911; 'Socialism Triumphant!' ibid., 30 Dec 1911; 'The Cotton War', ibid., 6 Jan 1912; 'End of the Cotton Lock-Out: the net result'. ibid., 27 Jan 1912; 'Our Party, our Aims, and our Methods', ibid., 4 May 1912; 'National Education: the BSP point of view', ibid., 25 May 1912; 'Socialism: the hope of the workers', ibid., 15 June 1912; 'The BSP Conference and after', ibid., 31 May 1913; 'Lessons of the recent Municipal Elections', ibid., 6 Dec 1913; 'There is no Wealth but Life', ibid., 30 July 1914; *The Failure of Capitalism* (1923) 8 pp. [although listed in BLPES author catalogue (vol. *3* of the *London Bibliography*) this pamphlet is now missing].

Sources: (1) MS: LRC letterbook, LP Library; Burnley School Board minutes, Burnley CL; Burnley and District Trades and Labour Council Archive DDX 1274 10/5, Lancashire CRO. (2) Other: County Borough of Burnley, *Minutes of the Proceedings of the Town Council and the Various Committees* (Burnley, 1889–1922); SDF, *Annual Conference Reports*; *Labour Annual* (1896); 'Our Representatives. I. – Dan Irving', *Social Democrat 3* (Jan 1899) 3–7; H. M. Hyndman, *Further Reminiscences* (1912); *Hansard*, 1919–23; M. Beer, *A History of British Socialism* (1921); *Dod* (1923); *Labour Who's Who* (1924); *WWW* (1916–28); S. Bryher, *An Account of the Labour and Socialist Movement in Bristol* (Bristol, 1929); H. W. Lee and E. Archbold, *Social-Democracy in Britain* (1935); W. Bennett, *The History of Burnley from 1850* (Burnley, 1951); C. Tsuzuki, *H. M. Hyndman and British Socialism* (1961); B. Simon, *Education and the Labour Movement 1870–1920* (1965); W. Kendall, *The Revolutionary Movement in Britain 1900–21* (1969); P. F. Clarke, *Lancashire and the New Liberalism* (Cambridge, 1971); L. Thompson, *The Enthusiasts: a biography of John and Katharine Bruce Glasier* (1971); D. Hardy, *Alternative Communities in Nineteenth Century England* (1979); S. Pierson, *British Socialists: the journey from fantasy to politics* (1979); D. Morris, 'Labour or Socialism?: opposition and dissent within the ILP 1906–14 with special reference to the Lancashire Division' (Manchester PhD, 1982); D. Howell, *British Workers and the Independent Labour Party 1888–1906* (Manchester, 1983). Biographical information: the late T. A. K. Elliott, CMG. OBIT. *Burnley News* and *Express and Advertiser*

[Burnley], 26 Jan 1924; *Times*, 4 Feb 1924. NOTE. The editors wish to acknowledge an earlier draft from Bob Whitfield, Bristol.

LAURENCE JACOBS
DAVID E. MARTIN

See also: Henry (Harry) QUELCH.

JENKINS, Arthur (1882–1946)
MINERS' LEADER AND LABOUR MP

Arthur Jenkins was born on 3 February 1882 at Varteg, near Pontypool in Monmouthshire, the son of John Jenkins, a coal-miner and his wife, Eliza (née Perry). Arthur attended the Varteg elementary school until the age of twelve, when he started work at Viponds' Colliery. Later he worked at two other local mines, Tirpentwys and Blaenserchan. At Blaenserchan he worked as a partner, driving headings, with the elder brother of Will Coldrick, later a Labour and Co-op. MP for Bristol North from 1945 to 1959, who also, briefly, worked alongside Arthur Jenkins as a collier's assistant.

In 1908 Jenkins won a scholarship from the Eastern Valley district of the South Wales Miners' Federation tenable at Ruskin College, Oxford. He was one of the first miners from South Wales to gain such an award and the importance of this experience he was to recall many years later on the occasion of his formal adoption as the Labour candidate to fight the Pontypool constituency in the 1935 general election:

> The miners gave me the first £30 to go to Ruskin College and I will be forever indebted to them. They made it possible for me to take a wider vision of affairs. There I met with a zeal for the cause, men who had helped to build up the great Labour movement throughout the land [Pontypool *Free Press*, 1 Nov 1935].

While at Ruskin College, Arthur Jenkins took part in the famous students' strike of 1909, which led to the creation of the Central Labour College, to which he transferred on its opening in the summer of 1909. He seems to have associated at this time, with some of the most radical and advanced sections of the student body; in March 1910 he made a successful defence of the Marxist 'theory of value' in the Labour College students' debating society. One of his closest friends at Ruskin and the Labour College was Frank Hodges, later general secretary of the Miners' Federation of Great Britain and a Labour minister, but at that time a miner scholar from Monmouthshire Western Valleys district. In the summer of 1910, together with Hodges, Arthur Jenkins set out on a visit to Paris which may have lasted some nine months, and was to have a profound influence on him. Hodges only stayed three months but in his autobiography he writes lyrically of this trip when two impecunious miners from South Wales sampled the delights of the French capital. They explored the city in the mornings, learnt French in the afternoons and met with members of the French Left, including Dr Paul Lafargue and his wife Laura, the daughter of Karl Marx, in the evenings [Hodges [1924?] Ch. 5]. Before returning to South Wales, Arthur Jenkins also visited the Belgian coalfields. His visit to the Continent established a great interest in France which he sustained until his death.

Jenkins returned to South Wales just as it was entering an unprecedented phase of rank-and-file militancy. He himself was certainly influenced by the semi-syndicalist ideas which were current at this time but it was the organisational side of the movement to which he devoted his efforts, and he became a man known for his conciliatory and mild-mannered attitudes. Soon after he returned to the Eastern Valley of Monmouthshire he became secretary of the Pontypool Trades and Labour Council; and he remained in this position until the end of the First World War. It was an office which involved him constantly in local disputes. He fought many ejectment orders for example, and acquired a very solid reputation as a dedicated activist for the basic rights of working people. He was particularly well known as an acknowledged expert on housing problems and the Rent Acts.

In 1918 Arthur Jenkins was elected as deputy miners' agent for the Eastern Valley, topping the first ballot and winning outright on the second. At that time the miners' agent for Pontypool was James Winstone and, upon his death in 1921, Jenkins was returned unopposed as Winstone's successor. His reputation was of an assiduous, well-briefed and thoroughly reliable union official. According to an interview with Will Coldrick (24 Sep 1973), who took over as deputy miners' agent, Arthur Jenkins was a rather poor speaker in his younger days, but much improved after his election as secretary of the Pontypool Trades Council and later was widely regarded as a competent public speaker. In 1926 Jenkins had the mantle of martyr thrust upon him. Throughout the General Strike and during the bitter months of lock-out which followed for the miners, he had sought to avoid confrontations with the authorities, checking the bitterness of his members towards over-zealous police-men, unsympathetic Poor Law officials and strike-breakers. On Monday, 30 August 1926, he addressed a meeting in Pontnewynydd of several hundred men on the question of some fifteen blacklegs who were working at the Quarry Level Colliery, just outside Pontypool. The meeting decided to mount a mass picket of the mine. By the time the straggling column reached Quarry Level, a detachment of fifteen policemen under the command of Superin-tendent Spendlove had stationed themselves at the colliery. For some reason Spendlove. a man well known for his hostility towards organised labour, decided to lead out the strike-breakers through the milling throng of locked-out miners. Following some minor scuffling and stone-throwing, Spendlove ordered his men to charge the crowd, batons drawn. Arthur Jenkins described the scene to a reporter of the local newspaper immediately after the event:

> I jumped on to the buffer of a rail wagon – I could see from the buffer of the truck that the truncheons were being freely used, hitting wildly at any man with whom they came into contact. I saw one constable deliberately hit two men lying on the ground. I shouted in an effort to stop the police making this ferocious attack upon the men and there were some women in the crowd. My shouts however could not be heard, and the result was that the policemen, using their truncheons forced their way through the crowd striking the men sitting on the bank [Pontypool *Free Press*, 3 Sep 1926].

Following this incident Jenkins and Coldrick along with six others were charged with riotous assembly, Jenkins being accused by Spendlove of inciting the crowd to use violence against the blacklegs. The case was heard at the Monmouth assizes late in November 1926, before Mr Justice Swift, a judge well known for his hostility to any kind of radical, who, after giving out sentences of nine months' imprisonment to Arthur Jenkins and three months' to Coldrick, launched into a paean of praise for the police action. The harshness of the sentence on Jenkins aroused much opposition from the Labour and trade union movement. Thomas Richards, a Privy Councillor and the long-serving general secretary of the SWMF, sharply criticised the sentences at a meeting of the Monmouthshire County Council, of which Richards, Jenkins and Coldrick were all members. Jenkins was the victim, Richards claimed, of a vendetta by the Chief Constable of Monmouthshire, Victor Bosanquet, against a highly critical police authority, of which Jenkins was a member. The County Council honoured the absent members by placing flowers on the seat where Jenkins and Coldrick usually sat. Coldrick was released within weeks, but it took a longer campaign, including a deputation of leading Labour and trade union officials, among them George Lansbury, Walter Citrine and George Hicks, to Lord Birkenhead, at the India Office (who was acting for the Home Secretary as Joynson Hicks was ill at the time) to secure the release of Jenkins. Arthur Jenkins returned to Pontypool early in March 1927, to an enthusiastic reception from all sections of the community.

His spell in prison served to enhance Arthur Jenkins' reputation as a labour leader. In

1934 he was elected vice-president of the SWMF, and he worked closely with the then president, James Griffiths, a man close in political terms to Arthur Jenkins. They led the struggle against the 'Spencer' non-political union and later they were close colleagues in the House of Commons. Both men belonged to the centre Right of the Labour Party; they were bedrock trade unionists and staunch supporters of the link between the unions and the Labour Party. As secretary of the Pontypool Trades and Labour Council, Arthur Jenkins had been responsible for the foundation of the Pontypool Constitutency Labour Party in 1918. He became its first president, a post he only relinquished after being selected as its prospective parliamentary candidate in December 1932. His commitment to the Labour Party was illustrated by a strenuous campaign he fought against an attempt by some of the Blaenavon lodges of the miners' federation to disaffiliate from the Labour Party in the aftermath of the 1921 stoppage. Jenkins' own political career in public office began on the Abersychan Urban District Council, and in the immediate post-war period he was elected to Monmouthshire County Council. In 1927 he was made a county alderman, a dignity he cherished until his death. He was always referred to in Labour Party meetings as the 'Alderman' long after his arrival in Westminster.

Arthur Jenkins served as a member of the Royal Commission on Licensing which was appointed in 1929 and presented its report in 1931. But his selection as the Labour candidate for Pontypool was not without some controversy. The division had been represented since 1918 by Tom Griffiths MP, who was sponsored by the British Iron and Steel and Kindred Trades Association (BISAKTA), whose rules prevented the sponsorship being continued for their MPs beyond normal retirement age. At a meeting of the constituency party in December 1931, Griffiths announced that this rule would prevent him from contesting the constituency again. At the same meeting the general secretary of the steelmen, Arthur Pugh, argued that the constituency ought to maintain its links with his union through the selection of another BISAKTA-sponsored candidate. Tom Griffiths was the only steelworkers' candidate to survive the 1931 general election and there was, at the time, a growing hostility to the domination of the coalfield constituencies by SWMF nominees. Arthur Jenkins was not, at this time, an officially endorsed miners' candidate, and indeed he was not adopted by them until after his selection. Pressure from BISAKTA failed to prevent Jenkins' selection in December 1932, and he won overwhelmingly on the first ballot. His hold on the local party and his standing in the community countered any impression that he had been foisted on the constituency by the Fed.

Arthur Jenkins served on the national executive of the Labour Party from 1925 to 1929, from 1931 to 1933 and again from 1935 to 1937. He does not appear to have played a particularly prominent role in the various internal disputes of these years, and he was a loyal supporter, as was his local party, of the leadership on most matters. The one issue where Arthur Jenkins was to some extent at odds with the Labour leadership was on the question of rearmament. He believed that the First World War had been an absolute disaster, particularly for working people, and that everything should be done to avoid another European conflict. In his 1935 election address Jenkins laid great emphasis on the need to strengthen collective security through the League of Nations, and he denounced the National Government's rearmament programme, fearing that it would result in a 'suicidal' arms race, leading inevitably to war. When, in 1937, the national executive committee of the Labour Party and the Parliamentary Labour Party dropped their opposition to rearmament, Arthur Jenkins was at the forefront of those seeking to reverse the decision.

He served as a member of the Labour Party Commission of Enquiry into the Distressed Areas and worked with Hugh Dalton, George Dallas, Barbara Gould and George Hall during 1936 and 1937 to produce the report relating to South Wales. His interest in international affairs took him in 1936, along with Jim Griffiths, on a visit to Danzig, where they experienced Nazi terror and subversion at first hand. Nevertheless he was unhappy about the drift to war with Germany and in this regard he accurately reflected opinion in his constituency party. Fearful of the consequences of a prolonged conflict, he spoke in the Commons in December 1939 of the need for the Government to lay down clear peace aims as well as war aims, and the risk of repeating the blunders of the Versailles settlement, which he still believed was responsible for this second war. He also argued for the war against Fascism abroad to be joined by an assault on poverty and inequality at home, articulating a frequent complaint within his local party that the workers had been cheated at the end of the previous war. Indeed, the only time Arthur Jenkins encountered any difficulties with his local party was when some members felt that the PLP was not exacting strong enough pledges on welfare reform as the price of their involvement in the Churchill Coalition.

Arthur Jenkins was particularly sensitive to such criticism following his appointment as parliamentary private secretary to Clement Attlee some years before the latter entered the Coalition Government as Lord Privy Seal. Highly regarded by Attlee, Jenkins served as a loyal and hard-working lieutenant. He accompanied Attlee on visits to North America in 1941 and 1942. In March 1945 Arthur Jenkins was appointed as parliamentary secretary to the Ministry of Town and Country Planning and, following the formation of the 1945 Labour Government, he was appointed parliamentary secretary to the Ministry of Education, a post he was forced to relinquish in November of the same year due to ill health.

Although it was widely believed that, had he lived and enjoyed good health, Arthur Jenkins would have seen high office, he is chiefly remembered as a strenuous servant of his constituency. He gained the seat in 1935 with a majority of over 11,000 votes; his agent at this election was Tom Proctor, later Labour MP for Eccles from 1945 to 1964. In 1945 Jenkins boosted the majority over his Conservative opponent to nearly 20,000. He served on innumerable local boards and committees, and he was recalled by many local politicians and colleagues who knew him as being an almost perfect constituency member, whom they credited with bringing much needed new industries to the Eastern Valley and with fighting tenaciously for his area and constituents.

Arthur Jenkins died in St Thomas's Hospital, London on 25 April 1946 following a serious operation a few days earlier. At his side was his wife Hattie, the daughter of William Harris, a Blaenavon steelworks manager, whom he had married in 1911. She was a regular chapel attender who provided her husband with an important link with the middle-class and professional sections of the Eastern Valley community. Arthur Jenkins' funeral took place at St James's Parish Church, Pontypool, and he was buried in the churchyard at Trevethin, near Pontypool. His estate was valued at £1631. He left one son, Roy Harris Jenkins, later to be deputy leader of the Labour Party, Home Secretary, Chancellor of the Exchequer, President of the EEC Commission and a founder and first leader of the Social Democratic Party. He was elected to represent the party in Parliament at a by-election at Hillhead, Glasgow, in 1982 and held the seat at the general election of 1983.

Writings: Press articles mainly on local government and coal-mining subjects; (with others) *Report of the Labour Party's Commission of Enquiry into the Distressed Areas*, no. 3: *South Wales* (1937) 32 pp.

Sources: (1) MS: Minutes of executive and general committees of the Pontypool LP made available by Councillor P. P. Murphy, LP secretary, Pontypool. (2) Other: F. Hodges, *My Adventures as a Labour Leader* [1924?]; *Labour Who's Who* (1927); *Hansard*, 1935–45; *WWW* (1941–50); *Dod* (1946); R. Jenkins, *Mr Attlee: an interim biography* (1948); C. R. Attlee, *As it happened* (1954); W. W. Craik, *The Central Labour College 1909–29* (1964); J. Griffiths, *Pages from Memory* (1969); H. Francis and D. Smith, *The Fed: a history of the South Wales Miners in the twentieth century* (1980). Biographical information: Dr H. Francis, South Wales Miners' Library, Swansea. Personal information: The Rt Hon. Roy

H. Jenkins, MP, son; interviews with former councillors F. Gifford and W. G. Thomas of Cwmbran, Gwent, and interview of Will Coldrick by R. Lewis and D. Egan, 24 Sep 1973 [text in South Wales Miners' Library, Swansea]. OBIT. *Times* and *Western Mail*, 27 Apr 1946; *Western Mail*, 30 Apr 1946; *Free Press of Monmouthshire*, 3 May 1946. NOTE. The editors wish to acknowledge the help given by the editor and staff of the Pontypool *Free Press*.

RICHARD LEWIS

See also: *Frank HODGES; †James WINSTONE.

JOYNES, James Leigh (1853–93)
GEORGEITE, SHELLEYAN AND SOCIALIST

James Leigh Joynes was born on 29 May 1853 at Eton, where his father, the Revd James Leigh Joynes, was an assistant master for many years. The latter was Swinburne's tutor and Stewart Headlam's housemaster, and his son Herman was classics tutor to Conrad Noel. When Noel was rusticated for a year from Corpus Christi, Cambridge, for heavy drinking and rowdyism, Herman persuaded Chichester Theological College to accept him. This was in 1893, and Noel did not return to Cambridge.

J. L. Joynes' career at Eton and Cambridge is discussed below in the memoir by H. S. Salt. Joynes, following his father's example, went back to Eton as an assistant master in 1876 and in the early 1880s began to be actively involved in politics. Henry George was the first major influence, and then Joynes, who was much affected by imperialist policies in Egypt, Africa and Ireland, joined the young Socialist movement. The previous year (1882) he had visited Ireland in company with Henry George and had been arrested, an episode that was widely publicised in England. It led to his resignation from Eton, and the following summer (1883) he signed the manifesto of the Democratic Federation, *Socialism made Plain*; at about the same time he was elected to the new EC of the organisation, along with H. H. Champion, Andreas Scheu, James Macdonald and William Morris [Thompson (1955) 350]. Joynes was already a member of the Fellowship of the New Life, and in the same year also he assisted Champion to edit the *Christian Socialist*, the journal of the Land Reform Union. In February 1884 Joynes, with Jack Williams, Macdonald, Morris and Hyndman, went to Blackburn in Lancashire to campaign on behalf of the textile workers on strike.

He was active in the Socialist movement for only a few years, but he made a powerful impression on his contemporaries. His *Socialist Catechism* enjoyed a wide circulation and was a powerful influence on many. Conrad Noel included it as one of the reasons why he became a Socialist. Joynes began studying medicine in 1887, fell seriously ill in the summer of 1889 and never recovered. He died on 13 January 1893 at West Hoathly, Sussex, where he was buried quietly on 16 January. He left effects valued at £3160.

Attached to this brief entry are two notices of Joynes published in the *Social-Democrat 1*, no. 8 (Aug 1897). The first is by H. S. Salt, who married Joynes's sister Kate and whose own autobiography, *Seventy Years among Savages*, was published in 1921. The second is by the well-known SDF militant Harry Quelch.

H. S. Salt

[After some introductory remarks Salt continued] When about twelve years old, he [Joynes] was elected to one of the [Eton] Foundation Scholarships, and after several years as a 'Colleger', went on to King's College, Cambridge, in 1871. His health had been delicate in boyhood, and owing to this he had lived much at home and was little known to his schoolfellows, in whose games and amusements he seldom took part. He was shy, silent and retiring; yet I think it was in the long run an advantage to him *not* to have caught the facile Etonian manner, for the true strength of his character lay in quite different qualities. Certainly for myself, who, though nominally his schoolfellow at Eton, had not really known him till we met at King's, it was a surprise and profit to see one so genuine and unsophisticated, who had not the least respect for the humbug of 'appearances', whose abruptness and angularity were in marked contrast to the Etonian polish, and whose bluntness of speech was only less notable than the kindliness of his heart.

I think we were brought together by our common impatience of the petty routine and respectability then dominant at King's; a system well calculated to make rebels and freethinkers. Imagine a small college, small in numbers and small in tone, with a code of unwritten yet tyrannical observances which it was 'bad form' to neglect, and you will understand why the conjunction of Learning and Silliness, so often found among the academical, was in 'the full bloom of the imbecility' in the King's College of a quarter-century ago. An epigrammatical professor once summed up a fellow-academician as 'a damned fool with a taste for the classics'. King's was pre-eminently a classical college, and the imbecility bacillus was rampant within its walls.

Amidst this cultured circle the 'freshman' Joynes, characteristically indifferent to 'what people thought', proceeded to take his own course with imperturbable serenity. Our friendship was a mutual alliance against the Respectables, pursued with a youthful regardlessness of consequences which, looking back, I feel to have been highly beneficial. While reading very hard on our own lines, we were guilty of every species of 'bad form'. We did not row on the odoriferous Cam (rowing was regarded as a patriotic duty), but devoted our afternoons to long country walks and the study of natural history, in which we always gave preference to those woods and fields where it was stated that 'Trespassers will be Prosecuted'. We wrote heretical articles in the *Undergraduates' Journal*. I have before me the number for November 19, 1873, containing an article by Joynes on compulsory chapel, in which he inveighs against the ordinance of full, choral service, where the unfortunate 'man without an ear' is doomed, for two long hours, 'to sit, stand, and kneel in wearisome succession'. When it was our turn, as King's Scholars, to read the lessons in chapel, we irreverently docked and shortened Holy Writ to suit our private purposes. 'Here endeth the Lesson', we cried, when we had read, perhaps, half-a-dozen out of a score or two-score verses; and immediately the great organ would sound and the pompous ceremonial continue. (I think they secretly blessed us for *that* illegality.) As a protest against the exclusiveness of the Senior Fellows, a few old gentlemen who allowed none but themselves to cross the College Lawn, we let out a mole; and no greater consternation could have been caused by the pollution of the Holy of Holies than by the appearance one morning of a chain of earth-heaps on the hitherto flawless expanse. In this outrage we had as an abettor a fellow-undergraduate who is now headmaster of an important school, but I forbear to publish his name for fear of injuring his reputation. I may mention, however, that when, a few years ago, this reverend gentleman discovered one of his pupils reading Socialist pamphlets, he could think of no more weighty warning against such pestilent heresies than to tell the boy that the only two Socialists whom *he* had known had both 'come to a bad end', and he did not scruple to name them.

In 1875 Joynes took his degree in the Classical Tripos (he was seventh in the first class, next on the list to Gerald Balfour, the present Irish Secretary), but he did not obtain a Fellowship at his college, as the Respectables, who had the award of such honours, seized this opportunity of paying off old scores, and avenging the memory of the mole. A little later we were both assistant Masters at Eton, and here the same revolutionary process went on, though in a less open manner, for the Eton Master is a more decorous and responsible person than the Cambridge undergraduate, and the atmosphere of the place, intellectually, is about as depressing as that of a London fog. For several years Joynes was an exemplary tutor, diligently doing for his pupils, in accordance with what is euphemistically known as the Eton 'tutorial system', the work which they were too lazy to do for themselves, and writing or revising about thirty thousand Latin verses per annum. This is the way to win golden opinions (and, what is more valuable, a large income) at Eton; but unfortunately we were both under suspicion as radicals and freethinkers, also we had adopted vegetarianism, which was felt to be a dangerous and immoral practice, and then, again, we rode tricycles, which was thought to be almost as bad. (Everyone cycles at Eton now.) So gradually our friend's affairs were drifting towards a crisis – and it came.

What brought matters to a head was the visit paid to England and Ireland by Henry George in 1882. We had all read *Progress and Poverty* and Joynes had been greatly impressed by it; and when, in the summer holidays of that year, he met and travelled with George in Ireland, a friendship at once sprang up between them which had an important influence on his life. It is unnecessary to tell at length a story that has been often told. By a ridiculous blunder of the Irish Constabulary, under the infamous Coercion Acts, the two travellers were arrested and locked up as dangerous conspirators; and though they were quickly discharged when the magistrate discovered the error, the whole Press of the country rang with amused comments, including a parody, by J. K. Stephen, of Gray's 'Ode on a Distant Prospect of Eton College', evidently written up to the one line, 'To snatch a fearful Joy(nes)'. The incident, however, was a serious one. The Government had to apologise to Henry George as an American citizen; and a brilliant account of the *fiasco*, written by Joynes, was published in the *Times* [on 4 Sep 1882] and caused great scandal in Etonian circles, where publicity is regarded – not without good reason – as the thing of all things to be deprecated. Great, then, was the horror of the Eton authorities when, a few weeks later, an advertisement announced Joynes' forthcoming volume, *Adventures of a Tourist in Ireland*. In hot haste he was informed by the headmaster, Dr. Hornby, that he must choose between his mastership and his book. He, of course, chose the latter, and resigned his post at Eton at the end of 1882. Then and there terminated his academical career, and his career as Socialist began. It was the 'bad end' to which his old fellow collegian, the headmaster of ——, so tearfully and tastefully alluded.

Probably if an estimate of Joynes' character were written by one of his academical colleagues, and were compared with another written by one of his Socialist fellow-workers of a later period, the contrast would be absolute and complete. The reason is that the escape from Eton, to a man of his sympathies, was something more than a mere change of occupation; it was a veritable passing from death-in-life to life. Everyone used to notice the surprising improvement in his health, spirits, and appearance; due to the fact that in Socialism he had at last found work in which he thoroughly believed. I say Socialism, because his clear mind necessarily did not stop short at Henry George's measure of Land Nationalisation. If I remember rightly, it was an invitation received by him from Champion and Frost, who wished to entertain him at a complimentary dinner after his retirement from Eton, that first brought him into contact with Socialists. The S. D. F. had been instituted in 1881, and Joynes threw himself with ardour into the work, attended the committee meetings at Westminster, and was on terms of friendly association with Hyndman, Champion, Frost, Bax, Morris, Quelch, Carpenter, Scheu, Burns, Burrows, Williams, Foulger and others well known in the movement. He was co-editor and founder of the *Christian Socialist* and *Today*, which were started respectively in 1883 and 1884, and he was also a contributor to *Justice* and the *Commonweal*, and author of *The Socialist Catechism*, one of the most successful pamphlets that have been issued by the Socialist press. In short, there was very little S. D. F. work at that early period in which Joynes did not take a part.

Others, as I have said, are better able to describe this phase of his character; but I think I am right in saying that it was his honesty, candour, and fearlessness that made him a valuable propagandist. If a thing, however disagreeable, had to be done, he would get up and do it, and what he undertook to do was never forgotten or neglected. These are the strong, sincere, homely qualities that make themselves respected, perhaps more than any others, in revolutionary propaganda, where there is generally so much profession that does not harden into practice. Even among the people who most disliked Joynes' views, and were irritated by his tart manner of expressing himself, I never knew one who personally distrusted him. Sincerity was written in every line of his face, and heard in every syllable that he uttered.

Nor was it to Socialism only that he gave his support, for there was scarcely an advanced cause to which he did not in some measure contribute. In addition to *Justice* and the *Commonweal*, he wrote at different times in a number of reform journals, besides those which he himself edited, such as *Progress*, *Our Corner*, *The Food Reform Magazine*, etc. For some years he was a regular diner at the vegetarian Wheatsheaf Restaurant in Rathbone Place, often in company with Bernard Shaw, for whom he always felt a strong regard and liking.

His literary work was pretty equally divided between poetry and prose. To be frank, I do not think his writings were the best part of him, though he had a clear, trenchant, analytical mind which made him at times a very damaging critic. His poems are very unequal; and in this respect the extreme facility of his pen was far from being an unmixed benefit to him; though one could not but admire the inexhaustible energy with which, at one period, he used to write almost every day a copy of verses for the *Pall Mall Gazette*. His *Socialist Rhymes* contained one or two good pieces; but in his later and more critical years he expressed to me the dissatisfaction he had felt on re-reading these early verses, and I think this judgment was a sound one. On the other hand, his translations from the German, *Songs of a Revolutionary Epoch*, have always seemed to me exceedingly good, and it is to be regretted that this volume is so little known among Socialists. Let us hope that it may some day be reprinted.

In 1884 and part of 1885 he carried out a long-cherished wish by travelling for some months on the Continent and making a lengthy stay in Germany, where he had relatives. (He was himself German on his mother's side.) During his absence there occurred the secession from the S. D. F. which led to the formation of the Socialist League; and after his return Joynes was less closely associated with the active work of the party. This was not owing to any change of feeling on his part, personal or political, for his views did not alter in any way, and he remained on most friendly terms with all his former comrades, in whichever branch of the party they might now be ranked. Indeed, I cannot remember an instance of anyone quarrelling with Joynes – it would scarcely have been possible to quarrel with one so disinterested and dispassionate by nature, so catholic in his friendships, and so determined to make the best of men and circumstances, whatever their attitude towards himself. While not in any degree devoid of strong feelings and emotions – he was, in fact, keenly sensitive – he possessed the most unruffled and dignified temper that I have ever seen. I must not forget to mention his love of nature and the country, of children, and of all simple and beautiful things [pp. 232–6].

Harry Quelch

I first met him in 1882, when I was first elected to the General Council of the S. D. F. – then the Democratic Federation. He and H. H. Champion were then acting as joint secretaries of the organisation. Previous to that I had, however, made his acquaintance through his writings and his adventures with Henry George in Ireland. At first I was disappointed in him. It was difficult to believe that this quiet, gentle, unobtrusive man, tall and fair, with rather stooping shoulders and ruddy, almost boyish, face, was the man who had written the letters and articles I had read; had been arrested as a 'suspect' in Ireland; had set himself in open opposition to all authorities; and had given up a good position and a career, rather than play the hypocrite and hide his opinion. I soon got to know him better, and to know that behind his almost timid reserve and kindly gentleness there was a sterling manly courage, a determination and a steadfastness of purpose which I have never seen surpassed. Tender and sympathetic as a woman to all who claimed his comradeship or counsel, he was stern and unbending wherever he came into contact with opposition or wherever a principle was in question. Yet I do not think he ever made an enemy. A more lovable man I have never met, and he had the love and respect of all the comrades with whom he worked. In the spring of 1884 E. Belfort Bax and I were elected to attend a Congress of the French Party at Roubaix, and our friend Joynes accompanied us. There was some talk at the time of the old law against the International – under which Kropotkin had been sentenced to five years' imprisonment in France – being enforced against us. As a matter of fact, there was some slight disorder once or twice, and we ran some risk of being arrested; but not the slightest hesitation or perturbation was manifested by our friend Joynes, who was calm and unexcited as when sitting on the lawn at a little cottage at Burnham Beeches, where I spent a few days with him a little later in the same year. That brief holiday will always be one of the brightest memories in my life.

To Joynes' work for the movement it is impossible to do justice. For several years, and these were years of stress and difficulty, and uphill pioneer work, he laboured unceasingly and indefatigably – lecturing at Radical clubs and other places, addressing open-air meetings, writing in *Justice*, the *Commonweal* and *To-day*. He was always doing something for the cause for which he had sacrificed so much. There is scarcely a number of *Justice* which appeared during those years but contains a contribution, either in prose or verse, from his pen.

The last time I saw him was at West Hoathly, only a few months before his death. He was kindly, cheerful, and sympathetic as ever, thinking more of others than of himself. It was hard to believe that he, with his youthful-looking ruddy face, was stricken for death, and would never be with us in the active work of the movement again [pp. 237–8].

Writings: (1) MS: Correspondence in the Henry George Coll., New York PL, the Socialist League archive, IISH, Amsterdam and some other locations. Most of William Morris' letters to Joynes are to be published in 1987 by the Princeton Univ. Press, in *The Collected Letters of William Morris*, vol. *2: 1881–1888*, ed. N. Kelvin (Princeton NJ). (2) Other: 'A Political Tour in Ireland', *Times*, 4 Sep 1882 [this was attributed to a 'correspondent' in an editorial comment that was published in the same issue and to which Henry George referred in a letter from him published in *The Times* on 6 Sep 1882 where he mentioned Joynes by name]; *The Adventures of a Tourist in Ireland* (1882); *The Socialist Catechism* (1884) 22 pp. [this was repr. with additions from *Justice* by the Twentieth Century Press in 1885 and again in·1895[?]]; *Socialist Rhymes* (1885) 15 pp.; (trans.) Karl Marx, *Wage–Labour and Capital* (1886; later eds as *Wages and Capital*); (compiler) of *Songs of a Revolutionary Epoch*, trans. from the German (1888); *Socialism analysed: being a critical examination of Mr Joynes's Socialist Catechism* [with the text] by W. Donisthorpe (Liberty and Property League, 1888); *On Lonely Shores and Other Rhymes* (1892). Joynes also edited (briefly) the *Christian Socialist* and, with Belfort Bax, started the magazine *To-day*. He also wrote for *Justice* and sent letters to the daily press.

Sources: *Times*, 4 Sep 1882; letters from Henry George to President Arthur on his arrests in Ireland, *Times*, 2 Oct 1882; E. B. Bax, *Reminiscences and Reflexions of a Mid and Late Victorian* (1918; repr. NY, 1967); H. S. Salt, *Seventy Years among Savages* (1921); idem, *Memories of Bygone Eton* (1928); May Morris, *William Morris, Artist, Writer, Socialist*, vol. *2* (Oxford, 1936); J. A. Venn (compiler), *Alumni Cantabrigienses*, pt 2, vol. *3* (Cambridge, 1947); *The Letters of William Morris to his Family and Friends*, ed. with an Introduction by

R. Henderson (1950); S. Winsten, *Salt and his Circle*, with a Preface by Bernard Shaw (1951); H. M. Pelling, *The Origins of the Labour Party, 1880–1900* (1954; 2nd ed. 1965); C. A. Barker, *Henry George* (NY, 1955); E. P. Thompson, *William Morris* (1955; 2nd rev. ed., 1977); P. d'A. Jones, *The Christian Socialist Revival, 1877–1914* (Princeton, NJ, 1968); C. Tsuzuki, *H. M. Hyndman and British Socialism* (1961); [G. B. Shaw], *Shaw: an autobiography 1856–1898*, selected from his writings by S. Weintraub (1969), J. Lindsay, *William Morris: his life and work* (1975); W. Wolfe, *From Radicalism to Socialism* (New Haven, Conn., 1975). Biographical information: P. R. Quarrie, Eton College Library, Eton. OBIT. *Justice*, 21 Jan 1893.

JOHN SAVILLE

See also: Henry Hyde CHAMPION; James MACDONALD; †Conrad le Despenser Roden NOEL; Henry (Harry) QUELCH; †John (Jack) Edward WILLIAMS.

LEYS, Norman Maclean (1875–1944)
CHRISTIAN SOCIALIST AND ANTI-IMPERIALIST

Norman Leys was born on 25 June 1875 at Willaston, Wirral, Cheshire, the son of John Leys, a barrister, and his wife Mary (née Munsie). His mother died giving birth to a second son, Kenneth, and the children were sent to live with their paternal grandparents. The grandfather was a Scottish Presbyterian minister, and the conversion of Norman's father and his second wife to Catholicism led to a major conflict over the custody of the children. The grandfather sent the boys to school in the United States in the care of two maiden aunts, Agnes and Eliza, and refused to disclose their location. The father brought a lawsuit to recover them and the grandfather was sent to prison for contempt of court. He received much public support for his action and the prison staff granted him every possible privilege. The father eventually relented and the grandfather returned to his manse. According to Gregory [(1962) 90], Leys spent much of his boyhood with the American evangelist Dwight L. Moody, and was educated at Moody's Mount Hermon School, Massachusetts.

The two boys returned to Britain in the nineties and Leys studied medicine at the University of Glasgow, specialising in obstetrics and graduating in 1900. While he was an undergraduate he joined the Fabian Society and also the Anti-Slavery and Aborigines Protection Society. He also became very close to Gilbert Murray, professor of classics at the University, and they remained friends for the rest of their lives. Leys had already decided, before graduation, to work outside Britain. He wrote to Gilbert Murray in January 1900:

> a man ought to do what most needs doing. And what I imagine the black and yellow people need most is not so much treatment for dyspepsia or rheumatism as something to make them stand up to the circumstances of the new civilization that is coming to them [quoted Cell (1976) 8].

Leys had a further year's study at the Liverpool School of Tropical Medicine where he obtained his Diploma in Public Health, and then went out in 1902 to medical practice in Portuguese East Africa. He first worked for the African Lakes Company in Chinde, a port at the mouth of the Zambezi River. After taking leave in Britain he joined the Colonial Service in 1904 and was posted to the British Central Africa Protectorate, known as Nyasaland from 1907. In that same year he was transferred to British East Africa (which became Kenya from 1920). In 1908, when stationed at Nakuru, Leys took part in a punitive expedition against the Kisii, and showed a curious unconcern compared with the reaction of the parliamentary under-secretary to the Colonial Office (Winston Churchill). 'It looks like a butchery . . .', Churchill minuted [quoted ibid., 320 n. 20]. The main documentation for Leys' early years in Africa is contained in the correspondence with Gilbert Murray, now deposited in the Bodleian Library, Oxford. Leys' only publication at this time was a series of physical measurements of Africans published in the *Journal of the Royal Anthropological Institute* in 1913.

Leys was transferred back to Nyasaland in 1913. This came as a result of the Masai affair which began in 1910. It concerned land on the Masai reserve which was coveted by white settlers. Leys was strongly opposed to the sympathy shown to the settlers by the Governor, Sir Percy Girouard. As a result of information Leys sent to Gilbert Murray, Ramsay MacDonald asked questions in the House of Commons, first in July 1911 and then again in April 1912. The Masai took legal action and the Colonial Office was convinced it was Leys who had initiated the decision to go to court: an interpretation that has been repeated by some historians. It would appear, however, as Leys himself always maintained, that his role was limited to contacting the lawyer for the application [Cell (1976) 321, n. 31]. The affair generated considerable bitterness, and for his part in the agitation Leys was moved from East Africa to Nyasaland in spite of his strenuous pleas to the local administration and to the Colonial Office to be allowed to stay.

It was in Nyasaland in 1915 that the Chilembwe rising took place. Those who were not executed were visited in gaol by Leys and partly on the basis of the statements he took down he wrote the chapter 'A Minor Rebellion in Nyasaland' in his book *Kenya*, published in 1924. The last two paragraphs of that chapter summarise Leys' own understanding and appreciation of the African situation; they are remarkable words:

Little likely, then, as any native rising may be for some years, either in Kenya or in Nyasaland, it is far from impossible that one may happen any day. If, some morning, the readers of this book open the morning paper over their breakfast coffee and read of some other Chilembwe or Thuku, they must not expect that some particular act of policy or the unwisdom of some Governor is the cause. They should look on the rising as a by-product of the system under which the very coffee they are drinking is produced. Nor must they blame Governor and Colonial Secretary for repressing the rising with slaughter. That is the kindest way of dealing with native risings. The fact that most of the people who engage in them are in no real sense criminally inclined makes it no less necessary to shoot them. Those who object to the shooting must go deeper.

There would be no native risings in Africa if most of the money raised by direct taxation of natives were spent on native education, if every family had as much rent-free land as it could use, and if those Africans who prefer to live and work at home were left undisturbed by Europeans who think Africans ought to work for them instead of developing land of their own [p. 350].

It remains to add that Dr Duncan Leys, his half-brother, told George Shepperson and Thomas Price that Norman Leys destroyed all his notes and records soon after writing *Kenya* [Shepperson and Price (1958) 508].

In 1918 Leys was home on leave, and it has been generally accepted that his health would not allow him to return to Africa, although there is some doubt about this and he may have retired under pressure [letter from Colin Leys to editors, 10 Feb 1985]. He bought a small, much run-down country practice in the village of Brailsford, near Derby, and remained there for nearly all the rest of his life.

During the early part of his leave, and before he took the decision not to return to Africa, Leys wrote a long and detailed letter to the Colonial Secretary about the existing situation in the Crown Colonies of East Africa. Cell published the complete letter in *By Kenya possessed* [(1976) 91–136], but Cell notes that it is not in the registry of official documents and that there is no copy of it in the PRO [Cell (1976) 329 n.89]. The letter contained a summary of most of the ideas about Africa that Leys ever had. It presented a powerful and cogent argument and among other things it led to a considerable correspondence with J. H. Oldham, which is an invaluable source for the way in which Leys elaborated his ideas.

J. H. Oldham was born in India in 1874; he became a missionary in India for a short time until ill health forced him back to Europe; and in 1921 he was elected one of the secretaries of the International Missionary Council – a forerunner of the World Council of Churches established in 1948. By the beginning of the inter-war years Oldham had contacts all over the world. He obtained a copy of Leys' letter to the Colonial Secretary through a friend of Gilbert Murray, and first wrote to Leys on 18 March 1918. Oldham was to dominate intellectually the Protestant missionary activity in Africa and was a major influence upon British policy on Africa during the years between the wars.

In his letters to Oldham, in articles and in his three books (*Kenya, A Last Chance in Kenya* and *The Colour Bar in East Africa*), Leys developed his ideas, attitudes and policies towards Africa and the Africans. He started from his Christian standpoint. Christianity, he insisted, was a radical set of beliefs; in a colonial situation Christianity could only mean the equality of black and white before God. On racial discrimination Leys argued that the early Christians were clear and explicit, and that racial equality was the message of all Christians to the contemporary world. This simple and highly seditious truth infused Leys's whole approach to the colonial problem and led him to argue that only a root-and-branch transformation of the colonial world – by the elimination of European Imperialism and its economic and political policies – would ensure the full development of freedom of the colonial peoples. But he did not recommend that the Europeans should just move out. He expected them to assist the processes of modernisation. Leys was critical of the policies of day-to-day reform; and he put his faith in the Labour Party in Britain backed by an educated public opinion. His views on the development of the African peoples themselves were sometimes contradictory and unusual. It is possible, for example, in spite of his knowledge of the Chilembwe rising, that he underestimated the resilience of African societies in the face of outside intervention.

Leys took his medical practice in Derbyshire seriously. His Socialism repelled the well-to-do in the village and in the surrounding countryside, but among the village tradesmen and the labouring families he found people he was happy and privileged to serve. His practice was never lucrative, but it was comfortable. And, above all, it left him time for his single-minded campaign on behalf of Kenya. Kenya became the testing ground for Africa's colonial problems, and it was Norman Leys' superb gifts as a writer and as a propagandist that made it so. He was indeed 'By Kenya possessed'.

It is not known exactly when Leys began working actively with the British Labour Party, but it was probably in 1920, when he was appointed to a sub-committee of the Labour Party's Advisory Committee on International Questions. The Labour Party established the Advisory Committee on International Questions in 1919; and in February 1920 it was decided to divide the Committee into three sub-committees, dealing with International Questions, International Economic Questions and Imperial Questions, respectively. Leonard Woolf was secretary of the Advisory Committee, and Leys, who was writing for the ILP and the left-wing press in general, submitted to the sub-committee memoranda on land tenure in Kenya and famine in East Africa.

Leys was, however, wide-ranging in his contacts in these early years. He had written in 1919 for the *International Review of Missions* and he wrote at least one pamphlet for the Student Christian Movement; in 1920 he drafted a proposal (with J. H. Harris, parliamentary secretary of the Anti-Slavery and Aborigines Protection Society and Liberal MP 1923–4) for the League of Nations Union Mandates Committee, of which Leys was a member; he was present at the second Pan-African Conference in Paris in 1921; and during the mid-1920s he lectured at ILP summer schools on African questions.

Leys always had great courage. well exhibited in the notorious controversy that E. D.

Morel had begun over the use of French Moroccan troops on the Rhine. Morel first used the columns of the *Daily Herald* on 10 April 1920, and later, after a visit to Germany in the summer of 1920, published a pamphlet, *The Horror on the Rhine*, in which stories of rape and sexual outrages committed by the black troops were again described in the most lurid terms. It was a racism that came strangely from the man who had carried on the campaign against Belgian exploitation of the Congo. Among the few who replied in critical terms to Morel's original *Daily Herald* article was Leys (17 Apr 1920), who sharply denied Morel's 'so-called physiological facts', declaring that they were 'one of the great sources of racial hatred and should never be given currency' [Reinders (1968) 17].

Leys' *Kenya* was to be one of the most influential pieces of writing on African colonialism during the inter-war years. It had a short Introduction by Gilbert Murray, a second edition in 1925 with a new Preface, and a third edition in 1926 with a much larger new Preface. A reprint edition was published in 1973 with an Introduction by George Shepperson of the University of Edinburgh. *Kenya* was first published by Leonard and Virginia Woolf at the Hogarth Press, and was a commercial success.

Leys had become increasingly close to William McGregor Ross (1877–1940), who was assistant engineer for the Uganda Railway (1900–4) and a director of public works in Kenya (1905–22). Ross, like Leys, developed a wide-ranging criticism of government policies and in 1927 he wrote *Kenya from within: a short political history*. Ross also became a member of the Labour Party's Advisory Committee and served on it continuously during the 1930s – unlike Leys, who resigned in 1931 but returned later.

The year before Leys' book on Kenya appeared the Conservative Government had published a White Paper, *Indians in Kenya*, setting out a policy which argued for the paramountcy of the native Africans, but gave no serious undertakings regarding the white settlers or the inviolability of the rich lands of the Highlands. The Labour Government which followed for most of 1924 had J. H. Thomas at the Colonial Office – 'doubtless the worst Colonial Secretary of State this century' [Brett (1973) 180]; and a special East Africa Commission was sent out in the middle of 1924. The Commission had the Conservative W. G. Ormsby-Gore as chairman; Major A. G. Church (general secretary of the National Union of Scientific Workers) as the Labour representative; and F. C. Linfield for the Liberals. Their Report could have been written by any leading representative of the white settlers, and it undoubtedly had a very considerable influence. Both Leys and McGregor Ross were exceedingly angry at this result of what had been a very perfunctory inquiry by the Commission, and Leys produced a highly critical memorandum for the Labour Party Advisory Committee on Imperial Questions. It must, however, be said that the 'dual policy' (complementary development of native and non-native communities in both economic and political spheres [Cmd 2904 (1927) 5]) which emerged as a counter to the idea of paramountcy of the native African, achieved a notable consensus of agreement among the leadership of all three main political parties, and critics on the Left, such as Leys and Ross, were somewhat marginalised in political terms. What criticism there was of government policy in East Africa came from a small group of Labour and Liberal MPs. Between 1925 and 1929, 258 out of a total of 325 questions asked on Kenya in the House of Commons were put by only six members, 103 of those by Josiah Wedgwood alone [Brett (1973) 60]. The Conservative Party tended to support the settler interest, and the Labour Party leadership showed little interest in the general problems of East Africa except in the matter of African labour. The Labour Party, in fact, had no alternative strategy of development for East Africa, and this became even more clear in the second Labour Government, of 1929–31.

By the time the Labour Party achieved office again, it had elaborated an African policy at least in general outline. In 1925 there was published the first comprehensive statement on the British Empire under the title *A Labour Policy for the British Commonwealth of Nations*; and the Party's election statement for 1929, *Labour and the Nation*, did prescribe a policy for the

Empire which reaffirmed its policies on land and insisted on full self-government 'at the earliest practical date'. At the same time the various official reports were notably vague on tropical Africa, including East Africa, and there was an absence of comment on or analysis of such issues as paramountcy or the dual policy. Once the second Labour Government took office, the Advisory Committee had remarkably little influence upon the Colonial Office, whose minister was Lord Passfield (Sidney Webb).

Before Labour came to office the Hilton-Young Commission had reported [*Report of the Commission on Closer Union of the Dependencies in Eastern and Central Africa*, Cmd 3234 (1929)]. The Commission was divided and there were two reports. The majority report was welcomed by a number of Labour specialists on colonial affairs – C. R. Buxton and Lord Olivier, for example – mainly because it was firm on the principles of trusteeship, subordinated federation to policies favouring the native Africans, and supported Indian demands for a common vote. The report, however, was vigorously condemned by the white settlers in Kenya. Norman Leys and J. H. Harris were also critical, and in particular were totally opposed to the report's suggestion of separate development for the white and black races. In this Leys found himself ranged against the majority of the Labour Party's Advisory Committee: 'What the other side forgets', Leys wrote:

> is that the minority of educated Africans, whom all the rest inevitably follow, will always refuse to accept anything less than equal rights. At the Advisory Committee Lord Olivier said that the policy of the report gave the natives more than equal rights. I answered that the trusteeship system had never worked whereas the equal rights policy had prevented oppression. To my mind the whole trusteeship policy, besides being hopelessly vague and sentimental, is a putting of natives into splints when what they need is to be allowed freedom. ... The Commissioners never entertained the idea that the result of all this regimenting will be not gratitude but resentment. ... I cannot understand why Olivier, who has actually operated the other plan in Jamaica, and Buxton, whom I had thought saw to the bottom of the whole problem, cannot see all that [Gupta (1975) 130; see also a letter from Leys in the *New Statesman*, 9 Feb 1929, 562–3].

The complicated story of the development of an African policy by Passfield, on behalf of the Labour Government, has been much written about [Gregory (1962); idem (1971) Chs 9 and 10; Gupta (1975) *passim*]. Leys was not satisfied with any of the proposals made, above all because there was no frontal attack upon racial discrimination. What political pressure from the Left achieved during the period of the second Labour Government was a limited retardation of the power of European immigrant groups, but it was only a temporary stay to a process of domination that would have required a much stronger personality than Passfield to achieve a more permanent change. In 1930 Leys published *A Last Chance in Kenya*, in which he analysed at length the complexity of the problems that bore very heavily upon the native Africans. It was an effective piece of writing which criticised sharply the second Labour Government, and it drew a very interesting review in the *Political Quarterly* from T. Drummond Shiels. Shiels had been under-secretary to Passfield at the Colonial Office and had been given a commendatory note by Leys in his book [p. 141, n. 1]. Shiels began his review by noting that Leys' first book on Kenya had 'created considerable stir' when it was first published; and Shiels was by no means wholly critical of Leys in this review of *A Last Chance in Kenya*, although he explicitly stated that he thought Leys had failed to appreciate what Labour had accomplished. In a letter to Winifred Holtby, however, he was a good deal more disparaging of Leys than in the *Political Quarterly* review [Shiels to Holtby, 3 Mar 1932, Winifred Holtby Coll., Hull CL]. He concluded his published comment:

> Dr Leys's book should be read. It is wholly sincere and high motived [*sic*], and its faults

are those of a handicapped and somewhat lonely fighter for human justice, who is shocked and dismayed at the apparent indifference to his message of hood-winked ministers and a callous bureaucracy, and who appeals to public opinion for support [Shiels (1932) 448].

Leys was so opposed to the Labour Government's approach to East Africa that he resigned from the Advisory Committee on Imperial Questions in April 1931. His memorandum on his resignation, to be found in the Labour Party archives, is a crucial document, both for his own career to that date and for a devastatingly critical analysis of the East African policies of the second Labour Government. He included the 'acquiescence' of the Advisory Committee in his general condemnation of the supineness of the Labour Government in the face of settler opposition to any variation of the policy of equal rights.

It has not been possible to determine how long Leys remained off the Advisory Committee. He submitted two memoranda in June 1932: 'Forced Labour in Kenya Colony' and 'East Africa: appointment of commissioners'. He was certainly in regular attendance in 1938 [but see Gupta (1975) 230] and it may be that prior to that date he only attended meetings when matters he was interested in were being discussed [letter, Stephen Bird, 10 Dec 1984]. History has vindicated Leys rather than his critics, but he and those who worked with him made little headway during the 1930s. Leys visited West Africa in company with C. R. Buxton in late 1932, and after his visit produced a memorandum on the Gold Coast for the Advisory Committee and an article entitled 'Kenya and the Gold Coast' [*New Statesman*, 15 Apr 1933]. He was very critical of indirect rule and strongly supported Achimota College, which he saw as producing a new generation of African intelligentsia. On East Africa it was hard to arouse any significant section of Labour opinion, let alone the wider public. In 1938 Leys, together with Leonard Barnes and Julius Lewin, had founded a Socialist journal, *Empire*, later taken over by the Fabian Colonial Bureau. In February 1939 Leys drafted a memorandum for the Labour Party which argued that the crucial issue was the elimination of the colour bar and that there could be 'no third alternative between equality and inferiority of status' [Gupta (1975) 265]. This memorandum was largely embodied in a draft produced later by Leonard Woolf in September 1941 which itself became an official Labour Party document in 1943: *The Colonies: the Labour Party's post-war policy for African and Pacific colonies*. Leys himself published a book on the same lines in 1941, *The Colour Bar in East Africa*.

In his last years Leys moved from Brailsford to Yalding, Kent, where he died on 15 August 1944. He was survived by his wife, Jane (née Donald) whom he had married in August 1904 at Johnstone, Renfrewshire (in his wife's home – a common practice at the time), and their daughter, Agnes, an only child. His funeral took place at Nettlestead Church, near Yalding and he left an estate valued at £1490. Leys and his brother Kenneth had been welcomed on their return from America by their father and step-mother and their family of two daughters and three sons. One of the sons, Duncan, became a paediatrician after the First World War, and his son, Professor Colin Leys, has become a specialist in African affairs.

The *New Statesman* obituary appeared in 'A London Diary', which was mostly written by Kingsley Martin, though it is likely that the paragraph on Leys was by Leonard Woolf. Leys was remembered here as a man of 'fanatical obstinacy and sincerity'. 'In ordinary life', the notice ended, 'he was the most simple, modest and kindly of men'.

Leys always remained a Christian Socialist. His fanaticism was of the reformist kind and he was never attracted by Communism. In 1928 he had published in the *New Leader* (7 Dec 1928) a short note explaining that he had joined the League Against Imperialism in the belief that it was 'an honest attempt to unite all the enemies of Imperialism . . . [but] I found that the only policy tolerated by the League is the policy of the Communist Party, and resigned'. Leys's achievement was summed up by George Shepperson in his Introduction to the 1968 reprint of *Kenya*:

> Half a century after it was written, Norman Leys' *Kenya* may still be read with profit. For students of history and sociology, it remains an important source for the study of the course of race relations in Kenya and Nyasaland. For students of literature, it is an example – better written than most – of the reformist writings which humanitarian British subjects in Africa have felt constrained to publish since the appearance in 1828 of Dr. John Philip's anti-Boer *Researches in South Africa*. For Africans, particularly of Kenya and Malawi (formerly Nyasaland), it helps the understanding of the processes which have led their countries to independence and it suggests some of the problems which still confront them; and it should remind them of the part played by Europeans like Norman Leys in the struggle for African freedom and dignity in the twentieth century. Above all, in such statements as the one quoted above on the danger of an inter-racial war; in its concern with 'the betrayal of Christ by the churches in Africa'; and in its anxiety about the future of underprivileged peoples in a world of potentially affluent societies, Norman Leys' *Kenya* continues to commend itself to the serious attention of all who are interested in human relationships outside as well as inside the confines of the continent from which he learned so much about men and to which he contributed so much in return [p. xiii].

Writings: Norman Leys was a prolific writer of articles to the daily and periodical press but it was particularly through his books and pamphlets that his ideas became more widely known. His first book, *Kenya*, published in 1924, was reprinted in 1925 and 1926; a fourth edition was published by Cass in 1973 with an Introduction by George Shepperson. *A Last Chance in Kenya* (1931) was followed by *The Colour Bar in East Africa* (1941). Apart from the Cass reprint of *Kenya*, all the books were published by the Hogarth Press, London. His pamphlets were: *Africa and the Nineteenth Century Reformation* (Student Christian Movement, 1920); *A Plan for Government by Mandate in Africa* (League of Nations Union, 1921) 20 pp.; *Land Law and Policy in Tropical Africa* (League of Nations Union, 1922) 16 pp.; *Why the Landworker is Poor* (ILP, 1925). His periodical writings included: (with T. A. Joyce) 'Note on a Series of Physical Measurements from East Africa', *J. of the Royal Anthropological Institute 43* (1913) 195–267; Fulani bin Fulani [pseud. N. M. Leys], 'Religion and Common Life: a problem in East African missions', *Int. Rev. Missions*, Apr 1919, 155–72; review of C. L. Temple's *Native Races and their Rulers*, ibid., 263–6; Fulani bin Fulani, 'Under a Mandate', *New Europe 11*, no. 142 (3 July 1919) 265–71, and no. 143 (10 July 1919) 300–6; 'Christianity and Labour Conditions in Africa', *Int. Rev. Missions*, Oct 1920, 544–51; Fulani bin Fulani, 'The Indian in Africa', *Church Missionary Rev.* (1921) 199–214; 'The Tropics and the League of Nations', *Soc. Rev.*, Jan–Mar 1921, 68–78; 'The Problem of Kenya', ibid. (May 1923) 205–12; 'The History of Kenya Colony', ibid. (Sep 1923) 129–33; 'New Style Imperialism in Kenya', *New Leader*, 25 May 1923, 6; 'Christianity and Socialism in the Tropics', ibid., 24 Apr 1925, 4; 'Civilisation, Capital and Soap: tales of African magic', ibid., 15 May 1925, 8; 'The Peril of the White', ibid., 30 Oct 1925, 4; 'West African Imperialism', ibid., 2 July 1926, 5; 'A Place in the Sun for the Native', ibid., 27 Aug 1926, 4; 'Towards Socialism: the next step', ibid., 8 Oct 1926, 3; 'The Education of the African' [letter], *Manchester Guardian*, 26 Oct 1926, 22; 'A New Policy for Missions', 13 Nov 1926, 4; 'Objects of Christian Education', ibid., 27 Nov 1926, 13; 'Education of the African' [letter], ibid., 18 Dec 1926, 11; 'The Scandal of Kenya', *New Leader*, 2 Dec 1927, 14; 'The Problem of Empire: what to do with the dependencies', *Soc. Rev.*, May 1928, 22–7; 'Labour and the Coloured Worker', *New Leader*, 21 Sep 1928; 'The League Against Imperialism' [letter], ibid., 7 Dec 1928, 9; 'Trusteeship', *West African Students' Union*, Jan 1929, 16–18; 'An Old Dragon not yet dead', *New Leader*, 5 July 1929, 4; 'The East Africa Report', *New Statesman*, 9 Feb 1929, 562–3; 'To him that hath', *New Leader*, 16 Jan 1931,

13; 'Professor Julian Huxley: Impertinence!' [review of Huxley's *Africa View*], ibid., 29 May 1931, 8; 'The Education of Africans' [letter in reply to 'Anthropologists and Africans', *West Africa*, 30 Jan 1932, 59–60, a letter critical of Leys], *West Africa*, 13 Feb 1932, 112; 'Kenya and the Gold Coast: a contrast', *New Statesman*, 15 Apr 1933, 471–2; 'A College in the Gold Coast', ibid., 22 Apr 1933, 499–500; 'The Report of the Kenya Land Commission', ibid., 28 July 1934, 116; 'Incident in Imperial History', ibid., 4 Jan 1936; 'The Kenya Labour Ordinance: robbing the Masai' [letter], *Manchester Guardian*, 2 June 1938, 20.

Sources: (1) MS: Gilbert Murray papers, Bodleian Library, Oxford; archives of the International Department of the LP, LP Headquarters, London; correspondence between T. D. Shiels and Winifred Holtby, Winifred Holtby Coll., Hull CL.
(2) Theses: J. H. Mower, 'The Development of the Colonial Policy of the British Labour Party, 1918–1939' (Harvard PhD, 1951); D. Wylie, 'Critics of Colonial Policy in Kenya with Special Reference to Norman Leys and W. McGregor Ross' (Edinburgh MLitt., 1974); C. J. Sansom, 'The British Labour Movement and Southern Africa 1918–1955: labourism and the imperial tradition' (Birmingham PhD, 1982).
(3) Official Publications: *Despatch . . . relating to Native Labour in Kenya Colony*, Cmd 873 (1920); *Despatch to . . . the Government of the Kenya Colony and Protectorate relating to Native Labour*, Cmd 1509 (1921); *Indians in Kenya*, Cmd 1922 (1923); *Report of the East Africa Commission*, Cmd 2387 (1924) [Ormsby-Gore Commission]; *Correspondence with the Government of Kenya relating to an Exchange of Land with Lord Delamere*, Cmd 2500 (1925); *Future Policy in Regard to Eastern Africa*, Cmd 2904 (1927); *Report of the Commission on Closer Union of the Dependencies in Eastern and Central Africa*, Cmd 3234 (1929); *Memorandum on Native Policy in East Africa*, Cmd 3573 (1930); *Statement of Conclusions of His Majesty's Government in the United Kingdom as regards Closer Union in East Africa*, Cmd 3574 (1930); Joint Select Committee on Closer Union in East Africa, vol. *I: Report*, HL 184 (1931), vol. *II: M of E*, HL 29 (1930), vol. *III: Appendices*, HL 29 (1930); *Report of the Kenya Land Commission*, Cmd 4556 (1934) [Carter Commission]; *Kenya Land Commission Report: summary of conclusions reached by His Majesty's Government*, Cmd 4580 (1934); *Report of the Commission appointed to enquire into and report on the Financial Position and System of Taxation of Kenya* (1936) [Pim Report].
(4) Other: W. McGregor Ross, *Kenya from within* (1927); A. G. Church, *East Africa. A new dominion: a crucial experiment in tropical development and its significance to the British Empire* (1928); T. D. Shiels, 'A Last Chance in Kenya' [review of Leys' book], *Pol. Q. 3*, no. 3 (July–Sep 1932) 444–8; *Dictionary of American Biography*, vol. *13* (1934); E. Huxley, *White Man's Country: Lord Delamere and the making of Kenya*, vol. *2: 1914–31* (1935; rev. ed. 1953, repr. 1956); M. R. Dilley, *British Policy in Kenya Colony* (NY, 1937; 2nd ed. 1966); *Medical Register* (1939); L. Barnes, *Empire or Democracy: a study of the colonial question* (Left Book Club, 1939); *Race and Politics in Kenya: a correspondence between Elspeth Huxley and Margery Perham*, with an Introduction by Lord Lugard (1944; rev. ed. 1946); *Observer*, 25 June 1950, 5; G. Shepperson and T. Price, *Independent African: John Chilembwe and the origins, setting and significance of the Nyasaland Native Rising of 1915* (Edinburgh, 1958); W. M. Macmillan, *The Road to Self-rule: a study in colonial evolution* (1959); R. G. Gregory, *Sidney Webb and East Africa: Labour's experiment with the doctrine of native paramountcy* (Berkeley, Calif., 1962); G. Bennett, *Kenya. A Political History: the colonial period* (Oxford, 1963); *History of East Africa*, vol. *2*, ed. V. Harlow and E. M. Chilver (Oxford, 1965); G. H. Mungeam, *British Rule in Kenya 1895–1912: the establishment of administration in the East Africa Protectorate* (Oxford, 1966); R. C. Reinders, 'Racialism on the Left: E. D. Morel and the "Black Horror on the Rhine"', *Int. Rev. Social Hist. 13* (1968) 1–28; M. Perham, *Colonial Sequence 1949–1969* (1970); R. G. Gregory, *India and East Africa: a history of race relations within the British Empire 1890–1939* (Oxford, 1971);

Rebellion in Black Africa, ed. with an Introduction by R. I. Rotberg (Oxford, 1971); E. A. Brett, *Colonialism and Underdevelopment in East Africa: the politics of economic change 1919–1939* (NY, 1973); P. S. Gupta, *Imperialism and the British Labour Movement, 1914–1964* (1975); *By Kenya possessed: the correspondence of Norman Leys and J. H. Oldham*, ed. and with an Introduction by J. W. Cell (Chicago, 1976); D. Wylie, 'Confrontation over Kenya: the Colonial Office and its critics, 1918–1940', *J. of African History 18*, no. 3 (1977) 427–47; idem, 'Norman Leys and McGregor Ross: a case study in the conscience of African Empire, 1900–39', *J. of Imperial and Commonwealth History 5*, no. 3 (1977) 294–309; idem, 'A Debate on Empire' [review of *By Kenya possessed*], *J. of African History 18*, no. 4 (1977) 633–4. Biographical information: Stephen Bird, archivist, LP. Personal information: Mrs Agnes Avery, daughter, London; Professor C. Leys, Queen's University, Kingston, Canada, half-nephew. OBIT. *Glasgow Herald*, 21 Aug 1944; *New Statesman*, 1 Sep 1944; *Lancet*, 2 Sep 1944. NOTE. The editors wish to acknowledge an earlier draft of this biography received from Diana Wylie and especially the details she supplied on the writings of Norman Leys.

JOYCE BELLAMY
JOHN SAVILLE
DIANA WYLIE

See also: Leonard John BARNES; Thomas Drummond SHIELS; *Josiah Clement WEDGWOOD.

MACDONALD, James (1857–1938)
SOCIALIST AND TRADE UNIONIST

Little is known of the early life and family of James Macdonald, other than that he was born in Glasgow in 1857. By early 1881 'Jimmy' or 'Jem', as he was often called, had settled in London and entered the West End tailoring trade. Within a short time he became one of the most popular and active labour leaders in London and won a reputation as the best orator in the British tailoring trade union movement. A Radical and an admirer of Gladstone when when he first lived in London, he joined a Scottish club which met in a public house in Tottenham Street. His own account of the stages in his political education to a Socialist position was given in *Justice*, 11 July 1896:

> one evening [in 1881] the landlord told us that there was a meeting being held in another room of some of the most red-hot Fenians and dynamiters in England. Some of us were curious to see these fellows, and eventually got introduced to them. There were Frank Kitz, James and Charles Murray, Garcia, Townsend, Butler and others. They were vehemently denouncing the Coercion Bill of the Liberal Government, and it was their opposition to this measure which had led to their being turned out of their former meeting place.

Macdonald and his friends argued with Kitz and his group, and gradually lost the argument. As a result they joined forces to form the Central Marylebone Democratic Association. Macdonald's acceptance of Socialism followed the reading of an article by Engels in the *Labour Standard* – probably 'A Fair Day's Wage' (7 May 1881) or 'The Wages System' (21 May 1881) – to which he had been introduced by the German Socialist Adam Weiler. Macdonald then got hold of a copy of Hyndman's *England for All* and about the same time he joined the German Club in Tottenham Street. It was not only Irish coercion that was moving Macdonald, and others, away from Liberalism; the Egyptian campaign was also important in this context. Macdonald's first public lecture was on 'Egyptian Iniquities'. He met the small group of Socialists in London – Hyndman, Champion, Williams – and thus became one of the few working-class men in the original group around Hyndman and the Democratic Federation.

At the conference held at Easter 1882 he was elected to the Democratic Federation executive and was a signatory of Hyndman's pamphlet *Socialism made Plain*, in which the Federation proclaimed its Socialism. As a member of the executive of the new Social Democratic Federation (SDF) in 1884 he was one of the chief spokesmen for the Socialist cause among the workers of London. A close reasoner and debater with an eloquent and pleasing manner, he stood near the centre of labour and Socialist politics in the metropolis for over thirty years. His approach to politics included an element of sectarianism and he had little patience with Lib–Lab co-operation or the Fabian policy of permeation. He could speak with exceptional power; on one occasion, according to Hyndman, he 'ripped up' the arguments of George Bernard Shaw [Hyndman (1912) 264]. Throughout his life Macdonald preached class warfare and the inevitability of class slavery under the capitalist system. He remained a staunch supporter of Socialist unity, a principle he was not willing to abandon for the labour alliance that was favoured by such figures as Keir Hardie and J. R. MacDonald. At the same time, he was prepared to work with Socialists of a more reformist kind, although he believed that emancipation of labour could come about only through the federation of all workers under Socialism. He was convinced that the growth of trusts, combines and finance capitalism was the natural outcome of the 'march of monopoly', and that the collapse of capitalism and the collective ownership of the means of production was inevitable.

In the dispute with William Morris and the subsequent split of the SDF Macdonald sided with Hyndman. In 1885, however, he left the SDF because of Hyndman's election policy (which had led to the 'Tory Gold' scandal) and formed the Socialist Union, only to return to the Federation in 1887. He was one of several SDF members who vigorously opposed schemes to relieve unemployment through working-class emigration. Throughout his life he opposed both emigration and restriction of alien (Jewish) labour as means of reducing the unemployment problem. During the cotton strike of 1884 he organised, with his friend Jack Williams, the first Lancashire branch of the SDF, in Blackburn. With Williams, John Fielding, Amie Hicks and H. H. Champion, he was arrested and convicted for obstruction in the Dod Street free-speech struggle of 1885 which grew out of the SDF's unemployment agitation. He was later a frequent spokesman for free speech during the anti-war demonstrations, of which he was a leader, in 1901.

Macdonald served as one of the strongest SDF voices in the Trades Union Congress, the London Trades Council and the Independent Labour Party. His philosophy was that Socialists must make use of all forms of government – municipal, parliamentary, local and trade unionist – and 'leaven the whole of them with the principles of socialism'. With Keir Hardie's encouragement, he stood as an Independent Labour and Scottish Labour candidate for Dundee in the general election of 1892. He polled 354 votes, far fewer than the four other candidates. In spite of Hyndman's policy of neutrality towards Hardie and the ILP, Macdonald represented the SDF at the founding conference of the ILP at Bradford in 1893 and became a member of the new party. In 1895 he stood again for Dundee, again finishing bottom of the poll, with 1313 votes, five per cent of the total cast. In the same year he supported merger negotiations between the SDF and the ILP, an attempt at labour unity that failed.

Macdonald was one of the four SDF representatives at the founding conference of the Labour Representation Committee in 1900. He moved the resolution that the new party be based upon 'a recognition of the class war' and have for its ultimate object the socialisation of the means of production, distribution and exchange, but that it should also be allowed to co-operate with other parliamentary parties 'that will support such measures, or will assist in opposing measures of an opposite character'. To this Alexander Wilkie moved an amendment which would have left the Labour MPs 'entirely free on all purely political questions': a position which the ILP in particular could not support. Keir Hardie therefore offered an alternative amendment, which Wilkie ultimately accepted [Bealey and Pelling (1958) 27–8; and *The Labour Party Foundation Conference* (1967 ed.) 11–13]. For many years SDF members claimed, mistakenly, that James Ramsay MacDonald was elected secretary of the Labour Representation Committee only because many of the delegates at the founding conference thought they were voting for 'our Jimmy' Macdonald. Macdonald's insistence on a Socialist and class-war position was repeated in 1903 when an attempt was made to form a London Labour Party, resulting in SDF withdrawal from the negotiations and thus again rendering labour unity in London an impossibility.

Macdonald's greatest influence on London politics grew from his role as head of the London Trades Council between 1896 and 1913. He was one of the few early SDF members who stood for a policy of Socialist involvement with the union movement, and it was through activists such as he that the LTC and other trades councils in London became Socialist strongholds. He regarded the trade councils as organisations that could mitigate the evils of industrial life as well as maintain the contest against the capitalists who were fighting to reduce living standards. In the summer of 1890 Macdonald had been one of the leaders of the 'new unionist' revolt within the LTC following the new militant unionism of 1888–9. Macdonald was elected to the Council's executive in December 1890. He replaced George Shipton, a member of the Lib-Lab 'old guard', as secretary of the Council in April 1896, at a salary of £156 per year. Under Macdonald the Council struggled through the collapse of many of the new unskilled unions and the employers' counter-attack. He mounted a disappointing campaign on behalf of the locked-out engineers and an inconclusive campaign to get a higher court to rule on the legality of picketing in the case of *Lyons* v. *Wilkins* [Saville (1960) esp. 346 ff.]. The LTC had some success in organising or reorganising semi-skilled and unskilled workers, so that the number of workers affiliated to it when Macdonald retired in 1913 was similar to the level reached in the early 1890s.

Guided by Macdonald, the LTC continually put pressure on the London County Council to establish a minimum wage for its workers and to set up a works department. The LCC was also urged to undertake the feeding of schoolchildren, municipal housing and other services that trade unionism was incapable of providing. The LTC supported political candidates only if they pledged themselves in favour of its wage and welfare reform proposals. At the same time it became the chief voice of the London unemployed. In 1904 it succeeded in getting the Local Government Board to establish a Central Committee on the Unemployed, which, in turn, led to the Unemployed Workmen Act of 1905. In September 1905 Macdonald organised a conference on the unemployed and supported a central workers' committee, the purpose of which was to agitate for the provisions of the Act to be carried out and to get workers on to the central and district bodies which managed the Act.

While secretary of the LTC, Macdonald founded and edited the penny monthly the *London Trades and Labour Gazette* (after 1904 the *Trades and Labour Gazette*). The paper became the official voice of the LTC and various other London unions and trades councils as well as a forum for Macdonald's Socialist views. In 1905 the paper's financial difficulties led to a scandal in which Macdonald was accused of soliciting and receiving subscription funds from Liberal Party politicians [*Trades and Labour Gaz.*, 15 Nov 1905]. As a result he was censured by the executive of the LTC, which assumed greater control of the paper. A serious illness removed him from his work for most of 1911. He resigned his position in February 1913 to devote more of his efforts to his tailors' trade union, although he continued as a member of the LTC executive until July 1915.

Macdonald used his position within the LTC to carry the new unionist and Socialist philosophy to the Trades Union Congress. He always believed that militant trades councils could become an alternative to the TUC and circumvent its Lib–Lab philosophy and leadership, or even, following the Taff Vale decision, compensate for the vulnerability of the unions by assuming a more militant role in the labour movement. At the TUC of 1890, held in Liverpool, he had joined Burns and others in attacking the pro-Liberal stance of Henry Broadhurst and the Parliamentary Committee. He then caused an uproar by proposing that the principle of collective ownership and control of the means of production be upheld by all political candidates supported by the TUC. This nationalisation-test amendment was defeated by 363 votes to 55, but was proposed again by Macdonald at subsequent congresses until it was adopted, by 137 votes to 97, at Belfast in 1893. The adoption of this motion contributed to the refusal of the non-Socialist leadership of the TUC to carry out the commitment to establish a Labour Representation Committee and a political fund. He further antagonised the older leadership in 1894 when he joined Keir Hardie to push through a resolution calling for the nationalisation of mines and mining royalties; the following year he once again pressed the question of Socialism by demanding that the Parliamentary Committee take action on the nationalisation resolution. At the TUC of 1895, however, the old guard hit back and trade councils were excluded from future congresses [Roberts (1958) Ch. 4].

Macdonald's career as a leading figure in the London tailoring trade union movement lasted for over thirty years. His strong belief in the autonomy of the local union and in the need to organise all workers, including women and Jews, often brought him into conflict with the national union. Tailoring in London was a highly seasonal trade with intense labour competition. The skilled craft unions had become increasingly weakened by new production methods, small-scale machinery and a ready supply of unskilled and unorganised workers who worked for sweated wages outside the traditional shop. Macdonald claimed that machinery was a danger to the trade because of the large number of unskilled workers it brought into competition with the educated workmen. Hence he saw that the real problem was not so much the master tailor as the unskilled worker who laboured for cut-throat wages in his home or in a small unregulated shop. Consequently Macdonald combined conservatism with militant unionism in an effort to keep skilled wages high, bring the unskilled into the union and destroy the practice of outworking. He moved against outworking in 1890 by proposing that the LCC should establish municipal workshops instead of dealing with clothing contractors. As head of the West End tailors and district secretary of the national union, the Amalgamated Society of Tailors, Macdonald launched London tailors on a campaign to organise the entire workforce, including women and Jewish workers. He also led an attempt to persuade employers to provide workshop space for all their workers. Even though in 1891 the AST passed Macdonald's resolution inviting Jewish unions to participate in the national union, it never fully agreed with Macdonald that it had no choice but to open its membership to all, even to aliens. For this reason Macdonald was unable to draw on the full support of either his own or the national union when he helped to lead the East End Jewish tailors' strike movement of 1888–91. He claimed that conflict between workers would continue to exist until the entire labour force came under a standard rate of wages, either enforced by the union or established by the state.

In these years he also aided the Women's Trade Union League and the Women's Industrial Council in their efforts to organise the thousands of women entering the tailoring trade. A tailoresses' branch of the men's union was established in 1891 and soon thereafter an East London branch for Jewish and English tailoresses was established. In 1894 Macdonald's West End branch formally reduced its entrance fee and was the first of the British tailoring unions to open its doors to women and aliens. Macdonald served on the executive of the Women's Trade Union League and also aided in the election of Frances Hicks, a fellow SDF member and a tailoress, as the first woman member of the LTC executive. Macdonald and the LTC supported the women unionists in their campaign for a state-enforced minimum wage in the sweated trades, a campaign that resulted, in 1909, in the first Trade Boards Act.

Macdonald's attempt to organise fully the London tailoring trade was hampered by disputes between the local and the national unions, often centring on the question of female membership. In the early 1890s the London tailors and the AST quarrelled over a plan for rejuvenating the union by admitting women workers, separating strike funds from benefit funds in order to allow 'trade only' memberships at lower dues, and eliminating superannuation benefits. In addition the AST refused to reimburse the Londoners for strike funds paid to some 800 women workers during the 1891 London tailors' strike. All this came on the heels of a London demand for increased local control of the policy on hours and wages. When the AST conference rejected their demands, the Londoners went ahead and passed new entrance rules allowing wider membership. Macdonald then outraged the AST by calling for the union's executive committee to be censured for their neglect of unorganised workers and moved that the union adopt a policy that 'the objects of this society are the protection and furtherance of the interests of its members and the complete emancipation of labour from the exploitation of capital'. (Macdonald's views at this time can be found in a long interview published in the *Workman's Times* on 14 November 1891.)

Subsequently he was expelled from the executive of the AST and the London West End branch broke from the union in 1893 to become the London Society of Tailors and Tailoresses. Macdonald and the London society remained critical of the AST's apathy on the problems of working conditions, long hours and the general problem of sweating. The London union rejoined the AST in 1901, when it appeared that the national union was willing to embark on a policy of aggressive and open unionism, only to break away again in 1905 following an attempt by the AST to dilute the militant influence of Macdonald and his union through a scheme of centralising all the London branches. Once again the West End branch officials accused the national union of being rigid, undemocratic and reluctant to fight against any breaches in the London wage agreements. Its membership, however, remained low. A jurisdictional dispute with the AST was waged for a number of years within the London Trades Council and the courts, although in the case of *Madden* v. *Rhodes* the summons issued by a trustee of the AST was dismissed by magistrates in 1905 and on appeal in 1906. In 1915 the London society, with several other unions, joined the Amalgamated Union of Clothing Operatives to form the United Garment Workers' Union, thereby uniting craft workers and factory workers. Macdonald remained secretary of the London branch until 1927.

On retirement he moved to Australia, returning to England a few years before his death, which occurred in Islington on 31 May 1938. He had married on 25 April 1892. His wife was an active member of the British Socialist Party Women's Council. The LTC recognised his contribution to the labour movement by setting up a memorial fund to be used for the support of his widow; by January 1939 it was reported that £78 had been collected. Macdonald's will has not been traced.

Writings: *Industrial Remuneration Conference: report of the proceedings and papers* (1885; repr. with an Introduction by J. Saville, NY, 1968) 242–3 [speech to the Conference, which Macdonald attended as one of three SDF delegates; note that in the text and index of the proceedings he is referred to as Mr *George* Macdonald, while in the list of participants he is given as Mr J. Macdonald] 'West End Tailoring-Men's Work' in *Life and Labour of the People*, vol. *4*, ed. C. Booth (1893) 142–9; 'How I became a Socialist', *Justice*, 11 July 1896; editorial notes in *Journeyman: a journal devoted to the interest of the workers in the clothing industry*, 1896–7; 'Apprenticeship' [lecture], *Master Tailor and Cutters' Gaz.*, May 1896, 98–9; 'Classification of Workmen' [lecture], ibid., Aug 1896, 140–1; *London Trades and Labour Gaz.*, 1901–4, and *Trades and Labour Gaz.*, 1904–13; tribute to Harry Quelch, *Justice*, 27 Sep 1913; 'Early Recollections of Jack Williams', ibid., 15 Nov 1917.

Sources: (1) MS: Webb Coll., BLPES; LTC minutes and records, TUC Library. (2) Other: *Justice*, 1890–1913, including 'J. Macdonald at Oxford – Socialism from a Workman's Standpoint' [report of an address to an SDF meeting on 21 Mar], 31 Mar 1900, 5; *Workman's Times*, 1890–4, including 'Interview with James Macdonald', 14 Nov 1891, 7; *J. of the Amalgamated Society of Tailors and Tailoresses*, 1898, 1901–9; *Trades and Labour Gaz.*, 15 Nov 1905; LCC, 'Fair Wages and Hours of Labour', *Report of the Fair Wage Committee for 1889–96* (1907); H. M. Hyndman, *Further Reminiscences* (1912); *Labour Who's Who* (1927); H. W. Lee and E. Archbold, *Social-Democracy in Britain* (1935); G. Tate, *London Trades Council 1860–1950* (1950); F. Bealey and H. Pelling, *Labour and Politics 1900–1906* (1958); B. C. Roberts, *The Trades Union Congress 1868–1921* (1958); J. Saville, 'Trade Unions and Free Labour: the background to the Taff Vale Decision', in *Essays in Labour History*, ed. A. Briggs and J. Saville (1960) 317–50; C. Tsuzuki, *H. M. Hyndman and British Socialism* (1961); H. A. Clegg *et al.*, *A History of British Trade Unions since 1889*, vol. *1: 1889–1910* (Oxford, 1964); M. Steward and L. Hunter, *The Needle is threaded* (1964); *The Labour Party Foundation Conference and Annual Conference Reports 1900–1905* (LRC, 1900–5; repr. 1967); P. Thompson, *Socialists, Liberals and Labour: the struggle for London 1885–1914* (1967); J. A. Garrard, *The English and Emigration 1880–1910* (1971); D. Howell, *British Workers and the Independent Labour Party 1888–1906* (Manchester, 1983); J. A. Schmiechen, *Sweated Industries and Sweated Labour: the London clothing trades, 1867–1914* (1984); E. Mappen, *Helping Women at Work: the Women's Industrial Council 1889–1914* (1985). Biographical information: Ms M. W. H. Schreuder, IISH, Amsterdam. OBIT. *Times*, 4 June 1938; *Tailor and Garment Worker 6* (June 1938); *LTC Annual Report* (1938); *TUC Report* (1938).

DAVID E. MARTIN
JAMES A. SCHMIECHEN

See also: Henry Hyde CHAMPION; †Amelia (Amie) Jane HICKS; †John (Jack) Edward WILLIAMS.

McSHEEDY, James Joseph (1852–1923)
SCHOOLMASTER, JOURNALIST AND RADICAL COUNCILLOR

James Joseph McSheedy was born in County Tipperary, Ireland, in 1852. Few details of his early life are known and he said little about his childhood in later years. McSheedy's father's occupation was given as stonemason on his marriage certificate. The family moved to Cardiff, where the young McSheedy became a pupil teacher at St Peter's School, gaining a Queen's Scholarship to St Mary's Training College, Hammersmith. There he was awarded a second-division certificate in 1871. As a Catholic, he obtained the post of headmaster of St Peter's School, Stalybridge, Cheshire. In 1873 he married a local headmistress, Mary Agnes Worth, the daughter of an inspector of canals, and settled in nearby Mossley.

From an early stage McSheedy was involved in Irish radical politics in Britain, organising meetings and presenting the Irish case in English newspapers. He travelled in the North of England for the Irish National League of Great Britain. Established in 1875, the League was a Parnellite organisation which campaigned for the Irish cause in British politics and organised the Irish vote in English constituencies. In 1885, with Parnell's instruction to Irish voters to support Conservative candidates in the general election, the activities of the League may have contributed to the loss of some fifty Liberal seats. At this time McSheedy strongly supported the Parnellite endorsement of Conservative candidates, although he never became an Irish Nationalist MP.

Probably owing to his parliamentary ambitions, McSheedy declined in 1885 the offer of an inspectorship and moved to London to take up a teaching post with the London School Board at Scawfell Street School, Hackney. He settled for the rest of his life in Walthamstow, where he became important in local radical politics in the town. During the last quarter of the nineteenth century, rapid and extensive suburban development in south-west Essex transformed Walthamstow from a fashionable residence for shipowners and financiers into a dormitory suburb of London. The enterprise of the estate developers and the Great Eastern Railway Company created the new, predominantly working-class, commuter suburb. The extension of the railway in 1870 and, in particular, the promotion of workmen's trains and 'half fares' caused a spectacular growth rate in Walthamstow. During the three decades from 1871 to 1901 the population of Walthamstow itself increased more than sevenfold, from 11,092 to 95,131. This rapid urban development made Walthamstow the second largest constituency in Britain, with an electorate of 19,845 voters at the 1897 by-election.

McSheedy soon established his political reputation as 'the stormy petrel of Walthamstow', on account of his activities in municipal affairs. In Walthamstow, 'McSheedyism' became well known as a style of 'Radical–Progressive' politics which was keenly anti-privilege in its attempts to reform local government. Though he was often accused of being a 'Socialist' or 'revolutionary', as the leader of the Radicals within the local Liberal Party, McSheedy was always sternly anti-Socialist. Instead, as a practitioner of Lib–Lab politics, he championed working-class and trade union interests and attacked his Socialist opponents as much as local Tories and certain Liberals in Walthamstow.

In particular, the Vestry became the battleground where McSheedy first became infamous to his opponents for his leading role in the late 1880s and early 1890s in pressing for reform of the administration of the local charities. As a Catholic in an area strong in Nonconformity, McSheedy led an attack on the Anglican control of the various eleemosynary charities, largely vested in the vicar of St Mary's Church, Walthamstow, the Revd T. Parry and his successor, the Revd W. H. Langhorne. Elected by open and plural voting, only a handful of people controlled the Vestry and the administration of the local charities.

In 1890 McSheedy led an investigating committee which examined the accounts of the Monoux Grammar School, the Walthamstow Charity Governors and Jane Sabina Collard charity and pressed the Charity Commissioners in London to undertake a local inquiry in Walthamstow. He pointed to the monopoly of local offices, such as Clerk to the Vestry, Clerk to the Charity Governors and similar positions, held by William Houghton senior and members of the Houghton family, who also had business interests as solicitors and auctioneers. Under their management of the various charities, McSheedy alleged, only a ridiculously small proportion of the charities went to the poor in Walthamstow. In 1891, in response to McSheedy's pressure, the Vestry assembled six times in two months. The meetings were characterised by lively discussions and outbursts of rowdyism, and McSheedy's opponents told the Charity Commissioners that Walthamstow was in a state of 'social revolution'.

McSheedy's ability to influence packed Vestry meetings at this time was evident in the dismissal of the Clerk to the Walthamstow Vestry, William Houghton, by the parishioners in October 1891. McSheedy took the leading part in making the case for an official inquiry into the administration of the Walthamstow parochial charities, which resulted in the appointment of Edward Bouverie, barrister-at-law and Assistant Charity Commissioner, to investigate the allegations of maladministration and corruption. McSheedy was the main critic at the inquiry, which cleared the trustees and governors of the charities 'of any want of integrity on the part of those who submitted the accounts', but found 'irregularities and confusion in the administration' and recommended 'the establishment of an authoritative scheme for their regulation'. This placed the administration of the Walthamstow parochial charities on a more democratic footing by increasing and widening the representative nature of the trustees.

By this time McSheedy's participation in local affairs extended beyond the Vestry into general party politics in Walthamstow. As leader of the Radical group within the Walthamstow Liberal Association, he pressed his local party to place its printing contracts with 'trade union' firms and he was the main force behind the attempts to alter its rules in order to contest local elections on party lines. However, in 1895, though the change of name to the Walthamstow Central Liberal and Radical Association reflected important developments within the local party, it did not conceal the bitter divisions among the different factions, especially those surrounding the activities of the party's stormy petrel, McSheedy.

In 1891, for instance, the *Star* carried anonymous letters (written by McSheedy) which alleged that certain Walthamstow Liberals, including W. B. Whittingham, the prospective Liberal parliamentary candidate, had acted in local affairs in co-operation with Tory candidates, an action which McSheedy later complained had cost the Liberals the working-class vote at the general election. After the 1892 election, McSheedy opposed the readoption of Whittingham as the Liberal parliamentary candidate. In 1894 a bitter dispute arose during the AGM of the Liberal Party between the different district associations about the legitimacy of internal elections. McSheedy was again at the heart of this feud, with the original minutes of the meeting being expunged from the records.

McSheedy's political support was drawn from the working-class areas in the constituency, such as the St James Street ward, which had expanded rapidly in the 1880s and 1890s and in 1894 returned McSheedy and five other working-class Radicals to the new Urban District Council. His activities as a councillor were publicised in his own local newspaper, the *Walthamstow Reporter*, 'a weekly Journal devoted to active Progressive Radicalism and Labour Interests'. In the 1897 municipal elections, the 'McSheedyites' gained control of the Council and, though McSheedy himself was defeated in 1901, during this period of 'Progressive' rule there were many local developments in Walthamstow, including the building of an isolation hospital and baths, the provision of electric lighting, municipal trams and the official opening of Lloyd Park, the former home of William Morris. On the council, McSheedy introduced trade union wages and conditions for municipal employees, while his opponents accused him and his supporters of municipal extravagance.

As demonstrated during his agitation in the Vestry, McSheedy's vivid and turbulent style of politics aroused demonstrations of great passion and hostility among supporters and opponents. As editor of the *Walthamstow Reporter* and local councillor, his temperament in local government led to a large number of legal cases, most of which he lost. In 1895, for instance, in *Cropley* v. *Walthamstow Reporter* in the Queen's Bench Division of the High Court, the jury found against him. McSheedy's career was characterised by a series of dramatic headlines in the local press, such as 'Stormy Scene in Council Chamber' and 'The Vicar Grossly insulted'. His attacks on the Herbert family, for example, brought the resignation of W. T. Herbert, Walthamstow's first librarian, but earned McSheedy the enmity of Herbert's father, who published the powerful *Walthamstow Guardian*.

While the group of working-class politicians around McSheedy gained increasing influence in municipal affairs in Walthamstow, from 1886 to 1897 the parliamentary constituency, which also included the villadoms of Leyton and upper-class Woodford, remained firmly in the grasp of the local Tory Party. But at a by-election in February 1897 Sam Woods, president of the Lancashire and Cheshire Miners' Federation and Secretary of the Parliamentary Committee of the TUC, became the official Liberal nominee and the first working man to contest and win the Walthamstow Division. McSheedy played a prominent role in Woods's dramatic victory, and Woods's term as the member for Walthamstow, with the Progressives' control of the District Council, introduced the Lib–Lab phase in Walthamstow politics.

During this period, McSheedy was a valuable asset to the Liberal Party. Besides his work on the District Council, his *Walthamstow Reporter* was an important organ for maintaining strong Liberal links with the growing working-class electorate. The paper reported fully both the activities of Sam Woods as the new Lib–Lab MP, and the Walthamstow Labour League, founded in Walthamstow in 1897 two years before the local Socialist-supported Trades Council.

In this way, McSheedy took a prominent part in maintaining the Lib–Lab alliance against increasing Socialist activities in Walthamstow, although there was a secession in the ranks of the Progressives in 1903 to support the organising secretary of the London Society of Compositors, A. E. Holmes, as the independent Labour parliamentary candidate. But McSheedy led a well-orchestrated campaign of opposition to Holmes to the extent that Ramsay MacDonald and the LRC executive had finally to receive McSheedy's deputation of trade unionists who were opposed to him. One of the deputation was W. V. Osborne, secretary of the Walthamstow branch of the Amalgamated Society of Railway Servants, whose active involvement in the protests was a prelude to his later political activities, resulting in the famous legal decision known as the 'Osborne Judgment'. With the eventual withdrawal of Holmes in 1905, the Labour Party did not run a parliamentary candidate in Walthamstow until after the First World War and did not capture this working-class constituency until Valentine la Touche McEntee (later Lord McEntee) became the member for West Walthamstow in 1922.

Instead, the strength of Liberalism was expressed in John (later Viscount) Simon's parliamentary victories in 1906 and in January, November (by-election) and December 1910, and in the Progressives' control of the Urban District Council until 1912. By this stage, McSheedy's own political career was in decline, for in 1903 he was declared bankrupt, his only creditor being Cllr C. T. Wilkinson, to whom he owed £750 damages from a libel case in the previous year. According to the bankruptcy hearing, McSheedy's only income was his salary of £150 p.a. from the London School Board. In 1899 Sam Woods had brought McSheedy's case to the attention of Herbert Gladstone, but it appears McSheedy received little assistance from official Liberal sources. As a result, a rift developed between McSheedy and the shareholders of the *Walthamstow Reporter*, and on 23 October 1903 McSheedy brought out instead the first edition of his *Walthamstow Recorder*. But in 1905 Wilkinson, as the trustee under the McSheedy bankruptcy order, went to court again; and the *Walthamstow Recorder* appeared for the last time in 1906.

In 1907 his name again caused a political storm in Walthamstow on his appointment as the headmaster of Winns Avenue School, though on his retirement in 1917 his teaching record was widely acknowledged. Though he continued to play a part in local affairs (he was agent for the prospective Liberal MP for Chelmsford, S. W. J. Robinson), McSheedy's political career was effectively over. He died on 25 May 1923 in Whipps Cross Hospital, Leytonstone, aged seventy. There was no will. The funeral ceremony was held at St Patrick's Roman Catholic Church, Blackhorse Road, Walthamstow, and he was buried in the same grave as his wife (who had died in 1916) in St Patrick's, Leyton, the only Catholic cemetery in East London. They had one son, who had emigrated to Australia, and one daughter (Mrs A. Collins) who ran a dancing school under her married name.

Writings: *Ten Years of Local Government in Walthamstow* (Walthamstow, 1898). McSheedy also wrote on the history of the Irish cause in the *Stalybridge Reporter*, 12, 19, 26 Sep, 30 Oct 1885. His views on local and national politics were extensively reported in his two newspapers, the *Walthamstow Reporter* (1894–1903) and *Walthamstow Recorder* (1903–6).

Sources: (1) MS Charity Commission files, 230700, Charity Commission Central Register

Office; LP archives, LRC, 11, 13, 28; Walthamstow Liberal and Radical Association, minute books (1888 to date) and annual reports (1886–1903), Vestry House Museum, Walthamstow; Viscount Gladstone papers, BL Add. MS 46483. (2) Other: *United Ireland*, 19, 26 Sep, 3 Oct 1885; *Stalybridge Reporter*, 12 Sep, 31 Oct 1885; *Star*, 2, 3, 4 Apr 1891; 'Dismissal of Mr. William Houghton ...' and 'Mr. Houghton's Reply to Mr. McSheedy's Charges' (Walthamstow, 1891) [copy in Walthamstow Charity Accounts, 1889–90, XA2 Churchwardens 1/15, Vestry House Museum]; *Walthamstow Reporter*, 7, 14, 21 Dec 1894; *Walthamstow Guardian*, 2 Nov 1894, 3 Jan 1896; *Walthamstow Whip*, 16, 23, 30 Jan, 6 Feb 1897; *Socialist Critic*, 24 Mar, 21 Apr 1900; *Daily Graphic*, 4 Nov 1902; *District Times*, 20 Nov 1903; *Walthamstow Guardian*, 31 May, 7 June 1907, 3 Aug 1917; R. G. C. Desmond, *Our Local Press: a short historical account of the newspapers of Walthamstow* (Walthamstow, 1955); J. A. Jackson, *The Irish in Britain* (1963); *London, Aspects of Change* (Centre for Urban Studies, 1964); P. Thompson, *Socialists, Liberals and Labour: the struggle for London 1885–1914* (1967); R. Wall, 'History of the Development of Walthamstow' (London MPhil., 1968); J. S. Shepherd, 'The Lib–Labs and English Working-Class Politics, 1874–1906' (London PhD, 1980); C. C. Pond, *The Walthamstow and Chingford Railway* (Walthamstow, rev. ed. 1982). Biographical information: D. Mander, Vestry House Museum, Walthamstow; C. Wilkins-Jones, Ashton-under-Lyne PL, Greater Manchester. Obit. *Walthamstow Guardian*, 1 June 1923.

JOHN S. SHEPHERD

See also: *Valentine la Touche McEntee.

MANN, James (1784?–1832)
CLOTHWORKER, BOOKSELLER AND RADICAL REFORMER

Very little is known about the early years of James Mann's life. His background and upbringing are as mysterious as they are obscure. He was probably born in Leeds around 1784, and married his wife, Alice, herself a native of Leeds, in the early 1810s. Two children, Alfred and Eliza, were born by 1819. He was probably apprenticed to a cropper in a local finishing mill in the early 1800s. It was undoubtedly through this trade that Mann was first thrown into the mainstream of radical politics.

As a young clothworker in Leeds, Mann witnessed the power of workshop organisation and trade union agitation. From the 1790s there was virtually total unionisation among the 1500 Leeds croppers. Their 'Clothworkers' Brief Institution' had developed by 1802 into an elaborate organisation with town societies all over the West Riding and with close contacts with the Wiltshire shearmen. Their campaign against gig mills and machine shears culminated in 1802–3 in a successful strike against Wormald and Gott, the largest Leeds woollen manufacturers. This brought to an end for a decade any attempts to introduce finishing machinery in the borough. In 1812 there was very little machine-breaking in Leeds because of the continued strength of the croppers' union there. Leeds, however, was reputedly a centre of organisation, the headquarters of the secret 'Committee of Trades'. Luddites claimed to have 'twisted in' 7000 in the borough. Mann may have been among them. E. P. Thompson points to the evidence of a Lancashire informer who claimed to have received a letter from one Mann of Leeds in April 1812 describing Luddite successes [Thompson (1968) 645, n. 3].

There is no proof that this was James Mann, but by 1817 he was certainly at the forefront of the 'insurrectionary' movement. Again Leeds was thought by the Home Office to be the headquarters of a secret committee of which Mann was a member. By the end of May 1817 there was much talk in the Leeds croppers' shops of a planned uprising. On 5 June, Mann set out to tramp to a secret rendezvous at Thornhill Lees, near Dewsbury, with 'Oliver the Spy' and the other Leeds 'delegate', the flax-dresser Thomas Murray. Both men fell straight into Oliver's trap. The meeting was surrounded by troops and all ten Yorkshire 'delegates' were arrested. Although acquitted of sedition, Mann continued to be held for some months under the suspension of Habeas Corpus.

Whereas until 1817 his political work had been secret, this revolutionary episode in Mann's career and his connection with the spy scandal which surrounded it gave him immediate public recognition. In his first public appearance since his arrest, at a meeting of 10,000 reformers on Hunslet Moor, he was announced as 'James Mann, cloth dresser, previously in one of Sidmouth's dungeons'. The second consequence of the Thornhill Lees experience was that it seems to have confirmed in Mann's mind the connection between the defence of the rights of labour and the need for political reform. Throughout his career as a radical reformer from 1819 to 1832, Mann never lost sight of the principle that labour organisation, particularly of the poorest workers and the unemployed, was a necessary corollary to political agitation.

In the summer of 1819, against the background of mass unemployment among croppers, faltering union resistance to finishing machinery, emigration schemes, soup kitchens and public relief funds, Mann and other radicals from 1816–17 succeeded in politically activating the Leeds labour movement. Between June and October 1819 Mann regularly appeared as a major speaker at public reform meetings. Crowds of up to 10,000 heard him demand universal suffrage, annual parliaments and vote by ballot. Chairing such a meeting on Hunslet Moor in July, Mann called for a 'National Union for the Recovery of their Constitutional Rights'. After Peterloo, Mann toured the borough helping to prepare for the massive protest meeting in Leeds at the end of September.

By October 1819 Mann's domestic situation had also changed. His eldest daughter Eliza had been born. With a wife and at least two children to support, and prospects in the finishing trade looking bleak, Mann set up as a bookseller at 68 Briggate, in a shop adjoining the Bull and Mouth Inn. This business was to run in his family for the next sixty years.

Mann was a retailer for the publications, among others, of Thomas Wooler and Richard Carlile. As a 'political pamphlet-vendor' with a shop in the main thoroughfare of central Leeds, a street where all classes mixed, Mann retained his high public profile. The Methodists censured their local preachers for looking in Mann's shop window at the 'unfruitful works of darkness'. Liberal manufacturers were offended by the booklets Mann sold giving contraceptive advice to mill girls.

Something of this high profile was lost when Mann moved his shop to Duncan Street in the mid-1820s. The Duncan Street site was on the edge of the Calls district, one of the poorest working-class areas in central Leeds. The shop, however, contained a small 'warehouse' for publications, and the business was supplemented by a stall in Leeds market. By 1830 Mann could advertise as a 'bookseller, stationer, publication warehouse and agent for London and provincial newspapers'.

Oddly, for someone so involved in the radical movement and in selling unstamped publications, Mann seems neither to have had much to do with the struggle against the Combination Laws in the mid-1820s, nor to have actively participated in Carlile's campaign for a free press. Yet he was acquainted with leading Leeds trade unionists like Joseph Oates, and was also closely connected with the group of Leeds reformers who had gone to gaol for Carlile in the early 1820s. In February 1829 Mann helped organise among Leeds radicals a support fund for Carlile and Revd Robert Taylor.

From the summer of 1829, however, Mann was subject to a number of attacks by Carlile in the *Lion*, as the former began, once again, to agitate for parliamentary reform. Carlile arraigned him for believing that suffrage reform could relieve the people's distress, and dismissed him as foolish, that 'Silly Mann', and among the 'minor fry of radicals'. Mann fell foul of Carlile's differences with Cobbett, Hunt, and John Foster, the editor of the *Leeds Patriot*. All four were 'utterly despicable as politicians', and were accused of trying again 'to play over the game of the radical era' [*Lion*, 17 July 1829].

It was Carlile, by now on the fringe of the radical movement, who was to be proved wrong. A new 'radical era' was about to begin. These final three years were the most politically active of Mann's life. At numerous reform meetings during 1830 and 1831 he repeated the demands of 1819: universal suffrage, annual parliaments and the ballot. He linked universal suffrage to the Magna Carta. It was 'a right which God and nature proclaim to belong to the people', [*Leeds Mercury*, 20 Mar 1830]. He helped organise radical political unions at Almondbury and Elland, and was a constant thorn in the side of the bourgeois reformers in Leeds, led by Edward Baines and the Hunslet glass-manufacturer Joshua Bower. One month before the July revolution in France, Mann told a meeting of 1500 radicals on Hunslet Moor, 'the times were pregnant with events, and some great change must soon take place', and he hoped that 'by united exertions, a Radical Reform would be obtained' [ibid., 5 June 1830].

The culmination of this agitation was the establishment in November 1834 of the Leeds Radical Political Union 'to watch over the interests of the labouring classes of society'. Known for a time as 'Mann's Political Union', it was a direct rival to the Leeds Political Union established at the same time by Baines and Bower. The formation of the latter was a calculated move by Baines and the bourgeois reformers to split decisively with Mann's radicals and carry with them a large section of the skilled working class. Immediately, however, the radicals began to combat the rival Political Union. They infiltrated its meetings. They held mass rallies to condemn the Liberal parliamentary candidates. They passed resolutions affirming the support for Hunt and calling for a Poor Law for Ireland, the abolition of tithes and the sale of Church and Crown land. Relying on his personal contacts, Mann invited to Leeds Henry Hunt, who urged the radicals to support Sadler and the Tory factory reformers. The opposition countered with an attack by Cobbett on Mann and his supporters as the 'dupes of Hunt'.

There is no doubt that during the spring of 1832 the LRPU gradually moved closer to a Tory–radical alliance. In April, Sadler's factory commission began hearing evidence from Leeds witnesses. In May, Tories and radicals together burnt an effigy of Baines in the streets. Radical leaders, Mann, William Rider, John Ayrey, joined with the secretary of the Leeds Trade Union, John Powlett, to defend the Union from attacks in the *Leeds Mercury*.

From May onwards the political radicals were overshadowed by trade union agitation in Leeds. The summer was marked by widespread union successes in enforcing wage increases, in spite of heavy unemployment among weavers and millworkers, and in the face of a raging cholera epidemic in the town. At the end of July, Mann led a meeting of 500 jobless on Woodhouse Moor. It was the first of a number of such rallies to be held, in a manner reminiscent of the unemployed croppers' campaign of 1819. It was, however, Mann's last public meeting. Four days later, at one o'clock in the morning of 2 August 1832, he suffered an attack of 'malignant cholera'. Eight hours later he was dead.

James Mann's widow, Alice, was only thirty-eight when he died. She was left with nine children, the youngest being less than two years old. Alice carried on her husband's business with vigour. She was the Leeds agent for the *Pioneer*, *Poor Man's Guardian* and Hobson's *Voice of the West Riding*, among other radical papers. Between 1833 and 1834 the shop in Duncan Street became a clearing-house for subscriptions and donations by the 'friends of the cause in Leeds' and for supporters of the Leeds Trade Union. By the autumn of 1834 she had set up as a letterpress printer and publisher, possibly in partnership with Joshua Hobson, who had recently moved to Leeds. By 1851 Alice Mann was employing five men in the Duncan Street shop, and two of her sons, Alfred and Arthur, were also trained as printers and compositors. Her various publications included Mann's *Historical Almanack*

(1835–69) grammar books, maps and tourist guides. Three influential volumes of *The Emigrant's Complete Guide* were published in 1849–50 and publicised by Joseph Barker in the *People*, at a time when many were turning to emigration as the only solution to the Chartist failure to achieve political reform at home. Alice Mann survived her husband by almost half a century. Her son Alfred was still running the stationery shop in Duncan Street in 1888.

James Mann was the leading radical reformer in Leeds between 1819 and 1832. He was important both locally and nationally not only because he spanned the generation between Luddism and the political reform movement of the 1830s, but also because he remained true to his principles. These principles were those with which he had set out with Oliver on the march to Thornhill Lees in 1817. He proclaimed to hundreds in the Leeds Cloth Hall yard in 1830 that 'as an individual who has been brought up in the ranks of the labouring classes I feel it to be my duty to advocate their cause' [*Leeds Mercury*, 20 Mar 1830]. His obituary echoed his own words: 'Mr Mann sprang from the people and he never for one moment would give up the people's rights' [*PMG*, 11 Aug 1832]. Mann's political creed was standard fare – annual parliaments, universal suffrage, vote by ballot – but he regarded these as inalienable rights and non-negotiable. 'During the late Reform Bill Mr Mann was too stubborn and sincere a Radical to give up all the principles he had suffered for, as so many did merely because it was then the fashion' [ibid.].

Undoubtedly Mann's Political Union failed to carry with it the bulk of the Leeds working class in the spring of 1832 in its opposition to the Reform Bill. However, Mann remained true to 'Real Reform'. Equally the drift towards the Tory–radical alliance did not essentially alter his political independence. The organisation of the unemployed, for instance, was not something undertaken by any other local radical at the time, though it was repeated by a handful of Chartists in the 1840s. Mann's loyalty to Hunt drew fierce attacks from Cobbett, Carlile and Baines, yet he himself bitterly resented the unfairness of being called a 'dupe'. At a meeting of the LRPU in February 1832 Mann had exhorted his members 'above all not to be influenced in their public proceedings by mere names, but to look at the conduct of individuals. These were the real friends of the poor, who advocated the rights of the working classes' [ibid., 4 Feb 1832]. It was his clarity of vision, his 'consistency in times of danger', his 'honesty' and loyalty to his own class which marked him out from the more vacillating of his fellow radicals. 'No person', began his obituary, 'will be more missed in Leeds than Mr Mann.'

Sources: (1) MS: HO 40/9, 10 (Oliver's Narrative) and 107/2321 (1851 Census, Leeds), PRO. (2) Newspapers: *Leeds Mercury*, 1817–34; *Lion*, 1829; *PMG*, 1832–3; *Pioneer*, 1833–4; *Voice of the West Riding*, 1833–4; *People*, 1849–50. (3) Other: Leeds directories, 1822–88; R. C. on the Employment of Children in Factories, *First Report*, 1833 XX, C2, evidence of Samuel Smith, 47; W. Hirst, *History of the Woollen Trade for the last Sixty Years* (Leeds, 1844); W. J. Linton, *James Watson: a memoir* (Manchester, 1880); A. S. Turberville and F. Beckwith, 'Leeds and Parliamentary Reform 1820–32', *Publications of the Thoresby Society 41* (1946) misc. 12, 1–88; A. Aspinall, *The Early English Trade Unions* (1949); A. Briggs, 'The Background of the Parliamentary Reform Movement in Three English Cities (1830–2)', *Cambridge Historical J. 10* (1952) 293–317; J. F. C. Harrison, 'Chartism in Leeds', in *Chartist Studies* ed. A. Briggs (1959) 66–97; M. Brook, 'Joseph Barker and the *People*, the True Emigrant's Guide', *Publications of the Thoresby Society 46* (1961) misc. 13, 331–78; E. P. Thompson, *The Making of the English Working Class* (1963; rev. ed. 1968); D. Fraser, 'The Fruits of Reform: Leeds politics in the 1830s', *Northern History 8* (1972) 89–111. OBIT. *Leeds Mercury and Leeds Patriot and Yorkshire Advertiser*, 4 Aug 1832; *PMG*, 11 Aug 1832.

NOTE. The editors wish to acknowledge the additional biographical information supplied by Professor F. K Donnelly, University of New Brunswick, Canada.

ROBIN PEARSON

See also: †Richard CARLILE; Joshua HOBSON.

MARSDEN, Richard (1802/3–58)
CHARTIST

Born in or near Manchester in 1802 or 1803, Marsden was a hand-loom weaver. He left Manchester in search of work during the slump of 1829, and settled with his family in the weaving township of Bamber Bridge, near Preston, Lancashire. He made his first recorded political speech at the inaugural meeting of the Preston Operative Radical Association in November 1837. He was secretary of the Preston committee which submitted evidence to the Royal Commission on Hand-loom Weavers, and was the principal witness before Commissioner R. M. Muggeridge during his visit to the town in May 1838. Besides reporting the specific grievances of the weavers, he argued for universal suffrage and the repeal of the Corn Laws. He was an active Chartist from the beginning, chairing the first public demonstration in Preston on 5 November 1838, when he introduced Feargus O'Connor, James Whittle and several local speakers. After making a fiery speech supporting the Charter, Marsden was elected to represent North Lancashire at the National Convention.

In London he was a consistent and unyielding advocate of 'ulterior measures'. Inside and outside the Convention he urged the need to prepare direct action for the day when the Chartist petition would be rejected by Parliament. He spoke in this vein with Julian Harney and William Rider at the celebrated meeting of the London Democratic Association on 28 February 1839; their implied criticism of the Convention provoked considerable resentment and an (unsuccessful) attempt to have them expelled. During the spring of 1839 Marsden travelled as an official missionary for the Convention in Sussex and the Welsh borders, toured Ireland on his own initiative, and returned for a brief speaking tour of North Lancashire. All this time he continued to assert the people's right to armed self-defence and became known as a prominent spokesman for 'physical force' Chartism, though he seems to have believed that its use would never be necessary. He was much affected by his visit to Ireland. He had long been fascinated by that country, puzzled by the weakness of Chartism there and the firm attachment of its people to Daniel O'Connell. He spent a few days in Dublin, then went on to Kilkenny, and was greatly moved by the poverty of the people: 'I had felt poverty in England', he wrote, 'but never shall I believe that we endure a thousandth part of the misery here undergone' [King (1981) 11].

In August 1839 Marsden returned to Preston for the unsuccessful 'national holiday'. Almost immediately he vanished to avoid arrest on a warrant relating to a violent speech that he had made in Newcastle at the beginning of the month. He was in Bradford during the abortive Chartist rising in January 1840, though the exact nature of his involvement is unknown. (The Bradford authorities were little better informed, offering a reward for the capture of 'James Marsden, supposed to be of Newcastle or Carlisle'). Marsden then moved to Bolton, where he lived under an assumed name and worked at his trade. Arrested there on 16 July 1840, he was taken to Bradford and then to Newcastle before being released two weeks later. The charges were dropped and the Chartists raised a national subscription for him. He remained in Bolton for almost a year, working at his loom and playing an active part in local Chartist affairs.

Prompted by Feargus O'Connor, the North Lancashire Chartists appointed Marsden as their paid itinerant lecturer. In July 1841 he moved back to Preston and spent the rest of the year in almost continuous speaking tours which, after his resignation from the North Lancashire post, took him to Cumberland and on into Scotland. When Chartist activity revived early in 1842, Marsden was again busy in his home area. 'Better die by the sword than of hunger,' he told a mass meeting on 29 May, 'and, if we are to be butchered, why not commence the bloody work at once?' [*Northern Star*, 4 June 1842]. Although in June 1842 the Preston Chartists advocated a standing joint conference of trade unionists and Chartists to fight for political reform, the great general strike of July and August was late in crossing the Ribble. Marsden was arrested in a confrontation between strikers and the military just outside Preston on 17 August, but no charges were pressed against him.

In the mid-1840s he rarely left Preston, but he remained an active Chartist and exerted a wider influence through a series of letters to the *Northern Star* which, along with a sustained correspondence with the *Preston Guardian* and the *Preston Chronicle*, defined his own political position. Unlike many more prominent national figures, Marsden became *less* liberal and more vigorously anti-capitalist after 1839. Formerly sympathetic to middle-class radicals like the famous Preston teetotaller and free trader Joseph Livesey, he came increasingly to stress that Chartism was a class movement aiming at the emancipation of working people. His sharp opposition to the Anti-Corn Law League brought him into conflict with the liberal-leaning majority of the Preston Chartists.

Marsden's isolation was increased by his rejection of O'Connor's Land Plan. At the Birmingham Convention in 1843 he 'asked Mr. O'Connor how they would get the Land from the landed aristocracy, and would it not be acknowledging . . . that they had a right to the land by purchasing it from them?' [*Northern Star*, 9 Sep 1843]. O'Connor brushed off the criticism, replying that no one objected to buying the wheat that was grown on the land and prophesying that the landlords would accept even Chartist money. For several years Marsden continued to regard the Land Plan as a diversion from the struggle for political reform, but by 1847 its sustained attractiveness for working people, at a time when political campaigning was proving so difficult, finally overcame his opposition to the scheme. Pragmatic support soon gave way to a more principled endorsement of the Land Plan as a means of strengthening the popular appeal of the Charter itself, and before long he was advocating the Plan as the only alternative to emigration and armed revolt.

He was never a 'nothing but the Charter' man. He involved himself with the Ten Hours Movement, with the 1844 campaign against proposed changes to the Master and Servant Laws, and then (through his organising activities for the National Association of United Trades for the Protection of Labour) with trade unionism in the cotton factories. At the end of 1845 Marsden was appointed secretary of the newly-formed Preston Power-loom Weavers' Union. His manifesto summarised his mature political beliefs: 'We are not inanimate machines; the power to think, to reason, and reflect is ours; sufficient at least, to enable us to discriminate between overpowering necessity on the one hand, and unfeeling inhuman avarice on the other. This power the tyrant may debase or brutalise, but while life exists, he can never wholly destroy.' But cotton unionism in Preston was notoriously feeble, and the weavers' union effectively disintegrated by the summer of 1847, when Marsden left Preston and moved to Blackburn to take charge of the more prosperous weavers' union there.

Marsden was again chosen to represent North Lancashire at the Chartist National Convention of 1848. In a sad echo of 1839 he was sent out as a missionary once more, this time to the North East and the Midlands. His speeches were now relatively subdued, both at the Convention and at the National Assembly which followed it. Marsden realised only too well how slim were the chances of success, and his last contribution to the Assembly, on 13 May 1848, was deeply pessimistic. He explained that he:

did not rise to blame the London men, or the Executive, or the Assembly; he exonerated them all, and himself too. Then they might ask him whom he would blame. The fact was, they were in leading strings, and they had not known it. Like wild colts they had gone to the end of their tether, and without knowing it, had started off still further. However, the pluck back which threw all together on the ground, let them know their condition. That was their position now, it was useless denying the truth, or to struggle against it.

To some extent Marsden's disillusionment was the product of a decade of unsuccessful struggle, compounded (we may suspect) by ill health. It was reinforced by the virtual collapse of Chartism in North Lancashire after April 1848, and by the absence of any revival, either in the summer of that year or subsequently. R. G. Gammage's careful investigation in 1853 found a small Chartist presence only in Padiham and Bacup; there was nothing in Preston or Blackburn [Jones (1975) 209]. Marsden's withdrawal from political life was almost immediate, and very nearly complete. His last, despairing letter to the *Northern Star* appeared on 10 June 1848, and for a few weeks thereafter his house was used for trade union and political gatherings. In 1850 he wrote to Julian Harney's *Red Republican* reaffirming his support for the Charter, but this seems to have been the limit of his involvement. After 1848 there is no record of his presence at public meetings, and the flow of letters to the local press ceased. Unlike many old Chartists, Richard Marsden played no part in the great Preston strike of 1853–4. Nothing more was heard of him, in fact, until his death in Bamber Bridge on 28 January 1858. No will has been located.

Writings: Marsden wrote long and cogent letters to the national Chartist and local press. Some autobiographical detail is given in his speeches, and in letters in the *Preston Chronicle* (2 June 1838), *Northern Star* (10 Sep 1842) and *Preston Guardian* (10 July 1847). His views on economic, political and social questions are given at length in letters to the *Northern Star* (8 Mar, 8 and 29 June 1839; 15 Aug, 3 and 24 Oct 1840; 9 Oct 1841; 18 June, 10 Sep 1842; 26 Aug, 23 Dec 1843; 29 Mar, 5 July 1845; 30 May, 6 June 1846; 16 Jan, 25 Sep, 4 Dec 1847), *Preston Chronicle* (16 Oct 1841; 22 Mar, 5 Apr 1845; 24 Dec 1846; 2 Jan 1847) and *Preston Guardian* (4 May, 24 Aug 1844; 17 May, 2 Aug, 13 Dec 1845; 7 Feb, 25 Apr, 4 July, 5 Dec 1846; 2 Jan, 3 Apr, 10 July, 7 Aug 1847; 29 Jan 1848). *See also* General Committee of the United Trades, *Remarks on the Proposed Reduction in the Wages of the Operatives* (Blackburn, Lancs [1848?]) [copy in Blackburn PL], which is most certainly written by Marsden. His last recorded public statement is in Harney's *Red Republican*, 28 Sep 1850.

Sources: (1) MS: The Home Office papers are generally unrevealing about Chartism in Preston, and add very little to our knowledge of Marsden. He does not seem to have left diaries or other personal papers.
(2) Newspapers and periodicals: Apart from the *Northern Star*, details of Marsden's Chartist activities in Preston may be found in the *Preston Chronicle*, which is improved upon (from 10 Feb 1844) by the *Preston Guardian*. His first arrest and its sequel are reported in the *Northern Liberator*, 1, 8, 15 Aug 1840. The second arrest is noted in the *Preston Pilot*, 3 Sep 1842. The last reference that has been traced (apart from an obituary) is in the *Red Republican*, 19 Oct 1850.
(3) Other: Reports of Assistant Hand-loom Weavers' Commissioners, pt V, 1840 XXIV; R. G. Gammage, *The History of the Chartist Movement, from its Commencement down to the Present Time* (1854–5; 2nd ed. Newcastle 1894, repr. with an Introduction by J. Saville, 1969); A. J. Peacock, *Bradford Chartism, 1838–1840* (Borthwick Papers, no. 36: York, 1969) 53 pp.; D. J. Rowe, 'Some Aspects of Chartism on Tyneside', *Int. Rev. Social Hist. 16*, pt 1 (1971) 38, n. 3, which cites an erroneous Home Office source claiming that Marsden fled to America early in 1840; D. J. V. Jones, *Chartism and the Chartists* (1975); H. I. Dutton and J. E. King, *'Ten Per Cent and No Surrender': the Preston strike, 1853–1854* (Cambridge, 1981); J. E. King, *Richard Marsden and the Preston Chartists, 1837–1848* (Univ. of Lancaster, Centre for North-West Regional Studies, Occasional Paper no. 10: Lancaster,

1981) 48 pp. Biographical information: R. Fyson, Newcastle-under-Lyne, Staffordshire. OBIT. *People's Paper*, 27 Feb 1858.

JOHN KING

MARTYN, Caroline Eliza Derecourt (1867–96)
CHRISTIAN SOCIALIST AND FEMINIST

Caroline Martyn was born on 3 May 1867 into a comfortably placed family in the city of Lincoln. Her father was James William Martyn, a police superintendent (later Deputy Chief Constable of Lincolnshire) and her mother Kate Eleanor (née Hewitt), who had nine children, Caroline being the eldest.

She had what was described as an 'excellent education' as a weekly boarder at Beaumont House School, Lincoln, from the age of thirteen to eighteen; and afterwards was a governess in a number of posts, none of which she found congenial. Subsequently she became a schoolteacher, first in a Church School at Belvedere, Kent, and then in a Board School at Reading (1890–1). Here she lived with an aunt, Mrs Bailey, whose radical Liberalism probably influenced Caroline Martyn, although she appears to have moved further to the left while still at Reading. There is an early letter she wrote to Sidney Webb on 10 July 1891 in which she sent him details of teachers' salaries paid by the School Board, and was signing herself 'Fabian'. Already her feminism was showing itself: 'I cannot think', she wrote, 'why women [teachers] should have to receive less pay for the same work – one reason may be that the regulation of the price of labour is in the hands of men.' She further noted in this letter that she had just become unemployed and that she was going back to her home in Lincoln for a month's holiday; but she was soon to be appointed a governess at the Royal Orphanage Asylum, Wandsworth Common, London. Here she was grossly overworked, and, after a year, a breakdown in health obliged her to resign during the summer of 1892.

Her acceptance of Fabian Socialism was a considerable break with her conservative Anglican upbringing. She always remained deeply religious, and her views on the relationship between religion and politics were those of many of her contemporaries. Thus in a letter written to a cousin in September 1893 she emphasised that 'The Socialist movement is distinctly and wholly a religious movement; it is the embodiment of the principle "Love thy neighbour as thyself".' During the period of her stay at Wandsworth she had joined the Guild of St Matthew.

In the early spring of 1893 she became a regular contributor to the *Christian Weekly*. This had originally been called *Religious Bits* and on 15 April 1893 the journal announced a change of name to the *Christian Weekly and Religious Bits*, although it seems thenceforth always to have been referred to by the first part of its title. In the same issue 'Miss Carrie Martyn' is introduced as a future contributor. Her writings in the *Christian Weekly* offered a good summary of her intellectual and political position. By this time she was also an articulate feminist. In the first of an important series of articles entitled 'Women's Work and Wages' (23 Sep–9 Dec 1893) Caroline Martyn began with these words:

After many centuries of repression woman is learning to use her human faculties. Eighteen hundred years have passed since Christ came to remove the curse of inferiority from the mothers of the generations. It has taken them all these centuries to recognise their salvation, and now they have commenced the struggle to realise it. The restoration of woman to her true position of comrade and helper of man, different, but of equal value, necessitates a real and complete social revolution, for her emancipation from dependence on man has as its corollary her entrance into all the paths in life where subsistence is to be found.

Caroline Martyn combined her feminism with her commitment to the labour movement. In the same article she argued the identity of interests of all workers against the wealth and power of the few in whose hands were their livelihood:

Women are awaking to facts, they are learning that they must insist on their rights or they will never obtain them; they are learning that individual effort is of little value, but that organisation is a lever whose force cannot be estimated. Men are beginning to understand that the interests of all workers are identical, and that women's labour will swamp their unions as unskilled labour would, unless their sister human is taken into fellowship and allowed to contribute her share to the triumph of right over might [ibid.].

The articles which followed this introduction in the *Christian Weekly* were concerned with a number of trades and occupations in which women formed a substantial part, or the whole, of the labour force: shop assistants, prison officials, schoolmistresses, private governesses, postal workers, journalists, boot and shoe operatives, flower girls, and factory workers in general. Together these articles form a useful collection for the social historian, for Martyn was a clear-sighted observer with a warm and sympathetic social conscience. She was also involved in lecturing and speaking – originally at the suggestion of Bruce Wallace of the Labour Church – and she came to rely increasingly on lecturing engagements for her income to the point where she employed an agent, a Mr Booth of Bradford. In a remarkably informative letter to her cousin Julia, already quoted above and written from London on 18 September 1893, Caroline said that her most useful work, which she did most successfully and with the greatest ease, was lecturing. Between the beginning of July and mid-September 1893 she had lectured forty times. 'The *Workman's Times* says I am the best woman speaker on Socialism in London. I often get rapturous notices in local papers and so on. . . . I prefer speaking in the open air to working men. At Southampton I had at one of my meetings an audience of at least 1000.' She made no claims for herself, believing that in this work she was 'used by God, "only an empty vessel", but used sometimes'.

Martyn continued her peripatetic lecturing life through 1894 and 1895 and she became a very well-known personality, being elected to the NAC of the ILP early in 1896. She was also writing in the *Labour Leader*, and among her last contributions were three articles on factory legislation (29 Feb, 28 Mar, 4 Apr 1896). In the February article she reviewed Beatrice Webb's Fabian pamphlet no. 67, *Women and the Factory Acts*, and warmly commended its approach.

During the campaign for the well-known by-election at Aberdeen in April–May 1896, Caroline Martyn acted as secretary to Tom Mann, and did a good deal of speaking directly on his behalf, since, for part of the time, Mann was suffering from a sore throat. She had already spoken for Mann when he contested Colne Valley in the general election of 1895 [Clark (1981) 68]. Soon after the Aberdeen campaign ended, in which Mann received 2479 votes, Martyn was appointed editor of *Fraternity*, the journal of the International Society for the Brotherhood of Man, by the Society's founder, the Scottish writer Mrs Isabella Fyvie Mayo (1843–1914), who was greatly struck by her 'oratorical impressiveness and beauty' [*Fraternity*, 1 July 1896, 7]. The July issue of *Fraternity* was the only issue under Martyn's editorship. She died suddenly of pleurisy in Dundee on 23 July 1896, and was buried there in Balgay Cemetery.

She had already agreed before her death to conduct a fortnight's campaign in Aberdeen for the organisation of mill and factory workers, and also to deliver a lecture under the auspices of the ILP; and she was especially mourned in that town. But her death was a shock to the whole movement. The *Labour Leader* gave over a whole page to her memory on 1 August 1896 and under a sketch of her was a poem by James Connell, author of 'The Red

Flag'. There was also published in this issue a letter from Mrs Mayo, written in her somewhat cloudy, rather verbose style, making the point which she later repeated in her autobiography [Mayo (1910) 225–9]: that Caroline Martyn greatly overtaxed her health by her heavy programme of speaking engagements all over the country. Mrs Mayo had the sense of a 'want of repose' arising from Martyn's failure to interiorise her beliefs, and she went so far as to give her opinion that Martyn's belief in her work as her best method of serving her kind wavered before her death. The causes of the physical weakness which contributed to Martyn's early death were identified by Mrs Mayo as long rail journeys, with little luggage, to meet a heavy programme of speaking engagements, for small fees and often with accommodation provided in the overcrowded houses of her poor supporters. Martyn's dissatisfaction with this nomadic lecturing life, to which Mrs Mayo refers, is borne out by views expressed in surviving letters to her cousin Julia Wallis. Shortly before her death Carolyn Martyn had decided she would accept the Fabian Society's offer of the Hutchinson Trust lectures and a study grant for three months.

She was a much-loved personality. Pelling described her as 'austere' [(1965 ed.) 155] and this may well be how many found her, for she was utterly dedicated and single-minded. Her death brought many tributes: as the *Labour Leader* wrote (1 Aug 1896), 'everyone feels that sense of vacuum and unsatisfied longing which only those who have lost a near relative can properly understand'. A requiem service was held for her at St John's Church, Great Marlborough Street, London. When the first Clarion Van (of 1895) was replaced by one suitable for mobile propaganda in 1897, subscribed to by *Clarion* readers, it was named in her honour [Pelling (1965 ed.) 178, n. 3, and photograph, 134].

Writings: A series of seven articles under the main title of 'Women's Work and Wages', in *Christian Weekly*, 23 Sep–9 Dec 1893, of which the individual titles are 'Do Women reduce Wages?' (n.s. no. 23, 23 Sep, 252–3), 'Women's Work behind the Counter' (no. 24, 30 Sep, 265–6), 'Prison Officials' (no. 25, 7 Oct, 285), 'Private Governesses' (no. 26, 14 Oct, 305–6), 'In the Post Office' (no. 27, 21 Oct, 325), 'Lady Journalists' (no. 28, 28 Oct, 345), 'In the Boot and Shoe Trade' (no. 30, 11 Nov, 385), 'Flower Girls' (no. 32, 25 Nov, 425–6) and 'In Factories' (no. 34, 9 Dec, 465); 'In Belgium', *Clarion*, 20 July 1895, 232; 'Annual Conference for Women's Trades' [letter], *Labour Leader*, 1 Feb 1896; 'Edith Lanchester', ibid., 15 Feb 1896; 'Women and the Factory Acts', ibid., 29 Feb 1896; 'Factory Legislation in Detail', ibid., 28 Mar and 4 Apr 1896; (ed.) *Fraternity 4*, no. 1 (1 July 1896).

Sources: (1) MS: Photocopies of six letters from Caroline Martyn, 1887–94, press cuttings and Lena Wallis, *Life and Letters of Caroline Martyn* (*Labour Leader*, 1898), deposited by R. F. S. Thorne (MSS 21/1738), MRC, Warwick Univ.; letter from Caroline Martyn to Sidney Webb, 10 July 1891, Webb Trade Union Coll., Section A, vol. *47*, item 29, fos 84–5, BLPES. (2) Other: *Clarion*, 22 and 29 Feb, 21 Mar, 25 Apr and 4 July 1896; 'Candidature of Tom Mann', *Aberdeen Evening Express*, 27, 28, 29, 30 Apr and 2 May 1896; *Labour Annual* (1896) 97 [portrait], 212 and (1897) 199; I. F. Mayo, 'Our New Editor: Caroline Martyn', *Fraternity 4*, no. 1 (1 July 1896) 7; idem, *Recollections of what I saw, what I lived through, and what I learned during more than Fifty Years of Social and Literary Experience* (1910); H. Pelling, *The Origins of the Labour Party* (1954; 2nd ed. Oxford, 1965); D. Clark, *Colne Valley: Radicalism to Socialism* (1981). Biographical information: Dr D. Rubinstein, Hull Univ. OBIT. *Aberdeen Evening Express*, 24 July 1896; *Labour Leader*, 25 July and 1 Aug 1896; *Clarion* [with portrait] and *Huntly Express*, 1 Aug 1896; *Glasgow Commonweal 7*, no. 5 (Aug 1896); *Fraternity 4*, no. 3 (1 Sep 1896).

JOHN SAVILLE
RICHARD STOREY

See also: Thomas HANCOCK for the Guild of St Matthew (**Special Note**).

MATHER, Joseph (1737–1804)
RADICAL SONGWRITER AND SINGER

Writing in 1862, John Wilson of Sheffield, a collector of Mather's songs, recorded one version of the singer's origins:

> Little is known of Joseph Mather's parentage or of his early history. If his obituary notice be correct he was born in 1737. ... he was ushered into this world in a locality that enjoyed the odoriferous name of 'Cack Alley'; my informant however, says that, 'vulgar people called it by a more expressive adjective'. This delightful region was a 'jennel' which led from Lambert-street to Westbar Green. Its name very probably accurately described its sanitary condition [Wilson (1862) vii].

According to another account, however, Mather was born in the village of Chelmorton, Derbyshire, and moved to Sheffield as a child. The town was then a compact community of some 10,000 people, largely dependent for their livelihood on the workshop-based cutlery trades. By the time of his death the metal trades were still pre-eminent, though changing in their organisation, and the population was over 45,000. During this period of economic change and, in the late eighteenth century, widespread political agitation, Mather's songs voiced the popular feelings of workers.

In the earlier part of his life Mather appears to have been untouched by any real sense of political and social injustice. He was apprenticed to the file trade during a period of relative prosperity. After serving his time he became a journeyman in the workshop of Nicholas Jackson, a file-manufacturer in Shemeld Croft. At some stage he rented his own workshop and was self-employed – a common practice in the metal trades – only to be overcome by debt. His autobiographical song 'The File Hewer's Lamentation' throws some light on his failure. His growing family stretched his resources:

> My income for me, Nelly,
> Bob, Tom, Poll, Bet, and Sally,
> Could hardly fill each belly,
> Should we eat salt and grains.

But he also blamed his hardships on the 'infernal ways' of 'knaves with power' who deserved to die:

> A hanging day is wanted;
> Was it by justice granted,
> Poor men distress'd and daunted
> Would then have cause to sing –
> To see in active motion
> Rich knaves in full proportion,
> For their unjust extortion
> And vile offences swing.

These sentiments were shared by many artisans, who resented the power of local merchants to reduce the prices paid for goods. One of Mather's most popular songs was directed against a master named Jonathan Watkinson, who required his men to make thirteen knives to the dozen. The chorus suggested a suitable fate for Watkinson, who was Master Cutler in 1787:

> And may the odd knife his great carcase dissect,
> Lay open his vitals for men to inspect,
> A heart full as black as the infernal gulph,
> In that greedy, blood-sucking, bone-scraping wolf.

It was said that on one occasion Watkinson was driven from the theatre when the gallery, led by Mather, burst into 'Watkinson's Thirteens'.

Mather's ability to articulate the robust artisan culture made him a popular tavern singer and entertainer. He wrote on a variety of subjects; his earlier songs often celebrated the everyday life of the local population, particularly its leisure-time pursuits. Sitting backwards on his donkey (according to folk memory, on a bull during race week), 'Old Joe' became a local character whose newest songs were keenly awaited. Some songs were printed as broadsheets and hawked about; others circulated orally and only later were written down – Mather himself apparently could read but not write – and not all have survived. Nor, of the fifty or so songs that have been recorded, are the tunes always known. The radical printer John Crome, made the first collection in 1811. When John Wilson published a fuller edition in 1862, he was able to record that Sheffield workmen still sang Mather's songs.

His later songs, especially those written during a prolific period in the 1790s, reflect the upsurge in radical ideas that was taking place. The disruption of trade caused by the American War of Independence led to severe hardships for Sheffield's workers. At the same time the merchants and larger manufacturers were intent on imposing a free market and breaking down the traditional regulation of wages and prices. In the struggle that followed, Mather was a champion of labour, although his interests were engaged wherever popular rights were challenged. His performances outside the Cutlers' Hall, where the magistrates as well as the increasingly exclusive masters and merchants met, drew the attention of the authorities. At one stage he was bound over to keep the peace for a year. On a number of occasions he was reputedly imprisoned in the town gaol – though unpaid debts rather than vocal agitation may have been the reason for this.

After 1789 interest in the French Revolution further heightened the political consciousness of Sheffield's citizenry. Within a few months of its establishment in 1791, the Sheffield Society for Constitutional Information had registered 2000 members. At its meetings members sang, to the tune of the national anthem, the Jacobin hymn 'God Save Great Thomas Paine', which Mather was said to have written. There is no doubt that the final verse was in keeping with his views:

> Despots may howl and yell,
> Tho' they're in league with hell
>> They'll not reign long;
> Satan may lead the van,
> And do the worst he can,
> Paine and his Rights of Man
>> Shall be my song.

Also of this period was his song 'Britons, Awake'. This was written to commemorate the Sheffield Jacobins' successful amendment to a motion brought before a town meeting to thank the King for his proclamation of May 1792 against seditious writings. Mather's lines attacked 'the vile crew' who met at 'Bang-beggar Hall' (the Cutlers' Hall) to deprive Britons of their liberties:

> A vile proclamation pick'd up at hell's mouth,
> That means to make libels or treason by truth –
> They met to give sanction, but I must confess
> I've seen a more excellent speech by an ass.

In a footnote on this verse in his edition of Mather's songs John Wilson pointed to the Book of Numbers Chapter 22 – the story of Balaam's ass. Whether or not Mather intended to make this allusion, he did have considerable biblical knowledge. When in 1790 George Wood, a scissors-manufacturer, was instrumental in having five grinders committed to prison, Mather dubbed him the 'Hallamshire Haman'. Mather's song compared the grinders' persecution by Wood with that of Mordecai by Haman in Chapter three of the Book of Esther; the chorus ran:

> Then Haman he vowed that all Israel should die;
> And Mordecai hang 'twixt the earth and the sky;
> But though he on plunder and rapine was bent,
> He never took discount at fifty per cent.

Mather's theological knowledge probably derived from his connection with Methodism. In spite of his admiration for Paine and his celebration of the roistering life of the public house and racecourse, he was an avid reader of the Bible. Crome wrote of his 'unimpeachable' moral character, though added he was 'too easily led by cheerful company into some excesses'. At one stage he was associated with the 'Thomas Paine' Kilhamite Methodist congregation at Scotland Street.

In 'True Reformers' Mather celebrated the leaders of the reform movement: among those mentioned in his verses were Thomas Hardy, Thomas Muir, Horne Tooke, Joseph Gerrald, John Thelwall and Henry Yorke. Part of the evidence in Hardy's trial stated that in Sheffield Joseph Gales, who printed the *Sheffield Register* as well as some of Mather's songs in broadsheet form, had arranged for pikes to be made. Gales fled to America and the *Register* was succeeded by the *Iris* under the editorship of James Montgomery. Soon Montgomery was arraigned and suffered two periods of imprisonment. The second of these was for libel after he had published an account of a riot that took place on 4 August 1795. Mather sang of the event in much more vehement terms but escaped prosecution, perhaps because the authorities regarded him as too disreputable to merit attention. A disturbance began when a crowd gathered by the parade ground where soldiers with a grievance over pay were refusing to disband. Radicals, who resented the garrison which had been stationed in the town in 1791, encouraged the soldiers to stand firm. When the onlookers refused to disperse, an officer, Colonel Althorpe, rode amongst them brandishing his sword. In the riot that followed local volunteers were called out. They fired into the crowd, killing two men and injuring several others. The anger of the populace was caught in two songs, 'Norfolk-street Riots' and 'Raddle-neck'd Tups'. In the eight doggerel verses of the first song Mather described the events surrounding the riot; in the second, his eight verses reviled the volunteers. The tone of the songs is conveyed by two verses from 'Norfolk-street Riots' (in the last line 'grunting swine' alludes to Burke's 'swinish multitude' – Mather, like other radicals, made much of the phrase):

> This arm'd banditti, filled with spleen,
> At his command, like bloodhounds keen,
> In fine, to crown the horrid scene,
>   A shower of bullets fired.

The consequence was deep distress,
More widows and more fatherless,
The devil blushed and did confess
    'Twas more than *he* required.

Corruption cried for this exploit
'His worship shall be made a knight,
I hold his conduct just and right,
    And think him all divine.'
Oppression need not fear alarms
Since tyranny has got such swarms
Of gallant heroes bearing arms,
    To butcher grunting swine.

One of his last political songs was 'He's out of Commission, Boys', written after the detested Althorpe ('Satan's agent') resigned his commission in 1799.

Any estimate of Mather's influence must be tentative. To some degree he was a popular entertainer in the tradition of the balladeer. His versifying probably gave expression to the feelings of the less articulate. Even his more outspoken songs tended to reflect rather than originate opinion, although John Crome, a few years after Mather's death, stated that his satirical pieces had forced reluctant masters to comply with the just demands of poor workmen. His gift was an ability to draw on the experiences of his community; the non-political works often sang of the older, declining culture. One historian has detected in his verses 'the pessimism of the rootless: the nihilism of the deracinated' [Armytage (1950) 320], and, although Mather was capable of writing vivid and humorous songs, there was in his life and times an element of what E. P. Thompson has termed the 'chiliasm of despair'. But his songs at the end of the American War of Independence had reflected a horror of war and militarism, and in the 1790s there was expressed a higher level of social and political comment: a popularisation of the emerging democratic ideology that characterised this decade. Mather's songs lasted for over half a century. John Wilson, who collected his songs in 1862, testified to their survival among the Sheffield working class of the middle decades of the century; but it was a radical heritage that was rapidly disappearing.

Mather died on 12 June 1804 and was buried in St Paul's churchyard, Sheffield. In his last years he had returned to the Wesleyans and sought solace in writing devotional works. His song 'Repentance', which became a popular hymn with local Methodists, ended:

When the battle's won,
And our race fully run,
We to mansions of glory shall fly;
There eternally praise
The blest Ancient of Days,
For His love made us ready to die.

Sources: (1) MS: 'Passages in the Life of Arthur Jewitt to the Year 1794', Edward Hall Coll., Wigan PL. (2) Other: *A Collection of Songs, Poems, Satires, etc. written by the late Joseph Mather of Sheffield* (Sheffield, 1811); J. Wilson, *The Songs of Joseph Mather* ... (Sheffield, 1862); R. E. Leader, *Reminiscences of Old Sheffield, its Streets and its People* (Sheffield, 1875); 'Joseph Mather', *South Yorkshire ... Notes and Queries 1*, no. 3 (Dec 1899) 159, no. 4 (Mar 1900) 230, and *2*, no. 7 (Dec 1900) 164–9; R. E. Leader, *Sheffield in the Eighteenth Century* (2nd ed., Sheffield, 1905); M. Walton, *Sheffield: its story and its achievements* (Sheffield, 1948); W. H. G. Armytage, 'Joseph Mather: poet of the filesmiths', *Notes and Queries 195* (22 July 1950) 320–2; A. L. Lloyd, *Folk Song in England* (1967); M.

Vicinus, *The Industrial Muse: a study of nineteenth century British working-class literature* (1974); W. Noblett, 'From Sheffield to North Carolina', *History Today 26*, no. 1 (Jan 1976) 23–31; J. L. Baxter, 'The Origins of the Social War in South Yorkshire: a study of capitalist evolution and labour class realization in one industrial region, *c.* 1750–1855' (Sheffield PhD, 1977); idem, 'Joseph Mather', *Holberry Soc. for the Study of Sheffield Labour History Bull.*, no. 1 (1978) 7–8. Obit. *Iris or Sheffield Register*, 14 June 1804.

JOHN L. BAXTER
DAVID E. MARTIN

MOLL, William Edmund (1856–1932)
CHRISTIAN SOCIALIST

Moll was born on 9 April 1856 at Heigham, Norwich. His father, William Moll, was a linen draper and his mother's name was Maria (née Chaplin); of their family life little seems to be known. The young Moll attended Norwich School and then went to Worcester College, Oxford, where he graduated with second-class honours in history in 1878. He was made deacon and then ordained priest in the diocese of St Albans. For the next decade and a half he served in London parishes: first at St Andrew's, Plaistow; then at Christ Church, Clapham, and St Thomas's, Regent Street; and for ten years at St Mary's, Charing Cross Road. In 1893 he went to Newcastle upon Tyne.

Moll was an early member of the Guild of St Matthew, an offshoot of the Catholic revival, imbued with the insight of F. D. Maurice and founded by Stewart Headlam in 1877. Scott Holland wrote of those who developed the work of the GSM:

> These men were kindled into splendid inspiration. They fused the message of Maurice with the Gospel learned from the Tractarians. They saw the vital efficacy of such a fusion and they carried their gospel abroad with a high courage and with direct effect. The worker found in them priests who were ready to identify themselves heart and soul with the cause of labour [quoted in Widdrington (1932) 216].

Moll joined the Guild immediately on leaving Oxford in 1878. Like so many of his generation, he came to Socialism through Henry George and served for a time as a committee member of the English Land Restoration League. Moll, however, moved beyond the single tax to his version of the Christian Socialism of the Anglican High Church. His parish of St Mary's became the centre of the causes supported by the GSM. It was the home of the Society of the Rosary, and the Church and Stage Guild. Moll trained C. L. Marson, and it was at St Mary's that Headlam said Mass when he was deprived of his licence to preach. Widdrington wrote of St Mary's:

> Ecclesiastical, political and other rebels gravitated towards the Clergy House. Cunninghame Graham, the stormy petrel of the House of Commons, arriving hot from a passage of arms with the Speaker, Michael Davitt, and left-wing radicals, members of the Metropolitan Radical Federation, Henry Georgites [*sic*] and persecuted Secularists, priests in trouble with reactionary vicars or congregations on account of unpopular opinions, struggling actors, poets, and artists, these, as well as the ordinary types you meet in a clergy house, found their way up the stairs to Father Moll's room [ibid., 217].

Moll was with Headlam in Trafalgar Square on 'Bloody Sunday' (13 Nov 1887), and he became both a close friend and a trusted lieutenant of Headlam. But Moll had become a

Socialist of a markedly egalitarian kind, and his politics increasingly diverged from those of Headlam and the GSM. As he announced to the English Church Union in 1885, when he avowed himself a Christian Socialist:

> As a Catholic I believe that the Church is the Body of Christ, filled with His Spirit, bound to do the works which He did on earth. .... As a Catholic I believe that the Church is the Kingdom of Heaven on earth – an organised society for the promotion of righteousness, and freedom, and truth among nations [quoted in Jones (1968) 124].

In 1893 Moll was nominated by the Prime Minister (W. E. Gladstone) to the Crown living of St Philip's, Elswick, Newcastle upon Tyne. The same year he married Edith Mann, who was also a member of the Guild of St Matthew. St Philip's was a large parish with a population of about 20,000, entirely working-class but with quite wide variations in the skill, income and regularity of employment of workers. There were considerable numbers of skilled workers employed at Armstrong's famous Elswick Works; about 500 miners at the one pit in the parish; and a large body of unskilled labourers and shopworkers. Moll was joined at St Philip's for some years by two curates who were among the most lively of all the Christian Socialists of their generation. The first, Percy Widdrington, came in the summer of 1897; and the second, Conrad Noel, who was to become the outstanding Socialist of the Anglican Church in the twentieth century, served from 1898 to 1900.

Moll remained at St Philip's for thirty-two years and for all that time he involved himself in the day-to-day politics of the Durham coalfield. He was for a number of years a member of the NAC of the ILP and on close terms with the leading Labour politicians. But his main work was in the mining villages of the North East. 'Moll is coming' was the signal for the local band of the mining village to go forth to meet him. Two or three nights a week Moll would be 'on the tramp for Christ'. During the Boer War Conrad Noel preached a sermon against the war, and in protest one of the local munitions workers wrote to Moll threatening to blow up St Philip's. Now, Moll had once described the church as 'the most abominable Churchwarden Gothic you can imagine' and said that he 'had never been in such a shamelessly ugly building'. To the threats of having his church blown up, he reacted positively, saying to Noel, 'My dear Noel, by all means let it go on, as it is the truth, and if we lose our church, which is the ugliest structure in Newcastle, we can build a new one with the insurance money' [Noel (1945) 57].

Moll's Socialism expressed itself in his support for the activities of any local militant. He became known as the 'Socialist Vicar of Newcastle' or the 'Red Flag Vicar'. At the beginning of the First World War he was soon in contact with Jim Middleton, secretary of the national Labour Party, on the issue of social benefits for soldiers' families; and when the war was over Moll was consistently active in promoting and supporting the parliamentary candidature of Charles Trevelyan, who was elected as Labour MP for the Central Division of Newcastle in 1922.

The most important new development in Moll's career as a Christian Socialist within the Anglican Church was his support for the Church Socialist League [for which see **Special Note** below]. The League arose out of discontent with the GSM and the Christian Social Union. It also expressed the enthusiasm for social change engendered by the general election results of 1906. Most of the clerical leaders were Anglo-Catholic, and, in its early years especially, the League encouraged the kind of political commitment to Labour which had already made Moll known as a Socialist parson.

In 1924 Moll was offered the position of Dean of Carlisle by Ramsay MacDonald. It was a controversial appointment, and, though Moll at first accepted, he almost immediately changed his mind on medical advice. The next year he was offered, and took, the parish of Chipping Barnet, St Albans, and he remained there quietly and happily until his death on 21 July 1932. He was survived by his widow and left effects valued at £2837.

Writings: (1) MS: Correspondence in 1914 on Relief Committee of Lord Mayor of Newcastle, LP archives, WNC 26/4/17–20, 28/8/48–50 and 52; correspondence and election material, Moll to C. P. Trevelyan, 1919–22, Trevelyan Family Papers, Special Colls, Newcastle upon Tyne Univ. Library. (2) Other: (Compiler) *St Mary's, Soho, Children's Prayer Book* [*c.* 1890?]; (with others) *Songs for the City of God* (St Philip's, Newcastle upon Tyne, 1899) 40 pp.; 'Stewart Headlam' [review], *Commonwealth*, Sep 1926, 276–8.

Sources: *Church Reformer 12*, no. 3 (Mar 1893) and ibid., no. 5 (May 1893); P. Stacy, 'The Church and Socialism', *Labour Leader*, 22 Jan 1906; 'New Dean of Carlisle: Labour Party supporter', *Church Times*, 7 Mar 1924, 256; J. F. S. L. Burn *et al.*, 'The Deanery of Carlisle' [letters], ibid., 14 Mar 1924, 288; J. Wilcockson, 'Sermon on the Mount Politics' [letter] ibid.; J. Clayton, *The Rise and Decline of Socialism in Great Britain 1884–1924* (1926); *Labour Who's Who* (1927); *Crockford's Clerical Directory* (1930); D. O. Wagner, *The Church of England and Social Reform since 1854* (NY, 1930); C. Noel, *An Autobiography*, ed. with a Foreword by Sidney Dark (1945); P. E. T. Widdrington, 'Those were the Days', *Christendom 15*, no. 65 (Mar 1947) 18–23; M. B. Reckitt, *P. E. T. Widdrington: a study in vocation and versatility* (1961); A. M. McBriar, *Fabian Socialism and English Politics, 1884–1918* (Cambridge, 1962); S. Mayor, *The Churches and the Labour Movement* (1967); P. d'A. Jones, *The Christian Socialist Revival, 1877–1914* (Princeton, NJ, 1968). Personal information: the late Mrs M. H. Gibb OBE, Cambo, Northumberland; T. Monaghan, Gateshead; Miss Elsie Purdy, Newcastle upon Tyne. OBIT. *North Mail and Newcastle Chronicle* and *Times*, 22 July 1932; *Church Times*, 29 July 1932; P. E. T. Widdrington, 'A Priest in Politics: William Edmund Moll, 1856–1932', *Christendom 2*, no. 5 (Mar 1932).

JOHN SAVILLE

See also: †Robert Bontine CUNNINGHAME GRAHAM; Thomas HANCOCK for the Guild of St Matthew **(Special Note);** †Stewart Duckworth HEADLAM; †Conrad le Despenser Roden NOEL; and below: the Church Socialist League.

The Church Socialist League

The Church Socialist League (CSL) was the third Anglican society to be founded in the phase of Christian Socialism that arose in the last quarter of the nineteenth century. It came into being at a conference at Morecambe on 13 June 1906. The germinal notion for such a society can be traced to a letter signed 'A Durham Priest' in the *Labour Leader* of 18 August 1905, itself a response to Keir Hardie's 'An Open Letter to the Clergy' published in the 23 June issue. The 'Durham Priest' was G. Algernon West, a Sunderland vicar. He remarked that there were many who were utterly dissatisfied with the Church's attitude to current social conditions, but they were isolated and without an organisation: there was a need, therefore, for some effort to bring together those clergy who were more or less in sympathy with the aims and methods of the ILP to decide on some common line of thought and action. 'We are Socialists because we are Churchmen', he declared. In the meantime the political campaigning preceding the general election of January 1906 showed that the number of clerics who were Labour sympathisers was very considerable, and Ramsay MacDonald paid tribute to the great assistance they had given. The election of twenty-nine members of the Labour Representation Committee was greeted with acclaim. Churchmen such as the veteran Socialist the Revd W. E. Moll of St Philip's, Newcastle, and the Revd

Lewis Donaldson, who had led the march of the Leicester unemployed in 1905, both of whom were to become leaders of the CSL, interpreted the Labour successes in religious categories. In May some 400 delegates from Lancashire and Yorkshire, drawn in roughly equal numbers from the clergy and from the ILP and SDF, attended a conference at the House of the Resurrection, the Anglican monastery at Mirfield in West Yorkshire. Meanwhile West, greatly encouraged by the campaigns and results of the general election, developed his ideas with Moll. A few weeks after the election, West and the Revd T. C. Gobat of Darlington, another future CSL leader, conducted a Parish Mission at More-cambe, and during this week they, with a handful of associates including the Revd Percy Widdrington, also to become prominent in the CSL, made arrangements for the conference at which the CSL was founded.

The Morecambe conference was attended by about sixty clergy (and a few laymen, added as an afterthought). The vast majority were parochial clergy from the North. Most of them already belonged to the Guild of St Matthew or the Christian Social Union or both, and the conference was addressed by the GSM's Warden, Stewart Headlam, but those present were convinced that for the particular work they had in mind a new society was required. The GSM was regarded as unsuitable because of its 'moribund' condition, its extreme and uncompromising Catholicism, its political stance and its involvement in what were regarded as irrelevant or peripheral activities. The CSU was rejected because it did not consist of 'definite Socialists'. The intention, however, was to complement the work of the existing societies, not to compete with them.

The conference drew up a written basis for the new society. The stated Principles were as follows:

1. The Church has a mission to the whole of human life, Social and Individual, Material and Spiritual.
2. The Church can best fulfil its social mission by acting in its corporate capacity.
3. To this end the members of the League accept the principles of Socialism [*Optimist*, Oct 1906].

The debate from which the Basis emerged featured three intertwined components of Christian Socialism which appear and reappear throughout the movement's history: a political element, in the form of Socialism; an intellectual element, exemplified in the call for 'an adumbration of Christian Sociology'; and an ecclesiastical element, illustrated by the assertion of the importance of a Catholic and sacramental basis. At Morecambe, in the enthusiasm engendered by the recent general election, supremacy went to Socialism. League members were to be convinced Socialists in the ordinary meaning of the word, 'moved by the conviction that the reconstruction of society on Socialist lines is the extension of God's kingdom on earth'. Entrance requirements, beyond the confession of Socialism, were kept to a minimum. While it was stressed that the CSL was a Church society, membership was open to any baptised (and therefore possibly 'nominal') member of the Church of England: the GSM and CSU were confined to communicants. However, although the novel and most striking feature of this latest society was its unambiguous declaration for Socialism, and, although sacramental Catholicism and 'intellectualism' found little expression in its written Basis, the CSL in reality was a kind of federation of elements. Catholicism and the intellectual aspect, if absent from the League's principles as originally set down, were still present in its membership. The interaction of these three forces – Socialism, Catholicism and 'intellectualism' – their relative strength and the degree to which they found expression, was to determine much of the internal history of the League. For the present the enthusiasm of the moment held them in a coalition transcending disruptive dissent, and a society emerged less Catholic than the GSM, less intellectual than the CSU, but more Socialist than either.

The infant CSL was faced with three tasks: to establish itself as an institution and to work out its relationship to the labour movement and to the rest of the Church. Reactions from the *Labour Leader* and the *Church Times* indicated that the League's future path would not be without problems: indeed they symbolised one of the central dilemmas which was to attend its course – was it essentially part of the labour movement, or part of the Church, or both, and, if the last, how were these two allegiances to be reconciled?

The new society emerged from the Morecambe Conference with a nucleus of thirty-five members, predominantly clerical in composition and Northern in base to set about the task of creating a national network of branches and a mass membership of both clergy and laity. The period 1906–9 was characterised by rapid expansion to a total of almost 1200 members in thirty-five branches, with the London branch accounting for almost a sixth of the total membership: thereafter the numbers remained relatively static for the next three years. Accompanying this phase there was also a shift in the League's centre of gravity from the North to the Midlands and the South East. Circumstances were propitious for advance in the early years. By 1909, however, conditions were less obviously favourable: post-election euphoria, for instance, faded as time passed and Labour's political performance occasioned doubts and dissatisfaction. Moreover, problems particular to the society – finance and constitutional arrangements – hampered its work. By 1909 the first vigorous burst was over, but problems and divisions were not yet sufficiently severe to cause decline and disruption.

During the League's history some fifty-four branches were established in Britain, three of these being in Wales and one in Scotland. There was also a branch in New Zealand. The Church Socialist League of the United States was a separate organisation. The largest number of branches in existence in any one year seems to have been thirty-five, in 1909, but some were very short-lived. After 1912 only nine new branches were founded. Predictably branches were found chiefly in the great industrial areas and urban centres, though there were some surprising gaps within them and unexpected developments outside them, such as branches at Bath and Taunton and in rural Essex and seaside Sussex. Institutionally the CSL succeeded partly in attaining its objectives. It established a national network of branches and it achieved what might be regarded as a 'respectable' membership roll: three times that of the GSM at its numerical peak and not beyond comparison with a body as influential as the Fabian Society. It did not, however, succeed in becoming a mass movement. It did not even become the largest of these Anglican societies: the mild social reformist CSU attracted five times the membership. The more extravagant hopes of the League's early leaders did not materialise.

Although laity overtook clergy in membership strength in the League's first year, the clergy dominated in directing its affairs. Lay people, however, were more prominent in the London branch and in the League's central affairs in its latter days. Leading clerical members included Algernon West, W. E. Moll and T. C. Gobat, all incumbents from the North East; Conrad Noel; Percy Widdrington (whose first wife was the Socialist campaigner Enid Stacy); her brother Paul; Lewis Donaldson; Paul Bull and Walter Frere, both members of the Community of the Resurrection, Mirfield; the Hon. J. G. Adderley; W. C. Roberts; and Harold Buxton. Hewlett Johnson and Ronald Knox, both to become notable later in different spheres, were also members for a period. The CSL clergy were broadly typical of the Anglican clergy in social and educational background. However, although several clergy possessed enterprise and ability, none achieved major promotion during the League's life and few after it; CSU members fared much better in this respect. Most CSL clergy had experience of working-class life, but their 'gentry culture' and professional group environ-ment made it virtually impossible for them to bridge the social gap between themselves and the working-class population.

Lay members came from a variety of backgrounds and occupations. Among them were two MPs, Thomas Summerbell and George Lansbury, chairman of the London branch from its inception to 1912, when he became League chairman for a year; the Countess of Warwick; Maurice Reckitt of the pharmaceutical firm family; R. H. Tawney; Henry Slesser;

Arthur Penty; and Cecil Chesterton. Leisured middle-class ladies occupied various offices. Clerks of various sorts were prominent, particularly in the London branch. Information on the rank and file is scant. For most of the lay members the CSL was only one interest among many: among the better-known laity, only Reckitt chose to give consistently over the years a priority to his Christian Socialist activities, thereby exerting an important influence on the CSL's direction in its later years.

The CSL's membership was not particularly well fitted to achieve the society's aims. The clergy effectively fell between two stools: among their number they had neither the dignitaries to promote the CSL cause in the councils of the Church, nor, though men such as Moll, Noel, West and Donaldson were active and apparently well-regarded in the labour movement, did they have clergy who were themselves working class and so able to be 'at one' with the people. Among the leading laity, too, there seems to have been a disappointingly small element drawn from the proletariat. In spite of its name, then, the CSL was not well placed, in terms of the composition of its membership, to have a major and lasting impact on either the Church or the labour movement. Though politically it was the most radical of the Anglican Christian Socialist societies, it remained clerical in direction and largely middle-class in atmosphere.

The League's activities at any given time were influenced by conditions and preoccupations in both the labour movement and the Church and the bearing these had on attempts to relate each to the other. Much energy went into public meetings, some of which attracted considerable support: 3000 people, for instance, attended a demonstration on unemployment held in Trafalgar Square in 1909. CSL branches frequently co-operated with local branches of the ILP, Social Democratic Party and British Socialist Party. Periodicals, pamphlets, manuals and manifestos were produced. From 1908 to 1921 the journals the *Optimist* (later renamed the *Church Socialist Quarterly*) and the *Church Socialist* served as the League's official organ. After 1921 the League resorted to an insert in the *Commonwealth*.

The life of the League was complicated not only by its dual allegiance to the Church and the labour movement but also by a certain ambivalence towards each. The CSL's explicit avowal of Socialism did not automatically result in its affiliation to the Labour Party. Differences of opinion on this issue were expressed by future leaders even before the League began. It was, however, a question which sooner or later the League would have to face. Its foundation documents stated expressly that it was 'a society within the Church composed exclusively of Socialists'. At its first annual conference it proceeded to a definition of Socialism, stating that:

> By Socialism is understood the fixed principle according to which the community shall own the land and capital collectively and use them for the good of all [Noel papers, Hull Univ.].

This definition was incorporated in the statements of the League's objects and rules. In 1909, the chairman, West, advocated the passing of a resolution that the League should seek affiliation to the Labour Party. It was rejected. The decision was, in effect, a turning-point in the League's history, ensuring that it would not become an integral and institutional part of the workers' political movement. The decision also had important consequences in that it led to the virtual secession of West and his League lieutenant Moll, thereby greatly weakening the activist Socialist element for the future. The issue was raised again from time to time, but affiliation was always rejected. The initiative was to pass to men such as Widdrington, who in 1913 declared, 'I am here to tell you that the League is not primarily a political society. It is committed to no political alliance.'

One of the reasons frequently given for the rejection of a political alignment was that party affiliation would impede the fulfilment of what some members conceived to be the

League's real purpose, the conversion of the Church. CSL members experienced a tension between allegiance and dissociation: they had both a sense of belonging to the Church and a desire to 'distance' themselves from some of its manifestations and to criticise them. The critical tone and propagandist activity of the early years led some members to feel uncomfortably alienated from the mainstream Church and so to desire a more harmonious and participatory relationship.

Not surprisingly, the superficial unity of the CSL proved precarious, and towards the end of 1912 the first signs of those divisions which were to change its direction, undermine its fragile cohesion and contribute to its disintegration began to manifest themselves. Some of those divisions had been implicit from the beginning, but now the League was subjected to increasing pressure from new developments in both theology and politics. In this phase of reappraisal and transition more emphasis, inevitably, was placed on study and less on action: the League had to take account of newly emerging political ideas, and the state of flux encouraged it to consider its roots in the Christian faith and its place in the Church. In the early days there was a desire to emphasise that League members *really* were Socialist; now, the desire to emphasise that they were *fully* Churchmen became more insistent, particularly as the nature and destiny of Socialism appeared less clear.

In this period the critique of state collectivism in Hilaire Belloc's book *The Servile State* (1912) made a considerable impact on some members, as did syndicalism and the pluralist philosophy of Father J. N. Figgis, but for an influential section of the League's membership it was Guild Socialism which held a particularly strong appeal. Its carefully devised structure appealed to the intellectuals, and its 'human scale', its emphasis on fulfilment in work, on fellowship, fraternity and participation, was consonant with a Christian assessment of the nature and dignity of man. The vigorous advocacy of Guild Socialism, particularly by Maurice Reckitt, editor of the *Church Socialist*, increased tensions. It was perhaps questionable how far Guild Socialism for some people could really be regarded as Socialist. 'The Guild idea', Reckitt wrote later, 'was far more like a revolt against Socialism than a re-interpretation of it' [(1941) 130]. These sentiments were a far cry from those of the League's early days, when it came close to Labour Party affiliation. When Socialism entered a stage of ferment and fragmentation, with state collectivism in a condition of disarray, it no longer presented a clear-cut model and programme for the League.

Moreover, in this situation members turned increasingly for illumination to the League's other constituent tradition, the Christian Faith. Far from helping to clarify the League's Socialist creed, this only served to produce further dissension. Dissension came from two sources: from the traditional divisions in theology and Churchmanship reflected in the CSL's membership, and from the impact of new theological developments, particularly in terms of the social implications of new thinking on eschatology and the concept of the Kingdom of God.

To these unresolved tensions, political and theological, were added the difficulties brought by war. Some members became combatants, others conscientious objectors: the impossibility of reaching a common official League policy on the war further threatened its precarious stability. The Russian Revolution caused further controversy. Meanwhile League activity, resources and membership declined rapidly, accelerating a trend discernible from the immediate pre-war period. The conduct of the League's affairs was left largely in the hands of the executive committee. As the activist Socialist element declined, activities favoured by the other elements – the 'intellectual' and the 'ecclesiastical' – increased: there was increasing emphasis on study and prayer. Indirectly the war also led to a more involved relationship with the 'official' Church: Donaldson and Lansbury were appointed to the Central Council of the National Mission of Repentance and Hope, launched in 1916, and Lansbury, R. H. Tawney and Fred Hughes were members of the committee set up by the Archbishops to inquire into industrial problems.

The League's latter years saw the resignation of Conrad Noel and the rise to prominence of what may be styled the Widdrington–Reckitt axis. As early as the founding conference, Noel, in speaking up for the GSM, was advocating a definite and extroverted Catholicism. In 1912 he gave notice that he expected the CSL ultimately to adopt his version of Catholicism or perish, and at a special conference in 1916 he made a last attempt to achieve his objective. He failed and resigned. Two years later he founded the Catholic Crusade to give institutional expression to his 'synthesis of uncompromising Catholicism and revolutionary Socialism'.

The way was now clearer for the 'intellectualist' approach of Widdrington and Reckitt and their supporters. As relations with the mainstream Church grew closer, this group turned its thoughts increasingly towards what it termed 'the re-discovery and enlargement of the social traditions of Christendom'. To this element the ILP sympathies and the Socialist formulations bestowed on the League by its founding fathers were not merely anachronistic or irrelevant: they were a positive obstacle to the fulfilment of the goals now envisaged. As the star of Christendom waxed, so the Socialist star waned. If the CSL's early struggles were concerned with establishing its Socialist credentials and promoting affiliation to the Labour Party, the later struggles were concerned with the removal of the word 'Socialism' from the League's name and objectives.

Since the 'Christian Sociology' expounded by the 'intellectualist' group was integrally related to Catholic dogma, there were further implications for the League's future. The 'intellectualists' became convinced that Catholicism must form the essential and only basis for the League, but this by no means put themselves in the same camp as Noel and his associates. Noel presented a synthesis of extroverted Catholicism and revolutionary Socialism; the Widdrington–Reckitt axis presented a combination of intellectualism and Catholicism. The note of 'traditional' Socialism was now so muted as to be almost inaudible. A transition from engagement to intellectualism, from activism to analysis, was completed.

By 1919 the word 'Socialism' had disappeared from all but the name of the League, but it was not until 1923 that the transformation was formally and finally effected with the dissolution of the CSL and the emergence of a successor body, the League of the Kingdom of God. Since there was considerable opposition to drastic change from the branches, the revisionists, who dominated the executive committee, attained their goal stage by stage through persistence and not without considerable manipulation. The Basis and Objects of the new League embodied the ideas and attitudes which Widdrington had long promoted: his plea for 'the adumbration of a Christian Sociology' made, and rejected, at the CSL's founding conference in 1906 now found expression in the LKG's official Objects, and, similarly, his theological preoccupation with the concept of the Kingdom of God was reflected in the new body's name and the first of its Objects.

The society, then, was captured by what was essentially a small pressure group of middle-class intellectuals. A fairly large minority which refused to forswear an explicitly Socialist allegiance went on to found the Society of Socialist Christians in February 1924. Unlike the CSL, the Society was non-denominational and to it came survivors of the Socialist Quaker Society and the Free Church Socialist League.

The total achievement of the CSL is difficult to estimate. Widdrington asserted that 'its usefulness consisted in allaying the suspicion entertained by the Labour Movement that the Church was hostile to the claims of social democracy' [*Commonwealth*, July 1927, 221–3] and he claims that it brought many men and women back to the practice of religion. He cited also its influence on the National Mission and on the report of the Archbishops' Committee of Inquiry into Industrial Problems (1918). At its lowest level it performed the 'biological' function of maintaining the Christian Socialist species and begetting the next generation.

The CSL was ultimately a failure in synthesis: the 'coalition' broke into fragments and the constituent elements regrouped. The three successor bodies can be characterised according to their attitudes to Socialism and Catholicism: for the Catholic Crusade, Catholicism, as its name implies, was central, but Socialism was seen as integrally bound up with it; for the League of the Kingdom of God, Catholicism was seen as ultimately connected with the formulation of a specifically Christian 'Sociology', but there was no attachment to Socialism; the Society of Socialist Christians provided an organisational home for the remaining Socialist minority from the CSL and, as a non-denominational society, lay outside the Catholic tradition as understood by Anglican Christian Socialism. The CSL's failure was not surprising given the fissiparous tendencies in both Socialism and Christianity, their different reference points, the particular traditions of the League's members and the circumstances and events of the period of its existence. It came into being at a time when Churchmen were conscious of the alienation of the working class. The process of alienation has continued and been progressively extended into other classes of society. The failure of the League, as of Christian Socialism in general, is, regardless of the innate difficulty of relating two ideologies and giving the relationship institutional expression in time and circumstance, an aspect of the wider failure of the Church.

Sources: (1) MS: There are no extant central records of the CSL, but the papers of prominent members contain CSL material. *See* Conrad Noel Coll., Brynmor Jones Library, Hull Univ., and Paul Stacy papers, Brotherton Library, Leeds Univ.
(2) Periodicals: The *Optimist* (1906–8), the *Church Socialist Q.* (1908–11), the *Church Socialist* (1912–21), and *Commonwealth* (CSL insert from 1921 to 1923) give valuable information.
(3) Thesis: The most comprehensive and detailed treatment of the CSL is to be found in I. Goodfellow, 'The Church Socialist League, 1906–1923: origins, development and disintegration' (Durham PhD, 1983).
(4) Other: C. Noel, *Socialism in Church History* (1910); *Christianity and Industrial Problems* (Report of the Archbishops' Fifth Committee of Inquiry, 1918); D. O. Wagner, *The Church of England and Social Reform* (NY, 1930); G. C. Binyon, *The Christian Socialist Movement in England* (1931) [Binyon was a member of the CSL]; M. B. Reckitt, *As it happened* (1941); idem, *P. E. T. Widdrington: a study in vocation and versatility* (1961); R. Groves, *Conrad Noel and the Thaxted Movement* (1967); P. d'A. Jones, *The Christian Socialist Revival 1877–1914* (Princeton, NJ, 1968).

IAN GOODFELLOW

MORLEY, Ralph (1882–1955)
EDUCATIONALIST AND LABOUR MP

Ralph Morley was born on 25 October 1882 at Chichester, the son of Thomas Walter Morley, a pharmacist, and his wife Mary. Educated at the local Modern School, he left at fifteen to become a pupil teacher at the Chichester Lancastrian School. He studied shorthand part-time at a technical school and then took a teaching course at the Hartley Institution (later Southampton University College). Entrance to a teacher training college, which he favoured, was only open at that time – as he later recalled – to members of the Church of England [*Schoolmaster and Woman Teacher's Chronicle*, 2 Apr 1931, 626].

Morley's teaching career began in London in 1903, but when his sisters moved to Itchen, Hampshire, he returned to the south coast and obtained a teaching post with Hampshire County Council at Portswood School, a position he held until the First World War. His political involvement with the labour movement developed during these years. Undoubtedly his Socialist sympathies were aroused by the poverty he encountered when he began to teach. One of his first pupils, born in the Southampton Workhouse in 1898, in recalling his own breakfast of porridge and dry bread, wrote that:

> very many poor children outside of the workhouse had No breakfast at all, and many had no boots, or stockings. It is here where Mr Morley comes into the picture. He always seem[ed] to have a distinguished and acute sensitivity of knowing which child had come to school without any breakfast. He would often bring from his own pocket, sandwiches, biscuits, and even chocolate and hand out to the more unfortunate children. I also recall, how long after school hours he, with other teachers would stay behind to mend, and repair (or try to repair) the children's much out-worn boots, and finding the leather, material, tools etc. and costs from their own pockets [private letter, E. H. Edmunds, 8 May 1983].

Ralph Morley had joined the Southampton branch of the Social Democratic Federation in 1906. Its secretary was Tommy Lewis [see *DLB 1*, 215–18], who in 1901 had become the town's first Labour councillor. Morley took over as secretary of the branch in February 1908, by which time it had adopted the organisation's new title of Social Democratic Party (the SDF became the SDP in October 1907); and in March 1908 Morley was reporting in the columns of *Justice* (14 Mar) on their leaflet campaign, on the formation of a Socialist Sunday School under the joint management of the SDP and the ILP, and on a series of lectures being held at the Labour Club. These included one by himself on 'The Education Programme and the SDP'. Plans were also being made for a propaganda campaign in the summer and for the formation of a branch at Winchester.

Morley continued his active Socialist career in the succeeding years. In 1912 a general meeting of all Socialists in Southampton was called to form a branch of the British Socialist Party (a union of the SDP and some ILP branches), and a Southern District Council of the BSP was established with Morley as secretary. At the Itchen council elections in 1913, Morley contested Pear Tree ward in the Socialist interest but was not elected. Morley was also active in the affairs of the Southampton Trades Council. He was president four times – the first occasion in 1911 – and remained a member until 1942. In 1914 he was president of the Southampton Class Teachers' Association. He was a staunch advocate of secular education – a controversial subject in the immediate pre-war years – and expressed his views in a *Justice* article of 21 September 1912 [Simon (1965) 277].

Soon after the outbreak of war Morley enlisted in the London Regiment and served on the Western Front from 1916 to 1919. On his return to civilian life he joined the ILP and in 1919 was elected for the Woolston ward of Itchen Urban District Council. He was Council chairman in 1920–1 and negotiated the amalgamation of the Urban District with Southampton Borough which took place at that time. Morley had returned to teaching and was much involved in the prolonged lock-out of the Southampton teachers in 1922. The Burnham Committee set up in 1919 by the President of the Board of Education produced a minimum scale for elementary school teachers from 1 January 1920. This was accepted by the Southampton Council, but when the Burnham Committee realised the scale was inadequate it produced a further report with a new scale. The Southampton Education Committee agreed this by a narrow majority, but the Council refused to accept it: the teachers withdrew their labour and the schools were then closed. It was a complicated issue and Morley predicted a long dispute. In spite of support from some members of the Council, including Tommy Lewis, there was, Morley wrote, 'a large element on the Council bitterly opposed to working-class education, some of whom have publicly declared that they care not whether the schools are open or shut' [*Justice*, 13 Apr 1922]. No other town in England of the size of Southampton was paying the minimum scale. The lock-out began on 3 April 1922, and, although Tommy Lewis attempted to reopen negotiations with the teachers, he was voted down by 34 to 15. The town was 'blacklisted' and eventually the President of the Board of Education intervened. The schools were reopened on 11 July after the teachers had agreed to wait until 1925 to receive the full benefit of the new scale. In the following year Morley became president of the Southampton Teachers' Association (a branch of the National Union of Teachers) and served in this capacity on two subsequent occasions in 1930 and 1933.

During the inter-war years Morley continued to be active in political and educational affairs. From 1925 to 1929 he was chairman of the Southampton ILP and represented the South of England on the federal council of the National Federation of Class Teachers from 1924 to 1931; he was president of the Federation in 1928–9 and treasurer from 1932 to 1937. From 1937 to 1945 he was the Federation's general secretary. Morley was also closely involved with the Southampton WEA both as an official and as a tutor, serving as vice-president (1925–8, 1932–3) and president (1928–31) and lecturing in economics, history and psychology. He also taught economics and economic history for courses organised by the WEA and Southampton University College and was well remembered as a speaker at the WEA Saturday Club, which was established about 1928.

At the 1929 general election Tommy Lewis and Ralph Morley contested the two-seat constituency of Southampton for Labour and both were successful – the first time the town had been represented by Labour members. It was Lewis's fifth attempt to enter Parliament, but both men lost their seats in 1931, were again unsuccessful in 1935 but were elected in 1945. They were good constituency MPs, but for Morley his special interest in educational matters predominated. During his first parliamentary period he wrote monthly articles in the *Schoolmaster and Woman Teacher's Chronicle*. He was highly critical of the rejection by the House of Lords in 1931 of a Bill which sought to raise the school-leaving age. He wrote of this episode:

After listening carefully to the greater part of the debate, I came away with the distinct impression that there is little chance for real educational advance until this assembly of irresponsible old gentlemen has been deprived of the power of putting barricades in the path of progress [*SWTC*, 5 Mar 1931].

Morley left teaching on his election to Parliament in 1929 but returned to his profession on losing his seat. For a time in the 1920s he had taught at the Central District School, but in the early 1930s he was at Sholing Boys' School in St Monica Road, Southampton, and then later at Swaythling Senior Boys' School. He did not, apparently, participate actively in the local projects during the Spanish Civil War – namely, a food ship for Spain and a camp for Basque children – but, according to Lord Maybray-King, both Morley and Lewis 'were sympathetic to what we were doing' [private letter, 31 Oct 1983]. In 1941 Morley was elected to the EC of the NUT and during the Second World War he undertook lecturing assignments for the Forces through the Extra-Mural Department of Southampton University College, of which he was a University Court member. He was also a JP for many years. From 1941 until 1945 he was secretary of the Southampton Teachers' Association.

When he was returned to Parliament in 1945 he was head of the Deanery Secondary School and vice-president of the NUT (of which he was president in the following year). He was also awarded an honorary degree by Reading University. A keen supporter of comprehensive schools, he served in 1950 on the Labour Party *ad hoc* sub-committee, chaired by Alice Bacon, to prepare a report on comprehensive education following a Labour Party resolution to encourage the Government to assist education authorities wishing to develop these schools [Barker (1972) 94–5]. Morley was regarded by the NUT as the teachers' representative in Parliament and was the first MP to become NUT president, after only four years on its executive committee. A member of the Burnham Committee,

Morley had long been a persistent advocate of the basic scale for teachers and was still concerned about the rights of the class teacher after he became a headmaster.

At the 1950 general election the previous two-seat constituency of Southampton was divided into two districts: Itchen and Test. Morley was elected for Itchen and Dr H. M. King (later Lord Maybray-King) for Test. Both held their seats in 1951, but Dr King's seat had become a marginal one, and, when, six weeks before the 1955 election, Morley resigned on health grounds, he had hoped that Anthony Crosland, MP for South Gloucestershire, would replace him, as the latter's seat had become marginal following boundary changes. This was not to be. Dr King switched to Morley's seat and Crosland was selected to contest Southampton, Test. In the event Crosland was unsuccessful, but King was elected for Itchen. Morley watched the election results from his hospital bed, where he died from cancer on 14 June 1955, three weeks after the election [private letter, Mrs A. Holmes, 8 May 1983].

Morley, a bachelor, was survived by three sisters, the Misses Marjorie and Frances Morley, with whom he lived, and Mrs Bertha Weston. His funeral, a secular one, was held at Stoneham Crematorium and his estate was valued at £6250. He left £100 to the Labour Party and £200 to the Southampton Education Committee for the award of prizes to a boy and a girl in maintained schools between the ages of thirteen and fifteen for the best essays in Morley's favourite subject – history. Shortly after his death a fund was established to perpetuate the memory of one of the city's outstanding educationalists. Miss Marjorie Morley was a member of the original committee for the fund and was succeeded by her sister Mrs Weston, a mathematics teacher in a local boy's school who was a trustee of the Ralph Morley Memorial Fund until her death at the age of ninety-five in 1980. Morley prizes are still (1985) being awarded to adult education students recommended by the University and La Sainte Union College and to local schoolchildren.

Ralph Morley was a much-loved and respected teacher and many tributes were paid to his lifelong crusade to improve conditions and opportunities for the underprivileged. His union praised the service he gave in the implementation of the 1944 Education Act and his loyalty to the causes he chose to serve. A close associate of Morley's in his WEA and Labour Party activities was E. G. Stride, who recalled a conversation he had with him after they had both spoken at a general management committee meeting of the Southampton LP: Morley had said, 'You know, you younger ones think I've become Right-wing but my views haven't changed at all. I was always regarded as Left-wing and I'm still the same. It's your generation that has different views' [private letter, 10 Oct 1983].

Writings: 'Report of Southampton SDP', *Justice*, 14 Mar 1908; 'The Class Teachers' Conference', ibid., 5 Oct 1912; 'Southern District Council', ibid., 12 Oct 1912; 'The Government and Education', ibid., 2 Aug 1913; 'Railway Nationalisation', ibid., 6 Dec 1913; 'The Teaching of Morality', ibid., 19 Feb 1914; 'The Recent Teachers' Strike', ibid., 12 Mar 1914; 'The "Business Government"', ibid., 25 Apr 1914; 'The Southampton Teachers' Lock-out', ibid., 13 Apr 1922; monthly articles in the *SWTC*, esp. 'Education in Parliament', 5 Mar 1931, and 'Parliament in March', 2 Apr 1931; 'Educate Children for a Changing World' [presidential address to the NUT], *Western Mail*, 25 Apr 1946, 4.

Sources: *Justice*, 1906–13, *passim* [for SDF/SDP/BSP activities in the Southampton area]; *Hampshire Independent*, 1 and 3 Mar 1913; *Southern Daily Echo*, 26 Mar 1913; *Southern Times*, 12 Apr 1913; *Southern Daily Echo*, 30 Mar 1922–11 July 1922, *passim* [for details of the Southampton teachers' lock-out]; *Labour Who's Who* (1927); *Times House of Commons* (1929); *Hansard*, 1929–31; *Schoolmaster*, 9 Apr 1942; *Hansard*, 1945–55; C. Bunker, *Who's Who in Parliament* (1946); 'Teachers' Press welcomes M. P. President', *Southern Daily Echo*, 3 May 1946; *Times House of Commons* (1950); *WWW* (1951–60); *Dod* (1954); 'Ralph Morley Prizes will perpetuate Name of Soton Educationist', *Southern Daily Echo*, 19 Oct

1956; 'Memorial Bookplate' [Ralph Morley Memorial Prize], ibid., 19 Dec 1957; B. Simon, *Education and the Labour Movement* (1965); 'Memories for Prize Pupils', *Southern Evening Echo*, 2 June 1967; R. Barker, *Education and Politics 1900–1951: a study of the Labour Party* (Oxford, 1972); I. R. Broad, 'A History of the Southampton Branch of the Workers' Educational Association 1907–1960' (dissertation in part fulfilment of a Southampton MA (Ed.), 1981); A. G. K. Leonard, 'MP Ralph served us all his Days', *Southern Evening Echo*, 4 Feb 1983; idem, 'Schools were closed for 101 Days', *Hampshire*, June 1984, 49–51; T. Bargate. 'A Strike that gave Pupils 101 Days off', *Southern Evening Echo*, 25 June 1984; 'Locked out', ibid., 29 June 1984; 'Absent-minded Morley', ibid., 2 July 1984; 'Memories of School', ibid., 5 July 1984; 'Scoffed', ibid., 7 July 1984. Biographical information: NUT, London; Southampton CL; C. Walker, British Gas Southern H.Q., Southampton. Personal information: H. T. Abbott, Mrs E. Eastman, E. H. Edmunds, E. C. Ford, Alderman W. Greenaway, J. Guilmant, Mrs A. Holmes, B. J. Howard, A. G. K. Leonard, the late Lord Maybray–King, Miss K. Smith, E. G. Stride, all of Southampton. Obit. 'Ralph Morley never spared himself in Cause he followed', *Southern Daily Echo*, 15 June 1955; *Times*, 16 June 1955; *SWTC*, 17 June 1955; *Labour Party Report* (1955). Note. The editors wish to acknowledge the helpful response from citizens of Southampton to an appeal for biographical information published in the *Southern Evening Echo*, 29 Apr 1983, and to other local residents who have assisted in a variety of ways.

Joyce Bellamy

See also: †Thomas (Tommy) Lewis; Henry (Harry) Quelch.

NEESOM, Charles Hodgson (1785–1861)
TRADE UNIONIST, CHARTIST, AND SECULARIST

Born 26 July 1785 at Scarborough on the coast of north Yorkshire, Charles Neesom was brought up by an aunt after both his parents died while he was still an infant. Receiving only a rudimentary education at a dame school in the town, he taught himself to read using Defoe's *Robinson Crusoe* and Bunyan's *Pilgrim's Progress* as primers. At the age of eleven he was apprenticed to a Scarborough tailor, a Paineite named Armstrong. His apprenticeship was a period of growing religious scepticism as he attended first a Baptist, then a Methodist, congregation before concluding that the Bible was 'a mass of improbabilities' [*National Reformer*, 20 July 1861, 6]. Completing his time, Neesom remained a further seven years in the North before moving to London in 1810. There he quickly found employment in Weston's, a Bond Street tailoring shop, and as quickly became immersed in radical politics, chiefly through reading the press – particularly Cobbett, Carlile and the *Independent Whig*. He changed employers twice, on the second occasion joining Ralph's in Cheapside. By 1819 he had joined the Polemic Society, direct successor to the Society of Spencean Philanthropists, at its meetings at the Mulberry Tree in nearby Moorfields. He was thus plunged into the midst of London Ultra-Radicalism, a conspiratorial group of infidels who openly 'boasted that the Government had been more annoyed by Individuals belonging to them than by any other body' [HO 40/8 (3), fo. 115]. Through membership of this group Neesom was, in his own words, 'very nearly implicated' in the Cato Street conspiracy of 1820. This reference is the only evidence we have of his contact with the Spenceans at this time, for there is no mention of his name in either the Home Office files or the Treasury Solicitor's papers. It may be presumed that he continued to maintain links with the Finsbury-based Spencean group within metropolitan radicalism, and it may also be assumed that he became acquainted with such personalities as the publisher James Watson and Allen Davenport. From the end of the 1820s information about his political activities becomes more specific. Neesom led Class 40 of the National Union of Working Classes, and took over the treasurership of the organisation in March 1833, when James Watson was imprisoned for selling the *Poor Man's Guardian*. He also regularly attended Robert Taylor's infidel services at the Rotunda, Blackfriars, and was secretary to the management committee of the Finsbury radical and secularist meeting-place, the Bowling Square Chapel in Lower White-Cross Street. Occasionally he spoke on the platform at Owen's Charlotte Street Institute. In addition he was deeply involved in the trade societies of the tailors – 'very active among them' in the words of an informer whom Neesom unwittingly proposed for membership of the Grand Lodge of Operative Tailors of London in February 1834. He was also active in the agitations on behalf of the lock-out of the Derby silk-weavers, which aroused wide public support, and also in the nationwide campaign in support of the Dorchester labourers.

In all his political activities at this time, Neesom's continuing ties of personal friendship and intellectual conviction to Spenceanism were readily apparent: 'property which had been acquired by the plunder of the people, he would encroach on when he could because he knew it to be his' [*PMG*, 8 June 1833, 181]. One of the more sensational episodes of this period was the violent break-up of an NUWC meeting in Cold Bath Fields by the Metropolitan Police on Monday 13 May 1833. James Mee, a Spencean, was proposed as chairman, but the police presence was so overwhelming that he proposed an adjournment, and the police then attacked in considerable force [*PMG*, 18 and 25 May 1833]. In the fighting which followed, a policeman named Robert Culley was stabbed to death, and a London jury, to the dismay and anger of the Coroner, declared at the inquest a verdict of 'Justifiable Homicide': a decision which was greeted with what the *Poor Man's Guardian* stated was 'indescribable delight' (25 May 1833). This particular episode remained for years in the memory of London radicals. Neesom was among a party of leading personalities of the NUWC who addressed a large protest meeting at Chatham.

Neesom had become closely associated with Allen Davenport, who came to live with him and his second wife Elizabeth at their home in Moor Lane, Cripplegate, in 1835. They greatly helped Davenport's recovery that year from a near-fatal illness. When, the following July, a dinner was organised to honour the memory of Spence (a biography of whom Davenport had just written), it was chaired by Charles Neesom and held at the Eastern Institution, Shoreditch. The two men had been instrumental in setting up this workers' mutual education organisation, and early the next year they were likewise involved in the East London Democratic Association: Neesom's name (misspelt 'Needham') appears on the latter's inaugural address. Besides serving on the committee of the Association, Neesom acted as secretary to a subscription fund in aid of Gale Jones and Thomas Preston, which evolved into the Metropolitan Society for the Relief of Distressed Patriots.

In the mid-1830s, dogged by increasingly defective sight, common among tailors, Neesom had abandoned the trade: he had tried for a short time to work on his own account but now, encouraged by his wife (whom he had married in 1830), he established a radical newsagent's shop. Elizabeth Neesom conducted a school on the same premises, in Brick Lane, Spitalfields. The business allowed them to devote more time to politics, and both played important parts in metropolitan Chartism. Charles Neesom served on the executive of the Central National Association, a short-lived attempt in 1837 to create a united Chartist organisation in the capital. He was, however, a figure of considerable controversy, still espousing Spencean views about property, attacking the 'black slugs' (clergy), 'the worst enemies we have', as well as taking a central role in the conduct of the republican East London Democratic Association. His membership of the other key Chartist organisation in the capital, the London Working Men's Association, was short-lived, however: in March 1838, incensed by its support for Daniel O'Connell, he resigned in order to revive, along with G. J. Harney and Thomas Ireland, the Democratic Association. Gammage's assessment of him at this time was barbed but not totally inaccurate: 'Neesom possessed no large amount of talent, or breadth of views, but the extreme language he employed was his passport to popularity. He made no secret of his prepossession in favour of a physical revolution.' [*History of the Chartist Movement* (1969 ed.) p. 68].

Neesom represented Bristol as a delegate to the Chartist Convention of 1839. Here he continued his close association with Harney and was particularly vocal in arguing that the proposed 'sacred month' should begin at the earliest possible date. The tendencies which Gammage noted were perhaps the reason why suspicion was harboured by a few moderate delegates that Neesom was a spy or *agent provocateur*. After the collapse of the Convention, Neesom was involved in another short-lived body, the London Association of United Chartists. He also returned to his native Yorkshire in November 1839, 'for the purpose of ascertaining how far the working classes are disposed as regards numbers to unite for the *People's Charter*' [*Northern Star*, 14 Dec 1839]. This visit was made on behalf of the London Democratic Association. However, Neesom's career as a revolutionary Chartist came to an abrupt end on 16 January 1840, when he was arrested following a police raid on a meeting at the Trades Hall, Bethnal Green, at which arms were found. Neesom's conduct as chairman was perhaps the only reason why the meeting dispersed peaceably. Nevertheless, after a night in the cells spent singing 'To Arms Ye Brave', Neesom appeared at Bow Street and was charged with sedition and conspiracy. With the terms for his bail totalling £1000, he had no alternative but committal to Newgate, where almost immediately he spent a spell in solitary confinement, and on bread and water, for refusal to attend chapel. An anonymous sympathiser having stood as surety, Neesom was released; but a few months later, after he had failed to answer a court summons, his goods were seized in distraint and he was committed to Queen's Bench Prison. His business declined disastrously as a result and, although all charges were eventually dropped, Neesom was profoundly unsettled by the whole affair.

The extent to which he emerged from this experience a changed man can perhaps be exaggerated. He could be found, for example, leading a boisterous Chartist invasion of an Anti-Corn Law League meeting in Deptford in March 1841; and he carried his secularist and republican principles with him to the grave. However, his outspoken support of the 'New Move', initiated by Lovett and Collins, earned him the enmity of O'Connor and his followers, especially after the *Northern Star* printed (albeit with great reluctance) a letter from Neesom attacking O'Connor. Like Allen Davenport, in 1842 he joined Lovett's National Association and it was the beginning of a cordial friendship. In his *Life and Struggles* Lovett recorded with distaste how 'my respected friend' and his wife were hounded from their radical newsagency and school by supporters of O'Connor because of their supposed treachery. Neesom was one of the signatories to the National Association's inaugural address, and in 1847 he took over from Lovett as its secretary. Prior to this he had represented the Tower Hamlets at the Complete Suffrage Union conference in Birmingham in 1842, and had been elected to the Union's council, where, however, he continued to espouse all six points of the Charter. On the periphery of metropolitan radicalism Neesom actively supported the National Land and Building Society, an ill-starred attempted rival to the Chartist Land Plan promoted by James Hill, an Owenite who was the father of the philanthropist, Octavia Hill. Neesom's most significant contribution to the radical movement in these years, however, was the part he played in promoting Teetotal Chartism. After October 1840 he announced he would refuse sugar until the Charter became law; then, in December the same year, he drew up (with Hetherington, Cleave, Hill and Vincent) an address arguing that teetotalism would assist the Chartists because the Government operated very largely through the vices of the poor. Widely reprinted, the address became virtually the manifesto of Teetotal Chartism. An East London Chartist Temperance Association, with Neesom as secretary, was formed the following year, closely followed by a women's counterpart led by Elizabeth Neesom. By 1848 the Neesoms had taken their dietary radicalism to the logical conclusion of becoming vegetarians.

The character of Neesom's political career, though not his general commitment, slackened during the 1850s, and he was content to play a largely passive role as a member of the London Secular Society. He was a close friend of the metropolitan secularist leader John Maughan, with whom he was involved in setting up the General Secular Benevolent Society in the autumn of 1860; but he had served on its committee for only four months before he himself needed the Society's support. During his final illness he was attended without charge by Doctor Viettinghof, an old comrade and member of an East End family of Polish exiles. On 8 June 1861 he died in his wife's arms, aged seventy-seven. Some 300 mourners attended his interment in the unconsecrated portion of Victoria Park Cemetery, Bethnal Green, on Sunday 16 June. Neesom's standing in metropolitan secularism is indicated by the fact that the occasion brought together Joseph Barker, Bradlaugh and Maughan – leading radicals more usually at odds with each other. William Lovett was another orator at the graveside. Bradlaugh and Maughan also led a memorial meeting at the Hall of Science, City Road. In Bradlaugh's words, 'another link had been lost which bound us to the past', and indeed longevity had contributed much to Neesom's reputation. More important, however, were the qualities identified by Maughan at this gathering: 'a firmness of character and unflinching integrity'. A collection at this memorial meeting was taken for Elizabeth Neesom, who survived her husband. His obituary [*National Reformer 2*, no. 62, 20 July 1861] speaks of Elizabeth Neesom as having 'seconded his efforts throughout'. More than this, as leader of the London Female Democratic Association she had made a distinctive and important contribution to radical politics in the capital. It is notable that Charles Neesom's peak years of activism followed his marriage to her in 1830. Furthermore, the obituary makes clear that it was she who largely ran the schoolroom and newsagency which supported them both when he ceased tailoring. Without his wife, Charles Neesom might well have had less time to devote to radicalism and free-thought, and perhaps even have been less motivated to do so.

Writings: Letter to the editor, *Gauntlet*, no. 14 (12 May 1833); letter (with Thomas Ireland), *Operative*, no. 9 (30 Dec 1838); letter, ibid., no. 10 (6 Jan 1839); 'Whig Tyranny and Persecution', *Northern Star*, 16 May 1840; letter (East London Total Abstinence and Mutual Instruction Association), *English Chartist Circular 1*, no. 5 (20 Feb 1841); letter to William Rider, *Northern Star*, 3 May 1841; two letters 'to the editor', ibid. In addition Neesom probably co-authored the address on 'Teetotal Chartism' which first appeared over his name, along with those of Vincent, Cleave, Hetherington and William Hill, in the *Northern Star*, 28 Nov 1840. It was several times reprinted: see *Chartist Circular* [Glasgow] 65 (19 Dec 1840), *English Chartist Circular 1*, no. 9 (20 Mar 1841), and *An Address to the Working Men of England, Scotland and Wales* [1841?].

Sources: (1) MS: PRO Kew: HO 40/8 (3), fo. 115; HO 64/12, 14 Aug 1832; HO 64/15, 27 Feb and 29 Apr 1833. BL, Dept of MSS: Add. MS 37773, fos 62, 74–5. BL, Dept of Printed Books: Place Coll., Set 56, Oct 1840–Feb 1841, fo. 29. (2) Other: *PMG*, nos 14 (8 Oct 1831) and 36 (18 Feb 1832); *Working Man's Friend*, 9 Feb 1833; *Cosmopolite, 2*, no. 52 (2 Mar 1833); *PMG*, nos 102 (18 May 1833), 103 (25 May 1833), 105 (8 June 1833), 109 (6 July 1833), 118 (7 Sep 1833) and 119 (14 Sep 1833); *Man*, 8 Dec 1833; *Cleave's Weekly Police Gazette*, 30 July 1836; *Prospectus of the East London Democratic Association* (Jan 1837; repr. in D. Thompson, *Early Chartists* (1971) 55–6); *London Dispatch*, no. 34 (4 June 1837); *London Mercury*, 18 June 1837; *London Dispatch*, nos 52 (10 Sep 1837) and 58 (22 Oct 1837); *Operative*, nos 3 (18 Nov 1838), 6 (9 Dec 1838), 8 (23 Dec 1838), 9 (30 Dec 1838), 17 (24 Feb 1839), 24 (14 Apr 1839) and 28 (12 May 1839); *Northern Star*, 14 Dec 1839; *Charter*, nos 52

(19 Jan 1840) and 53 (26 Jan 1840); *Southern Star*, 19 Jan 1840; *Northern Liberator*, 25 Jan 1840; *Southern Star*, 22 Mar 1840; *Northern Star*, 16 May, 6 June, 10 Oct and 28 Nov 1840, 30 Jan, 6 Mar, 1 and 8 May 1841; *Anti-Corn Law Circular*, 25 Mar 1841; *National Association Gaz.*, nos 1 (1 Jan 1842) and 13 (26 Mar 1842); *Brief Sketches of the Birmingham Conference* (1842); *Northern Star*, 17 Feb 1844; *The Life and Literary Pursuits of Allen Davenport ... written by himself* (1845); *National Reformer*, no. 14 (2 Jan 1847); *Reasoner 2*, no. 29 (Jan 1847); *Spirit of the Age*, no. 18 (25 Nov 1848); *Reasoner Gaz.*, *25*, nos 44 (28 Oct 1860), 47 (18 Nov 1860) and 50 (9 Dec 1860); *National Reformer 2*, no. 57 (15 June 1861); *Reasoner 26*, no. 24 (16 June 1861); *National Reformer 2*, no. 58 (22 June 1861); *Reasoner 26*, no. 26 (30 June 1861); 'Memoir of Mr C. H. Neesom compiled from an Autobiography left by himself and from other Sources', *National Reformer 2*, nos 62 (20 July 1861) and 63 (27 July 1861); R. G. Gammage, *The History of the Chartist Movement, from its Commencement down to the Present Time* (1854–5; 2nd ed. Newcastle, 1894; repr. with an Introduction by J. Saville, 1969); W. Lovett, *Life and Struggles ...* (1876; repr. in 2 vols with an Introduction by R. H. Tawney, 1920; another ed. minus the last three chapters, 1967); M. Hovell, *The Chartist Movement* (Manchester, 1918; 2nd ed. 1925); D. Thompson, *The Early Chartists* (1971); B. Harrison, 'Teetotal Chartism', *History 58*, no. 193 (June 1973) 193–217; E. Royle, *Victorian Infidels* (1974); D. J. V. Jones, *Chartism and the Chartists* (1975); T. Parssinen and I. J. Prothero, 'The London Tailors' Strike of 1834 and the Collapse of the Grand National Consolidated Trades' Union: a police spy report', *Int. Rev. Social Hist. 22*, no. 1 (1977) 65–107; I. J. Prothero, *Artisans and Politics in Early Nineteenth Century London* (Folkestone, Kent, 1979); E. Royle, *Chartism* (1981); J. Epstein, *The Lion of Freedom: Feargus O'Connor and the Chartist Movement, 1832–42* (1982); D. Goodway, *London Chartism 1837–41: a study in London Radicalism* (1982); J. Bennett, 'The London Democratic Association', in *The Chartist Experience: studies in working-class radicalism and culture 1830–60*, ed. J. Epstein and D. Thompson (1982) 87–119; I. J. Prothero, 'Charles Hodgson Neesom', in *Biographical Dictionary of Modern British Radicals*, vol. 2, ed. J. O. Baylen and N. J. Gossman (Brighton, 1984) 367–9; D. Thompson, *The Chartists* (1984). OBIT. *National Reformer 2*, nos 57 (15 June 1861) and 58 (22 June 1861); *Reasoner 26*, nos 24 (16 June 1861) and 26 (30 June 1861).

MALCOLM CHASE

See also: †Charles BRADLAUGH; †Richard CARLILE; †John CLEAVE; Allen DAVENPORT; †Robert George GAMMAGE; †Henry HETHERINGTON; †William LOVETT; Thomas PRESTON; Thomas SPENCE; †Henry VINCENT.

OLIVIER, Sydney Haldane (1st Baron Olivier of Ramsden) (1859–1943)
FABIAN, CIVIL SERVANT AND STATESMAN

Sydney Olivier was born on 16 April 1859 at Colchester, Essex. He was the second son and sixth of the ten children of the Revd Henry Olivier and his wife Anne Elizabeth (née Arnould). The Olivier family was Huguenot by origin who, after the revocation of the Edict of Nantes in 1685, went first to Holland and then came to England.

Olivier was educated at Tonbridge School and at Corpus Christi College, Oxford. There he became a close friend of Graham Wallas, whose father was also an Anglican parson of rigid evangelical persuasion. Their tutor at Corpus Christi was Thomas Case, a philosophical empiricist, an exponent of J. S. Mill's logic, and largely responsible for keeping the College free from the influence of Hegelian idealism in the 1880s. Olivier graduated in 1881, sat for the Civil Service examination in 1882 and headed the list of successful candidates. He entered the Colonial Office, and was to remain in government for many decades. Sidney Webb joined the Colonial Office in the same year as Olivier, and they too became close friends.

In the fragment of autobiography published after his death – the absence of a complete autobiography is much to be regretted – Olivier gave a vivid account of what working life was like:

I was put [he wrote] into the West India Department, the head of which was one of the old stagers, a pleasant non-excitable man who had been a University cricket blue, and who drove up to the office from a remote suburb every day in a dog-cart tandem, arriving about half-past twelve, after which he consumed a substantial lunch and went to sleep until tea-time. The clerk who did the work of the department was the Senior Second-class Clerk [Olivier (1948) 31].

The office also afforded Olivier a good deal of time for his own interests. He worked for Miss Gertrude Toynbee in a public health committee and at the same time began to be introduced to radical politics by his friends and acquaintances. Harold Cox, his future brother-in-law, was probably the most immediate influence. Cox was lecturing for the Democratic Federation and remained in the organisation after it added 'Social' to its title in 1884. Olivier was also influenced by Henry George. Soon after joining the Georgeite Land Reform Union in 1883, he made contact with H. H. Champion and J. L. Joynes, who were editing the *Christian Socialist*. This journal supported, among other aims, land reform and a moralistic version of Marxism. Olivier, however, was never seriously attracted to Marxism, although he was a member of the Hampstead Historic Society, which arose from a Marxist reading club [MacKenzie (1979) 65]. The philosopher he was much influenced by at this time was Auguste Comte – as were also both Graham Wallas and Sidney Webb. By the mid-1880s Olivier had arrived at a view of humanity which denied the old forms of individualism and which laid emphasis upon the 'social nature and propensity of man' [*Freedom*, Oct 1887].

Webb had been introduced to the Fabian Society meetings by Bernard Shaw in March 1885, and in May of the same year Webb and Olivier were admitted to membership. In the following year Graham Wallas joined [Shaw (1972) 490]. Of these four leading personalities of the early Fabian Society, Olivier is the least known to historians; and yet his colleagues clearly thought him a remarkable personality. At the age of eighty-eight in 1944 Shaw wrote a scintillating account of Olivier as the Preface to the memoir published by Margaret Olivier:

Olivier was an extraordinarily attractive figure, and in my experience unique; for I have never known anyone like him mentally or physically: he was distinguished enough to be unclassable. He was handsome and strongly sexed, looking like a Spanish grandee in any sort of clothes, however unconventional. . . .

It was fortunate for mankind that he was a man of good intent and sensitive humanity; for he was a law to himself, and never dreamt of considering other people's feelings, nor could conceive their sensitiveness on points that were to him trivial. . . . He had no apparent conscience, being on the whole too well disposed to need one; but when he had a whim that was flatly contrary to convention he gratified it openly and unscrupulously as a matter of course, dealing with any opposing prejudice by the method recommended by the American Mrs Stetson, of 'walking through it as if it wasn't there' [Olivier (1948) 9–10].

Olivier was certainly inclined to be impatient with stupidity, but what needs to be emphasised is what Shaw called his 'sensitive humanity'. This showed itself very plainly in his long periods of service in the Caribbean, and it shines through his correspondence. He and his young colleagues in the Fabian Society produced what became the most famous of all the Society's publications: *Fabian Essays* in 1889, edited by Shaw. Olivier wrote the essay on the moral basis of Socialism, in which he emphasised the varying morality grounded in class distinctions, and the 'effects of our present property system which work continuously for the destruction of the traditions of social morality in the capitalist class'. He ended with a typically Fabian conclusion:

it may have been sufficient in this paper to have shown some grounds for the conviction that Socialist morality, like that of all preceding systems, is only that morality which the conditions of human existence have made necessary; that it is only the expression of the eternal passion of life seeking its satisfaction through the striving of each individual for the freest and fullest activity; that Socialism is but a stage in the unending progression out of the weakness and the ignorance in which society and the individual alike are born, towards the strength and the enlightenment in which they can see and choose their own way forward – from the chaos where morality is not to the consciousness which sees that morality is reason; and to have made some attempt to justify the claim that the cardinal virtue of Socialism is nothing else than Common Sense [Olivier (1889) 161].

Olivier acted as honorary secretary to the Fabian Society between 1886 and 1889 and served on the Society's executive committee from 1887 to 1899. His professional career took a new turn when he was posted to British Honduras in 1890 as Colonial Secretary. On his return in April 1891 he was transferred to the position of principal clerk in the South African department of the Colonial Office. This was at a time when adventurers, scoundrels and respectable British companies were active in imposing their mercenary will upon the native peoples of South Africa. Olivier was greatly troubled by the proceedings of the South African Chartered Company and the activities of Cecil Rhodes. He remained much concerned with African affairs for the rest of his life, although apparently he never visited the continent. He was always vehement against racial prejudice and constantly warned against the violence that would build up in resentment of its application.

Soon after his return from British Honduras he and his wife, Margaret (they had married in 1885), began living in Limpsfield, near Oxted in the Weald of Kent; and a colony of progressively minded Liberals and Fabians began to settle in the area: the J. A. Hobsons, the Garnetts, the Peases, the Ford Hermann Heuffers. Only a little further away were Henry and Kate Salt, E. V. Lucas and Octavia Hill, who had a cottage on the edge of the countryside, nearer London. Olivier attended the Zurich Conference of the Labour and Socialist International in 1893 [*New Statesman*, 18 Aug 1928] and in 1895 was given a six-month appointment as Auditor-General of the Leeward Islands. On his return he went back to the West Indian department of the Colonial Office and at the end of 1896 went to the West Indies again as secretary to the Sugar Commission. He was sent in 1898 to Washington to assist in the negotiation of reciprocity agreements for the West Indies, and in the autumn of 1899 he was appointed Colonial Secretary to Jamaica.

During the periods he was in England he was always in close touch with his Fabian friends and colleagues, especially Wallas, Shaw and Webb. He was an early member of the Rainbow Circle, which had been first established in 1894 [Clarke (1978) 56 ff.] and when he was abroad he maintained contact by constant correspondence. He was vigorously opposed to the Boer War, and joined MacDonald and William Clarke in their struggle within the Fabian Society against the Webbs and Bernard Shaw.

The appointment to Jamaica as Colonial Secretary – he arrived there in 1900 – was the beginning of Olivier's very close association with the island. He was a most unusual colonial officer. He was, wrote a Jamaican contemporary, 'an entirely new element in the social life of the community and so strenuous was his energy, so original his point of view, that he soon began to affect most other receptive persons, thus gradually changing the *ethos* or character of Jamaica permanently' [de Lisser, in Olivier (1948) 231]. He actually walked to work: apparently a quite unprecedented habit. Olivier was in office until 1904 and acquired a remarkable reputation for efficient administration. He became deeply absorbed with Jamaica's problems, and established its finances on a sound basis. He also gave lectures on Socialism in the lecture hall of the Institute of Jamaica: a somewhat unusual event in the history of the British Empire.

He left Jamaica in September 1904 and resumed his position as principal clerk in charge of West Indian affairs at the Colonial Office. In January 1907 a great earthquake occurred in Jamaica, causing widespread damage and havoc. The Governor had already resigned, and a deputation of leading personalities, including the Archbishop of the West Indies, pressed strongly for Olivier's appointment; and after being appointed he was to remain in the office of Governor for five and a half years, retiring in January 1913. It was once more a highly successful tenure. On his return to England he became permanent secretary to the Board of Agriculture and Fisheries. In 1917 he entered the Treasury, and in 1920 he retired from the Civil Service.

Olivier's part in the modern history of Jamaica was of quite crucial importance. He was originally appointed to the position of Colonial Secretary by Joseph Chamberlain, with whose ideas on colonial policy he was in some sympathy. Olivier's main contributions to Jamaica were his use of positive government intervention – his Fabian background was of direct relevance here; his commitment of government to remunerative enterprises enabling a policy of progressive tax reduction, especially in the areas of indirect taxation; the extension of public services; and a consistent emphasis upon education. He won a very considerable co-operation from what traditionally had been a very conservative colony, with both 'a conservative oligarchy and a conservative peasantry' [Carroll (1973) 312], although the strong role of the convenor and the senior civil servants undoubtedly weakened the position of the elected members of the Legislative Council. The literature on Olivier's Jamaican administration is voluminous, and is usefully summarised in Carroll's 1973 thesis.

After his retirement Olivier lived for another twenty-three years, and was continually busy – above all in writing. He had published two books before the war: a short story, *The Empire Builder*, in 1905, and a serious analysis, *White Capital and Coloured Labour*, in 1906. Both were republished in the 1920s and the latter again in the 1970s. In 1927 he wrote *The Anatomy of African Misery* (repr. 1972); in 1933 *The Myth of Governor Eyre* – a relatively forgotten episode of the 1860s which wrote a shameful page in British colonial history; and in 1936 *Jamaica: the blessed island*. He also published a good deal in contemporary journals on a notably wide range of subjects, and in addition to political/social articles he also wrote extensively on colonial affairs. To the end of his life he maintained a firm, well-balanced and well-phrased English style.

During the 1920s Olivier's public life continued. In 1924 he became Secretary of State for India in Ramsay MacDonald's first minority Government. He was created a baron and a member of the Privy Council. His term of office was not a success, and there was little to distinguish the policy of the Labour Government from that of its Conservative predecessor. Gandhi was released from gaol after a severe illness, but there was no serious attempt at reconciliation. At the beginning of his short period in office (26 Feb 1924) Olivier spoke at length in the House of Lords of his own, and his Government's, attitude to Indian Home Rule. It was a somewhat equivocal statement. On the one hand he insisted that HMG had the same ultimate aim as the Indian Swaraj Party – namely, the achievement of responsible Dominion status; but he criticised the 'uncompromising intransigence' of the main body of Indian nationalists, and he turned down the suggestion that had come from India of a round table conference. Many years later he wrote he had come to the conclusion 'that the problem of India was insoluble'; and he seems to have regarded independence as a very long-term solution, if not an impossibility [Olivier (1948) 157].

In the second Labour Government he served as chairman of the West India Sugar Commission (1929–30), whose recommendations were rejected by Sidney Webb (Secretary of State for the Dominions and the Colonies) and the Labour Government. Olivier spoke sharply in the Lords against the Government [*Hansard*, 26 Nov 1930].

As he got older his whole life seemed to be centred upon the West Indies and Africa, and above all on Jamaica; and he spoke several times on Jamaican problems in the Lords. He continued to correspond throughout the 1930s with interested friends: Sir John Harris of the Anti-Slavery Society; Norman Leys; and W. M. MacMillan. Olivier had suffered bouts of ill health for many years before his death. The family – there were four daughters – had moved from Limpsfield to an Elizabethan manor house in north Oxfordshire in 1921, and in the last decade of his life he and his wife lived at Bognor on the south coast. They made short visits to Jamaica in 1938 and 1939, and Olivier was working, intermittently, on a book on Africa almost to his last days. He died on 15 February 1943 at Bognor and his funeral took place at Brighton Crematorium. One of his younger brothers was the painter H. A. Olivier; another was the Revd Gerald Kerr Olivier, the father of Lord Olivier, the actor.

Sydney Olivier had a considerable literary ability and wrote essays, stories and plays, and he had a felicitous gift for light verse. One of his plays, *Mrs Maxwell's Marriage*, was performed by the Stage Society on Sunday 21 January 1900. There was an amusing interchange of letters between Shaw, who praised the play highly ('as good as Ibsen'), and William Archer, who thought it 'dead as a doornail – therefore precisely fitted for a Sunday evening performance' [Shaw, *Collected Letters* (1972) 136, 140]. In 1911 the University of Edinburgh conferred on him an honorary LLD. The memoir published after his death by his widow contained many of Olivier's letters to H. G. Wells, who became a great friend after they first met in 1905, but relatively few to other correspondents not belonging to the family. A more complete selection of his correspondence would be very worthwhile. When Olivier died he was survived by his wife and three daughters. One married daughter, Brynhild, had died in January 1935. He left effects valued at £937.

Leonard Woolf, who became acquainted with Olivier when the latter was over sixty, wrote a remarkable obituary of him in the *New Statesman and Nation* for 27 February 1943. Olivier had been a member of the Labour Party's Advisory Committee on Imperial Questions, of which Woolf was secretary:

He was already in the eighties of last century a prominent Fabian Socialist. To be a Socialist and at the same time a civil servant, particularly a colonial civil servant, sixty years ago, was a remarkable, not to say an eccentric combination. To succeed in the Colonial Service, to become the Governor of a Colony, and to remain a Socialist, not merely in theory and academically, but in word and deed, as Olivier did, was an extraordinary phenomenon. Olivier's Socialism was both intellectual and emotional; it came from both his head and his heart. His head made him a Fabian. . . .

But it was his heart, his emotions, his likes and dislikes which also made him a Socialist, just as they made him a determined democrat, a life-long lover of freedom, an obstinate defender of all under-dogs. . . . This love of freedom and equality was, I say, not merely intellectual; there was nothing doctrinaire about it. It was instinctive in him. It was the thing that made him an eccentric Englishman. . . .

[And Woolf summed up his last years]

Olivier was one of those rare persons whose brain never hardened into conservatism. At the age of 80 his mind was as progressive and as open to new ideas as it was when he was 18. He never lost his enthusiasm, for what he thought to be politically right or socially desirable, for liberty, equality and Socialism.

Writings: Sydney Olivier was a prolific writer throughout his life as the following bibliography indicates. Listed here are his major works and a number of articles, mainly on political and colonial affairs, which have been located in contemporary journals and the weekly press. His plays have not been found. (With H. C. Campion) *Poems and Parodies* (1880) 24 pp.; 'John Stuart Mill and Socialism', *To-day 2* (1884) 490–504; 'Perverse Socialism', ibid. *6* (1886) 47–55, 109–14; 'A Champion of the Perverse', ibid., 175–8 [a reply to an article by H. H. Champion, 'Socialists of the Armchair', ibid., 146–51]; 'A Critic of Anarchism', *Freedom 2*, no. 13 (Oct 1887) 50–1; 'Socialism and Foreign Trade', *To-day 9* (1888) 70–82; 'Idols of the Sty', ibid. *10* (1888) 66–77, 94–100; *Capital and Land* (Fabian Tract no. 7: 1888; 5th ed. rev. 1896, repr. Kraus 1969) 15 pp.; 'The Moral Basis of Socialism', Ch. 4 in G. B. Shaw *et al.*, *Fabian Essays in Socialism* (1889; 6th ed. with a new Introduction by A. Briggs, 1962) 135–61; 'The Miners' Battle – and after', *Cont. Rev. 64* (Nov 1893) 749–64; 'Moths and Tulips: modulations upon a very ancient theme', ibid. *75* (Mar 1899) 343–9; 'Portraits and Phantoms', ibid. (May 1899) 687–701; 'An Empire Builder', ibid. *87* (May 1905) 692–704, repr. *The Empire Builder* (1927) 47 pp.; 'The White Man's Burden at Home', *Int. Q. 11* (1905) 6–23; 'The Beginnings of Leo Tolstoy', *Living Age 245* (1905) 698–701; '*A Modern Utopia*' [review of Wells' novel], *Fabian News 15* (Aug 1905) 38–9, repr. in *H. G. Wells: the critical heritage*, ed. P. Parrinder (1972) 110–12; 'Illumination in Art, Love and Revivalism', *Cont. Rev. 88* (Oct 1905) 495–515; 'Long Views and Short on White and Black' [on racial prejudice], ibid. *90* (Oct 1906) 491–504; *White Capital and Coloured Labour* (1906; rev. ed. 1929, repr. 1970 and 1971); 'The Government of Colonies and Dependencies', in *Universal Races Congress I* [papers on inter-racial problems] (1911) 293–301; *The League of Nations and Primitive Peoples* (1918) 16 pp.; 'The Muffled Mandates', *New Statesman 16* (25 Dec 1920) 360–1; 'Why not pay off the Floating Debt?' [letter], ibid. (12 Feb 1921) 555–6 [this was one of several letters from Olivier which gave rise to a lively correspondence on this issue]; 'Constitutional Development in the West Indies', ibid. *19* (24 June 1922) 316–17; 'Blowing the Gaff on the Landlords', *Nation 31* (23 Sep 1922) 816–17; 'A Financial Paradox' [letter], ibid. *32* (6 Jan 1923) 545–6; 'Vision of the Antechamber', *Hibbert J. 21*, no. 2 (Jan 1923) 367–74; 'Kingston Wharf', *Engl. Rev. 36* (Feb 1923) 157–63; 'The League and the Bondelswart Massacres', *New Statesman 21* (15 Sep 1923) 637–8; 'The Labour Party', *19th C. 95* (Jan 1924) 20–30; 'The Indian Reforms Enquiry', *New Statesman 24* (21 Mar 1925) 684–6; 'The "Saintliness" of Mr C. R. Das' [letters], ibid. *25* (27 June, 18 July 1925) 306–7, 391; 'Firing the Haystacks' [on South African Colour Bar Bill], ibid. *26* (20 Feb 1926) 576–7; 'Africanderus contra Mundum', ibid. (10 Apr 1926) 797–8; 'Segregation in Southern Rhodesia', ibid. *27* (26 June 1926) 287–8; 'Land in Rhodesia' [letter], ibid. (10 July 1926) 355; 'Lord Olivier on the Hindu–Moslem Quarrel', *Near East 30* (22 July 1926) 74–5; 'The Conversion of Kenya', *New Statesman 28* (27 Nov 1926) 200–1; *The Anatomy of African Misery* (1927; repr. 1972); 'Wisdom from British East', *New Statesman 29* (18 June 1927) 304–6; 'The Problem of South African Native Policy', *Labour Mag. 6* (July 1927) 107–11; 'Restore Stonehenge', *New Statesman 29* (13 Aug 1927) 564–5; 'The Second International at Brussels', ibid. *31* (18 Aug 1928) 584–5; 'Praise of Aargau', *Nation and Athenaeum 44*, no. 3 (20 Oct 1928) 105–7; 'An Uncharted Reef in South African Politics' [on colour bar, white labour policy and the Industrial and Commercial Workers' Union], *New Statesman 32* (17 Nov, 1 and 22 Dec 1928) 182–4 [letters] 250, 356; 'The Meaning of Imperial Trusteeship', *Cont. Rev. 136* (Sep 1929) 303–12, repr. as *Imperial Trusteeship* (Fabian Tract no. 230: 1929; repr. Kraus 1969) 14 pp.; 'The Fabulous Realm of Ameria' [on Kenya], *New Statesman 34* (12 Oct 1929) 6–7; 'The Government and our Sugar Colonies', *19th C. 108* (July 1930) 56–61; 'Sugar and British Colonies', *New Statesman 36* (22 Nov 1930) 198–200; (with D. M. Semple) *Report of the West Indian Sugar Commission 1929–30*, Cmd 3517 (HMSO, 1930); 'The Colour Bar: the economic basis', *Spec. 146* (9 May 1931) 727–8; 'The Kenya Land Committee', *New Statesman and Nation 3*, no. 67 (4 June 1932) 730 [in reply to a letter from J. Kenyatta of 28 May]; *The Myth of Governor Eyre* (1933); 'William Morris born March

24th 1834', *Spec. 152* (23 Mar 1934) 440–1; 'The End of an Epoch' [letter], *New Statesman and Nation 8* (29 Dec 1934) 965–6; 'Quelques souvenirs d'un noble voyage', *Illustration*, no. 4816 (22 June 1935) 299–302; *Jamaica: the blessed island* (1936); 'The Strikes in Jamaica' [letter], *New Statesman and Nation 15* (4 June 1938) 947; 'Democracy in the Colonial Empire', ibid. *20* (21 Dec 1940) 652; *Sydney Olivier: letters and selected writings*, ed. with a Memoir by Margaret Olivier with some impressions by Bernard Shaw (1948).

Sources: (1) MS: For details of Olivier papers see *A Guide to the Papers of British Cabinet Ministers 1900–1951*, compiled by C. Hazelhurst and C. Woodland (1974) 112; see also the Greenidge Coll., Rhodes House Library, Oxford. (2) Other: 'The Rent of Ability', *Practical Socialist 1*, no. 12 (Dec 1886) 187 [notes on a paper read by Olivier to the Fabian Society]; H. G. de Lisser, *Jane's Career: a story of Jamaica* (1914; new ed. 1972); *Hansard*, 1924; F. G. Bettany, *Stewart Headlam: a biography* (1926); *Hansard* (HL) vols *76–9, 81* (Feb 1930–June 1931) [for debates on the West Indian Sugar Industry]; *Statement of Policy in Regard to the West Indian and Mauritius Sugar Reports* (Cmd 3523, 1930); *Kelly* (1938); *DNB* (1941–50); H. Pearson, *Bernard Shaw: his life and personality* (1942; later eds); H. G. de Lisser, 'Notes on Lord Olivier's Official Career in Jamaica', in *Sydney Olivier: letters and selected writings*, ed. M. Olivier (1948) 231; *Shaw and Society* ed. C. E. M. Joad (1953); K. Martin, *Harold Laski* (1953); A. Freemantle, *This Little Band of Prophets: the British Fabians* (NY, 1960); M. I. Cole, *The Story of Fabian Socialism* (1961); A. M. McBriar, *Fabian Socialism and English Politics* (1962); M. Weiner, *Between Two Worlds* (1971); Bernard Shaw, *Collected Letters: 1874–1897* and *1898–1910*, ed. Dan H. Laurence (1965 and 1972); J. J. Carroll, 'The Government of Jamaica, 1900–1913, with Special Reference to the role of Sir Sydney Olivier' (London PhD, 1973); D. Wylie, 'Critics of Colonial Policy in Kenya with Special Reference to Norman Leys and W. McGregor Ross' (Edinburgh MLitt., 1974); W. Wolfe, *From Radicalism to Socialism: men and ideas in the formation of Fabian Socialist Doctrines, 1881–1889* (New Haven, Conn., 1975); S. B. Ward, 'Land Reform in England 1880–1914' (Reading PhD, 1976); N. and J. MacKenzie, *The First Fabians* (1977); P. Clarke, *Liberals and Social Democrats* (Cambridge, 1978); 'The Diary of Beatrice Webb 1873–1943', 57 vols (Cambridge, 1978) [on microfiche], and *Index to the Diary of Beatrice Webb 1873–1943* (1978); J. MacKenzie, *A Victorian Courtship: the story of Beatrice Potter and Sidney Webb* (1979); T. H. Qualter, *Graham Wallas and the Great Society* (1980); *The Diary of Beatrice Webb*, 4 vols, ed. N. and J. MacKenzie (1982–5). Obit. *Times*, 16 Feb 1943; *Banbury Advertiser*, 17 Feb 1943; *New Statesman*, 27 Feb 1943 [by Leonard Woolf].

JOHN SAVILLE

See also: Henry Hyde CHAMPION; †William CLARKE; James Leigh JOYNES; †James Ramsay MACDONALD; †Graham WALLAS; †Sidney James WEBB.

OUTHWAITE, Robert Leonard (1868–1930)
RADICAL LAND REFORMER AND LIBERAL MP

Outhwaite was born at Launceston, Tasmania, on 13 April 1868. He was the son of Robert Outhwaite, a sheep farmer, and Blanche Isabel (née Clerk). *The Times* obituary notice said that the father was a Yorkshire pastoralist who emigrated to Australia. The young Robert Outhwaite was educated at a Church of England grammar school and he may have become a journalist on the New Zealand *Examiner*; but the details of his early life are conflicting. His *Who's Who* entry, which he presumably wrote himself, spoke of his early life in 'country pursuits'. In 1898 he married Kathleen, the daughter of James Anderson, a New Zealand barrister, and a few years later, after the conclusion of the Boer War in 1902, he and his wife and their one son came to England. Outhwaite then went to South Africa (the date is not known) as correspondent of five Liberal papers to report on the Chinese labour problem: an issue that was becoming of major importance in British domestic politics in the last years of the Conservative Government before the general election of 1906. Certain of his articles, published in the *Echo* in the second half of 1905, were reprinted in pamphlet form under the title *Lord Milner's Record*. This was a searing indictment of Milner's administration in South Africa, and in particular Outhwaite documented the political manoeuvres by which Milner had prepared the way for the large-scale use of Chinese labour. He ended his pamphlet with the sub-heading 'Milner versus British Honour' and continued, 'So it comes about that Lord Milner's record is one of surrender of the interests of the many to the greed of the few, and of the betrayal of the good name and honour of Great Britain to degradation.'

In the general election of 1906 he contested West Birmingham as a Liberal, standing against Joseph Chamberlain. This was Chamberlain's home constituency. It was a predominantly working-class electorate [Pelling (1967) 182] and Outhwaite fought on the issues of the free breakfast table, abolition of the sugar bounties, the scandal of Chinese labour in South Africa, and taxation of land values. His reception was often hostile and on election day he polled just over 2000 votes against 7173 for Chamberlain.

Outhwaite had already become an advocate of the Henry George policy of a single tax on land and after the general election campaign he steadily increased his reputation as a radical land reformer. He published a series of six articles in the *Daily News* between January and March 1909 which were outspoken attacks upon aristocratic privilege and landed monopoly. In the light of his subsequent career it is to be noted that Outhwaite was always a good deal more radical – in his understanding of the economic and political struggle between classes, for example – than many of his contemporary Georgeites: certainly much more so than Frederick Verinder, for instance, although Outhwaite continued for many years to regard Socialism as misguided. In the general election of January 1910 Outhwaite stood as a Liberal at Horsham, Sussex, where the Conservative Party vote was always higher than the national average. It was an almost wholly rural constituency, with the influence of great landlords such as Lord Leconfield very powerful; and Outhwaite obtained only just over a third of the votes polled [Pelling (1967) 72–5]. In the following month Outhwaite was appointed an organiser for the recently established Gladstone League, whose aims and purposes were a systematic educational campaign on behalf of land reform [Peacock (1962) 226].

For the next two years Outhwaite continued his organising activities and published several pamphlets and articles; then, in May 1912, occurred the first of three by-elections which gave much heart to the land reformers: E. G. Hemmerde won Norfolk North-West. It was a constituency with a radical past in that Joseph Arch had won the seat in three general elections – 1885, 1892 and 1895 – retiring just before 1900. The constituency included part of the uplands of Norfolk, where farms were large and agricultural labourers were in large numbers receptive to the arguments of land reformers. Hemmerde's victory was followed by that of a Liberal land-taxer, Sydney Arnold, at Holmfirth, Yorkshire, and in July by an exciting by-election at Hanley, Staffordshire, which Outhwaite contested for the Liberals.

The Hanley constituency contained large numbers of potters and miners and was usually a safe Liberal seat. Enoch Edwards, a Lib–Lab miners' leader, had been defeated in 1900, but subsequent elections restored the Liberal majority. Outhwaite, who campaigned on a radical programme, to the left of official Liberalism, had a 654 majority over the Conservative candidate, with the Labour candidate, Samuel Finney, beaten into third place. Lloyd George had inaugurated his Land Enquiry Committee just before these three by-elections, and victory by the land-taxers was a very considerable encouragement to the radicals within the Liberal Party. Josiah Wedgwood wrote to a friend about the Hanley election, 'My friend Outhwaite stood as a Liberal and we polished off the Labour Party and the Tories too. All the single tax anarchists turned up with *Progress and Poverty* in their hands and won the election as though it was a religious revival' [Wedgwood (1951) 93]. Outhwaite publicly thanked Joseph Fels for his financial help. Fels was an American soap manufacturer who came to Britain in 1901 and was closely associated with George Lansbury, who advised him on the distribution of his surplus income in various good works – including co-operative smallholdings and colonies for the unemployed. Fels some-what later became an ardent supporter of the taxation of land values. In August 1912 the journal of the movement, *Land Values*, announced that Fels would match any contribution up to £20,000 raised to advance the land-tax cause; and Fels was always ready to help in the support of individuals or organisations whose aims he himself advocated. Hence his assistance to Outhwaite, and to Hemmerde before him.

Outhwaite's maiden speech in the House of Commons demonstrated the nature and quality of his radicalism. He spoke during the third reading of the Government of Ireland Bill, and provided strong support for the policy of Home Rule. He argued that the main opposition came from the landlord class, who assumed – very properly in Outhwaite's opinion – that an Irish Parliament would attack the privileged position of the landlords. He reported on a recent visit he had made to Belfast and the degrading conditions under which he had found women in the linen factories to be working; and he ended with a firm and enthusiastic endorsement of the cause of Irish nationalism.

One of the interesting, and often underestimated, aspects of the land-values movement was its firm and principled objection to the growth of government bureaucracy: a matter of much general concern in the years before the First World War. It was an important reason why radicals such as Outhwaite, who on most political and social issues were to the left of many in the Labour Party – certainly many in the PLP – kept an organisational distance from the Socialist movement. There was, as an additional reason, the hostility of most of Labour's leaders, including J. R. MacDonald, to the policy of land-value taxation. In these years, however, the land-taxers, and especially extreme radicals such as Outhwaite, were fighting within the Liberal Party for a land-tax programme; and it was the growing, painful recognition of the strength of the entrenched interests within the Liberal Party that slowly alienated the radical land reformers from their support for the traditional party of social progress. Outhwaite ended a leading article in *Land Values* (Aug 1914: the leader was written just before the outbreak of war) with the following words:

So we have reached this point – the land monopolists are promoting rebellion in Ulster in the hope to destroy the Liberal Government because of the work begun in the Land Clauses of the Budget of 1909. And out of the Budget of 1914 again emerges the dread issue.

That issue will not fail if the democracy but see eye to eye with the artistocracy, who realise that the taxation of Land Values involves the destruction of privilege and the coming of a new commonwealth founded on economic truth and social justice [p. 75].

The years of war advanced Outhwaite's radicalism. He was opposed to the party truce, was a member of the Union of Democratic Control by February 1915, argued for the financing of the war by land-value taxation, denounced conscription, was associated with the movement for a negotiated peace, and came out strongly against British intervention in Russia. He worked closely in Parliament with the radicals of the UDC, and with those in the PLP who fought against the jingoistic policies and attitudes of the wartime Coalition. What kept him from formally joining the Labour Party during the war years was the party's subservience to wartime government. In a trenchantly written booklet of 114 pages, *Land or Revolution* (1917), Outhwaite denounced the 'Bismarckian methods of State control and bureaucratic regimentation' [p. 77] to which the Labour Party lent their support:

> With the co-operation of members of the official Labour Party, Mr. Lloyd George has established bureaucratic control over the activities of the community, and a horde of officials are the masters of the people. The House of Commons has become a mere debating society, the only legislative function left to it being that of giving formal sanction to the decrees of the bureaucracy, whilst exercising less control over the conduct of affairs than the Reichstag itself [p. 79].

In the 'Coupon' election of 1918, because of his wartime radicalism and especially because of his opposition to war against Soviet Russia, Outhwaite was refused sponsorship by the Liberals at Hanley, and he stood as an Independent Liberal. J. A. Seddon, a former trade union leader, Labour MP, and now a member of the British Workers' League, won the seat against Labour and Liberal candidates. Outhwaite attracted only 2703 votes, although he was above the official nominee. Early in 1919 Outhwaite joined the ILP. His letter to Philip Snowden read as follows:

> My dear Snowden,
>   I was fortunate in having a splendid committee at Hanley, and it will interest you to hear that as they decided not to disband, I proposed that we should throw in our lot with the Independent Labour Party and form the Hanley Branch. I am glad to say that this suggestion was adopted. Personally I felt that having made my fight and fulfilled all obligations I could consult my own wishes and formally join those with whom I have been associated during the past four and a half bitter years. In the troublous days that lie ahead I desire to stand with those who in the supreme test have shown that they are not to be coerced or suborned into betraying the people to their enemies. That betrayal has now been consummated and they are in the grip of a Parliament of camp followers bent upon plunder. But the wheel will swiftly go round full circle. From the beginning I contended that the war would end in revolution born of hunger. So it has and half Europe is whirling back to the Dark Ages. The fire of revolution takes no heed of geographical boundaries, but will cleanse wherever the putridity created by war exists. And, as we see, hunger revolutions are directed towards economic emancipation. If we are to be spared the misery of futile civil strife it can only be by forestalling it by economic revolution and the destruction of sham democracy constituted of master class and slave class, of the privileged and the dispossessed. During the war ILP Branches have given me cordial welcome to their platforms and support for this view. I see nothing else worth doing in these days but this. Such experience has shown me that were the leaders of the ILP given the Parliamentary opportunity to strike a blow at land monopoly that the leaders of the Liberal Party were given they would not bamboozle and betray as the latter did. As a land taxer I would rejoice to see you Chancellor of the Exchequer. We are heading for chaos and if it were only a matter of the blood drunken crew one would pleasurably stand on one side and watch them be submerged. But the fate of others is involved. If a place in your endeavours can be found for me I hope I may be of service.
>   With best wishes,
>   Yours sincerely,
>   signed   R. L. Outhwaite
>   [*Labour Leader*, 16 Jan 1919]

By joining the ILP in the immediate post-war period Outhwaite was in line with many of his friends in the radical movement; and they brought a much-needed intellectual commitment to Labour politics. Outhwaite himself seems, however, to have withdrawn from public life in the 1920s, and the reason was ill health. Little has been discovered about the last ten years of his life. He died on 6 November 1930 at Birdham, near Chichester, Sussex, and left an estate of £1877. Probate was granted to his widow, Kathleen, and he was survived also by his son Cedric Robert Leonard, an engineer, who had won the Distinguished Service Cross at Zeebrugge.

Writings: (with C. H. Chomley) *The Wisdom of Esau: a tale* (1901); *Lord Milner's Record* [1905] 16 pp.; *Peer or Peasant: the ruin of rural England and the remedy* [1909] 52 pp.; *The Essential Reform: land values taxation in theory and practice* (1909); *Labour Unrest: the Young Liberal policy* (Dumfriesshire League of Young Liberals, 1911) 16 pp.; *Deer and Desolation: the Scottish land problem* [1911] 48 pp.; *The Rating of Land Values: the case for Hastings, Harrogate, Glasgow* (United Committee for the Taxation of Land Values, 1912) 18 pp.; *Wealth and the Worker: being an address delivered to the Carlisle Young Liberals in the Queen's Hall, Carlisle on 15 April 1912 under the title of 'Land Reform and Unrest'* (Dumfries, n.d.); 'Reply by R. L. Outhwaite' [to a letter repr. in the same issue of *Land Values* from the *Daily News* of 25 Mar 1912], *Land Values*, Apr 1912, 286; 'Battle with the Slum: why Glasgow wants to rate land values' [Repr. from the *Daily News* of 9 Apr 1912], *Land Values*, May 1912, 321–2; 'North-West Norfolk', ibid., July 1912, 50; 'The Duke's City: Sheffield's toll to Arundel. A tale of wrong. Industry in the grip of monopoly', ibid., 53–7; 'Hanley', ibid., Aug 1912, 98–9; 'A Warning from Scotland', ibid., Feb 1914, 358–9; 'The Government and Rating Reform', ibid., Aug 1914, 74–5; *The Ghosts of the Slain: a vision of the future*, with drawings by Joseph E. Southall (National Labour Press, Manchester, [1915]) 12 pp.; *The Land or Revolution* (1917); 'The Old Men and the War-without-end', *U. D. C. 3*, no. 8 (June 1918) 233; 'Demand for the Land', *Engl. Rev. 27* (Dec 1918) 433–41; 'Mr Outhwaite joins the I. L. P.' [letter], *Labour Leader*, 16 Jan 1919; *The Restoration of Hope* [a pamphlet on the ownership of land] (Commonwealth Land Party, [1924]) 31 pp. Outhwaite wrote frequently to the press, especially the *Daily News*, some of his articles being reprinted in *Land Values*.

Sources: *Birmingham Gazette and Express*, 2, 3, and 18 Jan 1906; *Birmingham Post*, 6, 10, and 12 Jan 1906; 'Liberal Win at Hanley', *Daily News*, 15 July 1912; *Hansard*, 1913–17; M. Fels, *Joseph Fels: his life-work* (1920); *WWW* (1929–40); J. Wedgwood, *Memoirs of a Fighting Life* (1940); C. V. Wedgwood, *The Last of the Radicals* (1951); E. P. Lawrence, *Henry George in the British Isles* (East Lansing, Mich., 1957); A. J. Peacock, 'Land Reform 1880–1919: a study of the activities of the English Land Restoration Leagues and the Land Nationalisation Society' (Southampton MA, 1962); C. A. Cline, *Recruits to Labour* (1963); H. Pelling, *Social Geography of British Elections 1885–1910* (1967); H. V. Emy, 'The Land Campaign: Lloyd George as a social reformer, 1909–14', Ch. 2 of *Lloyd George: twelve essays*, ed. A. J. P. Taylor (1971) 35–68; R. Douglas, *Land, People and Politics: a history of the Land Question in the United Kingdom 1878–1952* (NY, 1976); S. B. Ward, 'Land Reform in England 1880–1914' (Reading PhD, 1976); *Who's Who of British Members of Parliament*, vol. *2: 1886–1918*, ed. M. Stenton and S. Lees (Hassocks, Sussex, 1978). Biographical information: P. Drake, Social Sciences Dept, Birmingham Reference Library; A. Grangers, Hobart, Tasmania; A. J. Peacock, York; Mrs Tania Rose, London; Dr C. Wrigley, Loughborough Univ. OBIT. *Examiner* [Launceston, Tasmania] and *Times*, 10 Nov 1930.

JOHN SAVILLE

See also: *Edward George HEMMERDE; Frederick VERINDER; *Josiah WEDGWOOD; *James Dundas WHITE.

PRESTON, Thomas (1774–1850)
SPENCEAN, REVOLUTIONARY AND CHARTIST

Thomas Preston was born on 22 February 1774 in one of the crowded courts north of Cheapside in the City of London. It was one of the poorest and most wretched areas in the capital. Preston would later recount with some pride that among the family's neighbours had once been Elizabeth Brownrigg, a notorious murderess and exploiter of parish apprentices: this sense of having made good in spite of unpromising circumstances was a matter of much significance to Preston, who, however, never really overcame the burdens of family misfortune and poverty. His father died when Thomas was a babe in arms, and his mother soon remarried. As a result he was farmed out to a nurse, from whose negligence he suffered a permanently debilitating leg injury. He received a rudimentary education at a school in Aldersgate Street before being apprenticed to a City silversmith at the age of fourteen, but this was dramatically curtailed when he seriously injured himself while knife-polishing. He was next apprenticed to a shoemaker named Solway in the Somers Town (Kings Cross) area of London. He very soon ran away, first to Gravesend in Kent, where he worked for a few weeks, and then crossed the Thames into Essex to begin tramping. He moved north, through the Midlands to Manchester and Liverpool, where he embarked for Ireland. Preston worked in Dublin and then Cork, where he took a leading part in a strike by journeymen shoemakers. According to his *Life and Opinions* of 1817 (not always reliable), the masters of Cork conceded the claim on condition that Preston left the city; his fellow strikers therefore escorted him in triumph to the quayside, where he was presented with a purse collected by their subscriptions.

He returned to England in the spring of either 1793 or 1794. He arrived in Bristol and then tramped slowly back to London via Bath, Oxford and Maidenhead. Preston later recognised the three years he had spent on the tramp as his political apprenticeship: he had not had the opportunity to get involved in trade issues before his time in Cork and at all places on his route he became increasingly aware of the social and political questions of the day. The London Corresponding Society completed his political education. 'The arguments, the irresistible arguments laid down by the Corresponding Society had rivetted my heart to the cause of liberty' [*Life and Opinions*, 13]. It is unclear, though, how politically active Preston was on his return to the capital. Surviving records of the Corresponding Society have no reference to him, and a later claim that he was an associate of Horne Tooke was a rumour only, and somewhat improbable given what is known of the characters of the two men. The popular politics of these troubled years were not, however, contained within the Corresponding Society movement alone: tramping through major commercial centres and, more particularly, Ireland, Thomas Preston had wide opportunities for involvement in agitational and possibly insurrectionary activity. He again quitted London in 1797 or 1798 'in order to avoid imprisonment', working for a short time in Chatham before making a round trip to the West Indies as storekeeper of a merchant ship.

On his return once more to London (?1803) Preston married a Southwark widow and mother of three children and there were four more children of this marriage. The family established themselves first in Shoreditch, then in Clerkenwell. There they set up in business on their own account, subsequently opening additional shops in High Holborn and Swallow Street, Soho. Preston's position was precarious, however. Never having completed his training, he worked only as a 'translator' – that is, at revamping second-hand shoes for resale. The success of the business depended heavily on his more highly skilled wife, a 'closer' who supervised one of the shops on her own. In 1807 she left him and the family and sailed to America, in the company of a man who it seems had fathered one if not more of the four children Preston regarded as his own. Now facing the problem of raising a family of seven, Preston had no alternative but to give up the three shops and look elsewhere for employment – first in Brentford, then in Walworth on the Surrey side of the Thames, and finally from 1810 in central London.

The cumulative experience seems to have galvanised Preston into political action. He was an early member of the circle, grouped round Thomas Spence, which evolved into the Society of Spencean Philanthropists. Like Thomas Evans, who led the group after Spence's death, Preston argued for the inclusion of funded property in the Spencean programme, urging its abolition along with private property in the land. He belonged to the most senior of the Spencean Philanthropists' sections, meeting at the Mulberry Tree in Moorfields. It was the practical comradeship of this group, he freely admitted, which decisively sustained him through the grinding poverty he faced during the years 1811–17. He in turn was an indefatigable campaigner for Spenceanism, and one of the principal architects of its strategy of building a broadly based political movement to outflank 'respectable' Westminster radicalism, and promote Henry Hunt against Sir Francis Burdett. On behalf of the group Preston became involved in a committee of metropolitan trades delegates whose intention was to petition the Prince Regent to impose legal limits on the introduction of machinery. Having been elected its secretary, he called a 'Meeting of the Distressed Manufacturers, Mariners, Artisans, and Others' which became the nucleus of the first Spencean demonstration at Spa Fields on 15 November 1816. Spence's old associate Arthur Seale printed posters and leaflets for the occasion in such quantities that the committee, sensing matters had passed beyond their control, disowned the meeting and expelled their secretary: but by now the tight-knit Spencean circle had secured the momentum they required. The previous month a meeting had been held at Preston's home between the Spencean leadership and Henry Hunt. The latter's refusal to endorse the revolutionary agrarian memorial to the Prince Regent which the group had prepared caused Thomas Evans to withdraw from the project in disgust. Preston, Dr James Watson, and Arthur Thistlewood were more flexible, and acceded to Hunt's demands in order to secure their wider strategy; for their aim was not only to build a popular platform for Hunt in the capital, but also to initiate a mass meeting which might prove the signal for a general uprising.

The meeting on 15 November passed with some sporadic rioting, directed mainly at bread shops. It was the events on 2 December, when the meeting was to be reconvened ostensibly to consider the Regent's reply, that were expected to provide the springboard for insurrection. Plans were made to storm the Bank of England, prisons and the Tower of London. In the event, however, the greater part of the assembly remained peaceably at Spa Fields. Only two bodies left for the selected targets: one, led by the younger Watson, ran riot in the City, looting gunsmiths. The other, with Thomas Preston at its head, marched on the Tower, where, from the ramparts outside, its leader had to be content merely with haranguing the soldiery within.

Preston was arrested almost immediately for his part in the Spa Fields incident, but was bailed until formally committed for trial on a charge of High Treason in mid-February. His credit as a popular political leader was never higher than at this time: as Samuel Bamford (one of many provincial delegates then in London) later recalled, Preston's entry with Dr Watson into a radical meeting could transfix the assembly. However, while in the Tower following his committal, his family were evicted and Preston had to depend on the help of his fellow Spencean John Savidge to support them. To Savidge Preston entrusted the manuscript of what seems to have been his only sustained piece of political writing, 'The Peasant's Fate or the Griping Landlord humiliated'. He did so in the full expectation that it would have to be published posthumously; but it appears not to have been published at all. However its author's précis of it in his *Life and Opinions*, written around the same time, indicates a strongly Spencean satire:

Its object embraces with the Christian duties the manifestations of that misrule which characterises our internal agricultural situation. It is a mirror that faithfully reflects the whiggish virtue, that can prompt, at once, to support a Corn Bill, and abrogate a Property Tax, – for the benefit of generous magnanimous self. The idolators of the Sophistical MALTHUS must be dealt with gently, yet firmly, as all poor creatures that are insane require. The Spencean jacket is the best instrument to secure them from committing violence on themselves or others [pp. 32–3].

The successful defence of Preston's co-conspirator Watson, by discrediting the character of the Crown's principal witness, the spy John Castles, meant that Preston was never brought to trial. The experience confirmed Preston and other members of the Spencean group in their determination to persist with political agitation. This was in spite of the 1817 Seditious Meetings Act, recently passed by Parliament, which explicitly singled out Spencean groups not only as covert revolutionaries but also as having 'for their object the confiscation and division of the land, and the extinction of the funded property of the kingdom'. The credit for placing the last item on the Spencean agenda was almost entirely Preston's. The Act, however, did have important consequences for the group. First, regular Spencean meetings now reverted to the ostensibly more innocuous 'free and easy' form in which they had begun. Second, platform agitation with Hunt as its focus assumed (for the time being at least) a higher profile. Watson particularly was responsible for guiding the Spenceans in this direction; the organisations which he created, the Committee of Two Hundred and the Union of Non-Represented People, were only incidentally Spencean, though agrarian reform still featured prominently in their objectives and members of the Spencean circle occupied most positions of responsibility within them. To Watson, Thomas Preston gave considerable support and energy; but along with Arthur Thistlewood he was also the most prominent in favouring directly revolutionary tactics. Their aspirations in the latter respect hinged now on a plan to ferment widespread rioting during the Bartholomew Fair in September 1817, with the ultimate aim of storming the prisons and Bank. Nothing happened. The plot was real enough, but defeated by last-minute official precautions and the over-optimism of the protagonists:

Preston declared he was so disappointed, that if he had a Pistol by him, he thinks he should have blown out his brains. He took leave of his family on Friday Night, thinking he might never see them again. As nothing has been done he wishes to encourage the idea that nothing was intended [HO 42/170, 9 Sep 1817].

Since the Government was reluctant to become involved in further invidious controversy over its use of spies, none of the conspirators was arrested. The frustration of this attempted *coup d'état*, and others yet less tangible, to a great extent contributed to the evolution of the idea of a pre-emptive assassination of the main government figures. In this lay the origins of the Cato Street incident of January 1820, and in that, too, Preston was fully implicated.

Preston's energies were not, however, channelled exclusively into insurrection. Unlike Thistlewood especially, Preston recognised the need for political organisation on every level. He continued as a member of the Mulberry Tree Spencean group, now renamed the Polemic Society, at a time when Thistlewood was estranged from it. Preston attended Robert Owen's important City Tavern meetings in August 1817. Three months later he made a brief trip to the Midlands to rouse support for the Watsonite programme among Birmingham radicals. With Watson and his immediate circle, a meeting of the 'non-represented' was organised to be addressed by Hunt in Palace Yard during the latter's campaign for the Westminster election of September 1818. Preston was prominent, too, among the organisers of the great Smithfield meeting on 21 July 1819, one of the key metropolitan gatherings of that momentous year, and was a leading member of the Committee of Two Hundred. The latter, a broad and amorphous body of London radicals, sought to direct popular politics in the capital in the months around Peterloo; but the Two Hundred were dwarfed by Hunt, now no longer dependent on the support of Watson and his followers to mobilise the metropolis. An irrevocable split resulted on Hunt's public disavowal of the Spenceans following the triumphal procession into the capital largely organised by them in his honour after Peterloo. As Watson was committed to a debtors' prison for non-payment of the cost of a dinner arranged for the same purpose, it was left to Preston to act as spokesman for the group: he wrote an embittered letter to Hunt, accusing him of backsliding and betrayal.

The break with Hunt precluded any realistic moves at further organising a mass meeting which would be the signal for a general rising, though another attempt at this was made on 1 November 1819. Now, in the absence of Dr Watson's restraining influence, realistic steps were taken towards a *coup d'état*. The extent to which many sections of radical London waited on a signal for armed rising in the weeks leading up to Cato Street has not generally been appreciated. Regular armed drilling had for some time been taking place in several centres around the capital and, since his shop was in the West End, Preston took command of a band meeting at Chalk Farm. Several of the core group's planning meetings (at which it was decided to assassinate the Cabinet at one of its regular dinners) were held at Preston's home. It appears that his particular responsibility on the night of the rising was to seize cannon stored at the headquarters of the Honourable Artillery Company in Gray's Inn Lane; these were then to be dragged to the Mansion House, residence of the Lord Mayor, which was directly opposite the Bank of England. Preston had not arrived at the loft in Cato Street, Marylebone, when it was stormed by police on 23 February, and, although arrested very soon after, he was never brought to trial. He was held, however, for nearly three months in Tothill Fields prison.

More than most in the inner circle of Cato Street conspirators, Preston had held firmly to a defined political programme for the revolutionary regime they hoped to establish. For example, a few days before the affair was exposed, he was glimpsed at the Hope, Clare Market, 'speaking on the subject of the Spencean Plan and the division of Land, saying it was the Property of the People'. The strength of his revolutionary commitment can be gauged by his courageous appearance, in spite of the uncertainty surrounding his own position, to address memorial meetings on the night Thistlewood and four other conspirators were hanged and beheaded. He had better reason than most to adopt a low profile in the ensuing years; but more probably he remained active in the radical underworld of tavern politics. He was not well-placed, financially or socially, to participate in the co-operative or Owenite socialist movements; and like several others with a Spencean background Preston was deeply antipathetic to Owen himself. Moreover, while his economic position was consistently precarious, friends and opponents alike identified him as a heavy drinker – unusually so even by the standards of the time. His *Life and Opinions* reveals him to have been a considerable egoist and, interestingly, somewhat superstitious, which may partly explain his non-participation in the burgeoning infidel movement. Not that he was in any way reverential: among many minor incidents concerning him in government papers is an account of Preston seizing the chalice during a communion service at St George's in the Borough and downing the contents in one draft. He was much given to such burlesque gestures: for his mission to Birmingham in the autumn of 1817 he commissioned a special suit in the colours of the tricolour, with the addition of green for Ireland; and in 1819 he and his immediate followers proposed to raise a public subscription 'for purchasing an elegant Snuff box to be conveyed to the Prince Regent, as a present from the distressed Manufacturers – the box to be decorated, with various Revolutionary emblems, particularly the head of Charles 1st, and an Axe' [HO 42/194, 15 Sep 1819].

Preston's boisterous and avowedly disrespectable radicalism isolated him from many in the radical movement. Even his fellow Spencean the usually tolerant Allen Davenport thought him half-mad and a drunkard, while Carlile lampooned him in the *Republican*. Yet in other respects Preston is a very typical figure, though drawn from a strand in the labour movement with which historians have often failed to be concerned: unskilled rather than skilled, revolutionary rather than gradualist, intemperate rather than respectable. Unless effectively infiltrated by informers (as it had to a great extent been in the post-1815 period), this radical underworld is perhaps the most opaque area of any popular politics. It was back into this milieu that Preston almost disappeared in the 1820s. There he might have remained had it not been for the gathering momentum of the reform movement. Two things particularly seem to have reactivated his interest in more formal organisation at the end of the decade: first the French Revolution of 1830, news of which 'quite delighted him'; and second the formation of the National Union of the Working Classes. Like many of the Spencean rump he took a leading role in the affairs of the Union, both at their Finsbury base, the Philadelphian Chapel run by James Watson, and beyond it. He was a frequent public speaker, often warming to his old targets, the land and funded property; when he failed to persuade the NUWC officially to attend the funeral of Thomas Hardy (formerly leader of the London Corresponding Society), he took a prominent part personally. He was also a member of the sub-committee formed to co-ordinate the campaign for a National Convention. This was the group which organised the public meeting in May 1833 which culminated in the infamous Cold Bath Fields incident, and, with Davenport and John George, Preston was among the fiercest critics of police conduct on that occasion. He travelled, for example, to Chatham to address a protest meeting along with Charles Neesom. It is possible that one of the factors which induced the authorities to over-react at Cold Bath Fields was the unnerving spectacle of so many of the former Spencean group once more in collusion. Effectively, they controlled the National Convention campaign group: certainly it was Preston who did most to keep old revolutionary contacts and objectives alive. His premises were noted by informers as a gathering place for insurrectionary elements, and when Julian Thistlewood reappeared in London, pledged 'to avenge his father's death', it was in Preston's company. Informers also noted his persistent heavy drinking, usually in the Adam and Eve, Hoxton. This, like his inclination to violence, is thrown into stark and human perspective by his domestic situation: two of his daughters, together with the husband of another, had recently died, confronting Preston with the problem of supporting fifteen grandchildren.

By the autumn of 1835 Preston had been forced to vacate his shop premises, and was working from a cobbler's stall on the City Road. Personal problems did not, however, prevent him from continued political activism after the demise of the National Union of the Working Classes. He joined in the campaign for the unstamped press, speaking in support of Hetherington and Cleave when they were arrested in 1835. With James Walker, another former Watsonite and a member of the Cato Street defence committee, Preston promoted the ideas of Alexander Milne. The latter, one of several socialist (but non-Owenite) theorists active around this time, had written a pamphlet entitled *The Millenium or Social Circle* in 1834. It was 'an improvement of Spence and Owen's Plan, by going direct to Capital & Income', in the words of an informer who heard Preston speak on it at Walker's Coffee House in 1834 (HO 64/19, 20 Mar 1834]. Later the same year Preston put forward a plan of his own. Its decidedly gradualist character may well indicate a change on the part of its author; but it also reflects his perception of what, in the aftermath of 1832, was a feasible way forward for the radical movement. His plan was an amalgam of Spencean ideas with the pension proposals of Paine's *Agrarian Justice*. Its chief features were compulsory state acquisition of one acre in forty on the death of landowners, thereby ensuring a peaceable resumption of the land into public property; old-age pensions, paid from a levy on those in employment; and a death duty, on property of all kinds, of sixpence in the pound. By 1836 a Prestonian Association was meeting in the Sir John Barleycorn, Booth Street, Spitalfields, with possibly a further group at the Knave of Clubs in Club Row, Bethnal Green.

Now a very senior personality in the metropolitan labour movement, Preston (jointly with Gale Jones) was the beneficiary of a subscription fund organised in 1837. Davenport was among the collectors, Neesom acted as treasurer, and G. J. Harney was secretary. Like them, Preston was involved, though to a much lesser extent, in the East London Democratic Association. His age seems to have begun to tell, and further financial assistance had to be given by the movement in 1845 when Harney, Thomas Cooper and others launched the Veteran Patriots' Fund. He was still concerned, however, with the issue of property and, with William Benbow, was a fierce critic of Thomas Bowkett, whose building society promotions achieved some vogue in radical circles during the mid-1840s. Principally his political energies now focused on sporadic attempts to promote once more his own plan – most successfully in 1850, when it was taken up by Luke Hansard and Alexander Campbell during debates on the future of the socialist movement at the Regeneration Society, Leicester Square. However on 1 June of that year Thomas Preston died, aged seventy-six: his second wife, of whom little is known, survived him. It was reported that his last wish had been to see Julian Harney once more before he died. Harney jointly organised the funeral, Hansard making an oration at the graveside in which he mentioned the 'Preston Plan', a copy of a pamphlet on this being dropped on the coffin. In the *Northern Star* report of the funeral the comment was made that had the plan been adopted it 'must have improved the social condition of the whole labouring classes' [15 June 1850]. Continental exiles (exactly whom are not known) were among the 400 mourners who followed the coffin, draped in a red flag and accompanied by the banner of the Marylebone Chartists' 'Emmett League'.

Even among the radical funerals of its time, it is clear that this was quite a remarkable occasion. It reinforces a sense one derives from the details of Preston's career, that he had more than once hovered on the brink of national prominence. He was clearly a highly popular figure at the level of the rank and file, but perhaps temperamentally at odds with more prominent radicals who found his boisterousness and heavy drinking less to their taste. Ultimately, however, family responsibilities and poverty precluded him from sustaining the place in the movement which he had enjoyed during the aftermath of the Napoleonic Wars. His funeral though, was a fitting testimony to the standing he had acquired as a senior, even respectable, reformer, while reaffirming his undiminished stature as a revolutionary.

Writings: (1) MS: PRO, Kew: HO 42/177, letter to Fairbrother (expenses incurred during Birmingham mission), 1 June 1818, and letter to Lord Sidmouth (property allegedly stolen by the informer Castles) 18 June 1818; HO 42/195, letter to Henry Hunt (alleged betrayal), 17 Sep 1819; HO 44/5, fos 457–60, letter to Sidmouth (Cato Street), Mar 1820. (2) Other: *The Life and Opinions of Thomas Preston, Patriot and Shoemaker, containing much that is useful, more that is true, and a great deal more (perhaps) than is expected* (1817) 37 pp.; *A Letter to Lord Viscount Castlereagh, being a Full Development of All the Circumstances relative to the Diabolical Cato Street Plot* [1820] 12 pp.; 'Letter to Lord Sidmouth', *Black Dwarf*, 19 Apr 1820.

Sources: (1) MS: Preston figures extensively in Home Office papers (PRO, Kew), but see esp. HO 40/3 (3), fos 890, 908, 919, 920; HO 40/7 (1–4); HO 40/8 (3), fo. 128; HO 40/8 (4), fo. 168 (31 Jan 1818); HO 40/10 (3) fo. 320; HO 40/33 (3), fo. 194 (27 Nov 1835); HO 42/155, 12 and 14 Nov 1816); HO 42/158, 15 Jan 1817; HO 42/170, 9, 18 Sep 1817; HO 42/171, 15, 26 Nov 1817; HO 42 /177, 1, 18, 25, 27 June 1818; HO 42/179, 24, 25 Aug 1818; HO 42/181, 26 Oct 1818; HO 42/182, 10 Nov 1818; HO 42/188, 30 June 1819; HO 42/190, 29 Mar, 15 June, 29 July 1819; HO 42/191, 6, 8 Aug 1819; HO 42/194, 8, 15 Sep 1819; HO 42/195, 17, 22 Sep 1819; HO 42/196, 7 Oct 1819; HO 42/199, 30 Nov 1819; HO 42/200, 1 Dec 1819; HO 44/ 2, fo. 120 (10 May 1820); HO 44/4, fos 185 (13 Feb 1820) and 360–421 ('Testimony of John Castle'); HO 44/5, fos 23 (Mar 1820), 457–60 (n.d. [Feb or Mar 1820?]) and 482 (n.d. [Feb or Mar 1820]); HO 44/52, fo. 230 (23 Jan 1839); HO 64/11, 7 Aug, 11 and 25 Sep 1830; HO 64/ 12, 18 Jan, 7 Mar, 17 May, 14 Aug and 19 Oct 1832; HO 64/15, 'Monday morning' (?Feb 1834); HO 64/19, 20, 22 and 25 Mar 1834. See also the following Treasury Solicitors' papers

(PRO, Chancery Lane): TS 11/197/863, p. 74; TS 11/199/868, pt 1; TS 11/202/871, pt 2, 15 Jan 1817, BL, Dept of MSS: Place papers Add. MSS 27797, fos 11–20 and 27809, fo. 72. (2) Other: [W. Hone], *Hone's Riots in London Part II ... elucidating the Events of Monday, December 2, 1816. Including Original Memoirs and Anecdotes of Preston, Dyall, the Watson family, Thomas Spence ...* (1816) 2 pp.; Anon., *The Polemic Fleet of 1816* (1816); *Hansard,* 19 Feb 1817, cols 438–47; *Seditious Meetings Act,* 1817 (57 Geo. 3 c. 19); *Trials of Arthur Thistlewood, Gent ... James Watson the Elder, Surgeon, Thomas Preston, Cordwainer, and John Hooper, Labourer, for High Treason* (1817); [W. Hone], *Official Account Bartholomew Fair Insurrection, and the Pie-bald Poney Plot* (1817); H. Hunt, *Memoirs,* vol. *3* (1820); G. T. Wilkinson, *An Authentic History of the Cato-Street Conspiracy ...* (1820); A. Davenport, 'Agrarian Equality', *Republican 10,* no. 13 (1 Oct 1824) 390–417; *PMG,* nos 22 (19 Nov 1831), 35 (11 Feb 1832), 36 (18 Feb 1832), 61 (11 Aug 1832), 81 (22 Dec 1832), 103 (25 May 1833) and 108 (29 June 1833); *Gauntlet,* no. 26 (4 Aug 1833); *New Moral World,* 8 Nov 1834; *PMG,* no. 181 (22 Nov 1834); *London Dispatch,* no. 52 (10 Sep 1837); *Northern Star,* 31 Oct 1840; S. Bamford, *Passages in the Life of a Radical* (1844; later eds 1967, Oxford 1984); *Northern Star,* 18 Jan, 1 Mar and 20 Sep 1845; J. Stanhope, *The Cato Street Conspiracy* (1962); E. P. Thompson, *The Making of the English Working Class* (1963; 2nd ed. 1968); T. M. Parssinen, 'Thomas Spence and the Spenceans: a study of revolutionary Utopianism in the England of George III' (Brandeis PhD, 1968); idem. 'The Revolutionary Party in London, 1816–1820', *Bull. of the Institute of Historical Research 45* (Nov 1972) 266–82; idem, 'Association, Convention, and Anti-Parliament in British Radical Politics, 1771–1848', *Engl. Hist. Rev. 88* (1973) 504–33; D. Johnson, *Regency Revolution: the case of Arthur Thistlewood* (Salisbury, 1974); I. J. Prothero, 'William Benbow and the Concept of General Strike', *Past and Present,* no. 63 (May 1974) 132–71; J. C. Belchem, 'Henry Hunt and the Evolution of the Mass Platform', *Engl. Hist. Rev. 93* (1978) 739–73; I. J. Prothero, 'Thomas Preston', *Biographical Dictionary of Modern British Radicals,* vol. *1,* ed. J. O. Baylen and N. Gossman (Brighton, 1979) 389–91; idem, *Artisans and Politics in Early Nineteenth Century London: John Gast and his times* (Folkestone, Kent, 1979); J. Epstein, *Lion of Freedom: Feargus O'Connor and the Chartist movement, 1832–1842* (1982); J. A. Hone, *For the Cause of Truth: radicalism in London 1796–1821* (Oxford, 1982); M. S. Chase, 'The Land and the Working Classes: English agrarianism c. 1775–1851' (Sussex DPhil., 1985). Obit. *Northern Star,* 8, 15 June 1850.

MALCOLM CHASE

See also: †William BENBOW; †Richard CARLILE; †John CLEAVE; Allen DAVENPORT; Thomas EVANS; †Henry HETHERINGTON; Charles Hodgson NEESOM; Thomas SPENCE.

QUELCH, Henry (Harry) (1858–1913)
MARXIST, POLITICAL ACTIVIST AND JOURNALIST

Quelch was born on 30 January 1858 at Hungerford, Berkshire, and though given the name of Henry was always known as Harry. His father, who was an invalid for over twenty years before his death, was the son of a village blacksmith; his mother was the daughter of an agricultural labourer. The family was poor, and the young Quelch went to work full time at the age of ten at an upholsterer's shop. He then worked for a cattle-dealer and milk-seller, and at the age of fourteen he made his way to London. There he was first employed in a biscuit factory, then successively in a skinyard and an iron foundry. At the beginning of the 1880s, when his political career began, he was working in a wallpaper warehouse.

Quelch first joined the Bermondsey Radical Club in Keeton's Road, where he became acquainted with F. W. Soutter and Samuel Bennett and through them with the Ultra-Radical movement, which was especially opposed to the Liberal Government's coercion policy in Ireland. Soutter and Bennett, who had formed an Anti-Coercion Association, began to issue a small weekly paper, the *Radical*, in December 1880. The Democratic Federation (later the Social Democratic Federation) had been founded in June 1881, and early in 1883 it adopted a manifesto which for the first time called for the nationalisation of the means of production and distribution. Harry Quelch, James Macdonald, and John Burns were among the working-class recruits at this time. On 19 January 1884 the first number of *Justice* was published, in which the paper declared its independence from all existing parties and emphasised its own commitment to Socialism.

Harry Quelch was entirely self-educated, and he became one of the outstanding working-class intellectuals in the history of the modern labour movement. He taught himself French in order to read Marx's *Capital* which had not yet been translated into English, and he later learned German. He translated Marx's *The Poverty of Philosophy* from the French and this was published in 1900. He was extremely well-read and wrote over a wide range of political, social and cultural questions. In a number of mostly rather bitter short stories he depicted features of working-class life in fictional form.

His first signed article for *Justice*, 'Labour and Luxury, from a Labourer's Point of View', appeared in the issue of 16 February 1884; and in 1886 he became editor on the resignation from that position of H. M. Hyndman. In 1889 Quelch himself resigned when he was appointed secretary of the South Side Labour Protection League, but in 1891 he took up the position again and at the same time became manager of the newly established Twentieth Century Press (for which see the **Special Note** below). He remained editor of *Justice* until his death. The paper was lively and informative, although it reflected at times what Morris described as 'a pedantic tone of arrogance and lack of generosity' characteristic of certain attitudes within the SDF. *Justice* remains an invaluable source for much of the grass-roots history of the labour movement in the decades before 1914.

Quelch took his full share of the many-sided activity of a militant in the early years of the Socialist revival. He was not particularly successful in his first years as a public speaker. In his general attitudes he tended to be somewhat dour and gloomy, and his sombre manner was not especially attractive when he began to speak in public from the mid-1880s on. He later overcame most of these defects, becoming an effective debater with, at times, a good sense of humour. He was in all the well-known struggles of the early SDF, especially the unemployed marches, and on 'Bloody Sunday', 13 November 1887, he led the Bermondsey contingent into Trafalgar Square. His first international conference was that of the French Guesdists at Roubaix on 30 March 1884, in company with E. Belfort Bax, who became a lifelong friend. Quelch's speech to the Congress was translated by Paul Lafargue, and in the years that followed he attended every international conference for the SDF (Paris, 1889; Brussels, 1891; Zurich, 1893; London, 1896; Paris, 1900; Amsterdam, 1904; Stuttgart, 1907; Copenhagen, 1910). In his later years he began attending the Congresses of the German Social-Democratic Party as fraternal delegate from the SDF and BSP. He was expelled from the 1907 Stuttgart Congress by the Württemberg Government for referring to the second of The Hague Peace Conferences as a 'Thieves' Supper' (sometimes also referred to as a 'Thieves' Kitchen'): an incident which was long remembered in the European movement.

In the SDF Quelch was usually to the left of Hyndman and did not accept the latter's particular and peculiar aberrations, such as a tendency towards both chauvinism and anti-Semitism. But Quelch did have great respect for Hyndman and generally agreed with him on most important issues and policies. Their attitude towards trade unions, for example, was not quite as dogmatic as some writers have maintained, but they were both sceptical of the long-term importance of trade unions in the achievement of Socialism. Their theoretical analysis was based upon the Lassallean concept of the iron law of wages, whereby it was deemed impossible for unions to influence the general level of wages; although Hyndman himself, by 1901, at any rate, was somewhat guarded in its application [Hyndman in *Wilshire's Mag.*, Jan 1902, 42–5]. This led them, and many among the SDF, to regard the strike weapon as antiquated or useless. Marx had explicitly denied Lassalle's views in his comments on the Gotha Programme of 1875 and these were published in the *Neue Zeit* in 1891. Even so, when Belfort Bax and Quelch published *A New Catechism of Socialism* in 1902 the old view was affirmed with emphasis, to the effect that 'the "Iron Law of Wages" ... stands as firmly today as when stated by Lassalle' [Collins (1971) 52–3].

Quelch's own writings on trade unionism underlined the SDF's generally negative approach. In his pamphlet *Trade Unionism, Co-operation, and Social Democracy* (1892) he argued that unions were important mainly in mobilising the workers for political action, by developing solidarity and class-consciousness. He was writing, it should be recalled, in the aftermath of the New Unionism of 1889:

> Trade Unionism on the old lines is most useful to those who can best do without it. The skilled artisan, who is far better able to stand alone than is the unskilled labourer, is necessarily so much stronger in combination than is the latter. . . .
>
> Trade Unionism is not, for the unskilled worker, so much a weapon for fighting the capitalists as a means for securing a weapon wherewith to fight them. The utility of the 'New Unionism' lies less in the little gains of wages or leisure it has secured for the worker – of which, on the first opportunity, they may be deprived – than in its political effects. It represents the workers as a political force. It is in this direction mainly that the new unions must progress if they would succeed in achieving any permanent material advantage. They must become more political and revolutionary, not from a party, but from a class point of view. To go on following the old beaten paths of trade unionism is simply to go on exhausting the possibilities of error for an indefinite period. If the new unions are simply to play the part of regulators of wages, as trade and prices rise and fall, they will be of very slight advantage to the workers compared with what they might accomplish if they took a broader view of their opportunities and their duties. What they have to do, and that now, is to use the power which organisation gives them to get control of the political machinery of the country, and use it for the advancement of their class. By this means they could, if they chose, achieve as much in a year or two as would be gained in a century by the old methods of trade agitation and strikes [pp. 6–7].

Members of the SDF had played a major part in the upsurge of New Unionism from 1889, and Quelch himself was notably active in London south of the river. By 1889 only a single branch of the cornporters survived there from the earlier Labour Protection League, but this became the nucleus of a strike committee organised by Will Thorne, Quelch and other SDF members. After the strike Quelch formed a South Side Labour Protection League which recognised all other trade union tickets and which went outside the docks to recruit in Woolwich Arsenal and other factories [Thompson (1967) 51–2]. Quelch gave evidence before the Royal Commission on Labour on two occasions: the first (before Group A) when he discussed the organisation of workers in the Woolwich Arsenal, and the second – a much longer interview before Group B – on the dockside work of the South Side Protection League. Both provide much detailed information on all aspects of working conditions, but Quelch was also questioned on more directly political matters. In the Group A evidence, G. Livesey, the militantly reactionary chairman of the South Metropolitan Gasworks, put direct questions to Quelch about his social-democratic politics which were clearly beyond the terms of reference of the Commission, but to which Quelch answered in principled terms. In his appearance before Group B, Quelch was examined by Jesse Collings on the problems of working with non-unionists [Qs 2395 ff.]. The discussion foreshadowed the national debate on the issues of the closed shop and picketing which became so important with the increasing legal attack on trade unions, and which culminated in the Taff Vale judgment [Saville (1960) 317–50].

When the Twentieth Century Press was founded, Quelch resigned from his trade union work and went back to journalism and publishing. He then joined the Printers' Warehousemen and Cutters' Union, of which he later became treasurer. He was also a delegate to the London Trades Council (LTC) and its president from 1904 to 1906 and again from 1910.

Quelch was a Socialist candidate at many different types of election: Vestry, Board of Guardians, School Board, County Council and Parliamentary. His parliamentary contests were at Reading (1898, with 270 votes), Dewsbury (1902, 1597 votes), Southampton (1906, 2146 votes) and Northampton (Jan 1910, 1617 votes) [Pelling (1967) *passim* and see also *Labour Leader*, 17 June 1910]. He was one of the delegates of the SDF at the first conference of the Labour Representation Committee in 1900, and, after the SDF withdrew from the LRC in 1901, he regularly attended the conferences of the Labour Party, usually as a London Trades Council delegate, though in 1909 he represented his trade union.

Hyndman left the EC of the SDF in the summer of 1901, and it was Quelch who led the argument at the annual conference of August 1901 for a withdrawal from the LRC. At the second conference of the LRC in February 1901 Quelch had failed to carry his resolution endorsing class war; and he now persuaded a majority of the SDF delegates that the LRC was no place for a firmly committed Socialist organisation. The decision was a serious mistake. Among other consequences it severely handicapped the work of the SDF in London, where its influence had become considerable. Quelch favoured Socialist unity rather than the labour alliance, and so long as he lived the SDF, in the various forms it assumed, remained formally aloof from such an alliance. In 1914, within less than a year of his death, the British Socialist Party (the SDF in a new form) had reaffiliated, and what may be described as official hostility towards the London Labour Party ceased.

Quelch, as editor of *Justice* and one of the old guard, was involved in a central way in all the many disputes and debates in the decade before 1914. He was a vigorous opponent of the 'impossibilists' in Scotland and London [Tsuzuki (1961) 136 ff.] and with Hyndman was sceptical of most of the new political and industrial currents within the British labour movement. Quelch was anti-syndicalist and, for the most part, anti-suffragette. Certainly he was hostile to the Pankhursts and their organisation, and in 1910 he described the WSPU as 'anti-proletarian, anti-Socialist and anti-democratic'. But of all the controversial questions that divided the Socialist movement before 1914 none was more important than that of national defence and the attitude towards Germany.

The responses of Hyndman and Quelch to the political problems raised by imperialism were mixed. On India, for example, there was complete support for the demand for independence; and, when Tilak was being tried for sedition, *Justice* issued a special number devoted to the Indian struggle. The SDF also gave full assistance to the Russian revolutionaries fighting their illegal struggle against Tsarism, and in 1902, as Lenin recorded in his obituary notice of Quelch in 1913, when *Iskra* had to be printed in London, Quelch put the Twentieth Century Press printing and editorial facilities at the disposal of the Russians, who for a time included Lenin [*Lenin on Britain* (1934) 117–19]. In general both Hyndman and Quelch supported nationalism whenever it was asserting itself against foreign control or domination; but in the years prior to 1914 Germany began to dominate the question of war and peace. There were several strands to the SDF's approach. The first was summed up in a pamphlet by Quelch, *Social Democracy and the Armed Nation* [1900]. Quelch argued for a citizen army – the 'armed nation' – and the training of all citizens in the use of arms. Quelch offered the armies of the American War of Independence, the revolutionary armies of France and that of Garibaldi as examples of what he had in mind. In 1908 Will Thorne undertook, on behalf of the SDF, to introduce a 'Citizen Army' Bill into the Commons for 'compulsory military training under democratic safeguards' [Tsuzuki (1961) 203]; but there is no evidence that the Bill was actually introduced.

The other aspect of the defence policy of Hyndman and Quelch was a growing concern with what was thought to be the 'German menace'. Hyndman had been writing to conservative papers such as *The Times* and the *Morning Post* urging support for a larger Navy to counter German aims, and his authority inside the SDF was such that the opposition to his views only slowly came into the open. After the 1910 annual conference Theodore Rothstein wrote to Kautsky, 'I wonder if you could find time to write a letter to Quelch – Hyndman is past cure! – on the errors of his attitude' [quoted in Tsuzuki (1961) 209]. The first determined opposition inside the SDF to Hyndman and Quelch was at the annual conference of April 1911, when Zelda Kahan and W. P. Coates moved a resolution to oppose the call for additional armaments. Quelch moved the EC amendment which, while endorsing in principle the Second International resolution in favour of peace, disarmament and international arbitration, also included a demand for a national citizen army and an 'adequate Navy'. The executive amendment was carried by 47 votes to 33. The SDF was now irrevocably split; and the merging of the SDF into the new British Socialist Party made no difference to the fundamental disagreements between the two main groups.

For the last few years of his life Quelch suffered increasingly from ill health, especially from bronchitis and from a developing disease of the liver. When he became too ill to edit *Justice*, a small group, consisting of F. H. Gorle, Fred Knee, H. W. Lee and G. C. Swanson, was appointed as a temporary solution. Quelch died on Wednesday 17 September 1913; he had been twice married and his second wife survived him. No will has been located. The funeral, which took place on 20 September at Forest Hill Cemetery, was an imposing demonstration of affection and respect. *Justice* (27 Sep 1913) reported 10,000 mourners and spectators, and speakers included Jack Williams, Fred Knee, W. C. Anderson, Herbert Burrows, Louis de Brouckère and Hyndman. Among the later tributes published in *Justice* were those from Walter Crane, J. Hunter Watts, James Macdonald, Dan Irving, the Countess of Warwick and Belfort Bax. They also included one on behalf of the family from Lorenzo E. Quelch, Harry's brother, an organiser of the Berkshire Agricultural Labourers' Union in the 1890s and an active member of the Reading Trades Council. Harry's son Tom signed the Leeds Convention manifesto in 1917 and subsequently joined the Communist Party, from which he later resigned.

Writings: Quelch was a prolific debater in public and his major debates were printed in pamphlet form; details of his published debates are listed here chronologically, segregated from his other works.
(1) Debates: (with W. Simpson) *State Socialism: is it just and reasonable?* [rev. and repr. from *Burnley Gazette*] (1893) 20 pp.; (with W. C. Wright) *Socialism and the Single Tax* [1896] 16 pp.; (with J. Howes) *Socialism: what is it? How may it be brought about? Will it benefit the workers?* [1896?] 40 pp.; (with A. B. Moss) *Malthusianism v. Socialism* [1899?] 16 pp.; (with J. H. Roberts) *Liquor Municipalisation* [1905?] 32 pp.; (with J. H. Roberts) *Would Universal Total Abstinence reduce Wages?* [1905?] 36 pp.; (with C. Grant) *Should the Working Class support the Liberal Party?* (1906) 27 pp.; (with C. H. Moore) *Is Socialism advantageous to the Individual?* [1907?] 16 pp.; (with A. Bigland) *Tariff Reform v. Social-Democracy* [1908] 23 pp.; (with G. Lansbury) *The Poor Law Minority Report* [1910] 15 pp.; (with J. M. Robertson) *Is Socialism Impracticable?* [1910?] 20 pp.
(2) Other works (in addition to his numerous contributions to *Justice*): *Trade Unionism, Co-operation and Social-Democracy* (1892) 16 pp.; evidence before the R . C. on Labour, 1892 XXXV Group B, vol. I, Qs 2199–595, and 1893–4 XXXII Group A, vol. III, Qs 23697–992; *The Economics of Labour: a lecture delivered to the Economic Club of the Borough Polytechnic Institute, London* (1893; another ed. 1902 and later eds, 55th thous. [1912]) 16 pp.; *The Bimetallic Bubble* (1895; 2nd ed. 1896) 16 pp.; Ch. XI in *How I became a Socialist: a series of biographical sketches* (1896) 70–8; (trans. from the French) K. Marx, *The Poverty of Philosophy* (1900); *Social-Democracy and the Armed Nation* (1900) 16 pp.; 'The Working-

Class Movement in England', *Int. Soc. Rev. 1*, no. 2 (Aug 1900) 81–3; (with E. B. Bax) *A New Catechism of Socialism* (1902) 41 pp.; (with E. B. Bax and H. M. Hyndman) *Liberalism and Labour* [1903] 19 pp.; Introduction to H. Steele, *The Working Classes in France: a social study* (1904); (trans.) J. Jaurès, *Socialism and the Political Parties* (1905) 32 pp.; *The Social-Democratic Federation: its object, its principles and its work* (1905) 15 pp.; Introduction to *Deputation of Unemployed to the Rt. Hon. A. J. Balfour MP on November 6th 1905* (1905) 31 pp.; 'The Unemployed Agitation in England', *Int. Soc. Rev. 6*, no. 7 (Jan 1906) 390–4; 'Socialism and the Armed Nation', *Soc. Ann.* (1906) 48–50; 'The Socialist Movement in England', *Social Democratic Herald* [Milwaukee], 21 May 1910; *Social Democracy and Industrial Organisation* [1911] 16 pp.; 'The International Socialist Congress', *Soc. Ann.* (1911) 47–50; Introduction to B. Tillett, *History of the London Transport Workers' Strike, 1911* [1912]; 'To the Members of the British Socialist Party' [letter], *Justice*, 29 Mar 1913; 'The Balkan Question', *Soc. Ann.* (1913) 59–62; *The Crimes of Liberalism and Toryism* (n.d. [190–?]) 16 pp.; *The Co-partnership Snare* [1913?] 16 pp.; *Harry Quelch: Literary Remains*, ed. with a biographical introduction by E. B. Bax (1914).

Sources: *Labour Annual* (1896) 215; *The Encyclopedia of Social Reform*, ed. W. D. Bliss (1897) 1153; 'A Letter from Hyndman' (dated 11 Oct 1901), *Wilshire's Mag.*, no. 42 (Jan 1902) 42–5; 'Mr Harry Quelch', *Trades and Labour Gaz.*, Feb 1909, 9; *Reformers' Year Book* (1909); J. F. M., 'The Two Quelches', *Labour Leader*, 17 June 1910 [this was the beginning of a vigorous controversy between orthodox Labourites and Quelch over the Northampton election – see also Quelch's articles 'Furious Labourites dislike the Truth', *Justice*, 25 June 1910, and 'Furious Labourites again', ibid., 9 July 1910, and J. F. M.'s article 'Remember Northampton', *Labour Leader*, 1 July 1910]; H. M. Hyndman, *Further Reminiscences* (1912); P. Descours, review of *Harry Quelch: Literary Remains* in *Positivist Rev.*, 1 Feb 1915; E. B. Bax, *Reminiscences and Reflexions of a Mid and Late Victorian* (1918; repr. NY, 1967); *Lenin on Britain*, with an Introduction by Harry Pollitt (1934; 2nd ed. [repr. of 1934 ed. with a 2 pp. Preface] 1941); H. W. Lee and E. Archbold, *Social-Democracy in Britain* (1935); *Marx House: its history and traditions* n.d. [1945?] 8 pp.; 'Speech by H. Quelch to V Congress RSDLP, 16.5.1907', *Marx Memorial Library Q. Bull.*, no. 3 (July–Sep 1957) 3–4; F. Bealey and H. Pelling, *Labour and Politics, 1900–1906* (1958); C. Tsuzuki, *H. M. Hyndman and British Socialism* (Oxford, 1961); A. Rothstein, 'Harry Quelch', *Marx Memorial Library Q. Bull.*, no. 27 (July–Sep 1963) 4–6; H. Pelling, *Social Geography of British Elections 1885–1910* (1967); P. Thompson, *Socialists, Liberals and Labour: the struggle for London 1885–1914* (1967); W. Kendall, *The Revolutionary Movement in Britain, 1900–1921* (1969); C. J. James, *M. P. for Dewsbury* (Brighouse, Yorks, 1970); H. Collins, 'The Marxism of the Social Democratic Federation', in *Essays in Labour History, 1886–1923*, ed. J. Saville and A. Briggs (1971) 47–69; S. Pierson, *British Socialists: the journey from fantasy to politics* (1979). OBIT. *Justice*, 20 and 27 Sep 1913; A. S. Headingley, 'H. Quelch and the Working Class', *British Socialist 2*, no. 10 (15 Oct 1913) 433–6; Eliana Twynam, 'Harry Quelch: September 17, 1913: in ever grateful memory' [poem], ibid., 437; B. Tillett, 'A Soldier of Humanity–Harry Quelch', ibid., 438–40; *Pravda Truda*, 24 Sep 1913, tribute by V. I. Lenin printed in his *Collected Works 16* and reproduced in *Labour Monthly 35*, no. 9 (Sep 1953) 424–6. NOTE. The editors wish to acknowledge the assistance given by Graham Johnson in connection with this biography and the Special Note on the Twentieth Century Press which follows.

JOHN SAVILLE

See also: *Ernest Belfort BAX; †John Elliott BURNS; James MACDONALD; †William James

THORNE; †John (Jack) Edward WILLIAMS; and below: the Twentieth Century Press.

The Twentieth Century Press

The Twentieth Century Press was formed in 1891 as a result of the difficulties experienced by the Social Democratic Federation in the production of its newspaper *Justice*. In 1884 *Justice* had been set up with the aid of a £300 gift from Edward Carpenter. It was printed for a while by the Modern Press, owned by H. H. Champion, and with a loss amounting to £10 a week a heavy debt soon built up. The financial burden, along with developing political rifts with Champion, put an end to this as a source of support. The paper was then produced on a shoe-string budget with one paid compositor and the voluntary labour of other compositor members of the SDF; when this was no longer possible a *Justice* Guarantee Fund was set up to pay wages, but this also proved to be a failure. Like many labour-movement papers of the time it continued to be a financial liability, and in the years to 1891 H. M. Hyndman had financed the greater part of the losses. The dangers involved in dependence upon one individual were widely appreciated and demands were also being made within the SDF for *Justice* to be enlarged and its scope widened. A committee was formed by the general council of the Federation to consider the establishment of a press, and it proposed that a company be registered and the prospectus printed in *Justice*. The company was registered on 19 October 1891 with a nominal capital of £1000 divided into 4000 shares of five shillings each. The shares were divided into such small sums to encourage working-class members to take them up, and a scheme was devised whereby members could purchase 6*d* stamps on a regular basis, becoming the owners of a share when their stamps amounted to 5*s*.

The company prospectus first appeared in *Justice* on 14 November 1891, announcing that the aim was 'to establish a Printing and Publishing Press, adequately equipped and provided, in order to carry on the necessary printing of Socialist and Trade Union organisations in Great Britain, as well as to conduct the ordinary business of a Printing Office'. The long-term aim was to enlarge *Justice* and to widen its circulation from its current level of 2500. When appeals were first made in *Justice* for individuals to take up shares, a Free Speech Defence Fund was also established as well as a regular Propaganda Fund. The directors of the Press were E. Belfort Bax, H. M. Hyndman, H. W. Lee, H. Quelch and A. Taylor; the secretary was A. A. Watts.

At first it was hoped that the necessary finance would be raised by better-off supporters of the labour and Socialist movements. Rich sympathisers turned out to be in short supply, and *Justice* was soon talking of a 'Workman's Socialist Press' and boasting how the Press was 'the property of working men' [*Justice*, 1 Oct 1892]. The exigencies of running a business meant that the TCP was conducted as a capitalist concern, and that normal bargaining methods were accepted. The 1895 AGM for example, resolved that the employees' hours should be reduced to eight a day and that annual holidays be introduced. In appealing in 1897 for more shares to be taken up, the management stated that:

> We have never suggested that the Twentieth Century Press was an 'interesting experiment in practical Socialism', and have never claimed for it that it was any more than a business enterprise, carried on, as far as possible, on ordinary business lines, in order to assist Socialist propaganda, and to subsidise a Social-Democratic newspaper [ibid., 12 June 1897].

From 1898 a number of debenture shares were created and, while there is no surviving list of debenture holders, of the £695 of debentures in 1904, £200 were held by the Gasworkers' Union, the only union to invest in this way [ibid., 25 June 1904].

The Press always publicised itself as a good employer. In 1896 the directors gave the employees a 'wayze-goose (beanfeast)', and such celebrations, often held at seaside towns, became annual occasions, as did May Day holidays. At the beginning of 1900, the staff's weekly working hours were reduced from fifty-one to forty-eight, and this was done for the unskilled piece-workers as well as for the regular time-workers. This proud fact was incorporated into the heading of the Press after the title in many of the pamphlets and advertisements: it becoming 'The Twentieth Century Press Limited (Trade Union and 48 Hours)'. Good industrial relations were considered essential, and early in the new century when the Compositors' Union asked employers for an increase from 38s to £2 a week, the Press granted it immediately. An eventual compromise figure of 39s was agreed upon between employers and the Union, but the Press retained its £2 wage for compositors.

Initially the Press had a very limited growth. Members of the SDF who had enthusiastically bought shares in the belief that the Press would immediately enlarge *Justice* were disappointed and wrote letters of complaint to the paper. In the second year of its existence the TCP was, however, able to double the size of *Justice* to eight pages. By this time, although still under-capitalised, the Press had a firmer base in the movement; and it claimed to have been patronised by among others:

the Workers' Co-operative Production Society, the Gas Workers, the Journeymen Furriers, the Photographic Cabinet Makers, the Navvies, Bricklayers, and General Labourers, the South Side Labour Protection League, the Domestic Servants, the Borough Polytechnic, the Watermen and Lightermen, the Electrical Engineers, the French Polishers, the Brickmakers ... [ibid., 6 May 1893].

By the time of the first AGM, £428 5s 6d had been subscribed to the Press, and this limited capital enabled it to move to larger premises at 37a Clerkenwell Green in June 1893. The progress of the Press was slow and steady in the early nineties. In the first two years it had sustained a loss of £200, but by 1897 it could claim to be a paying concern and to possess 'assets to the full value of all the capital which has been subscribed' [ibid., 12 June 1897]. In the optimism of this year the AGM agreed to increase the capital to £5000 and renewed attempts were made to win shareholders. But all this enthusiasm and activity could only manage to raise £343 by the time of the following AGM, by which time the TCP 'had encountered depression in each section of our business' [ibid., 28 May 1898]. The next year saw a large increase in the amount of business done and large extensions to the company's premises. By 1900 the Press boasted a profit of £127, the most prosperous year it had had to date, with a turnover which increased within twelve months from £2415 to £3382.

The optimism of 1900 soon gave way to a more general pessimism. Quelch, who had been editor of *Justice* since the establishment of the Press and was its manager, continued to emphasise the lack of capital, and said at the AGM that in the main the Press's publishing activities resulted in a loss. Further attempts were made in 1901 to increase the amount of capital; 'credit notes' of sixpence were issued which could be saved up and redeemed for shares in the Press, or used to buy *Justice* or the *Social-Democrat*. The response to this scheme was discouraging. The volume of work done by the Press continued, however, to increase, but competition began to be felt more severely and the need for 'more work, more plant and more machinery' became increasingly apparent. This trend continued into the following years and, in particular, competition from the provinces was felt severely.

In 1905 there was a slight improvement, and 1906 saw an upturn in the TCP's fortunes; the balance sheet and report was declared to be the best it had ever had. The following year was even more successful, and there followed long-overdue expenditure on stock and an enlargement of the premises. The optimism of this period was such that Quelch, speaking at the AGM, 'looked forward to the day when they could make a grant to the SDF Propaganda Fund' [ibid., 29 June 1907]. This mood of expansive optimism was, however, short-lived. *Justice* was enlarged in 1905, and again in 1907, but from 1907 the Press began to make a substantial loss and continued to do so until its final crisis and collapse. In spite of this, *Justice* was expanded to sixteen pages in 1909.

The relationship between the Press and the SDF was close and many-sided. The initial attempts to attract outside support had been a failure. Among the first list of shareholders there were non-SDF members with large numbers of shares: the Indian nationalist Dadabhai Naoroji, for instance, had forty. The only really large holding besides Hyndman's was that of William Harris, a poultry farmer from Sussex who held 200 shares; but most of the shares were held in small amounts of individual 5s shares. It is safe to assume that the majority of these were SDF members responding to the appeals in *Justice* and purchasing shares, or collecting 6d stamps up to the value of a share. The TCP was considered by many to be the property of the SDF. There was a report on its relationship with the Press at the Federation's 1897 conference, and on the question of control it declared, 'It is obvious that the only collective influence the SDF as a body has over the TCP is through the 720 shares (equal to 90 votes) held by the Executive' [*Report* of SDF Conference, 1897]. The 720 shares were in fact the property of H. M. Hyndman, and, with a further £100, represented the price paid for the plant and materials of the old Justice Printery when taken over by the TCP in 1891.

It is doubtful if without the Press *Justice* could have been continued, and the paper proved to be the largest burden on the finances and resources of the business. Only in one year – 1895 – did the receipts from *Justice* exceed expenditure. Most of the time the loss on *Justice* and the fact that it was financed by the Press was accepted with resignation or pride, but there was also some criticism. At the 1894 AGM, Hunter Watts complained that *Justice* took up a great portion of the TCP's time and said that he considered the loss 'a great drawback'; in this year alone the loss amounted to £62, of which £30 was covered by profit on the business. The problems of financing the paper were inevitably exacerbated by its failure to attract advertising on any significant scale.

In years of prosperity the paper was enlarged and in moments of optimism Sunday editions and a daily newspaper were mooted, though neither ever materialised. By 1900 it was estimated that the Press had subsidised *Justice* to the amount of 'at least £500' [*Social-Democrat 4*, no. 5 (May 1900) 134] and by 1907 'no less than £1000' [*Justice*, 15 June 1907].

The printing of the paper took up valuable time on the business's equipment. While *Justice* was being printed 'the Press was but a quarter of itself, for any purpose of earning money, in printing'. In 1909, when the paper was expanded to sixteen pages and its circulation increased, the folly of using the antiquated machinery of the Press for newspaper production became evident:

> What was possible with 8,000 to 10,000 was not possible with 16,000, 20,000 upwards. A rotary machine, printing more quickly and folding at the same time, became a necessity, and as we could not afford to get one, we simply put out the machining until we are able to do it ourselves [ibid., 3 July 1909].

The production and finance of *Justice* was far from the only way in which the TCP subsidised the SDF. In 1897 the auditor strongly criticised the way credit was given to branches, and concluded in his report that in view of this 'the business was not run on sensible, business-like lines'. A regular criticism at Press AGMs was that the branches regularly failed to pay their debts. 'Not only did we stand the brunt of the loss on *Justice*', said Harry Quelch,

> but in other directions subsidised the movement. One way in particular was that Social-Democrats seemed to think that the TCP was the last creditor that should be paid. Work was brought to us and done which would not otherwise be able to be done if taken to other printers where an early payment was obligatory [ibid., 8 July 1899].

Complaining of the same thing in 1902, he said that outstanding accounts were about 25 per cent of the TCP's turnover, or two-thirds of its capital, and expressed his regret at the resultant shortage of cash [ibid., 5 July 1902]. In 1904, making the same point, he said that the 'ordinary means' of collecting debts were not available to the Press, 'as to a large extent the branches of the SDF are our debtors', the pressure from branches being particularly strong at election times [ibid., 25 June 1904].

The role of Harry Quelch in the history of the Press was a central one. He stepped down as secretary of the South Side Labour Protection League in order to take over the managing directorship of the Press at its inception; and he continued to hold this post and edit *Justice* for the next eighteen years. 'I am not speaking boastfully', he said at the 1902 AGM, 'but simply stating the fact when I say that almost the whole of the capital of the TCP, has been procured by my own personal efforts.' That most of the organisational work involved with the business fell on to his shoulders was widely recognised within the SDF. 'Our comrade Quelch is manifestly over-worked', said George Lansbury in his chairman's address to the 1896 conference of the Federation:

Not only has he to edit the paper, but he has to manage the business, in addition to which he is continually lecturing in all parts of the country. I feel it is a discredit to us to work him in this way, and I feel we should inform the TCP that we are prepared to take some share in the financial responsibility involved in appointing a manager in addition to an editor of *Justice* [Report of SDF Conference, 1896].

That this financial difficulty was a real and continuous one is suggested by a report that in 1902 Quelch was a creditor of the Press 'to about £87 by way of salary perforce, for a while, undrawn' [*Justice*, 12 July 1902]. In the same year he was to complain of the constant worry caused to him by the conduct of the paper, the running of the business and the shortage of cash. The strain, he told the shareholders, was telling on him, and if they had anyone to replace him he should be pleased to retire [ibid., 5 July 1902].

Not until 1909 did he feel able to retire. The work of editing the enlarged *Justice* and an expanding press were too much for one person. The managing directorship was handed over to Guy Bowman. The change proved to be disastrous. Intensive efforts were made to push the enlarged *Justice* along with the TCP's other publications, and a heavy loss built up. Bowman was replaced by W. A. Woodroffe early in 1910 and a salvage operation undertaken. The appointment of Bowman was heavily criticised at the following AGM. The directors said that they had gone 'outside' the TCP for a managing director because they had needed money and Bowman had promised capital [ibid., 11 June 1910]. The Press never recovered from its difficult position, sustaining a loss of £7 a week over the following year, and *Justice* was reduced to four pages. Although the long-term problems of the Press were more complex, including lack of capital and competition from larger firms, it is tempting to see its careful management in the hands of Quelch as a stabilising factor in its existence. A last attempt was made to save the Press in 1911. New appeals were made for capital, large advertisements appeared in *Justice* calling for £10,000 for a Socialist daily. The response to this bold appeal was insufficient for its continued survival. A receiver was appointed on 19 January 1912, and Quelch was personally declared bankrupt on 16 August 1912 [*Times*, 17 Aug 1912]. When the Press was reorganised with the formation of a new company, the Twentieth Century Press (1912) Ltd, the abridged prospectus listed as directors Thomas Kennedy, lecturer; Harry Quelch, journalist; David D. Irving, political agent, Burnley; Edwin C. Fairchild, general outfitter; Frank Colebrook, printer's valuer; with J. W. Gunnell as secretary [*Justice*, 15 Feb 1913]. There was no break in the continuity of its printing work and the firm still existed in 1982 as a commercial establishment.

Throughout its existence the original TCP was a relatively small concern. Foreign Socialists viewing the Press could not help being surprised at its limited size and scope. As the Press of organised Social Democracy in Britain, it was inevitably compared with Germany with its multitude of local Social Democratic presses, many of which published daily papers. Osip Pyatnitsky, an underground organiser for the Russian Social Democrats, recalled:

> I was profoundly astonished that the Social Democratic Federation had such a small weekly, the circulation of which was no larger than that of *Iskra*. The Russian SDP in a foreign country, far away from their native land, were publishing a paper which was no worse than that possessed by a legal party in Britain. For me at that time it was incomprehensible, all the more after the printing-presses, the newspaper circulations, the premises and bookshops, which I had seen in the hands of the German Social-Democrats [Rothstein (1966) 69].

British observers were more aware of the context in which the TCP operated and the difficulties of keeping it alive. Throughout its existence, those involved with the Press were proud of its achievements and its contribution to the Socialist movement. It had managed to keep alive *Justice* as a regular weekly Socialist paper, and in its periods of prosperity to increase its size and scope. It had directly and indirectly subsidised the SDF, proving a valuable asset to it at periods of national and local elections. Thousands of handbills were produced by the TCP and distributed by enthusiastic SDF members on a variety of general topics – in particular unemployment, but also on specific issues such as the Boer War. Books by leading SDF members including Hyndman and Bax, as well as less well-known figures like James Leatham, were made available to a wide audience. Most importantly, a wide range of Socialist pamphlets, most of them retailing at 1*d* or 2*d*, were published in their thousands. In this way some of the classics of Second International Marxism were made available to British Socialists for the first time. Works by Kautsky, Jaurès and Plekhanov, as well as such Socialist classics as Kropotkin's *An Appeal to the Young* were translated. Reports of international congresses were published, and Marx's *Wage Labour and Capital* was produced in pamphlet form. The final list was long and impressive, and the contribution to the richness of British Socialism was undeniable.

Sources: (1) MS: Twentieth Century Press company records, PRO, BT 31/15187–35009. (2) Other: Reports of the Press's AGMs appeared annually in *Justice*; other issues of *Justice* containing references to the TCP include those dated 1 Oct 1892, 6 May 1893, 12 June 1897, 28 May 1898, 8 July 1899, 5 July 1902, 25 June 1904, 29 June 1907, 3 July 1909 and 11 June 1910, plus those separately listed below. See further: Reports of the Sixteenth and Seventeeth Annual Conferences of the SDF (1896, 1897); 'The Story of a Socialist Press', *Social-Democrat 4*, no. 5 (May 1900) 132–4; 'H. Quelch: capitalist', *Justice*, 12 July 1902; 'The Story of a Socialist Press', ibid., 15 June 1907; F. Colebrook, 'My Note-book', ibid., 19 June 1909; *Times*, 17 Aug 1912; H. Quelch and J. Scurr, 'The New Twentieth Century Press', *Justice*, 7 Sep 1912; 'Abridged Prospectus of the New Twentieth Century Press', ibid., 15 Feb 1913; H. Quelch, 'For *Justice* and the Twentieth Century Press', ibid., 21 June 1913; Official Report of the Third Annual Conference of the British Socialist Party (1914); H. W. Lee and E. Archbold, *Social-Democracy in Britain* (1935); C. Tsuzuki, *H. M. Hyndman and British Socialism* (1961); A. Rothstein, *A House on Clerkenwell Green* (1966; repr. 1972; 2nd ed. 1983).

GRAHAM JOHNSON

RACKSTRAW, Marjorie (1888–1981)
LABOUR COUNCILLOR, FABIAN AND SOCIAL WORKER

Marjorie Rackstraw was born on 24 June 1888 in north London, the second of five daughters of Matthew Rackstraw and his wife Fanny (née Blofeld). Her father was the owner of a successful department store in Islington. He was a benevolent employer, much concerned with the welfare of his employees, and he and his sister, who was responsible for the staff's welfare, each donated a cottage as part of the Linen and Woollen Drapers' Scheme – still operating – at Mill Hill, London, for retired employees. The family also visited sick employees with baskets of food and medicaments. Marjorie Rackstraw was thus brought up in a socially conscious Anglican home, where she received her early education. She later attended the Grove School, Highgate, where, with her elder sister, she was a boarder. The latter went to Somerville College, Oxford, but Marjorie developed back trouble in her early teens and spent a year flat on her back at a Margate boarding school. For the rest of her life she suffered from a spinal disorder but refused to let it interfere with her subsequent activities.

After leaving school she spent a year in Paris with a French family and maintained a lifelong love of France, its people and culture. Although offered a place at Somerville on her return, the family decided that the Oxford climate would be unsuitable for her health, so she went to Birmingham University, where she graduated with a history degree. There she met and became a lifelong friend of Margery Fry, who was warden of University House, Birmingham, from 1908 to 1914. After a year at Bryn Mawr College, Pennsylvania, where she had been awarded a fellowship, Marjorie Rackstraw returned to become an assistant to Margery Fry.

During the First World War she joined the Quaker relief workers (organised by the Emergency and War Victims' Relief Committee) on the Marne Front, where Margery Fry was in charge of the operation from 1915 to 1918. Rackstraw worked at Sermaize-les-Bains and later at Châlons-sur-Marne Maternity Hospital. In religion she remained an Anglican, although in later life she was not a regular church-goer, but she maintained her connections with the Quakers and in 1920 volunteered for famine relief work in Russia at Buzuluk, where she was a district organiser. She spent two periods of service there and wrote of her experiences in the *Friend*. Francesca Wilson, writing in her book *In the Margins of Chaos* (1944) on famine relief in Russia, recalls how she met Marjorie Rackstraw in Warsaw *en route* for her second spell of duty and learned at first hand of the conditions there. 'I had heard from everybody,' she wrote, 'how much beloved she was by the Russian peasants and the other workers' [p. 141].

On her return to England Marjorie Rackstraw moved to Edinburgh, where she took an interest in local affairs, helped to found a nursery school and joined the Fabian Society. It is not known when she joined the Labour Party. She became warden of Masson Hall (part of the University of Edinburgh) in 1924 and held this appointment until 1937. From 1927 to 1937 she was also general adviser to women students in the University.

On leaving the University she returned to London, where she settled at 1 Keats Grove, her first and last home in Hampstead. Her house was always open to former students, family friends, refugees and strangers from at home and abroad and all walks of life. She believed rooms were meant to be occupied and acted accordingly. She then launched herself into voluntary and public work, but she only accepted a continued assignment where she could really contribute. She was particularly interested in children and old people. She linked up with the local Labour Party and continued her membership of the Fabian Society, but she was not a political activist and would be regarded by present-day standards as a moderate.

Immediately prior to the outbreak of the Second World War, Marjorie Rackstraw was helping the Quakers with refugee and associated problems and was on the last ship to leave

Bordeaux in 1939 before the Germans over-ran France. She then assisted with the evacuation of children in Britain and among other things started a local club for refugees in Hampstead. A member of the Hampstead Old People's Welfare Committee, she was, in 1940, a founder member of the National Old People's Welfare Council. At the end of 1944 she joined UNRRA and was in one of the first teams to enter Germany from France in 1945 to help care for, resettle or repatriate displaced Europeans. She became chief welfare officer for I Corps area of the British Zone.

She returned to England at the end of 1945. In her absence she had been elected to Hampstead Borough Council as a Labour councillor for the Belsize ward, one of fourteen Socialists against twenty-eight Conservatives elected to the Council. In 1946–7 she served on three committees (public libraries; trees, open spaces and cemeteries; and valuation) and in the following year sat also on the entertainments and cultural activities committees. From 1947 to 1950 she was also a Council representative on the Local Fuel Advisory Committee and the Hampstead Council of Social Services. She continued her committee work until she retired from the Borough Council in 1951.

During this period, however, she was the moving spirit in the development of the Hampstead Old People's Housing Trust, which was founded in 1947 and of which she was chairman until 1968 – her eightieth year – when she became president. She had been awarded the OBE in recognition of her public work, especially for the elderly. By 1977 the Trust was responsible for three homes and eight blocks of flatlets, one of which had been named Rackstraw House. In 1980 the three homes were accommodating seventy-five residents and the flatlets were housing 126 tenants [*34th Annual Report* of the Trust (1980) 14–15]. Marjorie Rackstraw had also maintained her interest in the Edinburgh University hall of residence of which she was warden and in 1965, when a new Masson Hall was opened, she generously helped to enhance its amenities and her name was commemorated in the Rackstraw Corridor and Rackstraw Bursary.

In spite of physical frailty and frustrating disabilities she never complained and had been on a country visit shortly before she died at her Hampstead home on 28 April 1981, aged ninety-two. Her funeral took place at Golders Green Crematorium on 5 May and she left an estate valued at £188,694.

In her work for the elderly especially, she had been associated with Henry Brooke and Anthony Greenwood. The latter, as Lord Greenwood of Rossendale, wrote in his obituary tribute in *The Times* (11 May 1981):

She will be remembered by thousands grateful for a lifetime of unbounded compassion and service. .... She seized the opportunity in 1945 to become a Labour councillor in Hampstead and succeeded brilliantly in making sure that the council used all its powers to help the old. Her all-Party Hampstead Old People's Housing Trust (with Lord Brooke of Cumnor and Lord Cottesloe as active members of its original management committee) has now 14 homes or blocks of flats [reprinted by permission of *The Times* and Lady Greenwood of Rossendale].

Writings: 'A Diary from Russia: bandits reported approaching', *Friend* n.s. *62* (23 June 1922) 445–6; 'In Russia – the Lighter Side', *International Service*, nos 22 (July 1922) 9–10, and 23 (Aug 1922) 8–9; 'An Old People's Hostel', *Social Work 3*, no. 1 (Jan 1944) 12–16.

Sources: Society of Friends' Emergency and War Victims' Relief Committee, *2nd Report* (Feb–Oct 1915) 8, *3rd Report* (Oct 1915–Sep 1916) 7, *4th Report* (Oct 1916–Sep 1917) 15, *5th Report* (Oct 1917–Sep 1918) 27, *8th Report* (Apr 1921–Mar 1922) 25, *9th Report* (Apr–Nov 1922) 20, *10th Report* (Apr–Nov 1923) 14; Society of Friends' Relief Missions in Europe,

International Service, no. 14 (Nov 1921) 7, and no. 18 (Mar 1922) 2; A. R. Fry, *A Quaker Adventure* (1926); W. P. and Z. Coates, *A History of Anglo-Soviet Relations* (1944); F. M. Wilson, *In the Margins of Chaos: recollections of relief work in and between three wars* (1944); E. H. Jones, *Margery Fry* (1966); W. R. Page *et al.*, *The First Thirty Years: the story of the Hampstead Old People's Housing Trust 1947–1977* (1977) [with portrait of Marjorie Rackstraw]; Hampstead Old People's Housing Trust, *34th Annual Report* (1980). Biographical information: Librarian, External Relations, Edinburgh Univ. Library; M. J. Holmes, Local History Library, London Borough of Camden; M. Thomas, Religious Society of Friends Library, London. Personal information: Marjorie Bucke, Theberton, Suffolk; John Curtis, Odiham, Hants, nephew; the late Lord Greenwood of Rossendale. OBIT. *Hampstead and Highgate Express*, 1 May 1981; *Times*, 11 May 1981; *Univ. of Edinburgh Bull. 17*, no. 5 (June 1981); *New Age* (Summer 1981).

JOYCE BELLAMY
MARJORIE BUCKE

RAWLINGS, Joseph (1894–1978)
COMMUNIST, TRADE UNIONIST AND UNEMPLOYED LEADER

Joe Rawlings was born the son of a miner in the small pit village of Willington in County Durham on 14 March 1894. When he was still a young child his twenty-two-year-old father was killed by a roof fall at the Brancepeth Colliery, leaving his widow to bring up two sons on a small pension provided by the Straker and Love Colliery Proprietors. Two years later an explosion at the same pit also killed Joe's grandfather and two uncles.

At five the family moved to Durham, where Rawlings attended the Blue Coat School, but when his mother married a brass-moulder a few years later they were on the move again, this time to Barrow-in-Furness, where Rawlings transferred to the Old Barrow council school. He left school at twelve to work on a milk round, but two years later joined the plan office at the Vickers shipyard. At this time Rawlings had his first taste of industrial action when his step-father was involved in a bitter dispute which began in 1907 and lasted for more than two years; at its conclusion many of the strikers were forced to leave Barrow, the Rawlings family among them. They returned to Willington, where Rawlings' step-father found employment as a navvy while the sixteen-year-old Joe went to work at the Brancepeth pit. Within eighteen months, however, his step-father had secured a job as a moulder at the Cammell Laird shipyard in Birkenhead and the family moved yet again.

Initially Rawlings, too, went to work at Laird's to serve his time as an engraver, but he did not take to the job and soon left to join Gordon-Alison's as an iron-moulder. On 28 June 1912 at the age of eighteen he joined the Friendly Society of Ironfounders, which in 1920 became the National Union of Foundry Workers and is now the Foundry Section of the Amalgamated Union of Engineering Workers.

Within two years, however, Britain was at war and a patriotic Rawlings joined up with the 9th Battalion of the Cheshire Regiment. After twelve months' training he was sent with the 19th Division to France where he saw his first action on the Western Front. But with his mining experience he was soon recalled and transferred to the 184th Tunnelling Corps, whose job was to construct tunnels beneath the German trenches, lay charges and explode them. He spent seventeen months in the Arras sector, ending up in Mulheim and Cologne.

It is not clear when Rawlings became a Socialist, at least in explicit terms. He once described his step-father as a man 'who boasted of his trade union principles and argued Toryism'. But during the army years Rawlings began to read political writings, and his mother sent him every week Robert Blatchford's *Clarion*. His political life did not, however, begin until he returned to Birkenhead in 1919. He rejoined his old company, Gordon-Alison's, only to find himself out on strike within a couple of months. The dispute lasted nineteen weeks, during which time Rawlings joined the Plebs League and the Birkenhead branch of the ILP. He also met and came under the influence of Jimmy Morton, a prominent local Socialist who was to be a founding member of the British Communist Party, and he began to attend classes in politics and economics. When the CPGB was formally established in 1920, Rawlings joined immediately, helping to form the Birkenhead branch. He was to remain a dedicated member of the same branch until his death fifty-eight years later.

In 1921 he was sacked shortly after being elected chairman of the Birkenhead branch of the Foundry Workers. For much of the next eighteen years he was out of work, blacklisted by employers, but did not allow this to curtail any of his political activities. Instead of organising workers he turned instead to the unemployed and in 1921 took part in the national hunger march to London. In 1922 he set up the Birkenhead branch of the newly formed National Unemployed Workers' Movement (NUWM), and became its organising secretary. He addressed the Manchester conference of the NUWM in 1922, and it is there he must have met Wal Hannington, although the latter was also on the hunger march of the previous year. It was about the same time, 1922, that he first made the acquaintance of Leo McGree of Liverpool. A year later, in 1923, Rawlings took part in the TUC–NUWM demonstration in London and he set up other branches of the NUWM on Merseyside. He soon became a well-known figure among the unemployed of Liverpool and Birkenhead, regularly speaking at the Pier Head and at the market-place in Birkenhead and becoming active on the Birkenhead Trades Council.

He paid the first of three visits to the Soviet Union in 1929, arriving in Leningrad on 2 November, just in time for the twelfth anniversary of the Revolution. He was greatly impressed by what he saw, and he never deviated from his enthusiastic support of the Soviet Union. His return home was to a Britain in which unemployment was increasing rapidly, and activity among the unemployed workers was to be his main political work. For a short period in 1932 Rawlings was a member of the national administrative council of the NUWM. In the autumn of 1932 Rawlings came to national prominence when unemployed riots tore the town of Birkenhead apart. Unemployment at that time in the town stood at 17,000, with one in three out of work at its peak. Unemployment benefit, which varied from borough to borough, was 12s 3d for a single man and 10s 6d for a single woman – considerably less than that paid by most other boroughs.

Events began quietly in August 1932 when a small demonstration marched from the park entrance to lobby the Conservative Council at its regular monthly meeting in the Town Hall. Organised by Rawlings through the NUWM, 2000 protesters handed a petition to the Council calling for the abolition of the means test, an extension of work schemes, a reduction in rents and an increase in benefits. Their demands, although heard sympathetically by the mayor, received no other response. A month later, on 7 September, Rawlings organised a second demonstration to petition the Council. This time the demonstration was considerably larger, with more than 5000 joining the march through the narrow streets to the Town Hall. But again they received no satisfaction and Rawlings warned the assembled crowd outside the Town Hall that 'next time, we'll make them listen and we won't be fobbed off as we have been today' [*Birkenhead News*, 10 Sep 1932]. The following week, on Tuesday 13 September, the NUWM marched again. But when the 5000 or so marchers reached the Town Hall they discovered that the police had erected barriers across the adjoining streets, making any approach to the building impossible. The barriers and the presence of so many police led to early skirmishes, and in an attempt to calm the situation the Council agreed to meet a deputation. 'Let me warn you', Rawlings told them, 'barriers and policemen will not be able to hold the unemployed back ... if you cannot see eye to eye with us in our programme of demands then all hell will be let loose in this town and every other town and city throughout the country' [ibid., 14 Sep 1932].

After some debate the Council reluctantly agreed with the NUWM's demand for the abolition of the Means Test and promised to petition the National Government in Parliament. But the Council could not go along with the demand to increase benefits, arguing that it was only in the remit of the Public Assistance Committee. Two days later, on Thursday 15 September, Rawlings helped organise the largest demonstration the town had ever witnessed: more than 15,000 marched to the offices of the Public Assistance Committee, which was scheduled to meet that day. After a short debate the PAC decided, rather unwisely, to let the matter lie on the table. It was a decision which was to spark off an uncontrollable series of events. Angry at the news, the large crowd dispersed in various directions, with 2000 of them setting off spontaneously towards the home of the PAC chairman, Councillor Alfred W. Baker. When they reached his home they were politely told that he was out but turned to find themselves confronting a line of baton-drawn policemen. 'The police struck out right and left and scores of men went down . . . it was an indescribable scene', reported the *Birkenhead News*, adding that 'scores of people lay about the roadway, holding bleeding heads and groaning in pain' [ibid., 17 Sep 1932].

News of the clash spread through the town, and as darkness fell that evening a rampage began which was to last four days and nights. Unemployed mobs swept down the main shopping street, smashing windows and looting. At the park entrance spiked railings were torn from their bases and hurled at the police along with a continual bombardment of bricks. Throughout the weekend the clashes between police and the Birkenhead workers gathered momentum. Police reinforcements were called in from Liverpool, Chester and Birmingham. Something approaching a state of siege took over. Gas lamps were smashed, manhole covers removed and trip wires laid across the roads. On two successive nights, 17 and 18 September, the police entered working-class homes and assaulted their inhabitants. Hannington, [*Unemployed Struggles* (1936) 235] gave his version of what happened:

In the investigations afterwards, carried out by the International Class War Prisoners' Aid, women stated that their husbands and sons were dragged from their beds by the police, and beaten into unconsciousness, and then flung into the waiting Black Marias, with blood streaming from head, face and body wounds. They were carried off to the courts to be charged with riotous behaviour and assaults on the police and then transferred to the hospitals to have their wounds dressed:

On the following Monday, 19 September, the PAC met to reconsider its position, and with 20,000 demonstrators crammed in the streets outside its office, the Committee agreed to increase the scale of benefits from 12s 3d to 15s for a single man and from 10s 6d to 13s 6d for a single woman, as well as announcing £170,000 worth of new work schemes. It was a considerable triumph for Rawlings and the Birkenhead unemployed. Rawlings, with other leading Communists, had been arrested during the disturbances, and on 25 October 1932 Joe Rawlings and six of his colleagues stood trial at Chester Assizes. In a court which clearly showed little sympathy for the unemployed, they were all given hefty terms of imprisonment. Rawlings received the heaviest sentence – twenty months' hard labour – and in passing sentence Judge Justice Charles told him:

you are the secretary of the NUWM and an organiser of these grave disturbances. I know from my experience having sat in other Assize courts on cases of this sort, of riots engineered, and deliberately engineered by the society of which you are secretary that they are the worst and most bitter enemies of decent workmen [*Birkenhead News*, 26 Oct 1932].

As Rawlings was dragged from the dock he shouted 'my body goes to prison but my spirit lives in Birkenhead'. Before the trial Rawlings had been held on remand for seven weeks at

Walton Prison, but on sentence was transferred to Strangeways in Manchester and later to Wakefield, which held twenty-six other members of the CPGB. Most of his time was spent in the ropery making string. He was allowed three books a week, as well as a monthly letter and a monthly visit.

On release from prison his life continued as before, and in 1936, together with twenty-five other Merseysiders, he took part in the Hunger March of that year: the largest and most successful of the four marches of the 1930s.

With the outbreak of Civil War in Spain, Rawlings found a new cause and in January 1937 persuaded twelve other Birkenhead men to join him and enlist with the International Brigade. They joined the British Battalion, where Rawlings became a sergeant, and almost immediately were thrown into one of the most crucial and bloodiest battles of the war, at Jarama. In three days' fighting the British suffered very heavy casualties. Among the many dead were Christopher Caudwell, Clem Beckett the Manchester speedway rider and Clifford Lawther of the well-known mining family [Alexander (1982) Ch. 8]. It was a grim and lasting experience for Rawlings, who at forty-two and with so many years of unemployment behind him was in no fit physical state to be a soldier, let alone endure the ardours of such a battle. For a brief spell he was attached to the political commissars, but already arguments were raging over the excess of Marxist education when what was most urgent was more equipment, ammunition and training. Rawlings had entered the struggle at one of the critical moments, and once the battle of Jarama was over he returned to England with many of the other survivors. He went back to Birkenhead, this time to warn against the growing threat of native Fascism. It was probably due to his forceful campaigning that the British Union of Fascists never gained support in Birkenhead.

At the outbreak of the Second World War the new demands for the armed forces began to create jobs and Rawlings found work at the Rowlands Foundry. But, as had been the case in the 1920s, he was again victimised and sacked. By 1940, however, he was in work again, at the propeller-manufacturers Manganese Marine Ltd, and was to remain with them until his retirement. He had been elected the Birkenhead branch president of the Foundry Workers and was again elected to the same office in 1942. He was secretary of the branch between 1948 and 1953 and was elected as a delegate to the district committee, becoming its secretary in 1949.

After the war his trade union activities continued, mainly on the district committee. He paid two further visits to the Soviet Union in 1950 and 1959 and in 1965 one of his final trades union duties was as a Foundry Workers' delegate to the annual conference of the TUC. He stood as a Communist Party candidate in Birkenhead at numerous municipal elections but always received a derisory vote. He never considered joining the Labour Party and was always scathing of its leaders. Rawlings remained faithful to the Communist Party to the end of his life, and, if he had any serious political doubts, he never made them public. In 1929 he had supported the new line of 'Class against Class' and he never deviated thereafter in his unswerving adherence to the party leadership.

In 1968 he suffered a heart attack, but recovered enough to help organise the Right to Work campaign. But in January 1978 he suffered a further heart attack and died on 13 January. He was survived by his wife as well as a son and daughter. He never received any financial benefits from his political activities, and every political position he held was as a lay official. A poor man all his life, Rawlings died penniless, living in a council house, and claiming a supplementary allowance to buy clothes.

Sources: *Annual Reports* of the Foundry Workers' Union and private papers; *Birkenhead News* (1932); *Liverpool Echo* (1932); W. Hannington, *Unemployed Struggles 1919–1936* (1936); H. J. Fyrth and H. Collins, *The Foundry Workers: a trade union history* (Manchester, 1959); R. C. Hayburn, 'The Response to Unemployment in the 1930s with Particular

Reference to South East Lancashire' (Hull PhD, 1970); J. Arnison, *Leo McGree: what a man ... what a fighter* (Union of Construction, Allied Trades and Technicians, 1980); B. Alexander, *British Volunteers for Liberty: Spain 1936–1939* (1982); P. Kingsford, *The Hunger Marchers in Britain 1920–1940* (1982); S. F. Kelly, *'Idle Hands, Clenched Fists': the depression in a shipyard town (Birkenhead)* (forthcoming, Nottingham, ?1987). Biographical information: AEU, Foundry Workers. Personal information: A. Calder, Leyland, Lancashire; J. Jones, London; M. Levine, Manchester.

STEPHEN F. KELLY

ROBINSON, Annot Erskine (1874–1925)
SUFFRAGIST AND SOCIALIST

Annot Erskine Wilkie was born on 8 June 1874 at Montrose, Scotland. Her birth certificate records her first name as 'Annie', but all her life she was known as Annot, and this is how she always signed herself. Her father, John Wilkie, was a laird's son who lost his money through unsuccessful railway investment, and her mother was Catherine Jane (née Erskine), a schoolmistress before her marriage. Five or six children survived infancy. John Wilkie's drapery business was never successful and eventually his wife took over the village school in nearby Westerton.

Annot Wilkie was educated at Montrose Academy and then commenced a four-year apprenticeship as a pupil teacher. She attended the Church of Scotland Training College in Edinburgh, apparently for two years; she also studied for (and obtained in 1901) the qualification of Lady Literate in Arts, an external diploma offered by the University of St Andrews. She worked as a teacher first in Fife and then in Dundee, and it was her personal experience of poverty in these areas, according to her daughter (Mrs Helen Wilson), that first aroused her interest in Socialism. But the main personal influence upon her was a Dundee dressmaker, Miss Agnes Husband, who was both a convinced Socialist and suffragist.

In 1905 Annot Wilkie became the first secretary of the Dundee branch of the Women's Social and Political Union; and she undertook speaking engagements on behalf of the WSPU's Scottish Council. She visited the Rhondda, where she met Sam Robinson of Manchester, and they were married on 2 January 1908.

Her husband came from a working-class Salford family and held a succession of unskilled jobs. Although a bad stammer debarred him from public speaking, he was a capable political organiser. By the time of his marriage he was a member of the Labour Church and in 1900 he had worked for the Manchester Transvaal Committee, an organisation which opposed the Boer War. Most of his political activity was on behalf of the ILP and the WSPU; and he held local and regional positions in the ILP, being a delegate to the national conference in 1907 and 1908. He was a staunch advocate of women's suffrage, and worked closely with the remarkable group of women in the Manchester and Lancashire area of the WSPU–among them the Pankhursts, Teresa Billington, Dora Walford, Mrs Wolstenholme Elmy, Annie Kenney and Mrs Morrisey.

On their marriage the Robinsons went to live in Ancoats, a poor working-class area of Manchester. Two months later, in February 1908, Annot was arrested for a 'raid' on the House of Commons and she spent six weeks in Holloway. She served a further three weeks' sentence in the following June. It appears that shortly afterwards she broke with the WSPU on the grounds that its militant activities were endangering life, and she was also highly critical of Mrs Pankhurst's dictatorial leadership. She had joined Manchester Central branch of the ILP in June 1907 and in the autumn and winter of 1908 she was active in the movement to publicise the issue of unemployment. She also became involved with the Women's Labour League and in January 1910 Ramsay MacDonald asked her to become a part-time organiser for the WLL in Lancashire. She also became a regular contributor to the 'Woman's Page' of the *Labour Leader*. She was a delegate both to regional and national conferences and between 1910 and 1914 she represented the ILP branch in Lochgelly, Fife, at the ILP's annual conferences (she had probably been a member while teaching in the area).

From May 1912 until the early months of 1915, Annot Robinson was a paid organiser for the Election Fighting Fund of the National Union of Women's Suffrage Societies (NUWSS). She was a capable organiser and an interesting speaker, with an attractive Scots accent. The work was mainly concerned with agitation for the suffrage in Labour constituencies in the Manchester area, since the Labour Party was the only political party which unequivocally supported women's suffrage. Her main constituencies were Manchester North East (J. R. Clynes), Manchester East (J. E. Sutton), Gorton (John Hodge), Stockport (G. J. Wardle), Blackburn (Philip Snowden) and Ince (Stephen Walsh). There were also two constituencies held by Liberal anti-suffragists: Accrington (Harold Baker) and Rossendale (Lewis Harcourt, who was Colonial Secretary). Harcourt was especially disliked, and Annot Robinson organised an intensive suffrage and Labour campaign in Accrington during the week of 20–26 October 1913. During 1914 these Labour constituencies were designated 'special nursing constituencies' and with Annot Robinson in the campaign was Ellen Wilkinson, with whom she developed a very close friendship. In the same year the Manchester Labour Party showed its appreciation by inviting Annot Robinson to sit as an EC member of the local Labour Representation Committee.

There were inherent tensions in the work she was doing for women's suffrage, and her Socialist loyalties. They arose largely out of organisational differences between the non-Socialist NUWSS and the ILP. These problems added to what was a very heavy physical and emotional commitment: in by-elections, special campaigns and constant speaking engagements. Probably her most enduring achievement was the successful appeal she was able to make to working-class groups and audiences. She was responsible, for example, for the passing of suffrage resolutions by fourteen branches of the Lancashire and Cheshire Miners' Federation; and she established a number of Labour and suffrage clubs in working-class districts. She helped form a Manchester and Salford branch of the Women's Labour League, with Ellen Wilkinson as secretary; and it was active during the early months of 1914.

The outbreak of the First World War in August 1914 marked a change in her activity. She supported the pacifist wing within the NUWSS but also helped develop relief work for working women, including the wives of those in the armed forces. Then, early in 1915, she returned to the NUWSS as a full-time election fund organiser. In May, after leaving her suffrage post, she initiated and organised the Manchester, Salford and District Women's War Interests Committee, again with Ellen Wilkinson as secretary. Their first investigation was into women's work in the munitions industry and the inquiry lasted from May 1915 to January 1916. The Committee also held conferences and organised deputations to government departments and various local committees. A conference of 12 June 1915 brought together eighty delegates, mainly from women's organisations, with Cllr Margaret Ashton taking the chair. Wages, hours and conditions of work were the subject for discussion, with Annot Robinson taking a strong feminist position. The *Labour Leader* reported her as saying that she was 'opposed to the idea that women should be displaced at the end of the war. Women should not be regarded as useful stop-gaps, and be thrown aside when no longer needed.' Two later conferences followed on 23 October 1915 and 18 December 1915. In July 1915 the War Interests Committee had sent a delegation to the trade union section of the Armaments Committee, to discuss minimum wage demands for women workers. They were asking for a guaranteed one pound wage for 48 hours' work, and time and a quarter for night work. On 6 February 1916 the War Interests Committee held a joint 'Equal Pay for Equal Work' conference with the United Suffragists. Annot Robinson shared the platform with Sylvia Pankhurst.

Annot Robinson slowly but steadily found herself in opposition to the majority opinion in the NUWSS over the crucial issue of pacifism and attitudes to the war. She wanted the National Union's suffrage work to be integrated with the demand for a permanent peace; and for militarism to be denounced as a way of diminishing further the position of women in society. Socialist pacifists such as she insisted upon the recognition of mutual rights and the principle of equality of men and women. The issue came to a critical point at the annual council meeting of February 1915 over the question of sending delegates to an international conference at The Hague. The proposal was rejected, and it was turned down again at the March meeting of the EC, by eleven votes to six. Annot Robinson, who had announced her intention of going to The Hague, was refused permission to leave the country by the Home Office.

The question of pacifism, and specific attitudes to the war, remained of major significance within the NUWSS; and at the half-yearly council meeting held in Birmingham on 17 and 18 June 1915 Annot Robinson, supported by, among others, Ellen Wilkinson, spoke against a resolution urging the Government to make more use of women in the war effort. The resolution was carried, and those who felt like Annot Robinson resigned, eventually regrouping as the Women's International League (WIL), the British section of the International Committee of Women for Permanent Peace. The British section was established at a founding conference in London from 30 September to 1 October 1915. Exactly what Annot Robinson's position in this organisation was before November 1918, when she was appointed organiser of the Manchester branch, has not been determined.

Remarkably little is known about Annot Robinson in the war years after the early months of 1916. There is an occasional reference in the press to her speaking, and it seems clear that she was still as active as ever within the labour movement. It is known, too, that she worked for the Women's Peace Crusade in 1917 and that she chaired a women's peace meeting in Stevenson Square, Manchester, on 22 July 1917. The speakers included Mrs Despard, Margaret Ashton, Mrs Bruce Glasier, Hannah Mitchell, Emily Cox and Mrs Watts. In November 1918 Ethel Snowden advised Women's Peace Crusade branches to merge with the WIL, and it is at this point that Annot Robinson became organiser of the flourishing Manchester premises at 1 Princess Street, Albert Square. Ellen Wilkinson's sister, Annie, was the branch secretary.

In May 1919 Annot Robinson attended the Zurich Congress of the WIL, but her main concern in the immediate post-war years was Ireland. On the initiative of the Manchester branch, a committee of inquiry went to Ireland, with Annot Robinson as one of its members. On her return she spoke at a number of meetings, and at the end of 1920 she and Ellen Wilkinson visited the USA to give evidence before the American Commission on Conditions in Ireland. The hearings were held in Washington, on 15 and 21 December 1920. In July 1921 Annot Robinson was a delegate to the WIL Vienna congress of the International Committee, after which she attended the summer school at Salzburg, where the theme was education for internationalism.

When she returned from Salzburg, she faced difficult problems in both her public and her private life. By the spring of 1922 she had left her WIL post as the branch could no longer afford a full-time organiser, and she existed on free-lance journalism. She was reluctant to return to teaching, but she managed to be invited by the American section of the WIL for a two-month intensive lecture tour, together with Gertrude Baer of Germany and Mlle Dejardin of France. She hoped to return the following year for a longer lecture tour, but the contract eventually fell through. When she returned to England she continued working for the WIL – it must have been on a part-time basis – for in October and November 1922 she was in the Netherlands, organising a conference planned for December. She was also, throughout these years, still active in the Manchester labour movement, and, according to her obituary notice in the *Northern Voice*, she contested unsuccessfully two municipal elections.

Her domestic life was difficult. For years she had been away from home on her political work, and her marriage with Sam Robinson had apparently been unsatisfactory for some time. Although she was never divorced, or legally separated, the marriage really ended when her husband came back from the Forces at the end of the war. There were two daughters of the marriage: Cathy, born in 1909, and Helen, born in 1911. During Annot's frequent absences from home, the girls were looked after by an elderly housekeeper, Mrs Edwards, helped by friends such as Mary Welsh or Annot's sister in Glasgow.

Annot Robinson was finally forced to return to teaching in order to earn a living. She first signed a two-year contract to teach at a school in the remote Gaelic-speaking hamlet of Aligon, near Loch Torridon; and then she obtained a position (with house attached) at Flisk, near Dundee. Her daughters had meanwhile remained with their aunt in Glasgow in order to continue their schooling, and the family was not reunited until 1925. Annot and the girls moved in at the end of June 1925, but in September she became ill, apparently with gallstones. She was taken by ambulance to Perth Infirmary, but died of heart failure during the operation, on 30 September 1925. She was fifty-one years old. She was buried in Flisk churchyard. As she had made no financial provision for her daughters (then aged fourteen and sixteen), the WIL opened the Annot Robinson Memorial Fund for this purpose. It eventually raised £177 14s 9d.

Annot Robinson had an assertive and vigorous personality, coupled with a rigid Calvinistic honesty and an intense intellectual commitment. She was both forceful and dominating, but these characteristics were moderated by a dry Scottish wit and personal warmth. Her inability to compromise, and occasional impatience with colleagues, were a handicap which limited her opportunities. She never found a completely congenial or permanent political base. Having left the militant WSPU over the issue of violence, and later the NUWSS over its wartime attitude to pacifism, she became a somewhat isolated figure. Equally her left-wing Socialist attitudes placed her outside the main stream of the ILP and labour movement. Contemporaries regarded her as one of the older generation of women activists, and one of the first to make a career as a professional organiser in the emergent labour and feminist movements during the first two decades of the twentieth century. It was a time when the opportunities for political work for educated and talented women – outside the traditional fields of nursing and teaching – were just beginning to be available. Perhaps Annot Robinson's most significant, if intangible, achievement lay in her personal example to younger women, who built upon her expertise and extended her pioneering role.

Writings: *Women's Enfranchisement* [1911?; NUWSS leaflet repr. from *Labour Leader*].

Sources: (1) MS: Papers of Annot Erskine Robinson, in the possession of Mrs Helen Wilson, Altrincham, Greater Manchester; information from student records 1891–1901, supplied by Mr R. N. Smart, Keeper of the Muniments, Univ. of St Andrews; Manchester Central ILP, minutes 1902–8, NUWSS, Manchester Society for Women's Suffrage, minutes 1914, and miscellaneous papers of Hannah Maria Mitchell (in Suffrage Coll.), all in the Archives Dept of Manchester PL. (2) Other: *Clarion*, 1899–1906, 1908; *Labour Leader*, 1900–22; *Common Cause*, 1912–15; NUWSS, Manchester Society for Women's Suffrage, Annual Reports 1912–17; *Blackburn Weekly Telegraph*, 4 Oct 1913; Manchester and Salford LP, Annual Reports 1914 and 1915; NUWSS, *Proceedings of the Special and Half Yearly Council, June 17th and 18th, 1915, at the Birmingham and Midland Institute, Birmingham* (1915); Manchester, Salford and District Women's War Interests Committee,

Women in the Labour Market (Manchester and District) during the War [Manchester?, 1916] n.p.; Commission of Enquiry into Industrial Unrest, No. 2 Division, *Report of the Commissioners for the North Western Area, including a Supplemental Report on the Barrow-in-Furness District* Cd 8663 (1917); Manchester and Salford Women Citizens' Association, *4th Annual Report* (1917); NUWSS, *7th Annual Report of the Manchester and District Federation. Presented at the Annual Meeting November 10th, 1917* [Manchester?, 1917] 58 pp.; *American Commission on Conditions in Ireland* 5th Report (Washington, DC, [1921?]) [evidence of Annot Robinson and Ellen Wilkinson printed in the *Nation* [New York] vol. *112*, no. 2907, section II (23 Mar 1921) 457–60 (Robinson) and 460–4 (Wilkinson)]; election address for Annot Robinson, contesting Blackley ward in the Manchester municipal elections, 1 Nov 1921; 'The National Conference of Labour Women: conference report', *Labour Woman*, 1 June 1921; H. Mitchell, *The Hard Way Up* (1968); C. A. N. Reid, 'The Origins and Development of the Independent Labour Party in Manchester and Salford, 1880–1914' (Hull PhD., 1981). OBIT. *Vote*, 16 Oct 1925; *Woman's Leader*, 6 Nov 1925; *Northern Voice*, 11 Dec 1925. Personal information: the late Dame Kathleen Courtney, London; Mrs Daisy Somerville, Manchester; Mrs Helen Wilson, Altrincham, Greater Manchester, daughter.

DAVID AND NAOMI REID

SAUNDERS, William (1823–95)
SINGLE-TAXER, JOURNALIST AND RADICAL

William Saunders was born 20 November 1823 at Russell Mill, Market Lavington, Wiltshire. He was the youngest son of Amram Edward Saunders, a miller and a farmer. The family was well known in the district. William Saunders was educated at school in Devizes, and then worked in his father's flour mills at Market Lavington and Bath. About 1844 he opened extensive stone quarries near the Box tunnel on the Great Western Railway. In 1852 he married Caroline, daughter of Dr Spender of Bath; and it was with the financial assistance of his father-in-law and the practical help of his brother-in-law Edward Spender that he began his journalistic promotions. The abolition of the tax on newspaper advertisements in 1853, of the stamp duty in 1855 and of the paper duty on 1 October 1861 provided the opportunities for a rapid growth in the popular press. Between 1855 and 1870 seventy-eight new provincial dailies appeared [Koss (1981) 121]. Saunders and Spender established the *Plymouth Western Morning News* in 1860. This was followed by other ventures: the *Western Express* at Exeter, the *Northern Daily Express* at Newcastle, and the *Eastern Morning News* in 1864 at Hull. The last named remained the only daily newspaper in Hull until 1884. It was edited by William Hunt, a West Country journalist, and until Saunders' death in 1895 it remained a radical paper of some note. Between 1886 and 1891 it was edited by J. A. Spender, nephew of Saunders, who was later to become famous as the editor of the *Westminster Gazette* [Lee (1980) 138–9].

In 1863 Saunders and Edward Spender had founded the Central Press Agency, the first central organisation supplying news and material for publication to provincial papers [Fox Bourne (1887)]. In circumstances which A. J. Lee described as obscure, it was sold to a Conservative group in 1870 while Saunders, 'apparently in breach of the sale agreement, founded another agency, the Central News' [Lee (1980) 153].

Throughout his life Saunders took a very strong interest in politics and social questions. He often referred to the poverty of the Wiltshire labourers of his youth. He was a strenuous advocate of temperance, and a prominent member of the United Kingdom Alliance. From his early days he was a radically-minded Liberal, and when Henry George published his

Progress and Poverty (1879) Saunders very soon became a fervent supporter of George's ideas. He was a founder member, along with Helen Taylor, Stewart Headlam and Philip Wicksteed, of the Land Reform Union in the early summer of 1883, and, when the Union merged into the newly-established English Land Restoration League (ELRL) a year or so later, Saunders soon became treasurer of the united organisation. He also started and edited, possibly at first with Helen Taylor and Michael Davitt, the *Democrat* and was the sole editor from December 1887 to September 1888. He was adopted as official Liberal candidate for Kingston upon Hull East at the general election of 1885 and was successful at the polls with a majority of 665 over his Conservative opponent, F. B. Grotrian. His most successful parliamentary performance was to introduce a motion in favour of the taxation of land values (designated as ground rents) which evoked a five-hour debate in the Commons [Ward (1976) 227; *Hansard*, 16 Mar 1886, cols 999–1049]. The subject was then referred to the S. C. on Town Holdings, before which Saunders gave evidence. He lost his seat, however, in the general election of 1886 (by 37 votes), there being some confusion over his attitude towards Irish Home Rule and his attitude towards Gladstone. Saunders was, in fact, a consistent radical in Irish affairs.

In the years after 1886 he devoted his attention largely to London politics. Together with Stewart Headlam and Frederick Verinder, he was involved with the Trafalgar Square incidents in November 1887. He was arrested on 11 November for attempting to address a meeting, but took no part in the events which resulted in 'Bloody Sunday' (13 Nov 1887). Saunders was charged at Bow Street Police Court on 17 November with disorderly conduct and obstructing the police while in the execution of their duty. The issue turned largely on the right of public meeting, and defending counsel was concerned to take the matter to a higher court. But the presiding magistrate dismissed the charge, and the opportunity of defining the legal position was thereby lost [*Right of Meeting in Trafalgar Square. Verbatim Report* [1887]]. Saunders was intensely interested in free speech and the right of public demonstration, and his book *The New Parliament* (1880) provided a detailed account of the many serious disturbances during the weeks of the 1880 general election.

Saunders was in close contact with Henry George from the time of George's first visit to England in 1882, and by the middle of the decade George regarded him as his most effective spokesman in Britain [Barker (1955) 523]. In May 1887 the English Land Restoration League in conjunction with the London Municipal Reform League established the United Committee for Advocating the Taxation of Ground Rents and Values, and Saunders became an executive member with Frederick Verinder as the organising secretary. At the first election to the newly-established London County Council in 1889 Saunders stood at Walworth as an official candidate of the Land Restoration League and defeated Lewis H. Isaacs (Conservative) and Harry Quelch (SDF). Saunders played a lively part in LCC affairs, especially in those matters connected with landlordism. He was able, for example, to secure the appointment of a special committee to consider the best method of assessing the value of land throughout the metropolitan area, as a first step towards the imposition of site value rating. And he worked with Sidney Webb on the difficult problem of the betterment principle included in the London Improvements Bill of 1893, which the House of Lords rejected. His successful parliamentary candidature for Walworth in 1892 was not least due to the vigorous support of the very active local branch of the SDF, and Saunders' ideas on land and landlordism were sympathetically received in the constituency.

In June 1890 the First International Congress on the Land Question was held in Paris. The preliminary circular had been signed by Saunders, Henry George and Michael Flürscheim. The last-named was an ironmaster from Baden Baden and a leader of the ten-year-old land reform movement in Germany [Barker (1955) 531]. The conference, with about 150 participants, led to the establishment of a central committee in Paris. Saunders was elected a vice-president, and Verinder secretary of the English group [Ward (1976) 237].

In the House of Commons Saunders took up an increasingly radical position. He found Gladstone's second Home Rule Bill even less satisfactory than the first, and he finally voted against it on the third reading. The result was a growing estrangement from the Liberal Party and, according to Ramsay MacDonald, who knew him, 'his views took too pronouncedly a socialistic complexion for his party' [DNB].

He was in ill health during the previous winter of 1894–5, most of which he spent in the South of France, and he died at his brother's home in Market Lavington on 1 May 1895. He had always been of independent views, with the taxation of land values the central political interest of the last period of his life. He was an excellent journalist, well known for his account of the first journey he made to America in 1878 – Through the Light Continent – and also for his history of the LCC published in 1892. He is an interesting example of a political figure, greatly influenced by the Georgeite movement of the 1880s, who became steadily more radical as he got older. He was survived by his wife, but no will has been located.

Writings: Evidence before the S. C. on the Telegraph Bill on 7 July 1868, M of E, 1867–8 XI, Qs 1359–97; The Postal Telegraph and the Retrograde Steps of the Treasury Commission [1875] 46 pp.; Through the Light Continent; or, the United States in 1877/8 (1879); Land Laws and their Results, at Home and Abroad (1880); The New Parliament, 1880 [1880]; Virtue rewarded etc. (Hull, [1884?]) 15 pp.; History of the Dauntsey Charity: showing how the Charity Commissioners and the City companies rob the poor [1887] 32 pp.; evidence before the S. C. on Town Holdings on 15 July 1887, M of E, 1887 XIII, Qs 11,548–957; The Land Struggle in London [1891]; History of the First London County Council 1889–1890–1891 (1892); Land Points etc. [1893?] 32 pp.; The Political Situation: how it strikes a Radical [1893] 31 pp.

Sources: Hansard, 16 Mar 1886; H. R. Fox Bourne, English Newspapers, vol. 2 (1887; repr. NY, 1966); ELRL, Annual Reports [Saunders' evidence before the S. C. on Town Holdings is summarised in the 1888 Report]; Right of Meeting in Trafalgar Square. Verbatim report of the proceedings at Bow Street against Mr William Saunders and Mr Corrie Grant's defence [1887] 16 pp.; DNB 17 [by J. R. MacDonald]; J. A. Spender, Life, Journalism and Politics (1927); W. Harris, J. A. Spender (1946); C. A. Barker, Henry George (Oxford, 1955); E. P. Lawrence, Henry George in the British Isles (East Lansing, Mich., 1957); A. H. Nethercot, The First Five Lives of Annie Besant (1961); A. J. Peacock, 'Land Reform 1880–1919: a study of the activities of the English Land Restoration League and the Land Nationalisation Society' (Southampton MA, 1962); H. Pelling, Social Geography of British Elections 1885–1910 (1967); P. Thompson, Socialists, Liberals and Labour: the struggle for London 1885–1914 (1967); A. J. Lee, The Origins of the Popular Press (1976; another ed. 1980); S. B. Ward, 'Land Reform in England 1880–1914' (Reading PhD, 1976); Who's Who of British Members of Parliament, vol. 2: 1886–1918, ed. M. Stenton and S. Lees (Hassocks, Sussex, 1978); S. Koss, The Rise and Fall of the Political Press in Britain: the nineteenth century (Chapel Hill, NC, 1981); D. C. Richter, Riotous Victorians (Athens, Ohio, 1981). Biographical information: A. J. Peacock, York. OBIT. Devizes and Wiltshire Advertiser, Eastern Morning News, Times and Western Morning News, 2 May 1895.

JOHN SAVILLE

See also: †Stewart Duckworth HEADLAM; Frederick VERINDER.

SAWYER, George Francis (1871–1960)
TRADE UNIONIST, LAND TAX ADVOCATE AND LABOUR MP

Sawyer was born on 25 June 1871 at Cuddesdon, a village five miles south-east of Oxford. The circumstances of his family are not entirely clear. Only his mother's name, Ann Sawyer, appears on the birth register, but in later life Sawyer gave his father's name as James Sawyer. He was baptised as George Sawyer on 1 December 1872 but was always known as George Francis Sawyer. Certainly there was a large Sawyer family presence in Cuddesdon at this period.

Sawyer was educated to fourth standard at the National School at Cuddesdon. He left school aged twelve and found work locally as an agricultural labourer, and later as a navvy and bricklayer's labourer. Details of his early work and political views are scanty, for Sawyer made little reference to them, but they were to prove central to his later political development. At the age of sixteen he joined a union, almost certainly the National Agricultural Labourers' Union, for he subsequently referred to helping Joseph Arch in the latter's campaigns. At the 1895 general election Sawyer expressed 'views of the old Radical type' and was in consequence blacklisted by the local farmers and employers. He left Oxfordshire and went to Birmingham, finding work as a porter with the London and North Western Railway at Curzon Street station. After a year he was promoted to goods guard, earning 25s a week. On 29 April 1899 he married Minnie Tadbrooke, the daughter of a labourer, John Tadbrooke, from Broadway, Worcestershire, at St Anne's Church, Vauxhall, Birmingham. They set up home in Howe Street, Duddeston, close to the station.

Sawyer soon became involved in railway trade unionism in Birmingham, joining the Amalgamated Society of Railway Servants, the forerunner of the National Union of Railwaymen. He was active in the All Grades Movement of 1907, was chairman of the Birmingham No. 1 branch for four years, and served on the London and North Western's Conciliation Board from 1912 to 1922. While he was prominent in the 1911 railway strike, Sawyer initially opposed the 1913 strike in Birmingham called after the dismissal of railwaymen for refusing to handle Dublin stout.

Sawyer joined the Labour Representation Committee in 1902, but it was not until 1915, when he was elected on to the Board of Guardians for St Batholomew's ward in Duddeston, that he became prominent. He served as a Guardian until 1930, energetically pursuing people's grievances. He campaigned to ensure that railwaymen's widows were not penalised by reduced allowances for their children when they were in receipt of the Orphan Fund benefit. By 1918 Sawyer was president of Duddeston Labour Party and in 1920 he was representing Duddeston on the Birmingham Labour Party executive. In 1921 he was elected to the City Council for Nechells and Duddeston ward. He was to retain his seat for the next twenty-four years. With both his Council and Guardians' responsibilities, Sawyer became exceptionally well known in Duddeston. His house became an unofficial advice centre for the area. By working nights on the railway and reducing his sleep to the minimum, he was able to devote most of his days to his political work. At the 1924 Council elections he achieved a record municipal poll of 4908 votes for a Birmingham Labour candidate.

Sawyer was chosen as the prospective parliamentary candidate for Duddeston after the 1922 general election. It proved more difficult to break through the Chamberlain tradition and Unionist supremacy at parliamentary level. Duddeston was Labour's best prospect, being essentially a working-class inner-ring constituency with poor housing and a substantial railway vote. Sawyer fought both the 1923 and 1924 general elections against the sitting MP and local industrialist Alderman John Burman, reducing the Unionist majority to 4413 in 1923 and to 515 in 1924.

The first Labour parliamentary success went to Robert Dennison in King's Norton in 1924. Sawyer's own contests with Burman were conducted in an atmosphere of goodwill,

Burman commenting that he could wish for 'no more honourable opponent than Mr Sawyer'. Sawyer fought both campaigns largely on his own record of service in the constituency.

The respect with which Sawyer was held by his political opponents sprang from his obvious sincerity and independence of mind. Combined with outspokenness, these qualities made Sawyer an uneasy colleague for fellow Labour councillors and trade unionists. He always fitted uneasily into the straitjacket of party policy, campaigning as 'the Labour man who votes and thinks for himself'. There were frequent clashes between Sawyer and his colleagues throughout his long political career. In 1922 the Birmingham Labour Party censured him for comments he made about some of his fellow Labour councillors. Again in 1926 he was rebuked, this time for attending a complimentary banquet for Sir Austen Chamberlain to celebrate the Foreign Secretary's award of the Freedom of the City, even though the Labour Council Group had voted against the honour.

Yet a few months later Sawyer was in the thick of the General Strike and was arrested for a speech he made in Duddeston. During it he described the special constabulary as 'nothing more than a body of traitors and each member should be looked upon as a suspicious person', adding 'but I must not say too much about them as I am a member of the Watch Committee and they serve under me' [*Birmingham Strike Bull.*, 10 May 1926]. Following his arrest a crowd of his supporters gathered outside the police station demanding his release. Sawyer was told by the police that he had made a statement likely to create disaffection between the police and the civilian population. He was released on bail and when the case came to court was bound over. Sawyer was also kept from returning to work till a week after his fellow railwaymen. The circumstances of his arrest were brought up in the Commons on 10 May by Morgan Jones, MP for Caerphilly, as an example of the Government's arbitrary assumption of power [*Hansard*, 10 May 1926].

Sawyer fought Burman again at the 1929 general election. The campaign centred on housing and unemployment and Sawyer was the beneficiary. The Labour vote rose by over 7000 and Sawyer was elected with a majority of 6565, the largest Labour majority of the six in Birmingham constituencies. The railway company granted him leave of absence from work for the length of the Parliament but he retained his Council seat. At the age of sixty it was unlikely that Sawyer would make a great impact on the Commons, especially in the circumstances of the 1929–31 Labour Government. He did serve on the S. C. on the Times of Sittings of the House in 1930. His questioning of witnesses indicated that he felt that MPs who were businessmen or lawyers should put their parliamentary duties first and that the Commons could start earlier in the day. Socially he found his companions among his fellow railwaymen. Although he felt the Government was not moving fast enough in some directions, Sawyer was never attracted by Mosley. He made two speeches in the Commons, on 12 February 1930 on housing and on 4 May 1931 supporting the land valuation tax provisions of the 1931 Finance Act. The choice was entirely typical of the man. His speech on housing illustrated his everyday experience of and commitment to the problems of his constituents. The taxation of land values was the political issue closest to Sawyer's heart. It was almost an obsession; George Sawyer and the taxation of land values were regarded in Birmingham as almost synonymous terms. The *Birmingham Evening Despatch* captured the right tone when it wrote of Sawyer's contributions to the Council, 'Every time he got up to speak in the Council Chamber, colleagues sat back and smiled, reporters dropped their pencils and went out for a cigarette. Everyone expected a speech on taxing the land and seldom were they wrong' [*Birmingham Evening Despatch*, 22 Oct 1945]. Sawyer saw the price of land with the wealth and power of landowners as the main evils of society and he advocated a gradual move towards land taxation of 20s in the pound as a universal panacea. He constantly advocated it as an alternative to nationalisation. His Commons speech of 4 May 1931 is as good a guide to Sawyer's political philosophy as any amount of newscuttings or interviews.

The 1931 landslide saw Sawyer losing by over 6000 votes to a new Unionist opponent, Oliver Simmonds. He returned to the railways. In 1932 he was censured yet again and warned about his future conduct by the Birmingham Labour Party executive after he had become involved in a fierce argument in the Council with the leader of the Labour Group, Alderman Ager. Sawyer fought Duddeston for the fifth and last time in 1935, again losing decisively to Simmonds. It was a particularly disappointing result, with Sawyer polling 1000 fewer votes than in 1931, though it was typical of all the Birmingham seats.

Sawyer would have been seventy-one at the next general election and he refused re-nomination as prospective candidate. He continued his Council work, however, although growing increasingly independent. In 1940 he officially rejected the Labour whip, claiming the Labour Group were plotting to replace him on the Watch Committee. At the 1945 municipal elections the Labour Party fielded three candidates for the three-member ward of Nechells and Duddeston, and Sawyer, running as an Independent Labour candidate on a 'tried and tested' ticket, finished above the Unionists but behind his erstwhile colleagues. This was the eighteenth and last election that Sawyer had contested in Duddeston, for the Board of Guardians, for the City Council and for Parliament.

Sawyer retired from the railway on 24 June 1936, the day before his sixty-fifth birthday, finishing his career as a ticket-collector at New Street station. It was his proud boast that in forty-one years' service he had never been late for work. As a result of his skilled advocacy of the workers' cause on the Conciliation Board, he was offered promotion, but, true to his independent character, he rejected it. He felt it would have been a breach of faith with his fellow railwaymen to accept advancement because his work on the Board had brought him to the notice of the railway executives. Sawyer firmly believed in the common cause of management and workers. On his retirement he remarked, 'I leave happy in the knowledge that a more amicable feeling exists between staff and management. They pull together now – more in unison than in the old days.' He was always a staunch advocate of railways as opposed to road transport.

It was plausibly claimed in the press that when Sawyer was elected an MP in 1929 it would have been impossible to find another MP living in humbler circumstances. He was still living in his cramped house in Howe Street in the middle of his constituency, although he had his name down on the municipal housing list. This lack of self-seeking, combined with his genuine devotion to his constituents – he claimed to know two-thirds of the electorate personally – led to his being popularly dubbed the 'George Lansbury of Duddeston'. He could be domineering and virtually impossible to interrupt when speaking, particularly in the Council chamber, where he was a master of procedure. He was never a Socialist, rather an old-fashioned radical Liberal who believed that trade unions had a role in politics but not in advocating Socialism. Socialism, he argued, 'may be alright in theory but is no good in practice'. Especially later in life he became quite conservative over developments in society, condemning the 1945–51 Labour Government for making life 'comfortable for the spivs, drones and artful dodgers'. Similarly, at work he had no sympathy for workers who did not pull their weight or for wage claims that employers could not afford. Sawyer appears to have had little interest in foreign policy and stood aside from the Right–Left disputes which divided the Labour Party in Birmingham in the 1930s. Free trade was another continuing thread in Sawyer's political philosophy – during the 1929 general election campaign he spoke strongly against protectionist measures. He was also a temperance advocate. Nevertheless, it was the taxation of land values, doubtless learned in his Oxfordshire days, but transplanted to Birmingham and advocated by Sawyer at every opportunity, which made him the distinctive politican he was. As for his personal qualities, a long-standing political opponent, Norman Tiptaft, summed up the respect in which Sawyer was held: 'Many modern Labour leaders stand higher in the political hierarchy of their party. None has a better record for sincerity and personal integrity than George Sawyer' [Tiptaft (1952) 175].

Sawyer died in hospital on 27 August 1960 aged eighty-nine. He was cremated at Perry Barr Crematorium. He left property and effects to the value of £1970. His wife had died two years before, shortly after they had celebrated their golden wedding. They had three sons, none of whom followed their father into politics, although one did become a railwayman.

Sources: (1) MS: Birmingham LP minutes, Birmingham PL. (2) Other: *Town Crier*, 19 Dec 1924, 23 Oct 1925, 14 June 1929, 20 June 1930, and 26 May 1933; *Birmingham Strike Bull.*, 10 May 1926; *Birmingham Gaz.*, 3 July 1929; *Birmingham Evening Despatch*, 24 June 1936 and 22 Oct 1945; *Sunday Mercury*, 6 Feb 1944; N. Tiptaft, *My Contemporaries* (Birmingham, 1952) 173–5; *Birmingham Post Yearbook and Who's Who* (1958–9) 870; R. P. Hastings, 'The Labour Movement in Birmingham 1927–1945' (Birmingham MA, 1959); C. J. Simmons, *Soap-Box Evangelist* (Chichester, 1972) 85; Birmingham PL and WEA, *The Nine Days in Birmingham: the General Strike 4–12 May 1926* (Birmingham, 1976) 43 pp. Biographical information: Oxfordshire CRO. Personal information: Mrs Ivy Sawyer, Birmingham, daughter-in-law. OBIT. *Birmingham Post*, 30 Aug 1960; *Birmingham Evening Despatch*, 31 Aug 1960.

PETER DRAKE

SCHOLES, Benjamin (1779?–1823)
RADICAL

Scholes was born around 1779, but nothing is known of his early life or family background. Possibly his political radicalism dates from the turbulent decade of the 1790s, but Scholes did not come to the attention of the authorities until April 1802, when Government informers reported that he was a member of a secret committee of radicals for Wakefield and Almondbury in the West Riding of Yorkshire. This committee was probably a part of the United Englishmen radical movement and there is some evidence suggesting a connection with Colonel Despard's conspiracy to overthrow the Government in London in November 1802.

Scholes was a joiner by trade, but also worked for a time at other jobs, including schoolmaster, valuer of work and auctioneer. From October 1811 until October 1812 he was deputy constable of the parish of Stanley-cum-Wrenthorp, near Wakefield, and from 1812 until 1814 he was also sub-collector of taxes for the parish. Various extremely hostile reports from local officials to the Home Office claim he was a bad, drunken character, idle in his work, but always active in the 'preaching of sedition'.

In November 1816 Scholes became a publican and leased the Joiners' Arms in New Street, Wakefield for £17 a year. In this venture he met with some success, owing to his policy of providing cheap beer for his working-class customers. A Hampden Club operated from his pub and admission to its meetings was by ticket only. The magistrates forced the club to move by threatening to revoke the pub's licence. According to a local informant:

Scholes was invariably introducing his Politics and plagued everyone who thought differently from himself constantly abusing the *Ins* as he called them and the Royal Family, and bitterly complaining that it was hard for him to be obliged to work and to be a slave to support them [Wood to Hobhouse, 4 Apr 1818].

In January 1817 at a large public meeting of Wakefield reformers, Scholes presented the resolutions of his Hampden Club and these were passed unanimously.

In the period April–June 1817 Scholes was implicated in the plots for an armed uprising that were revealed by the notorious government agent known in British history as Oliver the Spy. A confused state of affairs developed in early June 1817 in which Oliver was exposed in the press as a government spy and yet in spite of this two small uprisings took place at Pentrich in Derbyshire and near Holmfirth in Yorkshire. The Government suspended Habeas Corpus and arrested dozens of radicals, including Benjamin Scholes of Wakefield. His papers were seized, but these were found to contain only reform pamphlets, personal letters and old account books. Scholes was imprisoned in Cambridge Gaol from June until almost the end of December 1817 and, like other state prisoners of that year, was never brought to trial. He returned to Wakefield early in January 1818, but ill health began to restrict his activities. At the end of the year he had to put the public house up for rent and he also made some preliminary plans to emigrate to America. His premature death aged forty-four on 5 April 1823 was attributed to the effects of his confinement in Cambridge Gaol. In its obituary the local liberal newspaper described him as an 'active and useful member of society, in his humble station of life' who 'fell a victim to the fears of a weak and wicked Ministry, and the vile machinations of an unprincipled spy'.

His will of 11 March 1823 lists him as a surveyor, mentions his brother Charles and leaves an estate subsequently valued at £100 to his wife, Martha.

Sources: (1) MS: PRO: HO 40/9 (2), narrative of Oliver, 1817; HO 40/9 (3), papers of B. Scholes, 1817; HO 42/65, Colonel Fletcher to H. Pelham, 7 Jan and 3 Apr 1802; HO 42/174, H. J. H. to Lord Sidmouth, 21 Feb 1818; HO 42/176, J. Todd Nayler to H. Hobhouse, 1 Apr 1818, and Revd William Wood to H. Hobhouse, 4 Apr 1818. Borthwick Institute of Historical Research, York: will, 11 Mar 1823. (2) Other: *Leeds Mercury*, 25 Jan 1817; J. L. and B. Hammond, *The Skilled Labourer* (1919; later eds); E. P. Thompson, *The Making of the English Working Class* (1963; 2nd ed. 1968); F. K. Donnelly and J. L. Baxter, 'The Revolutionary "Underground" in the West Riding: myth or reality?', *Past and Present*, no. 64 (1974) 124–32; J. Stevens, *England's Last Revolution: Pentrich 1817* (Buxton, Derbys, 1977). OBIT. *Wakefield and Halifax J.*, 14 Apr 1823.

F. K. DONNELLY

See also: Thomas EVANS; Thomas FARRIMOND.

SHAW, Benjamin Howard (1865–1942)
LABOUR PARTY ADMINISTRATOR

Ben Shaw was born on 27 July 1865, the third of four sons of George Shaw and his wife, Mary-Jane (née Wilson). His father was a master cotton-spinner, the owner of Spring Gardens Mill, Milnsbridge, near Huddersfield, Yorkshire. About a mile from the mill, at Longwood, stood the family home, Stonelea House, which was set in ample gardens overlooking the industrial Colne Valley. Shaw attended the local school until the age of fourteen. He would have preferred to pursue his studies, but his father's intention was that he should enter the mill and, by working in various departments, acquire a practical knowledge of cotton-spinning so that he could follow the family business.

At eighteen he was allowed to return to formal education at the Huddersfield Technical College. He became interested in economic and social questions and nurtured an ambition to study at Oxford University. His father, however, was adamant that he should return to the factory, which he did after a year. At the same time he continued to read widely, being particularly attracted, like many serious-minded young men of his day, by the ideas of John Ruskin.

The writings of William Morris were another strong influence and by the early 1890s he had absorbed the Socialist doctrines of the Fabians and Keir Hardie. In January 1892 he joined the Colne Valley Labour Union. He was a founder member of a Labour Club established in Longwood on 11 November 1892, and in the following year he was also instrumental in forming a branch of the Labour Church in the village, of which he became the secretary. He was one of the first recruits to the ILP.

According to family tradition (as recalled by Ben Shaw's daughter in 1981), George Shaw, though regarding himself as a radical, told his son to 'drop this Socialist nonsense or get out'. Fortunately Shaw's activities had brought him into contact with Hardie, who, impressed by his skills as an organiser, wrote to him on 30 January 1894 with the offer of a post in Glasgow on the *Labour Leader*. 'You might feel sumptuous on 20/- [*s*] including lodgings', wrote Hardie; 'I accept it unreservedly', replied Shaw on the following day [NLS, Acc. 6471]. He was to spend the remainder of his life in Scotland, for the most part working on behalf of the Labour movement.

Shaw's position in the *Labour Leader* office was apparently managerial rather than journalistic, although all members of the small staff had to work flexibly in order to get out the paper. He was also involved with the *Glasgow Commonweal*, a Socialist monthly which survived for eight issues in 1896. It was said that Shaw met his future wife after she sent in a manuscript on the sweated conditions that women suffered in the tailoring trade. Her name was Joanna Bruce, the daughter of a farm-manager who on her father's death had moved to Glasgow with her mother. The marriage took place in June 1900 according to the forms of the Free Church of Scotland (though it has not been discovered whether Shaw had any set religious beliefs). Joanna Shaw was a strong believer in the emancipation of working-class women and shared her husband's political attitudes. The marriage was a happy one until she died in her early fifties in 1916.

When the printing of the *Labour Leader* was transferred from Glasgow, Shaw remained in Scotland and was able to get a post with the Civic Press Ltd, a firm that specialised in publishing labour and trade union literature. By all accounts Shaw's personality was retiring and unobtrusive, and only once did he stand for public office – in November 1905, when he was the unsuccessful ILP candidate for the Townhead ward in the Glasgow municipal elections. Behind the scenes he worked to greater effect. In 1897 he had helped to organise the election of George Mitchell to the City Council, and during the following thirty-five years he assisted in most local and parliamentary election campaigns in Glasgow. From January 1903 to January 1906 he was secretary of the Glasgow branch of the ILP.

Shaw's administrative abilities were also employed in the temperance movement. He was a staunch teetotaller and an active campaigner for regulation of the drink trade. Unlike many others in the Scottish temperance movement, however, he was not a Sabbatarian: another of the causes he supported was the Sunday opening of libraries and art galleries in Glasgow. Shaw believed in the ennobling influence of literature and art, which he wished to be more freely accessible to the working class. During 1905 he acted as corresponding secretary of a Plebiscite Committee that sought to organise support for Sunday opening.

Another area of activity was the Scottish TUC. He attended the annual congress at Falkirk in 1902, as a representative of the shop assistants' union. In 1909 he was a vice-chairman of the STUC. For about two years he was in charge of the insurance department of the Scottish Horse and Motormen's Association, which became an approved society under the terms of the National Insurance Act of 1911.

Though at the general election of December 1910 Adamson won West Fife, the Labour Party had only three MPs in Scotland – Barnes (Glasgow) and Wilkie (Dundee) were the other two – and the party's leadership resolved to strengthen organisation north of the border. Efforts were concentrated on Glasgow, one of the two major cities in which there was no central party (London was the other). There were special problems in Glasgow. The ILP Federation had twenty branches; there were five Labour Representation Committees; a lively Co-operative Society Defence Association which politically was Lib–Lab; and a Registration Committee which was expected to co-ordinate electoral registration. The situation was complex, with the trade unions as a further component, many with labourist attitudes. A meeting of trade unions and Socialist groups was called on 18 May 1911 and this was followed by the inaugural conference of the Glasgow Labour Party on 21 March 1912. The Co-operative Defence Association had already withdrawn and it was followed by the Social Democrats. Ben Shaw was appointed secretary of the city party, but, when Henderson promoted the Scottish Advisory Council (SAC), Shaw – apparently with great relief – retired from the Glasgow party to become secretary to the new Advisory Council in March 1914 [McKibbin (1974) 28 ff.]. At about this time he was appointed a Glasgow magistrate.

The outbreak of war delayed arrangements for the inaugural conference of the SAC. Moreover, the sort of problems that had occurred with the Glasgow Labour Party – questions of affiliation and rivalries between Trades Council and LRC delegates – had to be resolved. Eventually a conference was held in August 1915, a year later than originally intended, and, although an executive was elected, with Robert Smillie as chairman, there were indications of the magnitude of the task. For instance, at an organisation meeting on the eve of conference only MacDonald and Shaw attended [ibid. 42]. The war also created extra duties for Shaw in the form of 'emergency work' in Glasgow – advising on the liability of workers for conscription, monitoring rents and food prices, taking up the cases of servicemen's families, and so forth. His precise attitude to the war has not been discovered, but it is probable that he adopted a similar position to that of the majority of the ILP and that of his second wife Clarice McNab, who took the pacifist line. She was the Women's Labour League representative on the SAC executive committee. They were married in July 1918 at St Giles' Church, Edinburgh; it seems that this marriage too was built upon similar ideals and interests.

The SAC brought together representatives of trade unions, Trades Councils and the ILP and helped to unify the different elements of the labour movement. One issue that it became involved in was the imprisonment of John Maclean during 1918. Maclean was widely regarded as a political prisoner – Henderson referred to him as such in a letter to Shaw on 17 August 1918 – who should receive special treatment. Shaw visited Mrs Maclean to obtain the full details of the case and consulted J. S. Middleton, who helped to brief a deputation of Labour MPs to the Secretary of State for Scotland. When Maclean was again imprisoned, Shaw acted as corresponding secretary of a joint committee of the Parliamentary Committee of the STUC and the executive of the SAC. On 1 June 1921 he visited Barlinnie Prison to help arrange for food to be sent in from outside and to discuss with Maclean what might be done to secure his release. Maclean's tone, Shaw reported to Middleton, 'presently is one of great friendliness to the Labour Party'.

In the 1920s Labour quickly strengthened its position in Scotland. Twenty-nine Labour MPs were returned for Scottish constituencies in the general election of 1922 and at the election of 1923 thirty-four were successful. Along Clydeside in particular, the CPGB was also well established and Shaw was involved in trying to keep local Labour parties free of Communist influence. The most notable series of events occurred in Motherwell, where the Communist J. T. Walton Newbold had been elected in 1922, defeated in 1923 and reselected (in Shaw's presence) by Labour delegates in May 1924, only to resign his candidature in September. Shaw supervised another selection conference in October, when a candidate more to his taste, James Barr, was adopted and duly elected as MP in the general election held at the end of the month. (The full course of these negotiations is traced by McKibbin [(1974) 196–204].)

Until his retirement in October 1932 Shaw continued to travel extensively and to carry out the many administrative duties of his office. He also encouraged his wife in her political activities. In 1921 the couple moved to Troon, Ayrshire, where Clarice McNab Shaw became involved in local politics, and after his retirement he did much to assist her political career. They were regarded as one of the most successful partnerships in the Scottish Labour Party. He also maintained his long-standing connection with the Civic Press, which was then printing *Forward*, by acting as its secretary. However, he resigned from the ILP, after a membership of almost forty years, when it disaffiliated from the Labour Party in 1932.

A shy man, he nevertheless often spoke in public and was an effective indoor and outdoor speaker. His full, carefully trimmed beard gave him a quietly distinguished appearance. Though his methodical and sober manner caused some to lose their patience, he was always respected for his conscientiousness and devotion to duty. He was fond of reading and of classical music. Political affairs continued to interest him, but such was his despair when the Second World War broke out that he could hardly bear to hear the news on the radio. Shaw died suddenly, in his sleep, at his home in Troon on 27 October 1942. The funeral took place on 30 October at the Glasgow Crematorium. He left an estate valued at £2706. At the time of his death his wife was in poor health and, although she was elected as Labour MP for Kilmarnock in 1945, she died exactly four years after him, on 27 October 1946. A daughter of his first marriage, Marjorie, was trained as a teacher and spent part of the war in Moscow as a journalist.

Sources: (1) MS: Shaw papers, NLS Acc. 6471; Colne Valley LP papers, Huddersfield Polytechnic; LP EC minutes, LP Library, London. (2) Other: *YFT*, 31 Mar 1894 and 9 Jan 1904; D. Lowe, *From Pit to Parliament* (1923); *Daily Herald*, 13 Jan 1933; A. Tuckett, *The Scottish Carter: the history of the Scottish Horse and Motormen's Association 1898–1964* (1967); R. McKibbin, *The Evolution of the Labour Party 1910–1924* (Oxford, 1974); *A Catalogue of Some Labour Records in Scotland*, ed. I. MacDougall (Edinburgh, 1978); D. Clark, *Colne Valley: Radicalism to Socialism* (1981); *Scottish Labour Leaders 1918–1939*, ed. W. Knox (Edinburgh, 1984). Personal information: Lord Ross of Marnock; Marjorie Shaw, Edinburgh, daughter. OBIT. *Glasgow Herald*, 28 Oct 1942; *Forward*, 31 Oct 1942.

DAVID CLARK
HELEN CORR

See also: James BARR; †George GARSIDE; Clarice McNab SHAW.

SHAW, Clarice Marion McNab (1883–1946)
LABOUR MP

Clarice Marion McNab was born in Leith, near Edinburgh, on 22 October 1883, the eldest daughter of Thomas Charles McNab, a cloth weaver, and his wife Mary (née Fraser). Her father was an influential figure in local politics and during his lifetime was elected to Leith Town Council, gave service as a JP, and was a director of Leith Co-operative Association. He was influential in shaping his daughter's radicalism, although her political beliefs were to become more left wing than his.

Little is known about Clarice McNab's education except that she trained as a music teacher in Leith. It is probable that she acquired a teaching certificate by serving an apprenticeship as a pupil teacher until the age of eighteen and thereafter by attending a teacher training college. She became a founder member of the Glasgow Socialist Sunday School in the late 1890s. Some of her ideas stemmed from reading Keir Hardie's column for children in the *Labour Leader*. She joined a weekly discussion group and, alongside Socialists like Alex Gossip, also a founder member, played a leading role in building the Socialist Sunday School movement in Scotland. This contact with Socialists such as Lizzie Glasier and Gossip must have greatly strengthened her political convictions and affiliation to Labour politics.

Her involvement in education led to a particular interest in child welfare. She became a strong advocate of improved medical and welfare services for schoolchildren under the auspices of the state. Thus it was appropriate that her first entry into local government was her election to the Leith School Board on 22 April 1912. She was already active in the Women's Labour League – an organisation which was concerned with the employment and wages of female workers – and on the School Board she was closely identified as a champion of women's rights. She campaigned for equal pay for female teachers and the extension of employment opportunities for girls leaving school. Her range of responsibilities on the School Board echoed her own interests in broader social and economic issues. She was a member of the finance and law committee (an unusual appointment for a female member), the school attendance committee and the employment agency committee. In this way she was directly confronted with problems relating to truancy and the casual employment of children. Consequently she opposed the employment of children and called for the school-leaving age to be raised to sixteen. With similar conviction she argued for free books and stationery to be supplied to all children, not just those categorised as necessitous.

Clarice McNab continued throughout these years before 1914 as a committed Labour activist. On 3 November 1913 she was elected to Leith Town Council with a majority of 646. Her election gave her the distinction of being the first Labour woman member of a town council in Scotland and the only woman to serve on the Leith Council between 1913 and 1918. The greater part of her activities concerned medical and child-welfare schemes and in 1914 she was appointed convenor of the public health committee, which had special responsibility for disease and sickness among necessitous children.

Apart from official Council duties, Clarice McNab was extremely active in the work of the Women's Labour League. In 1916 she was appointed as representative of the League to the executive committee of the Scottish Advisory Council of the Labour Party. This appointment brought her into direct contact with her future husband, Benjamin Howard Shaw, the first secretary of the SAC. He was recovering from the death of his first wife, Joanna, who had died of cancer that year. For the next two years Ben Shaw and Clarice McNab worked together on issues connected with the industrial employment of women and in building up the organisation of the Labour Party. During this time Clarice McNab became vice-chairman of the EC of the SAC.

They were married on 3 July 1918 at St Giles' Church, Edinburgh, but chose to live in Glasgow since it was the centre of Ben Shaw's domestic and political life. The marriage was an exceptionally happy one and their ideals and tastes were similar. In addition to a common commitment to the Labour Party and Socialism, they had compatible views on other political and social issues. They were both staunch teetotallers and Clarice supported Ben Shaw's campaign for temperance reform during the First World War. They were also closely connected with the Socialist Sunday School Union, but in this case Clarice played a more prominent role, since she was for many years a leading personality in the movement. In February 1918 the *Labour Leader* published an interview with her, as honorary secretary of the Socialist Sunday School Union, which throws some light on her opinions at that time. She defined Socialism as 'a religion that means to us love and justice to every member of the great universal family of mankind'. From this it followed that the movement was opposed to all war:

Our aspirations, ideals, and teaching have from the beginning been based on Peace and the unity of the world's workers. This is the uncompromising attitude of the International

Socialist Young People's Organisation, which took its early inspirations from Karl Liebknecht, one of its revered founders [*Labour Leader*, 14 Feb 1918].

Shortly after her marriage Clarice McNab Shaw temporarily called a halt to some of her most pressing engagements in Edinburgh; she gave up her career as a music teacher and resigned from the Leith School Board and Town Council in 1918. This period of relative inactivity in public life was short-lived, because, when the couple moved to Troon, Ayrshire, in 1921, Clarice Shaw was elected to Troon Town Council and the Ayrshire County Council. During the 1920s and 1930s she enhanced her reputation as a competent civic administrator. She was also a magistrate in Ayrshire. Meanwhile, her close association with housing and health schemes led to her appointment as convenor of the Ayrshire public health committee. In these ways she persisted in her campaigns for state provision of hospital, maternity, medical and school-meal services; and in connection with her particular interest in child welfare and education she pioneered the opening of the first nursery school in Ayrshire. She served for thirteen years as a town councillor and was a member of the County Council until she died.

For many years her major ambition was to become a Labour MP, and in the parliamentary elections of 1929 and 1931 she unsuccessfully contested Ayr Burghs. During the early years of the 1930s she was closely involved in the international movement for peace, and she was almost certainly a pacifist. In 1935, for example, she and Agnes Dollan were among the main speakers at a Women's Peace Conference held at the Keir Hardie Institute. But, as the threat from the Fascist powers developed after 1933, she began to change her mind on the matter of armaments and national defence – as did the Labour Party nationally, of course – and she was in wholehearted support of the war against Germany when it began in September 1939. What her attitude was to the Spanish Civil War is not known, but during the war years she was regarded in the Labour Party as left of centre, and it is likely, therefore, that she supported Republican Spain.

By the time of the outbreak of the Second World War, Clarice McNab Shaw was a prominent figure in Scottish politics. She was chairman of the Scottish Labour Party in 1939, a Labour councillor, and a founder member of the Scottish Committee of Co-operative, Labour and Trade Union Women, established in 1934. Because of her connections with women's industrial organisations she had close links with the Scottish TUC and the Women's Co-operative Guild in England. Her abilities as a public speaker had contributed to her reputation, as had her capacity for efficient administration. This latter quality had led to membership of a number of bodies, including appointment as a commissioner under the Educational Endowments (Scotland) Act in 1935 and as a member of the local Price Regulation Committee early in the war. On 27 October 1942, however, she received a severe personal setback with the sudden death of her husband. Since his retirement from public life in 1932 he had given his wife much support in the advancement of her own political career. His death made no difference to her commitment to the Labour Party, although her health was far from sound.

McNab Shaw was a firm supporter of the Coalition Government from 1940, although she deplored the decision to defer the raising of the school-leaving age, and criticised as inadequate the control of food prices [*Forward*, 15 Mar 1941]. When the general election was called in the summer of 1945, she was selected as the Labour candidate for Kilmarnock. The summary of her election address put the complete defeat of Japan at the head of the list, followed by 'A Scottish Parliament for Scottish Affairs'. The remaining items related to the proposals for welfare provision and social security that were common to the national programme of the Labour Party. She won the seat with a 7537 majority in a straight fight with the Conservative.

In recognition of her services to the Labour Party, she was appointed secretary of the Scottish Parliamentary Group and a member of the Standing Committee on Scottish Bills.

Before she could begin work she became seriously ill and, although she was able formally to take her seat, she was never able to participate in the proceedings of the House of Commons. She was a woman of great courage and throughout her illness assiduously attended to her parliamentary correspondence. However, her hopes of improved health did not materialise and in September 1946 she reluctantly resigned her seat. She died at her home in Titchfield Road, Troon, on 27 October 1946, and the funeral took place in Glasgow on 31 October. Her estate was valued at £7765. There were no children of her marriage, although she was survived by a step-daughter, Marjorie. The by-election was held in December, when Willie Ross, who had been one of Clarice's Socialist Sunday School pupils, retained the seat for Labour [letter to editors from Lord Ross of Marnock, dated 2 Feb 1982].

Writings: 'War and the Schools: fair play for the children', *Forward*, 11 Nov 1939, 8; 'Meals for 9*d*: are they good enough?' [report of a speech by Bailie Mrs McNab Shaw at a women's conference of the Scottish Labour Party], ibid., 15 Mar 1941, 3.

Sources: (1) MS: Woman's Advisory Council, reports, NLS, ref. PGL 30/3. (2) Other: Leith School Board and Leith Town Council, minutes 1912–18, Edinburgh CL; 'What of our I. L. P. Children?' [an interview with Clarice McNab], *Labour Leader*, 14 Feb 1918; W. Stewart, *J. Keir Hardie: a biography* (1921); STUC, Annual Reports 1931-5; *WWW* (1941–50); election address 1945; *Times House of Commons* (1945); C. Bunker, *Who's Who in Parliament* (1946); *Who's Who of British Members of Parliament*, vol. 4: *1945–1979* ed. M. Stenton and S. Lees (Brighton, 1981); P. Brookes, *Women in Westminster* (1967); *Scottish Labour Leaders 1918–1939*, ed. W. Knox (Edinburgh, 1984). Biographical information: Ure Dargie, Largs, Ayrshire. Personal information: Lord Ross of Marnock; Marjorie Shaw, step-daughter; Robert Taylor, Bishopbriggs, Glasgow. OBIT. *Glasgow Herald*, 28 Oct 1946; *Ayrshire Advertiser*, 31 Oct 1946; *Ayrshire Post*, 1 Nov 1946; *Forward* and *Kilmarnock Standard*, 2 Nov 1946; *LP Report* (1947).

HELEN CORR
DAVID E. MARTIN
JOHN SAVILLE

See also: †Alexander GOSSIP; Benjamin Howard SHAW.

SHIELS, Sir Thomas Drummond (1881–1953)
LABOUR MP AND GOVERNMENT MINISTER

Thomas Drummond Shiels was born in Edinburgh on 7 August 1881, the second of the eight children of James Drummond Shiels and his wife Agnes (née Campbell). His father was a skilled worker, a lithographic printer, but the size of the family meant that times were often hard. At the age of twelve, after an elementary schooling in Glasgow (where his father worked for a period), he got a job with a firm of photographers, although he continued his education at night school. Later, when the children were more independent, Thomas, a brother and their father were able to set up a photographic studio in Lauriston Place, Edinburgh. Even after he became an MP, Shiels kept an interest in the business, which was managed by the brother.

In the First World War Shiels took a patriotic attitude, fought with the 9th (Scottish)

Division, rose to the rank of captain and was awarded the Military Cross and the Belgian Croix de Guerre. He was also mentioned in despatches following the battle of Arras in 1917, in which he was severely wounded. On leaving the Army he began to study medicine, partly it seems in order to gain a greater knowledge of public health problems. Before the war he had been active in the Edinburgh branch of the Fabian Society, of which he later became president. His keen interest in social problems led to membership of the City Council in 1919. At the same time he followed his medical courses at Edinburgh University, graduating in 1924 with degrees in Medicine and Surgery. At the general election of October 1924 he stood as Labour candidate for the Edinburgh East constituency. Since 1886 the seat had been held by the Liberals, but in 1924 Shiels defeated C. Milne, the Conservative, and J. M. Hogge, the sitting Liberal.

He served as an MP for seven years, during which time he became increasingly interested in colonial affairs. This interest led to a number of appointments. He was a member of the delegation which went to Australia in 1926 on behalf of the Empire Parliamentary Association. In August 1927 he became one of a four-man commission, set up under the chairmanship of the Earl of Donoughmore to report on the constitution of Ceylon and to consider proposals for its revision. The Commissioners spent several weeks in Ceylon during the winter of 1927–8. While there Shiels established an effective working relationship with A. E. Goonesinha, a prominent trade unionist who had been host to Ramsay MacDonald when the Labour leader visited Ceylon in 1926. Shiels briefed Goonesinha before the latter gave evidence to the Donoughmore Commission; in return Shiels obtained from Goonesinha detailed information about the constitutional situation and the aspirations of the local labour movement. In particular, he saw that a move towards responsible government should be coupled with the establishment of universal suffrage. Labour MPs such as Ellen Wilkinson and Fenner Brockway, who on most issues were to the left of Shiels, warmly approved the position he took on reforming the constitution of Ceylon [Jayawardena (1972) 275].

Shiels's interest in colonial affairs was recognised when the Labour Party took office in June 1929, and he was appointed under-secretary to Wedgwood Benn at the India Office. One of the difficult questions that was already in existence when they took office was the arrest and trial of a number of trade unionists in India who became known as the Meerut prisoners (after the town in which their trial took place: for which see the **Special Note** in *DLB 7*, 84–91). Fenner Brockway moved the reference back at the LP conference in October 1929 on this issue, and Shiels replied for the platform. He followed the official argument that the Meerut prisoners were not being tried for their trade union activities and he emphasised throughout the Communist affiliations of many of those on trial. The charge was, in fact, a political one of conspiracy, and one of his telling debating points, which undoubtedly swayed some votes, was that an official representative of the British Communist Party was being allowed to proceed to Meerut. This was J. R. Campbell, whose permission, however, was later withdrawn.

In December 1929 Shiels was moved to the Colonial Office, again as under-secretary, this time to Sidney Webb, now Lord Passfield. This led to a weekend at Passfield Corner which enabled Beatrice Webb to make one of her characteristic pen portraits. In her diary for 23 December 1929 she commented (and it must not be assumed that she was always accurate in her judgements):

This Scot is a ponderous man alike in body and mind – six feet and proportionally big in limbs, head and features; with a hard strong voice and a hard Edinburgh accent with which he argues and tells facetious stories too plentifully. He takes no exercise, eats and smokes heavily and at bedtime takes copiously of whisky. He is conceited and regards himself, his opinions, and his future as important to the world's history. He is well read and tough minded – he has an equal contempt for the revolutionary folly of the Clyde and reactionary conservatism of Govt officials . . . His wife is a good sort and intelligent but equally ponderous and over fed [Webb Diary microfiche 3922 pp. 4865–6 (vol. 43, 30 May 1929–27 Dec 1929)]

A somewhat similar impression of Shiels was conveyed in *A Hundred Commoners*, published in 1931. The author of this sketch characterised him as 'conscientious and intensely scrupulous', noted the 'strong metallic quality' of his voice and that 'determination is writ large all over his face and figure', and concluded that he 'might be called a drab personality' [Johnson (1931) 308–9]. Shiels apparently retained similar characteristics in later years, though his obituarist in the *Lancet* wrote in warmer terms:

In speech he was slow, deliberate, and almost ponderous, but he never took himself too seriously. If his demeanour was grave, his smile at once removed all traces of the funereal. His manner was tactful and persuasive, but that jowl of his denoted dour persistence: his humour was pawky rather than sly, for there was nothing but good nature behind it. At home in any company, he never forgot he was a Scot . . . [*Lancet*, 10 Jan 1953, 99].

Beatrice Webb had noticed Shiels's 'stiff obstinacy', and at the Colonial Office he often pressed for more radical policies than those favoured by Passfield. The older Fabian preferred to carry his permanent officials with him and avoid confrontation; he also, as Shiels noted many years later, lacked ruthlessness [Shiels (1949) 218]. Nevertheless, Shiels was able to invigorate the ministry on a number of issues. When he discovered that in North Borneo whipping was still inflicted as a punishment for natives in breach of employment contracts, he took up the question. Passfield had already begun to amend the operation of colonial master-and-servant laws and agreed with Shiels's proposals that certain standards, properly monitored, should be adopted wherever native labour was employed. However, it was May 1931 before a Colonial Labour Committee was established and, though it met frequently, it achieved little before the fall of the Labour Government, after which the new ministry was apathetic to colonial reform.

Shiels's policy was to encourage a gradual development of the civil rights of native populations, including membership of trade unions, so as to avoid unrest and more extreme demands. Thus, when it was reported that police in Gambia had used violent means during a labour dispute, he not only ordered an investigation into the alleged police brutality but also set up an inquiry into the underlying causes of the dispute. In Malaya Shiels pressed for a reduction in the powers of the local rulers and opposed the policies of Sir Cecil Clementi, the Governor, only to be overruled by Passfield, who minuted that Clementi 'had had the better of the argument' [Gupta (1975) 263].

Kenya was a major political issue during the whole period of the second Labour Government's term of office. This was largely due to the presence in England of a number of Labour activists committed to Africa and especially to East African affairs. Norman Leys, McGregor Ross and C. R. Buxton were especially important. The Governor of Kenya, Sir Edward Grigg, was reactionary and favoured the white settler interest. Passfield was always ready to compromise, and his well-known *Memorandum on Native Policy in East Africa* (Cmd 3573, 1930) is described by Gupta 'as a partial and somewhat grudging response to a humanitarian lobby' [(1975) 174]. Shiels was more liberal in his general approach, and persuaded Passfield, against the advice of his officials, to allow a meeting with Jomo Kenyatta while he was in England as a representative of the Kikuyu Central Association. The meeting took place on 23 January 1930, and Shiels was persuaded that Kenyatta, in spite of his contacts with the League Against Imperialism, would act constitutionally. When, soon after, Grigg began to move against the Kikuyu Central Association, Shiels was so angry that he wanted to send a sharp reprimand. Passfield, however, insisted that the Governor should be dealt with politely and given 'a regular lesson in administration' [ibid.,

194]. In November 1930 Passfield set up an all-party Joint Select Committee, of which Shiels was a member, to consider what constitutional changes should be made in East Africa. It issued its report in November 1931. Shiels believed the conclusions of the Joint Select Committee on Closer Union in East Africa [HL 184(1931)] were progressive, and gave a favourable account of the report in the *Political Quarterly* in 1932.

By this time he was out of Parliament. He left office on the formation of the National Government in August 1931 and lost his Edinburgh seat in October. Though he had to rely on his medical qualifications for his livelihood – he obtained a part-time post as London County Council medical officer – he maintained his involvement in colonial questions. In a review of Norman Leys's book *A Last Chance in Kenya* he countered Leys's criticisms by claiming that it was 'wise to try to get the sympathy and interest' of the white settlers [*Pol. Q.*, *3* (July–Sep 1932) 446]. Privately, writing to Winifred Holtby in a letter dated 15 January 1932, he charged Leys with lacking a sense of proportion and using unreliable information. In his book Leys had developed a vigorous criticism of Passfield's administration and, at the same time, indicated that Shiels might have done better [Leys (1931) 141]. He added a footnote stating, 'Dr. Shiels has a public record. Judging by that record, the author finds it impossible to believe that if Dr. Shiels had been Secretary of State instead of Under-Secretary, the Colonial Office would have taken the course it took between June 1929 and August 1931' [ibid., n. 1].

During the 1930s Shiels was associated with the Labour Party Advisory Committee on Imperial Questions. He was involved in making reports on Malaya in 1934 and on the West Indies in 1936. In common with many of his colleagues, he had no wish to dismantle the British Empire, although he favoured self-government for certain territories such as India and Ceylon. In other areas, such as East Africa, he called for enlightened and progressive policies which would benefit both native peoples and the economic interests of Britain; but he never really came to serious terms with the white settlers in Kenya and Southern Rhodesia (now Zimbabwe).

In domestic politics too, Shiels was towards the right of the Labour Party. He was highly critical of the Socialist League and especially of Stafford Cripps: in a letter to *Forward* (20 July 1935) he described Cripps and the Socialist League 'as a much greater hindrance to the increase of Socialist voters in this country than any of the anti-Labour forces', and characterised Cripps as 'the most valued contributor to the Tory propaganda department'. This was standard comment from the right wing of the Labour movement at this time, and Shiels was naturally an outspoken opponent of the United Front and the Popular Front.

Between 1933 and 1941 he acted as the medical secretary of the British Social Hygiene Council. In this capacity he wrote a number of pamphlets, issued by the Council, on such subjects as venereal disease and enuresis. In 1939 he was knighted and in the following year was appointed deputy secretary of the Empire Parliamentary Association. In 1946 he became an original member of the Colonial Economic and Development Council, an appointment made by the Colonial Secretary, Arthur Creech Jones, with whom Shiels had been associated in the 1930s. He also acted as public relations officer in the General Post Office from 1946 to 1949, in which year he was appointed secretary to the British group of the Inter-Parliamentary Union, a position he occupied until his death. He had joined the Royal Empire Society in 1928, was elected to its council in 1930 and appointed a vice-president (which he remained until death) in 1941. His pamphlet on the colonies was published on behalf of the Society in 1947.

Shiels was a stalwart of many other organisations, especially in the fields of medicine and colonial affairs. In addition to the bodies already mentioned, he was at various times a member of the East India Association, the Royal African Society, the Anti-Slavery and Aborigines Protection Society, the Dominions, India and Colonies Panel of the British Film Institute (of which he was chairman), the British Postgraduate Medical Federation, the Royal Society for the Prevention of Cruelty to Animals, the London Burns Club, the Royal

Society of Medicine and the Dominions Committee of the British Medical Association.

In 1904 Shiels had married Christian Blair Young, a schoolteacher and daughter of a joiner. She died in 1948. They had one child, a daughter. In 1950 he married Gladys Louise Buhler MBE, the secretary of the Imperial Studies Committee of the Royal Empire Society, in a Church of Scotland ceremony. Shiels died in Hammersmith Hospital on 1 January 1953. He was cremated privately, but a memorial service was held on 4 February at the Church of Scotland, Covent Garden. His widow, who died in 1968, was granted administration of his estate, which showed effects to the value of £718.

Writings: 'The East Africa Report', *Pol. Q. 3*, no. 1 (Jan–Mar 1932) 71–87; review of N. Leys, *A Last Chance in Kenya*, ibid., *3*, no. 3 (July-Sep 1932) 444–8; *Notes on the Venereal Diseases* [1934] 33 pp.; *Are we abolishing Venereal Disease?* [1935] 18 pp.; 'Dr. Drummond Shiels on Socialist League Tactics' [letter], *Forward*, 20 July 1935; *Bed-Wetting – Nocturnal Enuresis: notes for the use of superintendents, nurses and others* (1938) 21 pp.; *From Boyhood to Manhood*, 2 pts [1939, 1941]; *The Colonies Today and Tomorrow* (1947) 36 pp.; 'Sidney Webb as a Minister', in *The Webbs and their Work*, ed. M. Cole (1949) 201–18; (advisory ed.) *The British Commonwealth: a family of peoples* (1952).

Sources: (1) MS: Winifred Holtby Coll., Hull CL; Beatrice Webb Diary, BLPES (original) and on microfiche. (2) Other: *Hansard*, 1924–31; *Labour Who's Who* (1927); *Ceylon. Report of the Special Commission on the Constitution*, Cmd 3131 (1928); *Statement of Conclusions of His Majesty's Government in the United Kingdom as regards Closer Union in East Africa*, Cmd 3574 (1930); Joint Select Committee on Closer Union in East Africa, *Report*, HL 184 (1931); Anon., *The Scottish Socialists* (1931); J. Johnson, *A Hundred Commoners* (1931); N. Leys, *A Last Chance in Kenya* (1931); S. Namisivyam, *The Legislatures of Ceylon 1928–1948* (1951); *DNB* (1951–60) [by C. Jeffries]; *WWW* (1951–60); R. G. Gregory, *Sidney Webb and East Africa: a history of race relations within the British Empire 1890–1939* (Oxford, 1971); V. K. Jayawardena, *The Rise of the Labour Movement in Ceylon* (Durham, NC, 1972); P. S. Gupta, *Imperialism and the British Labour Movement* (1975); *Scottish Labour Leaders 1918–1939*, ed. W. Knox (Edinburgh, 1984). Biographical information: D. H. Simpson, Librarian, Royal Commonwealth Society. OBIT. *Scotsman* and *Times*, 3 Jan 1953; *Lancet*, 10 Jan 1953; *British Medical J.*, 10 and 24 Jan 1953; *United Empire* (Jan–Feb 1953). NOTE. The editors wish to acknowledge an earlier draft from Dr William Knox, Heriot Watt Univ., whose own entry was published in *Scottish Labour Leaders 1918–1939* (Edinburgh, 1984).

DAVID E. MARTIN
JOHN SAVILLE

See also: Leonard John BARNES; *Arthur Creech JONES; Norman Maclean LEYS; †Sidney James WEBB.

SPENCE, Thomas (1750–1814)
AGRARIAN REFORMER AND RADICAL BOOKSELLER

Thomas Spence was born on the Quayside, Newcastle upon Tyne, on 21 June 1750. His mother, a stockinger from Orkney, was the second wife of an Aberdonian net-maker; there were eighteen other children in the family. The young Thomas Spence was raised in an environment saturated in the biblical fundamentalism of Scottish Calvinism. He later recognised that the sessions spent as a child reading aloud and discussing the Scriptures at his father's work-bench were the most influential part of his education. Though informally schooled, Spence in time became a teacher; prior to this he had worked at net-making, at market gardening, and as a clerk. His introduction to radical politics began some time after 1865, when his family transferred its religious allegiances to the High Bridge Meeting House, where Thomas and his brother Jeremiah came under the influence of the new pastor there, James Murray (1732–82). Murray, a central figure in Newcastle radicalism during the second half of the eighteenth century, was one of the mediators between the 'Scottish Enlightenment' (he had graduated from Edinburgh in 1761) and indigenous Tyneside culture. He was the author of numerous Calvinist and radical works, among the latter a pro-rebellion history of the American War of Independence. In later life the two Spence brothers went separate ways, the one the legatee of Murray's radicalism, the other of his religion (leading the entire High Bridge congregation into Sandemanianism).

Thomas Spence's political views, however, were not the product of *émigré* Scottish Calvinism alone. The resolution of a protracted dispute concerning the enclosure of the Newcastle Town Moor in 1771 suggested to him a practical means of agrarian reform. The compromise evolved to compensate freemen for the common rights relinquished on enclosure was to devote rents from the land to charities for the freemen and their families. No less important than this episode, though, in stimulating Spence's political awareness was his membership of the informal artisanate intelligentsia which flourished around the premises of Newcastle's printers and allied trades. Of this group the *Memoir of Thomas Bewick, written by himself* contains a valuable cumulative portrait. Bewick first met Spence at one of the focal points of this lively culture, the workshop of the bookbinder Gilbert Gray: it was the beginning of a warm friendship as well of the collaboration (Bewick and his master, Ralph Beilby, supplying the type) which led to Spence's first publication, a phonetic dictionary. This, the first stage in a lifetime's devotion to the cause of language reform, was born of Spence's profound conviction that lack of education held down the poor and underpinned social and economic injustice. It was this same belief that impelled Spence to publish the text of a lecture on property which he gave to Newcastle Philosophical Society in November 1775. Several times reprinted, this lecture was to remain the keystone of Spence's political thought. Following Locke, Spence accepted as an axiom the equality of property in the state of nature. However, he rejected any notion of a social contract, arguing that private property in land was anathema: 'our boasted civilisation is founded alone on conquest'. If 'the country of any people, in a native state, is properly their common', then they jointly reap its fruits and advantages: 'For upon what must they live if not upon the productions of the country in which they reside? Surely to deny them that right is in effect denying them a right to live?' It follows from this that members of one generation cannot, through a personal appropriation of the land, deny the right they once enjoyed to those coming after them. 'For to deprive anything of the means of living, supposes a right to deprive it of life; and this right ancestors are not supposed to have over their posterity.' It is here that Spence broke free from the dominant interpretation of Locke; and it is from here that the radical thrust of his philosophy is derived, in the disavowal that time conferred innocence on private property in land. 'There is no living but on the land and its productions, consequently, what we cannot live without we have the same property in as our lives.' Any ascendancy over land was hence an ascendancy over people: therefore the issue of land-ownership lay at the root of all injustice, all economic exploitation, all social inequality. To the resolution of this issue Thomas Spence therefore devoted his political career.

The original lecture of 1775 hinged on education readily securing universal consent to a system of agrarian equality; it was to be some time before Spence sharpened his perception of the means which might be necessary to achieve the system he advocated. His perception of the ends, however, was unchanging – a parochial partnership of the residents of all ages and both sexes, equally dividing between them the revenue from the lease of the land to those who farmed it. Restrictions would be placed on the duration of leases, and on the size of holdings. Each parish would be self-governing, but joined with others in a federation to co-ordinate the defence of the nation by citizen militias. Spence reprinted his thesis, with only minimal amendments, at several points in his subsequent career – as *The Real Rights of Man* (1793), in the third volume of *Pigs' Meat* (1795) and as *The Meridian Sun of Liberty* (1796).

In Newcastle the lecture was greeted with immediate hostility, especially since Spence had published it in contravention of the Philosophical Society's regulations. In consequence he was expelled 'not for printing it only, but for printing it in the manner of a halfpenny ballad and having it hawked about the streets' [Mackenzie (1826) 5]. His ideas, though, were vigorously defended by his patron James Murray, as well as receiving the tacit endorsement of Thomas Saint, an important Newcastle publisher, who subsequently (1782) issued the political allegories, based on Swift and Defoe, in which Spence further elaborated his ideas. Yet for the remainder of his years on Tyneside – indeed, for the rest of his life – Spence was regarded as a pariah intellectual, not least because he declined to temper either the radical thrust of his views or the vigour with which he always stated them. They were a distinctive amalgam of seventeeth-century and enlightenment thought, iconoclastic Calvinism and indigenous English radicalism with strong millenarian overtones. Spence's politics were qualitatively different from the then customary radical critique of property as inducing effeminate and corrupting luxury, or of men of property for having abrogated their responsibilities to society at large. The hostility with which his 1775 *Lecture* was met most likely contributed to Spence's decision, shortly after, to move to Haydon Bridge, where he took the post of usher (a junior master) at the local grammar school. At such a distance (twenty-five miles) from Newcastle, it was difficult for him to capitalise on his new-found political notoriety, but on his appointment in April 1779 to an under-mastership at St Anne's School, Newcastle, Spence commenced a debating society at his rooms in Broad Garth in competition with the Newcastle Philosophical Society. He made little progress as a reformer, even his friend Bewick dissenting violently from his ideas; and he was further hampered by his lack of the status of freeman, which effectively precluded him from local politics. His isolation increased following Murray's death in 1782, and, shortly after, his marriage (to a Miss Elliott of Hexham) ended. In December 1787, dismissed from his teaching post, Spence determined to move to London.

The change in his circumstances was dramatic. His health had deteriorated – a stroke with ensuing speech difficulties perhaps explaining the end of his teaching career – and his early years in London were passed in considerable poverty. He was first dependent on casual earnings as a printer's number carrier (delivery man) for the publisher Charles Cooke of Paternoster Row, work he secured on the recommendation of Bewick's brother John, a London engraver. On the more positive side, however, Spence's residence in the capital embraced the years of the French Revolution, a powerful stimulus to political action. Even before this he had embarked on a new form of radical propaganda, the illegal counter-marking of crown currency with political slogans. By the autumn of 1792 he had gathered sufficient resources to become a seller of books and saloop (a cocoa-like beverage made from powdered sassafras bark) at a stall on the corner of Holborn and Chancery Lane. At about the same time he joined the London Corresponding Society. This was to prove a watershed in his life, as decisive even as the lecture of 1775 in which he had first developed his political philosophy. Though never an officer of the Corresponding Society, Spence was among the most active of its members at the grass-roots. He was member number one of the 30th Division and later, when he acquired permanent premises in Little Turnstile, High Holborn, host to the meetings of the 12th Division. He was a delegate to the General Committee and a member of the important Committee of Constitution (1794), of whose *Report*, the most explicit statement of the Society's principles, he was publisher. At his shop he received subscriptions and signatures to petitions, and sold tickets for Society events along with the full range of its publications. In March 1793 he was among the supporting signatories to the *Declaration* of the Friends of the Liberty of the Press. He also resumed publishing on his own account, notably further editions of his original lecture but also the remarkable *One Pennyworth of Pig's Meat*, issued in weekly parts from 1793 to 1795 and twice republished. This journal, which included extracts from Spence's own writings, also featured other radical authors, including Godwin, Harrington, Oliver Cromwell and Volney. Spence also began issuing his own token coins, thousands of which had entered general circulation by the end of the century. All bearing radical slogans, they drew from the *Gentleman's Magazine* the unintended compliment that Spence 'alone has done more harm to the coinage than any other persons in the aggregate' [(Feb 1798) 122].

There was a price to be paid for all this enterprise in the cause of radical politics, however, and Spence was arrested on two occasions in December 1792 for selling Paine's *Rights of Man*. Though acquitted of selling seditious material, he was subjected to verbal and physical abuse back at his stall, and on Christmas Eve he was evicted. He was four times arrested but not charged during the following months until, in May 1794, he was detained for examination before the Privy Council on suspicion of High Treason. He was specifically arraigned in connection with a shadowy radical military group, the Lambeth Loyal Association, which met for armed drilling in a room above his shop. The Government, unable to prove a conspiracy before the English courts, used the issue of the Association principally to embarrass the defence of Thomas Hardy, secretary to the London Correspondending Society. An indictment was prepared against Spence in anticipation that his conviction would be secured with ease once that of Hardy was carried: this strategy was frustrated by Hardy's acquittal and proceedings against Spence were dropped, but not before he had spent some seven months in prison. His obduracy before the Privy Council clearly ruled out any earlier release:

Spence said that the Plot for the Reform of Parliament will go on, notwithstanding all the Examination of persons and seizing of persons. He said, if the Burthens and Grievances were not attended to, they must look to the Consequences [PC 2/140, p. 177].

Spence maintained a highly vocal campaign after his release. Indeed, it is significant that he increased his own political activism just as government suppression was elsewhere taking effect. The year 1795 was one of his busiest as a radical publicist; furthermore, he made the first substantial revaluation of his ideas and, particularly, of the means by which his reforms might be secured. Henceforward all his writings conceded the probable necessity of physical force if reforms were to be achieved, as well as emphasising the distinctiveness of his political thought: 'There is another RIGHTS OF MAN by Spence, that goes farther than Paine's. . . . It is amazing that Paine and the other Democrats should level all their Artillery at Kings, without striking like Spence at this root of every abuse and grievance' [*End of Oppression* (1795) 5]. It was a controversial claim: not only did Spence now explicitly endorse the use of force to secure radical objectives; he also emphasised that chief among those objectives must be the destruction of the economic base of political power. To expound this, and at the same time attack Paine, was not calculated to endear him to important elements within metropolitan radicalism. Spence's publication a few months later of a mordantly satirical *Recantation of the 'End of Oppression'* points to a serious gulf between him and majority radical opinion.

Unabashed, Spence developed his critique of Paine further in the *Rights of Infants* (1797), which also contained an extensive argument in favour of women's rights, among which Spence included the vote. This concern to widen the constituency of radicalism was also reflected in his preoccupation with education, and it was here that he was content to focus his energies in popular politics. There is no evidence of his leading any specific group or faction during the 1790s, nor any to implicate him in the insurrectionary activities of the United Irish and English movements, in which several of his subsequent associates were involved. Nevertheless, he was regarded with sufficient suspicion to be arrested and detained in Cold Bath Fields Prison for a time in 1798.

Throughout the first two decades of the nineteenth century active conspirators in the capital were consistently associated with Spence's name. The first recorded meeting of any Spencean group took place in 1801, against a background of renewed United Irish activity and a few months before the exposure of the so-called 'Despard Conspiracy' [broadside, 18 Mar 1801]. There is no evidence linking them, but the formation of an avowed Spencean group at this critical juncture clearly derived impetus from renewed interest in insurrectionary politics. This was also a period of widespread food riots, which underlined the economic, and particularly agrarian, roots of contemporary grievances as stressed by Spence. He referred to this context of 'an unprecedented dearness of Provisions' in the course of his longest and most cogent work, *The Restorer of Society to its Natural State*, published the same year. Again he reiterated the justice of applying force to secure reform, this time invoking as exemplars the French and American revolutions, along with the naval mutinies of 1797. For so doing he was arrested and charged with seditious libel. Cobbett, who witnessed his trial in June 1801 in the Court of King's Bench, was impressed by his sincerity:

> He had no counsel, but defended himself and insisted that his views were *pure* and *benevolent*. . . . He was a plain, unaffected, inoffensive looking creature. He did not seem at all afraid of any punishment, and appeared much more anxious about the success of his *plan* than about the preservation of his life [*Political Register*, (14 Dec 1816) col. 634].

The trial confirmed Spence's reputation as a revolutionary thinker, and it ended with his removal to Shrewsbury Gaol to serve a twelve-month sentence. His involvement in politics upon his return was at first tentative, and, though he exploited the privileged status of legal proceedings to reissue both his defence speeches and the offending pamphlet, he did so initially only in an edition printed in his phonetic alphabet. Imprisonment had also brought an end to his bookselling business, and he very soon was forced to resume work as a number carrier. This, though, gave him the chance to hawk his pamphlets round the capital's workshops in the course of his deliveries. He also supplemented his income by taking in bookbinding at his new home in Princes Street, Soho. It was 1807 before he was again able to resume bookselling on a permanent basis, from 'a sort of caravan' stationed usually in Oxford Street or, more enterprisingly, in Parliament Street, Westminster.

Information concerning Spence's life in these years lacks the clarity of the Corresponding Society period. Among his known associates were several activists from the latter, notably Jonathan Panther, a member of Horne Tooke's circle; George Cullen, a friend of Thelwall and Hardy; and Thomas Evans, formerly secretary to the Society. Several others in Spence's circle had, like Evans, connections with the United Englishmen and other conspiratorial groups. Regular meetings of the Spenceans were being openly advertised by 1807, and in 1812 a formally constituted society was established 'at the Sign of the Fleece' in Little Windmill Street, Soho. Thomas Preston, whose radical career was to extend almost to the end of the Chartist period, was among the first to join. Probably the veteran Maurice Margarot was also a member. He had recently returned from serving a sentence of transportation in Australia and his *Proposal for a Grand National Jubilee* (1812) clearly revealed the influence of Spencean ideas. Some connection with a conspiratorial project – 'The Patriots' – during the following year also seems likely. It was proposed that Margarot, on behalf of this group, would make a clandestine trip to France in order to persuade Napoleon to invade Britain and restore the Saxon constitution. Besides Margarot, those involved included Thomas Hardy and a newcomer to London radical circles, Arthur

Thistlewood. The spy Edwards, who exposed the Cato Street conspiracy, recalled being introduced to the latter by Spence at about this time [Hone (1982) 233–4].

The activities of the radical underworld in the winter of 1812–13 are opaque in the extreme; but, as had happened ten years before, an increase in conspiratorial activity paralleled a surge of interest in Spence and his ideas. Three pamphlets of *Spence's Songs* were issued about this time, along with numerous other broadsides and ephemera. This flurry of Spencean publishing is particularly notable for two reasons. First, it reveals an undiminished determination on Spence's part to extend the circulation of radical ideas as widely as possible; and, about this time also, government informers reported an epidemic of Spencean graffiti around London. Second, in these popular publications Spencean ideology was further refined: 'shipping, Collieries, Mines and many other Great Concerns (which cannot be divided) can yet be enjoyed . . . in Partnership' [*Spence's Songs*, pt 3 (1812?)]. This programme of popular education was extended by the commencement, in 1814, of a new periodical imitative of *Pigs' Meat*, the *Giant Killer or Anti-Landlord*. Only two or three issues appeared, however, before Spence died on 1 September 1814 from a bowel complaint. His funeral at the New Burial Ground, Hampstead Road, brought the society he had founded into the public eye for the first time. The cortege was followed 'by a numerous throng of political admirers. Appropriate medallions were distributed, and a pair of scales preceded his corpse, indicative of his views' [HO 42/68, 18 Sep 1814]. William Snow, one of the most revolutionary of the Society of Spencean Philanthropists in the ensuing years, gave the graveside oration.

There is remarkable unanimity of opinion about Spence's character among those who knew him well. Men as diverse as Place, Cobbett and Bewick all spoke with warmth, even affection, for a person they nevertheless recognised as intolerant of criticism. 'He was above either concealment or disguise', recalled Place, 'and could not in any way compromise his opinions. He spoke his words freely without regard to the words he used or the person to whom he addressed them, and, notwithstanding that he was seldom intentionally uncivil, he was frequently when opposed not a little offensive' [BL Add. MS 27808, fo. 123]. Spence remained dedicated to revolutionary reform in spite of a life dogged by career disappointments, a brief first marriage and an unhappy second one, frequent poverty, and disabilities of speech and bearing consequent on a stroke suffered in the prime of life. He may have lacked the tact for compromise, but he left a legacy of ideas disproportionate both to the size of his following and the ephemeral nature of much of his published output. Though his work, unlike that of Paine and Hodgskin, went unpublished after his death, Spence's contribution to agrarian thought was one of substance, vitality and longevity. Out of the Society of Spencean Philanthropists emerged a cadre of dedicated propagandists, notably Thomas Evans in the years immediately after Spence's death, and subsequently Allen Davenport and George Petrie. The latter, who wrote (1833–4) under the pseudonymn of 'Agrarius' in the lively Ultra-Radical weekly the *Man*, had been on the fringes of the Spencean circle in the post-war years. Another significant factor in ensuring that agrarianism remained high on the radical agenda in the 1820s and 1830s was the disproportionately large number of ex-Spenceans who belonged to key labour organisations in those decades, among them the London Co-operative Society, the British Association for Promoting Co-operative Knowledge, and the National Union of the Working Classes.

In the absence of any reprinting of Spence's work, this assimilation of Spenceanism into radicalism through interpersonal connections was especially important: its function is most evident in the fact that the young G. J. Harney was introduced to Spence through Davenport. Because this, rather than the printed word, was the process by which Spence's posthumous influence was sustained, an acquaintance with his ideas on the part of many important figures can only be inferred. For example, Owen's only reference to Spence is in an illuminating anecdote about a mistaken stranger to whom he had been talking for some three hours during a coach journey: 'I am sure you are Spence, or else Owen' (this was in

1819); but a close acquaintance with Spencean thinking can reasonably be inferred from Owen's remarks on property in his *Revolution in the Mind and Practice of the Human Race* (1849). Likewise, certain phrases of Bronterre O'Brien, and his interest in the idea of parochial self-government in the late 1830s suggest that he knew Spence's ideas in some detail: again, Davenport's biography of 1836 may have stimulated this. Beyond the Chartist period, Spence's advocacy of the case for common ownership of the soil was a bench-mark to which a variety of reformers referred, including E. Belfort Bax, Ebenezer Howard and Henry George. The last-named owed his knowledge of Spence to H. M. Hyndman, who had virtually rediscovered him through a copy of *The Meridian Sun of Liberty* in the British Museum Reading Room. At George's insistence, Hyndman republished this 'practical and thoroughly English proposal for the nationalisation of the land' [*Nationalization of the Land in 1775 and 1882* (1882) 4]. It was the first of three important late nineteenth-century reissues of the Newcastle lecture, and reappraisals of Spence's thought, Hyndman being followed by the English Land Restoration League in 1896 and by the ILP's paper *Labour Leader* in 1900. In labelling Spence one of the 'precursors of Henry George and the single tax', these generalisations offered an unfairly restricted interpretation of Spence, but they ensured that, even at the close of the nineteenth century, Spence's ideas remained a central element of continuity in the agrarian tradition within the labour movement.

Writings: There is no comprehensive bibliography of Spence's writings. A nearly complete listing can be found in O. D. Rudkin's *Thomas Spence and his Connections* (1927), but there are divergencies of title and date between this and other catalogues, of which the most important are those of Goldsmiths' Library, London Univ. and the BL. The following list, including additional works located by the present author, represents a reassessment of publication dates. The list is divided into two parts: (1) traced writings and (2) writings known to have been published by Spence but not traced.

(1) Traced Writings: *The Grand Repository of the English Language* ... (Newcastle upon Tyne, 1775); *Real Reading made Easy: or foreigners' and grown-up persons' pleasing introductor to reading English* ... (Newcastle upon Tyne, 1782) 6 pp.; *A Supplement to the History of Robinson Crusoe* (standard English and phonetic eds, Newcastle upon Tyne, 1782); *Pronouncing and Foreigners' Bible* [1792?; a fragment only in BL Add. MS 27808, fo. 249]; *The Case of Thomas Spence, Bookseller ... to which is added an Extract of a Letter from His Grace the Duke of Richmond* ... [conventionally dated 1792 but believed to be 1793] 16 pp.; *The Case of Thomas Spence ... to which is added the Affecting Case of James Maccuddy, a Native of Ireland who was committed to Clerkenwell Bridewell for distributing Certain Seditious Papers, where he died in a Few Days* (1793) 16 pp.; *The Rights of Man, as exhibited in a Lecture read at the Philosophical Society in Newcastle, to which is now first added an Interesting Conversation between a Gentleman and the Author on the Subject of his Scheme with the Queries sent by the Rev. Mr J. Murray to the Society in Defence of the Same*, 4th ed. (1793) 40 pp.; (ed.) *One Pennyworth of Pig's Meat or Lessons for the Swinish Multitude* (undated, unnumbered weekly parts, 1793–5; 2nd ed. 1795; 3rd ed. 1796) [the later editions were titled *Pigs' Meat*]; *Copy of Thomas Spence's Commitment for High Treason* [broadside] (1794); letter in *Morning Chronicle*, 18 Dec 1794; *To the Public* [handbill] (1794); *Burke's Address to the 'Swinish Multitude'* [broadside] [1795?]; *The Coin Collector's Companion: being a descriptive alphabetical list of the modern provincial, political, and other copper coins* (1795) 50 pp.; *The End of Oppression, or a Quartern Loaf for Twopence: being a dialogue between an old mechanic and a young one concerning the establishment of the Rights of Man*, 1st ed. (1795) 7 pp., 2nd ed. (1795) 12 pp.; *A Letter from Ralph Hodge, to his Cousin Thomas Bull* [1795?] 12 pp.; letter in *Morning Chronicle*, 3 Jan 1795; *The Meridian Sun of Liberty, or the Whole Rights of Man displayed and most accurately defined in a Lecture read at the Philosophical Society in Newcastle on the 8th of November 1775, for printing of which the*

Society did the Author the Honour to expel him. To which is now first prefixed, by way of preface, a most important dialogue between the citizen reader and the author (1796) 12 pp.; *The Reign of Felicity, being a Plan for civilizing the Indians of North America; without infringing on their National or Individual Independence, in a Coffee House Dialogue, between a Courtier, an Esquire, a Clergyman and a Farmer* (1796) 12 pp.; *A Fragment of an Ancient Prophesy, relating, as some think, to the Present Revolutions [being the Fourth Part of the End of Oppression]* (1796) 12 pp.; *Spence's Recantation of the End of Oppression* [1796?] 4 pp.; *The Rights of Infants; or the Imprescriptable Right of Mothers to such a Share of the Elements as is Sufficient to enable them to suckle and bring up their Young, in a Dialogue between the Aristocracy and a Mother of Children, to which are added by way of Preface and Appendix Strictures on Paine's Agrarian Justice by T. Spence* . . . (1797) 16 pp.; *The Constitution of a Perfect Commonwealth: being the French Constitution of 1793, amended, and rendered entirely conformable to the Whole Rights of Man,* 1st ed. (1798) 18 pp., 2nd ed. with a Preface showing how to study Politics (1798) 24 pp.; *The Restorer of Society, to its Natural State, in a Series of Lectures to a Fellow Citizen with a Preface, containing the Objections of a Gentleman who perused the Manuscript, and the Answers by the Author* (1801) 41 pp.; *The Important Trial of Thomas Spence for a Political Pamphlet intitled 'The Restorer of Society to its Natural State' on May 27th 1801, at Westminster Hall, before Lord Kenyon and a Special Jury* (phonetic ed., 1803; 2nd ed., in standard English, 1807); *Something to the Purpose: a receipt to make a Millenium or Happy World, being extracts from the Constitution of Spensonia* [1805?] [a broadside of which there were earlier eds – possibly in 1803]; *Spence's Miscellanies: 'a new and infallible way to make peace' and 'Jubilee Hymn'* [broadside] [1812?]; *Spence's Songs: part the first* [1812?]; *Spence's Songs: part the second* [1812?]; *Spence's Songs: part the third* [1812?]; (ed.) *Giant-Killer and Anti-Landlord,* nos 1 (6 Aug 1814) and 2 (14 Aug 1814); *The Nationalization of the Land in 1775 and 1882. Being a lecture delivered at Newcastle-on-Tyne, by Thomas Spence, 1775,* repr. and ed. with Notes and Introduction by H. M. Hyndman (1882) 18 pp. [For other repr. writings of Spence, see **Sources** below].

(2) Untraced Writings: *Lecture to Newcastle Philosophical Society* (1st ed., 1775); *Repository of Common Sense and Innocent Amusement* (Newcastle upon Tyne, 1775); *Poor Man's Advocate* (2nd ed. of 1775 lecture); *Teacher of Common Sense* (1779); *Rights of Man in Verse* (1783); *Eye-salve* (1794); *Dictionary of the Spensonian Language* (1797); *Constitution of Spensonia* (1st ed. [1798?]; 3rd ed. 1803); *Important Trial of Thomas Spence* (1st standard English ed. [1804/5?]); *World turned upside down* (1805); (ed.) *Giant-Killer,* no. 3 (20 Aug 1814).

Sources: (1) MS: PRO, Kew: HO 42/136; HO 42/168; HO 42/156, 18 Sep 1814; HO 119/1, fos 39–41. PRO, Chancery Lane: PC 1/23/A38, 2/140; TS 11/939/3362, 951/3494, 953/3497, 955/3499, 958/3503, 959/3505, 956/3510A. BL, Dept of MSS: Add. MS 27808, fo. 138 ff.; Place papers, 'Collection for a Memoir of Thomas Spence', Add. MS 16922, fo. 152. 3. BL, Reference Division: MS note to a copy of Spence's *The End of Oppression* (1795), 1389 C 12; and MS note (George Cullen) to a copy of Spence's *Important Trial* (1807), 900 H 24 (i). BLPES: letter from Hone to Place, 6 Nov 1830, bound in with volume of Spencean tracts, R(SR) 422. Tyne and Wear Archives Department, Newcastle upon Tyne: Newcastle Common Council minute books, 4 Apr 1779 and 17 Dec 1787. Private Coll.: Hack MSS, letter from John Bewick to Thomas Bewick, 9 Apr 1788 [repr. in the 1975 ed. of *Thomas Bewick's Memoir . . . written by himself,* ed. I. Bain].

(2) Theses: T. M. Parssinen, 'Thomas Spence and the Spenceans: a study of revolutionary Utopianism in the England of George III' (Brandeis PhD, 1968); F. J. G. Robinson, 'Trends in Education in Northern England during the 18th Century: a biographical study' (Newcastle PhD, 1972); O. A. Smith, 'Politics of Language, 1790–1818' (Birmingham PhD, 1980); M. S. Chase, 'The Land and the Working Classes: English agrarianism *c.* 1775–1851' (Sussex DPhil., 1985).

(3) Other: *Newcastle Weekly Chronicle*, 9 July 1774, 25 Nov 1775 and 7 Dec 1787; *Newcastle J.*, 28 Oct 1775; J. Murray, *Impartial History of the Present War in America* (1778); *Newcastle Courant*, 12 Jan 1782; *Proceedings of the Friends of the Liberty of the Press* (1793); *Rules and Regulations to be observed by the Members of the Loyal Lambeth Association* (1794); *Report of the Committee of Constitution of the London Corresponding Society* [published by Spence himself in 1794] 8 pp.; *Trial of Thomas Hardy for High Treason*, vol. *1* (1794); *Morning Chronicle*, 3 Jan 1795; *Gentleman's Mag.*, Apr 1797, Jan, Feb, Mar and Sep 1798; *At a Meeting of the Real Friends to Truth, Justice and Human Happiness, it was resolved that the Principles of Citizen Spence's Theory of Society are as Immutable and Unchangeable as Truth and Nature on which they are built* [broadside] (18 Mar 1801); *Annual Register*, 13 June 1801; T. Evans, *A Humorous Catalogue of Spence's Songs* [1812?]; *Suitable Companion to Spence's Songs* [1812?]; M. Margarot, *Proposal for a Grand National Jubilee* (Sheffield, 1812); [R. Southey], 'Parliamentary Reform', *Q. Rev.*, Oct 1816, 225–78; *Cobbett's Weekly Political Register 31*, no. 24 (14 Dec 1816); R. Malthus, *Essay on the Principle of Population*, 5th ed. (1817); [W. Hone], *Hone's Riots in London Part II* (1816) 2 pp.; T. Preston, *The Life and Opinions of T. Preston, Patriot and Shoemaker* (1817) 37 pp.; T. Evans, *A Brief Sketch of the Life of Mr Thomas Spence, Author of the Spencean System of Agrarian Fellowship or Partnership in Land* (Manchester, 1821) 24 pp.; *Newcastle Mag.* n.s. *1*, no. 3 (Jan 1821); ibid., no. 4 (Mar 1821); ibid. n.s. *10*, no. 2 (Feb 1831); [E. Mackenzie], *Memoir of T. Spence. From Mackenzie's History of Newcastle* (Newcastle upon Tyne, 1826, privately printed); E. Mackenzie, *A Descriptive and Historical Account of the Town and county of Newcastle upon Tyne . . .* (Newcastle upon Tyne, 1827); A. Davenport, *The Life, Writings, and Principles of Thomas Spence* [1836]; idem, *The Life and Literary Pursuits of A. Davenport . . . written by himself* (1845); *Northern Star*, 30 Aug 1845, 13, 20 and 27 Jan 1849; R. Owen, *The Life of Robert Owen, written by himself*, vols *1* (1857) and *1A* (1858) [a supplementary appendix to vol. *1*] (repr. NY, 1967); T. Bewick, *Memoir of Thomas Bewick, written by himself* (1862; ed. with an Introduction by I. Bain, 1975; repr. with corrections, 1979); H. M. Hyndman, *Historical Basis of Socialism* (1883); J. Clephan, 'Thomas Spence', *Monthly Chronicle of North Country Lore and Legend 1*, no. 7 (Sep 1887) 296–302; J. Atkins, *The Tradesmen's Tokens of the Eighteenth Century* (1892); R. Welford, *Men of Mark 'twixt Tyne and Tweed*, vol. *3* (1895); F. Verinder, *Land for the Landless: Spence and 'Spence's Plan' (1775)*, with neo-Spencean Appendix compiled by J. Morrison Davidson (English Land Restoration League, 1896) 19 pp.; R. S. Watson, *The History of the Literary and Philosophical Society of Newcastle upon Tyne* (1897); J. M. Davidson, *Concerning Four Precursors of Henry George and the Single Tax . . .* (*Labour Leader* Publishing Dept, [1899]); H. S. Foxwell, Introduction to A. Menger, *The Right to the Whole Produce of Labour* (1899); E. Howard, *Garden Cities of Tomorrow* (2nd ed., 1902; later eds); G. Adler, 'Der ältere englische Sozialismus und Thomas Spence', in Thomas Spence, *Das Gemeineigentum am Boden* (Leipzig, 1904); H. George, 'Science of Political Economy', *Complete Works*, vol. 6 (1904) 185; A. W. Waters, *Notes gleaned from Contemporary Literature etc. respecting the Issuers of the 18th Century Tokens struck for the County of Middlesex* (Leamington Spa, Warwicks, 1906); R. Dalton and S. Hamer, *The Provincial Token Coinage of the 18th Century illustrated*, 3 vols (1910–18); A. W. Waters, *Trial of Thomas Spence in 1801 . . . also a Brief Life of Spence and a Description of his Political Token Dies* (Leamington Spa, Warwicks, 1917); *The Pioneers of Land Reform*, ed. with an Introduction by M. Beer (1920); O. D. Rudkin, *Thomas Spence and his Connections* (1927; repr. NY, 1966); G. R. Geiger, *The Philosophy of Henry George* (NY, 1933); M. Beer, 'Thomas Spence', *Encyclopedia of the Social Sciences*, vol. *15* (1934) 293–4; J. Eayrs, 'The Political Ideas of the English Agrarians, 1775–1815', *Canadian J. of Economic and Political Science 18* (1952) 287–302; A. W. Waters, *Notes on Eighteenth Century Trade Tokens* (1954); 'Land Nationalisation in Britain', *Our History 8* (1957); M. Roe, 'Maurice Margarot: a radical in two hemispheres, 1792–1815', *Bull. of the Institute of Historical Research 31* (1958)

68–78; D. Abercrombie, 'Forgotten Phoneticians' in *Studies in Phonetics and Linguistics* ed. D. Abercrombie (1965) 45–75; 'Selected Writings of Thomas Spence, 1750–1814', ed. with an Introduction by P. M. Kemp-Ashraf, Supplement to *Life and Literature of the Working Class: essays in honour of William Gallacher*, ed. P. M. Kemp-Ashraf and J. Mitchell (Humboldt Univ. Berlin, 1966) 271–354; C. Brunel and P. M. Jackson, 'Notes on Tokens as a Source of Information on the History of the Labour & Radical Movement. Part I', *Bull. Soc. Lab. Hist.*, no. 13 (Autumn 1966) 26–36; E. P. Thompson, *The Making of the English Working Class* (1963; 2nd ed. 1968); F. G. Black and R. M. Black, *The Harney Papers* (Assen, 1969); R. H. Thompson, 'The Dies of Thomas Spence', *British Numismatics J. 38* (1969) 126–63; idem, 'Additions and Corrections', ibid. *40* (1971) 136–8; R. Watkinson, 'Thomas Bewick, 1753–1828', *Luddites and Other Essays* ed. L. M. Munby (1971) 11–32; T. M. Parssinen, 'Thomas Spence and the Origins of English Land Nationalization', *J. of the History of Ideas 34* (1973) 135–41; S. Pierson, *Marxism and the Origins of British Socialism* (1973); A. F. Shields, 'Thomas Spence and the English Language', *Trans of the Philological Society for 1974* (1975) 33–64; T. R. Knox, 'Thomas Spence: the trumpet of jubilee', *Past and Present*, no. 76 (1977) 75–98; H. T. Dickinson, *Liberty and Property: political ideology in eighteenth-century Britain* (1977); T. M. Parssinen, 'Thomas Spence', *Biographical Dictionary of Modern British Radicals*, vol. *1*, ed. N. J. Gossman and J. O. Baylen (Brighton, 1979) 454–8; R. A. Franklin, 'Thomas Spence: the poor man's advocate', *Bull. of the North East Labour History Society*, no. 14 (1980) 1–18; J. Newmark, 'Tokens as Documents of the Industrial Revolution', *History Workshop J. 9* (Spring 1980) 129–42; E. and R. Frow, 'Charles Pigott and Richard Lee: radical propagandists', *Bull. Soc. Lab. Hist.*, no. 42 (Spring 1981) 32–5; G. Claeys, 'Four Letters between Thomas Spence and Charles Hall', *Notes and Queries 226* (Aug 1981) 317–21; S. Matszuka, 'Thought and Behaviour of Thomas Spence, 1750–1814: his millennialism and the English radicalism in the 1790s', *Seiyo-Shigaku* (1981); idem, 'Changing Views of Thomas Spence, 1750–1814: from radicalism to millennialism', *Shigaku-Zasshi* (1981); R. S. Neale, *Class in English History, 1680–1850* (Oxford, 1981); H. T. Dickinson, *Political Works of Thomas Spence* (Newcastle upon Tyne, 1982); R. A. Franklin, 'The Political Ideas of Thomas Spence', *J. of Local Studies 2*, no. 1 (Spring 1982) 42–56; J. A. Hone, *For the Cause of Truth: radicalism in London 1796–1821* (Oxford, 1982); *Pig's Meat: the selected writings of Thomas Spence, radical and pioneer land reformer, with an introductory essay and notes*, ed. G. I. Gallop (Nottingham, 1982); J. Barrell, *English Literature in History, 1730–1780: an equal, wide survey* (1983); M. Thale, *Selections from the Papers of the London Corresponding Society, 1792–1799* (Cambridge, 1983); P. M. Kemp-Ashraf, *The Life and Times of Thomas Spence* (Newcastle, 1983). OBIT. *Morning Post*, 10 Sep 1814; *Courier*, 12 Sep 1814; *Gentleman's Mag.*, Sep 1814, 300.

MALCOLM CHASE

See also: Allen DAVENPORT; Thomas EVANS; *Thomas HODGSKIN; †Robert OWEN; Thomas PRESTON.

STOKES, Richard Rapier (1897–1957)
BUSINESSMAN, LAND TAX ADVOCATE, AND LABOUR MP

Richard Stokes was born at Streatham, London, on 27 January 1897. He was the second son and fifth child in a family of eight children. His father, Philip Folliott Scott Stokes, was a barrister, and his mother, Mary Fenwick Rapier, belonged to the family which founded, with a Ransome, the Ipswich engineering firm of Ransomes and Rapier. Richard Stokes's grandfather had read theology at Cambridge, was much influenced by the Tractarian movement, and had been received into the Catholic Church. The young Richard therefore went to Downside School, where he was head of school and was prominent on the cricket and football fields. In 1915 he entered the Royal Military Academy and was commissioned in the Royal Artillery. He served on the Western Front, and retired as a Major in 1919 with an MC and bar, and a Croix de Guerre. Like so many of his contemporaries, he returned to civilian life with a deep horror and hatred of war.

On leaving the Army, Stokes entered Trinity College, Cambridge, where he took an engineering degree and gained a Rugby blue. He once played at Twickenham for England against the New Zealand All Blacks. He entered an engineering firm for experience, and in 1925 moved to the family business, of which he became managing director at the age of thirty. It was in the 1920s that he became converted to the ideas of Henry George – through Mr Charles Crompton, a business colleague – and Stokes remained for the rest of his life an ardent advocate of the taxation of land values. He published a pamphlet, *The Rating of Site Values* in 1955. Until the middle 1930s Stokes was mainly concerned with the direction of the family firm, a position which involved a good deal of international travel, especially in the Middle East. In 1937 he was decorated by King Fuad of Egypt with the Order of the Nile for his work on irrigation. Stokes joined the Labour Party some time in the mid-1930s. At the general election of 1935 he contested Central Glasgow as a Labour candidate but was defeated. When Abyssinia was invaded in 1935, Stokes telegraphed his protest to his Italian agent and cancelled all business with the Italian Government. In 1938 he won a notable by-election victory in his home town of Ipswich when he defeated Henry Willink, converting a 7250 Conservative majority into a Labour majority of 3161. Stokes retained the seat for the rest of his life.

Stokes's election material indicated his views at this time. He argued for a strong League of Nations and attacked the Government for being weak, vacillating and cowardly in the face 'of the empty blusterings of Fascist aggressors ... they have let down the name and reputation of Britain; they have seriously endangered my great ideal – a world free from war with trade barriers down and universal peace supreme and secure – a world where none dare wage war'. And he ended by extending his attack to the 'equal bankruptcy of decision and foresight' in domestic affairs.

Stokes had been an executive member of the League of Nations Union, and at this time he was on the Committee for Civil and Religious Peace in Spain. There was, however, no mention of Spain or the Spanish Civil War in his last election paper, produced just before voting day (Wednesday 16 Feb 1938). A year before, Stokes had suggested that his firm should make armaments at cost price, but the offer was rejected and his maiden speech in the House of Commons took up this and related issues in a Defence debate on 7 March 1938. Stokes began by stating his preference for the abolition of the private manufacture of armaments, or, if that could not be done, for the abolition of profit in their production. He referred to his firm's offer the previous year, and then proceeded to give a detailed statement of the cost and profit situation in the manufacture of shells. It was an impressive performance and was warmly commended by Winston Churchill, who followed him in the debate.

During the war years Stokes worked closely on the parliamentary back-benches with Aneurin Bevan, Sydney Silverman, Frank Bowles and others of the Labour Left in maintaining a vigorous critique of the policies of the Coalition Government. It involved much unpopularity with the leadership of his own Party and on one occasion Stokes was 'carpeted' by Attlee for voting against the Government after a debate on the conduct of the war. The small group of critics on the Labour back-benches were also severely criticised by most of the press. A. J. Cummings, a Liberal commentator in the liberal *News Chronicle* felt it necessary in 1942, in the course of an attack on Nye Bevan, to quote a rhyme sent him by A. A. Milne, the creator of Christopher Robin:

Goebbels, though not religious, must thank Heaven
For dropping in his lap Aneurin Bevan;
And doubtless, this pious mood invokes
An equal blessing on the trusty Stokes.
How well each does his work as a belittler
Of Germany's arch-enemy! Heil Hitler!

[Quoted in Foot (1962) 385]

In 1943 or 1944 – the date appears to be uncertain – Stokes went with Bevan to interview the Prime Minister of Eire, de Valera, in an unsuccessful attempt to obtain the use of Irish ports for British shipping. In the last years of the war Stokes opposed the practice of saturation bombing, and vigorously criticised the policy of 'unconditional surrender'. When the end of the war came, Stokes easily retained his seat in the general election of 1945. His election material emphasised what a conscientious and hardworking constituency MP he had been, and his majority was 8119 in a three-cornered fight. Stokes was thought too individualistic for Government office, and for the whole of this first Parliament he pursued his own concerns while in general sympathy with the Labour Government. He protested – in the end successfully – against the detention of German prisoners of war and opposed much of the policy in the British Occupied Zone of Germany. He was a notable critic of the American loan to Britain and of American international policies, not least of Bretton Woods; and, as would be expected from his pre-war career, he was an opponent of Government policy in Palestine, being single-mindedly pro-Arab. He was also against the increase in conscription.

After the 1950 general election, Attlee offered the Ministry of Works to Stokes. He proved an efficient administrator and became responsible for the completion of the Festival of Britain exhibition on London's South Bank. On one occasion he personally addressed strikers at the Festival site. In April 1951 Stokes was made Lord Privy Seal and in July Minister of Materials. Aneurin Bevan and Harold Wilson resigned from the Cabinet in April 1951 and Stokes had the responsibility of trying to prove them wrong over the rearmament issue. In the last months of the Labour Government, before the general election of late October 1951, Attlee sent Stokes on an emergency mission to Iran. A major crisis had developed with the new Prime Minister, Mossadeq, who was demanding nationalisation of the Anglo-Iranian Oil Company. Stokes went out in August 1951 and was recalled on 6 September with no agreement in sight. He reported to Attlee that the most sensible policy was to deal generously with the Iranians and to conduct serious negotiations with Mossadeq.

With the defeat of the Labour Party in October 1951, Stokes became shadow defence minister. By this time his political attitudes had changed somewhat. He had become increasingly anti-Communist, an attitude which he shared with very large numbers of his colleagues in the PLP, and on domestic issues he also moved towards the right. In the contest for the leadership of the PLP in December 1955 he supported Herbert Morrison, and, in a letter signed by ten MPs, including D. Grenfell, D. T. Jones, C. W. Key, C. L. Hale, F. Messer, W. Monslow, E. Shinwell and S. Viant, made a direct request to Aneurin Bevan to stand down. The letter asked Bevan to withdraw in order to allow Morrison to be returned unopposed, provided other candidates also withdrew [Williams (1979) 365–6]. Shinwell and Stokes were among Morrison's most active supporters and were probably the originators of the letter. Bevan, who welcomed the letter, immediately announced that he would withdraw providing Gaitskell did the same. But Gaitskell had no intention of resigning, and Stokes, although he gave his vote to Morrison, later supported Gaitskell. In the year following Stokes was severely criticised for supporting Hartley Shawcross in opposition to further nationalisation, for which Stokes was firmly opposed by the Left in his own constituency party.

Stokes had a motor-car accident on 21 July 1957. He was returning from London and, as he crossed a bridge, the car hit flood water and turned over. Stokes fractured six ribs and complications set in with the development of thrombosis. He died on Saturday 3 August 1957 at his home in London, leaving a net estate of £76,659.

Stokes never married, although he was engaged, briefly, twice. He was a very sociable man, a member of at least two London clubs, White's and the Garrick, and a great host at his house in 29 Palace Street, SW1. The comments about him all stress his personal warmth and selflessness. John Strachey wrote of his 'immense, unchecked flow of generosity to friend and opponent alike' [*Times*, 6 Aug 1957]. He was somewhat erratic in his political judgements at all stages of his career, and he was fearless in saying exactly what he thought, whatever embarrassment might be caused. What was never in doubt was his moral courage. His Catholicism did not often appear directly in his political life, although he never shirked the issue of Catholic schools. Without ostentatious piety Stokes throughout his adult life was a deeply religious man. It was from his religion (and also from his experiences in the trenches) that his devotion to the Labour ideals of social justice and international brotherhood came. He was completely loyal to the Labour Party, which he saw as a broad church with room for a wide spectrum of opinion sharing common ideals. There were two church requiems following his death: the first at Westminster Cathedral and the second at the Church of St Pancras, Ipswich. Stokes was buried at Withermarsh Church, near Ipswich.

Writings: (1) MS: Notes, diaries and letters in the Stokes papers, Bodleian Library, Oxford [see C. Hazelhurst and C. Woodland, *A Guide to the Papers of British Cabinet Ministers 1900–1951* (1974) 140–1]; correspondence between R. R. Stokes and A. W. Madsen (secretary of the UCTLV), 1946–51, relating to the rating of site values and the payment of development charges, UCTLV, London. (2) Other: election addresses 1938 and 1945, in *Ipswich Rapier*, Feb 1938 and July 1945 [copies in *DLB* Coll.]; *Some Amazing 'Tank' Facts. Sensational Indictment by a Serving Officer. The Truth about Guns and Armour* [1945]; 'British Zone' [letter], *New Statesman and Nation 32* (21 Dec 1946) 463; *Anglo-American Financial Discussions* [House of Commons speech, 13 Dec 1945] [1946] 5 pp.; *Gold-Dollar Price* [House of Commons speech, 30 Nov 1949] [1950] 6 pp.; *The Rating of Site Values* (LP Viewpoint Pamphlet, no. 2: 1955) 32 pp.

Sources: (1) MS: see **Writings** above. (2) Other: *Times*, 7 and 8 Oct 1935, 22 Apr 1937, 11 Jan 1938 and 9 Aug 1957; *Daily Worker*, 11 Feb 1938; *Hansard*, 1938–57, esp. 7 Mar 1938, 13 Dec 1945 and 30 Nov 1949; G. D. H. Cole, *A History of the Labour Party from 1914* (1948); *Illustrated London News*, 11 and 18 Aug 1951; *WWW* (1951–60); E. Shinwell, *Conflict without Malice* (1955); H. Dalton, *The Fateful Years: memoirs 1931–45* (1957) and *High Tide and after: memoirs 1945–60* (1962); E. J. Meehan, *The British Left Wing and Foreign Policy* (New Brunswick, NJ, 1960); M. Foot, *Aneurin Bevan*, vol. *1: 1897–1945* (1962); M. Sissons and P. French, *Age of Austerity 1945–51* (1963); B. Donoughue and G. W. Jones, *Herbert Morrison: portrait of a politician* (1973); P. Norton, *Dissension in the House of Commons* (1975); P. Williams, *Hugh Gaitskell* (1979); *The Backbench Diaries of Richard Crossman*, ed. J. Morgan (1981); K. Harris, *Attlee* (1982); Ipswich LP, *Ipswich Constituency LP Jubilee Year Book 1923–1983* [1983] [16 pp.]; E. M. S. Evans, 'In Old Age 1895– ' [typescript, 1985] 22 pp. Biographical information: Bryan Sadler, Warwick Univ. Personal information: Mrs Esther Evans, Feering, Colchester, Essex, sister; I. Grimwood,

Ipswich, Suffolk. OBIT. *Observer*, 4 Aug 1957; *Manchester Guardian*, 5 Aug 1957; *Times*, 5, 6, 8 and 14 Aug 1957; *Suffolk Chronicle*, 9 Aug 1957; *Land and Liberty*, Sep 1957, 125.

JOHN SAVILLE

See also: Frederick VERINDER.

THRING, Lillian Mary (1887–1964)
FEMINIST AND SOCIALIST

Lillian Thring – she always referred to herself by her surname – was born on 8 December 1887 at 15 Seaton Street, St Pancras, London, the daughter of Benjamin William Harris, a marine-store keeper, and his wife Elizabeth (née Tasker). Her forename, Lillian, was more commonly spelt as Lilian. As a young woman in the first decade of the century, she became a militant suffragette, and for a time worked as a shop assistant in Selfridges in Oxford Street. In 1911 she went to Australia. What prompted her to leave England is not known, but she continued her involvement with the women's movement in Melbourne (in March 1913 she was living at 6 Murray Street, Melbourne) and it was there that she seems first to have made contact with Socialist ideas and an active Socialist movement. In her papers there is a newspaper cutting of a talk she gave to a Socialist audience at the Gaiety Theatre, Melbourne, on 18 May 1913. Her subject was 'White Slaves and Militant Suffragettes', a theme she often returned to in later life. While in Australia she joined the International Workers of the World (IWW) and met the man who became her first husband. He was a white South African who apparently had no connection with the Socialist movement and she followed him in 1913 to the Sudan where they were married and where he worked as a postal official. In 1915 Thring returned to England, with one baby, and pregnant with a second (which she lost), but her husband died; and for most of the war years she was not active in politics.

It was towards the end of the war that Thring became involved in politics again, especially with Sylvia Pankhurst's Workers' Socialist Federation, which combined her own preoccupations with the women's movement and revolutionary Socialism. She also joined the North London Herald League. By 1918 she was a frequent speaker on left platforms, and became active in the 'Hands off Russia' campaign. In 1920 she became a foundation member of the Communist Party, and joined the Islington branch. By December of the same year she had become active in the unemployed movement, and she took a leading part in the seven-week occupation of the Essex Road Library, Islington, which attracted national publicity. This was in November 1920. In the spring following (April 1921) a conference was called establishing the National Unemployed Workers' Movement, with a national administrative council, and with Jack Holt, Percy Haye and Wal Hannington as chairman, secretary and organiser respectively. The conference met at the International Socialist Club, City Road, Hoxton, on 15 April 1921. Its central demand was 'Work or Full Maintenance at Trade Union Rates of Wages'. Six months after the founding conference 140 committees were affiliated, and its fortnightly paper, *Out of Work*, of which Lilian Thring was the first editor, reached a sale of 50,000.

The early years of the 1920s witnessed a great deal of militant activity on the part of the unemployed, including the campaign of the Labour councillors on Poplar Borough Council to equalise the rates between London boroughs. Thring was active throughout. She was a member of a small group who occupied a piano factory in St Pancras, the purpose being to try to persuade the workers to refuse to work overtime and the management to concede a wage increase. Factory occupations by the unemployed on these terms were a quite common agitation at this time. By the late summer of 1921 Thring was getting publicity in the national and London press as 'Red Rosa', the mystery woman with hypnotic eyes who was behind the unemployed agitation. At a very large unemployed demonstration on 4 October

1921, Thring was arrested and bound over to keep the peace in the sum of £5; and later, in December, she was arrested and fined for an article in *Out of Work* for alleged incitement to disaffection of the police. In August 1922 Thring lived in Huntingdon Street, Caledonian Road, Islington; her house was raided by the police, who found two German machine guns. Thring was charged with their possession and taken into custody, but later acquitted. While she was being held, the headquarters of the Finsbury unemployed was named Thring Hall in her honour.

In October 1922 she became a sub-agent for Shapurji Saklatvala, who successfully contested John Burns's old seat of Battersea North. Saklatvala was a Parsee, a member of the CPGB, but on this occasion stood as a Labour Party candidate, supported by the Battersea Trades and Labour Council (and backed by the NEC of the Labour Party). Among the active supporters of Saklatvala in this election was Mrs Charlotte Despard [*DLB* 6, 237].

In 1923 Thring left the Communist Party because of disagreements with its policies and attitudes. In March 1924 she was much involved in a famous by-election in the Abbey division of Westminster when Fenner Brockway was the Labour candidate and Winston Churchill campaigned as an independent anti-Socialist (designated Constitutionalist). Churchill lost by forty-three votes to the official Tory candidate and Brockway's large Socialist vote in Westminster caused a considerable sensation [Brockway (1942) 152–6]. Thring's own activity also attracted the attention of Labour Party organisations, and in 1927 she was approached by Westminster Labour Party to stand as their parliamentary candidate. She refused, as she was to refuse all subsequent offers.

During the 1926 General Strike she was a member of the Battersea Council of Action. She had moved to Battersea in 1923, or thereabouts, and in 1927 she married again and used her husband's name of Harvey. At other times she used either her maiden name or the pseudonyms of Thurston and Martin. The couple lived in Sonderburg Road, Islington. Thring began to be involved in the Women's Co-operative Guild, and continued her work among the unemployed. In the early 1930s she was active in anti-Fascist politics in north London, and she was also engaged in union organising, especially among women shop-workers. In 1934 she vigorously supported the successful resolution at the annual confer-ence of the Women's Co-operative Guild in favour of the legalisation of abortion. This resolution, passed with a miniscule minority against and 1340 votes in favour, was a landmark in the history of the campaign. Thring also won a resolution at this same conference on white slave traffic, 'asking the Government to provide adequate protection immediately, for girls and women going to unknown posts in London and other big cities, against the increased menace of the white slave traffic, and also urging for more stringent measures in dealing with those who destroyed the morality and purity of women and of the country' [*Co-op. News*, 16 June 1934].

In 1935 Thring moved to Ashingdon, near Rochford in Essex, with her companion George Tasker (no relation of her mother's family). They continued to live together until her death. Tasker was a men's hairdresser, and a member of the ILP. Thring herself at this time joined the ILP, and when the Second World War began in 1939 – to which she was in political opposition – she helped men on the run from conscription. When the war ended Thring was a strong supporter of the local squatters' movement, and she became secretary of the Rochford branch of the Agricultural Workers' Union, which she helped build into a strong local force. Between 1946 and 1948 she was an ILP councillor. During this period she led the homeless into the occupation of five army camps and a municipal building in Rochford. In 1950 she joined the Labour Party.

Lilian Thring died on 13 March 1964 after a long illness which had left her bedridden for her last three years. She was survived by her three children, Cyril, Nina and Rhona, and by George Tasker.

Sources: *Co-op. News*, 16 and 23 June 1934 [Co-op. congress reports]; F. W. Stella Browne, A. M. Ludovici and Harry Roberts, *Abortion* (1935); W. Hannington, *Unemployed Struggles 1919–1936* (1936); F. Brockway, *Inside the Left* (1942); N. Branson, *Poplarism 1919–1925* (1979); P. Kingsford, *The Hunger Marchers in Britain 1920–1940* (1982); K. Weller, *'Don't be a Soldier!': the Radical Anti-War Movement in north London 1914–1918* (1985). Biographical information: Mrs G. F. Lonergan, Co-op. Union Library, Manchester. Personal information: George Tasker, Ashingdon, Essex. OBIT. *Co-op. News*, 11 Apr 1964.

KEN WELLER

See also: *Wal HANNINGTON; †Shapurji Dorabji SAKLATVALA.

TURNER, Sir Ben (1863–1942)
TEXTILE WORKERS' LEADER AND LABOUR MINISTER

Turner was born at Boothhouse, Austonley, a hamlet standing above the Holme Valley about two miles from Holmfirth, Yorkshire, on 25 August 1863. His mother's family were small farmers and cloth-weavers; his father worked a woollen power-loom in a weaving shed. Family tradition held that a great uncle had been tried at York Assizes for his part in a Luddite rising. Both Turner's parents, Jonathan and Emma (née Moorhouse), were interested in politics. At the time of his birth their sympathies were with the Northern states in the American Civil War; in domestic politics they were advanced Liberals and readers of *Reynolds's News* and the *National Reformer*. 'My father', Ben Turner wrote in his autobiography, 'was a follower of Ernest Jones ... and would sing us Ernest Jones' "Chartist Hymn"' [Turner (1930) 28]. Jonathan Turner had a great fondness for dialect verse, which, along with his radicalism, he passed on to his son. He was also an active trade unionist and in 1872 was involved in an eleven-week strike in favour of a uniform piecework scale for weavers.

The family lived decently but poorly. Before he was ten Ben earned a few pence a week by helping an aunt, who was a hand-loom weaver, and by feeding a local farmer's pigs. At ten he began as a half-timer, working in a mill for 2s 6d a week. He had begun his education in a dame school before going to a Church school, at which Bible-reading had such import that he claimed to have twice read the entire Bible while there. At thirteen he worked in the mill full time, earning five shillings a week and receiving 2d of it as spending money. In 1877 the family moved to Huddersfield. There he became a piecer in a woollen mule-gate, with a weekly wage of nine shillings [ibid., 45–6].

Though only six miles from Austonley, Huddersfield provided Turner with a changed outlook. His father took him and his two brothers to the well-known Secular Sunday School. There he heard Charles Bradlaugh, then at the height of his influence, deliver lectures on both secularism and social questions. Among the other speakers he recalled were Annie Besant, Harriet Law, G. J. Holyoake, Charles Watts and Edward Aveling. The school also put on classes in singing and elocution and arranged debates and recitations. Besides learning to speak in public, Turner became an avid reader of newspapers and attended evening classes at the Mechanics' Institute. At eighteen he became secretary of the Secular Sunday School, but he did not reject religion as decisively as some free-thinkers. When he married at the age of twenty-one it was at the Unitarian Church, Huddersfield (on a Sunday, to avoid missing work). His wife, Elizabeth Hopkinson, was a cotton-spinner. They had five children, all girls. Turner was a resolute opponent of compulsory vaccination and received a number of fines when he refused to have his daughters vaccinated. He was involved in the local campaign to allow conscientious objectors exemption from having their children vaccinated and on several occasions appeared in the magistrates' court on behalf of parents. Later both Ben and Elizabeth Turner became magistrates, and it was said that between them they signed thousands of forms exempting parents who did not wish their children to be vaccinated [*Batley News*, 3 Oct 1942].

In 1882 Turner joined the Huddersfield-based Factory Operatives' Union, shortly after its revival as a 'fighting union'. In January 1883 he was elected as their delegate by the other workers in his weaving shed. Two months later the employers began a lock-out with a view to introducing a new scale of payments. The proposed scale amounted to a reduction in wages, particularly for women, but after eleven weeks the union was obliged to accept the employers' terms. In response to this Turner urged that lessons be learned from the organisation of the Lancashire cotton unions. He pressed his views on Allen Gee, the secretary of the West Riding of Yorkshire Power-loom Weavers' Association. This marked the beginning of a long working partnership between the two men. In 1886 Turner was made a member of the Weavers' Association's rules-revision committee, and in the following year he joined its executive committee. He was a delegate to the Huddersfield Trades Council and active in the eight-hour day agitation. Another interest was bimetallism, which involved him in the Trade Union Monetary Reform Association [for which see *DLB 3*, 83].

In November 1886 his workmates collected for him to visit London and report on the unemployment demonstration in Trafalgar Square; he also took the opportunity to see the Lord Mayor's procession in the morning and attend the theatre in the evening. The experience may have had an influence upon him, as he was for a time a member of the SDF; by his own account, he attended an SDF meeting in Oldham in 1887 [Turner (1930) 319] and in the same year H. W. Lee, the secretary of the SDF, wrote to him with advice about forming a local branch. At about this time local trade became depressed and in 1887 Turner was made redundant. He was, however, better fitted to face economic hardship than many workers: he was a teetotaller and believer in 'the duty each man owes to himself and family to make provision for sickness and unforeseen, but possible misfortunes' [ibid., 54–5]. Accordingly, he was a member of both the Manchester Unity of Oddfellows and the Royal Antediluvian Order of Buffaloes – bodies he praised for their comradely ethos as well as the friendly-society benefits they paid.

He had also developed an interest in journalism, which began through sending dialect poems and letters on political questions to the local press. From about 1886 he began to contribute to the *Cotton Factory Times*, and in 1889 he was offered a job in the projected *Yorkshire Factory Times*. He was then employed as an insurance agent and gladly accepted the post, which involved, in August 1889, a move to Leeds, where he worked under Joseph Burgess. The paper had a distinctly radical tone. Its contributors included Tom Maguire, Isabella Ford and Tom Paylor, whose accounts of working conditions, low wages and the autocratic behaviour of employers helped to prepare the ground for the newer labour politics. Turner, who wrote under the pseudonyms 'Mulegate Mussins' and 'Sweeper Up', was also active in recruiting trade union members. During the winter of 1890–1 he was much involved in the bitter Manningham Mills strike. It was a dispute that reverberated beyond the Bradford area, and for over four months Turner, Allen Gee and W. H. Drew were the 'strikers' triumvirate of leaders' [Pearce (1975) 57]. Though Turner concentrated on organising the textile workers, he also appeared on a variety of platforms. He was a member of the Leeds Socialist Party and the Leeds Trades Council. He spoke on behalf of the striking tailoresses of Leeds in 1889 and supported the gas workers in 1890. In his own words, he 'was young and active and in my element taking part in the advanced Labour and Socialist movement' [ibid., 79].

When on 11 November 1891, together with W. H. Drew, he gave evidence before the Royal Commission on Labour, he described himself as an employee of both the Batley district of the Yorkshire Weavers' Association and the *Yorkshire Factory Times*. In his evidence Turner stated that of some 13,000 workers in the district only about 1000 were in the union. Of these about 200 were men, the same proportion as in the trade as a whole. He believed that low wages were paid because of the large number of women workers. To A. J. Mundella's question 'where the women preponderate so largely the men are working at women's wages?', Turner replied 'Exactly' [Q. 5696]. He also expressed the view that it would be a good thing if the employers formed themselves into an association, as such a step would facilitate a greater uniformity of prices in the trade.

After about two years in Leeds, Turner moved in July 1891 to Batley, where he lived for the rest of his life. In his autobiography he gave the wish to live nearer the centre of the textile trade as a reason for the move, though it has been suggested he realised that in a smaller town he would be better able to pursue a career as a labour leader. If this did enter into his calculations the outcome must have been highly satisfactory to him, as, among other things, he was four times mayor of Batley (for three consecutive years, 1913–16, and in 1934–5) and eventually its MP. In 1896, at the opening of a new theatre, he apostrophised the town in a verse, the first eight lines of which indicate his civic pride and give a sense of his personal outlook:

Good old Batley! rich in story and song,
Improving, progressing as time rolls along;
A temple of Thespis created at last.
Good luck we all wish it; we glance at the past,
And the pages of history reveal to us all
That Batley was known to the great and the small.
More famous it grows, and to-night we proclaim
The honour, the glory, the worth of its name.

An inveterate versifier, he more often employed the dialect form, in which his homely philosophy of life received full play. His pieces were printed by local newspapers and some, such as 'Ther's now't but th' Workus, Lad', were issued as penny broadsheets.

Turner quickly became Batley's leading labour activist. His home was his workplace, for 'all the local Labour movements, both industrial and political' met there [Turner (1930) 162]. He was a founder of the Dewsbury Trades Council in 1891, the same year in which he became the first secretary of the Batley Fabian Society. In 1892 he was elected to the Batley School Board, and in 1893 to the Borough Council. He was present, as a delegate of the Batley Labour Party ('which always met at our house'), at the founding conference of the ILP in January 1893. At the 1894 conference of the ILP he seconded Leonard Hall's motion calling for closer co-operation between the ILP and the trade unions. This reflected his own career, which always combined both the political and industrial aspects of the labour movement.

He first attended the TUC in 1890, as a Leeds Trades Council delegate. Subsequently he became much involved in TUC activities. He spoke on numerous occasions, on such issues as the need for more factory inspectors (1893), Sunday working (1895), bimetallism (1899), a minimum wage (1913) and a national holiday for labour on 1 May (1919). In 1910 he was elected, with William Brace of the miners, as a delegate to the American Federation of Labor; but it was not until 1921 that he became a member of the General Council, on which he sat as a representative of the textile unions until 1928. He was TUC chairman in 1927–8.

At the local level, his main trade union work was in the textile trade. In 1892 he became secretary, at an initial salary of £12 a year, of the newly inaugurated Heavy Woollen District branch of the West Yorkshire Power-loom Weavers' Association; he was allowed one shilling a week office expenses, which went towards the upkeep of the front room of his house. By 1912, when he had done much to organise the trade, he was paid £2 a week. One of his main objects was to organise all grades of textile employees in the same union. He deplored the tendency of some groups, such as the spinners, to regard themselves as superior to less well-paid workers. Consequently he was particularly proud of his part in securing the 'willeyers' and fettlers' charter' in 1910, as hitherto these men, who did the hard preparatory work in woollen mills, had been among the least organised and lowest paid. One reflection of Turner's more open policy towards the less skilled was the change in the union's name to the General Union of Weavers and Textile Workers in 1900; in 1912 it became the General Union of Textile Workers. When the National Union of Textile Workers was formed in 1922 he became its president. He was also president, from 1917 to 1929, of the National Association of Unions in the Textile Trade. By 1919 his old paper the *Yorkshire Factory Times* had, under the title *Labour Pioneer*, become the official organ of the GUTW with Turner as its editor. As district secretary he arranged the purchase of social centres in Dewsbury and Batley; the latter served no alcohol, a restriction strongly approved of by Turner. His position was that, while he accepted the right of those who so wished to drink alcohol, teetotalism produced many benefits. He believed that Labour men and women knew how to enjoy themselves in a sober and sensible fashion, and that teetotallers were 'the jolliest of the lot' [ibid., 341]. This was certainly true of Turner personally; his fund of anecdotes and humorous dialect stories made him, in the words of the *Factory Times* (13 Mar 1910), 'the very soul of company'.

Unlike some of the Lancashire textile leaders, those of Yorkshire generally favoured the abolition of the half-time system. In November 1908 Turner gave evidence to this effect to an Inter-Departmental Committee sitting under the chairmanship of Charles Trevelyan. This was one of a number of occasions on which he appeared as a witness before official inquiries. He gave evidence to committees inquiring into fair wages and the truck acts, and was called before the Royal Commission on the Selection of Justices of the Peace. In July 1912 he was questioned with Allen Gee in the course of an inquiry, chaired by G. R. Askwith, into industrial agreements.

In common with many others, Turner was confused and saddened by the onset of war in 1914. At the congress of the Socialist International held at Basle in 1912 he had been among those labour leaders who pledged that they would call a general strike to prevent a European war. When the war began in August 1914, Turner, however, carried on his official duties as mayor of Batley. The account in his autobiography is somewhat equivocal, and on occasions Turner (who was writing in the late 1920s) sounded like a pacifist. He sat on the local tribunal concerned with objectors to military service and he wrote sympathetically about those with religious objections. He visited the battlefields of Flanders in January 1916, and accompanied the King and Queen on part of their visit to the West Riding in May 1918. In 1917 he was awarded the OBE.

Turner's support for the war was not unconditional. He was a Labour Party representative on the War Emergency Workers' National Committee and his political attitudes towards the conduct of the war seem to have hardened during its closing years. He was never a jingoist and he became increasingly convinced of the need to negotiate terms with Germany. Before the end of the war he had become a member of the Union of Democratic Control, although exactly when he joined is not known. In the Union's journal he wrote that the TUC of 1918 had shown the extent of support for peace by negotiations, and he ended with the declaration: 'Long live the Congress! Long live the "International"! Long live the Peoples' Party, and the Idealism of Peace by Reason!' [*U. D. C.*, Oct 1918, 269].

Alongside his trade union work, Turner was active in local and national politics. From 1893 until his death he sat on Batley Council; and from 1910 until 1942 he was a member of the West Riding County Council. He first tried to enter Parliament in 1906, when he was sponsored by the Heavy Woollen District Labour Representation Committee in a contest for the Dewsbury and Batley constituency, but he was defeated by Walter Runciman, the Liberal candidate. He made a second attempt for the same seat at a by-election on 23 April 1908, but his vote was slightly less than his poll in 1906. In December 1918 he contested the

Batley and Morley constituency, but was nearly 1500 votes behind the Liberal coalition candidate. He won this constituency in 1922, and again in 1923, but was defeated in the 'Zinoviev letter' campaign of October 1924. In 1929 he regained the seat, but was again defeated in the general election of October 1931. His parliamentary electoral history illustrates in microcosm the political problems confronted by the emerging Labour Party. Dewsbury and Batley, when he first fought the constituency in 1906, had a large number of miners on the register, an even larger body of male workers in the woollen industry, and a strong Catholic element among constituents. The Liberal tradition was strong and long-lasting [Pelling (1967) 300–1]. Turner chaired the Labour Party conference of 1912, held at Birmingham, and sat for eighteen years on the NEC.

In 1920 a British Labour Delegation went to Soviet Russia [for which see the **Special Note** below]. Ben Turner, representing the Labour Party, was chairman of the delegation, of which he gave some details in Chapter 18 of his autobiography. He had a private conversation with Lenin, which, according to his account, was mainly concerned with the question of violence in social change. 'Bloodshed is never justified', said Turner, to which Lenin replied, 'you will have bloodshed in England before you have a Socialist Government'. Turner added the comment, 'I was very much impressed with Lenin. He is one of the few big characters in the twentieth century. He created a new world and helped to destroy a wicked Russia' [Turner (1930) 220–1]. When Turner left Russia he was seen off personally by Chicherin, the Foreign Minister. They knew each other, having met at public meetings in England, and when Chicherin was in Brixton Gaol Turner had sent him books. Turner remained friendly towards the Soviet Union, and was always in favour of close diplomatic and trade relations.

He was on the General Council of the TUC for most of the 1920s, and in 1927–8 he was chairman: a position which involved him in the famous discussions with the employers known as the Mond–Turner talks. In his presidential address at the 1927 Edinburgh TUC, George Hicks made a public offer to British employers. Citrine suggested in the first volume of his memoirs that it was his initiative in the first place [(1964) 243–4] and on 23 November 1927 Sir Alfred Mond and twenty other signatories addressed a letter to the General Council of the TUC with the offer of a joint conference on industrial reorganisation and industrial relations. The first meeting was on 12 January 1928 at Burlington House, London, and a standing committee was appointed by the TUC to encourage future discussions. Arthur Cook violently opposed this new policy of 'Mondism', but he was in a small minority on the General Council [see *DLB 3*, 41]. There were sharp divisions on the employers' side, too [Middlemas (1979) 207 ff.] and the Mond–Turner initiative was largely ineffective, important only for the collaborationist attitudes that were exhibited among sections of business men as well as trade unionists; later initiatives were to be more productive.

It was probably Ben Turner's prominence during his year of office as president of the TUC that encouraged Ramsay MacDonald to offer him the position of Secretary for Mines in the second Labour Government, which took office in the summer of 1929. He was not regarded as a success in his department, and he was replaced at the end of a year, on the grounds of ill health, by Emanuel Shinwell. In 1931 he was knighted – he had been awarded the CBE the year previous – and for the remainder of his life he was on the margins of the labour movement. His role became that of the long-surviving pioneer, 'the grand old man of West Riding trade unionism' as he was sometimes acclaimed. With his full white beard he made a venerable figure and looked the part of a veteran leader. In 1930 he published his autobiography, *About myself*, a quite attractive volume especially useful for his early life, although, like so many memoirs of his time, its approach to the history of the labour movement was untheoretical and anecdotal, with the emphasis on the social advances that had been achieved during the writer's lifetime. Turner's lifelong moderation in industrial politics was emphasised in an interview he gave on becoming chairman of the TUC in 1927, in which he argued against the militant policy of 'always fighting' and for 'reasoning, argument, negotiation' [Tracey (1927) 293].

Turner maintained his friendship with Philip Snowden in spite of the events of 1931, and Snowden wrote the Preface to a volume of Turner's verses published in 1934. A year earlier he had retired from the presidency of the National Union of Textile Workers, but he continued as an alderman on the Batley and the West Riding councils, and as a magistrate. His wife, who had been an active suffragette, died in April 1939, and he himself on 30 September 1942, at his home in Batley. In the course of the funeral service, held at Batley Parish Church on 3 October, the Sermon on the Mount was referred to as his command-ments. After cremation his ashes were scattered over the family grave in Batley cemetery. His five daughters survived him. Turner's estate was registered as £400. Tributes emphasised his qualities of patience, courtesy and good humour. That in the annual report of the Labour Party noted how he had summed up his Socialism in a single verse:

God's been reit good and filled His world
Wi' baskets full to spare;
Ther's food and clothes an' ivvurything
If men 'ud nobbut share!

Writings: Evidence (with W. H. Drew) to R. C. on Labour, Group C, vol. I, 1892 XXXIV, Qs 5374–7 and 5667–842, to Departmental Committee on the Truck Acts, 1908 LIX, Qs 6767–7024; to Committee on Fair Wages, 1908 XXXIV, Qs 1264–443; and to Inter-Departmental Committee on Partial Exemption from School Attendance, 1909 XVII, Qs 1807–924; 'Should Half-Time Labour be abolished?', *Soc. Rev. 3* (1909) 19–24; *Dialect and other Pieces from a Yorkshire Loom* (Heckmondwike, Yorks, 1909); 'Profit-sharing: a splendid Huddersfield example', *Soc. Rev. 5* (1910) 267–71; evidence to R. C. on Selection of JPs, 1910 XXXVII, Qs 4824–95, and (with Allen Gee) to Industrial Council (Inquiry into Industrial Agreements), 1913 XXVIII, Qs 6819–7115; evidence to Departmental Committee on Juvenile Education in relation to Employment after the War, *Final Report*, vol. II 1917 XI, 39; *A Short Account of the Rise and Progress of the Heavy Woollen District Branch of the General Union of Textile Workers* (Dewsbury, Yorks, 1917); 'The Trades Union Congress and Peace', *U. D. C. 3*, no. 12 (Oct 1918) 269; *Short History of the General Union of Textile Workers* (Heckmondwike, Yorks, 1920); (with others) *British Labour Delegation to Russia 1920: Report* [1920]; 'Foreign Affairs and the Trades Union Congress', *Foreign Affairs 4*, no. 4 (Oct 1922) 87–8; *What is Socialism?: a symposium*, ed. D. Griffiths (1924) 77–8; 'A Labour View of the New Ministry', *Yorkshire Evening Post*, 30 Jan 1924; 'Don't be Downhearted: reminiscences of the past, faith and hope in the future', *Leeds Weekly Citizen*, 23 Apr 1926; 'The Factory Worker and Industrial Hygiene', *J. Royal Sanitary Institute 49* (Nov 1928) 286–90; *About myself 1863–1930* (1930); *Rhymes, Verses and Poems from a Yorkshire Loom* (Pontefract, Yorks, 1934). Turner had a regular column in *National Union of Textiles Monthly Record* [then *Quarterly Record* and finally *Record*] from its start in 1921 until his retirement in 1933.

Sources: (1) MS: Turner's scrapbook and miscellaneous papers, Huddersfield Local History Library; book of newspaper clippings on Turner and the National Union of Textile Workers, Dec 1932 to his retirement as president of the union in 1933, in papers of the Amalgamated Union of Dyers, Bleachers, Finishers and Kindred Trades, Bradford District Archives, 126 D77/136. (2) Other: *YFT*, 1889–1914, *Labour Who's Who* (1924 and 1927); 'Presentation to Councillor Ben Turner', *Reporter*, 21 May 1927; H. Tracey, 'An Apostle of Peace and Good Will', *Labour Mag. 6* (Nov 1927) 290–3; J. Johnston, *A Hundred*

Commoners (1931); 'Dialect Almanacks and Dialect Writers', *Trans Yorkshire Dialect Soc. 5* (1931) 9–13 [includes report of a lecture by Turner]; *WWW* (1941–50); W. Citrine, *Men and Work: an autobiography* (1964); *DNB* (1941–50) [by J. S. Middleton]; H. Morrison, *An Autobiography* (1960); H. A. Clegg *et al.*, *A History of British Trade Unions since 1889*, vol. *1: 1889–1910*, and (by Clegg alone) vol. *2: 1911–1933* (Oxford, 1964 and 1985); C. Cross, *Philip Snowden* (1966); H. Pelling, *Social Geography of British Elections 1885–1910* (1967); J. Waddington-Feather, 'Sir Ben Turner (1863–1942)', *Trans Yorkshire Dialect Soc. 12* (1969) 14–19; C. J. James, *M. P. for Dewsbury* (Brighouse, Yorks, 1970); M. Swartz, *The Union of Democratic Control in British Politics during the First World War* (Oxford, 1971); G. W. McDonald and H. F. Gospel, 'The Mond–Turner Talks 1927–33: a study in industrial co-operation', *Hist. J. 16* (1973) 807–29; C. Pearce, *The Manningham Mills Strike, Bradford, December 1890–April 1891* (Hull, 1975); J. Liddington and J. Norris, *One Hand tied behind us: the rise of the women's suffrage movement* (1978); H. F. Gospel, 'Employers' Labour Policy: a study of the Mond–Turner Talks 1927–33', *Business History 21* (1979) 180–97; R. K. Middlemas, *Politics in Industrial Society: the experience of the British system since 1911* (1979); *Who's Who of British Members of Parliament*, vol. *3: 1919–1945*, ed. M. Stenton and S. Lees (Hassocks, Sussex, 1979); J. Bornat, 'An Examination of the General Union of Textile Workers 1883–1922' (Essex PhD, 1980); J. A. Jowett and K. Laybourn, 'The Wool Textile Dispute of 1925', *J. of Local Studies 2*, no. 1 (Spring 1982) 10–27; K. E. Smith, 'Ben Turner', Ch. 4 of *West Yorkshire Dialect Poets* (Dialect Books, Wilsden, Yorks, 1982) 35–40; K. Laybourn and J. Reynolds, *Liberalism and the Rise of Labour* (1984); J. B. Hannam, 'The Employment of Working-Class Women in Leeds, 1880–1914' (Sheffield PhD, 1985). Biographical information: Dr J. Bornat, London; Mrs G. Snowden, Rotherham, Yorks; Dr C. Wrigley, Loughborough Univ. OBIT. *Batley News* and *Yorkshire Evening News*, 1 and 3 Oct 1942; *Huddersfield Daily Examiner,* 1 Oct 1942; *Yorkshire Observer*, 1 and 5 Oct 1942; *Daily Herald, Manchester Guardian, Yorkshire Post*, 2 Oct 1942; *Dewsbury Reporter*, 3 Oct 1942; *LP Report* (1943); *TUC Report* (1943).

DAVID E. MARTIN
BOB TURNER

See also: †William Henry DREW; Isabella Ormston FORD; †Allen GEE; and below: the British Labour Delegation to Russia, 1920.

The British Labour Delegation to Russia, 1920

The *Report* of the British Labour Delegation to Russia was dated July 1920 and signed by all members. Ben Turner, representing the Labour Party, was chairman of the group; Charles Roden Buxton and L. Haden Guest were joint secretaries; Margaret Bondfield, A. A. Purcell and H. Skinner represented the TUC, and Ethel Snowden, Tom Shaw and Robert Williams the Labour Party. The *Report* was also endorsed by R. C. Wallhead and Clifford Allen, who both accompanied the Delegation on behalf of the ILP. In an unofficial capacity Bertrand Russell also travelled with the Delegation.

The Delegation to Russia arose out of the campaign against the Allied military intervention against the Soviet Union. The agitation had been growing steadily in Britain throughout 1919. The 'Hands off Russia' movement had first appeared early in 1919 and was formally organised on a national basis in the late summer and autumn of that year. The Labour Party conference had met at Southport from 25 to 27 June 1919, and the chairman, J. McGurk, made the issue of intervention a central theme of his presidential address: 'We must resist military operations in Russia and the perpetuation of conscription at home.

There can be no peace so long as we continue to indulge in military adventures in Russia. Russia must be left free to work out its own political salvation...' [*LP Conference Report* (1919) 113].

The TUC held its annual conference three months later in Glasgow (8–13 Sep). A firm resolution on the Russian question was passed on 12 September with only one dissentient:

That this Congress, in view of the general desire of the country, and the repeated declarations of the Government prior to, during, and since the recent General Election, as reiterated to the deputation from the Parliamentary Committee which interviewed the leader of the House of Commons [Bonar Law] on the 22nd of May last, instructs the Parliamentary Committee to demand of the Government the repeal of the Conscription Acts, and the immediate withdrawal of British troops from Russia, and failing this, demands that a special Trades Union Congress be called immediately to decide what action shall be taken [*TUC Report* (1919) 333].

This resolution was moved by J. H. Thomas, the railwaymen's leader. The report of the deputation of the Parliamentary Committee was presented to a special TUC on 10 December 1919; and the conference demanded the right to send a delegation to Russia to make 'an independent and impartial enquiry into the industrial, economic and political conditions of Russia'. The composition of the delegation became a joint TUC–Labour Party affair, and it left England on 27 April 1920 and crossed the Russian–Estonian frontier on 10 May, arriving in Petrograd (now Leningrad) the following day. On the evening of 16 May the party left for Moscow, where it remained until 28 May. The delegation then went again by special train to Nijni-Novgorod, (as it was then spelt) where they embarked on the SS *Bielinsky* for the voyage down the Volga to Saratov. The weather was hot during the day and cold at night, and within twenty-four hours of leaving Nijni-Novgorod Clifford Allen, whose health had been seriously undermined by his experiences during the war [*DLB 2*, 3], became ill with pleurisy and pneumonia. At Saratov the majority of the party returned by train to Moscow, but Allen was too ill to be moved and Ethel Snowden, Bertrand Russell and Haden Guest remained on board as the boat continued the journey to Astrahkan on the Black Sea, and then back again to Saratov. By this time Allen had recovered sufficiently to return by a special railway coach. He was taken to a nursing-home at Reval in Estonia [Marwick (1964) Ch. 7]. The original party, who returned to Moscow, visited the Polish front near Smolensk, and reached England on 30 June 1920.

The *Report* consisted of a long agreed statement about conditions in Russia [pp. 5–27]; and there followed the greater part of the booklet which was made up of a large number of appendices. These included a series of official Russian statements, among them the Resolutions, in full, of the Ninth Congress of the Russian Communist Party (29 Mar–4 Apr 1920); then three critical statements – the first from L. Martov; the second a manifesto addressed to the British delegates by the Central Committee of the Social Revolutionary Party; and, third, a message from Kropotkin; and eleven separate reports from individual members of the delegation. These included App. XIII, 'Further Notes from the Diary of Margaret Bondfield'; App. XVI, 'Russian Militarism and the New Patriotism', by C. Roden Buxton and L. Haden Guest; App. XVII, 'The Blockade and its Effects', by Robert Williams; App. XXII, 'Visits to Educational Institutions', by L. Haden Guest. In an editorial note at the beginning of the *Report* Haden Guest noted that a large number of documents had been brought from Russia, and that those not published would be available at Labour Party headquarters for 'the use of accredited persons', but recent inquiries suggest these are not extant.

The Delegation's agreed *Report* covered, in summary form, almost all the social and political life of the Russian people. The privations and hardships were not underplayed, and on the issue of personal freedom the Delegation members were agreed that there was severe repression. The domination of the Communist Party was strongly emphasised. As will be noted below, the comments made by some individual members of the Delegation were a good deal more critical of the Russian system than the official *Report*, yet it could not be said that its approach was unrealistic or equivocal. What was important for the delegates' contemporaries, however, was the insistence that many statements about Russia in the West were thoroughly prejudiced and misleading; and that military intervention was a 'criminal folly' [p. 11].

Early in the *Report* the Delegation made its position clear on certain elementary matters:

We feel it necessary to begin by pointing out that most accounts of Soviet Russia which we had seen in the capitalist press of our own country proved to be perversions of the facts. The whole impression gained was of a different character from that presented by these accounts. We did not see any violence or disorder in the streets, though we walked about them freely at all hours of the day and night. We did not see people fall dead of starvation in the streets. We did not see any interference with the religious life of the people. We did not see any Chinese soldiers. We saw no evidence of extraordinary luxury on the part of the leading Commissars. We did not find that either women or children had been nationalised. We certainly did witness a widespread breakdown in the transport system with deplorable economic consequences, and we saw terrible evidences of under-feeding and suffering. These points have been dealt with, however, in the Reports already issued by the Delegation on the iniquitous policy of intervention and blockade [p. 6].

The reports 'already issued' by the Delegation were two interim reports. The first, undated, was probably published in the first days of July, very soon after the return of the Delegation to Britain, and was an appeal for the immediate ending of intervention and the blockade; and the second interim report, dated 7 July 1920, was a further appeal for an immediate peace and for free economic intercourse for Russia in order that the enormous privations and suffering of the Russian people could be alleviated. Ben Turner, the Delegation's chairman, told the Labour press on his return to England that the press stories of the Russian attempt to hoodwink the delegates were 'nonsense' and that it was not true that the country was in a condition of anarchy [White (1979) 14].

While the Delegation had been in Russia a number of important developments had occurred. The most dramatic was the *Jolly George* incident. On the day the Polish capture of Kiev was announced (10 May 1920) dockers refused to load munitions for Poland on to a ship bound for that country; and their action was supported by F. Thompson, the London District secretary of the Dockers' Union. It was an action that followed weeks of rank and file political activity in the London docks [for which see Pollitt (1940) Ch. 7]. A week after the incident Ernest Bevin, at a national conference at Plymouth of the Dockers' Union, moved a resolution which read:

this Triennial Conference makes emphatic protest against the export of arms to Poland and other Border States, which enables the Junkers of these countries to set the people at war in the interests of their financial paymaster. It congratulates our London members in refusing to have their labour prostituted for this purpose, and calls upon the whole of the movement to resist their labour being used to perpetuate these wicked ventures [*Daily Herald*, 19 May 1920; Hutt (1937) 36 ff.; Graubard (1956) 92–3; Bullock (1960) 133–4].

On 22 May 1920 there was published a manifesto, signed by a number of well-known trade union leaders, asking for a national conference to consider a twenty-four-hour strike in support of peace with Russia. Among the signatories were Robert Smillie (president, Miners' Federation of Great Britain), Tom Mann (general secretary, Amalgamated Society of Engineers), John Bromley (general secretary, Associated Society of Locomotive Engineers and Firemen), Alex Gossip (general secretary, Furnishing Trades Association), and A.

G. Cameron (general secretary, Amalgamated Society of Carpenters and Joiners). The appeal attracted considerable attention, and the 'Hands off Russia' Committee distributed several hundred thousand leaflets reproducing the text of the appeal. When the British Labour Delegation returned from Russia at the end of June there was, therefore, already a very considerable political ferment in the country; and its own *Report* was an important factor in the extension and hardening of public opinion against military intervention. The nationwide agitation continued until the Council of Action was formed in August 1920, and the Coalition Government began its retreat from direct military intervention [Calhoun (1976) 32 ff.].

This *Report* of the British Delegation had probably the most important impact of any single publication in the shaping of attitudes towards Russia in the matter of war and intervention. Three of the delegates produced their own books, although none had the merits of the *Report* itself. Ethel Snowden published *Through Bolshevik Russia* in September 1920 and it was reprinted twice before the end of the year. The book, which was not very well written and thoroughly hostile to Russia and to its Communist leaders, was critically received in ILP circles. As Graubard commented, 'The work actually merited slight attention; contradictory and simple, it revealed the operation of an undistinguished mind loosed from its parochial moorings' [(1956) 218]. Haden Guest, who, from internal evidence, had much to do with the shape and content of the official *Report*, published in 1921 *The Struggle for Power in Europe 1917–1921*, a text which covered conditions in Russia, Poland, Czechoslovakia, Austria, Hungary, Rumania and Bulgaria. On the Russian question Guest argued that the Bolsheviks had failed to convert the peasantry to their programme of agrarian reform; and he attacked the dictatorship of the Communist Party. Guest repeated his criticism in Chapter 4 of a small book he wrote in 1929 when he himself had renounced the Socialist ideal (*Is Labour leaving Socialism?*).

The third publication arising out of the 1920 Delegation's visit was Bertrand Russell's, *The Practice and Theory of Bolshevism* (1920). Before the visit Russell had written an article for the New York *Liberator* supporting the Bolshevik Government; and he entered Russia, so one of his biographers says, 'in a mood of unqualified optimism' [Clark (1978) 466]. He was granted a private interview with Lenin. Russell's book, which was written as soon as he returned to England, was severely critical of Russia and the Bolsheviks, much more so than the day-to-day journal he made during his journey [ibid., 467]. It has remained a well-known statement of the anti-Bolshevik position. [See also his *Autobiography*, vol. *2* (1968) 101–10].

Other relevant writings by members of the British Delegation are Margaret Bondfield's *A Life's Work* (1949), Ben Turner's *About myself* (1930), an unpublished manuscript by Clifford Allen [Allen Papers; in part printed in Marwick (1964) 62–4] and M. Gilbert's *Plough my own Furrow* (1965).

The two ILP members of the Delegation, R. C. Wallhead (ILP chairman) and Clifford Allen, had as their main purpose a discussion with the representatives of the Third International. At the 1920 conference of the ILP the central issue had been the relationship of British Socialism to the Bolsheviks; and the conference decided by 529 votes to 114 to end the ILP's connection with the Second International, and to inquire about the possibilities of affiliating to the Third International. Wallhead and Allen were therefore instructed to begin talks and they had a series of informal discussions with Radek, Lenin and other leaders. Allen was also granted a private interview with Lenin. Before the two ILP members left Moscow they submitted in writing twelve specific questions to the EC of the Communist International. Wallhead brought the International's answers back to London and they were published in a pamphlet, *The ILP and the 3rd International* (1920). The developments which followed the rejection by the ILP of the conditions laid down by the CI are related in a number of sources [see Dowse (1966) Ch. 4; Braunthal (1967); and Kendall (1969)].

Sources: (1) Reports: LP conferences, 1919 and 1920; TUC conferences, 1919 and 1920; ILP conferences, 1920 and 1921; *British Labour Delegation to Russia 1920: Report*, ed. L. Haden Guest [1920].
(2) Newspapers and Periodicals: *Times*, 10 June and 8 July 1920; *Labour Leader*, 17, 24 June and 22 July 1920; *Workers' Dreadnought*, 19 June and 3 July 1920; *Call*, 1 July 1920; *Plebs 12*, no. 11 (Nov 1920) 214–16.
(3) Other: *AEU Monthly J. and Report*, Aug 1920, 99–111; *British Labour Delegates in Red Petrograd* (Petrograd, 1920) 30 pp.; B. Turner, *About myself* (1930); C. Malleson [Colette], *After Ten Years* (1931); E. Goldman, *Living my Life* (1932); W. P. Maddox, *Foreign Relations in British Labour Politics* (Cambridge, Mass., 1934); M. E. Harrison, *Born for Trouble: the story of a chequered life* (1936); W. P. and Z. K. Coates, *Armed Intervention in Russia 1918–1922* (1935); A. Hutt, *The Post-War History of the British Working Class* (1937); A. Balobanova, *My Life as a Rebel* (1938); H. Pollitt, *Serving my Time: an apprenticeship to politics* (1940); W. P. and Z. K. Coates, *A History of Anglo-Soviet Relations* (1944); G. D. H. Cole, *A History of the Labour Party from 1914* (1948); S. R. Graubard, *British Labour and the Russian Revolution 1917–1924* (Cambridge, Mass., 1956); A. Marwick, *Clifford Allen: the open conspirator* (1964); R. E. Dowse, *Left in the Centre: the Independent Labour Party 1893–1940* (1966); R. P. Arnot, *The Impact of the Russian Revolution in Britain* (1967); J. Braunthal, *History of the International 1914–1943* vol. 2: *1914–1933* (1967); B. Russell, *Autobiography of Bertrand Russell*, vol. 2 (1968); W. Kendall, *The Revolutionary Movement in Britain 1900–21: the origins of British Communism* (1969); S. White, 'Labour's Council of Action 1920', *J. Cont. Hist. 9*, no. 4 (Oct 1974) 99–122; D. C. Calhoun, *The United Front: the TUC and the Russians 1923–1928* (Cambridge, 1976); R. W. Clark, *The Life of Bertrand Russell* (Penguin ed., 1978); S. White, *Britain and the Bolshevik Revolution: a study in the politics of diplomacy, 1920–1924* (1979); M. H. Cowden, *Russian Bolshevism and British Labor, 1917–1921* (NY, 1984). Biographical information: E. and R. Frow, Working Class Movement Library, Manchester.

JOHN SAVILLE

VERINDER, Frederick (1858–1948)
CHRISTIAN, RADICAL AND SINGLE-TAXER

Frederick Verinder was born on 14 October 1858 at Bethnal Green, in the East End of London. His father, of the same name, was a journeyman dyer and his mother was Eliza (née Haggis). The family had at some point migrated to London from Wiltshire, where Frederick Verinder's grandfather had been an agricultural labourer.

Frederick Verinder was educated at Parmiter Street School, near his home, and between 1872 and 1877 he was a pupil teacher at a National (i.e. Church of England) school in Bethnal Green. It was there that he met Stewart Headlam, who had been appointed a curate in the parish. Headlam quickly made friends with the pupil teachers – including Verinder – and this was the beginning of a very close relationship between the two men until Headlam's death in 1924. When the latter established the Guild of St Matthew in 1877 Verinder became its organising secretary. From 1878 to 1883 he was a master at Tottenham Grammar School while also studying at London University for a science degree under T. H. Huxley, who thought very highly of him, but Verinder decided to work in the field of social reform. He was out of employment for a time in the 1880s, but in 1881 he had read Henry George's

Progress and Poverty and he became passionately interested – as did Headlam – in land reform.

In 1883 there was formed the Land Reform Union and in the following year it was taken over by the Georgeites and changed its name to the English Land Restoration League (ELRL), following the example of the Scottish Land Restoration League, organised in late February 1884 [Barker (1955) 401–2]. Verinder became the secretary of the ELRL. This was in May 1884. Earlier in the same year, in January, he had become sub-editor of the *Church Reformer*, the monthly organ of the Guild of St Matthew.

Verinder became personally acquainted with Henry George in 1884, and he retained enormous respect for him. With the election of Verinder to the secretaryship of the ELRL the general level of agitational activity around the land question increased rapidly. Verinder was an outstanding organiser; his ideas were the ideas of others, but he proved a very effective publicist, with a clear and forthright style. The ELRL published a statement of aims in 1885:

> to abolish all the taxation which now bears on labour, improvement and thrift; to increase taxation on land until the whole annual value is taken for the public benefit. As a first step to this end, we shall demand of our representatives in Parliament a re-imposition of a tax of 4 shillings in the £ on the current value of land, irrespective of whether it is rented, used or kept idle by the holder [*Annual Report* of the EC of the ELRL, quoted in Ward (1976) 117].

The Land Restoration League was a proselytising body of considerable vigour. In its first years it especially directed its efforts towards the radical working men's clubs of London; leaflets were distributed by the hundred thousand and innumerable meetings were held [Ward (1976) 225]. The municipal reform movement in London was already under way, and as it gained strength and power from the middle of the decade the land-tax reformers decided to concentrate their efforts within the reform organisations. In 1887 there was established the United Committee for Advocating the Taxation of Ground Rents. It was a joint venture between the ELRL and the London Municipal Reform League. Verinder became the organising secretary and Sir Arthur Hobhouse (1819–1904), who was raised to the peerage in 1885, became the president [ibid., 228]. In the next year, 1888, Verinder acted as election agent for Headlam when the latter was elected as part of a Liberal–Socialist coalition to the London School Board for Hackney and Bethnal Green. It was an extremely lively election, with Headlam advocating School Board employment at trade union rates; free schooling for children; and the abolition of religious teaching in schools. He came fourth out of five successful candidates, and his victory was regarded as a considerable triumph for the radical cause.

The English Land Restoration League was much involved in the first LCC elections of 1889, distributing a quarter of a million copies of J. F. Moulton's pamphlet *The Taxation of Ground Values* [Ward (1976) 228–9]. In this period, too, Verinder also edited the *Democrat* (previously edited by William Saunders from 1884) and he also attended the First International Congress on the Land Question, held in Paris in June 1890, acting as secretary of the English delegation [ibid., 237].

During the early years of the 1890s the ELRL developed its Red Vans campaign. This was an attempt to politicise the English farm workers. The *Annual Report* for 1891 described the procedure:

> The van arrives at each village early in the forenoon and is stationed at some prominent position. A notice of the meeting is exhibited – the meeting being also advertised by placards in advance – and some large pictures representing the workings of landlordism are shown. A thorough distribution of suitable leaflets is made in the village. The meetings

are held in the open air at 7.30 and are attended by from 100 to 300 labourers [quoted in Douglas (1976) 106].

The main object of the campaign was general politicisation, and there were only a few attempts at establishing local branches. The campaign began in Suffolk and later extended to other parts of Southern England. There was inevitably a good deal of opposition from the local gentry and their supporters, and village innkeepers and shopkeepers were warned by local land agents against any indication of help. There were some examples of physical violence by roughs paid for ultimately by the landed classes; and the Liberty and Property Defence League, which had been formed in 1882 [Soldon (1974) 208], was especially active in countering the ideas of the land-taxers.

Verinder remained a radical Georgeite all his life, and his fundamental beliefs in the correctness of Henry George's analysis of society, and of the remedies he proposed, never wavered. While all single-taxers wanted a national solution to the problems of society, the configuration of British politics, in the last twenty years of the nineteenth century, meant that the issues of land values and their taxation were especially discussed and debated in local terms. The municipal land-tax movement began in Glasgow and London at the end of the 1880s and then spread rapidly throughout the rest of Britain. The issues became increasingly concentrated upon the right of local authorities to raise at least part of the rates by a tax on land values. In July 1895 a vote of 25 to 24 allowed Glasgow to petition Parliament in favour of a local tax, and in the municipal elections of 1896 forty-nine out of seventy-five Glasgow councillors were in favour of the land tax.

Glasgow was the most vigorous and most successful centre of the whole movement, but London, after the establishment of the LCC, remained also a major region for the agitation; and the urban land question was near the centre of the radical movement. Sidney Webb, for instance, was on the general committee of the ELRL from 1892 to 1898, while Tom Mann served from 1892 to 1897. Throughout the 1890s and down to the general election of 1906 the political pressures for the local taxation of land values continued to grow and expand. Verinder was inevitably involved on a day-to-day basis in this remarkably practical activity, and he was also a leading publicist for the League's ideas. By his radical contemporaries he was always reckoned, for example, to have got the better of Herbert Spencer in the attack upon land radicalism which Spencer carried on for most of the 1890s.

Verinder's energies were tightly stretched following the Liberal victory of 1906, when a substantial number of Government back-benchers supported the taxation of land values, and when parliamentary legislation seemed possible. In 1907 the English, Scottish and Irish Leagues came together to form the United Committee for Taxation of Land Values (UCTLV), and their support was especially given to the parliamentary Campaign Committee. The principle of land values taxation had now moved into the centre of domestic politics. In the April 1909 Budget Lloyd George included a tax of 20 per cent on unearned increment derived from the sale of land, and a further small levy on the capital value of underdeveloped land and minerals. A national valuation of land was to be undertaken immediately. The struggle over what became known as the 'People's' Budget, although its provisions fell very short of what the land-taxers had been advocating, occupied much of British politics until the passing of the Parliament Bill in the House of Lords in April 1911.

The years of the First World War saw the beginning of the end of the Liberal Party, and a parallel decline of the land-tax agitation. Verinder, like Stewart Headlam, was an interesting political mixture of radical Liberal and Labourist. They were both against land nationalisation, and in Verinder's case the experience of war considerably strengthened his prejudices against state control. A letter of 16 November 1918 sent by Verinder on behalf of the English League for Taxation of Land Values (ELTLV) to the Prime Minister and other leading politicians provided a lengthy argument in favour of taxation as against nationalisation; and it was this attitude, now much hardened, that alienated many within the growing

Labour Party from the pre-war radical movement. The history of the inter-war years is one of steady decline of land-tax ideas and their political expression, with the Labour Party, now the main Opposition Party, showing decreasing interest in the land-tax solution to the country's problems.

Stewart Headlam died in 1924, Verinder having acted as his election agent right through Headlam's political career in local government [Binyon (1931) 151]. Verinder himself continued to direct the organisational affairs of the League until within two years of his death on 19 November 1948 at the age of ninety. Verinder had married when quite young, and there were nine children of the marriage. His wife died before any of the children were grown up, and according to the testimony of one of his daughters, Frances [*Land and Liberty*, Jan 1949, 13], he was a loving and caring father. He remained a practising Christian all his life. He left effects valued at £2203.

Writings: Apart from his contributions to the periodicals with which he was directly associated, the *Church Reformer* and the *Democrat*, Verinder wrote a large number of pamphlets, conference papers, and articles and letters to the national press. Some of these works were reprinted in pamphlet form. The following list includes his three books and other principal writings, in addition to some from the organ of the single-tax movement, *Land Values*. This was originally published by the Scottish Land Restoration Union under the title of *Single Tax* in 1894; from 1903 it was retitled *Land Values* and from 1919 it was published as *Land and Liberty*. 'The Bible and the Land Question' [from a lecture], *Church Reformer* 4, no. 7 (15 July 1885) 152–4, no. 8 (15 Aug 1885) 177–9, and no. 9 (15 Sep 1885) 200–1; *Free Schools: a plea for a national system of schooling* [repr. from the *Church Reformer*] [1985] 13 pp; 'An Enquiry into the Extent, Causes and Effects of the Depopulation of the Rural Districts of England: X. The Causes of Rural Depopulation', *Church Reformer 11*, no. 1 (Jan 1892) 13–17, and no. 2 (Feb 1892) 38–42; *Land for the Landless: Spence and 'Spence's Plan' 1775, with neo-Spencean Appendix* compiled by J. Morrison Davidson (ELRL, 1896) 19 pp., 'A Just Basis of Taxation', *CWS Annual* (1900) 285–310 [repr. 1902 and 1907, 24 pp.]; *The Land Question, chiefly in its Relation to Labour and Taxation* (Manchester, 1901) 23 pp.; *The Great Problem of our Great Towns* [on the taxation of land values] (1908) 24 pp.; *Free Trade and Land Values* [paper read at the International Free Trade Congress, Antwerp] (*Land Values* Publication Dept, Glasgow and London, [1910]) 16 pp., new ed. (ELTLV, 1916) 20 pp.; *'Form IV'. What next?* (UCTLV, 1911) 28 pp.; *My Neighbour's Landmark: short studies in Bible land laws* ... (1911; reprints: Joseph Fels Fund, Cincinnati, 1915; Henry George Foundation, 1940; Memorial ed., 1950); 'The Rating of Sewers', *Land Values*, Jan 1912, 195; 'Housing and Destitution: I. About a conference', ibid., July 1912, 57–8; *Land, Industry and Taxation* (1914); *Land, Labour and Taxation after the War* (1915; 2nd ed. 1916) 16 pp; *'German Efficiency' versus British Liberty* (ELTLV, 1915) 16 pp.; *Methods of Land Nationalisation: a brief critical examination of some proposals of the Land Nationalisation Society* (ELTLV, 1918) 16 pp.; 'Taxation of Land Values' [copy of letter sent to the Prime Minister and Messrs Asquith, Bonar Law, Dillon, Henderson and Addison (Minister of Reconstruction), dated 16 Nov 1918, by Verinder on behalf of the committee of the ELTLV: copy in *DLB* Coll.]; *Is there a Cure for Unemployment?* (ELTLV, 1921) 16 pp.; *The Crying Injustice of our Rating System and the Remedy* (ELTLV, 1933; 2nd ed. 1937) 16 pp.; *Land and Freedom* (1935).

Sources:(1) MS: Papers relating to the various land taxation and nationalisation societies are in the UCTLV Coll., Institute of Agricultural History, Reading Univ.; see also C. Cook, *Sources in British Political History 1900–1951*, vol. *1* (1975) 272–3.
(2) Theses: Ping-ti Ho, 'Land and State in Great Britain 1883–1910' (Columbia PhD, 1951); A. J. Peacock, 'Land Reform 1880–1919: a study of the activities of the English Land

Restoration League and the Land Nationalisation Society' (Southampton MA, 1962); S. B. Ward, 'Land Reform in England 1880–1914' (Reading PhD, 1976).

(3) **Periodical Press:** *Church Reformer*, 1882–95; *Democrat*, 1884–90, then *Labour World*, 1890–1; *Single Tax*, 1894–1902, then *Land Values*, 1903–19, then *Land and Liberty*, 1919 to date.

(4) **Other:** H. George, *Progress and Poverty* (1879; later eds); *Mr Herbert Spencer and the Land Restoration League: correspondence ... mostly re-printed from the London Daily Chronicle, Aug, Sep and Oct 1894* (Land Restoration Tracts, no. 1: 1894) [microtext in Brynmor Jones Library, Hull Univ.]; *Labour Annual* (1895) 191; *Socialism and the Single Tax: a debate between Mr C. W. Wright (representing the English Land Restoration League) and H. Quelch of the SDF at Trades Hall, Birmingham, 20 June 1896* [1896] 16 pp.; W. D. P. Bliss, *Encyclopedia of Social Reform* (1897); *Labour Prophet*, Feb 1898, 159; 'Land Values – why and how they should be taxed', Ch. 5 of J. C. Wedgwood, *Essays and Adventures of a Labour M. P.* (1924) 71–115; F. G. Bettany, *Stewart Headlam* (1926); R. A. Sawyer, *Henry George and the Single Tax: a catalogue in the New York Public Library* (NY, 1926); D. O. Wagner, *The Church of England and Social Reform since 1854* (NY, 1930); G. C. Binyon, *The Christian Socialist Movement in England* (1931); C. A. Barker, *Henry George* (Oxford, 1955); E. P. Lawrence, *Henry George in the British Isles* (East Lansing, Mich., 1957); J. Saville, 'Henry George and the British Labour Movement: a select bibliography with commentary', *Bull. Soc. Lab. Hist.*, no. 5 (Autumn 1962) 18–26; P. Thompson, *Socialists, Liberals and Labour: the struggle for London 1885–1914* (1967); P. d'A. Jones, *The Christian Socialist Revival 1877–1914* (Princeton, NJ, 1968); *For Christ and the People*, ed. M. B. Reckitt (1968); H. J. Perkin, 'Land Reform and the Class Conflict in Victorian Britain', *The Victorians and Social Protest*, ed. J. Butt and I. F. Clarke (Newton Abbot, Devon, 1973) 177–217; N. Soldon, 'Laissez-Faire as Dogma: the Liberty and Property Defence League, 1882–1914', in *Essays in Anti-Labour History*, ed. K. D. Brown (1974) 208–33; R. Douglas, *Land, People and Politics: a history of the land question in the United Kingdom 1878–1952* (1976). Personal information: V. H. Blundell, UCTLV, London. OBIT. *Times*, 24 Nov 1948; 'In Memoriam: Frederick Verinder from a daughter in South Africa', *Land and Liberty*, Jan 1949, 13; Foreword to the Memorial ed. of *My Neighbour's Landmark* (1950).

JOHN SAVILLE

See also: Thomas HANCOCK for the Guild of St Matthew (**Special Note**); †Stewart Duckworth HEADLAM; *Edward George HEMMERDE; Robert Leonard OUTHWAITE; William SAUNDERS; *James Dundas WHITE.

WEDDERBURN, Robert (1762–c. 1835)
SPENCEAN AND ULTRA-RADICAL

Robert Wedderburn was born in Kingston, Jamaica, in 1762. His father, James Wedderburn of Inveresk, near Edinburgh, acquired extensive sugar plantations in East Jamaica and also practised there as a doctor and male midwife. He sired two children by Rosanna, an African born house slave, then resold her to her original owners while she was five months pregnant. The purchasers, James Sholto Douglas and his wife, agreed that Rosanna's mulatto baby, Robert, should be free from birth. He was baptised into the Church of England and given some elementary schooling, but this ceased on Lady Douglas's death when he was five. Rosanna was resold and the boy passed into the care of his slave grandmother, 'Talkee-Amy', a celebrated Kingston magic woman and a petty agent for merchant smugglers.

Though nominally a 'free coloured', Robert grew up in a slave environment and experienced many of its cruel and destructive consequences. His father's repeated rejections scarred the boy deeply and cost him the comfort, security, status and education given to his mulatto brothers and half-brothers. Illegitimacy and near-illiteracy were to hamper him for life. The Wedderburn family subsequently blamed Rosanna's frequent resales and occasional floggings on her 'rebellious and violent temper' [Wedderburn [1824] 9], but Robert's aunt and uncle were also sold against their will and transported to the United States. As a boy of eleven, he witnessed the public flogging of his seventy-year-old grandmother for alleged witchcraft on the orders of a young master whom she had helped to rear. Not surprisingly, Wedderburn grew up fearing that slave-owners could revoke his freedom whenever they chose. At the age of fifteen or sixteen he used the escape route of many Kingston mulattos and joined the Royal Navy.

The chronology of his subsequent naval career is unclear. He served an initial period aboard HMS *Polyphemus*, seeing action as a main gunner against the French and Spanish fleets. Later in life, perhaps during the depressed mid-1790s, he seems to have re-enlisted as a top-station hand aboard a privateer. He hints at having been present at the Nore Mutiny of 1797, but is not mentioned in any of the subsequent inquiries. Nor is there any evidence that he was influenced by Jacobin or United Irish sentiments at this time, though he later voiced the characteristic discontent of mutineers at the capriciousness and brutality of naval discipline. He also shared in the distress and disillusionment of many servicemen on being demobilised, an experience which pressed especially heavily on blacks and Lascars stranded without resources in a foreign land. According to one official in 1814, most ended up 'in the madhouse, poorhouse or Bridewell' [HO 42/141, Lieutenant-General Porter, 9 Oct 1814].

Wedderburn's life on first arriving in England around 1778 bore out this dictum. He drifted to London and to the rookeries around St Giles, where a substantial community of West Indians was congregated alongside other immigrant minorities, Jews, Lascars and Irish. Here he seems to have become part of an underworld of 'blackbirds', as they were known, who eked out a living by their wits, agility and strength. He later recorded having associated for seven years 'with an abandoned set of reprobates' [Wedderburn [1802?] 4]. His involvement in crime earned him one spell in Cold Bath Fields Prison, as well as a near miss on a charge of theft as late as 1813. He had also been a witness, at least, to the Gordon riots of 1780, and claimed later to have been friendly with one of the arrested ringleaders. He may have been one of the several blacks known to have participated; he was perhaps fortunate during these years not to have found himself among the numbers of West Indians transported from London to Van Diemen's Land (Tasmania) or Botany Bay.

Wedderburn was luckier than many of his countrymen, however, in having acquired the trade of journeyman tailor. When and how he did so is unclear. It is possible that he had begun an apprenticeship in Jamaica, perhaps on the plantation of his mother's sometime owners, the Campbells, with whom he maintained an affectionate contact, notwithstanding their omission from his polemical autobiography. He might equally have learned the rudiments of the trade at sea or in London itself. Since he claimed the right to call himself a 'flint' tailor, he probably gained registration in the book of trades. He was also to display many of the typical values of a late eighteenth-century artisan in craft and status, belief in the right to economic independence and social respect, and contempt for semi-skilled 'dung' tailors, who accepted sweated wages and conditions.

Competition from the last probably contributed to Wedderburn's degradation in the early nineteenth century. He became one of a considerable body of London artisans forced to supplement their income by such unrespectable means as charity or crime. Distress prompted him to make several attempts to beg from his father's family, who had returned to Britain, but he was refused help even when unemployed, with the quartern loaf at 1s 2½d and his wife pregnant. His involvement in petty theft during these years probably reflects the same pressures. He might also have suffered, like other artisans at this time, from the redefinition of traditional trade perquisites as crimes. An unsuccessful action against him in 1817 for stealing from a government-contracted master tailor could fit this category. By 1818 he was described in an intelligence report as 'a jobbing Taylor sitting in a kind of bulk near St Matthew's Church where he patches cloathes and vends cheap seditious publications' [HO 42/181, Stafford to Clive, 22 Oct 1818]. Shortage of work from master tailors forced him the following year into issuing an advertisement of his willingness to meet orders 'however small and trifling' at moderate prices [TS 11/45/167, handbill, c. Aug 1819].

Wedderburn was intellectually and spiritually ready for the levelling and restorative promises of popular radicalism, and it was an evangelical religious conversion that transformed his outlook. As a boy he had been subjected to both the ideas of Christianity as well as to his grandmother's magical practices. These lapsed on leaving Jamaica, until one day in 1786 when he stopped to listen to a Wesleyan preacher haranguing a crowd at Seven Dials. Vital plebeian Methodism seems to have carried echoes of the syncretic pagan–Christian beliefs Wedderburn had absorbed in the West Indies, including an emphasis on prophecy and dreams, a talismanic attitude to the Scriptures and a love of communal hymn-singing. At the same time, his conversion experience differed little from that of many indigenous English artisans. He was struck by feelings of deep sinfulness, followed by elation at receiving the gift of grace. He also received the characteristic surge of self-confidence that helps explain why early Methodism was so often feared as a seditious force.

By the early 1800s, when he produced his first published work, a small theological tract called *Truth Self-supported*, he had graduated through a variety of sects deploying Arminian, Calvinist and Unitarian ideas, and had reached a position independent and critical of both Established and Nonconformist Churches. His tract was still informed by Methodist piety, and contained no overt political opinions, but it revealed an almost antinomian belief in freedom from sin, a rationalist rejection of the Trinity, and a strong hint of millenarianism. The last possibly reflected the influence of London's most celebrated prophet, Richard Brothers. Wedderburn lived near him in the 1790s, employed one of Brothers' disciples to publish *Truth Self-supported* and later expressed strong sympathy for him. Millenarian ideas were, anyway, in common currency at this time of domestic and international upheaval. *Truth Self-supported* shows Wedderburn making a not-uncommon transition from plebeian Methodist to infidel prophet. He had begun to blend scriptural millenarianism and rationalistic anti-clericalism in ways that resembled both seventeenth-century and Jacobin religious radicalism. Becoming a licensed Unitarian preacher was the last stage in this process. His licence – later confirmed by the Government – was probably issued some time between 1802 and 1813, since it is not among those preserved after the Trinity Act of 1813. Whatever the date, it constituted an important psychological and social acquisition for someone of his deprived background.

Not long after, in 1813, he became a follower of Thomas Spence. As one of the few plebeian radical organisations to remain active in the decade after the Despard affair, the Spenceans benefited from a revival in reforming and free-thought interest after 1810. Wedderburn was part of an influx of new, non-Jacobin members who joined the circle in the wake of Spence's reorganisation and intensified propaganda campaign of 1812. By retaining the format of a tavern singing and debating club, Spence tapped a deep artisan attachment to mutualist, convivial and instructional practices; Wedderburn's background naturally predisposed him to enjoy these rough masculine fraternities. Spence's parish land-reform plan also seemed to offer degraded artisans a chance to recover lost rights, status and self-respect, and his skilful use of plebeian propaganda forms might also have proved attractive to someone of Wedderburn's limited literacy. A ragged street vendor himself, Spence could sympathise with social outcasts: 'Spence ... knew', wrote Wedderburn in 1817, 'that the earth was given to the children of men, making no difference for colour or character, just or unjust' [*Axe laid to the Root*, no. 1 (1817) 5]. There is no doubt, either, that Wedderburn's interest was kindled by Spence's enlightened enthusiasm for non-white peoples, particularly his equation of slavery abroad with aristocratic landed monopoly at home. This idea furnished Wedderburn with a critique which integrated his shaping experiences as disinherited slave offspring and degraded London artisan.

Initially at least, Wedderburn was also one of a number of Spencean recruits who viewed Spence more as a millenarian social prophet than a political radical. Spence's biblical imagery and language, his use of Christian communitarian models and his rationalist anticlericalism had much in common with the ideology of prophets such as Brothers. Wedderburn explicitly represented his adoption of Spenceanism as a prophetic calling. Writing several years later in his periodical, Axe laid to the Root – its title redolent of Paine, Spence and the Scriptures – he offered readers an ecstatic millenarian vision: 'Will not priests follow their princes and sing the solemn dirge of tyranny and corruption falling into contempt and hail the Kingdom of Christ forwarded by Spence, and experience the new birth "for a nation shall be borne in a day"' [Axe laid to the Root, no 2. (1817) 17].

When, after Spence's death in October 1814, his long-time disciple, Thomas Evans, consolidated the Society of Spencean Philanthropists (established formally in 1812) to perpetuate Spencean ideas, Wedderburn continued as 'an active and attentive member' [BL Add. MS 27808, fo. 322, Wedderburn to Place, 22 Mar 1831]. Wedderburn remained loyal to Evans and the Society when tactical and ideological divisions surfaced among Spenceans and Ultra-Radicals over the mass meetings and abortive uprising at Spa Fields in the winter of 1816. Evans refused to abandon the principles of land reform and continued to favour the structure and strategy of tavern debating clubs rather than the intimidatory mass platform or conspiratorial coup d'état preferred by his former followers, Dr James Watson and Arthur Thistlewood. Their consequent split from the Spenceans facilitated Wedderburn's rise to prominence in the Society.

Spies reported that he was a regular and consistently 'inflammatory' speaker at several of the Spencean tavern debating venues in the winter of 1816–17. But it was after the arrest of Evans and his son on 9 February 1817, and during their subsequent twelve-month imprisonment for suspected High Treason, that he emerged as leader. With Charles Jennison he assumed responsibility for attending and supporting the frightened debating sections and assisted Janet Evans to raise funds for her husband and son. During spring and summer 1817, when the Society had shrunk to a small residue which met under the alias of the Polemic Club at the Mulberry Tree tavern in Moorfields, it was Wedderburn again with Jennison who publicised Spencean ideas in the combative periodical Forlorn Hope and in Wedderburn's own Axe laid to the Root. By winter he had also revived the fortunes of the Mulberry Tree section with blasphemous and anti-clerical oratory that attracted capacity crowds, including influential radicals from the Freethinking Christian sect and from the British Forum debating club.

Wedderburn's success encouraged Evans, on his liberation early in 1818, to reorganise the Spenceans along the lines of an independent Dissenting sect using Wedderburn as preacher. During the spring or early summer, Evans and Wedderburn took out a joint licence to operate a chapel in the name of the Church of Christian Philanthropists in a large basement backroom at 6 Archer Street, Haymarket. By shifting venues from tavern to chapel, exploiting Wedderburn's legal protection as licensed preacher under the Trinity Act, renaming the twice-weekly debates 'conferences' and accentuating the Christian communitarian element of Spenceanism, it was hoped to enhance the Society's appeal and evade government prosecution. Spies reported that Spencean ideas continued to be expounded, but with an increased blasphemous and anti-clerical bias thanks to Wedderburn. Tensions soon developed, however, between those Spenceans, such as the Evans family, who wanted to present a reasonably cautious and respectable image and those who were captivated by Wedderburn's extremism. By November 1818 Wedderburn was flirting with Dr Watson's burgeoning Ultra-Radical union, and the Archer Street group split early the following year. Wedderburn left in characteristic style, taking many Spenceans and the chapel benches with him.

He took out a licence for a new Dissenting chapel on 25 April 1819. Hopkins Street Chapel, situated in a 'ruinous' Soho hayloft, immediately became one of the chief focal points of London Ultra-Radical activity. It attracted former followers of Evans, such as the veteran Jacobin William Carr, and the shoemaker poet Allen Davenport, as well as many extreme Watsonites who favoured insurrectionist tactics. Wedderburn also became 'Captain' of, and his chapel the venue for, the sixth section of Watson's reorganised radical union. Even before Peterloo, he and his section were foremost in urging the summoning of simultaneous armed mass meetings nationwide in order to intimidate the Government into granting radical reform or to provide a springboard for insurrection. It was Wedderburn who in September 1819 announced that London Ultra-Radicals intended to press for revolution on their own in view of Henry Hunt's equivocation and treachery as national leader. Over the next two months Wedderburn helped ensure that Hopkins Street became, in Thistlewood's opinion, the best-armed and best-trained Ultra-Radical division.

In early November, however, news of drilling at the chapel leaked to the newspapers, and a government raid was considered imminent. Defections and quarrels followed. The section broke up on the 22nd, shortly before Wedderburn was arrested on a charge of blasphemous libel. This saved him from almost certain involvement in Thistlewood's last desperate assassination plan, which culminated in the Cato Street raid. Wedderburn was always more realistic than Thistlewood and had criticised him sharply in September for exaggerating the extent of Ultra-Radical support. Nevertheless, Thistlewood believed that 'Bob' would have been 'in the front rank' had he been free [HO 42/199, 'w–r', 24 Dec 1819].

Wedderburn's premature arrest in December 1819 reflected the fact that the Home Office feared him more as a propagandist than as a conspirator. As early as August 1819, Lord Sidmouth had informed the Prince Regent that 'Wedderburne [sic], a Notorious Firebrand' was to be stopped by prosecution [Devon CRO, Addington MSS, Corr. 1819: 'Unrest', Sidmouth to the Prince Regent, 12 Aug 1819], but the charge of sedition had not been upheld. On the second attempt, in February 1820, the Solicitor-General argued that Wedderburn had to be silenced because he disseminated a particularly dangerous brand of propaganda which reached a low, vulgar audience and aimed to eradicate their morality and social respect.

Reports of Home Office spies and commissioned shorthand writers reveal that debating topics at Hopkins Street were often suggested by members of the audience and reflected their plebeian language and concerns. Speakers who attempted to use books or prepared papers were howled down; Wedderburn claimed to have spoken always 'on the spur of the moment' [Address of the Rev. Robert Wedderburn (1820) 3] and his language was coarse, violent and colloquial. Much of his effectiveness as a speaker derived from an ability to evoke flesh-and-blood villains set in a context familiar to his audience. He also exploited considerable talents as a performer, satirist and entertainer. He boasted that many came to the chapel because of his reputation as 'a strange curious sort of fellow' [HO 42/197, 18 Oct 1819]. His colour, burly physique and spectacular life echoed the themes and motifs of popular melodrama, just as his four-foot-high co-speaker, Samuel Waddington, resembled a pantomime imp. Together, the 'Black Prince' and 'Black Dwarf', as they were nicknamed, excelled at radical buffoonery and burlesque, continuing a long-established plebeian tradition of expressing protest in symbolic or ritualised forms. They frequently engaged in mock worship in order to demystify established religion. Their speeches were productive less of systematic political theory than of plebeian–populist rhetoric and theatrical effects, and were designed to impel action and debunk authority through shock, humour or pathos.

In so far as Wedderburn and his colleagues utilised political theory, they drew mainly on standard Paineite–Cobbettian critiques of 'Old Corruption', with special emphasis on the Spencean targets of fund-holders and private landlords. Wedderburn typically called for armed republican revolution, for the military to join the people and treat the Regent in the manner of Charles I, 'spit in his face and cut him off' [HO 42/196, 4 Oct 1819] and for some sort of restoration of land to the people. His most original contribution to Ultra-Radical ideology came from a systematic linking of West Indian slavery with working-class subjugation in England. This had been a dominant theme of his periodical articles of 1817 and was continued at Hopkins Street with such calculatedly double-edged topics as 'Has a Slave an Inherent Right to slay his Master who refuses him Liberty?' A handbill reported that this motion was affirmed 'without a dissenting voice, by a numerous and enlightened assembly, who exultingly expressed their desire of hearing of another Sable Nation freeing itself by the Dagger from the base Tyranny of their Christian masters' [HO 42/192, handbill, 16 Aug 1819]. On one occasion Wedderburn was supported in denouncing the cowardice of Methodist missionaries in Jamaica by two other West Indians, including William 'Black' Davidson, who was a regular attender at Hopkins Street and took part in the Cato Street conspiracy [HO 42/198, 10 Nov 1819]. All this throws doubt on the claims of some historians that working-class radicals had become alienated from the abolitionist cause because of its middle-class and evangelical support.

Religious subjects also featured prominently at Hopkins Street. Wedderburn gave zest to the familiar demonology of 'priestcraft', with scandalous local examples of clerical vice, corruption, cruelty and political subservience. On more speculative free-thought issues he combined earthy, common-sense materialism with deliberately outrageous blasphemy aimed at ridding his hearers of social deference and political passivity. 'We should think none greater than ourselves', he urged in a typical debate entitled 'Is the Bible the Word of God?' To prove his case he called Moses 'a whoremonger' and David a murderer like the Manchester magistrates [HO 42/195, 27 Sep 1819]. Yet biblical quotation was still a powerful political trope. He used scriptural authority automatically to justify such recourses as armed rebellion, regicide, the abolition of slavery and land restoration. As an advocate of non-resistance Jesus Christ was called 'a bloody spooney' [TS 11/45/67, *Rex* v. *Wedderburn*], but as an ancient levelling symbol Christ was enthusiastically harnessed to the Ultra-Radical cause.

> Times were bad then and Christ became a Radical Reformer. Now I never could find out where he got his knowledge but this much I know by the same book that he was born of very poor parents who like us felt with him the same as we now feel, and he says I'll turn Mr Hunt – and then when he had that exalted ride upon the Jackass to Jerusalem the people run before him crying out HUNT FOREVER! for that was the same as crying out Hosanna to the son of David . . . [ibid.].

He gave additional proof of the weight of scriptural authority by persuading a London Grand Jury on 21 September 1819 to throw out a charge of seditious libel on the grounds that he had simply been practising 'the true and infallible genius of prophetic skill' [*Times*, 22 Sep 1819, 3].

This was not an entirely cynical claim. In spite of his anti-clericalism and blasphemous scepticism, Wedderburn continued – along with many other supposed Hopkins Street infidels – to espouse a mixture of Christian supernatural and folk magical beliefs, reflected in frequent references to prophecy, portents, signs and providential interventions. But theoretical inconsistency did not lessen the sincerity and power of such beliefs. Hopkins Street infidelity sustained the Cato Street ringleaders at their execution on 10 May 1820 and Wedderburn himself the following day when he was sentenced to two years' imprisonment for blasphemous libel. 'I am so extremely poor', he retorted, 'that prison will be a home to me and as I am so advanced in life I shall esteem it an honour to die immured in a dungeon for advocating the cause of truth . . .' [*Address of the Rev. Robert Wedderburn* (1820) 12].

Wedderburn has been credited by some historians with considerable sophistication as a free-thinker on the basis of several pamphlets which appeared under his name in the years

1819–21, particularly *A Letter ... to the Rev. Solomon Herschell* [1819], *A Critical, Historical and Admonitory Letter to ... the Archbishop of Canterbury* [1820] and *High Heel'd Shoes for Dwarfs in Holiness* [1820]. Detailed textual and contextual investigation has shown, however, that these were largely the work of George Cannon, a lawyer–littérateur and fringe Ultra-Radical. Cannon, alias the Revd Erasmus Perkins, seems to have persuaded Wedderburn and several other working-class radicals to take responsibility for both authorship and publication of many of his own materialist–theist writings. Wedderburn was probably willing to accept the risk of prosecution in exchange for the opportunity to reach a more sophisticated audience and to present himself as 'Dr Wedderburn, V. D. M.' [*Verbi Dei Minister*: Preacher of the Word of God], a member of 'the republic of letters' [*Address of the Rev. Robert Wedderburn* (1820) 10–11]. Only the lively anti-clerical squib *Cast Iron Parsons* [1820], composed by Wedderburn in Dorchester Gaol and edited with some disclaimers by Cannon, bears the authentic stamp of Wedderburn's earthy, populist style – in marked contrast to the sly, donnish rationalism of the other pamphlets. Cannon also wrote a clever, philosophical defence plea which was read out for Wedderburn at his trial in February 1820. Unfortunately, this and a similar *Address* in mitigation merely antagonised the sentencing judge, Justice Bailey, who cited their erudition as evidence that Wedderburn possessed 'a perverted and depraved talent' and deserved a two-year prison sentence for 'aggravated offence' [ibid., 14–15].

At Dorchester Gaol Wedderburn made contact with another convicted infidel, the Paineite publisher Richard Carlile. Though critical of most fellow radicals, Carlile praised Wedderburn's courage and principle, and tried to help him by raising money for his indigent family, by providing him with materials so that he could fulfil his wish of learning to write in prison and by agitating unsuccessfully for him to be appointed prison chaplain. On leaving prison in 1823, Wedderburn seems to have been assisted also by a former Watsonite and Archer Street disciple, William Dugdale, who was beginning a long career as a publisher of infidel, libertine and eventually pornographic literature. It was from Dugdale's increasingly notorious premises, at 23 Russell Court, Drury Lane, that Wedderburn published his brief autobiography, *Horrors of Slavery*, in 1824. On 6 May 1824, at Dugdale's premises, Wedderburn was issued a printing licence for one year (he was also licensed to operate as a printer from there) [Todd (1972) 207]. This enabled him to print as well as to publish his autobiography, which was largely a compilation of a previous newspaper dispute between Wedderburn and his merchant half-brother, Andrew Colville, over the slave policies of their father, James Wedderburn. The timing and purpose of the autobiography reflects the revival of the English anti-slavery movement in 1823 and provides further evidence of that movement's plebeian reach and radical connections. According to Richard Carlile, Wilberforce visited Wedderburn in Dorchester Gaol some time towards the end of 1820, and 'subsequently pronounced him a honest and conscientious man' [*Republican*, 3 Mar [error for 'May'] 1822, 553].

Wedderburn's autobiography also signalled that he was one of a minority of Regency Ultra-Radicals in London whose political ardour remained undampened by the relative tranquillity of the mid-1820s: 'I am still in the same mind as I was before and imprisonment has but confirmed me that I was right' [*The Horrors of Slavery*, 4]. Throughout the 1820s he and a small circle of followers continued to attend the British Forum debating society at Lunt's coffee house, Clerkenwell Green, where veteran radical John Gale Jones and, for a time, the Evans family helped keep republican, infidel and, perhaps, Spencean ideas in circulation. Wedderburn's followers also encouraged and probably financed him in an attempt to open a new blasphemous Ultra-Radical chapel in 1828.

Unfortunately, 'The New Assembly Room', as Wedderburn called his chapel in White's Alley, Chancery Lane, closed at the end of June after only a few months' operation. It failed primarily because he could not adapt to the new style of popular radicalism that became imperative in the 1820s. Infidel preacher rivals such as Robert Taylor, Josiah Fitch and

Rowland Detrosier were able to meet the prevailing artisan appetite for moral and intellectual self-improvement by offering philosophic lectures and deist ritual at comfortable, respectable venues. The contrast with Wedderburn's chapel could hardly have been greater. Carlile's claim that Wedderburn's liturgy was a serious deist undertaking 'with nothing bordering on jest' [*Lion*, 28 Mar 1828] was undercut by its burlesque title, 'Holy Liturgy, or Divine Service upon the Principles of Pure Christian Diabolism'. Home Office intelligence noted that Wedderburn's services, held in what was actually an unlit carpenter's workshop, contained nothing but the old vulgar blasphemy of Hopkins Street days, and consequently attracted only a small circle of attendants, 'all very poor who have long known him' [HO 64/11, 'Police/Secret Service, 1827/8', n.d. fo. 86].

Spies also commented on the unrespectability of Wedderburn's congregation. By 1828 the Dugdale brothers and Cannon were already known pornographers, soon to be convicted, and the following year William Edgar, one of Wedderburn's closest disciples, was imprisoned for running a bawdy-house. Poverty seems to have driven Wedderburn to the same recourse. In the winter of 1830–1, at the age of sixty-eight, he was sentenced to two years' hard labour in Newgate Gaol on a similar charge. This marks the effective end of his career as a radical leader. What had once been a fairly commonplace method of supplementing income among the rough artisans of his youth now seemed embarrassing to a new generation of radicals influenced by respectable *mores*.

Yet it would be wrong to presume from this that Wedderburn left no legacy. The early 1830s saw a revival of mass political radicalism in London and a resurgence in prestige for many of his former colleagues, such as Preston, Waddington, Davenport, Neesom, Jennison and Mee. Under their leadership, radical blasphemous chapels similar to Hopkins Street once again became key agents of Spencean Ultra-Radical propaganda, theatrical effects, education and political mobilisation. Even the charismatic infidel preacher Robert Taylor, who had conceded Wedderburn's 'measure of talent' in 1828 [*Lion*, 28 Mar 1828], began increasingly to imitate his style of blasphemous burlesque. And it was at one of Taylor's flamboyant services, held at Benbow's Theobalds Road chapel in 1834, that a spy recorded the last sighting of 'Wedderburn, the coloured and others of that school' [HO 64/19, 'Secret Service, 1834', 17 Mar 1834]. It is not certain when Wedderburn died, but it is thought that it might have been sometime between 1834 and 1836. Fifteen years of GRO registers (from 1837) were checked without result and there is no record of him in the register of the Kensal Green Cemetery, where many of his colleagues were buried. The 1841 Census was also checked without result. Unlike some of his Regency colleagues, he did not live long enough to become an active Chartist, but he did see the passage of the Reform Act of 1832 and the abolition of West Indian slavery two years later. This must have provided some consolation for a man whose credo had always been 'I am a West Indian, a lover of liberty, and would dishonour human nature if I did not show myself a friend to the liberty of others' [*Axe to laid to the Root*, no. 1 (1817) 8–9].

Writings: *Truth Self-supported: a refutation of certain doctrinal errors generally adopted in the Christian Church* [n.d., BL estimate 1790, my estimate *c.* 1802]; *Forlorn Hope, or Call to the Supine*, nos 1–3 [1817], published by Charles Jennison, largely written by Wedderburn; *Axe laid to the Root, or a Fatal Blow to the Oppressors: being an address to the planters and negroes of the Island of Jamaica*, nos 1–6 [Nov–Dec 1817]; *Christian Policy; or Spence's Plan in Prose and Verse*, by a Spencean Philanthropist [1818]; *Essay on Printing, by a Spencean Philanthropists* [*sic*] [1818]; *A Few Plain Questions to an Apostate* [in HO 42/190 'A', 15 Apr 1819] and *A Few Lines for a Double-faced Politician* [in HO 42/202]; *A Letter addressed to the Rev. Solomon Herschell, the High Priest of Israel ... concerning the Origin of the Jewish Prophecies and their expected Messiah* [1819]; *A Critical, Historical and Admonitory Letter to the ... Archbishop of Canterbury* [1820?]; *Trial of the Reverend Robert Wedderburn ... for*

Blasphemy . . . containing a Verbatim Report of the Defence, ed. Erasmus Perkins [1820]; *Address of the Rev. Robert Wedderburn to the Court of the King's Bench on appearing to receive Judgement for Blasphemy . . . May 1820*, ed. Erasmus Perkins [1820]; *Cast Iron Parsons: or, hints to the public and the legislature on political economy . . .* [1820]; *High Heel'd Shoes for Dwarfs in Holiness, being Plain Directions to Weak Christians how they may escape the Snares of the Devil and the Dreadful Gulphs of Scepticism and Infidelity* [1821]; *The Horrors of Slavery; exemplified in the Life and History of the Rev. Robert Wedderburn . . .* [1824] [there is an engraving of Wedderburn in the front of this work].

Sources: (1) MS: PRO: TS 11/45/167, *Rex* v. *Wedderburn*, Briefs for the Crown; TS 11/201/ 876, 202/875–6, 204/875 (Spencean tavern meetings 1816–17); HO 40/7 (3); HO 40/8 (4); HO 41/25, 'Entry Book, London Disturbances 1815–20'; HO 42/164, Apr 1817, 'List of Persons mentioned by Mr Caldecott' (Wedderburn's theft); HO 42/177 (Spencean tavern meetings, 1816–17); HO 42/180–3 (Archer Street Chapel); HO 42/188, 190–9, and 44/1–3 (Watsonite meetings and Hopkins Street Chapel); HO 49/7, 'Law Offices Entry Book, 1817–30'; HO 64/ 11, 'Police/Secret Service 1827–8' (New Assembly Room); HO 64/19, 'Secret Service, 1834' (Theobalds Road Chapel). Corporation of London RO: 'Index to London Indictments, 1793–1820'. Guildhall Library: MS 9580/5, 'Register of Dissenters' Meeting Houses', 23 Apr 1819. Devon CRO: Addington papers, Corr. 1819: 'Unrest', Lord Sidmouth to the Prince Regent, 12 Aug 1819. BL: Place papers, Add. MS 27808, fo. 322, R. Wedderburn to F. Place, 22 Mar 1831. (2) Other: *Times*, 22 Sep 1819, 3 [trial of Wedderburn for Sedition]; ibid., 27 Jan 1820, 3, 26 Feb 1820, 3, and 10 May 1820, 2 [trial of Wedderburn for blasphemy]; *Annual Register* (1820) 56–7; *Republican*, 20 Oct 1820 [Dorchester Gaol] and 3 Mar [error for 'May'] 1822; *Lion*, 21 Mar 1828 [contains extract of Wedderburn's *Holy Liturgy, or Divine Service upon the Principles of Pure Christian Diabolism . . .*]; *Lion*, 28 Mar 1828; *Deists' Mag.* (1819–20) 71–2, 172; W. H. Wickwar, *The Struggle for the Freedom of the Press 1819–1832* (1928); J. M. Robertson, *A History of Free Thought in the Nineteenth Century* (1929); T. N. Parssinen, 'The Revolutionary Party in London, 1816–20', *Bull. Institute of Historical Research 45* (1972) 266–82; W. B. Todd, *A Dictionary of Printers and Others in Allied Trades, London and Vicinity 1800–40* (1972); I. J. Prothero, *Artisans and Politics in Early Nineteenth-Century London: John Gast and his Times* (Folkestone, Kent, 1979); J. Ann Hone, *For the Cause of Truth: Radicalism in London, 1796–1821* (Oxford, 1982); J. H. Wiener, *Radicalism and Freethought in Nineteenth-Century Britain: the life of Richard Carlile* (Westport, Conn., 1983); P. Fryer, *Staying Power: the history of black people in Britain* (1984); I. D. McCalman, 'A Radical Underworld in Early Nineteenth Century London: Thomas Evans, Robert Wedderburn, George Cannon and their circle, 1800–1835' (Monash DPhil., 1984). Biographical information: Dr M. Chase, Leeds Univ.

IAIN MCCALMAN

See also: †William BENBOW; Allen DAVENPORT; †Richard CARLILE; Thomas EVANS; Charles Hodgson NEESOM; Thomas PRESTON; Thomas SPENCE.

WHITTAKER, James (1865–1940)
LABOUR COUNCILLOR AND AGENT

James ('Jimmy') Whittaker was born in Glasgow in 1865, the son of James Whittaker, a plumber who came from Littleborough, Lancashire, and his wife, Margaret. While he was a child, his parents moved to Southport, where, in 1874, James Whittaker senior set up in business as a plumber at 2 East Street, moving in 1881 to 91 Sefton Street.

Of James's childhood and upbringing nothing is known, except that on 10 May 1877 he joined the 'Youthful Effort' Juvenile Tent of the Independent Order of Rechabites, thus beginning an attachment which he cherished throughout his life, and which led him to an abiding interest in social and political affairs. He also became involved, at an early age, in the Pleasant Sunday Afternoon (PSA) movement. (The origin of Rechabitism – including the use of the term 'tent' instead of the more familiar 'lodge' or 'branch' – is in Jeremiah 35.)

Whittaker was apprenticed into the same occupation as his father, moving in 1884 from Lancashire to Bilston in Staffordshire, to 'finish his time'. In 1891 he left Bilston for Wolverhampton, where he entered the service of the water department, ultimately rising to the position of foreman plumber. An active trades unionist, he became in turn secretary of the Wolverhampton lodge and Birmingham district of the United Operative Plumbers' Association, the Birmingham Area Apprenticeship Council and the Wolverhampton Building Trades Federation.

A man of strong religious principles, James Whittaker attended Darlington Street Wesleyan Methodist Church, which he served long and loyally as a lay preacher (from 1885), a Sunday School teacher, and also secretary of the Home Mission Society. For many years he preached the annual 'Temperance Sunday' sermon. The Independent Order of Rechabites, however, remained Whittaker's main focus of voluntary activity. He was secretary to the 'Albert Victoria' Tent, Wolverhampton, and delegate to the Birmingham district, holding a number of subordinate offices, before twice becoming District Chief Ruler in 1901 and 1930.

Whittaker's involvement in the affairs of the voluntary societies of Wolverhampton was complemented by his political commitment. During the 1890s he became an active member, and later secretary, of the Wolverhampton ILP and Trades Council. In 1903 he was co-opted on to the borough education committee and elected president of the Trades Council, an office he held until 1919. In November 1903 he was elected to Wolverhampton Borough Council as a Labour representative for St John's ward, retaining his seat for the next eight years. He became a JP in 1906.

As the Labour Party struggled to become a significant political force in Wolverhampton, James Whittaker made a major organisational contribution. He acted as agent in January 1906 when T. F. Richards won Wolverhampton West by a majority of 168 votes, and again in January 1910, when Richards was defeated by the Conservative candidate, Alfred Bird. In May 1911, Whittaker again agreed to act as electoral registration officer, a task which imposed such demands upon his time that he resigned his Council seat in November.

In February 1912, a new prospective parliamentary candidate was selected to contest Wolverhampton West: Alexander Walkden, the secretary of the Railway Clerks' Association, who accepted 'financial responsibility for working and fighting the constituency' on behalf of his union. This commitment included funding the salary of a full-time organiser, a post for which Whittaker was selected from a short list of three in March 1912. Under Whittaker's direction, political organisation continued apace; rooms were rented at 35 Queen Street, and a monthly newspaper, the *Wolverhampton Worker*, was launched in April 1913. The *Worker* was the only newspaper ever produced on a regular basis by the Wolverhampton Labour movement, and contained a lively combination of national and local news, scathing attacks on the Conservative–Independent group of councillors who controlled Wolverhampton, and reports of Labour and trade union activities. During the summer of 1913, considerable space was devoted to a campaign by the Wolverhampton Tenants' Defence League, of which Whittaker was chairman, to resist rent rises.

The war years halted the growth of Labour strength in Wolverhampton, but during the eight years following the extension of the suffrage in 1918 the party doubled its municipal representation from six to twelve councillors. Whittaker's efforts remained devoted to parliamentary contests. After a by-election in March 1922, however, when Walkden failed again to win Wolverhampton West (he had stood in 1918), Whittaker suffered a major breakdown in health. In May he resigned as agent.

Whittaker returned to political life in November 1924, when he won Graiseley ward with a majority of 152 on a 64 per cent poll. In March 1927 he was elected chairman of the Wolverhampton West Constituency Labour Party, and he was still in office four years later when W. J. Brown, who had won the seat for Labour in May 1929, left the Party at the same time as Sir Oswald Mosley. In the crisis precipitated by Brown's secession, Labour lost many active members in Wolverhampton and much of its grass-roots support. As an 'elder statesman' and leader of the reconstituted Labour group from March 1934, Whittaker played an important part in nursing the party through the lean years of the 1930s.

In November 1935 Jimmy Whittaker was elected mayor of Wolverhampton. His elder daughter, Mrs A. Swift, acted as mayoress, as his wife had died in 1934. In September 1937 he became an alderman. During his second period of Council service, Whittaker was one of the most respected members of the local authority, being especially expert in matters pertaining to standing orders and their interpretation. He was chairman of the committee for the care of the mentally defective from 1924 until 1940, and also sat on the education committee throughout this period. In pursuance of this latter duty, he was a member of a party of borough councillors and officers who set out by car on 3 April 1940 to visit teacher training colleges in the South of England in order to interview a number of prospective Wolverhampton teachers. Between Ascot and Reading the vehicle, driven by the chairman of the education committee, Alderman J. Clark, was in collision with an omnibus, and Whittaker received multiple injuries that proved fatal.

Representatives of the many public and voluntary organisations with which Jimmy Whittaker was connected filled Darlington Street Methodist Church for his funeral on 8 April. The service was conducted by the Revd P. B. Jenkinson, and six Socialist colleagues acted as pall-bearers. He was survived by two daughters and a nephew and left effects valued at £372.

Jimmy Whittaker has been described as 'a little round-shouldered man, slightly hunch-backed, patently honest'. Photographs show that he wore a heavy, characteristically Edwardian moustache. He is still (1986) remembered with kindness and respect by his former associates.

Sources: (1) MS: 1871 Census, Schedule 28, Enumeration District 11 (Southport). Wolver-hampton Borough Archives, Wolverhampton PL: minutes of Wolverhampton LRC (1907–14), Wolverhampton LP (1918–30) and West Wolverhampton LP (1930–42), published in microfilm with an Introduction by J. Rowley (Microform Ltd, Wakefield, 1983); minutes of Darlington Street Wesleyan Methodist Sunday School committee, 1900–13. 'Mr James Whittaker' (biographical notes, c. 1930, author unknown) 6 pp. [located in *Express and Star* Newspaper Library, Wolverhampton]. (2) Other: *Southport Directories*, 1874–86; *Wolverhampton Chronicle*, 1903–12; *Wolverhampton Red Book*, 1903–40 [portrait in 1906 ed. opposite p. 32]; *Wolverhampton Worker*, 1913–15; *Express and Star*, 1903, 1924–37; 'Bro. Councillor James Whittaker J. P. District Chief Ruler' [article in untitled Rechabite periodical, 1930]; J. H. Lear Caton, *Birmingham District's Century 1839–1939* [of the Independent Order of Rechabites] (Birmingham, 1939); J. Harrison, *Independent Order of Rechabites (Salford Unity) Friendly Society – the Emblem of the Order: a textbook for temperance knowledge examinations* (Manchester, 1968) 40 pp.; G. W. Jones, *Borough Politics: a study of the Wolverhampton Town Council 1888–1964* (1969). Personal informa-tion: W. N. Jacob, Cllr H. E. Lane OBE, the late Mrs A. Onions and Mrs D. Southwick, all of Wolverhampton. Obit. *Express and Star*, 4, 8 Apr 1940; *Labour Organiser*, June 1940, 94; *Wolverhampton Red Book* (1940–1) 217.

JOHN ROWLEY

See also: †Thomas Frederick (Freddy) RICHARDS; †Alexander George WALKDEN.

Consolidated List of Names

Volumes I–VIII

ABBOTTS, William (1873–1930) I
ABLETT, Noah (1883–1935) III
ABRAHAM, William (Mabon) (1842–1922) I
ACLAND, Alice Sophia (1849–1935) I
ACLAND, Sir Arthur Herbert Dyke (1847–1926) I
ADAIR, John (1872–1950) II
ADAMS, David (1871–1943) IV
ADAMS, Francis William Lauderdale (1862–93) V
ADAMS, John Jackson (1st Baron Adams of Ennerdale) (1890–1960) I
ADAMS, Mary Jane Bridges (1855–1939) VI
ADAMS, William Edwin (1832–1906) VII
ADAMS, William Thomas (1884–1949) I
ADAMSON, Janet (Jennie) Laurel (1882–1962) IV
ADAMSON, William (1863–1936) VII
ADAMSON, William (Billy) Murdoch (1881–1945) V
ALDEN, Sir Percy (1865–1944) III
ALDERSON, Lilian (1885–1976) V
ALEXANDER, Albert Victor (1st Earl Alexander of Hillsborough) (1885–1965) I
ALLAN, William (1813–74) I
ALLEN, Reginald Clifford (1st Baron Allen of Hurtwood) (1889–1939) II
ALLEN, Robert (1827–77) I
ALLEN, Sir Thomas William (1864–1943) I
ALLINSON, John (1812/13–72) II
ALLSOP, Thomas (1795–1880) VIII
AMMON, Charles (Charlie) George (1st Baron Ammon of Camberwell) (1873–1960) I
ANDERSON, Frank (1889–1959) I
ANDERSON, William Crawford (1877–1919) II
APPLEGARTH, Robert (1834–1924) II

ARCH, Joseph (1826–1919) I
ARMSTRONG, William John (1870–1950) V
ARNOLD, Alice (1881–1955) IV
ARNOLD, Thomas George (1866–1944) I
ASHTON, Thomas (1841–1919) VII
ASHTON, Thomas (1844–1927) I
ASHTON, William (1806–77) III
ASHWORTH, Samuel (1825–71) I
ASKEW, Francis (1855–1940) III
ASPINWALL, Thomas (1846–1901) I
ATKINSON, Hinley (1891–1977) VI
AUCOTT, William (1830–1915) II
AYLES, Walter Henry (1879–1953) V

BAILEY, Sir John (Jack) (1898–1969) II
BAILEY, William (1851–96) II
BALFOUR, William Campbell (1919–73) V
BALLARD, William (1858–1928) I
BAMFORD, Samuel (1846–98) I
BARBER, Jonathan (1800–59) IV
BARBER, [Mark] Revis (1895–1965) V
BARBER, Walter (1864–1930) V
BARKER, George (1858–1936) I
BARKER, Henry Alfred (1858–1940) VI
BARMBY, Catherine Isabella (1817?–53) VI
BARMBY, John [Goodwin] Goodwyn (1820–81) VI
BARNES, George Nicoll (1859–1940) IV
BARNES, Leonard John (1895–1977) VIII
BARNETT, William (1840–1909) I
BARR, James (1862–1949) VIII
BARRETT, Rowland (1877–1950) IV
BARROW, Harrison (1868–1953) V
BARTLEY, James (1850–1926) III
BARTON, Alfred (1868–1933) VI
BARTON, Eleanor (1872–1960) I
BASTON, Richard Charles (1880–1951) V
BATES, William (1833–1908) I
BATEY, John (1852–1925) I

277

BATEY, Joseph (1867–1949) II
BATTLEY, John Rose (1880–1952) IV
BAYLEY, Thomas (1813–74) I
BEATON, Neil Scobie (1880–1960) I
BECKETT, John (William) Warburton (1894–1964) VI
BEER, Max (1864–1943) VII
BELL, George (1874–1930) II
BELL, Letitia (1890–1981) VIII
BELL, Richard (1859–1930) II
BENBOW, William (1784–?) VI
BENNISON, Thomas Mason (1882–1960) V
BENTHAM, Ethel (1861–1931) IV
BERKELEY, Frederick Charles (1880–1938) VII
BESANT, Annie (1847–1933) IV
BING, Frederick George (1870–1948) III
BIRD, Thomas Richard (1877–1965) I
BLAIR, William Richard (1874–1932) I
BLAND, Hubert (1855–1914) V
BLAND, Thomas (1825–1908) I
BLANDFORD, Thomas (1861–99) I
BLATCHFORD, Montagu John (1848–1910) IV
BLATCHFORD, Robert Peel Glanville (1851–1943) IV
BLYTH, Alexander (1835–85) IV
BOND, Frederick (1865–1951) I
BONDFIELD, Margaret Grace (1873–1953) II
BONNER, Arnold (1904–66) I
BOSWELL, James Edward Buchanan (1906–71) III
BOWER, Sir Percival (1880–1948) VI
BOWERMAN, Charles William (1851–1947) V
BOYES, Watson (1868–1929) III
BOYLE, Hugh (1850–1907) I
BOYNTON, Arthur John (1863–1922) I
BRACE, William (1865–1947) I
BRADBURN, George (1795–1862) II
BRADLAUGH, Charles (1833–91) VII
BRAILSFORD, Henry Noel (1873–1958) II
BRANSON, Clive Ali Chimmo (1907–44) II
BRAUNTHAL, Julius (1891–1972) V
BRAY, John Francis (1809–97) III
BRIDGEMAN, Reginald Francis Orlando (1884–1968) VII
BRIGGS, William (Billy) Layton (1876–1957) VIII
BROADHEAD, Samuel (1818–97) IV
BROADHURST, Henry (1840–1911) II

BROCKLEHURST, Frederick (1866–1926) VI
BROOKE, Willie (1895/6?–1939) IV
BROWN, Alfred Barratt (1887–1947) VIII
BROWN, George (1906–37) III
BROWN, Herbert Runham (1879–1949) II
BROWN, James (1862–1939) I
BROWN, William Henry (1867/8–1950) I
BRUFF, Frank Herbert (1869–1931) II
BUCHANAN, George (1890–1955) VII
BUGG, Frederick John (1830–1900) I
BURNETT, John (1842–1914) II
BURNS, Isaac (1869–1946) IV
BURNS, John Elliott (1858–1943) V
BURT, Thomas (1837–1922) I
BUTCHER, James Benjamin (1843–1933) III
BUTCHER, John (1833–1921) I
BUTCHER, John (1847–1936) I
BUTLER, Herbert William (1897–1971) IV
BUXTON, Charles Roden (1875–1942) V
BUXTON, Noel Edward (1st Baron Noel-Buxton of Aylsham) (1869–1948) V
BYRON, Anne Isabella, Lady Noel (1792–1860) II

CAIRNS, John (1859–1923) II
CAMPBELL, Alexander (1796–1870) I
CAMPBELL, George Lamb (1849–1906) IV
CANN, Thomas Henry (1858–1924) I
CANTWELL, Thomas Edward (1864–1906) III
CAPE, Thomas (1868–1947) III
CAPPER, James (1829–95) II
CARLILE, Richard (1790–1843) VI
CARPENTER, Edward (1844–1929) II
CARTER, Joseph (1818–61) II
CARTER, William (1862–1932) I
CASASOLA, Rowland (Roland) William (1893–1971) IV
CATCHPOLE, John (1843–1919) I
CHADWICK, William Henry (1829–1908) VII
CHALLENER, John Ernest Stopford (1875–1906) V
CHAMPION, Henry Hyde (1859–1928) VIII
CHANCE, John (1804–71) VI
CHARLTON, William Browell (1855/7?–1932) IV
CHARTER, Walter Thomas (1871–1932) I
CHATER, Daniel (Dan) (1870–1959) IV

CHATTERTON, Daniel (1820–95) VIII
CHEETHAM, Thomas (1828–1901) I
CHELMSFORD, 3rd Baron and 1st Viscount Chelmsford. *See* THESIGER, Frederic John Napier V
CHEW, Ada Nield (1870–1945) V
CIAPPESSONI, Francis Antonio (1859–1912) I
CLARK, Fred (1878–1947) I
CLARK, Gavin Brown (1846–1930) IV
CLARK, James (1853–1924) IV
CLARK, Thomas (1821?–57) VI
CLARKE, Andrew Bathgate (1868–1940) I
CLARKE, (Charles) Allen (1863–1935) V
CLARKE, John Smith (1885–1959) V
CLARKE, William (1852–1901) II
CLAY, Joseph (1826–1901) I
CLEAVE, John (1795?–1850) VI
CLERY, William Edward (1861–1931) VII
CLIMIE, Robert (1868–1929) VII
CLUSE, William Sampson (1875–1955) III
COCHRANE, William (1872–1924) I
COLMAN, Grace Mary (1892–1971) III
COMBE, Abram (1785?–1827) II
COMSTIVE, William (1792–1834) VIII
COOK, Arthur James (1883–1931) III
COOK, Cecily Mary (1887/90?–1962) II
COOK, Samuel (1786–1861) VI
COOK, Samuel Quartus (1822–90) VI
COOMBES, Bert Lewis (Louis) (1893–1974) IV
COOPER, George (1824–95) II
COOPER, Robert (1819–68) II
COOPER, William (1822–68) I
COPPOCK, Sir Richard (1885–1971) III
CORMACK, William Sloan (1898–1973) III
COULTHARD, Samuel (1853–1931) II
COURT, Sir Josiah (1841–1938) I
COWEN, Joseph (1829–1900) I
COWEY, Edward (Ned) (1839–1903) I
CRABTREE, James (1831–1917) I
CRAIG, Edward Thomas (1804–94) I
CRANE, Walter (1845–1915) VI
CRAWFORD, William (1833–90) I
CREMER, Sir William Randal (1828–1908) V
CROOKS, William (1852–1921) II
CRUMP, James (1873–1960) V
CUFFAY, William (1788–1870) VI
CULLEN, Alice (1891–1969) VII
CUMMINGS, David Charles (1861–1942) VI

CUNNINGHAME GRAHAM, Robert Bontine (1852–1936) VI
CURRAN, Peter (Pete) Francis (1860–1910) IV

DAGGAR, George (1879–1950) III
DALLAS, George (1878–1961) IV
DALLAWAY, William (1857–1939) I
DALY, James (?–1849) I
DARCH, Charles Thomas (1876–1934) I
DAVENPORT, Allen (1775–1846) VIII
DAVIES, Margaret Llewelyn (1861–1944) I
DAVIES, Stephen Owen (1886–1972) VIII
DAVIS, William John (1848–1934) VI
DAVISON, John (1846–1930) I
DEAKIN, Arthur (1890–1955) II
DEAKIN, Charles (1864–1941) III
DEAKIN, Jane (1869–1942) III
DEAKIN, Joseph Thomas (1858–1937) III
DEAN, Benjamin (1839–1910) I
DEAN, Frederick James (1868–1941) II
DEANS, James (1843/4?–1935) I
DEANS, Robert (1904–59) I
DENT, John James (1856–1936) I
DIAMOND, Charles (1858–1934) VIII
DICKENSON, Sarah (1868–1954) VI
DILKE, Emily (Emilia) Francis Strong, Lady (1840–1904) III
DIXON, George Henry (1902–72) VII
DIXON, John (1828–76) I
DIXON, John (1850–1914) IV
DOCKER, Abraham (1788/91?–1857) II
DODDS, Ruth (1890–1976) VII
DOUSE, William John (1842?–1927) VII
DRAKE, Henry John (1878–1934) I
DREW, William Henry (Harry) (1854–1933) IV
DUDLEY, Sir William Edward (1868–1938) I
DUNCAN, Andrew (1898–1965) II
DUNCAN, Charles (1865–1933) II
DUNN, Edward (1880–1945) III
DUNNING, Thomas Joseph (1799–1873) II
DYE, Sidney (1900–58) I
DYSON, James (1822/3–1902) I

EADES, Arthur (1863–1933) II
EDWARDS, Alfred (1888–1958) IV
EDWARDS, Allen Clement (1869–1938) III
EDWARDS, Ebenezer (Ebby) (1884–1961) V
EDWARDS, Enoch (1852–1912) I

EDWARDS, John (1861–1922) VII
EDWARDS, John Charles (1833–81) I
EDWARDS, Wyndham Ivor (1878–1938) I
ELVIN, Herbert Henry (1874–1949) VI
ENFIELD, Alice Honora (1882–1935) I
EVANS, George (1842–93) VI
EVANS, Isaac (1847?–97) I
EVANS, Jonah (1826–1907) I
EVANS, Thomas (1763–182–?) VIII
EWART, Richard (1904–53) IV

FAIRBOTHAM, Harold (1883–1968) VI
FALLOWS, John Arthur (1864–1935) II
FARMERY, George Edward (1883–1942) V
FARRIMOND, Thomas (1766–1828?) VIII
FENWICK, Charles (1850–1918) I
FINCH, John (1784–1857) I
FINLEY, Lawrence (Larry) (1909–74) IV
FINNEY, Samuel (1857–1935) I
FISHWICK, Jonathan (1832–1908) I
FLANAGAN, James Aloysius (1876–1953) III
FLANAGAN, James Desmond (1912–69) IV
FLEMING, Robert (1869–1939) I
FLYNN, Charles Richard (1882–1957) III
FORD, Isabella Ormston (1855–1924) VIII
FORGAN, Robert (1891–1976) VI
FORMAN, John (1822/3–1900) I
FOSTER, William (1887–1947) I
FOULGER, Sydney (1863–1919) I
FOWE, Thomas (1832/3?–94) I
FOX, James Challinor (1837–77) I
FOX, Thomas (Tom) (1860–1934) II
FOX, Thomas (Tom) Samuel (1905–56) V
FOX, William (1890–1968) V
FRITH, John (1837–1904) I

GALBRAITH, Samuel (1853–1936) I
GALLAGHER, Patrick (Paddy the Cope) (1871–1966) I
GAMMAGE, Robert George (1820/1–88) VI
GANLEY, Caroline Selina (1879–1966) I
GARSIDE, George (1843–1907) VII
GEE, Allen (1852–1939) III
GIBB, Margaret Hunter (1892–1984) VIII
GIBBS, Charles (1843–1909) II
GIBSON, Arthur Lummis (1899–1959) III
GILL, Alfred Henry (1856–1914) II
GILLILAND, James (1866–1952) IV
GILLIS, William (1859–1929) III
GLOVER, Thomas (1852–1913) I

GLYDE, Charles Augustus (1869–1923) VI
GOLDSTONE, Sir Frank Walter (1870–1955) V
GOLIGHTLY, Alfred William (1857–1948) I
GOODALL, William Kenneth (1877–1963) V
GOODY, Joseph (1816/17–91) I
GOSLING, Harry (1861–1930) IV
GOSSIP, Alexander (Alex) (1862–1952) VII
GOSSLING, Archibald (Archie) George (1878–1950) V
GOULD, Barbara Bodichon Ayrton (1886–1950) VII
GOULD, Gerald (1885–1936) VII
GRAHAM, Duncan MacGregor (1867–1942) I
GRAHAM, Robert Bontine Cunninghame. *See* CUNNINGHAME GRAHAM, VI
GRANT, Cyril David (1892–1980) VII
GRAY, Jesse Clement (1854–1912) I
GRAY, John (1799–1883) VI
GREENALL, Thomas (1857–1937) I
GREENING, Edward Owen (1836–1923) I
GREENWOOD, Abraham (1824–1911) I
GREENWOOD, Joseph (1833–1924) I
GRIBBLE, James (1868–1934) VII
GRIFFITHS, George Arthur (1878–1945) III
GROSER, St John Beverley (John) (1890–1966) VI
GROVES, Thomas Edward (1882–1958) V
GROVES, William Henry (1876–1933) II
GRUNDY, Thomas Walter (1864–1942) III
GUEST, John (1867–1931) III
GUEST, Leslie Haden (1st Baron Haden-Guest of Saling) (1877–1960) VIII
GURNEY, Joseph (1814–93) V

HACKETT, Thomas (1869–1950) II
HADDOW, William Martin (1865–1945) VII
HADEN-GUEST, 1st Baron Haden-Guest of Saling. *See* GUEST, Leslie Haden VIII
HADFIELD, Charles (1821–84) II
HALL, Frank (1861–1927) I
HALL, Fred (1855–1933) II
HALL, Fred (1878–1938) I
HALL, George Henry (1st Viscount Hall of Cynon Valley) (1881–1965) II
HALL, Joseph Arthur (Joe) (1887–1964) II
HALL, Thomas George (1858–1938) II

HALLAM, William (1856–1902) I
HALLAS, Eldred (1870–1926) II
HALLIDAY, Thomas (Tom) (1835–1919) III
HALSTEAD, Robert (1858–1930) II
HAMILTON, Mary Agnes (1882–1966) V
HAMPSON, Walter ('Casey') (1866?–1932) VI
HAMSON, Harry Tom (1868–1951) V
HANCOCK, John George (1857–1940) II
HANCOCK, Thomas (1832–1903) VIII
HANDS, Thomas (1858–1938) II
HARDERN, Francis (Frank) (1846–1913) I
HARDIE, David (1870–1939) VII
HARES, Edward Charles (1897–1966) I
HARFORD, Edward (1837/8–98) V
HARKER, John (1864–1908) VII
HARKNESS, Margaret Elise (1854–1923) VIII
HARRIS, Samuel (1855–1915) III
HARRISON, Frederic (1831–1923) II
HARRISON, James (1899–1959) II
HARTLEY, Edward Robertshaw (1855–1918) III
HARTSHORN, Vernon (1872–1931) I
HARVEY, William Edwin (1852–1914) I
HASLAM, James (1842–1913) I
HASLAM, James (1869–1937) I
HAWKINS, George (1844–1908) I
HAYHURST, George (1862–1936) I
HAYWARD, Sir Fred (1876–1944) I
HEAD, Albert (Bert) Edward (1892–1978) VII
HEADLAM, Stewart Duckworth (1847–1924) II
HEATH, David William (1827/8?–80) V
HEMM, William Peck (1820–89) VI
HENDERSON, Arthur (1863–1935) I
HENSHALL, Henry (Harry) (1865–1946) VI
HENSON, John (Jack) (1879–1969) V
HEPBURN, Thomas (1796–1864) III
HERRIOTTS, John (1874–1935) III
HETHERINGTON, Henry (1792–1849) I
HEYWOOD, Abel (1810–93) VI
HIBBERT, Charles (1828–1902) I
HICKEN, Henry (1882–1964) I
HICKS, Amelia (Amie) Jane (1839/40?–1917) IV
HIGDON, Annie Catharine (1864–1946) VII
HIGDON, Thomas George (1869–1939) VII

HILL, Howard (1913–80) VII
HILL, John (1862–1945) III
HILLIARD, Robert (1835–1904) VII
HILTON, James (1814–90) I
HINDEN, Rita (1909–71) II
HINES, George Lelly (1839–1914) I
HIRST, George Henry (1868–1933) III
HOBSON, Charles (1845–1923) VII
HOBSON, John Atkinson (1858–1940) I
HOBSON, Joshua (1810–76) VIII
HODGE, John (1855–1937) III
HODGSON, Sir Mark (1880–1967) VII
HOGAN, Luke (1885–1954) VII
HOLBERRY, Samuel (1814–42) IV
HOLE, James (1820–95) II
HOLLIDAY, Jessie (1884–1915) III
HOLWELL, Walter Charles (1885–1965) V
HOLYOAKE, Austin (1826–74) I
HOLYOAKE, George Jacob (1817–1906) I
HOOSON, Edward (1825–69) I
HOPKIN, Daniel (1886–1951) IV
HORNER, Arthur Lewis (1894–1968) V
HOSKIN, John (1862–1935) IV
HOUGH, Edward (1879–1952) III
HOUSE, William (1854–1917) II
HOWARTH, Charles (1814–68) I
HOWELL, George (1833–1910) II
HUCKER, Henry (1871–1954) II
HUDSON, Walter (1852–1935) II
HUGHES, Agnes Paterson (Nan Hardie) (1885–1947) VII
HUGHES, Edward (1856–1925) II
HUGHES, Hugh (1878–1932) I
HUGHES, Will (1873–1938) V
HUMPHREYS, George Hubert (1878–1967) VI
HUTCHINGS, Harry (1864–1930) II

IRONSIDE, Isaac (1808–70) II
IRVING, David Daniel (Dan) (1854–1924) VIII

JACKSON, Henry (1840–1920) I
JACKSON, Thomas Alfred (1879–1955) IV
JARVIS, Henry (1839–1907) I
JENKINS, Arthur (1882–1946) VIII
JENKINS, Hubert (1866–1943) I
JENKINS, John Hogan (1852–1936) IV
JEWSON, Dorothea (Dorothy) (1884–1964) V
JOHN, William (1878–1955) I
JOHNS, John Ernest (1855/6–1928) II

JOHNSON, Henry (1869–1939) II
JOHNSON, John (1850–1910) I
JOHNSON, William (1849–1919) II
JOHNSTON, James (1846–1928) V
JONES, Benjamin (1847–1942) I
JONES, Joseph (Joe) (1891–1948) V
JONES, Patrick Lloyd (1811–86) I
JOWITT, William Allen (1st Earl Jowitt of Stevenage) (1885–1957) VII
JOYNES, James Leigh (1853–93) VIII
JUGGINS, Richard (1843–95) I
JUPP, Arthur Edward (1906–73) IV

KANE, John (1819–76) III
KEELING, Frederic Hillersdon (1886–1916) VII
KELLEY, George Davy (1848–1911) II
KENDALL, George (1811–86) VI
KENYON, Barnet (1850–1930) I
KESSACK, James O'Connor (1879–1916) VI
KILLON, Thomas (1853–1931) I
KING, William (1786–1865) I
KNEE, Fred (1868–1914) V
KNIGHT, Albert (1903–79) VII
KNIGHT, Robert (1833–1911) VI
KUMARAMANGALAM, Surendra Mohan (1916–73) V

LACEY, James Philip Durnford (1881–1974) III
LANG, James (1870–1966) I
LANSBURY, George (1859–1940) II
LAST, Robert (1829–?) III
LAW, Harriet Teresa (1831–97) V
LAWRENCE, Arabella Susan (1871–1947) III
LAWSON, John James (1st Baron Lawson of Beamish) (1881–1965) II
LAWTHER, Sir William (Will) (1889–1976) VII
LEE, Frank (1867–1941) I
LEE, Peter (1864–1935) II
LEES, James (1806–91) I
LEICESTER, Joseph Lynn (1825–1903) III
LEONARD, William (1887–1969) VII
LEWINGTON, William James (1862–1933) VI
LEWIS, Richard James (1900–66) I
LEWIS, Thomas (Tommy) (1873–1962) I
LEWIS, Walter Samuel (1894–1962) III
LEYS, Norman Maclean (1875–1944) VIII

LIDDLE, Thomas (1863–1954) I
LINDGREN, George Samuel (Baron Lindgren of Welwyn Garden City) (1900–71) II
LINNEY, Joseph (1808–87) VI
LISTER, David Cook (1888–1961) VI
LITTLEWOOD, France (1863–1941) VI
LLOYD, Charles Mostyn (1878–1946) VII
LOCKEY, Walter Daglish (1891–1956) V
LOCKWOOD, Arthur (1883–1966) II
LONGDEN, Fred (1886–1952) II
LOVETT, Levi (1854–1929) II
LOVETT, William (1800–77) VI
LOWERY, Matthew Hedley (1858–1918) I
LOWERY, Robert (1809–63) IV
LUCRAFT, Benjamin (1809–97) VII
LUDLOW, John Malcolm Forbes (1821–1911) II
LUNN, William (Willie) (1872–1942) II

MABEN, William (1849–1901) VI
McADAM, John (1806–83) V
MACARTHUR, Mary (1880–1921) II
McBAIN, John McKenzie (1882–1941) V
MACDONALD, Alexander (1821–81) I
MACDONALD, James (1857–1938) VIII
MacDONALD, James Ramsay (1866–1937) I
MacDONALD, Margaret Ethel Gladstone (1870–1911) VI
MACDONALD, Roderick (1840–94) IV
McELWEE, Andrew (1882–1968) V
McGHEE, Henry George (1898–1959) I
McGHEE, Richard (1851–1930) VII
McGURK, John (1874–1944) V
McHUGH, Edward (1853–1915) VII
McKEE, George William (1865–1949) V
MACPHERSON, John Thomas (1872–1921) V
McSHANE, Annie (1888–1962) IV
McSHEEDY, James Joseph (1852–1923) VIII
MADDISON, Fred (1856–1937) IV
MALONE, Cecil John L'Estrange (1890–1965) VII
MANN, Amos (1855–1939) I
MANN, James (1784?–1832) VIII
MANN, Jean (1889–1964) VI
MANNING, (Elizabeth) Leah (1886–1977) VII
MARCROFT, William (1822–94) I
MARLOW, Arnold (1891–1939) I
MARSDEN, Richard (1802/3–58) VIII

MARTIN, Emma (1812–51) VI
MARTIN, James (1850–1933) I
MARTYN, Caroline Eliza Derecourt (1867–96) VIII
MATHER, Joseph (1737–1804) VIII
MATHERS, George (1st Baron Mathers of Newton St Boswells) (1886–1965) VII
MATTHEWS, Sir James (Henry John) (1887–1981) VII
MATTHIAS, Thomas Davies (1823–1904) VII
MAXWELL, Sir William (1841–1929) I
MAY, Henry John (1867–1939) I
MELL, Robert (1872?–1941) V
MELLOR, William (1888–1942) IV
MERCER, Thomas William (1884–1947) I
MERCHANT, Emmanuel (1854–1924) VII
MESSER, Sir Frederick (Fred) (1886–1971) II
MIDDLETON, Dora Miriam (1897–1972) IV
MIDDLETON, George Edward (1866–1931) II
MILLERCHIP, William (1863–1939) I
MILLIGAN, George Jardine (1868–1925) V
MILLINGTON, Joseph (1866–1952) II
MILLINGTON, William Greenwood (1850–1906) III
MITCHELL, John Thomas Whitehead (1828–95) I
MITCHISON, Gilbert Richard (Baron Mitchison of Carradale) (1890–1970) II
MOLESWORTH, William Nassau (1816–90) I
MOLL, William Edmund (1856–1932) VIII
MOLYNEUX, Sir John (Harry) (1882–1968) VII
MOORHOUSE, Thomas Edwin (1854–1922) I
MORGAN, David (Dai o'r Nant) (1840–1900) I
MORGAN, David Watts (1867–1933) I
MORGAN, John Minter (1782–1854) I
MORLEY, Iris Vivienne (1910–53) IV
MORLEY, Ralph (1882–1955) VIII
MOSLEY, Cynthia Blanche, Lady (1898–1933) V
MOTT, William Henry (1812–82) VI
MUDIE, George (1788?–?) I
MUGGERIDGE, Henry Thomas Benjamin (1864–1942) V
MUIR, John William (1879–1931) VII

MUNRO, William John (Jack) (1873–1948) VII
MURDOCH, Mary Charlotte (1864–1916) V
MURNIN, Hugh (1861–1932) II
MURRAY, Robert (1869–1950) I
MYCOCK, William Salter (1872–1950) III

NEALE, Edward Vansittart (1810–92) I
NEESOM, Charles Hodgson (1785–1861) VIII
NEWCOMB, William Alfred (1849–1901) III
NEWTON, William (1822–76) II
NICHOL, Robert (1890–1925) VII
NICHOLLS, George (1864–1943) V
NOEL, Conrad le Despenser Roden (1869–1942) II
NOEL-BUXTON, 1st Baron Noel-Buxton of Aylsham. See BUXTON, Noel Edward V
NOEL-BUXTON, Lucy Edith Pelham, Lady (1888–1960) V
NORMANSELL, John (1830–75) I
NUTTALL, William (1835–1905) I

OAKEY, Thomas (1887–1953) IV
O'GRADY, Sir James (1866–1934) II
OLIVER, John (1861–1942) I
OLIVIER, Sydney Haldane (1st Baron Olivier of Ramsden) (1859–1943) VIII
O'NEILL, Arthur George (1819–96) VI
ONIONS, Alfred (1858–1921) I
ORAGE, [James] Alfred Richard (1873–1934) VI
OUTHWAITE, Robert Leonard (1868–1930) VIII
OWEN, Robert (1771–1858) VI

PALIN, John Henry (1870–1934) IV
PARE, William (1805–73) I
PARKER, James (1863–1948) II
PARKINSON, John Allen (1870–1941) II
PARKINSON, Tom Bamford (1865–1939) I
PARROTT, William (1843–1905) II
PASSFIELD, 1st Baron Passfield of Passfield Corner. See WEBB, Sidney James II
PATERSON, Emma Anne (1848–86) V
PATTERSON, William Hammond (1847–96) I
PATTISON, Lewis (1873–1956) I
PEASE, Edward Reynolds (1857–1955) II

PEASE, Mary Gammell (Marjory) (1861–1950) II

PEET, George (1883–1967) V

PENNY, John (1870–1938) I

PERKINS, George Leydon (1885–1961) I

PETCH, Arthur William (1886–1935) IV

PHILLIPS, Marion (1881–1932) V

PHIPPEN, William George (1889–1968) V

PICKARD, Benjamin (1842–1904) I

PICKARD, William (1821–87) I

PICTON-TURBERVILL, Edith (1872–1960) IV

PIGGOTT, Thomas (1836–87) II

PILLING, Richard (1799–1874) VI

PITMAN, Henry (1826–1909) I

PLUNKETT, Sir Horace Curzon (1854–1932) V

POINTER, Joseph (1875–1914) II

POLLARD, William (1832/3?–1909) I

POLLITT, James (1857–1935) III

PONSONBY, Arthur Augustus William Harry (1st Baron Ponsonby of Shulbrede) (1871–1946) VII

POOLE, Stephen George (1862–1924) IV

POSTGATE, Daisy (1892–1971) II

POSTGATE, Raymond William (1896–1971) II

POTTER, George (1832–93) VI

POTTS, John Samuel (1861–1938) II

PRATT, Hodgson (1824–1907) I

PRESTON, Thomas (1774–1850) VIII

PRICE, Gabriel (1879–1934) III

PRICE, Thomas William (1876–1945) V

PRINGLE, William Joseph Sommerville (1916–62) II

PRIOR, John Damrel (1840–1923) VI

PRYDE, David Johnstone (1890–1959) II

PURCELL, Albert Arthur (1872–1935) I

QUELCH, Henry (Harry) (1858–1913) VIII

RACKSTRAW, Marjorie (1888–1981) VIII

RAE, William Robert (1858–1936) II

RAMSAY, Thomas (Tommy) (1810/11–73) I

RAWLINGS, Joseph (1894–1978) VIII

READE, Henry Musgrave (1860–?) III

REDFERN, Percy (1875–1958) I

REED, Richard Bagnall (1831–1908) IV

REEVES, Samuel (1862–1930) I

REEVES, William Pember (1857–1932) II

REYNOLDS, George William MacArthur (1814–79) III

RICHARDS, Thomas (1859–1931) I

RICHARDS, Thomas Frederick (Freddy) (1863–1942) III

RICHARDSON, Robert (1862–1943) II

RICHARDSON, Thomas (Tom) (1868–1928) IV

RICHARDSON, William Pallister (1873–1930) III

RITSON, Joshua (Josh) (1874–1955) II

ROBERTS, George Henry (1868–1928) IV

ROBERTS, John (Jack) (1899–1979) VII

ROBINSON, Annot Erskine (1874–1925) VIII

ROBINSON, Charles Leonard (1845–1911) III

ROBINSON, Richard (1879–1937) I

ROBSON, James (1860–1934) II

ROBSON, John (1862–1929) II

ROEBUCK, Samuel (1871–1924) IV

ROGERS, Frederick (1846–1915) I

ROGERSON, William Matts (1873–1940) III

ROTHSTEIN, Theodore (1871–1953) VII

ROWLANDS, James (1851–1920) VI

ROWLINSON, Ernest George (1882–1941) VI

ROWLINSON, George Henry (1852–1937) I

ROWSON, Guy (1883–1937) II

RUDLAND, Frederick William (1866–1941) VII

RUST, Henry (1831–1902) II

RUTHERFORD, John Hunter (1826–90) I

SAKLATVALA, Shapurji Dorabji (1874–1936) VI

SAMUELSON, James (1829–1918) II

SAUNDERS, William (1823–95) VIII

SAWYER, George Francis (1871–1960) VIII

SCHOFIELD, Thomas (1825–79) II

SCHOLES, Benjamin (1779?–1823) VIII

SCOTTON, Amos (1833–1904) VII

SCRYMGEOUR, Edwin (1866–1947) VII

SCURR, John (1876–1932) IV

SEDDON, James Andrew (1868–1939) II

SEWELL, William (1852–1948) I

SHACKLETON, Sir David James (1863–1938) II

SHAFTOE, Samuel (1841–1911) III

SHALLARD, George (1877–1958) I

SHANN, George (1876–1919) II

SHARP, Andrew (1841–1919) I
SHARP, Clifford Dyce (1883–1935) VII
SHAW, Benjamin Howard (1865–1942) VIII
SHAW, Clarice Marion McNab (1883–1946) VIII
SHAW, Fred (1881–1951) IV
SHEPPARD, Frank (1861–1956) III
SHIELD, George William (1876–1935) III
SHIELS, Sir Thomas Drummond (1881–1953) VIII
SHILLITO, John (1832–1915) I
SHORROCKS, Peter (1834–86) VI
SHURMER, Percy Lionel Edward (1888–1959) II
SIMPSON, Henry (1866–1937) III
SIMPSON, James (1826–95) I
SIMPSON, William Shaw (1829–83) II
SITCH, Charles Henry (1887–1960) II
SITCH, Thomas (1852–1923) I
SKEFFINGTON, Arthur Massey (1908–71) V
SKEVINGTON, John (1801–51) I
SKINNER, (James) Allen (1890–1974) V
SLATER, Harriet (1903–76) VII
SLOAN, Alexander (Sandy) (1879–1945) II
SMILLIE, Robert (1857–1940) III
SMITH, Albert (1867–1942) III
SMITH, Alfred (1877–1969) III
SMITH, Herbert (1862–1938) II
SMITHIES, James (1819–69) I
SOUTHALL, Joseph Edward (1861–1944) V
SPARKES, Malcolm (1881–1933) II
SPENCE, Thomas (1750–1814) VIII
SPENCER, George Alfred (1873–1957) I
SPENCER, John Samuel (1868–1943) I
STANLEY, Albert (1862–1915) I
STANTON, Charles Butt (1873–1946) I
STEAD, Francis Herbert (1857–1928) IV
STEADMAN, William (Will) Charles (1851–1911) V
STEPHEN, Campbell (1884–1947) VII
STEVENS, John Valentine (1852–1925) II
STEWART, Aaron (1845–1910) I
STEWART, James (1863–1931) VII
STOKES, Richard Rapier (1897–1957) VIII
STOTT, Benjamin (1813–50) IV
STRAKER, William (1855–1941) II
STRINGER, Sidney (1889–1969) V
SULLIVAN, Joseph (1866–1935) II
SUMMERBELL, Thomas (1861–1910) IV

SUTHERLAND, Mary Elizabeth (1895–1972) VI
SUTHERS, Robert Bentley (1870–1950) IV
SUTTON, John Edward (Jack) (1862–1945) III
SWAN, John Edmund (1877–1956) III
SWANWICK, Helena Maria Lucy (1864–1939) IV
SWEET, James (1804/5?–79) IV
SWIFT, Fred (1874–1959) II
SWINGLER, Stephen Thomas (1915–69) III
SYLVESTER, George Oscar (1898–1961) III

TAYLOR, John Wilkinson (1855–1934) I
TAYLOR, Robert Arthur (1866–1934) IV
TEER, John (1809?–83?) IV
THESIGER, Frederic John Napier, 3rd Baron and 1st Viscount Chelmsford (1868–1933) V
THICKETT, Joseph (1865–1938) II
THORNE, William James (1857–1946) I
THORPE, George (1854–1945) I
THRING, Lillian Mary (1887–1964) VIII
TILLETT, Benjamin (Ben) (1860–1943) IV
TOOLE, Joseph (Joe) (1887–1945) VII
TOOTILL, Robert (1850–1934) II
TOPHAM, Edward (1894–1966) I
TORKINGTON, James (1811–67) II
TOYN, Joseph (1838–1924) II
TRAVIS, Henry (1807–84) I
TREVOR, John (1855–1930) VI
TROTTER, Thomas Ernest Newlands (1871–1932) III
TROW, Edward (1833–99) III
TUCKWELL, Gertrude Mary (1861–1951) VI
TURNER, Sir Ben (1863–1942) VIII
TWEDDELL, Thomas (1839–1916) I
TWIGG, Herbert James Thomas (1900–57) I
TWIST, Henry (Harry) (1870–1934) II

VARLEY, Frank Bradley (1885–1929) II
VARLEY, Julia (1871–1952) V
VEITCH, Marian (1913–73) III
VERINDER, Frederick (1858–1948) VIII
VINCENT, Henry (1813–78) I
VIVIAN, Henry Harvey (1868–1930) I

WADSWORTH, John (1850–1921) I
WALKDEN, Alexander George (1st Baron

Walkden of Great Bookham) (1873–1951) V

WALKER, Benjamin (1803/4?–83) I

WALLAS, Graham (1858–1932) V

WALLHEAD, Richard [Christopher] Collingham (1869–1934) III

WALLWORK, Daniel (1824–1909) VI

WALSH, Stephen (1859–1929) IV

WALSHAM, Cornelius (1880–1958) I

WARD, George Herbert Bridges (1876–1957) VII

WARD, John (1866–1934) IV

WARDLE, George James (1865–1947) II

WARNE, George Henry (1881–1928) IV

WARWICK, Frances Evelyn (Daisy), Countess of (1861–1938) V

WATKINS, William Henry (1862–1924) I

WATSON, William (1849–1901) III

WATSON, William Foster (1881–1943) VI

WATTS, John (1818–87) I

WEBB, Beatrice (1858–1943) II

WEBB, Catherine (1859–1947) II

WEBB, Sidney James (1st Baron Passfield of Passfield Corner) (1859–1947) II

WEBB, Simeon (1864–1929) I

WEBB, Thomas Edward (1829–96) I

WEDDERBURN, Robert (1762–c.1835) VIII

WEIR, John (1851–1908) I

WEIR, William (1868–1926) II

WELLOCK, Wilfred (1879–1972) V

WELSH, James Carmichael (1880–1954) II

WEST, John (1812–87) VII

WESTWOOD, Joseph (1884–1948) II

WHEATLEY, John (1869–1930) VII

WHEELER, Thomas Martin (1811–62) VI

WHITE, Arthur Daniel (1881–1961) III

WHITE, Charles Frederick (1891–1956) V

WHITEFIELD, William (1850–1926) II

WHITEHEAD, Alfred (1862–1945) I

WHITEHOUSE, Samuel Henry (1849–1919) IV

WHITELEY, William (1881–1955) III

WHITTAKER, James (1865–1940) VIII

WIGNALL, James (1856–1925) III

WILKIE, Alexander (1850–1928) III

WILLIAMS, Aneurin (1859–1924) I

WILLIAMS, David James (1897–1972) IV

WILLIAMS, Sir Edward John (Ted) (1890–1963) III

WILLIAMS, John (1861–1922) I

WILLIAMS, John (Jack) Edward (1854?–1917) VI

WILLIAMS, Ronald Watkins (1907–58) II

WILLIAMS, Thomas (Tom) (Baron Williams of Barnburgh) (1888–1967) II

WILLIAMS, Thomas Edward (1st Baron Williams of Ynyshir) (1892–1966) III

WILLIS, Frederick Ebenezer (1869–1953) II

WILSON, Cecil Henry (1862–1945) VI

WILSON, John (1837–1915) I

WILSON, John (1856–1918) II

WILSON, Joseph Havelock (1858–1929) IV

WILSON, William Tyson (1855–1921) III

WINSTONE, James (1863–1921) I

WINTRINGHAM, Thomas Henry (Tom) (1898–1949) VII

WINWOOD, Benjamin (1844–1913) II

WOODS, Samuel (1846–1915) I

WOOLF, Leonard Sidney (1880–1969) V

WORLEY, Joseph James (1876–1944) I

WRIGHT, Oliver Walter (1886–1938) I

WYLD, Albert (1888–1965) II

ZEITLIN, Morris (1873–1936) VII

General Index

Compiled by Joyce Bellamy with assistance from Wendy P. Mann, V. J. Morris and Barbara Nield

Numbers in bold type refer to biographical entries and Special Notes